D1361593

SCIENTIFIC AND EXPERT EVIDENCE

ASPEN PUBLISHERS

SCIENTIFIC AND EXPERT EVIDENCE

JOHN M. CONLEY
WILLIAM RAND KENAN JR. PROFESSOR OF LAW
UNIVERSITY OF NORTH CAROLINA SCHOOL OF LAW

JANE CAMPBELL MORIARTY
ASSOCIATE PROFESSOR OF LAW
UNIVERSITY OF AKRON SCHOOL OF LAW

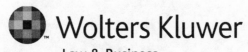

Wolters Kluwer
Law & Business

AUSTIN   BOSTON   CHICAGO   NEW YORK   THE NETHERLANDS

To contact Customer Care, e-mail customer.care@aspenpublishers.com,
call 1-800-234-1660, fax 1-800-901-9075, or mail correspondence to:

> Aspen Publishers
> Attn: Order Department
> PO Box 990
> Frederick, MD 21705

Printed in the United States of America.

1 2 3 4 5 6 7 8 9 0

ISBN 978-0-7355-5799-4

Library of Congress Cataloging-in-Publication Data

Conley, John M.
    Scientific and expert evidence/John M. Conley, Jane Campbell Moriarty.
        p. cm.
    Includes index.
    ISBN 978-0-7355-5799-4
    1. Evidence, Expert—United States. I. Moriarty, Jane Campbell. II. Title.
    KF8961.C665 2007
    347.73′67—dc22

                                                2007019825

About Wolters Kluwer Law & Business

Wolters Kluwer Law & Business is a leading provider of research information and workflow solutions in key specialty areas. The strengths of the individual brands of Aspen Publishers, CCH, Kluwer Law International and Loislaw are aligned within Wolters Kluwer Law & Business to provide comprehensive, in-depth solutions and expert-authored content for the legal, professional and education markets.

CCH was founded in 1913 and has served more than four generations of business professionals and their clients. The CCH products in the Wolters Kluwer Law & Business group are highly regarded electronic and print resources for legal, securities, antitrust and trade regulation, government contracting, banking, pensions, payroll, employment and labor, and healthcare reimbursement and compliance professionals.

Aspen Publishers is a leading information provider for attorneys, business professionals and law students. Written by preeminent authorities, Aspen products offer analytical and practical information in a range of specialty practice areas from securities law and intellectual property to mergers and acquisitions and pension/benefits. Aspen's trusted legal education resources provide professors and students with high-quality, up-to-date and effective resources for successful instruction and study in all areas of the law.

Kluwer Law International supplies the global business community with comprehensive English-language international legal information. Legal practitioners, corporate counsel and business executives around the world rely on the Kluwer Law International journals, loose-leafs, books and electronic products for authoritative information in many areas of international legal practice.

Loislaw is a premier provider of digitized legal content to small law firm practitioners of various specializations. Loislaw provides attorneys with the ability to quickly and efficiently find the necessary legal information they need, when and where they need it, by facilitating access to primary law as well as state-specific law, records, forms and treatises.

Wolters Kluwer Law & Business, a unit of Wolters Kluwer, is headquartered in New York and Riverwoods, Illinois. Wolters Kluwer is a leading multinational publisher and information services company.

SUMMARY OF CONTENTS

CONTENTS

We bring to this book a mixture of academic and practical experience with scientific evidence, a blend that we hope is reflected in the book itself. For each of us, the book represents a logical next step in a lengthy relationship with the topic. Both of us spent substantial apprenticeships as big-firm litigators, during which we dealt extensively with expert witnesses, both friendly and hostile. We both have also dealt with the judiciary on these issues, Conley as director of a "judging science" program and a teacher of law and social science at the University of Virginia's Graduate Program for Judges, and Moriarty as clerk to a state supreme court justice with a special interest in questions of law and science. And both of us have written on law and science, Moriarty primarily on psychological and "forensic science" issues, and Conley on anthropology and statistics.

At about the time that *Daubert* brought new urgency to the topic, each of us began teaching a course on scientific evidence. Although we were not in consultation at the time, each of us concluded that, to be an intelligent and critical consumer of scientific evidence, a lawyer needs a grounding both in the relevant legal doctrines and in the basic scientific principles that underlie various types of evidence — not that a lawyer needs to function as a scientist (neither of us fits that description), but it is not sufficient to treat the "scientific" part of scientific evidence as a black box to be managed by the experts. We have both believed from the outset that mastery of a relatively few overarching scientific concepts and processes can greatly enhance a lawyer's effectiveness. Accordingly, as we assembled, tested, and revised our own *ad hoc* teaching materials, we particularly sought cases and other sources that deal with scientific issues in some depth, in a way that is both accurate and straightforward.

The completion of the *Daubert* trilogy; the burgeoning academic literature about the theoretical, practical, and policy implications of the trilogy; the revision of Federal Rule of Evidence 702; and, most importantly, the proliferation of significant cases that seem to turn on the admissibility and sufficiency of scientific evidence acted in concert to persuade us that the time had come to turn our *ad hoc* teaching materials into a casebook. In simplest terms, scientific evidence had become part of the basic literacy of every courtroom lawyer, whether civil or criminal, and that reality seemed to call for a course with a "real" book.

We hope that law students and their teachers will find this to be a challenging yet non-intimidating introduction to the scientific techniques that regularly enter the courtroom and the evidentiary principles that govern their use. If we, who majored in Latin literature (Conley) and philosophy (Moriarty), have been able to achieve elemental literacy, then so can you. We hope that this book will make your journeys a good deal less painful than ours have been.

John M. Conley
Jane Campbell Moriarty

May 2007

I owe special thanks to my research assistant, Rhiannon D'Agostin, a member of the class of 2008 at the University of North Carolina School of Law. An adept law student as well as a graduate biologist, she went far beyond the usual RA duties in helping me to define topics, find and edit cases and materials, and insure the accuracy of the biological material.

My longtime friend David Peterson also deserves a particular expression of gratitude. A forensic statistician whose work has been relied on by the Supreme Court in multiple cases, David has been my mentor (and frequent collaborator) on all things statistical since I began teaching in 1983. He generously read and commented on the statistical components of this book, and, even more generously, wrote an essay on regression analysis that appears in Chapter 3, Statistical Inference.

Jake Barnes, Scott Baker, and Richard Myers were kind enough to read and comment on portions of the manuscript within their respective areas of expertise, as were the anonymous reviewers solicited by Aspen. My students (including many judges) over the years have also been astute reviewers of the materials as they have developed.

And above all, thanks to my wife, Paula, for everything.

J.M.C.

Many thanks to my colleagues, and the librarians and staff at the University of Akron School of Law who have been helpful and encouraging, for which I am most grateful. Most particularly, Dean Richard L. Aynes, Associate Dean Elizabeth Reilly, and Faculty Research Director Tracy Thomas have provided encouragement, support, and assistance during the last few years while I worked on this project. Thank you all so much.

Michael Saks, John Conley, Will Huhn, Simon Cole, Bill Thompson, Michael Perlin, Adina Schwarz, Mindy Mechanic, Maureen O'Connor, Michael Risinger, Mark Brodin, and David Faigman have helped shape my thoughts on various aspects of expert evidence over the last several years. I'm grateful to each of you. Thanks to the anonymous reviewers solicited by Aspen who provided many helpful suggestions and new ways to think about issues.

Many thanks to Alex Pachos, a member of the 2008 class of the University of Akron School of Law, who has put in long (and tedious) hours to help complete this project. A number of students over the years at Akron have used portions of this book in its draft form and have been instrumental in helping me refine my thoughts on the contents. I thank you all.

As always, love and gratitude to my husband, Gary Zimmerman. You're as constant as the northern star.

J.C.M.

We would also like to acknowledge the authors, publishers, and copyright holders of the following publications for permission to reproduce excerpts herein:

Angell, Marcia, Editorial: Do Breast Implants Cause Systemic Disease? — Science in the Courtroom, 330 New England J.Med. 1784 (1994), reprinted with permission of Massachusetts Medical Society and the author. Copyright 1994 Massachusetts Medical Society. All rights reserved.

Childs, John C., Toxicogenomics: New Chapter in Causation and Exposure in Toxic Tort Litigation, 69 Defense Counsel J. 441 (2002), reprinted with permission of Defense Counsel Journal.

Fradella, Henry F., Why Judges Should Admit Expert Testimony on the Unreliability of Eyewitness Testimony, 2006 Fed. Cts. L. Rev. 3, reprinted with permission of the Federal Courts Law Review and the author.

Moriarty, Jane C., and Michael J. Saks, Forensic Science: Grand Goals, Tragic Flaws and Judicial Gatekeeping, published in Judges' Journal, Volume 44, No. 4, Fall 2005. Copyright © 2005 by the American Bar Association. Reprinted with permission.

Peterson, David W., A Note Regarding Pay Discrimination (2006), reprinted with permission of the author.

Thomson, William C., and Dan E. Krane, DNA in the Courtroom, in Jane Campbell Moriarty, Psychological and Scientific Evidence in Criminal Trials (2003), reprinted with permission of Thomson/West and the authors.

Tire illustration, as contained in Kumho Tire Co. v. Carmichael (1999), reprinted with permission of Kumho Tire USA.

SCIENTIFIC AND EXPERT EVIDENCE

CHAPTER 1

INTRODUCTION TO SCIENCE AND THE LEGAL PROCESS

"Scientific evidence" is a far more complicated phrase than it might appear at first glance. To lawyers, it usually means "expert testimony based on scientific knowledge and inquiry that is offered in litigation"—in other words, *evidence,* in the legal sense, whose source is *scientific.* A lawyer's concern is typically with the legal questions of whether scientific evidence will be admitted in court and how much weight it will be given, as well as with the practical question of its persuasive impact.

To a scientist, however, the phrase and its constituent words are all likely to mean something quite different—although exactly what is not clear. To start with, "the word *evidence* is used much more loosely in science than in the law. The law has precise rules of evidence that govern what is admissible and what isn't. In science the word merely seems to mean something less than 'proof.'" David Goodstein, *How Science Works,* in *Reference Manual on Scientific Evidence* 80. (Federal Judicial Center, 2d ed. 2000). And the question of what counts as "scientific" has been debated by philosophers of science for centuries, with no resolution in sight. So science lacks a precise, universally accepted definition of either "scientific" or "evidence."

Why should lawyers care about these philosophical and linguistic issues? Until 1993, most American courts, both state and federal, applied the "*Frye* test" and admitted purportedly scientific evidence if the subject matter had "gained general acceptance in the particular field to which it belongs." Frye v. United States, 293 F. 1013, 1014 (D.C. Cir. 1923). A trial judge had only to look to the expert's community of practice and decide, aided by testimony and/or published works, the straightforward factual question of whether the work being offered had achieved broad acceptance. Whether it was deserving of such acceptance was irrelevant. Now, however, that simple determination is not enough. In the federal courts and the majority of the states, trial judges must now evaluate whether "scientific" evidence is really scientific, *according to the standards of science.* Under the "*Daubert* trilogy" of United States Supreme Court cases — Daubert v. Merrell Dow Pharmaceuticals, Inc., 509 U.S. 579 (1993); General Electric Co. v. Joiner, 522 U.S. 136 (1997); and Kumho Tire Co. v. Carmichael, 526 U.S. 135 (1999) — and the state decisions that have adopted their standards, trial judges are required to make an independent determination of whether proffered scientific testimony is "ground[ed] in the methods and procedures of science." *Daubert,* 509 U.S. at 590. Judges must therefore have some understanding of what "the methods and procedures of science" are.

The legal requirements imposed by the *Frye* and *Daubert* tests are dealt with in great detail in Chapter 2. The purpose of this chapter is to introduce, in general terms, the problems that can arise when judges must apply scientific standards that they may not adequately understand, and about which scientists themselves may not agree. The cases and materials that follow will address such issues as the judge's duty to identify scientific knowledge, how scientists define what is "scientific," how judges think science works, and what can happen when the two are in conflict.

I. *THE JUDGE AS ARBITER OF SCIENCE*

Daubert v. Merrell Dow Pharmaceuticals, Inc.

509 U.S. 579 (1993)

JUSTICE BLACKMUN delivered the opinion of the Court.

In this case we are called upon to determine the standard for admitting expert scientific testimony in a federal trial.

I

Petitioners Jason Daubert and Eric Schuller are minor children born with serious birth defects. They and their parents sued respondent in California state court, alleging that the birth defects had been caused by the mothers' ingestion of Bendectin, a prescription antinausea drug marketed by respondent. Respondent removed the suits to federal court on diversity grounds.

After extensive discovery, respondent moved for summary judgment, contending that Bendectin does not cause birth defects in humans and that petitioners would be unable to come forward with any admissible evidence that it does. [The District Court held that the petitioners' expert testimony was inadmissible under the *Frye* general acceptance standard and the Ninth Circuit affirmed. The Supreme Court reversed, holding that Federal Rule of Evidence 702 requires independent judicial scrutiny of the reliability and relevance of scientific evidence.]

... [U]nder the [Federal] Rules [of Evidence] the trial judge must ensure that any and all scientific testimony or evidence admitted is not only relevant, but reliable.

The primary locus of this obligation is Rule 702, which clearly contemplates some degree of regulation of the subjects and theories about which an expert may testify. "*If scientific*, technical, or other specialized *knowledge will assist the trier of fact* to understand the evidence or to determine a fact in issue" an expert "may testify *thereto*." (Emphasis added.) The subject of an expert's testimony must be "scientific ... knowledge."[8] The adjective "scientific" implies a grounding in the methods and procedures of science. Similarly, the word "knowledge" connotes more than subjective belief or unsupported speculation. The term "applies to any body of known facts or to any body of ideas inferred from such facts or accepted as truths on good grounds." Webster's Third New International Dictionary 1252 (1986). Of course, it would be unreasonable to conclude that the subject of scientific testimony must be "known" to a certainty; arguably, there are no certainties in science. See, *e.g.*, Brief for Nicolaas Bloembergen et al. as *Amici Curiae* 9 ("Indeed, scientists do not assert that they know what is immutably 'true' — they are committed to searching for new, temporary, theories to explain, as best they can, phenomena"); Brief for American Association for the Advancement of Science et al. as *Amici Curiae* 7-8 ("Science is not an encyclopedic body of knowledge about the universe. Instead, it represents a *process* for proposing and refining theoretical explanations about the world that are subject to further testing and refinement" (emphasis in original)). But, in order to qualify as "scientific knowledge," an inference or assertion must be derived by the scientific method. Proposed testimony must be supported by appropriate validation — *i.e.*, "good grounds," based on what is known. In short, the requirement that an expert's testimony pertain to "scientific knowledge" establishes a standard of evidentiary reliability. ...

8. Rule 702 also applies to "technical, or other specialized knowledge." Our discussion is limited to the scientific context because that is the nature of the expertise offered here. [The Court developed a more flexible standard for nonscientific experts in *Kumho Tire*, the third case in the *Daubert* trilogy. See Chapter 2.]

Faced with a proffer of expert scientific testimony, then, the trial judge must determine at the outset, pursuant to Rule 104(a),[10] whether the expert is proposing to testify to (1) scientific knowledge that (2) will assist the trier of fact to understand or determine a fact in issue.[11] This entails a preliminary assessment of whether the reasoning or methodology underlying the testimony is scientifically valid and of whether that reasoning or methodology properly can be applied to the facts in issue. We are confident that federal judges possess the capacity to undertake this review. Many factors will bear on the inquiry, and we do not presume to set out a definitive checklist or test. But some general observations are appropriate.

Ordinarily, a key question to be answered in determining whether a theory or technique is scientific knowledge that will assist the trier of fact will be whether it can be (and has been) tested. "Scientific methodology today is based on generating hypotheses and testing them to see if they can be falsified; indeed, this methodology is what distinguishes science from other fields of human inquiry." Green, Expert Witnesses and Sufficiency of Evidence in Toxic Substances Litigation: The Legacy of *Agent Orange* and Bendectin Litigation, 86 Nw. U. L. Rev. 643, 645 (1992). See also C. Hempel, Philosophy of Natural Science 49 (1966) ("The statements constituting a scientific explanation must be capable of empirical test"); K. Popper, Conjectures and Refutations: The Growth of Scientific Knowledge 37 (5th ed. 1989) ("The criterion of the scientific status of a theory is its falsifiability, or refutability, or testability") (emphasis deleted).

Another pertinent consideration is whether the theory or technique has been subjected to peer review and publication. Publication (which is but one element of peer review) is not a *sine qua non* of admissibility; it does not necessarily correlate with reliability, see S. Jasanoff, The Fifth Branch: Science Advisors as Policymakers 61-76 (1990), and in some instances well-grounded but innovative theories will not have been published, see Horrobin, The Philosophical Basis of Peer Review and the Suppression of Innovation, 263 JAMA 1438 (1990). Some propositions, moreover, are too

10. Rule 104(a) provides:

"Preliminary questions concerning the qualification of a person to be a witness, the existence of a privilege, or the admissibility of evidence shall be determined by the court, subject to the provisions of subdivision (b) [pertaining to conditional admissions]. In making its determination it is not bound by the rules of evidence except those with respect to privileges."

These matters should be established by a preponderance of proof.

11. Although the *Frye* decision itself focused exclusively on "novel" scientific techniques, we do not read the requirements of Rule 702 to apply specially or exclusively to unconventional evidence. Of course, well-established propositions are less likely to be challenged than those that are novel, and they are more handily defended. Indeed, theories that are so firmly established as to have attained the status of scientific law, such as the laws of thermodynamics, properly are subject to judicial notice under Federal Rule of Evidence 201.

particular, too new, or of too limited interest to be published. But submission to the scrutiny of the scientific community is a component of "good science," in part because it increases the likelihood that substantive flaws in methodology will be detected. See J. Ziman, Reliable Knowledge: An Exploration of the Grounds for Belief in Science 130-133 (1978); Relman & Angell, How Good Is Peer Review?, 321 New Eng. J. Med. 827 (1989). The fact of publication (or lack thereof) in a peer reviewed journal thus will be a relevant, though not dispositive, consideration in assessing the scientific validity of a particular technique or methodology on which an opinion is premised.

Additionally, in the case of a particular scientific technique, the court ordinarily should consider the known or potential rate of error, see, *e.g.*, *United States* v. *Smith*, 869 F.2d 348, 353-354 (CA7 1989) (surveying studies of the error rate of spectrographic voice identification technique), and the existence and maintenance of standards controlling the technique's operation, see *United States* v. *Williams*, 583 F.2d 1194, 1198 (CA2 1978) (noting professional organization's standard governing spectrographic analysis), cert. denied, 439 U.S. 1117, 59 L. Ed. 2d 77, 99 S. Ct. 1025 (1979).

Finally, "general acceptance" can yet have a bearing on the inquiry. A "reliability assessment does not require, although it does permit, explicit identification of a relevant scientific community and an express determination of a particular degree of acceptance within that community." *United States* v. *Downing*, 753 F.2d at 1238. See also 3 Weinstein & Berger P702[03], pp. 702-41 to 702-42. Widespread acceptance can be an important factor in ruling particular evidence admissible, and "a known technique which has been able to attract only minimal support within the community," *Downing*, 753 F.2d at 1238, may properly be viewed with skepticism. . . .

CHIEF JUSTICE REHNQUIST, with whom JUSTICE STEVENS joins, concurring in part and dissenting in part.

[The dissenters concurred in the judgment that the *Frye* test should be superseded, but disagreed with some of the majority's "general observations" about how the new standard should be applied.] The Court speaks of its confidence that federal judges can make a "preliminary assessment of whether the reasoning or methodology underlying the testimony is scientifically valid and of whether that reasoning or methodology properly can be applied to the facts in issue." *Ante*, at 592-593. The Court then states that a "key question" to be answered in deciding whether something is "scientific knowledge" "will be whether it can be (and has been) tested." *Ante*, at 593. Following this sentence are three quotations from treatises, which not only speak of empirical testing, but one of which states that the " 'criterion of the scientific status of a theory is its falsifiability, or refutability, or testability.' " *Ibid.*

I defer to no one in my confidence in federal judges; but I am at a loss to know what is meant when it is said that the scientific status of a theory depends on its "falsifiability," and I suspect some of them will be, too.

I do not doubt that Rule 702 confides to the judge some gatekeeping responsibility in deciding questions of the admissibility of proffered expert testimony. But I do not think it imposes on them either the obligation or the authority to become amateur scientists in order to perform that role. I think the Court would be far better advised in this case to decide only the questions presented, and to leave the further development of this important area of the law to future cases.

NOTES AND QUESTIONS

1.   *Daubert* holds that, to satisfy Rule 702, "[t]he subject of an expert's testimony must be 'scientific . . . knowledge,'" and that "in order to qualify as 'scientific knowledge,' an inference or assertion must be derived by the scientific method." Thus, Rule 702 requires trial judges to determine whether the inferences and assertions of scientific experts are derived from the application of the scientific method. But how are they to know the scientific method when they see it? In other words, what is the Supreme Court's philosophy of science?

2.   Although the Court did "not presume to set out a definitive check-list or test," it did presume, under the guise of "general observations," to set out what have become famous as the "four *Daubert* factors": (1) whether the theory or technique "can be (and has been) tested," or falsified; (2) "whether the theory or technique has been subjected to peer review and publication"; (3) "the known or potential rate of error" of the technique; and (4) general acceptance, demoted from controlling factor to secondary consideration. One widespread practical criticism of these factors is that they call on trial judges to do too much. Whereas the majority was "confident that federal judges possess the capacity to undertake this review," the dissent was skeptical about trial judges functioning as "amateur scientists." To illustrate the problem, Chief Justice Rehnquist observed that "I am at a loss to know what is meant when it is said that the scientific status of a theory depends on its 'falsifiability,' and I suspect some of them will be, too." (If he had thought about it further, he might have been even more confused about what "error rate" means — see Section II.B *infra*.) There continues to be controversy over who was right. As frequent teachers of judges, the authors can affirm that the trial bench takes the *Daubert* duty seriously and works hard at it. Practicing lawyers and testifying experts report wide variation in judges' ability to know the scientific method when they see it. Earlier in the *Daubert* era, one federal district judge observed, somewhat sourly, that "[t]hings have changed in recent years. The language problem has expanded and not merely because world

commerce brings more languages into our courts. Rather, there are dozens of areas of scientific and technical expertise, and those who offer such testimony often speak in the functional equivalent of Urdu, and translation is impossible without understanding some principles of the relevant science." United States ex rel. Kokoraleis v. Director of the Ill. Dep't of Corrections, 963 F. Supp. 1473, 14— (N.D. Ill. 1997) (Zagel, J.).

3. A second, more substantive criticism of the *Daubert* factors is that they are too narrow. The contention is that the four factors properly apply only to science on the physics model, in which (at least ideally; see the next reading) hypotheses are developed and then tested in rigorous experiments—what is often called positivist, or "hard" science. Consequently, it is argued, the strict application of the factors may lead to the rejection of many kinds of expert analysis that fail to meet the standards of physics but are nonetheless "scientific" in the commonly understood meaning of the term (for example, the testimony of clinical physicians about the causes of disease, discussed in Chapter 8, Economic Analysis of Liability and Damages). The rest of this chapter is devoted to the exploration of this critique. We will explore alternative conceptions of the meaning of science, beginning with those of scientists themselves and then turning to those expressed by judges. The goal is to develop a general understanding of science and the scientific method that can serve as background for the study of specific scientific disciplines in the subsequent chapters.

II. HOW SCIENTISTS THINK ABOUT SCIENCE

A. The Philosophy of Science

How Science Works

Reference Manual on Scientific Evidence 69-75 (Federal Judicial Center, 2d ed. 2000)
David Goodstein

II. THEORIES OF SCIENCE . . .

A. FRANCIS BACON'S SCIENTIFIC METHOD

. . . If one asks a scientist the question, What is science?, the answer will almost surely be that science is a process, a way of examining the natural world and discovering important truths about it. In short, the essence of science is the scientific method.

That stirring description suffers from an important shortcoming. We don't really know what the scientific method is. There have been many attempts at formulating a general theory of how science works, or at least how it ought to work, starting, as we have seen, with Sir Francis Bacon's [the

Lord Chancellor of England in the early 1600s — a lawyer, not a scientist!].
Bacon's idea, that science proceeds through the collection of observations
without prejudice, has been rejected by all serious thinkers. Everything
about the way we do science — the language we use, the instruments we
use, the methods we use — depends on clear presuppositions about how
the world works. Modern science is full of things that cannot be observed
at all, such as force fields and complex molecules. At the most fundamental
level, it is impossible to observe nature without having some reason to choose
what is worth observing and what is not worth observing. Once one makes
that elementary choice, Bacon has been left behind.

B.   KARL POPPER'S FALSIFICATION THEORY

In [the twentieth] century, the ideas of the Austrian philosopher Sir
Karl Popper have had a profound effect on theories of the scientific method.
In contrast to Bacon, Popper believed all science begins with a prejudice, or
perhaps more politely, a theory or hypothesis. Nobody can say where the
theory comes from. Formulating the theory is the creative part of science,
and it cannot be analyzed within the realm of philosophy. However, once the
theory is in hand, Popper tells us, it is the duty of the scientist to extract from
it logical but unexpected predictions that, if they are shown by experiment
not to be correct, will serve to render the theory invalid.

Popper was deeply influenced by the fact that a theory can never be
proved right by agreement with observation, but it can be proved wrong by
disagreement with observation. Because of this asymmetry, science makes
progress uniquely by proving that good ideas are wrong so that they can be
replaced by even better ideas. Thus, Bacon's disinterested observer of nature
is replaced by Popper's skeptical theorist. The good Popperian scientist
somehow comes up with a hypothesis that fits all or most of the known
facts, then proceeds to attack that hypothesis at its weakest point by extracting from it predictions that can be shown to be false. This process is known as
falsification.

Popper's ideas have been fruitful in weaning the philosophy of science
away from the Baconian view and some other earlier theories, but they fall
short in a number of ways in describing correctly how science works. The first
of these is the observation that, although it may be impossible to prove a
theory is true by observation or experiment, it is nearly just as impossible to
prove one is false by these same methods. Almost without exception, in order
to extract a falsifiable prediction from a theory, it is necessary to make additional assumptions beyond the theory itself. Then, when the prediction turns
out to be false, it may well be one of the other assumptions, rather than the
theory itself, that is false. To take a simple example, early in the twentieth
century it was found that the orbits of the outermost planets did not quite
obey the predictions of Newton's laws of gravity and mechanics. Rather than
take this to be a falsification of Newton's laws, astronomers concluded the

orbits were being perturbed by an additional unseen body out there. They were right. That is precisely how the planet Pluto was discovered.

The apparent asymmetry between falsification and verification that lies at the heart of Popper's theory thus vanishes. But the difficulties with Popper's view go even beyond that problem. It takes a great deal of hard work to come up with a new theory that is consistent with nearly everything that is known in any area of science. Popper's notion that the scientist's duty is then to attack that theory at its most vulnerable point is fundamentally inconsistent with human nature. It would be impossible to invest the enormous amount of time and energy necessary to develop a new theory in any part of modern science if the primary purpose of all that work was to show that the theory was wrong.

This point is underlined by the fact that the behavior of the scientific community is not consistent with Popper's notion of how it should be. Credit in science is most often given for offering correct theories, not wrong ones, or for demonstrating the correctness of unexpected predictions, not for falsifying them. I know of no example of a Nobel Prize awarded to a scientist for falsifying his or her own theory.

C.   THOMAS KUHN'S PARADIGM SHIFTS

Another towering figure in the twentieth century theory of science is Thomas Kuhn. Kuhn was not a philosopher but a historian (more accurately, a physicist who retrained himself as a historian). It is Kuhn who popularized the word *paradigm,* which has today come to seem so inescapable.

A paradigm, for Kuhn, is a sort of consensual world view within which scientists work. It comprises an agreed upon set of assumptions, methods, language, and everything else needed to do science. Within a given paradigm, scientists make steady, incremental progress, doing what Kuhn calls "normal science."

As time goes on, difficulties and contradictions arise that cannot be resolved, but one way or another, they are swept under the rug, rather than being allowed to threaten the central paradigm. However, at a certain point, enough of these difficulties have accumulated so that the situation becomes intolerable. At that point, a scientific revolution occurs, shattering the paradigm and replacing it with an entirely new one.

The new paradigm is so radically different from the old that normal discourse between the practitioners of the two paradigms becomes impossible. They view the world in different ways and speak different languages. It isn't even possible to tell which of the two paradigms is superior, because they address different sets of problems. They are incommensurate. Thus, science does not progress incrementally, as the science textbooks would have it, except during periods of normal science. Every once in a while, a scientific revolution brings about a paradigm shift, and science heads off in an entirely new direction.

in commensurate', -

Kuhn's view was formed largely on the basis of two important historical revolutions. One was the original scientific revolution that started with Nicolaus Copernicus and culminated with the new mechanics of Isaac Newton. The very word *revolution,* whether it refers to the scientific kind, the political kind, or any other kind, refers metaphorically to the revolutions in the heavens that Copernicus described in a book, *De Revolutionibus Orbium Caelestium,* which was published as he lay dying in 1543. Before Copernicus, the dominant paradigm was the world view of ancient Greek philosophy, frozen in the fourth century B.C. ideas of Plato and Aristotle. After Newton, whose masterwork, *Philosophiae Naturalis Principia Mathematica,* was published in 1687, every scientist was a Newtonian, and Aristotelianism was banished forever from the world stage. It is even possible that Sir Francis Bacon's disinterested observer was a reaction to Aristotelian authority. Look to nature, not to the ancient texts, Bacon may have been saying.

The second revolution that served as an example for Kuhn occurred early in the twentieth century. In a headlong series of events that lasted a mere twenty-five years, the Newtonian paradigm was overturned and replaced with the new physics, in the form of quantum mechanics and Einstein's relativity. The second revolution, though it happened much faster, was no less profound than the first.

The idea that science proceeds by periods of normal activity punctuated by shattering breakthroughs that make scientists rethink the whole problem is an appealing one, especially to the scientists themselves, who know from personal experience that it really happens that way. Kuhn's contribution is important. It gives us a new and useful structure (a paradigm, one might say) for organizing the entire history of science.

Nevertheless, Kuhn's theory does suffer from a number of shortcomings as an explanation for how science works. One of them is that it contains no measure of how big the change must be in order to count as a revolution or paradigm shift. Most scientists will say that there is a paradigm shift in their laboratory every six months or so (or at least every time it becomes necessary to write another proposal for research support). That isn't exactly what Kuhn had in mind.

Another difficulty is that even when a paradigm shift is truly profound, the paradigms it separates are not necessarily incommensurate. The new sciences of quantum mechanics and relativity, for example, did indeed show that Newton's laws of mechanics were not the most fundamental laws of nature. However, they did not show that they were wrong. Quite the contrary, they showed why Newton's laws of mechanics were right: Newton's laws arose out of new laws that were even deeper and that covered a wider range of circumstances unimagined by Newton and his followers, that is, things as small as atoms, or nearly as fast as the speed of light, or as dense as black holes. In more familiar realms of experience, Newton's laws go on working just as well as they always did. Thus, there is no ambiguity at all about which paradigm is better. The new laws of quantum mechanics and relativity subsume and enhance the older Newtonian world.

D.   AN EVOLVED THEORY OF SCIENCE

If neither Bacon nor Popper nor Kuhn gives us a perfect description of what science is or how it works, nevertheless all three help us to gain a much deeper understanding of it all.

Scientists are not Baconian observers of nature, but all scientists become Baconians when it comes to describing their observations. Scientists are rigorously, even passionately honest about reporting scientific results and how they were obtained, in formal publications. Scientific data are the coin of the realm in science, and they are always treated with reverence. Those rare instances in which data are found to have been fabricated or altered in some way are always traumatic scandals of the first order.

Scientists are also not Popperian falsifiers of their own theories, but they don't have to be. They don't work in isolation. If a scientist has a rival with a different theory of the same phenomena, the rival will be more than happy to perform the Popperian duty of attacking the scientist's theory at its weakest point. Moreover, if falsification is no more definitive than verification, and scientists prefer in any case to be right rather than wrong, they nevertheless know how to hold verification to a very high standard. If a theory makes novel and unexpected predictions, and those predictions are verified by experiments that reveal new and useful or interesting phenomena, then the chances that the theory is correct are greatly enhanced. And even if it is not correct, it has been fruitful in the sense that it has led to the discovery of previously unknown phenomena that might prove useful in themselves and that will have to be explained by the next theory that comes along.

Finally, science does not, as Kuhn seemed to think, periodically self-destruct and need to start over again, but it does undergo startling changes of perspective that lead to new and, invariably, better ways of understanding the world. Thus, science does not proceed smoothly and incrementally, but it is one of the few areas of human endeavor that is truly progressive. There is no doubt at all that twentieth century science is better than nineteenth century science, and we can be absolutely confident that what will come along in the twenty-first century will be better still. One cannot say the same about, say, art or literature.

To all this, a couple of things must be added. The first is that science is, above all, an adversary process. It is an arena in which ideas do battle, with observations and data the tools of combat. The scientific debate is very different from what happens in a court of law, but just as in the law, it is crucial that every idea receive the most vigorous possible advocacy, just in case it might be right. Thus, the Popperian ideal of holding one's hypothesis in a skeptical and tentative way is not merely inconsistent with reality, it would be harmful to science if it were pursued. As I discuss shortly, not only ideas, but the scientists themselves engage in endless competition according to rules that, although they are nowhere written down, are nevertheless complex and binding.

In the competition among ideas, the institution of peer review plays a central role. Scientific articles submitted for publication and proposals for funding are often sent to anonymous experts in the field, in other words, peers of the author, for review. Peer review works superbly to separate valid science from nonsense, or, in Kuhnian terms, to ensure that the current paradigm has been respected.[11] It works less well as a means of choosing between competing valid ideas, in part because the peer doing the reviewing is often a competitor for the same resources (pages in prestigious journals, funds from government agencies) being sought by the authors. It works very poorly in catching cheating or fraud, because all scientists are socialized to believe that even their bitterest competitor is rigorously honest in the reporting of scientific results, making it easy to fool a referee with purposeful dishonesty if one wants to. Despite all of this, peer review is one of the sacred pillars of the scientific edifice.

NOTES AND QUESTIONS

1. Goodstein is a physics professor and senior administrator at Caltech, and thus at the center of "hard" scientific research. His article is a remarkably concise (if, in his term, "irreverent") survey of the history and philosophy of science. Which of the theories of science that Goodstein describes did the Supreme Court seem to adopt in *Daubert?* Here is Goodstein's answer to that question:

> In reading these four illustrative criteria mentioned by the Court, one is struck immediately by the specter of Karl Popper looming above the robed justices. (It's no mere illusion. The dependence on Popper is explicit in the written decision.) Popper alone is not enough, however, and the doctrine of falsification is supplemented by a bow to the institution of peer review, an acknowledgment of the scientific meaning of error, and a paradigm check (really, an inclusion of the earlier *Frye* standard).

11. The Supreme Court received differing views regarding the proper role of peer review. *Compare* Brief for Amici Curiae Daryl E. Chubin et al. at 10, Daubert v. Merrell Dow Pharms., Inc., 509 U.S. 579 (1993) (No. 92-102) ("peer review referees and editors limit their assessment of submitted articles to such matters as style, plausibility, and defensibility; they do not duplicate experiments from scratch or plow through reams of computer-generated data in order to guarantee accuracy or veracity or certainty"), *with* Brief for Amici Curiae New England Journal of Medicine, Journal of the American Medical Association, and Annals of Internal Medicine in Support of Respondent, Daubert v. Merrell Dow Pharms., Inc., 509 U.S. 579 (1993) (No. 92-102) (proposing that publication in a peer-reviewed journal be the primary criterion for admitting scientific evidence in the courtroom). *See generally* Daryl E. Chubin & Edward J. Hackett, Peerless Science: Peer Review and U.S. Science Policy (1990); Arnold S. Relman & Marcia Angell, *How Good Is Peer Review?* 321 New Eng. J. Med. 827-29 (1989). As a practicing scientist and frequent peer reviewer, I can testify that Chubin's view is correct.

All in all, I would score the decision a pretty good performance. The justices ventured into the treacherous crosscurrents of the philosophy of science — where even most scientists fear to tread — and emerged with at least their dignity intact. Falsifiability may not be a good way of doing science, but it's not the worst a posteriori way to judge science, and that's all that's required here. At least they managed to avoid the Popperian trap of demanding that the scientists be skeptical of their own ideas. The other considerations help lend substance and flexibility. The jury is still out (so to speak) on how well this decision will work in practice, but it's certainly an impressive attempt to serve justice, if not truth.

Id. at 82.

2.   The word "positivism" is often associated with the Popperian theory of science. Goodstein suggests that it is generally inadequate to account for how science is actually practiced. But is it a better fit for some scientific enterprises than others? In considering the adequacy of the positivist model, would it make sense to distinguish Goodstein's own physics from, say, clinical psychology? Is it a question of degree — are some sciences more Popperian than others? We return to this question in Section III *infra*.

3.   Other scientists are more sanguine ("reverent," perhaps?) about achieving the Popperian ideal than Goodstein. They tend to see a greater divide between scientific and legal approaches to proof, and to take a less generous view of the latter. See, for example, the *New England Journal of Medicine*'s post-*Daubert* editorial, which discusses ongoing litigation over the safety of breast implants:

> [W]hile the FDA was considering whether to remove breast implants from the market, public concern was mounting. When the implants were banned, the concern did not abate, because of the many women who already had breast implants. Frightening stories about the effects of breast implants swept through the media and were reified by repetition. The fact that implants occasionally leaked or ruptured, causing local problems, was well known, but the new stories focused primarily on anecdotes of serious systemic effects. Breast implants were said to cause arthritis or polymyositis or systemic lupus erythematosus. Since these are chronic disorders that are not always easily diagnosed and since they clearly can occur in women who do not have breast implants as well as in those who do, the postulated associations were very difficult to evaluate, and until now there has been little attempt to do so systematically.
>
> Despite the lack of published epidemiologic studies, the accumulated weight of anecdotes was taken by judges and juries as tantamount to proof of causation. Multimillion-dollar settlements followed, along with poignant stories in the media and appearances by plaintiffs on talk shows. All this added to the weight of the anecdotes, which in a circular way became accepted by the courts and the public as nearly incontrovertible evidence. Three manufacturers of breast implants finally decided that a lump settlement would be

anecdotes →

less expensive than to go on losing cases one by one, so they agreed to a class-action settlement, establishing a fund of $4.2 billion. . . .

What does this tell us about the way scientific issues are settled in the courtroom? As readers of the Journal know, scientific conclusions cannot be based on argument and opinion. There must be data. Yet, in the courtroom, acceptance of expert testimony on scientific questions usually turns on the "credibility" of the witness, not the validity of the evidence on which the witness's opinion is based. Furthermore, expert witnesses are selected by the contesting lawyers, often paid by them, and their testimony is reviewed in advance—circumstances unlikely to ensure objectivity or even competence. The resulting judgments are sometimes manifestly ludicrous. For example, one court awarded damages to a woman who claimed that she lost her psychic powers because of a computed tomographic scan. (This decision was later overturned.)

Marcia Angell, M.D., Editorial: *Do Breast Implants Cause Systemic Disease?—Science in the Courtroom*, 330 New England J. Med. 1748 (1994).*

B. The Scientific Ideal in Practice

Of Cherries, Fudge, and Onions: Science and Its Courtroom Perversion

64 Law & Contemporary Problems 213 (2001)
David W. Peterson and John M. Conley

II. A SCIENTIFIC IDEAL: THE DESIGNED EXPERIMENT

A. THE SALK VACCINE TRIALS

As of the early 1950s, the poliomyelitis virus was a scourge of America's children; hundreds of thousands were afflicted, and many were disabled for life. Among several vaccines under development, the one produced by √ Dr. Jonas Salk showed considerable promise.[23] The United States Public Health Service decided to conduct a very large-scale experiment to determine its effectiveness. Ultimately, about two million school children were involved in the tests, though only a fraction of them actually received the vaccine.

In designing the experiment, the Public Health Service attempted to take account of a variety of special considerations. The first was the nature of the disease itself. Polio is a hygiene-related disease: children who live in unhygienic environments are more likely to contract polio than those who live in cleaner environments. Perversely, it is the latter children who are most severely affected when they do contract the disease; the former are likely to be exposed early to the polio virus, so they tend to suffer only mildly

*Reprinted with permission of Massachusetts Medical Society and the author.
23. See David Freedman et al., *Statistics* 3[-7] (2d ed. 1991).

and to develop an immunity to further harm. Polio is also contagious, so that if one second-grader is infected, there is an increased chance that his or her classmates will be infected. Furthermore, polio is epidemic, so the incidence is much greater in some years than in others.

Second, there were ethical and technical considerations distinct from the nature of the disease. Clearly, one could not ethically require that any particular child be vaccinated with the experimental vaccine without permission from the child's parents or guardian. But it is possible that children whose parents would grant permission would differ in some material and systematic ways from children whose parents would withhold permission. For example, it might be that well-educated and relatively affluent parents would tend to grant permission, while less well-educated and less affluent parents would not. A potential result is that relatively many children living in hygienic circumstances would be permitted to take part in the study, and relatively few of those living in less hygienic conditions. This imbalance could seriously skew the results of the study.

There is also the problem that the behavior of the child or the parents might be influenced by the fact that the child had been vaccinated. A child thus protected need not be quite as cautious in avoiding possible exposure to polio, and therefore might tend to engage in riskier behavior than his non-vaccinated neighbor. This too could seriously distort the study results. Moreover, since polio comes in both mild and severe forms, it is not always clear whether a child has contracted the virus. As a result, a clinician examining a child who had been vaccinated might be less inclined to diagnose polio for that child than for her unvaccinated neighbor.

Sorting through this web of considerations, the Public Health Service decided upon the following course of action. First, it selected schools across the nation where the incidence of polio was relatively high. It then sought the permission of parents of first, second, and third graders for their children to be vaccinated as part of the study. Half of the participating children were selected *at random* and injected with the Salk vaccine. The other half of the subjects were injected with a placebo, a saline solution designed to have no medical effect whatsoever. The children and guardians did not know whether a child received the vaccine or the placebo. All of the children — both those who received the Salk vaccine and those who received the placebo — were monitored over the ensuing months by clinicians who also were not told which of the children had received which treatment.

An experiment of this sort is termed randomized and double-blind. It is randomized because the choice of whom to give the real vaccine is made by the toss of a coin or some other equally detached chance process. This process virtually guarantees that there will be no systematic difference between the group of children given the real vaccine and those who are given the false vaccine. It is blind in the first instance because the children and their parents are unaware of whether they have actually been vaccinated.

Consequently, there is virtually no chance that the vaccinated children, as a group, will behave any differently from those who were given the false vaccine. It is blind in the second instance because the people evaluating the health of the children do not know which of their subjects received the Salk vaccine and which received the placebo. As a result, it is virtually certain that the same methods and standards for diagnosis will be used for the vaccinated group as for the placebo group.

In all, about 200,000 students received the Salk vaccine and about 200,000 received the placebo in this phase of the experiment. The incidence of polio among the vaccinated group was approximately twenty-eight cases per 100,000, while that among the placebo group was about seventy-one cases per 100,000. Given the randomized, double-blind construction of this experiment, there are only two possible explanations for these results. The first is that the Salk vaccine really differed from the placebo in its effect on polio and that the difference was in the direction of reducing polio. The second is that the Salk vaccine was no different from the placebo in its effect on polio, and that the observed reduction in the incidence in polio was due solely to the manner in which children were assigned to the treatment groups. In other words, the children who contracted polio were destined to get it regardless of their treatment and the fact that most of them were placed in the group given the placebo was due purely to the luck of the coin toss. . . .

Part of the genius of this experimental design is that one can calculate the probability that, if indeed the Salk vaccine were identical to the placebo in its effect on the polio virus, the coin toss mechanism would result in so many of the children predestined to contract polio being assigned to the placebo group. That probability is about one in a billion. Thus, it seems safe to say that the difference in the incidence of polio between the Salk group and the placebo group cannot reasonably be attributed to the random assignment of children to treatment and placebo groups. The only remaining possibility is that the difference was caused by the greater effectiveness of the Salk vaccine. . . .

This is the logic of the ideal scientific experiment. The design features of random assignment and double-blinding virtually rule out the possibility of systematic differences between the experimental and control groups other than exposure to the suspected causal agent. When [statistical testing] indicates that chance is too unlikely an explanation for an observed disparity in outcomes, the only alternative is to conclude that the agent's causal effect is real.

The problem is that few questions, scientific or otherwise, can be settled with the elegant finality of the Salk trials. This is particularly true in legal contexts, where the evidence is almost never so neat. In many instances, logistical or ethical barriers preclude a true experiment. Researchers are relegated to uncontrolled observational studies or after-the-fact data analysis. In all such cases, the focus on the suspected causal agent can never be as sharp as in the ideal, well-designed experiment.

These situations have proved to be particularly troubling for courts under the *Daubert* regime. When the only scientific evidence of causation falls short of the Salk trials' gold standard, as it does in most cases, does it comport sufficiently with the scientific method to be admissible? That is, is it sufficiently reliable to be translated into legal causation? This is precisely the question that troubled the courts that heard the *Daubert* case itself as they wrestled with the issue of whether Bendectin could be reliably shown to cause birth defects.

NOTES AND QUESTIONS

1.   Do you see why the authors describe the Salk vaccine trials as the scientific "gold standard"? Does this research at least approximate the Popperian ideal? What was the researchers' hypothesis? How did they test it? Why did they reach the conclusion that they did? As you will see in Chapter 3, the methods of statistical inference introduce some complexities into the hypothesis-testing process that are not discussed in this excerpt.

2.   Assume that a qualified scientist wished to testify in a federal court that the Salk vaccine is effective in preventing polio. Assume that the results of the vaccine trials had been published in a peer-reviewed journal. How would the expert's assertion fare under the other three *Daubert* factors? Has it been tested/falsified? What might "error rate" mean here? How would you assess "general acceptance"?

3.   As Peterson and Conley contend, the "gold standard" is rarely achieved in science, and particularly the science that experts regularly testify about. As the next section illustrates, scientific evidence offered in court is often less Popperian. As the next two cases illustrate, judges have recognized this problem and struggled to deal with it.

III.   HOW THE COURTS UNDERSTAND SCIENCE: IRRECONCILABLE DIFFERENCES?

The problem of dealing with scientific evidence is not new:

The federal judiciary's love-hate relationship with scientific evidence dates back to at least 1908. In that year, in *Muller v. Oregon*,[1] the Supreme Court received the eponymous "Brandeis brief." Louis Brandeis, defending

1. 208 U.S. 412 (1908).

an Oregon statute that limited the working hours of women, submitted "a very copious collection" of authorities purporting to show the particular vulnerability of women in the turn-of-the-century workplace.[2] The Court upheld the law, commenting on Brandeis' submission with sibylline brevity: "It may not be amiss, in the present case, before examining the constitutional question, to notice the course of legislation as well as expressions of opinion from other than judicial sources"[3] Drawing on Brandeis' brief, the Court found "[t]hat woman's physical structure and the performance of maternal functions place her at a disadvantage in the struggle for subsistence."[4]

Since *Muller*, the courts' attitudes toward science in the courtroom have run the gamut from uncritical enthusiasm to dismissive Luddism, with stops at all intermediate points. Just nineteen years after *Muller*, Oliver Wendell Holmes, Jr. led the Supreme Court into the depths of evangelical credulity with his infamous opinion in *Buck v. Bell* upholding the compulsory sterilization of "imbeciles" on the basis of turn-of-the-century theories of intelligence testing.[5] A generation later, in footnote eleven of its opinion in *Brown v. Board of Education*, the Court turned to science to support its finding of constitutional fact that separate education is inherently unequal.[6] In the 1970s, as employment discrimination litigation proliferated, the Court plunged into detailed questions of scientific method, endorsing particular tests of the statistical significance of racial disparities in hiring.[7] Over the last ten years, particularly in its death penalty jurisprudence, the Court has displayed a more skeptical attitude toward scientific evidence. Sometimes this skepticism has expressed itself in the form of detailed critiques of particular research;[8] at other times, Court majorities have questioned whether broad-based scientific studies can ever be probative of individual constitutional violations.[9] Categorizing trends in the lower court's reception of scientific evidence would be a book-length undertaking. For background purposes, suffice it to say that one can find case support for almost any side of nearly every scientific question that has ever come before the courts.

2. *Id.* at 419.
3. *Id.*
4. *Id.* at 421.
5. 274 U.S. 200, 207 (1927).
6. 347 U.S. 483, 494 n.11 (1954).
7. Hazelwood Sch. Dist. v. United States, 433 U.S. 299, 308 n.14 (1977) (endorsing the proposition that employer's denial of discrimination will be "suspect" where representation of protected group in employer's workforce is more than two or three standard deviations below what would be expected on basis of population data); Castenada v. Partida, 430 U.S. 482, 466 n.17 (1976) (same).
8. *See e.g.,* Lockhart v. McCree, 476 U.S. 162, 170-73 (1976) (criticizing studies intended to show bias of guilt-phase juries in capital cases).
9. *See e.g.,* McClesky v. Kemp, 481 U.S. 279, 292-95 (1987) (questioning whether social science data can ever prove sentencing to be racially discriminatory in any particular case).

John M. Conley and David W. Peterson, *The Science of Gatekeeping: The Federal Judicial Center's New* Reference Manual on Scientific Evidence, 74 N.C.L. Rev. 1183, 1184-85 (1996).

The first of the two cases that follow lays out a strongly Popperian understanding of "hard" science, and then attempts to categorize the work of the practicing physician. The second discusses the special problems of dealing with the "soft," statistically based social sciences. Be sure to consult the notes after the cases, as each has an unusual and significant history, and each is treated in further detail in subsequent chapters.

— hard sciences vs. soft science

Moore v. Ashland Chemical, Inc.

126 F.3d 679 (5th Cir. 1997), *superseded by* 151 F.3d 269
(5th Cir. 1998)(en banc)

[Moore claimed that his rare lung disease was caused by exposure to toluene on the job and sued his employer. In attempting to prove causation, he relied primarily on the opinions of the clinical physicians who cared for him. The district court rejected these opinions under *Daubert*. In this, its initial opinion, the Fifth Circuit reversed, holding that the district court had abused its discretion in excluding the doctors' testimony.]

[C]linical medicine (as opposed to research and laboratory medical science) is not a hard science discipline; its goals, subject matter, conditions of study and well developed methodology are sui generis and quite different from that of hard science and its methodology. . . .

A. HARD SCIENTIFIC KNOWLEDGE

Speaking specifically of "scientific knowledge," the [*Daubert*] Court stated that the adjective " 'scientific' implies a grounding in the methods and procedures of science." 509 U.S. at 592. The Court elaborated:

'Science is not an encyclopedic body of knowledge about the universe. Instead, it represents a *process* for proposing and refining theoretical explanations about the world that are subject to further testing and refinement. . . . '
But, in order to qualify as 'scientific knowledge,' an inference or assertion must be derived by the scientific method. . . .

Thus, the *Daubert* Court defined "scientific knowledge" in terms of "hard science" or "Newtonian science" i.e., knowledge obtained and tested through "the scientific method," of which Sir Issac Newton was the leading exponent. . . .

The methodology of hard or Newtonian science is what distinguishes it from other fields of human inquiry. See Michael D. Green, *Expert Witnesses and Sufficiency of Evidence in Toxic Substances Litigation: The Legacy of Agent*

Orange and Bendectin Litigation, 86 NW.U.L.REV. 643, 645 (1992). "Scientific methodology today is based on generating hypotheses and testing them to see if they can be falsified. . . . Theoretically, therefore, hypotheses are not affirmatively proved, only falsified. Of course, if a hypothesis repeatedly withstands falsification, one may tend to accept it even if conditionally true." *Id.* at 645-646 (citing Karl R. Popper, *The Logic of Scientific Discovery* (1965); David L. Faigman, *To Have and Have Not: Assessing the Value of Social Science to the Law as Science and Policy,* 38 EMORY L.J. 1005, 101517 (1989); *Interdisciplinary Panel on Carcinogenicity, Criteria for Evidence of Chemical Carcinogenicity,* 225 SCI. 682, 683 (1984)). . . .

In *Daubert,* the Court indicated that, (1) "scientific knowledge" within Rule 702 means principles, theories, techniques or inferences derived by the scientific method or by a body of sound scientific methods; and (2) that the proffered expert's opinion, inference, or testimony based on scientific knowledge, in order to have evidentiary reliability or trustworthiness, must be derived or inferred by the same methods. *Id.* at 590 n.9; *see also* the court's "general observations" on principal scientific methods. *Id.* at 593-594.

By the same token, we conclude that, under Rule 702, an opinion based on other technical or specialized knowledge, must be grounded in the principles, methods and procedures of the particular field of knowledge involved. Every discipline employs a body of methods, rules, and postulates, i.e., methodology, both in its ordinary functions and in developing and adopting new concepts, techniques, and analogues. Therefore, the "knowledge" of each discipline, under Rule 702, is both its principles and methodology and the theories, techniques or inferences produced through its methodology. Thus, the proffered opinion of any expert in a field of knowledge, in order to be evidentiarily reliable, must either be based soundly on the current knowledge, principles and methodology of the expert's discipline or be soundly inferred or derived therefrom. . . .

F. THE *DAUBERT* "FACTORS" ARE HARD SCIENTIFIC METHODS THAT GENERALLY ARE INAPPROPRIATE FOR THE RELIABILITY ASSESSMENT OF CLINICAL MEDICAL TESTIMONY.

After declaring that evidentiary reliability of an expert's scientific opinion depends on whether it is soundly grounded in the the scientific method, the *Daubert* Court identified several individual methods or techniques within the body of hard or Newtonian scientific methodology as appropriate for trial judges' use in testing the methodology-relatedness of particular hard scientific opinion proffers. *Daubert,* 509 U.S. at 593. These hard scientific methods, now sometimes called "*Daubert* factors," are empirical testing, peer review and publication, known or potential rate of error, the existence and maintenance of operational standards, and acceptance within a relevant scientific community. *Id.* at 593-94.

Because the objectives, functions, subject matter and methodology of hard science vary significantly from those of the discipline of clinical medicine, as distinguished from research or laboratory medicine, the hard science techniques or methods that became the *"Daubert* factors" generally are not appropriate for assessing the evidentiary reliability of a proffer of expert clinical medical testimony.

First, the goals of the disciplines of clinical medicine and hard or Newtonian science are different. In hard science, the usual motive is inquiring: to gain a new understanding of some mechanism of nature. Alvan R. Feinstein, *Clinical Judgment* 22 (1967) [hereinafter Feinstein]. In contrast, the care and treatment of the individual patient is the ultimate, specific act that characterizes a clinical physician. *Id.* at 27; Pellegrino and Thomasma, *For The Patient's Good* 71 (1988); Pellegrino and Thomasma, *A Philosophical Basis of Medical Practice* 120 (1981) ("The whole process is ordained to a specific practical end—a right action for a particular patient—and . . . this end must modulate each step leading to it in important ways."). The clinical physician, therefore, must take account of the immediacy of the problem confronting her for she bears an essential relationship to each patient. Additionally, she has many human values to consider—ethics, compassion, and must have a willingness to take responsibility in the face of the unknown. Edmond A. Murphy, *The Logic of Medicine* 6 (1976) [hereinafter Murphy]. The pursuit of these different goals—of hard science and clinical medicine—serves to shape the distinct objectives of the scientific experiment and the clinical treatment of a patient:

> In clinical treatment, the main motives are remedial, or prophylactic: to change what nature has done or to prevent what it may do. In laboratory work, the premise is innovative: the goal is to test a new hypothesis or a new procedure. In ordinary clinical treatment, the premise is repetitive: the goal is to reproduce (or surpass) the best results of experiments conducted before in similar circumstances. A clinician chooses treatment in a new situation by reviewing what was done and what happened in previous situations that resembled the one at hand; he then selects whatever mode of treatment had the most successful outcome in the past. *Id.* at 22.

In ordinary clinical treatment, the purpose is not to gain new knowledge but to repeat a success of the past. *Id.* at 23.

Second, the subject matter and conditions of study are different. "In laboratory work, the experimental material is an intact animal, a part of a person or of an animal, or an inanimate system; in clinical treatment, the material is an intact human being." *Id.* at 22. The hard scientist initiates the experiment at a time of his own convenience and chooses the material usually without regard to its desire or consent for participation. *Id.* In clinical medicine, the patient initiates the treatment, choosing the time, place, duration, and clinician. *Id.* "The physician is not studying the properties of chemical compounds in a test tube; he cannot postpone dealing with cancer in a patient for fifty years because he hopes by then to have a much clearer insight into the nature of the disorder." *Id.*

Finally, clinical medicine and hard science have markedly different methodologies. A clinician observes at least three types of data for each patient who undergoes treatment: A disease in morphologic, chemical, microbiologic, physiologic, or other impersonal terms; the host in whom the disease occurs and his environmental background, including his personal properties (such as age, race, sex, and education) and external surroundings (such as geographic location, occupation, and financial and social status) before the disease began; and the illness that occurs in the interaction between the disease and its environmental host, consisting of clinical phenomena: the host's subjective sensations, or "symptoms," and "signs," which are findings discerned objectively during the physical examination. Feinstein, at 24-25.

Using these data, the clinician determines a present diagnosis (which gives the disease a name and tells what is wrong), a past etiology and pathogenesis (or how it got that way), and a future prognosis and therapy (or what to do about it). *Id.* at 25. Some of the data used by the clinician can often be obtained by examining the patient's fluids, cells, tissues, excreta, roentgenograms, graphic tracings, and other derivative substances. The patient's personal environmental data can often be elicited by nurses, secretaries, social workers, or other interviewers. But the history-taking, physical examination, and the determination of symptoms and signs can properly be done only by a doctor skilled in the clinical procedures described above. *Id.* "Moreover, the [clinical physician's] capacity to make judgments in cases of a kind which he has never seen before must depend ultimately on a cultivated capacity to see equivalences between quite disparate things, that is, on analogy." Murphy, at 9.

In sum, hard or Newtonian scientific knowledge does not comprehend all subjects that theoretically might be subjected to its methodology. It is knowledge of a particular and limited kind, gathered or tested by a particular and characteristic method. T.H. Savory, *The Language of Science* (1953). Although clinical medicine utilizes parts of some hard sciences, clinical medicine and many of its subsidiary fields are not hard sciences. The purposes, criteria, values and methods of hard or Newtonian science and clinical medicine are far from identical. Fred A. Mettler, *The Medical Sourcebook* xxxiv (1959). Consequently, the *Daubert* factors, which are hard scientific methods selected from the body of hard scientific knowledge and methodology generally are not appropriate for use in assessing the relevance and reliability of clinical medical testimony. Instead, the trial court as gatekeeper should determine whether the doctor's proposed testimony as a clinical physician is soundly grounded in the principles and methodology of his field of clinical medicine.[2]

McCleskey v. Kemp

753 F.2d 877 (11th Cir. 1985), *aff'd,* 481 U.S. 279 (1987)

[McCleskey was convicted of murder and sentenced to death in the Georgia state courts. In a federal habeas corpus petition, he challenged the conviction and sentence on several grounds. In support of a constitutional argument, he offered a now-famous "regression analysis" (a statistical technique that is discussed in Chapter 3, Statistical Inference; the regression analysis in this case is also discussed) that purported to show that the odds of receiving the death sentence were substantially higher for black than white defendants, especially when the victim was white. The petition was rejected at every level.]

SOCIAL SCIENCE RESEARCH EVIDENCE

To some extent a broad issue before this Court concerns the role that social science is to have in judicial decisionmaking. Social science is a broad-based field consisting of many specialized discipline areas, such as psychology, anthropology, economics, political science, history and sociology. *Cf.* Sperlich, *Social Science Evidence and the Courts: Reaching Beyond the Advisory Process,* 63 Judicature 280, 283 n. 14 (1980). Research . . . is conducted under both laboratory controlled situations and uncontrolled conditions, such as real life observational situations, throughout the disciplines. The broad objectives for social science research are to better understand mankind and its institutions in order to more effectively plan, predict, modify and enhance society's and the individual's circumstances. Social science as a *nonexact* science is always mindful that its research is dealing with highly complex behavioral patterns and institutions that exist in a highly technical society. At best, this research "models" and "reflects" society and provides society with trends and information for broad-based generalizations. The researcher's intent is to use the conclusions from research to predict, plan, describe, explain, understand or modify. To utilize conclusions from

2. The *Daubert* factors may be relevant and appropriate, however, in assessing other types of expert evidence outside the realm of hard science. For example, this court and others have recognized the utility of testing as a factor for assessing the reliability of proffered expert engineering testimony in alternative design cases. *Watkins v. Telsmith, Inc.,* 121 F.3d 984 (5th Cir. 1997); *Cummins v. Lyle Industries,* 93 F.3d 362 (7th Cir. 1996); *Peitzmeier v. Hennessy Industries, Inc.,* 97 F.3d 293 (8th Cir. 1996). It is self evident, of course, that an engineer's proffered conclusion as to a feasible alternative design lends itself to verification by controlled testing or experimentation, whereas a medical patient usually cannot practicably, ethically or humanely be subjected to experimentation under conditions like those believed by a clinical physician to have caused the patient's disease simply to verify the doctor's proffered opinion.

such research to explain the specific intent of a specific behavioral situation goes beyond the legitimate uses for such research. Even when this research is at a high level of exactness, in design and results, social scientists readily admit their steadfast hesitancies to conclude such results can explain specific behavioral actions in a certain situation.

The judiciary is aware of the potential limitations inherent in such research: (1) the imprecise nature of the discipline; (2) the potential inaccuracies in presented data; (3) the potential bias of the researcher; (4) the inherent problems with the methodology; (5) the specialized training needed to assess and utilize the data competently; and (6) the debatability of the appropriateness for courts to use empirical evidence in decisionmaking. *Cf.* Henry, *Introduction: A Journey into the Future — The Role of Empirical Evidence in Developing Labor Law,* 1981 U. Ill. L. Rev. 1, 4; Sperlich, 63 Judicature at 283 n. 14.

Historically, beginning with "Louis Brandeis' use of empirical evidence before the Supreme Court . . . persuasive social science evidence has been presented to the courts." Forst, Rhodes & Wellford, *Sentencing and Social Science: Research for the Formulation of Federal Guidelines,* 7 Hofstra L.Rev. 355 (1979). *See Muller v. Oregon,* 208 U.S. 412, 28 S. Ct. 324, 52 L. Ed. 551 (1908); *Brown v. Board of Education,* 347 U.S. 483, 74 S. Ct. 686, 98 L. Ed. 873 (1954). The Brandeis brief presented social facts as corroborative in the judicial decisionmaking process. The Brandeis brief "is a well-known technique for asking the court to take judicial notice of social facts." Sperlich, 63 Judicature at 280, 285 n. 31. "It does not solve the problem of how to bring valid scientific materials to the attention of the court. . . . Brandeis did not argue that the data were valid, only that they existed. . . . The main contribution . . . was to make extra-legal data readily available to the court." *Id.*

This Court has taken a position that social science research does play a role in judicial decisionmaking in certain situations, even in light of the limitations of such research. Statistics have been used primarily in cases addressing discrimination.

Statistical analysis is useful only to show facts. In evidentiary terms, statistical studies based on correlation are circumstantial evidence. They are not direct evidence. *Teamsters v. United States,* 431 U.S. 324, 340, 97 S. Ct. 1843, 1856, 52 L. Ed. 2d 396 (1977). Statistical studies do not purport to state what the law is in a given situation. The law is applied to the facts as revealed by the research.

In this case the realities examined, based on a certain set of facts reduced to data, were the descriptive characteristics and numbers of persons being sentenced to death in Georgia. Such studies reveal, as circumstantial evidence through their study analyses and results, possible, or probable, relationships that may exist in the realities studied. The usefulness of statistics obviously depends upon what is attempted to be proved by them. If disparate impact is sought to be proved, statistics are more useful than if the causes of that impact must be proved. Where intent and motivation must be proved, the statistics have even less utility. This Court has said in discrimination cases, however, "that while statistics alone usually cannot establish intentional discrimination, under certain limited circumstances they might." *Spencer v. Zant*, 715 F.2d 1562, 1581 (11th Cir. 1983), *on pet. for reh'g and for reh'g en banc*, 729 F.2d 1293 (11th Cir. 1984). These limited circumstances are where the statistical evidence of racially disproportionate impact is so strong as to permit no inference other than that the results are the product of a racially discriminatory intent or purpose. . . .

Much has been written about the relationship of law and the social science. "If social science cannot produce the required answers, and it probably cannot, its use is likely to continue to lead to a disjointed incrementalism." Daniels, *Social Science and Death Penalty Cases*, 1 Law & Pol'y Q. 336, 367 (1979). "Social science can probably make its greatest contribution to legal theory by investigating the causal forces behind judicial, legislative and administrative decisionmaking and by probing the general effects of such decisions." Nagel, *Law and the Social Sciences: What Can Social Science Contribute?*, 356 A.B.A.J. 356, 357-58 (1965).

With these observations, this Court accepts social science research for what the social scientist should claim for it. As in all circumstantial evidence cases, the inferences to be drawn from the statistics are for the factfinder, but the statistics are accepted to show the circumstances.

NOTES AND QUESTIONS

1.   In *Moore*, the court confronted the problem of how to categorize the diagnostic opinions of clinical physicians ("differential diagnosis," as it is termed in medicine) under *Daubert*. Most people would probably describe the practice of Western allopathic medicine as "scientific," and the doctors who conduct it as informed by scientific research, even though they may not be active researchers themselves. The dilemma for the courts is that an individual diagnosis does not — literally, at least — possess *any* of the four identifying features of positivist science that *Daubert* identified. It is not testable: If the single patient fails to recover, that does not "falsify" the diagnosis, no more than the patient's recovery would validate it; most patients get better regardless of what the doctor does. Individual diagnoses are almost never published. An individual diagnosis has no "error rate." And although differential diagnosis is itself generally accepted in the medical community, that label cannot be meaningfully applied to a single case. Courts are thus left with two choices: to reject differential diagnosis as failed or "bad" positivist science, or to accept it as a "good" example of a hybrid: a complex, judgmental art that is nonetheless strongly rooted in a vast body of evolving scientific knowledge. In the opinion above, the Fifth Circuit opted for the second approach, explaining with considerable sophistication how and why

differential diagnosis diverges from the positivist model. It was willing to admit the evidence as long as the "doctor's proposed testimony as a clinical physician is soundly grounded in the principles and methodology of his field of clinical medicine." Is this an invitation to unreliable expert testimony? Can a speculative diagnosis be admitted as long as the doctor says, "I did what clinical physicians do, and here's what I think"? Or does the court's standard presume that there will be a close nexus between the underlying science and the physician's ultimate judgment? In its en banc opinion in *Moore* the next year (reproduced in Chapter 8, Economic Analysis of Liability and Damages), the Fifth Circuit did a 180-degree turn, effectively relegating differential diagnosis to the "failed positivism" category. As discussed in Chapter 8, opinions of treating physicians continue to fall through the evidentiary cracks, leading to inconsistent decisions on very similar facts.

2.   The differential diagnosis dilemma is an aspect of a more general problem: what to do with experts who are in some sense "scientific" but whose work cannot satisfy the positivist standards of *Daubert*. Some of these experts — civil engineers, for example — are like the clinical physicians in *Moore*. They are practitioners of a discipline that exists independent of the law who make individualized judgments on the basis of indisputably "scientific" knowledge. Other types of experts have developed their disciplines specifically to answer questions posed by the legal system, and those disciplines vary widely with respect to how scientific their foundations are. (See, for example, the treatment of the various "forensic sciences" in Chapter 5, Expert Testimony about Behavioral Science.) To some of these latter experts, footnote 8 in *Daubert*, which limits the holding to "scientific" experts, presented a temptation: Renounce any claim to being "scientific," thereby evading the four-factor *Daubert* analysis, and seek admissibility instead under some other, presumably lower, standard for "technical, or other specialized knowledge." As we will see in the next chapter, in its 1999 *Kumho Tire* opinion, the Supreme Court held that trial courts must scrutinize such evidence for reliability but may apply the *Daubert* factors in a flexible way. When you study *Kumho Tire*, ask yourself whether the first *Moore* opinion anticipated the Supreme Court's approach.

3.   *McCleskey*, a pre-*Daubert* case, dealt with the special problems presented by social science evidence. The social sciences include psychology, sociology, anthropology, linguistics, and (by some definitions) economics. Much social science is qualitative and interpretive. For example, anthropologists and some sociologists interpret culture on the basis of observation and interviews, some clinical psychologists use interviews and case histories to diagnose and treat patients, and "forensic linguists" interpret crucial language in such varied contexts as criminal conspiracies and ransom demands. Such work, which tends to focus on the behavior of individuals, is clearly non- (or even aggressively anti-) positivist, falling well outside *Daubert's* four-factor definition of "scientific." Other social science, however — for

example, experimental psychology, quantitative sociology, and much of economics — is classically positivist, with hypotheses subjected to rigorous statistical testing. The regression analysis in *McCleskey* is in this tradition. The Eleventh Circuit's problem (the Supreme Court majority later said almost the same thing) was not that the research was "unscientific," but that its implications were too general: "Even when this research is at a high level of exactness, in design and results, social scientists readily admit their steadfast hesitancies to conclude such results can explain specific behavioral actions in a certain situation." (Post-*Daubert,* this objection would probably be made under the heading of relevancy.) Is the court putting social science in a head's-I-win-tails-you-lose bind? It seems to be demanding that social science evidence focus more specifically on the individual case at hand. But such evidence would likely have to be interpretive, and the positivist "high level of exactness" found in this case would therefore be diminished.

4. After reading the next chapter, as well as Chapter 3, Statistical Inference, and Chapter 5, Expert Testimony About Behavioral Science, ask yourself whether the *Daubert* regime has made it harder or easier to admit social science evidence in general. Consider the following:

> If a case concerning nightmares had arisen during Freud's time, would the *Daubert* standard have permitted him to testify? . . . Freud's elaborate theory of dream process . . . did depend upon repeated empirical observations of patients in psychoanalysis, but not in a replicable way. It depended more heavily on Freud's non-replicable interpretation of those observations. Freud asserted that psychoanalysis could trace most dreams to sexual issues or, as he put it, to 'erotic wishes'. . . . It is difficult to conceive an experiment that would falsify these theories. Therefore, even though Freud might have had much to say that might assist a jury in his time, *Daubert* probably would not have permitted him to say it.

David Crump, *The Trouble with* Daubert-Kumho: *Reconsidering the Supreme Court's Philosophy of Science,* 68 Mo. L. Rev. 1, 24 (2003).

5. The best general source on social science evidence is John Monahan & Laurens Walker, *Social Science in Law* (6th ed. 2002); for shorter treatments that focus on linguistics and psychology see John M. Conley & William M. O'Barr, *Just Words: Law, Language, and Power* (2d ed. 2005), ch. 10, and Lawrence M. Solan & Peter M. Tiersma, *Speaking of Crime* (2006).

CHAPTER 2
EXPERT EVIDENCE:
RULES AND CASES

This chapter is divided into three parts. The first part provides an in-depth consideration of the essential evidentiary concerns relative to both the Federal Rules of Evidence and cases interpreting those rules (and similar state rules) that regulate the admission of expert testimony. The second part considers the special standards that have been judicially created to govern the admission of expert testimony. This second section addresses the *Frye* general acceptance standard, the *Daubert* reliability standard, and the Supreme Court's trilogy of cases on expert evidence. The third part of the chapter concludes with a review of additional considerations and rules that govern opinion testimony.

I. FRE 702 AND GENERAL CONSIDERATIONS

Before or during trial, the trial judge decides whether the proposed expert testimony meets the minimum requirements to be admissible. These requirements include the following:

- The expert's opinion must be based on specialized knowledge;
- The expert must be sufficiently qualified;

- The testimony must be helpful to the jury to decide or understand an issue;
- There must be a sufficient foundation for the expert's opinion; and
- The proposed testimony must meet reliability standards.

Rule 702 of the Federal Rules of Evidence governs the admission of expert evidence in federal trials:

FRE 702, Testimony by Experts:

> If scientific, technical, or other specialized knowledge will assist the trier of fact to understand the evidence or to determine a fact in issue, a witness qualified as an expert by knowledge, skill, experience, training, or education, may testify thereto in the form of an opinion or otherwise, if (1) the testimony is based upon sufficient facts or data, (2) the testimony is the product of reliable principles and methods, and (3) the witness has applied the principles and methods reliably to the facts of the case.

The requirements of specialized knowledge, relevance and helpfulness, and qualifications are addressed in the first part of the chapter. Reliability issues are addressed in the second part.

A. *Specialized Knowledge and Helpfulness*

For expert evidence to be admissible, the Rule language requires expert testimony to be of a specific type: "scientific, technical, or other specialized knowledge." While there may be little dispute that a chemist's expert testimony is both scientific and specialized, there is a great deal more disagreement about whether the testimony is specialized when it involves a bookkeeper or a plumber. Whether proposed expert testimony is "specialized knowledge" is important because the jury may be more convinced by testimony from an expert than from a lay witness.

Expert testimony is "helpful" if it either assists the jury in understanding the evidence or determining a fact in issue. In Daubert v. Merrell Dow Pharmaceuticals, Inc., 509 U.S. 579, 591-592 (1993), discussed at length in the next section, the Supreme Court described the relevance/helpfulness inquiry as follows:

> Rule 702 further requires that the evidence or testimony "assist the trier of fact to understand the evidence or to determine a fact in issue." This condition goes primarily to relevance. "Expert testimony which does not relate to any issue in the case is not relevant and, ergo, non-helpful." . . . The consideration has been aptly described . . . as one of "fit." "Fit" is not always obvious, and scientific validity for one purpose is not necessarily scientific validity for other, unrelated purposes. The study of the phases of the moon, for example, may provide valid scientific "knowledge" about whether a certain night was dark,

and if darkness is a fact in issue, the knowledge will assist the trier of fact. However (absent creditable grounds supporting such a link), evidence that the moon was full on a certain night will not assist the trier of fact in determining whether an individual was unusually likely to have behaved irrationally on that night. Rule 702's "helpfulness" standard requires a valid scientific connection to the pertinent inquiry as a precondition to admissibility.

The two cases following consider the specialized knowledge and helpfulness requirements of expert testimony.

Kopf v. Skyrm

993 F.2d 374 (4th Cir. 1993)

K.K. HALL, Circuit Judge:

Ada Kopf appeals a judgment entered after a jury verdict in favor of the defendant police officers and a subsequent summary judgment for the defendant county in this 42 U.S.C. § 1983 action alleging excessive use of force during the arrest of Kopf's deceased son. We reverse and remand for a new trial. [Plaintiff's son and two others were involved with a pizza-shop robbery. The robbers were quickly discovered and one man apprehended. The other two — a pregnant woman and Casella (Plaintiff's son) were chased on foot, and were hiding behind a garage in the backyard of a nearby house. The hiding place was an extremely narrow passage between the wall of the garage and a fence around the yard. One end of the passage was obstructed by a post and the other by a woodpile.]

Prince George's County officer Joseph Wing arrived with his police dog "Iron." After one unsuccessful track around the neighborhood, Iron located Casella and Obloy's hiding place. According to Wing, he announced in a loud voice that he would release the dog unless the suspects surrendered. Obloy testified that she heard no warning. Wing released Iron. He testified that he did so because it was more reasonable to subject the dog rather than an officer to the possibility of being shot. Iron ran to the garage and went into the passage. Wing followed. With his flashlight, Wing could see Iron bite Obloy. Casella kicked Iron. According to Obloy, Casella yelled to the officers to tell them she was pregnant and to get the dog off of her. Wing did not recall Iron. Rather, he repeatedly ordered Casella and Obloy to raise their hands, but they did not. Iron released Obloy and began biting Casella.

Two more county policemen, Steven Kerpelman and James Skyrm, arrived. They climbed over the woodpile and grabbed Casella; the dog continued to assist by biting. Casella was screaming and flailing his arms around. Skyrm could see that Casella did not have a gun in his hands, and he holstered his own weapon and grabbed his slapjack. He testified that he struck Casella a number of times, and that he may have hit him on the head.

By this time, Wing also knew that Casella was unarmed. Still, he did not order Iron to release; instead, he ran around the garage to the more accessible (woodpile) end in order to assist Kerpelman and Skyrm. Iron began biting Casella in the thigh and groin. Casella was flailing his arms and legs around. According to Wing, Casella's arm hit him, and he responded with a slapjack blow to Casella's upper body, unintentionally striking Casella's head. According to Obloy, just before the first blow struck Casella's head, an officer said angrily, "Don't touch my dog." Obloy was subdued and removed from the woodpile. Finally, Wing commanded Iron to release Casella.

From a hunched over position between standing and kneeling, Casella lunged forward. Kerpelman interpreted this movement as an attempt to grab Skyrm's holstered gun. Kerpelman struck Casella with his slapjack, again in the head, again, according to the officer, unintentionally. At some point, one of Casella's flailing blows struck Kerpelman, causing a minor cut on his forehead.

Soon the officers had pulled Casella out into the open yard. The struggle (or, according to the plaintiff, the beating) continued. Kerpelman struck Casella with his flashlight and, after it broke, his slapjack.

Casella was eventually reduced to senselessness. Emergency medical personnel were summoned to the scene. According to one of the paramedics, Wing walked up to Casella as he lay on a stretcher and said, "You son of a bitch, you kicked my dog." Wing denied making this statement. . . .

[Casella's] skull was fractured, and he had an epidural hematoma, which required immediate surgery. Dog bites adorned Casella's lip, right arm, chest, knee, thigh, and scrotum. The five-inch-long thigh wound was deep and involved muscle. The skin covering Casella's scrotum was avulsed "in a jagged fashion," though the scrotal sac was intact. [He] . . . spent five months in a brain injury rehabilitation program at Mount Vernon Hospital. He suffered several cognitive deficits from his head injuries, the most serious of which was aphasia — an impairment in the ability to express oneself verbally. Though he made progress, he never fully recovered.

Casella pled guilty to armed robbery and was sentenced to state prison. He later brought this suit against Wing, Kerpelman, Skyrm, and Prince George's County. He alleged a claim under 42 U.S.C. § 1983 against all defendants and pendent state-law claims for battery and negligence.

On July 31, 1989, Casella was attacked in prison and killed. Ada Kopf, his mother, is his personal representative and was substituted as plaintiff.

Following discovery, the district court granted summary judgment for the defendants. Kopf appealed, and this court reversed and remanded. . . . Then, in the central ruling on appeal, the district court ruled in limine that two expert witnesses Kopf expected to call — Thomas Knott and Robert diGrazia — would not be permitted to testify. Kopf sought a writ of mandamus from this court to compel the district court to permit the testimony. We denied the writ. . . .

A jury trial was held. Because of the total exclusion of her expert witnesses, Kopf was forced to call Wing [the defendant who was in charge of the police dog] as an adverse witness and to ask him about the standards for and the particular use of the dog. Wing did not give the answers Kopf would have liked, and she was unable to rebut them. On the use of slapjacks, Kopf introduced a lesson plan for county officers, which stated, "[n]ever strike your aggressor's head, neck, or throat." The court permitted the author of this report to contradict it with testimony that the head was not a "primary target area," but "there may be a time in [a] police officer's career where a blow to the head is necessary." Again, Kopf's experts were not permitted to rebut these assertions.[1]

The jury returned a verdict for the defendants. On the county's motion, summary judgment was then entered for it as well. Kopf appeals.

II. A.

Fed. R. Evid. 702 provides:

> If scientific, technical, or other specialized knowledge will assist the trier of fact to understand the evidence or to determine a fact in issue, a witness qualified as an expert by knowledge, skill, experience, training, or education, may testify thereto in the form of an opinion or otherwise.

Article VII of the Federal Rules of Evidence eliminated many formalistic barriers imposed by the common law on the introduction of opinion and expert testimony. Rule 702 is broadly interpreted, and helpfulness to the trier of fact is its "touchstone". . . . Testimony from an expert is presumed to be helpful unless it concerns matters within the everyday knowledge and experience of a lay juror. *Persinger v. Norfolk & Western Railway Co.*, 920 F.2d 1185, 1188 (4th Cir. 1990) (testimony about how difficult it is to lift heavy things is not "helpful" and is thus excludable). Even then, the erroneous admission of such testimony is usually harmless: an astronomer's explanation that the days are longer in the summertime may not assist the jury, but it is also not likely to cause an erroneous finding of fact. "Trouble is encountered only when the evaluation of the commonplace by an expert witness might supplant a jury's independent exercise of common sense." *Scott v. Sears, Roebuck & Co.*, 789 F.2d 1052, 1055 (4th Cir. 1986).

The witness' qualifications to render an expert opinion are also liberally judged by Rule 702. Inasmuch as the rule uses the disjunctive, a person may qualify to render expert testimony in any one of the five ways listed: knowledge, skill, experience, training, or education. . . . Where the expert's

---

1. This testimony was purportedly offered as a firsthand account of the officers' training, rather than *Rule 702* expert opinion. The transcript reveals that the attorneys and witness had a difficult time maintaining the distinction.

qualifications are challenged, the test for exclusion is a strict one, and the purported expert must have neither satisfactory knowledge, skill, experience, training nor education on the issue for which the opinion is proffered. One knowledgeable about a particular subject need not be precisely informed about all details of the issues raised in order to offer an opinion.

The subject matter of Rule 702 testimony need not be arcane or even especially difficult to comprehend. If, again in the disjunctive, the proposed testimony will recount or employ "scientific, technical, or other specialized knowledge," it is a proper subject. There is no gap between the "specialized knowledge" that is admissible under the rule and the "common knowledge" that is not. The boundary between the two is defined by helpfulness. . . .

B.

The plaintiff's proposed experts were Thomas Knott, a retired canine unit trainer for the Baltimore city police and head of that department's canine unit for sixteen years, and Robert diGrazia, former Chief of Police of Montgomery County, Maryland, and Police Commissioner of Boston and St. Louis.

Knott would have testified that Wing's actions were unreasonable and violated accepted police practices. According to Knott, the purpose of a police dog is to locate suspects, not to apprehend or bite them. Inasmuch as several officers were on the scene, all of whom were trained to make arrests, it was improper, in Knott's opinion, to permit the dog to bite and cause serious injury.

Both Knott's explanation of the purpose of a police dog and his ultimate opinion would have directly refuted Wing, who testified that the dog's role was to encounter a dangerous situation in lieu of officers. DiGrazia would have corroborated Knott that the primary purpose of a police dog is to locate suspects; when that mission is accomplished, it is the officers', and not the dog's, role to make the arrest.

On the use of slapjacks, diGrazia would have testified that

> the use of blackjacks or slapjacks by all three officers [was] brutal and excessive. With three officers present to make an arrest, and many more nearby, there was no necessity to strike the suspect. The officers should have grabbed and held Casella without striking him in the head. The use of blackjacks to strike the head is potentially lethal and is universally prohibited. The blows delivered to Casella's head appear to have been delivered with maximum force, causing a skull fracture, with resulting epidural hematoma. . . . I [do not] agree that the head was the only available area which could be struck.

Even if it were, it would not be an appropriate area to strike unless the loss of life was an acceptable method of securing Casella's arrest, which I reject.

C.

The district court held that the excessive force standard—"objective reasonableness"—is comprehensible to a lay juror and that expert testimony would therefore not assist the trier of fact. We review the district court's decision to admit or exclude expert testimony for an abuse of discretion. . . .

We find an abuse of discretion here. As a general proposition, the "objective reasonableness" standard may be comprehensible to a lay juror. On the other hand, any "objective" test implies the existence of a standard of conduct, and, where the standard is not defined by the generic—a reasonable person—but rather by the specific—a reasonable officer—it is more likely that Rule 702's line between common and specialized knowledge has been crossed.

The district court seems to have deduced a blanket rule that expert testimony is generally inappropriate in excessive force cases from *Wells v. Smith*, 778 F. Supp. 7 (D. Md. 1991). To the contrary, expert testimony has often been admitted in such cases. . . . Nonetheless, a blanket rule that expert testimony is generally admissible in excessive force cases would be just as wrong as a blanket rule that it is not.

The facts of every case will determine whether expert testimony would assist the jury. Where force is reduced to its most primitive form—the bare hands—expert testimony might not be helpful. Add handcuffs, a gun, a slapjack, mace, or some other tool, and the jury may start to ask itself: What is mace? What is an officer's training on using a gun? How much damage can a slapjack do? Answering these questions may often be assisted by expert testimony.

A dog is a more specialized tool than a gun or slapjack. How to train a poodle to sit or roll over is not everyday knowledge and could be explained by an expert in a case where it was relevant. How to train and use a police dog are even more obscure skills. Both Knott and diGrazia were qualified to testify about this specialized knowledge by their long experience.

DiGrazia's proffered testimony about the use of slapjacks is a closer issue. A club and the damage it can cause when it strikes a person's head are easily understood by most laymen. Still, diGrazia should clearly have been permitted to testify as to the prevailing standard of conduct for the use of slapjacks, even if he had been precluded from giving an opinion on the ultimate issue of whether the use in this case was reasonable. The total, in limine exclusion of Knott and diGrazia's testimony was an abuse of discretion.

United States v. Vallejo

237 F.3d 1008 (9th Cir. 2001)

WARDLAW, Circuit Judge:

Guillermo Vallejo appeals his conviction under 21 U.S.C. §§ 841(a)(1), 952, and 960 for importation and possession with intent to distribute marijuana. . . . We . . . conclude that . . . the district court abused its discretion by excluding both the expert testimony of Vallejo's school psychologist. . . . We reverse and remand to the district court for a new trial.

I.   BACKGROUND

[The defendant, a youth, was stopped and questioned as he attempted to cross the border from Mexico into the United States. He was asked questions in both English and Spanish and answered in both. He did not express a preference for either language and was given Miranda warnings in English. During a search of the car, marijuana was discovered. Statements made during the interrogation were admitted at trial against the defendant.] . . .

B.   EXPERT TESTIMONY OF THE SCHOOL PSYCHOLOGIST

Vallejo argues that the district court abused its discretion when it excluded the expert testimony of his high school's psychologist and director of special education at trial. The expert was prepared to testify about Vallejo's long-standing, severe language disorder, documented by more than ten years of school and special education records, and the difficulties he experienced understanding and expressing English. The testimony was offered to explain the discrepancies between Vallejo's and the Agents' recollection of the communications which occurred during the interrogation.

The district court never clearly articulated why it excluded this evidence. First, the court appeared to misconstrue the import of the proposed testimony, stating, "I'm not going to permit a psychologist to say he would have been more comfortable [speaking] in Spanish." When Vallejo clarified that the proposed testimony was offered to explain how high school children like Vallejo cope with communication problems—especially in "pressure" situations like interrogations—the court was not swayed, ruling that the testimony was "totally irrelevant and remote." The court indicated that if Vallejo had trouble perceiving specific questions and answers, he might rule otherwise. Without specific examples, however, the court failed to see why answering interrogation questions was so complex or difficult that it required an expert's explanation. The court reasoned that determining what was actually said during the interrogation and the reasons for any discrepancies were matters that the jury could and should decide for itself.

It was also reluctant to allow testimony from an expert who had never personally examined Vallejo.[5]

Vallejo asserts that the proffered testimony was admissible under Rules 702 and 703 of the Federal Rules of Evidence, and was not rendered inadmissible by application of Rule 403. We agree.

The proposed expert testimony was admissible under Rule 702. . . .

Expert testimony must be both relevant and reliable. *Daubert v. Merrell Dow Pharms., Inc.*, 509 U.S. 579, 597, 113 S.Ct. 2786, 125 L.Ed.2d 469 (1993). To be admissible, expert testimony must (1) address an issue beyond the common knowledge of the average layman, (2) be presented by a witness having sufficient expertise, and (3) assert a reasonable opinion given the state of the pertinent art or scientific knowledge. . . . The district court is accorded broad latitude in determining the reliability of expert testimony. *Kumho Tire Co. v. Carmichael*, 526 U.S. 137, 142, 119 S.Ct. 1167, 143 L.Ed.2d 238 (1999).

The proposed testimony of the school psychologist addressed an issue beyond the common knowledge of the average layperson: the special problems that former special education students have when attempting to communicate in English in high pressure situations. His testimony would have explained how two people, like Vallejo and Agent Pina, could have very different perceptions of what occurred during the interrogation, yet could both be correct from a communications standpoint. The expert would have described Vallejo's communication difficulties to help the jury understand how he struggled to comprehend and communicate during the interrogation and why he appeared to struggle while testifying at trial.

There was no dispute that the witness had sufficient expertise, based on his degree in psychology and his current job as the High School's director of special education. The expert witness's opinion was reliable. In preparation for trial, as custodian of the school records, he extensively reviewed ten years of school documentation regarding Vallejo's language skills and his progress in special education classes. Although the district court, in its haste to find "closure," prevented defense counsel from fully explaining what the records contained, we can discern some of the records' contents from what defense counsel was permitted to argue. Apparently the records would have shown that Vallejo had been in special education classes since kindergarten, but that he had been taken out of those classes in the past couple years.

---

5. The court said:

> If you had an examining doctor who could give a medical opinion, psychological opinion, because of his examination of the Defendant, his IQ scores, and his testing that he's done with him—and I've permitted those people to testify. This guy—this person hasn't done any of these things and I'm not going to permit him to start rambling off into the "toolies" about things that he doesn't know specifically apply to this Defendant or not. So the answer is no.

The records would also have shown that Vallejo was in the lowest, i.e. the first, second, or third, percentiles in many verbal categories.

The First Circuit found similar testimony to be both relevant and reliable in *United States v. Shay*, 57 F.3d 126 (1st Cir. 1995). Defending against charges of conspiracy and aiding and abetting an attempt to blow up his father's car, Shay sought to introduce expert testimony explaining that his inculpatory statements resulted from a mental disorder called "pseudologica fantastica," a condition which causes people to create intricate lies in order to place themselves in the center of attention. . . . Although the district court excluded the testimony on the grounds that the jury could easily determine the reliability of Shay's statements by listening to the testimony of other trial witnesses, the First Circuit reversed, holding that the jury was unqualified to determine whether the false statements were made because the defendant suffered from a mental disorder. *See id.* at 133. Specifically, the expert testimony was needed to explain why the defendant would make "false statements even though they were inconsistent with his apparent self-interest" when "[c]ommon understanding conforms to the notion that a person ordinarily does not make untruthful inculpatory statements." *Id.*

We have also admitted expert testimony to explain inconsistencies in an individual's testimony. In *United States v. Bighead*, 128 F.3d 1329 (9th Cir. 1997), we held that expert testimony regarding the characteristics of "delayed disclosure" and "script memory," commonly found in victims of child abuse, would assist the trier of fact in determining whether the victim was abused as a child and would not infringe on the jury's role of determining witness credibility. *Id.* at 1330-31. We emphasized that "the jury was free to determine whether the victim delayed disclosure or simply fabricated the incidents". . . .

Here, the expert testimony was intended to explain why Agent Pina remembered Vallejo saying that his friend, Francisco, decided not to drive Bebo's car because he suspected it contained drugs, while Vallejo claimed he never said such a thing. We agree with the First Circuit's reasoning in *Shay*, and conclude that the expert testimony was necessary to assist the jury in determining whether the inconsistencies resulted from Vallejo's recognized language difficulties. As we stated in *Bighead*, allowing the expert testimony would not displace the role of the jury because, after hearing the expert testimony, the jury was free to decide that the reason for the discrepancy was Vallejo's lack of credibility—not his communications disorder. We therefore hold that the expert testimony was admissible under Rule 702.

NOTES AND QUESTIONS

1. Was the court in *Kopf* correct that expert testimony might not be necessary had the officer only used his hands to strike the arrestee, as

opposed to using a weapon or a dog? Do you agree with the court's conclusion here that handling a police dog was indeed specialized knowledge? Of the various types of expert evidence discussed, which would be the most helpful to the jury? Which would be the least helpful?

2.   In a lawsuit about whether hot-glue fumes caused throat polyps and irritation, the defendant challenged the proposed testimony of the plaintiff's expert, who intended to testify that the concentration of the fume particles was reduced as one moved farther from the source of the fumes. Should this testimony be disallowed on the grounds that it is knowledge any layman would have? *See* McCullock v. H.B. Fuller Company, 61 F.3d 1038, 1042-1044 (2d Cir. 1995).

3.   In federal criminal cases such as bank robberies, the prosecution may introduce testimony from a forensic photographic expert to compare a photograph of an item with a sample of an item. For example, in United States v. McKreith, 140 Fed. Appx. 112 (11th Cir. 2005), Dr. Vorder Bruegge compared a shirt and bag seized at the defendant's house with the surveillance photos at the crime scene. He concluded:

"[a]ll of the characteristics of this shirt matched the class characteristics of the shirt worn by the bank robber in those cases that we could see the shirt," which was seven of the eight robberies captured by surveillance images. Vorder Bruegge also testified that the black bag seized from McKreith's residence was "indistinguishable" from the bag seen in the photos at one of the bank robberies. He further testified that by examining the bank surveillance images, he was able to identify that "there are similarities" between McKreith and the person depicted in those images, including "the shape of the nose, mouth and chin."

Id. at *2. Do you agree that this testimony is helpful? Is it appropriate to introduce expert testimony when the jury is able to compare the items with the photographs without assistance? Is the experience-based knowledge of the expert helpful to the jury since he routinely compares photographs with people and items and likely is more skilled at such an endeavor? *See also* United States v. Martin, 46 Fed. Appx. 119 (3d Cir. 2002) (same type of expert testimony).

4.   Some state courts permit experts to testify only when the subject is one "beyond the ken of the jury." *See e.g.*, Rule 702 of the Pennsylvania Rules of Evidence, requiring experts to have "specialized knowledge beyond that possessed by a lay person." Many courts have rejected such a standard. New Jersey, for example, has rejected the old standard, noting that the question is not whether the proposed evidence is beyond the ken of the jury, but "whether the witnesses offered as experts have peculiar knowledge or experience not common to the world which renders their opinions founded on such knowledge or experience any aid to the court or jury in

determining the questions at issue." State v. Berry, 658 A.2d 702, 707 (N.J. 1995), citing, inter alia, 3 Jack B. Weinstein & Margaret A. Berger, *Weinstein's Evidence* ¶ 7.02[02], at 702-715 (1988) ("Must a court exclude expert testimony if the subject is within the comprehension of the average juror? Such a test is incompatible with the standard of helpfulness expressed in Rule 702.").

5.   One voiced concern is that jurors may overvalue expert testimony, particularly where it is of a sophisticated or complicated nature. *See e.g.,* United States v. Addison, 498 F.2d 741, 744 (D.C. Cir. 1974) (stating that scientific evidence may "assume a posture of mythic infallibility in the eyes of a jury of laymen"). The Supreme Court recognized that the trial judge's role is especially significant in regulating expert testimony because the expert's opinion "can be both powerful and quite misleading because of the difficulty [for the jury] in evaluating it." Daubert v. Merrell Dow Pharms., Inc., 509 U.S. 579, 595 (1993). Should courts be concerned primarily with scientific testimony that is exceptionally technical — such as DNA profiling or statistical evidence — or does such a concern have equal weight in cases such as the photograph comparison cases?

6.   Courts generally do not permit expert testimony that vouches for the truthfulness of witnesses. *See e.g.,* United States v. Scop, 846 F.2d 135, 142 (2d Cir. 1988), stating "[t]he credibility of witnesses is exclusively for the determination by the jury, . . . and witnesses may not opine as to the credibility of the testimony of other witnesses at the trial." Thus, expert opinions that constitute evaluations of witness credibility, even when . . . rooted in scientific expertise, are impermissible. . . . Nimely v. City of New York, 414 F.3d 381, 398 (2d Cir. 2005). Does the testimony in *Vallejo* cross the line from being acceptably helpful to being an unacceptable comment on credibility? What about the two cases discussed in that *Vallejo* case? Many forms of expert testimony touch on issues that concern credibility; for example, eyewitness identification experts testifying about common problems associated with eyewitness' observation and memory. Some courts exclude such expert testimony on the ground that it impermissibly infringes upon the proper role of the jury. *See e.g.,* United States v. Carter, 410 F.3d 942, 950 (7th Cir. 2005) (credibility of eyewitness testimony is generally not appropriate expert testimony "because it influences a critical function of the jury — determining the credibility of witnesses"). Although the Court of Appeals for the Seventh Circuit has been somewhat hostile to such testimony on this and other grounds, it still recognizes that expert testimony about eyewitness identification may be both helpful and critically necessary in some cases. *Id.* at 950-951. While some expert testimony treads closer than others to comments on credibility — for example, testimony that "children never lie about abuse," — doesn't all expert testimony comment in some form on the credibility of witnesses?

B.   Expert Qualifications

FRE 702 states, "a witness qualified as an expert by knowledge, skill, experience, training, or education, may testify thereto in the form of an opinion or otherwise. . . ." The Rule is written in the disjunctive, thus recognizing that an expert may be qualified by experience, training, *or* education. Thus, a physician who has just completed her residency may be qualified to testify about medical matters on the basis of her education and training while a businessperson may testify as an expert based solely on his experience. More commonly, however, experts generally possess a combination of education, training, and experience.

The types of expertise are wide ranging and include not only the professions, but skilled persons as well. The 1972 Advisory Committee Notes to Rule 702 explain:

> The fields of knowledge which may be drawn upon are not limited merely to the "scientific" and "technical" but extend to all "specialized" knowledge. Similarly, the expert is viewed, not in a narrow sense, but as a person qualified by "knowledge, skill, experience, training or education." Thus within the scope of the rule are not only experts in the strictest sense of the word, *e.g.*, physicians, physicists, and architects, but also the large group sometimes called "skilled" witnesses, such as bankers or landowners testifying to land values.

Historically, the minimum standard for expert qualifications has been a low hurdle to clear. The Third Circuit Court of Appeals has stated "at a minimum, a proffered expert witness . . . must possess skill or knowledge greater than the average layman. . . ." Elcock v. Kmart Corp., 233 F.3d 734, 741 (3d Cir. 2001). The Seventh Circuit posits that "[a]nyone with relevant expertise enabling him to offer responsible opinion testimony helpful to judge or jury may qualify as an expert witness." Tuf Racing Products, Inc. v. American Suzuki Motor Corp., 223 F.3d 585, 591 (7th Cir. 2000).

This low standard, however, is tempered with realistic interpretation. As a general rule, the more technical the specialty, the more likely that courts will require substantial expertise before finding a person minimally qualified to testify as an expert. For example, in medical malpractice cases, a court will not allow a nurse to testify as an expert on the standard of care for a physician — even if that nurse has 20 years of experience working with doctors. Claims of professional negligence must be supported by expert testimony from individuals licensed in that specific profession.

Moreover, since the Supreme Court now requires the proponent of expert testimony to establish reliability prior to its admission (as does FRE 702), the standards for expertise have become both more precise and stringent in many fields. Thus, even though an expert may be qualified to testify in one field, he may not be deemed sufficiently qualified in another, closely related field. Although the "liberal thrust of the Federal Rules" favors the admission of testimony, as the Supreme Court noted in Daubert v. Merrell Dow Pharmaceuticals, Inc., 509 U.S. 579, 588 (1993), many courts exercise their gatekeeping responsibility to exclude the testimony of experts whom they deem insufficiently qualified.

Consider how the court resolves the issue of qualifications in the following case.

Ralston v. Smith & Nephew Richards, Inc.

275 F.3d 965 (10th Cir. 2001)

GARTH, Circuit Judge.

Plaintiff-appellant Karen Ralston appeals the district court's grant of summary judgment in favor of defendant-appellee Smith & Nephew, Inc. For the reasons discussed below, we will affirm the judgment.

I.

Ralston was diagnosed with cancer of her left femur in 1986. That year, she underwent a series of operations and procedures to treat her cancer, including six weeks of intensive preoperative radiation therapy, removal of bone tissue, and additional postoperative radiation. These treatments significantly reduced the strength of her left leg bone.

In April 1996, Ralston tripped and fractured portions of her lower left femur extending into the knee area. Ralston was treated by Dr. William Bohn, who implanted a multihole nail (the "MultiHole Nail") manufactured by Smith & Nephew in the broken femur. The purpose of the nail was to hold fractured bone fragments in the proper position to permit healing of the bone. According to Dr. Bohn's deposition testimony . . . , one advantage of the MultiHole Nail was its ability to deal with multiple fractures, by binding several pieces of fractured bone in place for healing.

In October 1996, six and a half months after having the MultiHole Nail implanted, Ralston twisted her leg while at work, causing pain and weakness in her left leg. Upon examination, it was discovered that the MultiHole Nail had broken, and that another fracture was found in her left femur, although it was not the same fracture as had occurred before. Dr. Bohn performed a bone graft and removed the MultiHole Nail, replacing it with a longer titanium intramedullary nail that extended up Ralston's hip. Ralston continued to have problems with her left leg, and in March 1998, Dr. Bohn performed another bone graft to relieve her continuing pain. He also referred Ralston to Dr. Howard Rosenthal, a physician specializing in oncologic orthopedics. Upon examination, he concluded that the original fractures of April 1996 had not yet healed, but that the failure of the MultiHole Nail did not prevent that original fracture from healing. In June 1999, Dr. Kimberly Templeton, an orthopaedic surgeon and associate professor at the University of Kansas Medical School, performed a total knee replacement by removing the titanium nail and the fractured femur, and implanting a piece of metal with a hinge in their place.

In April 1998, Ralston filed suit against Smith & Nephew alleging (i) design defect, (ii) manufacturing defect, (iii) various FDA violations, and (iv) negligence, including a failure to warn. Moreover, she claimed that Dr. Bohn, as her treating physician, was not properly warned that another kind of nail manufactured by Smith & Nephew—a five hole nail (the "Five Hole Nail") —was more durable than the MultiHole Nail, and may have been more appropriately used.

In June and July 1999, Smith & Nephew filed its motion for summary judgment as well as a motion to strike Ralston's only expert at that time, Dr. Christopher Ramsay. In a hearing before the district court on September 27, 2000, Ralston's counsel agreed to Smith & Nephew's motion to strike Dr. Ramsay, substituting Dr. Templeton as their new expert. Moreover, counsel advised the court that Ralston would abandon her product defect and FDA claims, and pursue only the failure to warn cause of action. Consequently, the district court granted Ralston additional time to file a supplemental opposition to Smith & Nephew's summary judgment motion based on the "failure to warn" theory. . . .

A final hearing was held before the district court on November 7, 2000, after which the court ruled in favor of Smith & Nephew, finding no material issue of fact as to the inadequacy of the warnings provided by Smith & Nephew. In so ruling, the district court excluded Dr. Templeton's testimony under Fed. R. Evid. 702 on the grounds that she was unqualified to render an opinion on the subject-matter of Ralston's theory, and because her opinions were not reliable under the principles set forth in *Daubert v. Merrell Dow Pharmaceuticals, Inc.*, 509 U.S. 579, 113 S.Ct. 2786, 125 L.Ed.2d 469 (1993). . . .

In this appeal, Ralston first challenges the district court's exclusion of Dr. Templeton's expert testimony. . . . The district court's decision to admit or exclude evidence generally, including expert testimony, is typically reviewed under an abuse of discretion standard. . . . A district court abuses its discretion "when it renders an arbitrary, capricious, whimsical, or manifestly unreasonable judgment". . . . "A trial court's decision will not be disturbed unless [this Court has] a definite and firm conviction that the [trial] court has made a clear error of judgment or exceeded the bounds of permissible choice in the circumstances". . . .

A.

Fed. R. Evid. 702 imposes upon the trial judge an important "gatekeeping" function with regard to the admissibility of expert opinions. . . . In order to determine whether Dr. Templeton's expert opinion is admissible, the district court had to undergo a two-step analysis. First, the court had to determine whether Dr. Templeton, the expert, was qualified by "knowledge, skill, experience, training, or education" to render an opinion. *See* Fed. R. Evid. 702. Second, if Dr. Templeton was so qualified, the court had to determine whether her opinions were "reliable" under the principles set forth under *Daubert*, 509 U.S. 579, 113 S.Ct. 2786, 125 L.Ed.2d 469, and *Kumho Tire Co., Ltd. v. Carmichael*, 526 U.S. 137, 119 S.Ct. 1167, 143 L.Ed.2d 238 (1999). Because we find that Dr. Templeton's testimony was properly excluded on the ground that she was unqualified, we have no need to address the reliability of her conclusions under *Daubert.*

Dr. Templeton herself admits that she is not an expert on intramedullary nailing. Throughout her deposition testimony, she conceded several times that she knew little — if anything — about the subject. She admits that she has done no research with intramedullary nailing and that she was asked to testify in the Ralston litigation in order to opine on the subject of bone healing, not to discuss the adequacy of warnings.

> I do absolutely no research with intramedullary nailing. My expertise is in oncology and in this instance was to bring in expertise as far as the treatment or the healing and problems with healing of a radiated bone.

She has never been published in any matter, and the two articles that were accepted for publication had nothing to do with intramedullary nailing. Indeed, Dr. Templeton admits to never having researched the MultiHole Nail at issue in this appeal. ("I've not done any research specifically looking at this nail.")

Moreover, on the issue of the adequacy of warnings generally, Dr. Templeton testified that she had never drafted, nor has ever been asked to draft, a surgical technique or warning of a product of any kind. . . . (Q: "Have you drafted a warning that you think is appropriate for this particular device in this case?" A: "No. . . ." Q: "Have you ever been asked to draft a surgical technique or warnings for a product of any kind?" A: "No.") She also testified that she had never seen a warning for any device that was similar to the form in the warning provided by Smith & Nephew in its "Warnings and Precautions Page," noting instead that the only warnings she had ever observed were "very brief warning[s]" that "they'll put down at the bottom of the page."

The only reason advanced by Ralston that Dr. Templeton is qualified to testify as an expert is because she is a board certified orthopaedic surgeon and is therefore entitled to rely upon general orthopaedic and surgical principles and concepts. Ralston cites *Compton v. Subaru of*

America, Inc., 82 F.3d 1513, 1519-20 (10th Cir. 1996) in support of this proposition.[2]

Ralston's reliance upon *Compton* is misplaced. That case holds only that "[a]s long as an expert stays 'within the reasonable confines of his subject area,' our case law establishes 'a lack of specialization does not affect the admissibility of [the expert] opinion, but only its weight.'" *Id.* at 1520. . . . The dispositive question becomes, therefore, whether the issue of the adequacy of the warning with regard to Smith & Nephew's intramedullary nail is "within the reasonable confines" of Dr. Templeton's subject area. As demonstrated by Dr. Templeton's own admissions discussed above, it is evident that the district court did not abuse its discretion in finding that intramedullary nailing was not within the reasonable confines of her subject area.

Moreover, *Compton*'s citation to *Wheeler v. John Deere* for the precept that reliance upon general principles and concepts is sufficient for admissibility of expert testimony is itself questionable as *Wheeler* is a pre-*Daubert* opinion. While this Court has not had the occasion to discuss that particular issue, the district courts in this Circuit have held after *Wheeler* and *Compton,* and we agree, that merely possessing a medical degree is not sufficient to permit a physician to testify concerning any medical-related issue. . . .

Finally, the *Compton* court merely held that the trial court did not abuse its discretion when it admitted expert testimony based upon the expert's familiarity with general engineering principles and concepts. That is a far cry from suggesting that a district court always abuses its discretion when it excludes an expert who may have some marginal familiarity with general concepts in the relevant field. Accordingly, our decision in *Compton* erects no bar to the District Court's exclusion of Dr. Templeton's testimony below.

Thus, the district court's determination that Dr. Templeton did not possess the requisite qualifications to render an expert opinion concerning the adequacy of the warnings with respect to the MultiHole Nail was not "'arbitrary, capricious, whimsical, or manifestly unreasonable'" so as to constitute an abuse of discretion. . . . On the contrary, as we have just pointed out, Dr. Templeton's lack of qualifications to testify to the issue of "warnings" is well supported in the record.

---

2. The viability of *Compton* has been questioned generally by some district courts given the fact that it was based on the premise that a *Daubert* analysis was inapplicable to expert opinions not based on a particular methodology or technique. See, e.g., *Alexander v. Smith & Nephew,* PLC, 98 F. Supp. 2d 1310, 1315 n. 1 (N.D. Ok. 2000). That premise has since been rejected by *Kumho,* 526 U.S. at 141, 119 S.Ct. 1167 (holding that district court's gatekeeping function "applies not only to testimony based on 'scientific' knowledge, but also to testimony based on 'technical' and 'other specialized' knowledge.").

NOTES AND QUESTIONS

1. Who would be the properly qualified witness to discuss the warnings on a surgical nail? Why does the court decide that it is not within the general scope of expertise of an orthopaedic surgeon to address the adequacy of these warnings? For whom are these warnings intended? Has the *Ralston* court split hairs too finely? Or, has the *Ralston* court acted appropriately in its gatekeeping role to keep testimony from an unqualified witness away from the jury?

2. The Court notes that the physician in question had never written a warning. Should that be an important inquiry in a case like this? Would a witness who routinely reads the warnings, such as an orthopaedic surgeon, be equally or better qualified?

3. Prior to Daubert v. Merrell Dow Pharmaceuticals, Inc., 509 U.S. 579 (1993), many courts permitted physicians broad leeway to testify about medical-related subjects, even if not within their specialty. Some states still permit physicians to opine on a variety of medical subjects, holding that the physician's expertise is a matter of weight, not admissibility. *See e.g.*, Ayers v. Debucci, 738 N.E.2d 101, 104 (Ohio App. 2000) ("Under Ohio law, any doctor licensed to practice medicine is competent to testify on medical issues, including the relationship of medical expenses to a particular injury or cause. The fact that the doctor has a specialty of pathology, rather than some other specialty such as radiology, bears only upon the weight to be given the evidence, not its admissibility."). *But see* Ohio Rev. Code Ann. § 2743.43, imposing more particularized requirements for experts in medical claims cases. Is the approach the *Ralston* court takes more compelling than the Ohio approach?

McCullock v. H.B. Fuller Co.

61 F.3d 1038 (2d Cir. 1995)

Before: McLaughlin, Cabranes, and Parker, Circuit Judges.
McLaughlin, Circuit Judge:
Geraldine McCullock won a jury verdict for $75,000 in a diversity action for negligence and strict liability in the United States District Court for the District of Vermont (Lee P. Gagliardi, Judge, sitting by designation), against H.B. Fuller Company ("Fuller"), a manufacturer of hot-melt glue. McCullock persuaded the jury that: (1) Fuller failed to warn her about the health hazards associated with the use of its glue; and (2) the glue fumes caused her respiratory health problems, including throat polyps.

On appeal, Fuller argues that the district court: (1) erroneously admitted the testimony of two expert witnesses. . . . Because the expert testimony was properly admitted, . . . we affirm.

BACKGROUND

For approximately 16 years Geraldine McCullock toiled at The Book Press, a company that binds and prints books in Brattleboro, Vermont. Then, in 1986, The Book Press began purchasing Fuller's hot-melt glue, HM-949, for use in two of its three binding machines. From 1986 to 1990, McCullock worked as a "pocket filler" on the "HC binder," a binding machine that used Fuller's glue. Her work station was 30 feet from the unventilated "glue pot." McCullock and other employees could smell the glue fumes, especially when the glue pot overheated.

There is no question that Fuller was aware of health problems associated with exposure to the hot-melt glue's vapors. [It provided The Book Press with a "Material Safety Data Sheet" ("MSDS") that included warnings.]

Additionally, affixed to each hot-melt glue container was a warning label. . . .

Significantly, both warnings noted that there were health problems associated with the glue, and recommended that it be used only with adequate ventilation. Contrary to Fuller's written recommendations, The Book Press did not place a local ventilation system over the glue pot on the HC binder, although there were ventilation systems over all its other glue pots. . . .

Between 1986 and 1990, McCullock developed respiratory symptoms, which gradually developed into throat polyps. In September 1988, Dr. David Fagelson surgically removed a vocal cord polyp. McCullock's health problems forced her to quit her job in March 1990. Thereafter, she had polyps removed on three separate occasions. She has also experienced hoarseness, irritation, and thickening of her vocal cords. . . .

McCullock sued under theories of negligence and strict liability (failure to warn), alleging that unventilated fumes from the hot-melt glue caused her throat polyps and respiratory problems.

The case was first tried in March 1992. McCullock sought to introduce the testimony of two experts, Jack Woolley and Dr. Robert Fagelson. Woolley, a consulting engineer, would opine as to the adequacy of Fuller's warnings about the dangers of the glue fumes. Dr. Fagelson would testify that the glue fumes caused her ailments. The district court (Franklin S. Billings, Jr., Judge) admitted Fagelson's testimony but refused to qualify Woolley as an expert, finding that he lacked the necessary qualifications to testify about the adequacy of Fuller's warnings.

At the close of McCullock's case, the district court granted Fuller's motion for judgment as a matter of law, holding that a manufacturer had no duty to warn a purchaser's employees about the dangers of its product. We reversed and remanded for a new trial. . . .

At the retrial in July 1994, McCullock established Woolley's credentials, which included: Master of Science degree in Industrial Engineering from Purdue University; courses in plant design and industrial safety; Safety

Consultant for Bureau of Industrial Research at Norwich University (fifteen years); experience with issues concerning vapors or fumes in an industrial workplace (a "couple of dozen times"); years of practical experience as a consulting engineer; and experience designing ventilation systems. Woolley then testified that McCullock was within the zone of exposure or the "breathing zone" of the fumes emitted from the unventilated glue pot.

As in the first trial, Dr. Fagelson testified as a medical expert to prove medical causation, i.e., the fumes caused McCullock's injury. His qualifications included: Medical Degree from Loyola University of Chicago and internship at St. Joseph's Hospital in Chicago (1960); training residency at the Illinois Eye and Ear Infirmary and the Veteran's Administration Hospital in Hines, Illinois; specialty in otolaryngology (diseases of the ears, nose, throat and upper respiratory system) since 1966; certified by the American Board of Otolaryngology in 1966; clinical practice in Brattleboro, Vermont since 1975. He provided the following opinion:

> With reasonable medical certainty my opinion is that Mrs. McCullock's vocal-cord polyps were the result of chronic repeated irritation from fumes resulting from the hot-glue pot; inhalation of the fumes from the hot-glue pot.

The jury returned a verdict for $75,000 on both the negligence and strict liability counts. Fuller now appeals.

DISCUSSION

EXPERT TESTIMONY

Fuller argues that the district court failed to perform its "gatekeeper" function under *Daubert v. Merrell Dow Pharmaceuticals, Inc.,* ... and Fed. R. Evid. 702. Specifically, it contends that both Woolley and Fagelson were unqualified to testify as experts, and that their opinions were not based on scientific knowledge. We disagree. . . .

A.   WOOLLEY

Notwithstanding that we previously stated that Woolley could provide expert testimony regarding whether McCullock was within the "breathing zone" of the glue fumes, ... Fuller contends that the consulting engineer is unqualified because (1) he has no formal education related to fume dispersal patterns, and (2) he has no experience performing or interpreting air quality studies. Moreover, it argues that, on cross-examination, Woolley did not know the chemical constituents of the hot-melt glue, the chemical constituents of any fume emitted by the glue, or the concentration level of the fumes. Finally, it maintains that Woolley's "expert" testimony consisted of a fact that any layman knows—that the concentration of fume particles was reduced as one moved farther from the source of the fumes.

We find that Woolley's testimony easily qualifies for admission under Daubert. Fuller's argument ignores Woolley's extensive practical experience. . . . Woolley's background and practical experience qualify as "specialized knowledge" gained through "experience, training, or education," Fed. R. Evid. 702, and his testimony was properly admitted. . . . Fuller's quibble with Woolley's academic training in fume dispersal and air quality studies, and his other alleged shortcomings (lack of knowledge regarding the chemical constituents of the fumes or the glue vapor's concentration level), were properly explored on cross-examination and went to his testimony's weight and credibility—not its admissibility. . . .

Woolley had both the practical experience and necessary academic training to testify whether McCullock was in the breathing zone of the glue fumes. The district court therefore did not err, let alone manifestly err, by admitting Woolley's expert testimony.

NOTES AND QUESTIONS

1. Clearly, there is a range of perspectives on where to draw the admissibility line in judging expert qualifications. Are the two cases you just read reconcilable?

2. As a policy matter, should juries hear evidence from questionably qualified experts? Is it properly a question of weight, not admissibility, once the court determines the witness has minimal qualifications? Some courts favor that approach. "If the expert meets liberal minimum qualifications [under Rule 702], then the level of the expert's expertise goes to credibility and weight, not admissibility." In re Unisys Savings Plan Litigation, 173 F.3d 145, 166 n.11 (3d Cir. 1999). Although the Supreme Court and the rules favor liberal admission, judges are still obligated to act as gatekeepers of expert testimony. As one court has noted, "[t]he shift under the Federal Rules to a more permissive approach to expert testimony, however, did not represent an abdication of the screening function traditionally played by trial judges." Nimely v. City of New York, 414 F.3d 381, 396 (2d Cir. 2005). The court reasons that decisions concerning expert qualification are critical, since experts are given "substantially more leeway" in offering opinions than are lay witnesses. Does either the McCullock or Ralston case find the proper balance between liberal admission rules and gatekeeping obligations?

3. When considering complicated areas of expert testimony as occurred in Ralston, some courts require very precise qualifications before permitting an expert to testify to the jury. Where the type of expertise is less complicated, some courts have been more flexible in holding experts are sufficiently qualified. For example, in State v. Watson, 599 A.2d 385, 386-387 (Conn. App. Ct. 1991), the court held a witness with one year's experience counseling battered women sufficient to qualify her as an expert on the issue

of why battered women delay reporting abuse. The witness had only a bachelor's degree and lacked any advance degree in psychology or sociology. What policy arguments favor or detract from such an approach?

4.   As you read through the chapter, consider the intersection between qualifications of witnesses and proof of reliability or general acceptance of the proposed evidence.

II.   STANDARDS OF ADMISSIBILITY

A.   The "General Acceptance" Standard

Frye v. United States

293 F. 1013 (C.A. D.C. 1923)

Before SMYTH, Chief Justice, VAN ORSDEL, Associate Justice, and MARTIN, presiding Judge of the United States Court of Customs Appeals.

VAN ORSDEL, Associate Justice.

Appellant, defendant below, was convicted of the crime of murder in the second degree, and from the judgment prosecutes this appeal.

A single assignment of error is presented for our consideration. In the course of the trial counsel for defendant offered an expert witness to testify to the result of a deception test made upon defendant. The test is described as the systolic blood pressure deception test. It is asserted that blood pressure is influenced by change in the emotions of the witness, and that the systolic blood pressure rises are brought about by nervous impulses sent to the sympathetic branch of the autonomic nervous system. Scientific experiments, it is claimed, have demonstrated that fear, rage, and pain always produce a rise of systolic blood pressure, and that conscious deception or falsehood, concealment of facts, or guilt of crime, accompanied by fear of detection when the person is under examination, raises the systolic blood pressure in a curve, which corresponds exactly to the struggle going on in the subject's mind, between fear and attempted control of that fear, as the examination touches the vital points in respect of which he is attempting to deceive the examiner.

In other words, the theory seems to be that truth is spontaneous, and comes without conscious effort, while the utterance of a falsehood requires a conscious effort, which is reflected in the blood pressure. The rise thus produced is easily detected and distinguished from the rise produced by mere fear of the examination itself. In the former instance, the pressure rises higher than in the latter, and is more pronounced as the examination proceeds, while in the latter case, if the subject is telling the truth, the pressure registers highest at the beginning of the examination, and gradually diminishes as the examination proceeds. . . .

Counsel for defendant, in their able presentation of the novel question involved, correctly state in their brief that no cases directly in point have been found. The broad ground, however, upon which they plant their case, is succinctly stated in their brief as follows:

'The rule is that the opinions of experts or skilled witnesses are admissible in evidence in those cases in which the matter of inquiry is such that inexperienced persons are unlikely to prove capable of forming a correct judgment upon it, for the reason that the subject-matter so far partakes of a science, art, or trade as to require a previous habit or experience or study in it, in order to acquire a knowledge of it. When the question involved does not lie within the range of common experience or common knowledge, but requires special experience or special knowledge, then the opinions of witnesses skilled in that particular science, art, or trade to which the question relates are admissible in evidence.'

Numerous cases are cited in support of this rule. Just when a scientific principle or discovery crosses the line between the experimental and demonstrable stages is difficult to define. Somewhere in this twilight zone the evidential force of the principle must be recognized, and while courts will go a long way in admitting expert testimony deduced from a well-recognized scientific principle or discovery, the thing from which the deduction is made must be sufficiently established to have gained general acceptance in the particular field in which it belongs.

We think the systolic blood pressure deception test has not yet gained such standing and scientific recognition among physiological and psychological authorities as would justify the courts in admitting expert testimony deduced from the discovery, development, and experiments thus far made. The Judgment is Affirmed.

NOTES AND QUESTIONS

1. The court states that the "thing from which the deduction is made must be sufficiently established to have gained general acceptance in the particular field in which it belongs." In the *Frye* case, what is "the thing" to which the court refers? Is it the relationship between deception and changes in blood pressure? Or is "the thing" something else?

2. The second inquiry mandated by *Frye* requires a determination of the "particular field to which it belongs." Which field(s) would that be in this case? Is this usually a clear-cut decision? In the *Ralston* case in the previous section, what might be the "particular field" implicated in that case? *See* State v. Superior Court In and For Cochise County, 718 P.2d 171 (Ariz.

1986) (holding that a field sobriety test, horizontal gaze nystagmus, which is related to amount of alcohol consumed and measures eye movement, meets the general acceptance standard. In this case, the State argued that the relevant scientific community included law enforcement, highway safety agencies, and behavioral scientists). Does that accurately define the "field to which it belongs"?

3. Many concerns have arisen with the use of the *Frye* case, including the problems posed by the questions above. Some courts have rejected the *Frye* test as simply "nose-counting"; tallying up how many experts agree and determining that if a sufficient number do, then the proposed evidence is "generally accepted." *See* United States v. Downing, 753 F.2d 1224, 1238 (3d Cir. 1985). Does the following contemporary interpretation of *Frye* resolve any of the concerns that the general acceptance test poses? Does it create new problems?

Grady v. Frito-Lay, Inc.

839 A.2d 1038 (Pa. 2003)

Before RALPH J. CAPPY, C.J., and CASTILLE, NIGRO, NEWMAN, SAYLOR, and LAMB, JJ.

Chief Justice Cappy,

In the present case, we consider whether the Superior Court correctly reversed the trial court's decision to exclude expert scientific evidence. We also consider whether to retain the rule announced in *Frye v. United States*, 293 F. 1013 (D.C. Cir. 1923), for determining whether such evidence is admissible. We conclude that Frye continues to provide the rule for decision in Pennsylvania. We also conclude that the Superior Court erred in reversing the trial court's ruling.

On April 5, 1995, Carl R. Grady ("Mr. Grady") and his wife, Diana Grady (collectively, "Appellees") commenced a lawsuit against the appellant, Frito-Lay, Inc. ("Frito-Lay"). In their complaint, Appellees alleged that Mr. Grady ate several Doritos brand Tortilla Chips ("Doritos") that Frito-Lay designed, manufactured, and sold; that Mr. Grady felt as though chips had lodged in his throat; that Mr. Grady sought emergency hospital care; that medical procedures showed that Mr. Grady suffered an esophageal tear that resulted in serious physical injuries; and that the Doritos Mr. Grady had eaten caused the esophageal tear. Alleging further that Frito-Lay's Doritos are unsafe and defective because they fracture into hard, sharp fragments that are capable of lacerating the esophagus when eaten, Appellees set forth claims in negligence, strict liability, and breach of warranty. . . .

In their response to Frito-Lay's Motion for Summary Judgment, Appellees filed two expert reports. One of the reports (the "Beroes Report") was prepared by Charles Beroes, Ph.D., P.E., an associate professor emeritus of chemical engineering at the University of Pittsburgh. In his report, Dr. Beroes stated that Doritos possessed "several hidden-hazardous physical-strength and physical-shape properties" and described the tests he had performed on several types of Doritos, including Doritos that came from the bag of chips that Mr. Grady had eaten, to quantify these propensities. . . .

In one series of tests, Dr. Beroes measured the compressive strength of dry Doritos. In these tests, Dr. Beroes held a Dorito in his hand and pressed its triangular tip down on a platform gram balance that was covered with a pad until the chip snapped. He calculated the downward force needed to break each Dorito in grams, converted that force to pounds, and set forth "the average pressure that develop[ed] under the chip tips" and "the average breaking force [he had] applied to the tips". . . . Dr. Beroes summarized this series of tests as establishing that "[l]arge pressures result when a few pounds of force are applied to the triangular shaped chips. The chip points were able to endure high pressures before fracturing. The sharp triangular chips can readily pierce the esophagus when driven into the walls of the esophagus by peristaltic action."

In a second series of tests, Dr. Beroes measured the time it took saliva to soften Doritos. These tests were conducted in the same manner as the dry chip test, except that Dr. Beroes used Doritos that he had wetted with saliva by holding them in his mouth for 15 seconds, 30 seconds, 45 seconds, and 60 seconds. According to Dr. Beroes, these tests showed that "the tips of the triangular chips did not soften sufficiently to prevent laceration of the esophagus after 60 seconds of exposure of saliva. Each triangular chip fractures into smaller triangular chips with sharp tips. These tips resemble spears. Enormous pressures occur on these needle sharp tips which can lacerate almost any tissues in the digestive tract."

Based on his tests, Dr. Beroes concluded that the Doritos were dangerous and defective because they broke into smaller triangular chips that were too sharp, too thick, and too hard for safe passage in the esophagus. He also opined within a reasonable degree of scientific certainty that Frito-Lay failed to warn of the dangers of eating Doritos; that it failed to conduct the appropriate safety studies; that it failed to produce and sell Doritos with uniform compressive strength and hardness; that Doritos were not fit for safe consumption; that Doritos were negligently designed and manufactured; and that their uneven and dangerous characteristics caused Mr. Grady's esophageal tear and resulting injuries.[1] . . . [The trial court granted Frito-Lay's motion for compulsory non-suit holding that the Bereos methodology was "akin to 'junk science' and did not meet the *Frye* test."]

1. Appellees also filed an expert's report prepared by Augusto N. Delerme, M.D., F.A.C.S. in response to Frito-Lay's Motion for Summary Judgment. In his report, Dr. Delerme opined that the Doritos that Mr. Grady ate lacerated his esophagus on their passage to his stomach, and that the laceration caused Mr. Grady's injuries.

motion in limine—

On appeal, the majority of the Superior Court en banc reversed the trial court's order granting Frito-Lay's Motions in limine, vacated the judgment of non-suit, and remanded for trial. . . .

This appeal followed, limited to whether the Superior Court correctly applied the law in reversing the trial court's decision to exclude Dr. Beroes' expert testimony on certain physical characteristics of Doritos. . . .

The *Frye* test, . . . adopted in Pennsylvania . . . is part of Rule 702. Under *Frye*, novel scientific evidence is admissible if the methodology that underlies the evidence has general acceptance in the relevant scientific community. . . .

After *Daubert* was decided, a number of state courts adopted the Daubert standard. We, however, have continued to follow *Frye*. . . . After careful consideration, we conclude that the *Frye* rule will continue to be applied in Pennsylvania. In our view, *Frye*'s "general acceptance" test is a proven and workable rule, which when faithfully followed, fairly serves its purpose of assisting the courts in determining when scientific evidence is reliable and should be admitted.

One of the primary reasons we embraced the *Frye* test in [*Commonwealth v. Topa*, 369 A.2d 1277 (Pa. 1977)] was its assurance that judges would be guided by scientists when assessing the reliability of a scientific method. . . . Given the ever-increasing complexity of scientific advances, this assurance is at least as compelling today as it was in 1977, when we decided that case. We believe now, as we did then, that requiring judges to pay deference to the conclusions of those who are in the best position to evaluate the merits of scientific theory and technique when ruling on the admissibility of scientific proof, as the *Frye* rule requires, is the better way of insuring that only reliable expert scientific evidence is admitted at trial.

We also believe that the *Frye* test, which is premised on a rule — that of "general acceptance" — is more likely to yield uniform, objective, and predictable results among the courts, than is the application of the *Daubert* standard, which calls for a balancing of several factors. Moreover, the decisions of individual judges, whose backgrounds in science may vary widely, will be similarly guided by the consensus that exists in the scientific community on such matters.

Thus, as we are persuaded of the wisdom and efficacy of *Frye*'s "general acceptance" rule, we hold that it continues to control in Pennsylvania.[12]

We now turn to the importance of *Frye*'s proper application, and make the following points. First, consistent with our traditional adherence to the general evidentiary tenet that the proponent of a proposition bears

___

12. Our reasons for adhering to the *Frye* rule are among the reasons that other courts have given for their respective views that the rule is sensible and effective. *See e.g., People v. Kelly,* 17 Cal.3d 24, 130 Cal.Rptr. 144, 549 P.2d 1240, 1244-45 (1976); *Stokes v. State,* 548 So.2d 188, 193-94 (Fla. 1989); *State v. Copeland,* 130 Wash.2d 244, 922 P.2d 1304, 1312-1315 (1996); *Goeb v. Tharaldson,* 615 N.W.2d 800, 812-814 (Minn. 2000).

the burden of proving it, ... Second, in applying the *Frye* rule, we have required and continue to require that the proponent of the evidence prove that the methodology an expert used is generally accepted by scientists in the relevant field as a method for arriving at the conclusion the expert will testify to at trial.

methodology not conclusion. [handwritten]

This does not mean, however, that the proponent must prove that the scientific community has also generally accepted the expert's conclusion. We have never required and do not require such a showing. This, in our view, is the sensible approach, for it imposes appropriate restrictions on the admission of scientific evidence, without stifling creativity and innovative thought.

Third, under Pa.R.E. 702, the *Frye* requirement is one of several criteria. By its terms, the Rule also mandates, inter alia, that scientific testimony be given by "a witness who is qualified as an expert by knowledge, skill, experience, training or education. . . ." Pa.R.E. 702. Whether a witness is qualified to render opinions and whether his testimony passes the *Frye* test are two distinct inquiries that must be raised and developed separately by the parties, and ruled upon separately by the trial courts.

Fourth and finally, as to the standard of appellate review that applies to the *Frye* issue, we have stated that the admission of expert scientific testimony is an evidentiary matter for the trial court's discretion and should not be disturbed on appeal unless the trial court abuses its discretion. . . .

It now remains to apply these principles to the present case. . . .

Therefore, we will consider whether the trial court abused its discretion when it decided to exclude Dr. Beroes' testimony because it did not satisfy Frye.

In reaching its decision, the trial court viewed Dr. Beroes' testimony, and hence his tests, as aimed at evaluating certain physical characteristics of Doritos while in the process of being chewed and swallowed. Based on this perspective, the trial court concluded that Dr. Beroes' testimony was inadmissible because it was not shown that the means he used to evaluate those characteristics was generally accepted by scientists who evaluate food safety.

Appellees argue that the trial court's determination cannot stand because the trial court failed to understand that Dr. Beroes measured the crush strength of Doritos by applying the standard calculations that any scientist would use to test the crush strength of a material. Frito-Lay asserts that Appellees' exclusive focus on the allegedly standard nature of the calculations Dr. Beroes used in his tests is beside the point, insofar as it fails to account for the fact that Dr. Beroes' conclusions went to the hardness and shape of Doritos as they are eaten, not their physical condition in a vacuum.

We agree with Frito-Lay that Appellees' argument regarding Dr. Beroes' methodology misses the mark, in light of the conclusion about Doritos that Dr. Beroes was going to present to the jury at trial. That conclusion was not, as Appellees' position implies, the average downward force that it takes to break various types of Doritos. Rather, it was that Doritos remain too hard

abuse of discretion ⇒ [handwritten]

and too sharp when being chewed and swallowed for safe eating. While
Dr. Beroes' calculations may in fact represent a standard method that scientists use to reach a conclusion about the downward force needed to break
Doritos, they are not also necessarily a generally accepted method that scientists in the relevant field (or fields) use for reaching a conclusion as to
whether Doritos remain too hard and too sharp as they are chewed and
swallowed to be eaten safely. It was, therefore, incumbent upon Appellees
to prove that scientists in the relevant field (or fields) generally accept Dr.
Beroes' methodology as a means for arriving at such a conclusion. Appellees,
however, filed no evidence whatsoever in this regard. Thus, Appellees failed
to satisfy their burden of proving that Dr. Beroes' evidence met the *Frye* rule.
Accordingly, we conclude that the trial court did not abuse its discretion in
deciding that Dr. Beroes' testimony was inadmissible, and hold that the
Superior Court erred in reversing the trial court's ruling.[15]

NOTES AND QUESTIONS

1. The court does not give any guidance on how the proponent of the
evidence should establish that the expert's methodology is generally
accepted. How should the proponent of such evidence establish general
acceptance? What else could have been done in this case?

2. Although Pennsylvania rejects *Daubert* and its focus on reliability,
does the state supreme court seem to be influenced by the reliability requirement? The Pennsylvania court finds that the consensus of scientific opinion
is a good guide for the courtroom. Moreover, the court notes that there must
be general agreement by scientists with the methodology employed by the
court. When you read the *Daubert* decision, *infra*, consider whether there is
much difference between the modern interpretation of the general acceptance test and *Daubert*'s reliability standard. For further commentary on
Daubert's effect on state courts, see Edward K. Cheng and Albert H. Yoon,
Does Frye *or* Daubert *Matter? A Study of Scientific Admissibility Standards*, 91 Va.
L. Rev. 471, 503 (2005) (data suggests that *Daubert* has created a greater
awareness of the problems of poor-quality scientific evidence, regardless
of whether the jurisdiction follows *Frye* or *Daubert*).

3. While a substantial minority of states continue to use *Frye*, many of
those jurisdictions have begun to weave a reliability requirement into their
general acceptance test. For example, the Kansas Supreme Court has
defined the *Frye* general acceptance test as one requiring that "before expert

15. We observe that in its opinion, the trial court did not only conclude that Appellees
failed to show that Dr. Beroes' evidence satisfied the *Frye* rule. The trial court also affirmatively
concluded that Dr. Beroes' methodology is "junk science" and essentially, not generally
accepted by scientists in the relevant field. The record does not support this conclusion.
Frito-Lay did not prove that Dr. Beroes' method is not generally accepted by scientists in
the relevant field, nor was it required to do so. As we point out, it was Appellees' burden to
prove that *Frye* was satisfied, not Frito-Lay's burden to prove otherwise.

scientific opinion may be received into evidence, the basis of the opinion must be shown to be *generally accepted as reliable* within the expert's particular scientific field." Kuhn v. Sandoz Pharmaceuticals Corp., 14 P.3d 1170, 1178 (Kan. 2000) (emphasis supplied).

4.   Do you agree with the Pennsylvania Supreme Court's distinction between methodology and conclusions? In Daubert v. Merrell Dow Pharmaceuticals, Inc., the Supreme Court notes the focus should be solely on the principles and methodologies employed, not the conclusions generated. Subsequently, the Court softened the distinction in General Electric Co. v. Joiner, noting that "conclusions and methodologies are not entirely distinct." 522 U.S. 136, 146 (1997). Why would a court distinguish between methodology and conclusions? Should courts make this distinction? Which approach makes the most sense to you?

5.   Although there are a number of states that continue to follow *Frye*, there is a great deal of variability in their approaches. Kansas continues to follow the *Frye* general acceptance test but has held that the test applies only in "circumstances where a new or experimental scientific technique is employed by an expert witness." Kuhn v. Sandoz Pharmaceuticals Corp., 14 P.3d 1170, 1178 (Kan. 2000). In a more recent case, the Kansas court limited *Frye's* applicability even further, exempting "pure opinion testimony," which the court defined as "an expert opinion developed from inductive reasoning based on the expert's own experiences, observations, or research." State v. Patton, 120 P.3d 760, 783 (Kan. 2005). *See also* Logerquist v. McVey, 1 P.3d 113, 123 (Ariz. 2000) (*Frye* test only applies to novel scientific evidence and does not apply to observation and experience-based expert testimony); Ibar v. State, 938 So. 2d 451, 467-468 (Fla. 2006) (excluding handwriting and shoe print comparison from a *Frye* analysis because they had been accepted for so many decades by the court); and State v. MacLennan, 702 N.W.2d 219, 232-233 (Minn. 2005) (distinguishing between scientific evidence derived from a specific test or diagnosis that must meet the *Frye* standard and expert testimony about syndromes that offers an explanation for a person's behavior. For the latter category, the court only uses a helpfulness analysis). Should a general acceptance analysis apply to all expert testimony or only to scientific or novel testimony? Do you agree that testimony about behaviors should not need to meet a general acceptance standard? Why are courts exempting categories of testimony? What is the effect of grandfathering-in testimony such as handwriting comparison? Do concerns about judicial economy justify courts' willingness to exempt categories of evidence?

6.   In Logerquist v. McVey, 1 P.3d 113 (Ariz. 2000), the plaintiff alleged that her pediatrician sexually abused her from 1971 through 1973. She claimed amnesia about the event until 1991, when a television commercial featuring a pediatrician triggered the memory of abuse. The parties introduced competing expert opinions at the *Frye* hearing: The plaintiff relied on a clinical psychiatrist who testified that, based on his observations and

experiences, repressed and recovered memory exists in some patients. By contrast, the defendant's expert, a research psychologist, claimed that the research data did not support the repressed memory theory.

The Supreme Court of Arizona, citing its own decisions about behavioral science and the decisions of other courts, rejected a reliability test and held that *Frye* "has been strict enough to enable our trial judges to reject the truly questionable while enabling them to admit those principles and techniques based on generally accepted scientific theory." *Id.* at 128. The court then declined to broaden *Frye*'s historical reach in Arizona to "behavioral or experience-based testimony." *Id.* at 129. The court noted some skepticism about the theory of repressed memory, but indicated that "we believe the evidentiary testimony should come from the adversary system and be decided by the jury . . . we believe jurors can handle this problem." *Id.* at 134.

The dissent in *Logerquist,* however, notes that the majority bypasses *Frye* by deciding that repressed memory is not based upon scientific theory, noting that the "phenomenon of repressed memory . . . remains woefully short of being empirically verified and, indeed, heralds from a non-rigorous school of psychology in which empirical validation is not a core test." *Id.* at 138, quoting 1 David L. Faigman, David H. Kaye, Michael J. Saks & Joseph Sanders, *Modern Scientific Evidence: The Law and Science of Expert Testimony* § 13-1.5, at 534-535 (1997). Does this case suggest some of the shortcomings of the *Frye* test? The subject of repressed and recovered memory is dealt with in more detail in Chapter 9, Expert Testimony About Memory. For critical commentary on the *Logerquist* case, *see* Margaret A. Berger, *When is Clinical Psychology Like Astrology?* 33 Ariz. St. L. J. 75 (2001); and David L. Faigman, *Embracing the Darkness: Logerquist v. McVey and the Doctrine of Ignorance of Science Is an Excuse,* 33 Ariz. St. L.J. 87 (2001).

7. Consider the reasons why the Supreme Court of Pennsylvania rejects the *Daubert* test of reliability in favor of the general acceptance test. When you read *Daubert,* consider those reasons and compare the benefits and drawbacks of the general acceptance analysis versus the reliability analysis.

B. The Reliability Standard — The Supreme Court Trilogy on Expert Evidence

Daubert v. Merrell Dow Pharmaceuticals, Inc.

509 U.S. 579 (1993)

Justice BLACKMUN delivered the opinion of the Court.

In this case we are called upon to determine the standard for admitting expert scientific testimony in a federal trial.

I

Petitioners Jason Daubert and Eric Schuller are minor children born
with serious birth defects. They and their parents sued respondent in
California state court, alleging that the birth defects had been caused by
the mothers' ingestion of Bendectin, a prescription antinausea drug marketed by respondent. Respondent removed the suits to federal court on
diversity grounds.

After extensive discovery, respondent moved for summary judgment,
contending that Bendectin does not cause birth defects in humans and that
petitioners would be unable to come forward with any admissible evidence
that it does. In support of its motion, respondent submitted an affidavit of
Steven H. Lamm, physician and epidemiologist, who is a well-credentialed
expert on the risks from exposure to various chemical substances. Doctor
Lamm stated that he had reviewed all the literature on Bendectin and
human birth defects—more than 30 published studies involving over
130,000 patients. No study had found Bendectin to be a human teratogen
(i.e., a substance capable of causing malformations in fetuses). On the basis
of this review, Doctor Lamm concluded that maternal use of Bendectin
during the first trimester of pregnancy has not been shown to be a risk factor
for human birth defects.

Petitioners did not (and do not) contest this characterization of the
published record regarding Bendectin. Instead, they responded to respondent's motion with the testimony of eight experts of their own, each of
whom also possessed impressive credentials. These experts had concluded
that Bendectin can cause birth defects. Their conclusions were based upon
"in vitro" (test tube) and "in vivo" (live) animal studies that found a link
between Bendectin and malformations; pharmacological studies of the
chemical structure of Bendectin that purported to show similarities between
the structure of the drug and that of other substances known to cause birth
defects; and the "reanalysis" of previously published epidemiological
(human statistical) studies.

The District Court granted respondent's motion for summary judgment. The court stated that scientific evidence is admissible only if the
principle upon which it is based is " 'sufficiently established to have general
acceptance in the field to which it belongs.' " . . . The court concluded that
petitioners' evidence did not meet this standard. Given the vast body of
epidemiological data concerning Bendectin, the court held, expert opinion
which is not based on epidemiological evidence is not admissible to establish
causation. . . . Thus, the animal-cell studies, live-animal studies, and
chemical-structure analyses on which petitioners had relied could not
raise by themselves a reasonably disputable jury issue regarding causation. . . . Petitioners' epidemiological analyses, based as they were on recal-
culations of data in previously published studies that had found no causal

link between the drug and birth defects, were ruled to be inadmissible because they had not been published or subjected to peer review. . . .

The United States Court of Appeals for the Ninth Circuit affirmed. . . . Citing *Frye v. United States*, . . . the court stated that expert opinion based on a scientific technique is inadmissible unless the technique is "generally accepted" as reliable in the relevant scientific community. . . . The court declared that expert opinion based on a methodology that diverges "significantly from the procedures accepted by recognized authorities in the field . . . cannot be shown to be 'generally accepted as a reliable technique.' " . . .

We granted certiorari, 506 U.S. 914, 113 S.Ct. 320, 121 L.Ed.2d 240 (1992), in light of sharp divisions among the courts regarding the proper standard for the admission of expert testimony. . . .

II A

In the 70 years since its formulation in the *Frye* case, the "general acceptance" test has been the dominant standard for determining the admissibility of novel scientific evidence at trial. E. Green & C. Nesson, Problems, Cases, and Materials on Evidence 649 (1983). Although under increasing attack of late, the rule continues to be followed by a majority of courts, including the Ninth Circuit.

The *Frye* test has its origin in a short and citation-free 1923 decision concerning the admissibility of evidence derived from a systolic blood pressure deception test, a crude precursor to the polygraph machine. In what has become a famous (perhaps infamous) passage, the then Court of Appeals for the District of Columbia described the device and its operation and declared: "Just when a scientific principle or discovery crosses the line between the experimental and demonstrable stages is difficult to define. Somewhere in this twilight zone the evidential force of the principle must be recognized, and while courts will go a long way in admitting expert testimony deduced from a well-recognized scientific principle or discovery, *the thing from which the deduction is made must be sufficiently established to have gained general acceptance in the particular field in which it belongs.*" 54 App. D.C., at 47, 293 F., at 1014 (emphasis added).

Because the deception test had "not yet gained such standing and scientific recognition among physiological and psychological authorities as would justify the courts in admitting expert testimony deduced from the discovery, development, and experiments thus far made," evidence of its results was ruled inadmissible. . . .

The merits of the *Frye* test have been much debated, and scholarship on its proper scope and application is legion. Petitioners' primary attack, however, is not on the content but on the continuing authority of the rule. They contend that the *Frye* test was superseded by the adoption of the Federal Rules of Evidence. We agree.

We interpret the legislatively enacted Federal Rules of Evidence as we would any statute. . . . Rule 402 provides the baseline: "All relevant evidence is admissible, except as otherwise provided by the Constitution of the United States, by Act of Congress, by these rules, or by other rules prescribed by the Supreme Court pursuant to statutory authority. Evidence which is not relevant is not admissible."

"Relevant evidence" is defined as that which has "any tendency to make the existence of any fact that is of consequence to the determination of the action more probable or less probable than it would be without the evidence." Rule 401. The Rule's basic standard of relevance thus is a liberal one.

Frye, of course, predated the Rules by half a century. In *United States v. Abel*, 469 U.S. 45, 105 S.Ct. 465, 83 L.Ed.2d 450 (1984), we considered the pertinence of background common law in interpreting the Rules of Evidence. We noted that the Rules occupy the field, *id.*, at 49, 105 S.Ct., at 467, but, quoting Professor Cleary, the Reporter, explained that the common law nevertheless could serve as an aid to their application: " 'In principle, under the Federal Rules no common law of evidence remains. "All relevant evidence is admissible, except as otherwise provided. . . ." In reality, of course, the body of common law knowledge continues to exist, though in the somewhat altered form of a source of guidance in the exercise of delegated powers.' " *Id.*, at 51-52, 105 S.Ct., at 469.

We found the common-law precept at issue in the *Abel* case entirely consistent with Rule 402's general requirement of admissibility, and considered it unlikely that the drafters had intended to change the rule. . . . In *Bourjaily v. United States*, 483 U.S. 171, 107 S.Ct. 2775, 97 L.Ed.2d 144 (1987), on the other hand, the Court was unable to find a particular common-law doctrine in the Rules, and so held it superseded.

Here there is a specific Rule that speaks to the contested issue. Rule 702, governing expert testimony, provides:

> "If scientific, technical, or other specialized knowledge will assist the trier of fact to understand the evidence or to determine a fact in issue, a witness qualified as an expert by knowledge, skill, experience, training, or education, may testify thereto in the form of an opinion or otherwise."

Nothing in the text of this Rule establishes "general acceptance" as an absolute prerequisite to admissibility. Nor does respondent present any clear indication that Rule 702 or the Rules as a whole were intended to incorporate a "general acceptance" standard. The drafting history makes no mention of *Frye*, and a rigid "general acceptance" requirement would be at odds with the "liberal thrust" of the Federal Rules and their "general approach of relaxing the traditional barriers to 'opinion' testimony." *Beech*

Aircraft Corp. v. Rainey, 488 U.S., at 169, 109 S.Ct., at 450 (citing Rules 701 to 705). *See also* Weinstein, Rule 702 of the Federal Rules of Evidence is Sound; It Should Not Be Amended, 138 F.R.D. 631 (1991) ("The Rules were designed to depend primarily upon lawyer-adversaries and sensible triers of fact to evaluate conflicts"). Given the Rules' permissive backdrop and their inclusion of a specific rule on expert testimony that does not mention " 'general acceptance,' " the assertion that the Rules somehow assimilated *Frye* is unconvincing. *Frye* made "general acceptance" the exclusive test for admitting expert scientific testimony. That austere standard, absent from, and incompatible with, the Federal Rules of Evidence, should not be applied in federal trials.

B

That the *Frye* test was displaced by the Rules of Evidence does not mean, however, that the Rules themselves place no limits on the admissibility of purportedly scientific evidence. Nor is the trial judge disabled from screening such evidence. To the contrary, under the Rules the trial judge must ensure that any and all scientific testimony or evidence admitted is not only relevant, but reliable.

The primary locus of this obligation is Rule 702, which clearly contemplates some degree of regulation of the subjects and theories about which an expert may testify. "*If scientific,* technical, or other specialized *knowledge will assist the trier of fact* to understand the evidence or to determine a fact in issue" an expert "may testify *thereto.*" (Emphasis added.) The subject of an expert's testimony must be "scientific . . . knowledge."[2] The adjective "scientific" implies a grounding in the methods and procedures of science. Similarly, the word "knowledge" connotes more than subjective belief or unsupported speculation. The term "applies to any body of known facts or to any body of ideas inferred from such facts or accepted as truths on good grounds." Webster's Third New International Dictionary 1252 (1986). Of course, it would be unreasonable to conclude that the subject of scientific testimony must be "known" to a certainty; arguably, there are no certainties in science. *See, e.g.,* Brief for Nicolaas Bloembergen *et al.* as *Amici Curiae* 9 ("Indeed, scientists do not assert that they know what is immutably 'true' — they are committed to searching for new, temporary, theories to explain, as best they can, phenomena"); Brief for American Association for the Advancement of Science et al. as *Amici Curiae* 7-8 ("Science is not an encyclopedic body of knowledge about the universe. Instead, it represents a *process* for proposing and refining theoretical explanations about the world that are subject to further testing and refinement" (emphasis in original)). But, in order to qualify as "scientific knowledge," an inference or assertion

---

2. Rule 702 also applies to "technical, or other specialized knowledge." Our discussion is limited to the scientific context because that is the nature of the expertise offered here.

must be derived by the scientific method. Proposed testimony must be supported by appropriate validation — i.e., "good grounds," based on what is known. In short, the requirement that an expert's testimony pertain to "scientific knowledge" establishes a standard of evidentiary reliability.[3]

Rule 702 further requires that the evidence or testimony "assist the trier of fact to understand the evidence or to determine a fact in issue." This condition goes primarily to relevance. "Expert testimony which does not relate to any issue in the case is not relevant and, ergo, non-helpful." 3 Weinstein & Berger ¶ 702[02], p. 702-18. *See also United States v. Downing,* 753 F.2d 1224, 1242 (CA3 1985) ("An additional consideration under Rule 702 — and another aspect of relevancy — is whether expert testimony proffered in the case is sufficiently tied to the facts of the case that it will aid the jury in resolving a factual dispute"). The consideration has been aptly described by Judge Becker as one of "fit." *Ibid.* "Fit" is not always obvious, and scientific validity for one purpose is not necessarily scientific validity for other, unrelated purposes. *See* Starrs, *Frye v. United States* Restructured and Revitalized: A Proposal to Amend Federal Evidence Rule 702, 26 Jurimetrics J. 249, 258 (1986). The study of the phases of the moon, for example, may provide valid scientific "knowledge" about whether a certain night was dark, and if darkness is a fact in issue, the knowledge will assist the trier of fact. However (absent creditable grounds supporting such a link), evidence that the moon was full on a certain night will not assist the trier of fact in determining whether an individual was unusually likely to have behaved irrationally on that night. Rule 702's "helpfulness" standard requires a valid scientific connection to the pertinent inquiry as a precondition to admissibility.

That these requirements are embodied in Rule 702 is not surprising. Unlike an ordinary witness, see Rule 701, an expert is permitted wide latitude to offer opinions, including those that are not based on firsthand knowledge or observation. *See* Rules 702 and 703. Presumably, this relaxation of the usual requirement of firsthand knowledge — a rule which represents "a 'most pervasive manifestation' of the common law insistence upon 'the

3. We note that scientists typically distinguish between "validity" (does the principle support what it purports to show?) and "reliability" (does application of the principle produce consistent results?). *See* Black, 56 Ford. L. Rev., at 599. Although "the difference between accuracy, validity, and reliability may be such that each is distinct from the other by no more than a hen's kick," Starrs, *Frye v. United States* Restructured and Revitalized: A Proposal to Amend Federal Evidence Rule 702, 26 Jurimetrics J. 249, 256 (1986), our reference here is to evidentiary reliability — that is, trustworthiness. Cf., e.g., Advisory Committee's Notes on Fed. Rule Evid. 602, 28 U.S.C. App., p. 755 (" '[T]he rule requiring that a witness who testifies to a fact which can be perceived by the senses must have had an opportunity to observe, and must have actually observed the fact' is a 'most pervasive manifestation' of the common law insistence upon 'the most reliable sources of information' " (citation omitted)); Advisory Committee's Notes on Art. VIII of Rules of Evidence, 28 U.S.C. App., p. 770 (hearsay exceptions will be recognized only "under circumstances supposed to furnish guarantees of trustworthiness"). In a case involving scientific evidence, evidentiary reliability will be based upon *scientific validity.*

most reliable sources of information,' " Advisory Committee's Notes on Fed. Rule Evid. 602, 28 U.S.C. App., p. 755 (citation omitted) — is premised on an assumption that the expert's opinion will have a reliable basis in the knowledge and experience of his discipline.

C

Faced with a proffer of expert scientific testimony, then, the trial judge must determine at the outset, pursuant to Rule 104(a), whether the expert is proposing to testify to (1) scientific knowledge that (2) will assist the trier of fact to understand or determine a fact in issue.[11]

This entails a preliminary assessment of whether the reasoning or methodology underlying the testimony is scientifically valid and of whether that reasoning or methodology properly can be applied to the facts in issue. We are confident that federal judges possess the capacity to undertake this review. Many factors will bear on the inquiry, and we do not presume to set out a definitive checklist or test. But some general observations are appropriate.

Ordinarily, a key question to be answered in determining whether a theory or technique is scientific knowledge that will assist the trier of fact will be whether it can be (and has been) tested. "Scientific methodology today is based on generating hypotheses and testing them to see if they can be falsified; indeed, this methodology is what distinguishes science from other fields of human inquiry." Green 645. *See also* C. Hempel, Philosophy of Natural Science 49 (1966) ("[T]he statements constituting a scientific explanation must be capable of empirical test"); K. Popper, Conjectures and Refutations: The Growth of Scientific Knowledge 37 (5th ed. 1989) ("[T]he criterion of the scientific status of a theory is its falsifiability, or refutability, or testability") (emphasis deleted).

Another pertinent consideration is whether the theory or technique has been subjected to peer review and publication. Publication (which is but one element of peer review) is not a *sine qua non* of admissibility; it does not necessarily correlate with reliability, see S. Jasanoff, The Fifth Branch: Science Advisors as Policymakers 61-76 (1990), and in some instances well-grounded but innovative theories will not have been published, see Horrobin, The Philosophical Basis of Peer Review and the Suppression of Innovation, 263 JAMA 1438 (1990). Some propositions, moreover, are too particular, too new, or of too limited interest to be

---

11. Although the *Frye* decision itself focused exclusively on "novel" scientific techniques, we do not read the requirements of Rule 702 to apply specially or exclusively to unconventional evidence. Of course, well-established propositions are less likely to be challenged than those that are novel, and they are more handily defended. Indeed, theories that are so firmly established as to have attained the status of scientific law, such as the laws of thermodynamics, properly are subject to judicial notice under Federal Rule of Evidence 201.

published. But submission to the scrutiny of the scientific community is a component of "good science," in part because it increases the likelihood that substantive flaws in methodology will be detected. *See* J. Ziman, Reliable Knowledge: An Exploration of the Grounds for Belief in Science 130-133 (1978); Relman & Angell, How Good Is Peer Review?, 321 New Eng. J. Med. 827 (1989). The fact of publication (or lack thereof) in a peer reviewed journal thus will be a relevant, though not dispositive, consideration in assessing the scientific validity of a particular technique or methodology on which an opinion is premised.

Additionally, in the case of a particular scientific technique, the court ordinarily should consider the known or potential rate of error, *see, e.g.,* *United States v. Smith*, 869 F.2d 348, 353-354 (CA7 1989) (surveying studies of the error rate of spectrographic voice identification technique), and the existence and maintenance of standards controlling the technique's operation, *see United States v. Williams*, 583 F.2d 1194, 1198 (CA2 1978) (noting professional organization's standard governing spectrographic analysis), *cert. denied*, 439 U.S. 1117, 99 S.Ct. 1025, 59 L.Ed.2d 77 (1979).

Finally, "general acceptance" can yet have a bearing on the inquiry. A "reliability assessment does not require, although it does permit, explicit identification of a relevant scientific community and an express determination of a particular degree of acceptance within that community." *United States v. Downing*, 753 F.2d, at 1238. *See also* 3 Weinstein & Berger ¶ 702[03], pp. 702-41 to 702-42. Widespread acceptance can be an important factor in ruling particular evidence admissible, and "a known technique which has been able to attract only minimal support within the community," *Downing*, 753 F.2d, at 1238, may properly be viewed with skepticism.

The inquiry envisioned by Rule 702 is, we emphasize, a flexible one.[12] Its overarching subject is the scientific validity and thus the evidentiary relevance and reliability—of the principles that underlie a proposed submission. The focus, of course, must be solely on principles and methodology, not on the conclusions that they generate.

Throughout, a judge assessing a proffer of expert scientific testimony under Rule 702 should also be mindful of other applicable rules. Rule 703 provides that expert opinions based on otherwise inadmissible hearsay are to be admitted only if the facts or data are "of a type reasonably relied

---

12. A number of authorities have presented variations on the reliability approach, each with its own slightly different set of factors. *See, e.g., Downing*, 753 F.2d, at 1238-1239 (on which our discussion draws in part); 3 Weinstein & Berger ¶ 702[03], pp. 702-41 to 702-42 (on which the Downing court in turn partially relied); McCormick, Scientific Evidence: Defining a New Approach to Admissibility, 67 Iowa L. Rev. 879, 911-912 (1982); and Symposium on Science and the Rules of Evidence, 99 F.R.D. 187, 231 (1983) (statement by Margaret Berger). To the extent that they focus on the reliability of evidence as ensured by the scientific validity of its underlying principles, all these versions may well have merit, although we express no opinion regarding any of their particular details.

upon by experts in the particular field in forming opinions or inferences upon the subject." Rule 706 allows the court at its discretion to procure the assistance of an expert of its own choosing. Finally, Rule 403 permits the exclusion of relevant evidence "if its probative value is substantially outweighed by the danger of unfair prejudice, confusion of the issues, or misleading the jury. . . ." Judge Weinstein has explained: "Expert evidence can be both powerful and quite misleading because of the difficulty in evaluating it. Because of this risk, the judge in weighing possible prejudice against probative force under Rule 403 of the present rules exercises more control over experts than over lay witnesses." Weinstein, 138 F.R.D., at 632.

III

We conclude by briefly addressing what appear to be two underlying concerns of the parties and *amici* in this case. Respondent expresses apprehension that abandonment of "general acceptance" as the exclusive requirement for admission will result in a "free-for-all" in which befuddled juries are confounded by absurd and irrational pseudoscientific assertions. In this regard respondent seems to us to be overly pessimistic about the capabilities of the jury and of the adversary system generally. Vigorous cross-examination, presentation of contrary evidence, and careful instruction on the burden of proof are the traditional and appropriate means of attacking shaky but admissible evidence. *See Rock v. Arkansas*, 483 U.S. 44, 61, 107 S.Ct. 2704, 2714, 97 L.Ed.2d 37 (1987). Additionally, in the event the trial court concludes that the scintilla of evidence presented supporting a position is insufficient to allow a reasonable juror to conclude that the position more likely than not is true, the court remains free to direct a judgment, Fed. Rule Civ. Proc. 50(a), and likewise to grant summary judgment, Fed. Rule Civ. Proc. 56. Cf., *e.g., Turpin v. Merrell Dow Pharmaceuticals, Inc.*, 959 F.2d 1349 (CA6) (holding that scientific evidence that provided foundation for expert testimony, viewed in the light most favorable to plaintiffs, was not sufficient to allow a jury to find it more probable than not that defendant caused plaintiff's injury), *cert. denied,* 506 U.S. 826, 113 S.Ct. 84, 121 L.Ed.2d 47 (1992); *Brock v. Merrell Dow Pharmaceuticals, Inc.*, 874 F.2d 307 (CA5 1989) (reversing judgment entered on jury verdict for plaintiffs because evidence regarding causation was insufficient), *modified,* 884 F.2d 166 (CA5 1989), *cert. denied,* 494 U.S. 1046, 110 S.Ct. 1511, 108 L.Ed.2d 646 (1990); Green 680-681. These conventional devices, rather than wholesale exclusion under an uncompromising "general acceptance" test, are the appropriate safeguards where the basis of scientific testimony meets the standards of Rule 702.

Petitioners and, to a greater extent, their *amici* exhibit a different concern. They suggest that recognition of a screening role for the judge that allows for the exclusion of "invalid" evidence will sanction a stifling and repressive scientific orthodoxy and will be inimical to the search for truth. . . . It is true that open debate is an essential part of both legal and scientific analyses. Yet there are important differences between the quest for truth in the courtroom and the quest for truth in the laboratory. Scientific conclusions are subject to perpetual revision. Law, on the other hand, must resolve disputes finally and quickly. The scientific project is advanced by broad and wide-ranging consideration of a multitude of hypotheses, for those that are incorrect will eventually be shown to be so, and that in itself is an advance. Conjectures that are probably wrong are of little use, however, in the project of reaching a quick, final, and binding legal judgment—often of great consequence—about a particular set of events in the past. We recognize that, in practice, a gatekeeping role for the judge, no matter how flexible, inevitably on occasion will prevent the jury from learning of authentic insights and innovations. That, nevertheless, is the balance that is struck by Rules of Evidence designed not for the exhaustive search for cosmic understanding but for the particularized resolution of legal disputes.[13]

IV

To summarize: "General acceptance" is not a necessary precondition to the admissibility of scientific evidence under the Federal Rules of Evidence, but the Rules of Evidence—especially Rule 702—do assign to the trial judge the task of ensuring that an expert's testimony both rests on a reliable foundation and is relevant to the task at hand. Pertinent evidence based on scientifically valid principles will satisfy those demands. The inquiries of the District Court and the Court of Appeals focused almost exclusively on "general acceptance," as gauged by publication and the decisions of other courts. Accordingly, the judgment of the Court of Appeals is vacated, and the case is remanded for further proceedings consistent with this opinion.

It is so ordered.

Chief Justice REHNQUIST, with whom Justice STEVENS joins, concurring in part and dissenting in part.

The petition for certiorari in this case presents two questions: first, whether the rule of *Frye v. United States*, 54 App.D.C. 46, 293 F. 1013 (1923), remains good law after the enactment of the Federal Rules of Evidence; and second, if *Frye* remains valid, whether it requires expert

13. This is not to say that judicial interpretation, as opposed to adjudicative factfinding, does not share basic characteristics of the scientific endeavor: "The work of a judge is in one sense enduring and in another ephemeral. . . . In the endless process of testing and retesting, there is a constant rejection of the dross and a constant retention of whatever is pure and sound and fine." B. Cardozo, The Nature of the Judicial Process 178, 179 (1921).

scientific testimony to have been subjected to a peer review process in order to be admissible. The Court concludes, correctly in my view, that the *Frye* rule did not survive the enactment of the Federal Rules of Evidence, and I therefore join Parts I and II-A of its opinion. The second question presented in the petition for certiorari necessarily is mooted by this holding, but the Court nonetheless proceeds to construe Rules 702 and 703 very much in the abstract, and then offers some "general observations." *Ante*, at 2796.

"General observations" by this Court customarily carry great weight with lower federal courts, but the ones offered here suffer from the flaw common to most such observations — they are not applied to deciding whether particular testimony was or was not admissible, and therefore they tend to be not only general, but vague and abstract. This is particularly unfortunate in a case such as this, where the ultimate legal question depends on an appreciation of one or more bodies of knowledge not judicially noticeable, and subject to different interpretations in the briefs of the parties and their *amici*. Twenty-two *amicus* briefs have been filed in the case, and indeed the Court's opinion contains no fewer than 37 citations to amicus briefs and other secondary sources.

The various briefs filed in this case are markedly different from typical briefs, in that large parts of them do not deal with decided cases or statutory language — the sort of material we customarily interpret. Instead, they deal with definitions of scientific knowledge, scientific method, scientific validity, and peer review — in short, matters far afield from the expertise of judges. This is not to say that such materials are not useful or even necessary in deciding how Rule 703 should be applied; but it is to say that the unusual subject matter should cause us to proceed with great caution in deciding more than we have to, because our reach can so easily exceed our grasp.

But even if it were desirable to make "general observations" not necessary to decide the questions presented, I cannot subscribe to some of the observations made by the Court. In Part II-B, the Court concludes that reliability and relevancy are the touchstones of the admissibility of expert testimony. *Ante*, at 2794-95. Federal Rule of Evidence 402 provides, as the Court points out, that "[e]vidence which is not relevant is not admissible." But there is no similar reference in the Rule to "reliability." The Court constructs its argument by parsing the language "[i]f scientific, technical, or other specialized knowledge will assist the trier of fact to understand the evidence or to determine a fact in issue, . . . an expert . . . may testify thereto. . . ." Fed. Rule Evid. 702. It stresses that the subject of the expert's testimony must be "scientific . . . knowledge," and points out that "scientific" "implies a grounding in the methods and procedures of science" and that the word "knowledge" "connotes more than subjective belief or unsupported speculation." *Ante*, at 2794-95. From this it concludes that "scientific knowledge" must be "derived by the scientific method." *Ante*, at 2795. Proposed testimony, we are told, must be supported by "appropriate validation." *Ante*, at 2795. Indeed, in footnote 9, the Court decides that "[i]n a case involving scientific evidence, *evidentiary reliability* will be based upon *scientific validity*." *Ante*, at 2795, n. 9 (emphasis in original).

Questions arise simply from reading this part of the Court's opinion, and countless more questions will surely arise when hundreds of district judges try to apply its teaching to particular offers of expert testimony. Does all of this dicta apply to an expert seeking to testify on the basis of "technical or other specialized knowledge"—the other types of expert knowledge to which Rule 702 applies—or are the "general observations" limited only to "scientific knowledge"? What is the difference between scientific knowledge and technical knowledge; does Rule 702 actually contemplate that the phrase "scientific, technical, or other specialized knowledge" be broken down into numerous subspecies of expertise, or did its authors simply pick general descriptive language covering the sort of expert testimony which courts have customarily received? The Court speaks of its confidence that federal judges can make a "preliminary assessment of whether the reasoning or methodology underlying the testimony is scientifically valid and of whether that reasoning or methodology properly can be applied to the facts in issue." *Ante*, at 2796. The Court then states that a "key question" to be answered in deciding whether something is "scientific knowledge" "will be whether it can be (and has been) tested." *Ante*, at 2796. Following this sentence are three quotations from treatises, which not only speak of empirical testing, but one of which states that the " 'criterion of the scientific status of a theory is its falsifiability, or refutability, or testability,' " *Ante*, at 2796-97. I defer to no one in my confidence in federal judges; but I am at a loss to know what is meant when it is said that the scientific status of a theory depends on its "falsifiability," and I suspect some of them will be, too.

I do not doubt that Rule 702 confides to the judge some gatekeeping responsibility in deciding questions of the admissibility of proffered expert testimony. But I do not think it imposes on them either the obligation or the authority to become amateur scientists in order to perform that role. I think the Court would be far better advised in this case to decide only the questions presented, and to leave the further development of this important area of the law to future cases.

NOTES AND QUESTIONS

1. The Supreme Court granted certiorari in this case to determine whether the *Frye* general acceptance test was superceded by the adoption of the Federal Rules of Evidence and concludes it was. Consider the reasons why the Court reaches such a holding. Are you convinced by the Court's reasoning? Is there a competing rationale that supports an opposite conclusion?

2. The holding in *Daubert* is that the *Frye* general acceptance test did not survive the enactment of the Federal Rules: "that austere standard, absent from, and incompatible with, the Federal Rules of Evidence, should not be applied in federal trials." Why doesn't the Court simply stop there? Is the rest of the opinion just *dicta*, as Justice Rehnquist argues in his concurring and dissenting opinion?

3. Although the Court determines that the general acceptance test does not survive the enactment of the Rules, it lists it as a factor to be considered in determining whether evidence is reliable. "Widespread acceptance can be an important factor in ruling particular evidence admissible, and 'a known technique which has been able to attract only minimal support within the community,' may properly be viewed with skepticism." Is the Court's inclusion of general acceptance in this section consistent with their reasoning that *Frye* did not survive the enactment of the Federal Rules?

4. In his dissenting portion of his opinion, Justice Rehnquist worries about the role the Court is carving out for federal judges:

> I defer to no one in my confidence in federal judges; but I am at a loss to know what is meant when it is said that the scientific status of a theory depends on its "falsifiability," and I suspect some of them will be, too. I do not doubt that Rule 702 confides to the judge some gatekeeping responsibility in deciding questions of the admissibility of proffered expert testimony. But I do not think it imposes on them either the obligation or the authority to become amateur scientists in order to perform that role.

In the Court of Appeals decision in *Daubert* upon remand, Judge Kozinski, speaking for the panel, writes under the title of "Brave New World,"

> [a]s we read the Supreme Court's teaching in *Daubert*, therefore, though we are largely untrained in science and certainly no match for any of the witnesses whose testimony we are reviewing, it is our responsibility to determine whether those experts' proposed testimony amounts to "scientific knowledge," constitutes "good science," and was "derived by the scientific method. . . ."
>
> Our responsibility then, unless we badly misread the Supreme Court's opinion, is to resolve disputes among well-respected, well-credentialed scientists about matters squarely within their expertise, in areas where there is no scientific consensus as to what is and what is not "good science," and occasionally to reject such expert testimony because it was not "derived by the scientific method." Mindful of our place in the hierarchy of the federal judiciary, we take a deep breath and proceed with this heady task.

Daubert v. Merrell Dow Pharmaceuticals, Inc., 43 F.3d 1311, 1316 (9th Cir. 1995) (on remand). Do you agree with these concerns or do you think the *Daubert* test is a workable standard for federal court? Has the Ninth Circuit panel exaggerated the difficulty of complying with the *Daubert* mandate?

As you continue reading cases herein, consider whether *Daubert* has indeed required judges to become amateur scientists and if so, whether that is a role suitable for the court. Is the *Frye* general acceptance case a more court-friendly approach to complicated scientific evidence or does *Daubert* provide a better standard?

5.   What does "falsifiability" mean? The Court quotes Karl Popper's *Conjectures and Refutations: The Growth of Scientific Knowledge* 37 (5th ed. 1989) ("[T]he criterion of the scientific status of a theory is its falsifiability, or refutability, or testability"). As Popper stated elsewhere in that text, "[A] system is to be considered as scientific only if it makes assertions which may clash with observations; and a system is, in fact, tested by attempts to produce such clashes, that is to say by attempts to refute it. Thus testability is the same as refutability, and can therefore likewise be taken as a criterion of demarcation." *Id.* at 256. But many scientists take issue with the Popperian model of science. For further discussion and critique of Popper's view of science, see Adina Schwartz, *A Dogma of Empiricism Revisited: Daubert v. Merrell Dow Pharmaceuticals, Inc., and the Need to Resurrect the Philosophical Insight of Frye v. United States*, 10 Harv. J. Law & Tech. 149, 165-189 (1997). Is the falsifiability concept too complex for the legal system to manage? Is general acceptance a more courtroom-friendly concept? Chapter 1, Introduction to Science and the Legal Process, provides an in-depth analysis of many issues raised in these Notes and Questions.

6.   While many scholars and commentators envisioned a more liberal approach to the admission of expert testimony post-*Daubert*, there is a real question of what effect *Daubert* has had on judges' decision making about the admissibility of expert testimony in civil cases. In the more than ten years since *Daubert* has been decided, many would posit that federal courts are quite willing to grant summary judgment in defendants' favor in toxic tort cases, where courts rule as a matter of law the plaintiffs have not established that their proposed evidence is sufficiently reliable. In *Uncertainty and Informed Choice: Unmasking* Daubert, 104 Mich. L. Rev. 257 (2005), Professors Margaret A. Berger and Aaron D. Twersky discuss the difficulty plaintiffs have in prevailing in toxic tort cases post-*Daubert* and conclude that "proving causation in many toxic tort cases is well-nigh impossible." *Id.* at 267. For an empirical evaluation of the impact of *Frye* on civil cases in state courts, see Edward Cheng & Albert H. Yoon, *Does* Frye *or* Daubert *Matter? A Study of Scientific Admissibility Standards*, 91 Va. L. Rev. 471 (2005) (noting that while *Daubert* has been a boon to defendants in civil toxic tort cases, state court civil cases do not seem to display much effect from *Daubert*).

In criminal cases, some judges and many scholars have complained that the courts are unwilling to seriously apply *Daubert*'s factors to forensic science, allowing virtually any evidence into court, regardless of its dubious quality. *See e.g.*, D. Michael Risinger, *Navigating Expert Reliability: Are Criminal Standards of Certainty Being Left on the Dock?*, 64 Alb. L. Rev. 99 (2000) (discussing the remarkable frequency with which defendants lose their challenges to the reliability of prosecutorial expert evidence); and Jane Campbell Moriarty & Michael J. Saks, *Forensic Science: Grand Goals, Tragic Flaws & Judicial Gatekeeping*, 44 Judges' J. 16, 28 (2005) ("[t]here is almost no [prosecutorial] expert testimony so threadbare that it will not be admitted if it comes to a criminal proceeding under the banner of forensic science.").

7.   For data-based analyses of the effects of the *Daubert* standard, see Henry F. Fradella *et al.*, *The Impact of* Daubert *on Forensic Science*, 31 Pepp. L. Rev. 323 (2004); and Jennifer Groscup et al., *The Effects of* Daubert *on the Admissibility of Expert Testimony in State and Federal Criminal Cases*, 8 Psych. Pub. Pol'y & L. 339 (2002).

8. In the *Daubert* remand decision, the court added another consideration:

> One very significant fact to be considered is whether the experts are proposing to testify about matters growing naturally and directly out of research they have conducted independent of the litigation, or whether they have developed their opinions expressly for purposes of testifying. That an expert testifies for money does not necessarily cast doubt on the reliability of his testimony, as few experts appear in court merely as an eleemosynary gesture. But in determining whether proposed expert testimony amounts to good science, we may not ignore the fact that a scientist's normal workplace is the lab or the field, not the courtroom or the lawyer's office.

43 F.3d 1311, 1317 (9th Cir. 1995).

How important should this additional consideration be in determining whether the proposed testimony is reliable? The Court of Appeals for the Ninth Circuit also mentions in a footnote that such a consideration should not apply to forensic science, such as fingerprint analysis, where the courtroom is the "principal theatre of operations." *Id.* at n.5. Do you agree with the distinction? In 2000, FRE 702 was amended to incorporate *Daubert*'s reliability standard. The Advisory Committee Notes include the factors mentioned in *Daubert* as well as others:

(1)   Whether experts are "proposing to testify about matters growing naturally and directly out of research they have conducted independent of the litigation, or whether they have developed their opinions expressly for purposes of testifying."

(2) Whether the expert has unjustifiably extrapolated from an accepted premise to an unfounded conclusion.

(3) Whether the expert has adequately accounted for obvious alternative explanations.

(4) Whether the expert "is being as careful as he would be in his regular professional work outside his paid litigation consulting."

(5) Whether the field of expertise claimed by the expert is known to reach reliable results for the type of opinion the expert would give.

Consider these factors in the cases you read and decide how much weight other courts give them.

9. The majority of state courts have either adopted *Daubert* or, if not expressly adopting it, make use of it. Like *Frye* states, however, some *Daubert* states have exempted certain types of evidence from a reliability review. In Marron v. Stromstad, 123 P.3d 992, 1004 (Ala. 2005), the Alaska Supreme Court limited its application of *Daubert* to "expert testimony based on scientific theory, as opposed to testimony based upon the expert's personal experience." The Supreme Court, however, as you will read in Kumho Tire Co. v. Carmichael, 526 U. S. 137 (1999), applies the gatekeeping obligation to all expert evidence.

10. Scholars, lawyers, and judges have written thousands of articles and chapters about *Daubert.* For a small sample of some of the significant articles, see Edward J. Imwinkelried, *The* Daubert *Decision on the Admissibility of Scientific Evidence: The Supreme Court Chooses the Right Piece For All the Evidentiary Puzzles,* 9 St. John's J. Legal Comment. 5 (1993); Margaret A. Berger, *Procedural Paradigms for Applying the* Daubert *Test,* 78 Minn. L. Rev. 1345 (1994); Paul C. Giannelli, Daubert: *Interpreting the Federal Rules of Evidence,* 15 Cardozo L. Rev. 1999 (1994); Bert Black et al., *Science and the Law in the Wake of* Daubert: *A New Search for Scientific Knowledge,* 72 Tex. L. Rev. 715 (1994); David L. Faigman, *Mapping the Labyrinth of Scientific Evidence,* 46 Hastings L. J. 555 (1995); Adina Schwartz, A *"Dogma of Empiricism" Revisited: Daubert v. Merrell Dow Pharmaceuticals, Inc. and the Need to Resurrect the Philosophical Insight of Frye v. United States,* 10 Harv. J.L. & Tech. 149, 196-198 (1997); Erica Beecher-Monas, *The Heuristics of Intellectual Due Process: A Primer for Triers of Science,* 75 N.Y.U. L. Rev. 1563 (2000); Michael J. Saks, *The Aftermath of* Daubert: *An Evolving Jurisprudence of Expert Evidence,* 40 Jurimetrics J. 229 (2000); and David G. Owen, *A Decade of* Daubert, 80 Denv. U. L. Rev. 345 (2002).

The *Daubert* decision generated numerous issues for the lower courts to resolve, leading to conflicting opinions among the federal courts. The questions included:

• What the appropriate standard of review should be of a court's decision to admit or exclude expert evidence;

- Whether the trial court should be permitted to consider the reliability of the conclusions generated as part of its gatekeeping role;
- Whether the trial court should have discretion to disregard the suggested *Daubert* factors or are they mandatory inquiries; and
- Whether the *Daubert* test of reliability and relevance applies to all expert evidence or only to scientific expert evidence.

Between 1997 and 1999, the Supreme Court decided two cases that allowed them to respond to these unanswered questions.

General Electric Co. v. Joiner

522 U.S. 136 (1997)

REHNQUIST, C. J., delivered the opinion for a unanimous Court with respect to Parts I and II, and the opinion of the Court with respect to Part III, in which O'CONNOR, SCALIA, KENNEDY, SOUTER, THOMAS, GINSBURG, AND BREYER JJ., joined. BREYER, J., filed a concurring opinion, STEVENS, J., filed an opinion concurring in part and dissenting in part.
Chief Justice REHNQUIST delivered the opinion of the Court.

We granted certiorari in this case to determine what standard an appellate court should apply in reviewing a trial court's decision to admit or exclude expert testimony under *Daubert v. Merrell Dow Pharmaceuticals, Inc.*, 509 U.S. 579, 113 S.Ct. 2786, 125 L.Ed.2d 469 (1993). We hold that abuse of discretion is the appropriate standard. We apply this standard and conclude that the District Court in this case did not abuse its discretion when it excluded certain proffered expert testimony.

I

[Respondent Robert Joiner began work as an electrician, which required him to work with and around the city's electrical transformers, which used a mineral-oil-based dielectric fluid as a coolant. Joiner often had to stick his hands and arms into the fluid to make repairs. The fluid would sometimes splash onto him, occasionally getting into his eyes and mouth. The fluid in some of the transformers was contaminated with polychlorinated biphenyls (PCBs). PCBs are widely considered to be hazardous to human health. Congress, with limited exceptions, banned the production and sale of PCBs in 1978. . . .

Joiner was diagnosed with small-cell lung cancer in 1991 and filed suit, claiming that the exposure to the PCBs and their derivatives "promoted" his cancer. Had he not had such exposure, he argued, he would not have developed cancer for many years, if at all. There was a history of lung cancer in the family and he was a smoker.]

II

Petitioners challenge the standard applied by the Court of Appeals in reviewing the District Court's decision to exclude respondent's experts' proffered testimony. They argue that that court should have applied traditional "abuse-of-discretion" review. Respondent agrees that abuse of discretion is the correct standard of review. He contends, however, that the Court of Appeals applied an abuse-of-discretion standard in this case. As he reads it, the phrase "particularly stringent" announced no new standard of review. It was simply an acknowledgment that an appellate court can and will devote more resources to analyzing district court decisions that are dispositive of the entire litigation. All evidentiary decisions are reviewed under an abuse-of-discretion standard. He argues, however, that it is perfectly reasonable for appellate courts to give particular attention to those decisions that are outcome determinative.

We have held that abuse of discretion is the proper standard of review of a district court's evidentiary rulings. . . . Indeed, our cases on the subject go back as far as *Spring Co. v. Edgar*, 99 U.S. 645, 658, 25 L.Ed. 487 (1879), where we said that "[c]ases arise where it is very much a matter of discretion with the court whether to receive or exclude the evidence; but the appellate court will not reverse in such a case, unless the ruling is manifestly erroneous." The Court of Appeals suggested that *Daubert* somehow altered this general rule in the context of a district court's decision to exclude scientific evidence. But *Daubert* did not address the standard of appellate review for evidentiary rulings at all. It did hold that the "austere" *Frye* standard of "general acceptance" had not been carried over into the Federal Rules of Evidence. But the opinion also said:

"That the *Frye* test was displaced by the Rules of Evidence does not mean, however, that the Rules themselves place no limits on the admissibility of purportedly scientific evidence. Nor is the trial judge disabled from screening such evidence. To the contrary, under the Rules the trial judge must ensure that any and all scientific testimony or evidence admitted is not only relevant, but reliable." 509 U.S., at 589, 113 S.Ct., at 2794-2795 (footnote omitted).

Thus, while the Federal Rules of Evidence allow district courts to admit a somewhat broader range of scientific testimony than would have been admissible under *Frye*, they leave in place the "gatekeeper" role of the trial judge in screening such evidence. A court of appeals applying "abuse-of-discretion" review to such rulings may not categorically distinguish between rulings allowing expert testimony and rulings disallowing it. Compare *Beech Aircraft Corp. v. Rainey*, 488 U.S. 153, 172, 109 S.Ct. 439, 451, 102 L.Ed.2d 445 (1988) (applying abuse-of-discretion review to a lower court's decision to exclude evidence), with *United States v. Abel, supra*, at 54, 105 S.Ct., at 470 (applying abuse-of-discretion review to a lower court's decision to admit evidence). We likewise reject respondent's argument that because the granting of summary judgment in this case was "outcome determinative," it should have been subjected to a more searching standard of review. On a motion for summary judgment, disputed issues of fact are resolved against the moving party—here, petitioners. But the question of admissibility of expert testimony is not such an issue of fact, and is reviewable under the abuse-of-discretion standard.

We hold that the Court of Appeals erred in its review of the exclusion of Joiner's experts' testimony. In applying an overly "stringent" review to that ruling, it failed to give the trial court the deference that is the hallmark of abuse-of-discretion review. . . .

III

[The court reviews the plaintiffs' expert reports and explains why the District Court's analysis was proper. The Supreme Court's discussion of causation is reprinted in Chapter 7, Medical Causation.]

Respondent points to *Daubert*'s language that the "focus, of course, must be solely on principles and methodology, not on the conclusions that they generate." 509 U.S., at 595, 113 S.Ct., at 2797. He claims that because the District Court's disagreement was with the conclusion that the experts drew from the studies, the District Court committed legal error and was properly reversed by the Court of Appeals. But conclusions and methodology are not entirely distinct from one another. Trained experts commonly extrapolate from existing data. But nothing in either *Daubert* or the Federal Rules of Evidence requires a district court to admit opinion evidence that is connected to existing data only by the *ipse dixit* of the expert. A court may conclude that there is simply too great an analytical gap between the data and the opinion proffered. . . . That is what the District Court did here, and we hold that it did not abuse its discretion in so doing.

We hold, therefore, that abuse of discretion is the proper standard by which to review a district court's decision to admit or exclude scientific evidence. We further hold that, because it was within the District Court's discretion to conclude that the studies upon which the experts relied were not sufficient, whether individually or in combination, to support their conclusions that Joiner's exposure to PCB's contributed to his cancer, the District Court did not abuse its discretion in excluding their testimony. . . .

Justice BREYER, concurring:

The Court's opinion, which I join, emphasizes *Daubert*'s statement that a trial judge, acting as "gatekeeper," must " 'ensure that any and all scientific testimony or evidence admitted is not only relevant, but reliable' ". . . . This requirement will sometimes ask judges to make subtle and sophisticated determinations about scientific methodology and its relation to the conclusions an expert witness seeks to offer — particularly when a case arises in an area where the science itself is tentative or uncertain, or where testimony about general risk levels in human beings or animals is offered to prove individual causation. Yet, as *amici* have pointed out, judges are not scientists and do not have the scientific training that can facilitate the making of such decisions. See, *e.g.*, Brief for Trial Lawyers for Public Justice as *Amicus Curiae* 15; Brief for New England Journal of Medicine et al. as *Amici Curiae* 2 ("Judges . . . are generally not trained scientists").

Of course, neither the difficulty of the task nor any comparative lack of expertise can excuse the judge from exercising the "gatekeeper" duties that the Federal Rules of Evidence impose — determining, for example, whether particular expert testimony is reliable and "will assist the trier of fact," Fed. Rule Evid. 702, or whether the "probative value" of testimony is substantially outweighed by risks of prejudice, confusion or waste of time, Fed. Rule Evid. 403. To the contrary, when law and science intersect, those duties often must be exercised with special care.

Today's toxic tort case provides an example. The plaintiff in today's case says that a chemical substance caused, or promoted, his lung cancer. His concern, and that of others, about the causes of cancer is understandable, for cancer kills over one in five Americans. See U.S. Dept. of Health and Human Services, National Center for Health Statistics, Health, United States 1996-97 and Injury Chartbook 117 (1997) (23.3% of all deaths in 1995). Moreover, scientific evidence implicates some chemicals as potential causes of some cancers. See, *e.g.*, U.S. Dept. of Health and Human Services, Public Health Service, National Toxicology Program, 1 Seventh Annual Report on Carcinogens, pp. v-vi (1994). Yet modern life, including good health as well as economic well-being, depends upon the use of artificial or manufactured substances, such as chemicals. And it may, therefore, prove particularly important to see that judges fulfill their Daubert gatekeeping function, so that they help assure that the powerful engine of tort liability, which can generate strong financial incentives to reduce, or to eliminate, production, points toward the right substances and does not destroy the wrong ones. It is, thus, essential in this science-related area that the courts administer the Federal Rules of Evidence in order to achieve the "end[s]" that the Rules themselves set forth, not only so that proceedings may be "justly determined," but also so "that the truth may be ascertained." Fed. Rule Evid. 102.

I therefore want specially to note that, as cases presenting significant science-related issues have increased in number, see Judicial Conference of the United States, Report of the Federal Courts Study Committee 97 (Apr. 2, 1990) ("Economic, statistical, technological, and natural and social scientific data are becoming increasingly important in both routine and complex litigation"), judges have increasingly found in the Rules of Evidence and Civil Procedure ways to help them overcome the inherent difficulty of making determinations about complicated scientific, or otherwise technical, evidence. Among these techniques are an increased use of Rule 16's pretrial conference authority to narrow the scientific issues in dispute, pretrial hearings where potential experts are subject to examination by the court, and the appointment of special masters and specially trained law clerks . . . [citations omitted].

In the present case, the New England Journal of Medicine has filed an *amici* brief "in support of neither petitioners nor respondents" in which the Journal writes:

> "[A] judge could better fulfill this gatekeeper function if he or she had help from scientists. Judges should be strongly encouraged to make greater use of their inherent authority . . . to appoint experts. . . . Reputable experts could be recommended to courts by established scientific organizations, such as the National Academy of Sciences or the American Association for the Advancement of Science."

Brief, *supra*, at 18-19. Cf. Fed. Rule Evid. 706 (court may "on its own motion or on the motion of any party" appoint an expert to serve on behalf of the court, and this expert may be selected as "agreed upon by the parties" or chosen by the court); see also Weinstein, *supra*, at 116 (a court should sometimes "go beyond the experts proffered by the parties" and "utilize its powers to appoint independent experts under Rule 706 of the Federal Rules of Evidence"). Given this kind of offer of cooperative effort, from the scientific to the legal community, and given the various Rules—authorized methods for facilitating the courts' task—it seems to me that *Daubert's* gatekeeping requirement will not prove inordinately difficult to implement, and that it will help secure the basic objectives of the Federal Rules of Evidence, which are, to repeat, the ascertainment of truth and the just determination of proceedings. Fed. Rule Evid. 102.

NOTES AND QUESTIONS

1. The question of appellate review of evidentiary decisions is an important one that can determine the outcome of a case on appeal.

Traditionally, decisions by trial judges have been divided into three categories for purposes of appellate review: questions of law, reviewable "de novo"; questions of fact, reviewable for "clear error"; and matters of discretion, reviewable for "abuse of discretion."

The first category, "de novo review[,] is review without deference," or review that is "independent and plenary." Under de novo review, the appellate court will thus "look at the matter anew, as though it had come to the courts for the first time."

The other two categories involve different degrees of deference to the trial court, with abuse of discretion usually thought to be the more deferential of the two. A finding of fact is said to be " 'clearly erroneous' when although there is evidence to support it, the reviewing court on the entire evidence is left with the definite and firm conviction that a mistake has been committed." Under clear error review, the appellate court cannot reverse the trial court's determination merely because it would have found the facts differently had it been sitting as the trier of fact: "[w]here there are two permissible views of the evidence, the fact finder's choice between them cannot be clearly erroneous."

A district court vested with discretion on a matter "is not required by law to make a particular decision. . . . [but instead] is empowered to make a decision — of its choosing — that falls within a range of permissible decisions." Sometimes, the trial court's exercise of its discretion is based on a weighing of factors, in which case an abuse of discretion will be found only if the trial court failed to consider the appropriate factors, considered improper factors, or made a " 'clear error of judgment' " in weighing the correct factors.

The appellate court cannot under this standard of review merely substitute its own judgment for that of the trial court. In general, an abuse of discretion will be found only if the trial court's decision is "arbitrary," "irrational," "capricious," "whimsical," "fanciful," or "unreasonable." Furthermore, the trial court's exercise of its discretion will not be disturbed unless it can be said that " 'no reasonable person would adopt the district court's view.' "

Peter Nicholas, *De Novo Review in Deferential Robes?: A Deconstruction of The Standard of Review of Evidentiary Errors in the Federal System*, 54 Syr. L. Rev. 531, 532-533 (2004) (footnotes to citations omitted). Did the Supreme Court select the correct standard of review for decisions reviewing the admissibility of expert testimony? What are the competing reasons for and against such a choice? For further commentary, see David L. Faigman, *Appellate Review of Scientific Evidence Under* Daubert *and* Joiner, 48 Hastings L. J. 969 (1997); and Christopher B. Mueller, Daubert *Asks the Right Questions: Now Appellate Courts Should Help Find the Right Answers*, 33 Seton Hall L. Rev. 987 (2003).

2. The *Joiner* decision softened *Daubert*'s sharp distinction between methodology and conclusions, where the Court stated that the "focus, of course, must be solely on principles and methodology, not on the conclusions that they generate." 509 U.S., at 595, 113 S.Ct., at 2797. In *Joiner*, the Court adds that "nothing in either *Daubert* or the Federal Rules of Evidence

requires a district court to admit opinion evidence that is connected to existing data only by the *ipse dixit* of the expert. A court may conclude that there is simply too great an analytical gap between the data and the opinion proffered." 522 U.S. at 146.

The "*ipse dixit*" problem, as it is often called, has posed formidable challenges for courts evaluating expert testimony. The Court of Appeals for the Second Circuit describes the gatekeeping inquiry as follows:

> In undertaking this flexible inquiry, the district court must focus on the conclusions the expert has reached or the district court's belief as to the correctness of those conclusions. . . .
>
> Thus, when an expert opinion is based on data, a methodology, or studies that are simply inadequate to support the conclusions reached, *Daubert* and Rule 702 mandate the exclusion of that unreliable opinion testimony. . . . This is not to suggest that an expert must back his or her opinion with published studies that unequivocally support his or her conclusions. [Citations omitted.] . . . [W]e [have] affirmed the district court's admission of medical expert testimony despite the fact that the expert "could not point to a single piece of medical literature" that specifically supported the expert's opinion. . . . Where an expert otherwise reliably utilizes scientific methods to reach a conclusion, lack of textual support may "go to the weight, not the admissibility" of the expert's testimony. . . . A contrary requirement "would effectively resurrect a *Frye*-like bright-line standard, not by requiring that a methodology be 'generally accepted,' but by excluding expert testimony not backed by published (and presumably peer-reviewed) studies." . . . Such a bright-line requirement would be at odds with the liberal admissibility standards of the federal rules and the express teachings of *Daubert*. . . .
>
> The flexible *Daubert* inquiry gives the district court the discretion needed to ensure that the courtroom door remains closed to junk science while admitting reliable expert testimony that will assist the trier of fact. To warrant admissibility, however, it is critical that an expert's analysis be reliable at every step. As Chief Judge Becker of the Third Circuit has explained, the *Daubert* "requirement that the expert testify to scientific knowledge—conclusions supported by good grounds for each step in the analysis—means that any step that renders the analysis unreliable under the *Daubert* factors renders the expert's testimony inadmissible."
>
> In deciding whether a step in an expert's analysis is unreliable, the district court should undertake a rigorous examination of the facts on which the expert relies, the method by which the expert draws an opinion from those facts, and how the expert applies the facts and methods to the case at hand. A minor flaw in an expert's reasoning or a slight modification of an otherwise reliable method will not render an expert's opinion per se inadmissible. "The judge should only exclude the evidence if the flaw is large enough that the expert lacks 'good grounds' for his or her conclusions."
>
> This limitation on when evidence should be excluded accords with the liberal admissibility standards of the federal rules and recognizes that our adversary system provides the necessary tools for challenging reliable, albeit

debatable, expert testimony. As the Supreme Court has explained, "[v]igorous cross-examination, presentation of contrary evidence, and careful instruction on the burden of proof are the traditional and appropriate means of attacking shaky but admissible evidence." *Daubert*, 509 U.S. at 596, 113 S.Ct. 2786; *accord* Weinstein, § 702.05[3] at 702-76.

Amorgianos v. National R.R. Passenger Corp., 303 F.3d 256, 266-267 (2d Cir. 2002). Does this explanation help flesh out the way the proponent of the expert evidence can bridge the ipse dixit gap? Determining whether the inference is properly inferred from the data poses a challenge for many courts. *See e.g.*, McLean v. Metabolife Int'l, Inc., 401 F.3d 1233, 1239-1252 (11th Cir. 2005) (expert substituted own opinion for scientific proof that use of defendant's supplements caused plaintiffs' strokes and heart attack); Norris v. Baxter Healthcare Corp., 397 F.3d 878, 886-887 (10th Cir. 2005) (plaintiff experts' opinions that silicone breast implants caused autoimmune diseases not reliably grounded on existing data); and Valentine v. Conrad, 850 N.E.2d 683 (Ohio, 2006) (compare majority and dissenting opinions debating whether the expert's testimony finding a causal relationship between chemical exposure and brain tumor was based on sufficiently reliable scientific data).

3.   The Seventh Circuit Court of Appeals describes the abuse of discretion standard in more fanciful terms: "We review the district court's determination for abuse of discretion, noting that [a]ppellants who challenge evidentiary rulings of the district court are like rich men who wish to enter the Kingdom: their prospects compare with those of camels who wish to pass through the eye of the needle." United States v. Coleman, 179 F.3d 1056, 1061 (7th Cir. 1999).

4.   Several state decisions employing a *Frye* standard have used the more expansive *de novo* standard of review to consider whether novel scientific evidence was generally accepted and thus properly admitted or excluded. *See* Jane Campbell Moriarty, *Psychological and Scientific Evidence in Criminal Trials*, § 10:30, n. 8 (West, 1996, 2006) (collecting cases). Many states only apply the *Frye* standard to novel scientific evidence and most states that use a *Daubert* standard apply it to all types of expert evidence. In light of that distinction, is there a rational explanation for the different standard of review?

5.   An inherent complication of the abuse of discretion standard to govern decisions about reliability of evidence is the potential for inconsistent decisions by different trial courts within the same jurisdiction: Both can be affirmed under an abuse of discretion standard. *Compare* United States v. Hines, 55 F. Supp. 2d 62, 69-70 (D. Mass. 1999) (finding handwriting comparison expertise not sufficiently reliable to permit expert to testify about conclusions, although able to testify about points of comparison) *with* United States v. Mooney, 315 F.3d 54, 63 (1st Cir. 2002) (affirming

the trial court's decision finding handwriting comparison reliable and not-ing that the *Hines* decision did not compel a different outcome). Does this type of problem suggest a different standard of review might be more appro-priate for decisions about the reliability of expert evidence?

6. Some state and federal courts are taking judicial notice of the reliability of expert evidence. *See e.g.*, Holmes v. State, 135 S.W.3d 178, 195 (Tex. App. 2004) (taking judicial notice of the reliability of blood spatter analysis); and United States v. Llera Plaza, 188 F. Supp. 2d 549, 551 (E.D. Pa. 2002) (taking judicial notice of the uniqueness and perma-nence of fingerprints). *But see* United States v. Mitchell, 365 F.3d 215, 252 (3d Cir. 2004) (holding it was error for the district court to take judicial notice of the uniqueness and permanence of fingerprints. "[I]f the question merited such an extensive *Daubert* hearing, it surely was not suitable for resolution by judicial notice." Nonetheless, the court deemed the error harmless.). FRE 201(b) describes the types of facts of which a court may take judicial notice:

> (b) Kinds of facts. A judicially noticed fact must be one not subject to reason-able dispute in that it is either (1) generally known within the territorial juris-diction of the trial court or (2) capable of accurate and ready determination by resort to sources whose accuracy cannot reasonably be questioned.

Does challenged expert testimony ever seem to be the proper type of fact of which the court may take judicial notice?

Kumho Tire Co. v. Carmichael

526 U.S. 137 (1999)

BREYER, J., delivered the opinion of the Court, Parts I and II of which were unanimous, and Part III of which was joined by REHNQUIST, C.J., and O'CONNOR, SCALIA, KENNEDY, SOUTER, THOMAS, and GINSBURG, JJ. SCALIA, J., filed a concurring opinion, in which O'CONNOR and THOMAS, JJ., joined. STEVENS, J., filed an opinion concurring in part and dissenting in part.

Justice BREYER delivered the opinion of the Court.
In *Daubert v. Merrell Dow Pharmaceuticals, Inc.*, 509 U.S. 579, 113 S.Ct. 2786, 125 L.Ed.2d 469 (1993), this Court focused upon the admissibility of scientific expert testimony. It pointed out that such testimony is admissible only if it is both relevant and reliable. And it held that the Federal Rules of Evidence "assign to the trial judge the task of ensuring that an expert's testimony both rests on a reliable foundation and is relevant to the task at hand." . . . The Court also discussed certain more specific factors, such as testing, peer review, error rates, and "acceptability" in the relevant scientific

community, some or all of which might prove helpful in determining the reliability of a particular scientific "theory or technique."

This case requires us to decide how *Daubert* applies to the testimony of engineers and other experts who are not scientists. We conclude that *Daubert's* general holding—setting forth the trial judge's general "gate-keeping" obligation—applies not only to testimony based on "scientific" *Rule* knowledge, but also to testimony based on "technical" and "other" specialized" knowledge. See Fed. Rule Evid. 702. We also conclude that a trial court may consider one or more of the more specific factors that *Daubert* mentioned when doing so will help determine that testimony's reliability. But, as the Court stated in *Daubert*, the test of reliability is "flexible," and *Daubert's* list of specific factors neither necessarily nor exclusively applies to all experts or in every case. Rather, the law grants a district court the same broad latitude when it decides how to determine reliability as it enjoys in respect to its ultimate reliability determination. See *General Electric Co. v. Joiner*, 522 U.S. 136, 143, 118 S.Ct. 512, 139 L.Ed.2d 508 (1997) (courts of appeals are to apply "abuse of discretion" standard when reviewing district court's reliability determination). Applying these standards, we determine that the District Court's decision in this case—not to admit certain expert testimony—was within its discretion and therefore lawful.

I

[Plaintiffs were either killed or seriously injured following a tire blowout of their minivan. They sued the manufacturer and distributor of the tire, alleging it was defective. Despite the fact that the tire was old and well-traveled, the plaintiffs' expert claimed it was defective and described in a deposition the methodology he used to reach that conclusion. His methodology and conclusions were disputed.]

Kumho Tire moved the District Court to exclude Carlson's testimony on the ground that his methodology failed Rule 702's reliability requirement. The court agreed with Kumho that it should act as a *Daubert*-type reliability "gatekeeper," even though one might consider Carlson's testimony as "technical," rather than "scientific." The court then examined Carlson's methodology in light of the reliability-related factors that *Daubert* mentioned, such as a theory's testability, whether it "has been a subject of peer review or publication," the "known or potential rate of error," and the "degree of acceptance . . . within the relevant scientific community". . . . The District Court found that all those factors argued against the reliability of Carlson's methods, and it granted the motion to exclude the testimony (as well as the defendants' accompanying motion for summary judgment).

The plaintiffs, arguing that the court's application of the *Daubert* factors was too "inflexible," asked for reconsideration. And the court granted that motion. . . . After reconsidering the matter, the court agreed with the plaintiffs that *Daubert* should be applied flexibly, that its four factors were simply illustrative, and that other factors could argue in favor of admissibility. It conceded that there may be widespread acceptance of a "visual-inspection method" for some relevant purposes. But the court found insufficient indications of the reliability of "the component of Carlson's tire failure analysis which most concerned the Court, namely, the methodology employed by the expert in analyzing the data obtained in the visual inspection, and the scientific basis, if any, for such an analysis."

It consequently affirmed its earlier order declaring Carlson's testimony inadmissible and granting the defendants' motion for summary judgment.

The Eleventh Circuit reversed. . . . It "review[ed] . . . de novo" the "district court's legal decision to apply *Daubert*." *Id.*, at 1435. It noted that "the Supreme Court in *Daubert* explicitly limited its holding to cover only the 'scientific context,'" adding that "a *Daubert* analysis" applies only where an expert relies "on the application of scientific principles," rather than "on skill- or experience-based observation." *Id.*, at 1435-1436. It concluded that Carlson's testimony, which it viewed as relying on experience, "falls outside the scope of *Daubert*," that "the district court erred as a matter of law by applying *Daubert* in this case," and that the case must be remanded for further (non-*Daubert*-type) consideration under Rule 702. . . .

Kumho Tire petitioned for certiorari, asking us to determine whether a trial court "may" consider *Daubert*'s specific "factors" when determining the "admissibility of an engineering expert's testimony". . . . We granted certiorari in light of uncertainty among the lower courts about whether, or how, *Daubert* applies to expert testimony that might be characterized as based not upon "scientific" knowledge, but rather upon "technical" or "other specialized" knowledge. . . .

II

A

In *Daubert*, this Court held that Federal Rule of Evidence 702 imposes a special obligation upon a trial judge to "ensure that any and all scientific testimony . . . is not only relevant, but reliable." 509 U.S., at 589, 113 S.Ct. 2786. The initial question before us is whether this basic gatekeeping obligation applies only to "scientific" testimony or to all expert testimony. We, like the parties, believe that it applies to all expert testimony. . . . For one thing, Rule 702 itself says:

> "If scientific, technical, or other specialized knowledge will assist the trier of fact to understand the evidence or to determine a fact in issue, a witness qualified as an expert by knowledge, skill, experience, training, or education, may testify thereto in the form of an opinion or otherwise."

This language makes no relevant distinction between "scientific" knowledge and "technical" or "other specialized" knowledge. It makes clear that any such knowledge might become the subject of expert testimony. In *Daubert*, the Court specified that it is the Rule's word "knowledge," not the words (like "scientific") that modify that word, that "establishes a standard of evidentiary reliability". . . . Hence, as a matter of language, the Rule applies its reliability standard to all "scientific," "technical," or "other specialized" matters within its scope. We concede that the Court in *Daubert* referred only to "scientific" knowledge. But as the Court there said, it referred to "scientific" testimony "because that [wa]s the nature of the expertise" at issue. . . . Neither is the evidentiary rationale that underlay the Court's basic *Daubert* "gatekeeping" determination limited to "scientific" knowledge. *Daubert* pointed out that Federal Rules 702 and 703 grant expert witnesses testimonial latitude unavailable to other witnesses on the "assumption that the expert's opinion will have a reliable basis in the knowledge and experience of his discipline." *Id.*, at 592, 113 S.Ct. 2786 (pointing out that experts may testify to opinions, including those that are not based on firsthand knowledge or observation). The Rules grant that latitude to all experts, not just to "scientific" ones.

Finally, it would prove difficult, if not impossible, for judges to administer evidentiary rules under which a gatekeeping obligation depended upon a distinction between "scientific" knowledge and "technical" or "other specialized" knowledge. There is no clear line that divides the one from the others. Disciplines such as engineering rest upon scientific knowledge. Pure scientific theory itself may depend for its development upon observation and properly engineered machinery. And conceptual efforts to distinguish the two are unlikely to produce clear legal lines capable of application in particular cases. Cf. Brief for National Academy of Engineering as *Amicus Curiae* 9 (scientist seeks to understand nature while the engineer seeks nature's modification); Brief for Rubber Manufacturers Association as *Amicus Curiae* 14-16 (engineering, as an "'applied science,'" relies on "scientific reasoning and methodology"); Brief for John Allen et al. as *Amici Curiae* 6 (engineering relies upon "scientific knowledge and methods").

Neither is there a convincing need to make such distinctions. Experts of all kinds tie observations to conclusions through the use of what Judge Learned Hand called "general truths derived from . . . specialized experience." Hand, Historical and Practical Considerations Regarding Expert Testimony, 15 Harv. L. Rev. 40, 54 (1901). And whether the specific expert testimony focuses upon specialized observations, the specialized translation of those observations into theory, a specialized theory itself, or the application of such a theory in a particular case, the expert's testimony often will rest "upon an experience confessedly foreign in kind to [the jury's] own." *Ibid.* The trial judge's effort to assure that the specialized testimony is reliable and relevant can help the jury evaluate that foreign experience, whether the testimony reflects scientific, technical, or other specialized knowledge.

We conclude that *Daubert*'s general principles apply to the expert matters described in Rule 702. The Rule, in respect to all such matters, "establishes a standard of evidentiary reliability". . . . It "requires a valid . . . connection to the pertinent inquiry as a precondition to admissibility". . . . And where such testimony's factual basis, data, principles, methods, or their application are called sufficiently into question, see Part III, *infra*, the trial judge must determine whether the testimony has "a reliable basis in the knowledge and experience of [the relevant] discipline". . . .

B

Petitioners ask more specifically whether a trial judge determining the "admissibility of an engineering expert's testimony" may consider several more specific factors that *Daubert* said might "bear on" a judge's gatekeeping determination. Brief for Petitioners i. These factors include:

- Whether a "theory or technique . . . can be (and has been) tested";
- Whether it "has been subjected to peer review and publication";
- Whether, in respect to a particular technique, there is a high "known or potential rate of error" and whether there are "standards controlling the technique's operation"; and
- Whether the theory or technique enjoys " 'general acceptance' " within a " 'relevant scientific community.' "

Emphasizing the word "may" in the question, we answer that question yes.

Engineering testimony rests upon scientific foundations, the reliability of which will be at issue in some cases. See, *e.g.*, Brief for Stephen N. Bobo et al. as *Amici Curiae* 23 (stressing the scientific bases of engineering disciplines). In other cases, the relevant reliability concerns may focus upon personal knowledge or experience. As the Solicitor General points out, there are many different kinds of experts, and many different kinds of expertise. See Brief for United States as *Amicus Curiae* 18-19, and n. 5 (citing cases involving experts in drug terms, handwriting analysis, criminal modus operandi, land valuation, agricultural practices, railroad procedures, attorney's fee valuation, and others).

Our emphasis on the word "may" thus reflects *Daubert*'s description of the Rule 702 inquiry as "a flexible one". . . . *Daubert* makes clear that the factors it mentions do not constitute a "definitive checklist or test". . . . And *Daubert* adds that the gatekeeping inquiry must be " 'tied to the facts' " of a particular "case" (quoting *United States v. Downing*, 753 F.2d 1224, 1242 (C.A.3 1985)). We agree with the Solicitor General that "[t]he factors identified in *Daubert* may or may not be pertinent in assessing reliability, √

depending on the nature of the issue, the expert's particular expertise, and the subject of his testimony". . . . The conclusion, in our view, is that we can neither rule out, nor rule in, for all cases and for all time the applicability of the factors mentioned in *Daubert*, nor can we now do so for subsets of cases categorized by category of expert or by kind of evidence. Too much depends upon the particular circumstances of the particular case at issue.

Daubert itself is not to the contrary. It made clear that its list of factors was meant to be helpful, not definitive. Indeed, those factors do not all necessarily apply even in every instance in which the reliability of scientific testimony is challenged. It might not be surprising in a particular case, for example, that a claim made by a scientific witness has never been the subject of peer review, for the particular application at issue may never previously have interested any scientist. Nor, on the other hand, does the presence of *Daubert*'s general acceptance factor help show that an expert's testimony is reliable where the discipline itself lacks reliability, as, for example, do theories grounded in any so-called generally accepted principles of astrology or necromancy.

At the same time, and contrary to the Court of Appeals' view, some of *Daubert*'s questions can help to evaluate the reliability even of experience-based testimony. In certain cases, it will be appropriate for the trial judge to ask, for example, how often an engineering expert's experience-based methodology has produced erroneous results, or whether such a method is generally accepted in the relevant engineering community. Likewise, it will at times be useful to ask even of a witness whose expertise is based purely on experience, say, a perfume tester able to distinguish among 140 odors at a sniff, whether his preparation is of a kind that others in the field would recognize as acceptable. We must therefore disagree with the Eleventh Circuit's holding that a trial judge may ask questions of the sort *Daubert* mentioned only where an expert "relies on the application of scientific principles," but not where an expert relies "on skill- or experience-based observation". . . . We do not believe that Rule 702 creates a schematism that segregates expertise by type while mapping certain kinds of questions to certain kinds of experts. Life and the legal cases that it generates are too complex to warrant so definitive a match.

To say this is not to deny the importance of *Daubert*'s gatekeeping requirement. The objective of that requirement is to ensure the reliability and relevancy of expert testimony. It is to make certain that an expert, whether basing testimony upon professional studies or personal experience, employs in the courtroom the same level of intellectual rigor that characterizes the practice of an expert in the relevant field. Nor do we deny that, as stated in *Daubert*, the particular questions that it mentioned will often be appropriate for use in determining the reliability of challenged expert testimony. Rather, we conclude that the trial judge must have considerable leeway in deciding in a particular case how to go about determining whether particular expert testimony is reliable. That is to say, a trial court should consider the specific factors identified in *Daubert* where they are reasonable measures of the reliability of expert testimony.

C

The trial court must have the same kind of latitude in deciding how to test an expert's reliability, and to decide whether or when special briefing or other proceedings are needed to investigate reliability, as it enjoys when it decides whether or not that expert's relevant testimony is reliable. Our opinion in *Joiner* makes clear that a court of appeals is to apply an abuse-of-discretion standard when it "review[s] a trial court's decision to admit or exclude expert testimony". . . . That standard applies as much to the trial court's decisions about how to determine reliability as to its ultimate conclusion. Otherwise, the trial judge would lack the discretionary authority needed both to avoid unnecessary "reliability" proceedings in ordinary cases where the reliability of an expert's methods is properly taken for granted, and to require appropriate proceedings in the less usual or more complex cases where cause for questioning the expert's reliability arises. Indeed, the Rules seek to avoid "unjustifiable expense and delay" as part of their search for "truth" and the "jus[t] determin[ation]" of proceedings. Fed. Rule Evid. 102. Thus, whether *Daubert*'s specific factors are, or are not, reasonable measures of reliability in a particular case is a matter that the law grants the trial judge broad latitude to determine. See *Joiner, supra.* . . . And the Eleventh Circuit erred insofar as it held to the contrary.

III

[The Supreme Court's analysis of the reliability of Plaintiff's proposed expert testimony is set forth in Chapter 10, Accident and Crime Scene Reconstructions, Defective Products, and Experiments.]

. . . Respondents additionally argue that the District Court too rigidly applied *Daubert*'s criteria. They read its opinion to hold that a failure to satisfy any one of those criteria automatically renders expert testimony inadmissible. The District Court's initial opinion might have been vulnerable to a form of this argument. There, the court, after rejecting respondents' claim that Carlson's testimony was "exempted from *Daubert*-style scrutiny" because it was "technical analysis" rather than "scientific evidence," simply added that "none of the four admissibility criteria outlined by the *Daubert* court are satisfied." 923 F. Supp., at 1521. Subsequently, however, the court granted respondents' motion for reconsideration. It then explicitly recognized that the relevant reliability inquiry "should be 'flexible,'" that its "'overarching subject [should be] . . . validity' and reliability," and that "*Daubert* was intended neither to be exhaustive nor to apply in every case". . . . And the court ultimately based its decision upon Carlson's failure to satisfy either *Daubert*'s factors or any other set of reasonable reliability criteria. In light of the record as developed by the parties, that conclusion was within the District Court's lawful discretion.

In sum, Rule 702 grants the district judge the discretionary authority, reviewable for its abuse, to determine reliability in light of the particular facts and circumstances of the particular case. The District Court did not abuse its discretionary authority in this case. Hence, the judgment of the Court of Appeals is Reversed.

Justice SCALIA, with whom Justice O'CONNOR and Justice THOMAS join, concurring.

I join the opinion of the Court, which makes clear that the discretion it endorses — trial-court discretion in choosing the manner of testing expert reliability — is not discretion to abandon the gatekeeping function. I think it worth adding that it is not discretion to perform the function inadequately. Rather, it is discretion to choose among *reasonable* means of excluding expertise that is *fausse* and science that is junky. Though, as the Court makes clear today, the *Daubert* factors are not holy writ, in a particular case the failure to apply one or another of them may be unreasonable, and hence an abuse of discretion.

NOTES AND QUESTIONS

1. In 2000, the text of FRE 702 was amended to reflect the changes brought about by the preceding Supreme Court opinions. The new rule added three requirements related to reliability and now reads as follow:

> If scientific, technical, or other specialized knowledge will assist the trier of fact to understand the evidence or determine a fact in issue, a witness qualified as an expert by skill, experience, training, or education, may testify thereto in the form of an opinion or otherwise, if (1) the testimony is based upon sufficient facts or date, (2) the testimony is the product of reliable principles or methods, and (3) the witness has applied the principles and methods reliably to the facts of the case.

The Advisory Committee Notes to the 2000 Amendment provide that the Rule was amended in response to *Daubert* and cases applying *Daubert*, including *Kumho Tire*. The Notes indicate that no attempt was made to codify the specific factors and remarks that "*Daubert* itself emphasized that the factors were neither exclusive nor dispositive," and indicates that the standards set forth in the amendment are "broad enough to require consideration of any or all of the specific *Daubert* factors where appropriate." Does Rule 702 have different requirements than the *Daubert* trilogy? If so, how do they differ?

2.   Was the Supreme Court right to extend the *Daubert* reliability standard to all evidence? Since the *Daubert* factors tend to apply more readily to matters that fit within the traditional scientific testing method, such as medical causation, how should the factors be applied when considering non-scientific types of expertise, such as projections made by economists, loss of goodwill damages, negligent construction testimony, and psychological opinions about insanity? As you read post-*Daubert* cases in the following chapters on such subjects, consider whether the application of such factors is a sensible one in the different disciplines. Some federal and state courts have rejected a strict application of the *Daubert* factors in cases involving behaviors of gang members, code words used by criminals, and psychological and syndrome testimony. *See e.g.,* United States v. Padilla, 387 F.3d 1087, 1094 (9th Cir. 2004) (finding testimony about street gangs reliable on the basis of witness' extensive experience investigating street gangs). Is this appropriate?

3.   FRE 403 also applies to expert testimony, as *Daubert* and other cases recognize. *See Daubert,* 509 U.S. at 595. The Rule prohibits admission of testimony when the probative value is substantially outweighed by the danger of unfair prejudice, confusion of issues, or misleading the jury as well as by considerations of undue delay, waste of time, or needless presentation of cumulative evidence. Although Rule 403 objections to expert testimony are generally unsuccessful at excluding expert testimony, there are exceptions. *See e.g.,* United States v. Pineda-Torres, 287 F.3d 860 (9th Cir.), *cert. denied,* 537 U.S. 1066 (2002) (reversing a defendant's conviction in part on FRE 403 grounds, where government introduced expert evidence about the structure of drug trafficking in a case where the defendant was charged only with transporting contraband across the border. There was no conspiracy charged and no evidence of any drug trafficking operation.).

4.   In *Kumho Tire,* the Court opines that the *Daubert* factors may or may not be pertinent to all types of expertise, remarking "we can neither rule out, nor rule in, for all cases and for all time the applicability of the factors mentioned in *Daubert,* nor can we now do so for subsets of cases categorized by category of expert or by kind of evidence. Too much depends upon the particular circumstances of the particular case at issue." Does this standard provide the right amount of flexibility to address the various types of expertise or is it so flexible as to vest virtually unlimited discretion in the trial judge?

5.   In addition to requiring the trial judge to serve as gatekeeper for all expert evidence, another focus of *Kumho Tire* was to "make certain that an expert, whether basing testimony upon professional studies or personal experience, employs in the courtroom the same level of intellectual rigor that characterizes the practice of an expert in the relevant field." Is the court suggesting that the less particular the practice, the less intellectual rigor required to prove reliability? When you consider the approaches between

such complex areas as medical causation and handwriting comparison, for example, was such an interpretation possibly intended?

6. These Supreme Court cases grant discretion to the trial court both to determine whether to apply the *Daubert* factors and to decide which of those factors are appropriate: Can you square such discretion with the following phrase from *Kumho Tire*? "[W]e conclude that the trial judge must have considerable leeway in deciding in a particular case how to go about determining whether particular expert testimony is reliable. That is to say, a trial court should consider the specific factors identified in *Daubert* where they are reasonable measures of the reliability of expert testimony." Does this statement suggest that the specific factors should apply unless the trial court determines they are not reasonable measures of reliability of expert testimony?

7. Although a number of state courts have adopted both *Daubert* and *Kumho Tire,* some have adopted *Daubert* and rejected *Kumho Tire. See e.g.,* Marron v. Stromstad, 123 P.3d 992, 1004 (Alaska 2005) ("we have never adopted *Kumho Tire*'s extension of *Daubert* to all expert testimony and we now explicitly decline to do so"). For thoughtful commentary on *Kumho Tire,* see Joseph Sanders, Kumho *and How We Know,* 64 L. & Contemp. Probs. 373 (2001); and David Crump, *The Trouble with* Daubert-Kumho: *Reconsidering the Supreme Court's Philosophy of Science,* 68 Mo. L. Rev. 1 (2003).

C. Alternative Approaches to Admissibility Standards

Searles v. Fleetwood Homes of Pennsylvania, Inc.

878 A.2d 509 (Me. 2005)

LEVY, J.

This case arises from Ronald and Debra Searles's purchase of a home from Schiavi Homes, LLC, that was manufactured by Fleetwood Homes of Pennsylvania, Inc. After experiencing a series of problems with the home, including the growth of extensive mold, the Searleses filed a complaint seeking damages. Following a jury trial, the Superior Court (York County, Brennan, J.) entered a judgment awarding money damages in favor of the Searleses. Fleetwood and Schiavi assert that the court erred by (1) failing to exclude the testimony of the Searleses' expert witness. We affirm the judgment.

I. BACKGROUND

Viewed in a light most favorable to the jury's verdict, the record establishes the following facts.

A. THE SEARLESES' PROBLEMS WITH THEIR HOME

The Searleses purchased their home in November 2000. Soon after they and their three young children moved into the home, the Searleses compiled a list of repairs that needed to be made. During a subsequent walk-through, a Schiavi representative assured the Searleses that somebody would contact them and that the repairs would be made.

The Searleses did not hear from anyone and had to follow up with Schiavi to inquire about the repairs. In the interim, they were having a condensation problem with their windows. [Despite repeated requests, the defendants did not repair the problems throughout the winter–summer period of 2001.] That fall, condensation from the Searleses' daughter's bedroom window soaked her bed, and the Searleses discovered mold growing on the bedpost, up the side of the window, on the trim, and on the inside of the curtains.

[Ultimately], a Fleetwood representative visited the Searleses' home. The representative concluded that at least five, and possibly all, of the windows in the home needed to be replaced and that the mold needed to be remedied. Before leaving, the representative assured the Searleses that he would place the order for the windows himself and return to take care of their problems. The representative never returned. From January to April 2002, the Searleses repeatedly called Fleetwood to inquire when their windows would be replaced. On two separate occasions contractors were sent to the home, but the windows were not replaced either time.

In April 2002, a Fleetwood contractor replaced the Searleses' windows. In the process of replacing the windows, the contractor discovered that mold was growing on the windowsills and frames, on the studs used to frame the windows, in the insulation near the windows, on and under the home's vinyl siding, and under the roof. After obtaining approval from Fleetwood, the contractor started replacing some of the mold-damaged studs and insulation. The contractor soon realized that the scope of the mold problem was beyond his ability to repair and, upon Fleetwood's instruction, stopped those efforts and simply replaced the windows.

Fleetwood sent experts to the Searleses' home to do mold testing in May 2002. Their investigations documented active mold growth in the home and heightened airborne mold levels, as compared with levels outside. The Searleses subsequently sent Fleetwood a letter revoking their acceptance of the home. In response, Fleetwood offered to remediate the home and to pay for the family's lodging while the work was being done. The Searleses rejected the offer because Fleetwood never provided them with a detailed remediation plan and because they no longer trusted the company.

B. PROCEDURAL BACKGROUND AND TRIAL

The Searleses filed a complaint in October 2002 seeking damages on theories of, among other things, revocation of acceptance, unfair trade practices, and negligence. A jury trial was held in March 2004. Prior to the trial, Fleetwood and Schiavi (Fleetwood) filed a motion in limine requesting the court to exclude the testimony of one of the Searleses' expert witnesses, Dr. Susan Upham. The motion focused on evidence related to the Searleses' respiratory problems. The Searleses developed respiratory problems shortly after moving into their home. Their symptoms included coughing, postnasal drip, and sinus and chest congestion. Dr. Upham was expected to testify that the Searleses' symptoms were caused by an irritant reaction to volatile organic compounds (VOCs) emitted by the mold in their home. Invoking the Daubert standard, . . . Fleetwood asserted that there was "no evidence in the record demonstrating that [Dr. Upham's] opinion [was] based on any scientific testing [or methodology] that has been subject to peer review or that is otherwise generally accepted in the relevant scientific community." Accordingly, Fleetwood asked the court to exclude Dr. Upham's testimony.

At the outset of the trial, the court preliminarily ruled that it would permit Dr. Upham to testify. Before she testified, however, the court gave Fleetwood an opportunity to reargue that her testimony should be excluded. Fleetwood reiterated its objections to Dr. Upham's testimony based on the arguments set forth in its motion in limine. The court then formally denied Fleetwood's motion. To counter Dr. Upham's testimony, Fleetwood offered expert testimony that the mold in the Searleses' home could not have caused their medical problems.

The jury found [in favor of the Searleses and awarded] damages. . . . This appeal followed.

II. DISCUSSION

A. EXPERT TESTIMONY

Fleetwood contends that the Superior Court erred in admitting Dr. Upham's testimony because no peer-reviewed, scientifically verified, and generally accepted studies support her conclusion that VOCs emitted by mold can cause irritant reactions of the type experienced by the Searleses.

The Maine Rules of Evidence provide, "If scientific, technical, or other specialized knowledge will assist the trier of fact to understand the evidence or to determine a fact in issue, a witness qualified as an expert by knowledge, skill, experience, training, or education, may testify thereto in the form of an opinion or otherwise." M.R. Evid. 702. A proponent of expert testimony must establish that (1) the testimony is relevant pursuant to M.R. Evid. 401, and (2) it will assist the trier of fact in understanding the evidence or determining a fact in issue.[2]

"To meet the two-part standard for the admission of expert testimony, the testimony must also meet a threshold level of reliability." In cases where expert testimony "rests on newly ascertained, or applied, scientific principles," a trial court may consider whether "the scientific matters involved in the proffered testimony have been generally accepted or conform to a generally accepted explanatory theory" in determining whether the threshold level of reliability has been met. General acceptance is not a prerequisite for admission, however. A court has latitude to admit "proffered evidence involving newly ascertained, or applied, scientific principles [that] have not yet achieved general acceptance . . . if a showing has been made [that] satisfies the [court] that the proffered evidence is sufficiently reliable to be held relevant."

Indicia of scientific reliability may include the following: whether any studies tendered in support of the testimony are based on facts similar to those at issue, whether the hypothesis of the testimony has been subject to peer review, whether an expert's conclusion has been tailored to the facts of the case, whether any other experts attest to the reliability of the testimony, the nature of the expert's qualifications, and, if a causal relationship is asserted, whether there is a scientific basis for determining that such a relationship exists.

We review a court's foundational finding that expert testimony is sufficiently reliable for clear error. Assuming that a court finds that there is a proper foundation, its decision whether to admit the testimony is a matter of discretion. The question in the present case — whether Dr. Upham's testimony should have been excluded because it was not sufficiently supported by the medical literature — speaks to whether her testimony was sufficiently reliable. Therefore, we review the court's finding that it was for clear error.

In response to Fleetwood's motion in limine, the Searleses provided the court with eight scientific articles in support of Dr. Upham's position that airborne VOCs emitted by mold can cause a nonallergic irritant reaction in some individuals. Fleetwood argues that the eight articles

---

2. Fleetwood contends that we should adopt the *Daubert* standard, *v. Merrell Dow Pharmaceuticals, Inc.*, 509 U.S. 579, 589-95, 113 S.Ct. 2786, 125 L.Ed.2d 469 (1993), based on its contention that we effectively eliminated consideration of "general acceptance" as an element to be considered when determining whether scientific evidence is admissible in *State v. Williams*, 388 A.2d 500 (Me. 1978). Contrary to Fleetwood's argument, however, the *Williams* standard does not preclude the court from considering the question of general acceptance in undertaking its evaluation of challenged testimony. *Id.* at 504. Moreover, Fleetwood concedes that the result in this case would be the same whether we apply *Daubert* or *Williams*. Accordingly, we decline Fleetwood's invitation to adopt the *Daubert* standard in the present case.

demonstrate that Dr. Upham's position is "unproven, not clinically tested, and tenuous at best." To support its argument, Fleetwood quotes selected passages from the articles that suggest that Dr. Upham's opinion regarding causation is not generally shared in the scientific community: "One of the major reasons that residential indoor standards have not been established is the absence of scientific evidence for adverse health effects in occupational settings with high concentrations of airborne fungi";[3] "[I]t has proven quite difficult to quantitate exposure to fungal allergens";[4] and "It is important to note that a link between [fungal VOCs] and any health effects is, at present, tenuous."[5]

Whether a proposition has achieved general acceptance is a relative question. The challenged articles demonstrate that the relevant scientific community has not adopted generally accepted numerical benchmarks by which it can be determined what levels of exposure to airborne fungi will produce nonallergic irritant reactions in humans. Those articles, however, also reveal that many in the community have concluded that a causal relationship likely exists. For example, in one of the articles that Fleetwood quotes, the author states within that same paragraph, "It is considered likely that, where present, fungal VOCs can contribute to the mucosal irritation associated with some of the irritant or 'annoyance' forms of 'tight' or sick building syndrome."[6] Likewise, another article observes that "[f]ungi contain or produce many agents that can have irritant or toxic effects[,] . . . [and] can cause irritant-type health effects in high concentration and have been implicated in building-related symptoms."[7]

Thus, this is not a situation, such as we encountered in [*State v.*] *Black*, in which there is "no scientific basis" for determining that a causal relationship

3. Emil J. Bardana, Jr., M.D., *Indoor Air Quality and Health, Does Fungal Contamination Play a Significant Role?*, 23 IMMUNOLOGY & ALLERGY CLINICS OF N. AM. 291, 294 (2003).

4. Robert E. Esch & Robert K. Bush, *Aerobiology of Outdoor Allergens*, in MIDDLETON'S ALLERGY: PRINCIPLES AND PRACTICE 529, 541 (6th ed., Mosby 2003).

5. W. Elliott Homer, Ph.D., et al., *Fungi*, 14 IMMUNOLOGY & ALLERGY CLINICS OF N. AM. 551, 562 (1994).

6. W. Elliott Horner, Ph.D., et al., *Fungi*, 14 IMMUNOLOGY & ALLERGY CLINICS OF N. AM. 551, 562 (1994).

7. Christine A. Rogers, Ph.D., *Indoor Fungal Exposure*, 23 IMMUNOLOGY & ALLERGY CLINICS OF N. AM. 501, 504 (2003) (citations omitted). *See also* Bardana, *supra* note 3, at 295 ("In the absence of chemical contamination, there is evidence that indoor fungal contamination could cause transient, irritational symptoms.") (citation omitted); Horner, *supra* note 5, at 558 ("The presence of fungi or conditions that are conducive to fungal growth have long been associated with adverse respiratory health effects.") (citation omitted); Robert E. Dales et al., *Adverse Health Effects Among Adults Exposed to Home Dampness and Molds*, 143 AM. REV. OF RESPIRATORY DISEASE 505, 509 (1991) ("In summary, increased respiratory (and other) complaints have been associated with the presence of home dampness and molds among both children and adults. . . ."); B. Flannigan et al., *Allergenic and Toxigenic Microorganisms in Houses*, 70 J. OF APPLIED BACTERIOLOGY SYMP. SUPPLEMENT 61S, 61S (1991) ("[S]everal surveys have noted a strong relationship between reported mould growth and respiratory symptoms.") (citations omitted).

exists. 537 A.2d 1154, 1157 (Me. 1988).[8] Even if the proposition that fungal VOCs can cause an irritant reaction of the type experienced by the Searleses has not gained general acceptance, Dr. Upham's testimony and the journal articles submitted by the Searleses indicate that the proposition cannot be discounted as the marginal view of a handful of members of the relevant scientific community.

It was also established that Dr. Upham has extensive experience in diagnosing environmental health problems in a variety of settings; performs toxicology work associated with indoor air quality; has completed a two-year fellowship in environmental occupational medicine; and has practiced in the field for twelve years. If Dr. Upham were not a specialist with extensive experience in the field, there might be reason to scrutinize more closely her characterization and interpretation of the scientific literature. *See* DAVID H. KAYE ET AL., THE NEW WIGMORE: A TREATISE ON EVIDENCE, EXPERT EVIDENCE § 2.5.4 at 68 (Richard D. Friedman ed., 2004) ("Courts have been much too liberal about allowing doctors to testify to causation of injury outside the malpractice arena. Few doctors are trained in relevant disciplines."). Dr. Upham, however, is a specialist who has been trained to diagnose and treat people who have been exposed to substances such as molds.

In addition, Dr. Upham's opinion was not formed in the abstract; it was tailored to the facts of this case. She personally examined Debra Searles, reviewed the relevant medical records, considered the reports of the experts who did mold testing at the Searleses' home, and completed a differential medical diagnosis.

Based on the foregoing, several factors support the trial court's foundational finding that Dr. Upham's testimony was sufficiently reliable. Dr. Upham's qualifications established her as an expert in environmental occupational medicine, her conclusion that the Searleses experienced an irritant reaction to VOCs emitted by the mold in their home was based on the facts of this case, and there is support in the relevant scientific community for her opinion regarding causation. Because the record supports the court's finding that Dr. Upham's testimony was sufficiently reliable, the finding cannot be said to be clearly erroneous.

Having established that the testimony was sufficiently reliable, the next question is whether the court erred in admitting it. Resolving close questions regarding the admission of expert testimony properly rests with the discretion of the trial judge. In contrast to our appellate review, the trial judge had

---

8. In *State v. Black*, 537 A.2d 1154, 1157 (Me. 1988), a mental health professional was prepared to testify that a victim of sexual abuse had also been sexually abused in the past based on certain "indicators" alleged to occur frequently in sexually abused children. We concluded that her testimony demonstrated no scientific basis for determining that a causal relationship exists between sexual abuse and clinical features of sexual abuse because, inter alia, the summary of symptoms encountered in her population of patients was impaired by selection bias and no testing was done with children who were not victims of sexual abuse to determine whether they exhibited similar indicators.

the opportunity to observe Dr. Upham in person and to assess whether her effort to relate a body of unsettled scientific knowledge to the issue of causation was sufficiently coherent and cogent so as to be of assistance to the jury. In view of all of the circumstances, the court acted within the bounds of its discretion by treating the unsettled state of the relevant science as bearing on the weight to be afforded Dr. Upham's testimony, but not as precluding its consideration by the jury.[9]

NOTES AND QUESTIONS

1. In *Searles*, Maine declines to adopt *Daubert* but requires that novel evidence must be generally accepted, conform to a generally accepted explanatory theory, or meet a reliability standard. Does this hybrid approach strike a better balance than either the *Frye* or *Daubert* approach? What potential problems can you envision with such a flexible approach?

2. Maine requires the proponent to establish a scientific basis for the causal relationship, if the proponent claims such a relationship exists. This is often a formidable burden in toxic tort cases, as set forth in Chapter 7, Medical Causation.

Some expert evidence implies a causal relationship without explicitly proving it, as occurs commonly with syndrome evidence that alleges behaviors of victims that are causally related to some form of criminal violence. In State v. Black, 537 A.2d 1154, 1157 (Me. 1988), the Supreme Court of Maine reversed a conviction where the expert testified about "indicators" of child sexual abuse — behaviors clinicians claim are consistent with abuse. The court held that the testimony failed to meet the required standard:

> The validity of the summary of symptoms encountered in the population of her patients is seriously impaired by selection bias. No comparison testing was done with children who were not victims of sexual abuse to determine whether they also demonstrated like indicators. Her testimony demonstrates no scientific basis for determining that a causal relationship exists between sexual abuse and the "clinical features of sexual abuse," nor is there demonstrated even a positive correlation between the two. In the absence of any demonstration of scientific reliability, we reject the testimony of the mental health expert identifying John as a victim of child sexual abuse.

Contrary to the analysis of the Maine court, many other courts have not required explicit proof of causation in these cases. For an interesting study,

---

9. In a related argument, Fleetwood contends that causation of damages in this case was impermissibly speculative. *See Crowe v. Shaw*, 2000 ME 136, ¶ 10, 755 A.2d 509, 512. Because Dr. Upham's testimony was the only evidence in the record establishing that the mold in the Searleses' home caused their medical problems, this argument hinges upon a finding that Dr. Upham's testimony was erroneously admitted. Because we affirm the trial court's admission of Dr. Upham's testimony, causation of damages was not impermissibly speculative.

see Veronica B. Dahir, *et al., Judicial Application of* Daubert *to Psychological Syndrome and Profile Evidence,* 11 Psychol. Pub. Pol'y & L. 62 (2005).

3. Should jurors or judges be deciding whether the expert testimony is sufficiently reliable? Some critique *Daubert's* focus on the gatekeeping role of judges, arguing that the jury should properly decide whether the evidence is sufficiently reliable. The North Carolina Supreme Court in Howerton v. Arai Helmet, Ltd., 597 S.E.2d 674, 692 (N.C. 2004) expressed concern that one effect of *Daubert* was to strip the jury of its right to decide controversies, allowing judges in civil cases to decide matters by summary judgment. "[W]e are concerned that trial courts asserting sweeping pre-trial "gatekeeping" authority under *Daubert* may unnecessarily encroach upon the constitutionally-mandated function of the jury to decide issues of fact and to assess the weight of the evidence. . . ." The *Howerton* decision has itself been the subject of commentary. *See, e.g.,* John M. Conley & Scott W. Gaylord, *We Are Not a* Daubert *State — But What Are We? Scientific Evidence in North Carolina After* Howerton, 6 N.C. J. L. & Tech. 289 (2005). For further discussion about the effects of *Daubert* on decisions about the sufficiency of expert testimony in tort litigation, see Lucinda M. Finley, *Guarding the Gate to the Courthouse: How Trial Judges Are Using Their Evidentiary Screening Role to Remake Tort Causation Rules,* 49 DePaul L. Rev. 335 (1999); and Margaret A. Berger, *Upsetting The Balance Between Adverse Interests: The Impact Of The Supreme Court's Trilogy on Expert Testimony in Toxic Tort Litigation,* 64 L. & Contemp. Probs. 289 (2001).

III. ADDITIONAL RULES AND CONSIDERATIONS

A. Distinguishing Between Lay and Expert Opinions: FRE 701 and Cases

Courts must occasionally determine whether proposed testimony is an expert or lay opinion. FRE 701 and 702 provide guidance in making this determination. Rule 701 governs non-expert opinion testimony, commonly termed "lay opinion evidence." Since witnesses generally are limited to testifying about facts and may not render opinions, the lay opinion rule provides a narrow exception to the general rule and limits those opinions to ones based solely upon the witness' perception.

Expert opinions, unlike other lay opinions, need not be based on the witness' percipient knowledge of the facts of the case. That is to say, expert witnesses may still testify, even when they have never met the parties to the case nor visited the scene of the accident or the crime. Because of this special exemption expert witnesses are given, courts are required to screen the experts to make sure they meet Rule 702's explicit requirements.

To understand where opinion evidence divides between lay opinion and expert opinion, review the language of FRE 701, Opinion Testimony by Lay Witnesses, which provides:

> If the witness is not testifying as an expert, the witness' testimony in the form of opinions or inferences is limited to those opinions or inferences which are (a) rationally based on the perception of the witness, (b) helpful to a clear understanding of the witness' testimony or the determination of a fact in issue, and (c) not based on scientific, technical, or other specialized knowledge within the scope of Rule 702.[4]

Thus a lay witness opinion must be both rationally based upon his perception and not the type of matter about which an expert would testify. Additionally, the matter must be helpful to the jury. In the following examples, can you determine whether the proposed witness' testimony would be lay opinion or expert? What questions must you ask in order to answer these hypotheticals?

- In a malpractice case, testimony from an operating room nurse that the surgeon did not appear to be concerned about the plaintiff's blood pressure and that such a lack of concern was unusual
- In a malpractice case, testimony from the hospital receptionist that the patient appeared to be intoxicated when she arrived at the hospital
- In a speeding arrest case, testimony from a police officer about the speed of the defendant's vehicle when it passed the police officer. In this case, the police officer had no radar but stated that the defendant "was driving far in excess of the speed limit."
- In a speeding arrest case, testimony from a police officer about the speed of the defendant's vehicle clocked on radar as it passed the police officer
- In a construction litigation case, testimony from a plumber about the types of shower tiles that were installed and why they were not appropriate for the project in question
- In a drug case, testimony from an officer that the defendant appeared nervous and was sweating profusely

4. In 2000, Rule 701 was amended for the purpose of drawing a clearer distinction between FRE 702 expert testimony and 701 lay opinion testimony, so as to "eliminate the risk that the reliability requirements set forth in Rule 702 will be evaded through the simple expedient of proffering an expert in lay witness clothing." *See* Advisory Committee Notes to the 2000 FRE Amendments. Subsection (c) was added to expressly distinguish between lay and expert opinion evidence.

The amended Federal Rules of Evidence require that courts draw a bright line between opinions requiring specialized knowledge (expert opinions) and opinions that do not require such knowledge (lay opinions).

The lay/expert distinction distinguishes between the types of testimony; not between the types of witnesses. Thus, a single witness can provide both lay and expert opinions. For example, a police officer may testify about his observations of the participants in a drug conspiracy case. He may opine — in his role as a fact witness — that the defendant appeared to be nervous. That officer may also testify as an expert witness about how drugs are packaged, delivered, and how code words are substituted for drugs in phone conversations.

In other cases, a treating physician may testify about whether the plaintiff in a car accident appeared to be in pain — generally a lay opinion — and may testify about the plaintiff's prognosis for recovery — generally an expert opinion.

In the following cases, did the respective courts correctly rule on the admissibility of the opinion evidence under FRE 701?

United States v. Martinez-Figueroa

363 F.3d 679 (8th Cir. 2004), *reversed and remanded on sentencing grounds,* Martinez-Figueroa v. U.S., 543 U.S. 1100 (2005)

LOKEN, Chief Judge.

Missouri state highway patrol officers stopped Luciano Martinez-Figueroa driving a tractor-trailer rig on Interstate 44 near Joplin, Missouri. A consent search of the refrigerated trailer revealed a load of cheddar cheese and 537 kilograms of marijuana. Figueroa was charged with conspiracy to distribute marijuana and possession of marijuana with the intent to distribute. . . . [Appellant was convicted and the Court of Appeals affirms.]

At trial, undercover narcotics agent James Musche described how he infiltrated the drug trafficking conspiracy by offering to store marijuana near Joplin. When the time came for a delivery, Musche met confidential informant Edward Raifsnider at a truck stop near Interstate 44. Musche testified that conspirator Jamie De La Pena was in the front passenger seat of Raifsnider's vehicle and Figueroa was in a rear seat. After a brief conversation, De La Pena told Figueroa to "go get the truck." Narcotics agents followed the truck when it left the truck stop and contacted the highway patrol officers, who stopped the truck soon thereafter.

Officer Banasik testified that he questioned Figueroa at the scene of the arrest after giving Miranda warnings. Figueroa first denied but then admitted knowing that he was hauling marijuana. Banasik used Figueroa's trucking logbook in questioning him about the circuitous route he had traveled from California, where the cheese was loaded, toward Crawfordsville, Indiana, where it was scheduled to be delivered. The logbook showed that Figueroa had lingered in California for two days and then traveled the same route through New Mexico to Texas on two consecutive days. The government also introduced evidence that there was no seal on the trailer door when the truck was stopped, contrary to a bill of lading for the cheese. After the government rested, Figueroa took the stand. He admitted keeping a false logbook to evade government trucking regulations. He denied being at the truck stop or knowing either De La Pena or Raifsnider. Figueroa accused the highway patrol officers of removing the seal from his trailer. . . .

II. The Logbook Testimony.

At trial, Officer Banasik testified that, after questioning Figueroa about the course of his travels, "I went up to the tractor unit to obtain the bill of lading [and] his logbook . . . to see if I could determine if there were any discrepancies in what he told me and what the paperwork stated." After identifying a government exhibit as the logbook he used, Banasik was asked, "What is the purpose of a logbook?" The court overruled Figueroa's timely objection, and Banasik responded:

> The logbook has several purposes. One, truckdrivers are regulated by law how long they can drive, how long they have to sleep. They're very regulated on how much they can drive and stuff. The logbook basically records their activities so if they are stopped by law enforcement purposes, the law enforcement officer can go back and ensure that they are not in violation of federal or state law, overdriving and stuff.
>
> Companies use it also to verify that their drivers picked up a load, and sometimes it verifies how many miles they have driven, how many loads they have taken. Then it also verifies their trip. If they have a bill of lading that says they're from somewhere and they get stopped and it verifies — the logbook should show that they had stopped there to pick up a load and stuff.

On appeal, Figueroa argues that the district court abused its discretion by permitting Officer Banasik to testify as an expert witness when the government had not given the notice required by Rule 16(a)(1)(G) of the Federal Rules of Criminal Procedure.*

Rule 701 of the Federal Rules of Evidence limits opinion testimony by lay witnesses "to those opinions or inferences which are . . . (c) not based on scientific, technical, or other specialized knowledge within the scope of Rule 702," which deals with the admissibility of testimony by expert witnesses. This limitation is designed to prevent a party from using lay opinion

---

*Fed. R. Crim. P 16 (a)(1)(G) requires the government to provide a written summary of the testimony of any expert witnesses the government intends to call at trial, if defendant has filed a request for such information. — Ed.

testimony to "subvert[ ] the disclosure and discovery requirements of Federal Rules of Criminal Procedure 26 and 16 and the reliability requirements for expert testimony." United States v. Peoples, 250 F.3d 630, 641 (8th Cir. 2001). In general, unless a law enforcement officer is qualified as an expert, opinion testimony "is admissible only to help the jury or the court to understand the facts about which the witness is testifying and not to provide specialized explanations or interpretations that an untrained layman could not make if perceiving the same acts or events". . . .

In this case, Officer Banasik had firsthand knowledge based upon his use of the logbook to interrogate Figueroa after his arrest. The above-quoted testimony was in the nature of foundation to explain to the jury why Banasik was able by reason of his training and experience as a highway patrol officer to use the logbook to verify or refute Figueroa's description of his travels. The explanation required a knowledge of trucking regulations that an untrained layman might lack. But it was not particularly technical. Indeed, a prior witness, patrol officer Mory McKnight, had given testimony that reflected knowledge of how truckers keep logbooks without objection, and Figueroa gave later testimony regarding the regulatory purposes of his logbook that was consistent with Officer Banasik's explanation. In these circumstances, the district court did not abuse its Rule 701 discretion by permitting Banasik to offer this lay opinion testimony. In any event, the challenged testimony was cumulative, and thus any error was harmless.

The judgment of the district court is affirmed.

NOTES AND QUESTIONS

1. The court above reasoned that the officer's explanation in court "required a knowledge of trucking regulation that an untrained layman might lack. But it was not particularly technical." Is that the correct test?

Bank of China, New York Branch v. NBM, LLC

359 F.3d 171 (2d Cir. 2004)

SCHEINDLIN, District Judge

I. BACKGROUND

Bank of China alleged that the defendants defaulted on their loan obligations and perpetrated a massive fraud on Bank of China, beginning in 1991 and continuing until mid-2000. In sum, Bank of China claimed that various defendants borrowed huge sums from the Bank through false and misleading representations, and in many cases, forged documents. In violation of representations and contractual undertakings, the borrowed funds were converted into different currencies and transferred into accounts held by other defendants, which were represented to the Bank to be independent businesses; in fact, the "third-party businesses" were controlled by the borrowing defendants. The borrowed funds were then falsely represented to Bank of China to be "trade debt" owed to the borrowing defendants, thus creating the illusion that the borrowing defendants and the "third-party businesses" were thriving businesses with sufficient cash flows to sustain the borrowing limits approved by the Bank. The borrowed funds were also disguised as "collateral" for further loans, creating further indebtedness to the Bank. Finally, additional monies were drawn down against letters of credit issued under the increased credit facilities by the presentation of false and forged documents for non-existent transactions. The success of the fraud was dependent, in part, on bribes paid to defendant Patrick Young, then a deputy manager at Bank of China who handled defendants' transactions with the Bank.

B.   TESTIMONY OF HUANG YANGXIN

At trial, the District Court allowed plaintiff's witness Huang Yangxin, a Bank of China employee, to testify to the following: (1) that certain transactions between defendants . . . did not comport with the business community's understanding of normal, true, trade transactions between a buyer and seller; (2) the concept of a "trust receipt," and how it works in the context of an international commercial transaction; and (3) that it is considered fraud when an importer presents a trust receipt to a bank to obtain a loan knowing that there are no real goods involved. The District Court found that Huang's testimony was admissible based on his many years of experience in international banking and trade,[10] and concluded that the testimony satisfied the requirements for lay opinion testimony under Federal Rule of Evidence 701.

The admission of this testimony pursuant to Rule 701 was error because it was not based entirely on Huang's perceptions; the District Court abused its discretion to the extent it admitted the testimony based on Huang's

---

10. Huang testified for several days, and his testimony spans nearly 1000 pages of the trial transcript. Defendants objected to much of the testimony, including Huang's description of a "trust receipt" and his conclusions concerning the defendants' transactions. At times, defendants did not specify the nature of their objections, including their objections to much of the "trust receipt" testimony, and the District Judge did not explain why he allowed the testimony. *See* Tr. at 247-50. In overruling one of the objections, the District Judge noted that Huang had years of experience in the international banking business. *See id.* at 259. However, he also said that Huang's testimony was "common sense," thus suggesting that he may not have relied entirely on Huang's experience in international banking in overruling the objection. *See id.* In any event, because defendants consistently objected to the testimony, their objections were preserved. Moreover, although the district judge's reasoning for allowing some of the testimony is not entirely clear, we conclude that admission of the testimony was an abuse of discretion because the testimony was, in large part, not clearly based on Huang's perceptions.

experience and specialized knowledge in international banking. Subsection (c) of Rule 701, which was amended in 2000, explicitly bars the admission of lay opinions that are "based on scientific, technical, or other specialized knowledge within the scope of Rule 702". . . . The Advisory Committee explained that the purpose of Rule 701(c) is "to eliminate the risk that the reliability requirements set forth in Rule 702 will be evaded through the simple expedient of proffering an expert in lay witness clothing". . . . That is, in part, what happened here.

Testimony admitted pursuant to Rule 701 must be "rationally based on the perception of the witness". . . . To some extent, Huang's testimony was based on his perceptions. As a Bank of China employee, Huang was assigned to investigate defendants' activities at the tail-end of their scheme and after Bank of China stopped doing business with them. Huang's senior role at the Bank and his years of experience in international banking made him particularly well-suited to undertake such an investigation and was likely a factor in the Bank's decision to assign the task to him. The fact that Huang has specialized knowledge, or that he carried out the investigation because of that knowledge, does not preclude him from testifying pursuant to Rule 701, so long as the testimony was based on the investigation and reflected his investigatory findings and conclusions, and was not rooted exclusively in his expertise in international banking. "Such opinion testimony is admitted not because of experience, training or specialized knowledge within the realm of an expert, but because of the particularized knowledge that the witness has by virtue of his [ ] position in the business." Fed. R. Evid. 701 advisory committee's note. Thus, to the extent Huang's testimony was grounded in the investigation he undertook in his role as a Bank of China employee, it was admissible pursuant to Rule 701 of the Federal Rules of Evidence because it was based on his perceptions. *See United States v. Glenn,* 312 F.3d 58, 67 (2d Cir. 2002) ("[A] lay opinion must be rationally based on the perception of the witness. This requirement is the familiar requirement of first-hand knowledge or observation.")

However, to the extent Huang's testimony was not a product of his investigation, but rather reflected specialized knowledge he has because of his extensive experience in international banking, its admission pursuant to Rule 701 was error. Thus, Huang's explanations regarding typical international banking transactions or definitions of banking terms, and any conclusions that he made that were not a result of his investigation, were improperly admitted. Of course, these opinions may, nonetheless, have been admissible pursuant to Rule 702 because "[c]ertainly it is possible for the same witness to provide lay and expert testimony in a single case." Fed. R. Evid. 701, advisory committee's note. . . . But before such testimony could have been proffered pursuant to Rule 702, Bank of China was obligated to satisfy the reliability requirements set forth in that Rule, and disclose Huang as an expert pursuant to Rule 26(a)(2)(A) of the Federal Rules of Civil Procedure.

NOTES AND QUESTIONS

1. The court here states that "[t]he fact that Huang has specialized knowledge, or that he carried out the investigation because of that knowledge, does not preclude him from testifying pursuant to Rule 701, so long as the testimony was based on the investigation and reflected his investigatory findings and conclusions, and was not rooted exclusively in his expertise in international banking." The Advisory Committee Notes point out the long-recognized distinction between expert opinions and those based upon the "particularized knowledge that the witness has by virtue of his or her position in the business." The court here drew a distinction between the type of testimony that was permissible under 701 (investigation results) and that which was impermissible under 701 (specialized knowledge based upon extensive experience in the banking industry). *See also* National Hispanic Circus, Inc. v. Rex Trucking, Inc., 414 F.3d 546, 551-552 (5th Cir. 2005) (stating that Rule 701 "does not exclude testimony by corporate officers or business owners on matters that relate to their business affairs, such as industry practice and pricing"). Is this distinction as straightforward as it might seem upon first consideration? Is it consistent with the respective purposes of Rules 701 and 702?

2. There are two primary purposes for the Rules' new sharp distinction between lay opinion and expert opinion testimony: (1) to prevent litigants from avoiding the disclosure requirements of the federal civil and criminal rules of procedure by simply calling the testimony lay opinion evidence; and (2) to require litigants to comply with the reliability requirements of Rule 702 when introducing expert testimony. Were such purposes met in the preceding cases?

3. For additional examples of judicial interpretation of FRE 701, *see e.g.*, Bryant v. Farmers Ins. Exchange, 432 F.3d 1114, 1124 (10th Cir. 2005) (holding that testimony about the calculation of the average of 103 numbers was aptly characterized as lay opinion under 701, since it was a "mathematical calculation well within the ability of anyone with a grade school education."); and United States v. Pinillos-Prieto, 419 F.3d 61, 71 (1st Cir. 2005) (testimony about the dangerous nature of drug organizations was appropriately admissible as lay opinion evidence).

B. Basis of Knowledge for an Expert's Opinion: FRE 703 and Cases

FRE 703 governs the use of facts or data that an expert relies upon in forming her opinion and provides as follows:

> The facts or data in the particular case upon which an expert bases an opinion or inference may be those perceived by or made known to the expert at or before the hearing. If of a type reasonably relied upon by experts in the

particular field in forming opinions or inferences upon the subject, the facts
or data need not be admitted. Facts or data that are otherwise inadmissible
shall not be disclosed to the jury by the proponent of the opinion or inference
unless the court determines that their probative value in assisting the jury to
evaluate the expert's opinion substantially outweighs their prejudicial effect.[5]

The Rule permits the expert to be provided "facts or data" both prior to
testifying and at the hearing itself. Thus, an expert may actually listen to a
witness testifying as part of the information upon which he bases an opinion.
Not all facts upon which an expert relies need to be admissible; for example,
a specialist physician may rely on the various medical records of the patient
that contain hearsay information. Although those records might not be
admissible because of hearsay problems, the information may form the
basis for the expert's opinion, since it is the type "reasonably relied upon
by experts in the particular field in forming opinions." Before such
"otherwise inadmissible" evidence is disclosed to the jury, the court engages
in a balancing, determining whether the probative value substantially outweighs the prejudicial effect. The court determines whether the probative
value of that underlying information "substantially outweighs" their prejudicial effect.

Most of the concerns about the application of Rule 703 involve a
question of whether the underlying evidence is of the type "reasonably
relied upon" by experts in that field. Consider the following court's interpretation of that issue.

Ferrara & DiMercurio v. St. Paul Mercury Insurance Company

240 F.3d 1 (1st Cir. 2001)

Before SELYA, Circuit Judge, COFFIN and CAMPBELL, Senior Circuit Judges.
LEVIN H. CAMPBELL, Senior Circuit Judge.

I. BACKGROUND

On July 3, 1993, the commercial fishing vessel F/V TWO FRIENDS was
destroyed by a fire. Plaintiff-Appellant Ferrara & DiMercurio ("F&D"),
owner of the vessel, sought to recover insurance under a Hull Policy issued
by defendant-appellee St. Paul Mercury Insurance Company ("St. Paul").

---

5. This Rule, like FRE 701 and 702, was amended in 2000. The Advisory Notes explain
the purpose of the amendment: "Rule 703 has been amended to emphasize that when an
expert reasonably relies on inadmissible information to form an opinion or inference, the
underlying information is not admissible simply because the opinion or inference is
admitted."

St. Paul denied coverage after its investigation ended with a determination of arson, which it understood to be excluded from coverage under the policy. Thereafter, F&D brought an action in the district court claiming that St. Paul's refusal to pay was a breach of the insurance contract and constituted "bad faith" in violation of Massachusetts General Laws ch. 93A. After a first trial ended in a hung jury, a second trial ended with the court directing a verdict in favor of the plaintiff.

At the time the district court directed a plaintiff's verdict, the court accepted that St. Paul would not be liable could it prove its affirmative defense that the fire was deliberately set by the insured. But the court ruled that the evidence put forward was legally insufficient for a jury to find that plaintiff had deliberately set its boat on fire. St. Paul had also asserted that it would be exempt from liability were the fire found to have been deliberately set by an unknown third party, relying upon the language of an exclusion for "malicious acts" found in the so-called Strikes, Riots, and Civil Commotions ("SR&CC") clause. However, the court construed that provision as excluding from coverage only those fires deliberately set by third parties in the context of civil unrest, a setting absent here.

On appeal, this court disagreed with the district court's rulings, reversing and remanding the case for a third trial. . . .

The parties returned to district court to prepare for a third trial, this time before yet a third judge, Judge Harrington. Based upon their mutual understanding of this court's decision in *Ferrara I*, both parties agreed that the following single question would be submitted to the jury to be answered "Yes" or "No": "Do you find that the defendant, St. Paul Mercury Insurance Company, has established by a preponderance of the evidence that the fire was of an incendiary nature or deliberately set?". This question was apparently meant to incorporate both holdings of *Ferrara I*, entitling St. Paul to the defense of arson by third parties as well as to the defense of arson-by-the-insured. The jury returned a verdict in favor of defendant St. Paul, answering "Yes" to the special verdict. F&D appeals.

Unlike in *Ferrara I*, when we were faced with, among other issues, the task of construing somewhat unusual language in the insurance policy, this time the issues presented are more commonplace. F&D claims reversible error on the basis of certain evidentiary rulings, any one of which, F&D argues, entitles it to a fourth trial. We disagree. F&D also appeals from the district court's denial of plaintiff's post-trial motion for sanctions. For the reasons that follow, we affirm all of the rulings below.

II. Legal Analyses of Evidentiary Issues

The three evidentiary issues are as follows: . . . (B) the propriety of admitting into evidence against F&D the expert testimony of John Malcolm regarding the cause and origin of the fire; . . .

A.   JOHN MALCOLM'S EXPERT TESTIMONY AS TO CAUSE AND ORIGIN

Much of the two-week trial before Judge Harrington was a battle between the experts concerning whether the fire was accidental or of incendiary origin. Defendant's expert, John Malcolm, concluded that the fire on the TWO FRIENDS had three points of origin and was deliberately set. Plaintiff's expert, Paul Sullivan, testified that an accidental electrical fire started in the lower electrical panel and exploded in a so-called flash-over igniting everything in the super-heated compartments of the vessel.

Beyond the conflicting expert opinions, the battle also raged over whether John Malcolm should be allowed to testify as St. Paul's cause-and-origin expert. It is on this issue that F&D appeals. F&D contends that John Malcolm should not have been permitted to render an expert opinion as to cause and origin because (1) his opinion was based on unreliable data, viz, data not collected by him personally and (2) St. Paul failed to supplement its expert disclosures to include Malcolm's testimony regarding cause and origin. Before going into the merits of these arguments, we recount the history of Malcolm's involvement in this case.

As soon as four days after the fire, St. Paul had hired Fred O'Donnell as its expert to investigate the origin and cause of the fire. Fred O'Donnell then hired John Malcolm as an electrical systems expert to assist him in that investigation. On July 8, 1993, the two men began their investigation on site in Gloucester where the boat remained moored. O'Donnell and Malcolm worked closely with each other. Malcolm testified that together, sometimes with Malcolm holding the measuring tape for O'Donnell, the two took measurements of the vessel in preparation for producing scale drawings to assist in the investigation and their report. Although Malcolm's job for which O'Donnell had retained him was to pay close attention to the boat's electrical system, the two men worked in tandem, often double-checking each other's observations and analyses by calling each other over to various burn sites on the vessel to coordinate their data collection and inquiries.

During the first two trials, O'Donnell and Malcolm both testified as experts, O'Donnell as to the fire's cause and origin and Malcolm as to related but narrower questions concerning the fire and the boat's electrical system. Unfortunately, however, between the first appeal and the third trial, O'Donnell died. For the third trial, then, instead of replacing O'Donnell with an outside cause-and-origin expert, defendant decided that Malcolm would testify as St. Paul's only fire expert, providing opinions on both cause and origin and the vessel's electrical system. This decision is the source of F&D's objection regarding the admissibility of Malcolm's testimony. F&D argued to the district court, as it does to us now, that Malcolm was not competent to testify as to cause and origin as his testimony was principally based not on his own observations but on those made by O'Donnell. F&D

also argues that designating Malcolm as a cause-and-origin expert so close to trial unduly prejudiced their case against St. Paul. At least, F&D contends, St. Paul should have supplemented its interrogatory answers and expert reports to include Malcolm's anticipated expanded testimony. . . .

F&D's next objection, although not crafted as such, is essentially a Rule 703 objection. F&D claims that Malcolm's opinion as to cause and origin was based on unreliable data, viz, data provided by the late Fred O'Donnell and not that which was collected through Malcolm's own personal observation.

A major problem with this argument is that Malcolm himself had visited the fire scene and examined the evidence there side by side with O'Donnell. Besides looking at burn patterns and studying the electrical system, he took measurements and photographs and wrote his own report. He also interviewed the vessel's engineer. Many photographs of evidence at the scene were entered into evidence by stipulation. Hence, it is simply not the case that Malcolm's cause-and-origin opinion rested mainly upon O'Donnell's investigations.

To be sure, Malcolm's opinion coincided with O'Donnell's and he testified that he read O'Donnell's report in preparation for his expert testimony, along with the report of the local fire department. But the opinion he rendered was his own, and, as said, he had first-hand knowledge of the fire scene and the observable facts there upon which to base that opinion. Federal Rule of Evidence 703 allows Malcolm to have taken O'Donnell's report and opinion into account when forming his own expert opinion. So long as the basis of Malcolm's opinion did not extend beyond facts or data "of a type reasonably relied upon by experts in the particular field in forming opinions or inferences upon the subject, the facts or data need not be admissible in evidence." Fed. R. Evid. 703. We think a cause-and-origin expert like Malcolm could be expected to examine the report of another expert like O'Donnell as well as the fire department's report in the course of forming his own opinion derived from a variety of sources, including his own first-hand knowledge of the primary evidence at the fire scene. . . .

This court has said that when an expert relies on the opinion of another, such reliance goes to the weight, not to the admissibility of the expert's opinion. . . . *See also Newell Puerto Rico, Ltd. v. Rubbermaid Inc.*, 20 F.3d 15, 21 (1st Cir. 1994) ("When the factual underpinning of an expert opinion is weak, it is a matter affecting the weight and credibility of the testimony—a question to be resolved by the jury."). In the present case, the jury understood that Malcolm's observations coincided with those of the deceased expert hired by defendant and that, until recently, Malcolm's only job was to advise and supplement O'Donnell's conclusions as to the cause and origin of the fire with his own opinion concerning the role of the vessel's electrical system in the fire. Thus, in weighing and evaluating Malcolm's opinion, the jury was able to determine whether it was in some way weakened by reliance upon O'Donnell's.

We find no error in the district court's ruling that Malcolm's opinion as to cause and origin was properly admitted.

NOTES AND QUESTIONS

1. Although litigating Rule 703 issues is not as common as disputes over Rule 702, some courts have drawn firm lines, finding that the underlying facts or data were not of a type reasonably relied upon by experts in the particular field in forming opinions or inferences upon the subject. For instance, in United States v. Tran Tron Cuong, 18 F.3d 1132, 1143 (4th Cir. 1994), the court of appeals held it was error for one doctor in a case to testify that he relied on an inadmissible opinion prepared by another physician for the purpose of litigation, noting it was doubtful that report would qualify as data "of a type reasonably relied upon by experts in the particular field." The court remarked that since the "report was prepared at the request of the prosecution," it constituted a forensic opinion or report in a criminal case. The court questioned whether a physician would usually rely upon forensic medical opinions or reports in forming his opinions in family medicine. Can you explain the different outcomes in the preceding case and in *Tran Tron Cuong?*

C. Ultimate Issue Testimony: FRE 704

1. FRE 704(a)

Historically, courts did not permit expert opinion evidence about the ultimate opinion in a case, believing that such evidence was an impermissible infringement on the jury's role as factfinder. This "ultimate issue" objection had lost ground over time and was not well received, even before the enactment of FRE 704. *See* Christopher B. Mueller & Laird C. Kirkpatrick, *Federal Evidence, Second Edition*, § 360, n.4 (2006), citing cases. Rule 704 was enacted in 1984 and subsection (a) of that Rule provides as follows:

Rule 704. Opinion on Ultimate Issue

(a) Except as provided in subdivision (b), testimony in the form of an opinion or inference otherwise admissible is not objectionable because it embraces an ultimate issue to be decided by the trier of fact.

One court describes the effect of Rule 704(a) as follows:

Federal Rule of Evidence 704(a) provides that, with certain exceptions not relevant here, "testimony in the form of an opinion or inference otherwise admissible is not objectionable because it embraces an ultimate issue to be decided by the trier of fact." Rule 704(a) was designed specifically to abolish the "ultimate issue" rule. Fed. R. Evid. 704 advisory committee's notes. The rule, however, "does not lower the bars so as to admit all opinions." *Id.* "As a condition to admissibility under Rule 704(a), testimony on ultimate issues must be otherwise admissible under the Rules of Evidence." Weinstein's Federal Evidence § 704.03[1] (2d ed. 2001). Therefore, although opinion testimony that embraces an ultimate issue cannot be excluded under Rule 704(a), it may be excludable on other grounds. . . . [u]nder Rule 701 and 702, opinions must be helpful to the trier of fact, and Rule 403 provides for exclusion of evidence which wastes time. These provisions afford ample assurances against the admission of opinions which would merely tell the jury what result to reach, somewhat in the manner of the oath-helpers of an earlier day.

United States v. Barile, 286 F.3d 749, 759-760 (4th Cir. 2002).

Many courts, however, have stated that expert witnesses are not entitled to give opinions about legal conclusions or opinions about the ultimate issue of law, since such opinions are not deemed helpful to the jury in making a decision but rather seek to substitute the expert's judgment for the jury's. *See e.g.*, Elsayed Mukhtar v. California State University, Hayward, 299 F.3d 1053, 1065 n.10 (9th Cir. 2002).

2. FRE 704(b)

In the early 1980s, John Hinckley shot and seriously wounded President Ronald Reagan. Hinckley was able to successfully invoke the insanity defense in his trial, which resulted in his confinement in a mental institution rather than being sentenced to a federal prison. This jury verdict provoked a storm of controversy, which resulted in a wholesale change to the federal law of insanity and also led to the enactment of Rule 704(b), which provides:

(b) No expert witness testifying with respect to the mental state or condition of a defendant in a criminal case may state an opinion or inference as to whether the defendant did or did not have the mental state or condition constituting an element of the crime charged or of a defense thereto. Such ultimate issues are matters for the trier of fact alone.

Most courts have interpreted this Rule to preclude testimony by a mental health expert that a defendant did or did not "appreciate the wrongfulness of his conduct" — which is the legal standard for insanity.

However, Rule 704(b) has been held to apply to other types of federal criminal cases, where mens rea is an element of the crime. For example, in several cases, courts have commented critically on expert testimony about whether the defendant possessed contraband with intent to distribute. Frequently, the prosecution will call an expert to discuss packaging and paraphernalia as evidence that the contraband was not possessed for personal use, but to distribute. Occasionally, the expert testimony crosses the line and becomes prohibited expert opinion evidence of the defendant's intent — which as an element of the crime is not susceptible to expert opinion. *See e.g.*, United States v. Watson, 260 F.3d 301, 310 (3d Cir. 2001).[6]

D. Disclosure of Facts or Data Underlying Expert Opinion: FRE 705

FRE 705 provides that the expert may testify in terms of opinion or inference and give reasons therefor without first testifying to the underlying facts or data, unless the court requires otherwise. The expert may in any event be required to disclose the underlying facts or data on cross-examination.

This rule, which should be read in tandem with Rule 703, permits an expert to give an opinion without first laying out the predicate facts or data upon which the opinion rests, unless the court so requires. According to the 1993 Advisory Committee Notes "[i]f a serious question is raised under Rule 702 or 703 as to the admissibility of expert testimony, disclosure of the underlying facts or data on which opinions are based may, of course, be needed by the court before deciding whether, and to what extent, the person should be allowed to testify."

---

6. United States v. Romero, 189 F.3d 576 (7th Cir. 1999), reprinted in Chapter Five, Expert Testimony About Behavioral Science, includes a discussion of FRE 704(b).

CHAPTER 3

STATISTICAL INFERENCE

The process of *statistical inference* lies at the core of much scientific evidence. In simplest terms, the problem is what practical sense to make of quantitative information; more specifically, it is a method for testing hypotheses. Suppose, for example, that in a certain county 79 percent of the jury-eligible population was Mexican-American, but only 39 percent of the people called for jury duty over a period of time were Mexican-American. Is this admissible evidence of discrimination on the part of the county court officials? If so, is this evidence sufficient to support a prima facie case?

Before answering those questions, it might be helpful to think about the possibility of random variation. That is, assume that the court officials did not discriminate. On the contrary, they put the name of every jury-eligible person on a ping-pong ball and put all the balls into a huge drum. Every time they needed to summon a jury pool, they rotated the drum and then, while blindfolded, withdrew the requisite number of ping-pong balls.

If we examined many pools summoned using this technique, we would probably expect the percentage of Mexican-American jurors to be about 79 percent. If, for example, over the course of ten years only 390 out of the 1,000 jurors who were summoned were Mexican-American (versus the expected 790), we would be surprised and probably suspicious of the county officials' story. We would not have the same expectation about any single pool, however. In that case, we might not be suspicious if, say, only four of ten jurors (versus the expected eight [10 × .79]) were Mexican-American. But where would we draw the line? At what point would we become suspicious — how about 39 out of 100, or 195 out of 500? And what would be the basis for our decision?

Most non-statisticians would probably say that the 4-out-of-10 evidence shouldn't be taken too seriously because of the possibility of random variation in drawing the ping-pong balls. On the other hand, random variations should even out over the course of a large number of draws. We might analogize to flipping a coin: We would expect 1,000 flips to produce something close to 500 heads (and suspect the fix was in if they didn't), but would acknowledge that almost anything might happen over only ten flips.

All of the questions posed thus far — and, indeed, most of the statistical questions that the law regularly confronts — can be restated in a more general form: When what we observe deviates from what we expect, how big does the deviation have to be before we reject chance as an explanation and begin entertaining other hypotheses? In the jury example, our expectation — shaped by our knowledge of the jury-eligible population — was that about 79 percent of the jurors would be Mexican-American. How far do the data have to stray from that expectation before we reject the chance explanation and think about things like discrimination?

Examples of related questions might include:

- In a study to test the efficacy of a new vaccine for a certain disease, 100,000 people receive the vaccine and another 100,000 receive a placebo. Among the vaccinated group, there are 28 cases of the disease; among the placebo group, 71 cases. Should the Food and Drug Administration conclude that the vaccine is "effective" to prevent the disease?
- An employer uses a written test as part of its application process. Eighty-two percent of the Caucasian applicants pass but only 61 percent of the African-Americans pass. Can the test be said to have a discriminatory impact?
- The employer defends its use of the test, saying that it has a strong positive correlation with job performance. How would one prove or test this assertion?
- In an employment case, an expert statistician for the plaintiff class testifies that on average, African American employees are paid only 68 percent as much as "comparably qualified" Caucasian employees. On what basis can a statistician make such an assertion? How might the lawyer for the defendant employer prepare to cross-examine and/or rebut this evidence?

The science of statistics offers an intellectual framework for dealing with such questions. Although statistics rarely offers bright-line answers, it does provide a set of analytical techniques, guidelines for applying them, and principles for interpreting results. This chapter presents some of the statistical techniques that have been used most frequently in the courts. In the cases that follow, statistical analysis is the explicit basis for interpreting quantitative evidence and reaching a legal decision. It is important to remember, though, that statistics plays an important role — sometimes explicit and sometimes implicit — in almost every branch of science that is discussed in this book. For that reason, understanding the material discussed in this chapter is an essential prerequisite to a full understanding of the scientific approaches covered in the subsequent chapters.

The topics to be covered in this chapter include data collection, with emphasis on the principles of sampling from larger populations; confidence intervals and estimation; the assessment of the statistical significance of observations that deviate from expectations, with specific reference to null hypotheses, standard deviations, and p-values; and regression analysis, a widely used technique for creating statistical models.

I. COLLECTING DATA: POPULATIONS AND SAMPLES

An initial question in any statistical problem is often whether the right data, or pieces of information, have been gathered. The terms *population* and *sample* frequently come up. The population is the universe (courts often use "population" and "universe" interchangeably) that the analyst wants to study or measure. Sometimes, it is possible to include the whole population in the analysis. If, for example, the case involves the promotion of men and women in a company's workforce over a specified period, the company's records may permit the litigants to collect data on every affected employee. In other situations, however, it is impossible to study the whole population, so it is necessary to take a sample of the larger group. Consider the exit polls that the television networks rely on to project the winners of elections. It would be impossible to interview every voter coming out of every voting precinct, so the networks (1) choose a sample of precincts in the relevant state and then (2) interview a sample of voters as they emerge from the polls.

An obvious next question is the appropriateness of the sample. Specifically, is the sample sufficiently *representative* of the population from which it was drawn to support inferences being made about that population? Think about the exit polls again: What we really want to know is how the population of voters is behaving. Whether the exit polls will accurately predict their behavior depends on whether the sample of voters who have been interviewed is representative of voters as a whole. In many cases, the best way to insure representativeness is to take a random sample of the population. A sampling procedure is *random* if every member of the population has an equal probability of being selected. The ping-pong ball method of drawing of jurors described at the beginning of this chapter would qualify. As will be described in Section II, the statistician's confidence in the representativeness of a random sample generally increases with the size of the sample.

In other cases, however, random sampling is either infeasible or undesirable. In those situations, the researcher exercises judgment to try to insure representativeness. To return to exit polling, the networks choose the voters to be interviewed at a given precinct on a random basis. But they choose the precincts that have a track record of accurately predicting state-wide results — in other words, they make an informed, non-random judgment about the representativeness of the chosen precincts. In trademark infringement cases, the litigants often offer surveys of shoppers to prove or refute the proposition that the plaintiff's and defendant's trademarks are confusingly similar. These surveys usually involve selecting one or more stores where the relevant products are sold, interviewing every willing shopper (a so-called *opportunity sample*), showing them the two marks, and asking questions designed to ferret out possible confusion. Not surprisingly, these cases routinely produce disputes over whether the competing surveys have targeted the correct population of shoppers and whether the survey methods have produced representative samples of the relevant population. The next two cases raise questions about the legal use of, respectively, random and non-random samples.

United States ex rel. Free v. Peters

806 F. Supp. 705 (N.D. Ill. 1992)

[Petitioner Free brought this federal habeas corpus proceeding to set aside his Illinois state court conviction for murder and sentence of death. Free argued that the death sentence violated the Eighth Amendment because the jurors did not understand their instructions concerning the role of mitigating factors in sentencing. To demonstrate this lack of comprehension, Free relied in large part on surveys of jurors in Cook County, Illinois conducted in 1990 and 1992 by Professors Zeisel and Rossi.]

[The court addressed the prosecution's contention that] it is improper to draw conclusions about the universe sampled from, *i.e.,* all eligible jurors in Cook County, because Free has not demonstrated the representativeness of the samples. . . .

1. REPRESENTATIVENESS OF SURVEY SAMPLE

As noted by respondents, general difficulties may arise when a researcher depends on limited data from samples to answer general questions about populations. It is axiomatic that samples ordinarily are not identical to the populations from which they come. Hence stems the concept of sampling error, i.e., the difference between a sample and its population. Further, samples themselves are variable. For instance, if we were to take two samples from the same population, the composition of those samples will differ, as will the results generated. Nonetheless, we can be reasonably assured that a sample is representative of its population if (1) it is obtained by a process of random sampling, and (2) it is sufficiently large.

That the survey samples were randomly selected is supported by the overwhelming weight of the evidence. A random sample is one in which each individual in the population has an equal chance of being selected. Professor Zeisel testified that, to ensure a random sample, he used actual jurors called to service at the Daley Center on the days that the surveys were administered. Further, according to the uncontradicted testimony of attorney James Bailinson, the survey respondents were grouped by jury officials in the same manner as those jurors sent to courtrooms for actual jury service. Upon arriving at the Daley Center, the potential juror handed in her summons and pulled from a basket a folded up piece of paper which contained a panel number. Once the juror received her panel number, she waited in Room 1700 of the Daley Center until her panel number was called. Zeisel and his assistants "were given jurors from the assignment room just as the judges would get in batches from there." Such a random sampling procedure is not only representative, but appears to be as good a probability sample of potential Cook County jurors that could be designed.

Amstar Corp. v. Domino's Pizza, Inc.

615 F.2d 252 (5th Cir. 1980)

Amstar Corporation brought this suit asserting trademark infringement and unfair competition against Domino's Pizza, Inc. (DPI) and several of its franchisees to enjoin their use of Amstar's federal registration of the "Domino" trademark [used on sugar and condiments]. The complaint is based on allegations that defendants' use of the mark "Domino's Pizza" in connection with the sale of fast-food delivered hot pizza pies constitutes trademark infringement and a false designation of origin or representation . . . [and] that said use constitutes unfair competition . . . and dilutes the distinctive quality of plaintiff's mark "Domino" . . . The district court ruled in favor of plaintiff, dismissed defendants' counterclaim, and permanently enjoined defendants' use of the names "Domino" or "Domino's Pizza." Defendants then filed this appeal. We reverse because we find that the district court's decision was fundamentally erroneous since it was predicated on a holding that there was a likelihood of confusion between the use of "Domino's Pizza" by defendants in connection with pizza store services and the use of "Domino" by plaintiff in connection with the sale of sugar and individual packets of condiment items. . . .

Plaintiff's claims against defendants, except the dilution claim, therefore, turn on the determination of whether defendants' use of the mark "Domino's Pizza" is likely to cause confusion, mistake, or deception. . . .

At trial, both parties introduced survey evidence on the issue of likelihood of confusion. The trial court characterized the defendants' survey as "about as contrived a survey as I have ever run across," but found plaintiff's survey "properly conducted and fair." Our own examination of the survey evidence convinces us that both surveys are substantially defective.

Plaintiff's survey was made by Dr. Russ Haley, Professor of Marketing at the University of New Hampshire. It was conducted in ten cities among female heads of households primarily responsible for making food purchases. Each participant was shown, in her own home, a "Domino's Pizza" box and was asked if she believed the company that made the pizza made any other product. If she answered yes, she was asked, "What products other than pizza do you think are made by the company that makes Domino's Pizza?" Seventy-one percent of those asked the second question answered "sugar."

While the possible confusion level shown by the Haley study is high, there are several defects in the survey which significantly reduce its probative value. First, one of the most important factors in assessing the validity of an opinion poll is the adequacy of the "survey universe," that is, the persons interviewed must adequately represent the opinions which are relevant to the litigation. The appropriate universe should include a fair sampling of those purchasers most likely to partake of the alleged infringer's goods or services. Of the ten cities in which the Haley survey was conducted, eight had no "Domino's Pizza" outlets, and the outlets in the remaining two had been open for less than three months. Additionally, the persons interviewed consisted entirely of women found at home during six daylight hours who identified themselves as the member of the household primarily responsible for grocery buying. As plaintiff's sugar is sold primarily in grocery stores, participants in the Haley survey would have been repeatedly exposed to plaintiff's mark, but would have had little, if any, exposure to defendants' mark. Furthermore, the survey neglected completely defendants' primary customers, young, single, male college students. Thus, we do not believe that the proper universe was examined, and the results of the survey must therefore be discounted. . . .

The trial court discounted defendants' survey for largely the same reasons just discussed — it was conducted on the premises of "Domino's Pizza" outlets and therefore did not examine a proper survey universe, and the questioning procedures used were improper. Thus, defendants' survey is likewise not probative of the presence or absence of confusion.[13]

NOTES AND QUESTIONS

1. The *Amstar* court is not especially precise in its use of the terms "universe" (usually, "population") and "sample." Recall that the issue is whether consumers are likely to be confused by the pizza company's use of the "Domino" trademark. What is the appropriate universe of consumers? Did the Haley survey define its universe properly? Or was the problem a failure to take a representative sample ("a fair sampling," in the court's words) of the relevant universe? Or both? If you were Haley, whom would you have attempted to survey?

2. For practical reasons, trademark surveys almost never involve random sampling. A consequence of this is that the samples cannot be subjected to statistical analysis in the way that random samples are (see Section II below). Courts must therefore make judgments about raw numbers without the benefit of statistical evidence. Footnote 13 illustrates one such judgment: deciding whether a particular level of confusion amounts to a "likelihood." (An underlying problem that footnote 13 also reflects is the use of the undefined and imprecise term "confusion level." The term may mean different things when applied to the two surveys.) Assume that the defendant's survey had not been flawed, and that the plaintiff's interpretation ("6.8% confusion level") was correct. If that means that 6.8 percent of the relevant consumers are confused, is that enough to prove likelihood of confusion? The trademark case law offers little consistent help on this issue. For a clear and comprehensive review of survey research in legal contexts, see Shari Seidman Diamond, *Reference Guide on Survey Research,* in *Reference Manual on Scientific Evidence* (Federal Judicial Center, 2d ed. 2000); and Shari Seidman Diamond, Legal Applications of Survey Research, 1 David L. Faigman et al. (eds.), *Modern Scientific Evidence* 185 (1997).

---

13. The actual results of defendants' survey are disputed. Plaintiff argues the survey shows a 6.8% confusion level, and the court in copying plaintiff's proposed Findings of Fact, adopted that argument. Defendants argue the survey showed an actual confusion level of only 0.4%. They contend the 6.8% figure can be derived only by eliminating all respondents to the survey who were either not familiar with "Domino" sugar or who responded "don't know" when asked if the same entity made both "Domino" sugar and "Domino's Pizza." They argue that such a procedure is as unwarranted as excluding the percentage of "undecided" voters in a political poll. While we note the conflict between plaintiff and defendants on this issue, our holding discounting the survey evidence in this case makes it unnecessary for us to resolve it.

II. ANALYZING SAMPLES: CONFIDENCE INTERVALS

If a data set consists of a sample rather than an entire population, an obvious question arises: Just how accurately does the sample reflect the population? If, for example, an exit poll early on election night indicates that the Democratic candidate will get 52 percent of the vote and the Republican 48 percent, should the Democrats start their victory party, or should they wait for all the actual votes to be counted? In a variation on the same theme, suppose that a random sample of African-American workers in a given county shows an average (or *mean;* the sum of the values of all the individual cases divided by the number of cases) income of $29,000, whereas a random sample of Caucasian workers reveals an average of $31,200. Do we conclude that, across the whole population of the county, Caucasian workers earn more than their African-American counterparts?

The answer will lie in the degree of *confidence* that we have in the sample mean as an *estimate* of the population mean. An amount of $29,000 is not all that different from $31,200. So if we suspect that the samples provide only rough estimates of the population means, then we might take a cautious approach and refuse to conclude that the average incomes of the two populations are in fact different—maybe they are the same, or perhaps African-Americans actually earn more than whites. In making such an intuitive judgment, we are likely to be factoring in several concerns. Was the sampling procedure as random as we thought? Or might it have been biased in some way? Maybe high-income whites are more willing to talk to pollsters than high-income African-Americans. Even if the sample was random, is it big enough to insure representativeness? Recall that seven or eight heads in ten coin flips wouldn't be all that surprising.

The calculation of a statistic called the *confidence interval* provides a more precise response to these general concerns. As the following case explains, it is a band or range around the mean of a random sample (for example, the $29,000 figure in the preceding paragraph) within which the population mean will lie to some specified probability. If the "95% confidence interval" (the most commonly used probability) for the $29,000 estimate turned out to be +/−$1,500, then we would have 95 percent confidence that the mean of the population was between $27,500 and $30,500.[1] We could take the next step and calculate the 95 percent confidence interval for the $31,200 estimate as well. Suppose it was +/−$1,800, yielding a 95 percent confidence interval of $29,400 to $33,000. Note that the two intervals overlap substantially. Because of that, we could *not* express 95 percent confidence that the two *population* means are actually different. Under widely applicable statistical conventions,

---

1. This is the customary phrasing in legal contexts. To be technically correct, one would say that if the population were randomly sampled an infinite number of times, the population mean would be captured by the estimated range 95 percent of the time.

we would reject the hypothesis that they are different, instead ascribing the differences in the sample means to some kind of sampling error.

United States ex rel. Free v. Peters

806 F. Supp. 705 (N.D. Ill. 1992)

[Having dealt with the question of randomness in the portion of the opinion excerpted in Section I above, the court turned to the issue of extrapolating from samples to populations. In a footnote, it defined "confidence interval" as follows:]

In circumstances where we cannot measure the precise value of the quantity in question, we must approach the quantity in terms of estimates. Take as an example the mean I.Q. of females residing in Cook County on any particular day, a value that would be too costly to measure precisely. A point estimate, for example, is a single number which represents our best guess at the true value of the unknown quantity. Thus, we may estimate that the mean I.Q. for females residing in Cook County on the day in question is 150. Often, we express our guess in terms of an interval. For example, we might estimate that, on the relevant date, the mean I.Q. for females residing in Cook County is between 145 and 155. When an interval estimate is accompanied with a specific level of confidence (or probability), it is termed a confidence interval. A 99% confidence interval, for instance, is an indication that if we repeated our measurement 100 times under identical conditions, 99 times out of 100 the point estimate derived from the repeated experimentation will fall within the initial interval estimate — in our example, between 145 and 155.*

[Having thus defined confidence interval, the court put the concept to use to respond to some of the objections raised by the prosecution.]

The law of large numbers states that the larger the sample size, the more probable that the sample mean will be close to the population mean. After removing those jurors who did not meet the requirements of Witherspoon v. Illinois, 391 U.S. 510, 88 S. Ct. 1770, 20 L. Ed. 2d 776 (1968) [jurors who are disqualified from sitting on capital cases because of an unwillingness to impose the death penalty], the April 1990 survey sample consisted of 96 potential jurors, and the January 1992 survey sample included 95. According to Professor Zeisel, any concern that the sample size was too small to be representative is allayed not only by computation of a confidence interval for each question, but also by the results of a split-half reliability analysis. Zeisel essentially divided the samples from each survey into two halves as they arrived in seriatim and treated them as independent samples. As a

---

*[The last clause of this sentence might have been more correctly phrased as follows: ". . . 99 times out of 100 the population average will fall within the interval constructed from the point estimate." — EDS.]

comparison of the answering patterns for the two half samples of each survey revealed that they were nearly identical, we can conclude, and respondents have not rebutted, that the sample sizes were sufficiently large to ensure that the samples were representative of the population.

[A further issue was whether the 1992 survey results were consistent with those reached in 1990.]

Respondents maintain that a comparison of the 1992 survey results with the confidence intervals predicted on the basis of the 1990 survey demonstrates a mark of inconsistency or "volatility." We disagree.

More than one confidence interval was calculated on the basis of the 1990 survey. Professor Zeisel calculated 95% confidence intervals based on percentages of incorrect answers, while Professor Rossi calculated 99% confidence intervals based on percentages of correct answers. Each eliminated those questions for which no correct answer existed (questions 1, 13, 14, 15 and 16), as well as question 6, which was not included in the 1990 results because of a typographical error. Comparing the 1992 results to the Zeisel intervals, "the 1992 results fell within the predicted confidence intervals for 3 questions, fell slightly outside (1% to 2%) for 2 questions, outside by 4% to 6% for 3 questions and outside by 9% to 12% for 2 questions." "Using Rossi's confidence intervals, the 1992 results fell within predicted confidence intervals for 3 questions, slightly outside for 1 question, outside by 5% to 8% for 5 questions, and outside by 12% for 1 question."

As an empirical matter, we agree with Magistrate Judge Weisberg and Professor Rossi that the levels of deviation in the 1992 survey from the results predicted on the basis of the 1990 survey (i.e., the confidence intervals) are "modest." According to Professor Rossi, that the two surveys were not identical accounts for this modest deviation. Indeed, the predictive quality of the confidence interval rests on the assumption of identical surveys being given under identical conditions. In any event, the fact that both surveys, with few exceptions, depict very high levels of misunderstanding buttresses the Magistrate Judge's conclusion that the surveys are valid and reliable. . . .

The conclusion to be drawn from the Zeisel survey is apparent: The Illinois statute, as implemented through [the relevant jury instructions], permits the arbitrary and unguided imposition of the death sentence. As such, Free's sentence was imposed in violation of the Eight and Fourteenth Amendments of the United States Constitution.

NOTES AND QUESTIONS

1. An excerpt from another portion of the opinion gives the flavor of the survey results:

Questions 13 and 15 were designed to test juror comprehension respecting who, if anyone, bears the burden of persuasion:

13. After hearing all of the evidence in this case, a juror is not persuaded one way or another as to whether there are or are not mitigating factors sufficient to preclude the death penalty. Because the juror has not found that there is a mitigating factor sufficient to preclude death, the juror votes for the death penalty.

Has that juror followed the judge's instructions?

* 1992 Survey—Yes (50.5%); No (42.1%); Don't know (7.4%)
* 1990 Survey—Yes (62.5%); No (31.3%); Don't know (6.3%)

15. The jury in stage one found the defendant eligible for death. Which, if any, of the following four statements are correct and which if any are incorrect under the instructions given by the judge in this case:

(A) Once the jury finds the defendant is eligible for death, the prosecution must prove that mitigating factors do not exist; unless it does, the jury must vote against the death penalty.

* 1992 Survey—Correct (32.6%); Incorrect (58.9%); Don't know (7.4%)
* 1990 Survey—Correct (29.2%); Incorrect (62.5%); Don't know (8.3%)

(B) Once the jury finds the defendant is eligible for death, the defendant must prove that mitigating factors exist; unless he does, the jury must vote for the death penalty.

* 1992 Survey—Correct (49.5%); Incorrect (40.0%); Don't know (6.3%)
* 1990 Survey—Correct (45.8%); Incorrect (44.8%); Don't know (8.3%)

(C) Once the jury finds the defendant is eligible for death, the prosecution must prove that the death penalty should be imposed; unless it does, the jury must vote against the death penalty.

* 1992 Survey—Correct (36.8%); Incorrect (54.7%); Don't know (6.3%)
* 1990 Survey—Correct (37.5%); Incorrect (56.3%); Don't know (5.2%)

(D) Once the jury finds the defendant is eligible for death, the defendant must prove to the jury that the death penalty should not be imposed; unless he does, the jury must vote for the death penalty.

* 1992 Survey—Correct (37.9%); Incorrect (54.7%); Don't know (6.3%)
* 1990 Survey—Correct (41.7%); Incorrect (51.0%); Don't know (7.3%)

2.   As should be clear from *Free,* the confidence interval is derived from a calculation; it is not an arbitrary or hypothetical set of numbers chosen by the statistician. What the statistician chooses is the level of probability for which the confidence interval is calculated (most often, as in *Free,* 95 and/or 99 percent). In the authors' experience, judges and lawyers are sometimes confused on this point.

3.   As the *Free* opinion also suggests, confidence interval calculations are sensitive to sample size. Generally, the bigger the sample, the narrower the chosen confidence interval will be. This is common sense: The bigger the sample I compile, the more "confident" I'll be about my estimate of the population mean.

4.   Test your understanding by examining the way that the court used confidence intervals to decide whether the 1990 and 1992 surveys were consistent. Earlier in the opinion, the court used confidence interval in the conventional way: to estimate the range within which the average survey

scores of the 1990 population of potential jurors would probably fall, based on a sample of 96 potential jurors. Then it asked a separate question: Did the results from the (slightly different) *1992* survey fall within the *1990* confidence intervals? Because they did (more or less, anyway), the court concluded that the 1990 and 1992 survey results were essentially the same. This is a quick and useful approach to the question. But do you have any concerns about this reasoning process? Can you think of another way to address the problem of the consistency of the two surveys?

5.   Why would it be inappropriate to calculate a confidence interval for the survey results in *Amstar*?

III. *STATISTICAL SIGNIFICANCE: STANDARD DEVIATIONS AND p-VALUES*

"Statistical significance" refers to a set of conventions that statisticians and other scientists use for deciding when a discrepancy between what is observed and what is expected is too big to be reasonably attributable to chance. To begin to explore this concept, think again about the jury pool example with which this chapter began, which was based on an actual Supreme Court case. In theory, the county officials were taking repeated random samples from a population that was 79 percent Mexican-American. But over the course of the 11 years at issue in the real case, only 39 percent (339 out of 870) of the jurors who were summoned were Mexican-American. Is this too big a discrepancy to be written off to chance? In concluding that it was — and thus permitting an inference of discrimination — the Supreme Court invoked *standard deviation.*

For present purposes, think of standard deviation as the usual or typical amount by which members of a group will deviate from the group average. If we come across one or several individuals that differ from the group average by about the standard deviation, we would probably ascribe the difference to random fluctuations. But if we come across a subgroup whose members are many standard deviations from the average, we may conclude that it is "really" different in some way. Try to follow this logic through the Supreme Court's exposition of what came to be called the "two-or-three standard deviation rule."

Castenada v. Partida

430 U.S. 482 (1977)

MR. JUSTICE BLACKMUN delivered the opinion of the Court. . . .

Respondent, Rodrigo Partida, was indicted in March 1972 by the grand jury of the 92d District Court of Hidalgo County for the crime of burglary of a private residence at night with intent to rape. Hidalgo is one of the border counties of southern Texas. After a trial before a petit jury, respondent was convicted and sentenced to eight years in the custody of the Texas Department of Corrections. He first raised his claim of discrimination in the grand jury selection process on a motion for new trial in the State District Court. In support of his motion, respondent testified about the general existence of discrimination against Mexican-Americans in that area of Texas and introduced statistics from the 1970 census and the Hidalgo County grand jury records. . . .

The disparity proved by the 1970 census statistics showed that the population of the county was 79.1% Mexican-American, but that, over an 11-year period, only 39% of the persons summoned for grand jury service were Mexican-American. This difference of 40% is greater than that found significant in *Turner v. Fouche,* 396 U.S. 346 (1970) (60% Negroes in the general population, 37% on the grand jury lists). Since the State presented no evidence showing why the 11-year period was not reliable, we take it as the relevant base for comparison. The mathematical disparities that have been accepted by this Court as adequate for a prima facie case have all been within the range presented here. For example, in *Whitus v. Georgia,* 385 U.S. 545 (1967), the number of Negroes listed on the tax digest amounted to 27.1% of the taxpayers, but only 9.1% of those on the grand jury venire. The disparity was held to be sufficient to make out a prima facie case of discrimination. See *Sims v. Georgia,* 389 U.S. 404 (1967) (24.4% of tax lists, 4.7% of grand jury lists); *Jones v. Georgia,* 389 U.S. 24 (1967) (19.7% of tax lists, 5% of jury list). We agree with the District Court and the Court of Appeals that the proof in this case was enough to establish a prima facie case of discrimination against the Mexican-Americans in the Hidalgo County grand jury selection.[17]

17. If the jurors were drawn randomly from the general population, then the number of Mexican-Americans in the sample could be modeled by a binomial distribution [this describes the properties of the data being studied; see Note 1 following the case]. Given that 79.1% of the population is Mexican-American, the expected number of Mexican-Americans among the 870 persons summoned to serve as grand jurors over the 11-year period is approximately 688. The observed number is 339. Of course, in any given drawing some fluctuation from the expected number is predicted. The important point, however, is that the statistical model shows that the results of a random drawing are likely to fall in the vicinity of the expected value. The measure of the predicted fluctuations from the expected value is the standard deviation, defined for the binomial distribution as the square root of the product of the total number in the sample (here 870) times the probability of selecting a Mexican-American (0.791) times the probability of selecting a non-Mexican-American (0.209). Thus, in this case the standard deviation is approximately 12. As a general rule for such large samples, if the difference between the expected value and the observed number is greater than two or three standard deviations, then the hypothesis that the jury drawing was random would be suspect to a social scientist. The 11-year data here reflect a difference between the expected and observed number of Mexican-Americans of approximately 29 standard deviations. A detailed calculation reveals that the likelihood that such a substantial departure from the expected value would occur by chance is less than 1 in 10^{140}.

NOTES AND QUESTIONS

1. The logic of the standard deviation calculation in footnote 17 is quite simple; the calculation, which is only slightly more complicated, is discussed in the next Note. As the Court points out, the expected number of Mexican-American jurors over the 11-year period — 79.1 percent of the total of 870 — was 688. The actual total was only 339. It is possible to calculate the standard deviation for that expected number: that is, the average kind of variation one might expect as a matter of chance alone, even if the jury selection really was random. That standard deviation was 12. So we would probably not be surprised if there had been 676 Mexican-American jurors, or 700 (in a case like this the standard deviation works both ways, or $+/-$). However, the discrepancy was not 12, but 349 (688 − 339) or more than 29 times 12! The Court refused to believe in chance as an explanation, and instead found a prima facie case of discrimination.

2. For those who are interested in the calculations: The Court refers to the "binomial distribution." *Distribution* is the way that a phenomenon being measured and studied (a *variable*) occurs in the world. Different distributions dictate different standard deviation formulas. In a binomial distribution, the variable has two possible values and there are multiple independent trials with fixed probabilities. "Independent" means that the result of one trial is unaffected by the results of any others. The classic example is the variable "number of heads in a series of coin flips": the variable can have the values "heads" and "not heads" (or tails), there are multiple flips, the results of each flip is not influenced by the others, and there is a constant probability of 50 percent. (Another common distribution, the normal distribution (the familiar bell curve), is explored in the next case.) Do you understand why the variable "number [or percentage] of Mexican-American jurors" is also described by the binomial distribution? (Note: The Court has apparently adopted an ethnic breakdown of "Mexican-American" and "non-Mexican-American." The latter category could, of course, contain multiple racial/ethnic groups, but the case does not treat those distinctions as legally significant.) Does this depend on any assumptions about the juror selection process? The standard deviation formula for the binomial distribution that the Court follows can be described as follows: Start with the total number in the sample; multiply that number by the probability of one value of the variable (here, Mexican-American) and then by the probability of the other (non-Mexican-American); then take the square root of that result.

3. The most-quoted statement in *Castenada* is that "if the difference between the expected value and the observed number is greater than two or three standard deviations, then the hypothesis that the juror drawing was random would be suspect to a social scientist." Several important statistical concepts are implicated. The first is the "hypothesis that the juror drawing was random": this is often called the *null hypothesis*. Strictly speaking, it is the

hypothesis that Mexican-American jurors are chosen from the eligible population on exactly the same basis as are other jurors, and that any difference between the observed and expected numbers of Mexican-American jurors is due to chance alone. When the Court found the discrepancy of 29 standard deviations too big to attribute to chance, it *rejected the null hypothesis*. In statistical terms, it excluded chance as a reasonable explanation, and opened the door to all other possible explanations, including discrimination. But note that rejecting the null hypothesis does not *prove* any particular non-chance explanatory hypothesis, but simply permits consideration of such explanations. When the Court translated the rejection of the null hypothesis into a prima facie case of discrimination, it was stating a principle of discrimination law, not of statistics.

4. Lawyers sometimes wonder about the *two-or-three standard deviation* criterion of significance that the Court endorsed. Was it an arbitrary choice? Why two or three rather than three or four? And why the imprecision of two *or* three? Aren't they different? The case of Palmer v. Shultz, presented later in this section, addresses these issues.

5. When, as in *Castenada*, appropriate statistical testing leads to rejection of the null hypothesis, the results are often said to be *statistically significant*. So another way to phrase what the Court said in footnote 17 is that "if the difference between the expected value and the observed number is greater than two or three standard deviations, then that difference is statistically significant." Statistical significance is sometimes expressed in terms of a number called the *p-value*, or just *p*. It is usually defined as the probability of getting results of the magnitude of those obtained solely by chance, or the probability of obtaining such results if we assume that the null hypothesis is true. As a probability, it can always be written as a number between 0 and 1: If the probability of chance occurrence is 1 in 20, then $p = .05$. On the *Castenada* facts, *p* would be the probability of finding a difference as big as that discovered even if the jury selection process had been random. The Court was presenting a *p*-value when it stated at the end of footnote 17, "[a] detailed calculation reveals that the likelihood that such a substantial departure from the expected value would occur by chance is less than 1 in 10^{140}." The figure 10^{140} is 1 followed by 140 zeroes, so one chance in that many is a very tiny probability indeed. The case that follows is an especially detailed judicial exposition of these concepts, in the context of an age discrimination claim.

Allard v. Indiana Bell Tel. Co.

1 F. Supp. 2d 898 (S.D. Ind. 1998)

[Class action plaintiffs alleged that Indiana Bell had violated the federal Age Discrimination in Employment Act by disproportionately selecting workers over 40 for termination during a "workforce resizing program," or WRP. In this opinion on the defendant's summary judgment motion, the court considered the admissibility of several expert affidavits submitted by the plaintiffs. In the excerpts that follow the court focuses on the admissibility of a set of reports prepared by an economist named Richard Wertheimer.]

The probative value of [Wertheimer's] questionable methodology, incomplete research, and shaky conclusions, would be substantially outweighed by the distinct possibility of confusing the jury about the relevant issues. It would also be outweighed by the danger of misleading them into inferring causation from the fact that an expert found the disparity in selection rates "statistically significant."

Statistical significance is an expression of the probability of achieving a certain result by chance. It is often measured by p-values. When a statistician computes the p-value for any set of data, he or she is determining the probability of getting, just by chance, test data as extreme as the actual data obtained, given that the null hypothesis is true. Moore's Federal Practice: Reference Manual on Scientific Evidence 402 (Fed. Jud. Ctr. 1995) ("Moore's Reference Manual"). A "null hypothesis" is the hypothesis that there is no difference between two groups from which samples are drawn. *Id.* at 401. For example, the null hypothesis in this case would be that there is no difference between Indiana Bell employees who are under forty and those forty or more in terms of the criteria used to select them for termination. Thus, if the selection rates found in samples of the two age groups at Indiana Bell are not the same, then the p-value would give the probability that this data resulted from "the luck of the draw." *See* Moore's Reference Manual 378.

Large p-values are consistent with the null hypothesis, and small p-values undermine the hypothesis. *Id.* at 402. However, *p* does not express anything about the accuracy of the null hypothesis, or the probability that it is true. Rather, it is computed by *assuming* the hypothesis is true. *Id.* In this case, a small p-value would be consistent with a disparate impact by the selection process. *Id.* Wertheimer's report indicates the p-value for the difference in the termination rates between the two age groups was quite small (0.0000004). If the null hypothesis is true, then the following conclusions drawn from Wertheimer's analysis might be useful.

Wertheimer found the disparity in termination rates between the two age groups "highly statistically significant." Use of the term "significant" in this context describes the degree of difference between the expected results, in light of the null hypothesis, and those actually obtained. Essentially it is just a label for certain kinds of p-values. *Id.* at 380. Its meaning is no different from, and it is subject to the same limitations as, p-values. *Id.* "Significant differences are evidence that something besides random error is at work, but they are not evidence that this 'something' is legally or practically important." *Id.* That is why statisticians distinguish between statistical and practical significance. *Id.* "Significance comes no closer to expressing the probability that the null hypothesis is true than does the underlying p-value." *Id.* at 381.

In other words, by first assuming that the two age groups will have equal rates of being selected for termination, Wertheimer tested for the actual selection rates. Next, he compared the actual results to the expected results, given his underlying assumption of no difference between the two age groups, and found the observed difference in selection rates "statistically significant." Although Wertheimer's conclusion is internally consistent with the model he structured, it simply means that, given the hypothesis of equality, the fact that the outcome was different suggested that something besides random error was at work. For him to take the next step and conclude that the results he obtained are consistent with the claim that Indiana Bell's WRP *error* treated older workers differently goes beyond the realm of scientific methodology and into speculation. . . .

For all these reasons, the Court finds that Wertheimer's reports are inadmissible, and cannot form the foundation on which the plaintiffs build their theory of recovery under the ADEA. Because [a second expert's] report is a mirror of Wertheimer's results, it is also inadmissible. Defendant's motion to strike all of the experts' reports, opinions and testimony is GRANTED.

NOTES AND QUESTIONS

1. Test your knowledge of the critical statistical concepts in the case by answering a series of questions. What was Wertheimer's null hypothesis? Why did he reject the null hypothesis? What p-value did he compute? How would you state the meaning of that p-value in simple prose?

2. There are a variety of ways to calculate p-values. Some of the more commonly used are the Z, t, and chi-square tests, and the binomial formula (as in *Castenada*). Deciding which to use depends on many factors, including the distribution of the phenomenon being studied. For an introduction to the various approaches to significance testing, see David W. Barnes & John M. Conley, *Statistical Evidence in Litigation* §§ 3.11 to 3.17 (1986).

3. Tests of statistical significance are sensitive to sample size. In other words, the formula will take account of the size of the sample being studied. As a general rule, the smaller the sample size, the bigger the difference that will be required to yield a statistically significant p-value. So if you see a small sample and a low p-value, expect a very large difference. At the other extreme, the converse is also true: With huge sample sizes, very small raw differences can produce highly significant p-values. This can sometimes raise questions about the *practical significance* of statistically significant results. That is, even if we reject the chance explanation, do we think the results

have any practical value? For example, a medical study of large numbers of people might show a statistically significant difference in rates of heart attacks between people who eat ice cream and people who don't. But upon closer examination, it turns out that the raw difference in rates is only 1 percent. Statistically significant or not, is that a compelling basis for denying oneself one of life's sublime pleasures? Consider this recent discussion of standard deviations, statistical significance, and sample size in another employment discrimination case, Carpenter v. Boeing Co., No. 04-3334 (10th Cir. Aug. 7, 2006):

> There is no dispute that the [plaintiffs'] Siskin Study's regression analysis reflected a difference in the amount of overtime worked by men and women that was many standard deviations removed from equality. The Siskin Study computed departures from equal treatment of men and women whose statistical significance ranged from 7.95 standard deviations (weekend overtime during 2002) to 38.03 (weekday overtime during 1999). That statistical significance, however, does not necessarily mean that the departure from equality was large. For example, the Siskin Study calculated that women worked an average of 19% fewer hours of weekday overtime in 1999, 17% fewer in 2000 and 2001, and 11% fewer in 2002. For weekend overtime it calculated that women worked an average of 18% fewer overtime hours in 1999, 19% fewer in 2000, 18% fewer in 2001, and 10% fewer in 2002. Although notable, these are not what most would call "massive disparities" — it is nothing like men receiving proportionately even twice as much overtime as women. . . .
>
> What the large number of standard deviations means is that the departure from equality, whatever its magnitude, is highly unlikely to be random. Of course, when there are massive disparities, the difference may be many standard deviations. But when, as here, there is a great deal of data, even a relatively small difference may be highly statistically significant (that is, unlikely to be random). Consider an experiment involving 1,000,000 flips of a coin. The canonical result, of course, would be 500,000 heads and 500,000 tails. Say, the results were 510,000 heads and 490,000 tails. Although the magnitude of the difference is small, only about 4% more heads than tails, the odds of such a difference occurring in the absence of a weighted coin are exceedingly small — the departure from equality is 20 standard deviations. The difference strongly indicates *some* influence on the results other than the operation of pure chance.

4. Why did the *Allard* court reject Wertheimer's report? Did the court think he made some error in statistical method, or overreached in interpreting his results, or both? Focus on the following passage:

Although Wertheimer's conclusion is internally consistent with the model he structured, it simply means that, given the hypothesis of equality, the fact that the outcome was different suggested that something besides random error was at work. For him to take the next step and conclude that the results he obtained are consistent with the claim that Indiana Bell's WRP treated older workers differently goes beyond the realm of scientific methodology and into speculation.

Did the court get this right? Once Wertheimer had rejected random error, was it really "speculation" to opine that his results were "consistent" with differential treatment of older workers? If this was too speculative, how might Wertheimer have rephrased it?

5. The next case brings together the concepts introduced in *Castenada* and *Allard* and explores them in considerably greater depth. Among other things, it explains the basis for the two-or-three standard deviation rule and connects *p*-values and standard deviations.

Palmer v. Shultz

815 F.2d 84 (D.C. Cir. 1987)

In this action, a class of women plaintiffs allege various forms of unlawful employment discrimination in the Foreign Service from 1976 to 1983. After a trial, the District Court found that no unlawful discrimination had occurred . . . [W]e reverse, and remand for further proceedings in accordance with this opinion. . . .

This appeal followed from the District Court's failure to find sex discrimination in seven different types of personnel practices. [The practices at issue included initial job assignments, subsequent selection for more prestigious assignments, evaluation, and the awarding of honors.]

With respect to each of these seven personnel practices, the appellants offered data showing a disparity between men and women, along with a statistical analysis designed to demonstrate the improbability that a disparity of that scale could result from chance. The data and analysis, they allege, provide a strong basis for inferring that this disparity was the product of unlawful discrimination.

. . . In discounting the probative force of appellants' statistics, the District Court said that their statistical studies rested on faulty data, or flawed methodology, or omitted a crucial variable that would explain the disparity between men and women in a nondiscriminatory way. The District Court also said that some of the statistical evidence focused on too narrow a segment of Foreign Service personnel practices. As we shall explain, the District Court's treatment of the appellants' evidence was in some instances contrary to law and in other respects clearly erroneous as a matter of fact. . . .

A "disparate impact" claim alleges that the defendant based an employment decision on a criterion that although "facially neutral" nevertheless impermissibly disadvantaged individuals of one sex more than the other. This case is a "classic" example of a disparate impact claim in which plaintiffs allege that the defendant based employment decisions on the results of a test for which members of one sex on average received lower scores than members of the other sex. . . .

Proof of the disparity itself is based upon a comparison of the proportion of those women eligible for selection who were actually selected with the corresponding proportion of eligible men who were actually selected. Plaintiffs establish a disparity disfavoring women if the evidence demonstrates that the selection rate for eligible women was less than the selection rate for eligible men. Sometimes, the disparity is expressed as the difference between the number of women actually selected and the number of women one would expect to have been selected, assuming equality in the selection rates for men and women. . . .

Proof that the observed disparity was caused by an unlawful bias against women need not be direct. Circumstantial evidence that the disparity, more likely than not, was a product of unlawful discrimination will suffice to prove a pattern or practice disparate treatment case. Indeed, this circumstantial evidence may itself be entirely statistical in nature . . .

A disparity between the selection rates of men and women for a particular job or job benefit has one of three possible causes. *See* D. Baldus & J. Cole, *Statistical Proof of Discrimination* 291 (1980). First, the disparity may be a product of an unlawful discriminatory animus; this is what plaintiffs are attempting to prove. Second, the disparity may have a legitimate and nondiscriminatory cause. For example, prior experience of a certain type may be an important factor in making certain employment decisions, and if it happened to be true that women on the average have less of this experience than men, one would expect, that women could be selected less frequently. Third, the disparity may simply be a product of chance. . . .

A statistical analysis of a disparity in selection rates can reveal the *probability* that the disparity is merely a random deviation from perfectly equal selection rates. Statistics, however, cannot entirely rule out the *possibility* that chance caused the disparity. Nor can statistics determine, if chance is an unlikely explanation, whether the more probable cause was intentional discrimination or a legitimate nondiscriminatory factor in the selection process. *See id.* at 290-92. . . .

The preliminary question for a court, then, is at what point is the disparity in selection rates sufficiently large, or the probability that chance was the cause sufficiently low, for the numbers alone to establish a legitimate inference of discrimination. . . . The Supreme Court has twice stated that "as a general rule for . . . large samples, if the difference between the expected value and the observed number is greater than two or three standard deviations, then the hypothesis that [the disparity] was random would be suspect to a social scientist." But many lower courts and commentators have noted that the difference between two and three standard deviations is considerable and that, therefore, the Supreme Court's statement falls short of establishing an exact legal threshold at which statistical evidence, standing alone, establishes an inference of discrimination.

This court, using different terminology, has stated that statistical evidence meeting "the .05 level of significance ... [is] certainly sufficient to support an inference of discrimination." *Segar v. Smith,* 738 F.2d 1249, 1283 (D.C. Cir. 1984). "The .05 level," the *Segar* opinion explained, "indicates that the odds are one in 20 that the result could have occurred by chance." *Id.* at 1282. (This statement is somewhat imprecise and has predictably led to confusion, as we discuss *infra.*) The *Segar* court justified the consistency of its statement with the statements of the Supreme Court by observing that "[a] level of two standard deviations corresponds to statistical significance at the .05 level." *Id.* at 1283 n.28. In this case, the District Court cited *Segar* in its Conclusions of Law, stating: "The Court adopts the .05 level for establishing that a [statistical] study is statistically significant." But the District Court then went on to say that "the .05 level generally corresponds to 1.65 standard deviations."

How can a 5% probability of randomness correspond both to a measurement of two standard deviations and a measurement of 1.65 standard deviations, one may reasonably ask? There is a legitimate answer: it depends on whether one is using a "one-tailed" or a "two-tailed" test of statistical significance. A disparity measuring 1.65 standard deviations corresponds to a 5% probability of randomness under a one-tailed test. A disparity measuring two standard deviations (to be more precise, 1.96 standard deviations) corresponds to a 5% probability of randomness under a two-tailed test. ...

Appellants' and appellee's evidence on the underpromotion of women ... measures 1.88 and 1.76 standard deviations, respectively. (The difference results from the use of some different data.) Whether one adopts the appellants' or the appellees' number as the better evidence, it falls between 1.65 and 1.95 standard deviations. Therefore, if one tests the statistical significance of this number using the *Segar* standard of a 5% probability of randomness, the outcome turns on whether one uses a one-tailed or two-tailed test. Under a one-tailed test, the number is statistically significant (because it is larger than 1.65 standard deviations, which corresponds to a 5% probability of randomness under a one-tailed test) and therefore by itself establishes a prima facie case of disparate treatment. Under a two-tailed test, the number does not quite reach the statistically significant threshold (because it is smaller than 1.96 standard deviations, which corresponds to a 5% probability of randomness using a two-tailed test) and therefore by itself does not raise an inference of discrimination.

Given the unavoidability of embarking upon a journey into the statistical maze, we begin with the terms "one-tailed" and "two-tailed"; they refer to the "tails" or ends of the bell-shape curve, which represents in graph form a "random normal distribution." *E.g.,* W. Curtis, *Statistical Concepts for*

Attorneys 72-73 (1983); *see* Diagram 1 copied from *id.* In these random distributions, the area under any segment of the bell curve measures the probability of that range of results occurring randomly. *Id.* Furthermore, the percentage area underneath the bell curve within one standard deviation ([the Greek letter] sigma) distance from the mean ([the Greek letter] mu) of a normal distribution is always the same for all normal distributions (regardless of the specific value of sigma or mu, or the units in which these terms are measured). Thus, the probability of a result randomly occurring that measures within one standard deviation of the mean of the distribution (either greater or lesser than the mean) is the same for all normal distributions: 68.26%. *Id.* Indeed, this relationship holds true for any distance from the mean, measured in numbers of standard deviations. For example, the probability of a result occurring within two standard deviations from the mean is 95.44% and the probability of a result occurring within three standard deviations is 99.73%. *See* Diagram 1. Thus, for all normal distributions, the probability of randomness is directly associated with a measurement in numbers of standard deviations.

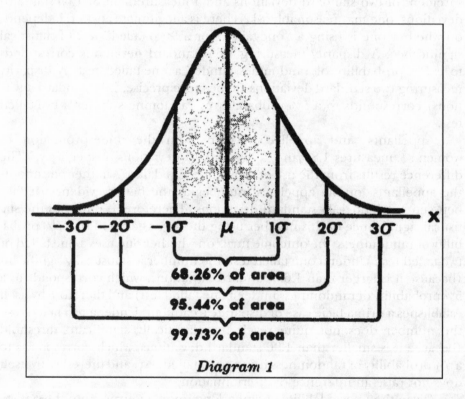

Diagram 1

But for every deviation from the mean of a normal distribution, measured in a certain number of standard deviations, there are two distinct ways of referring to the probability of that result occurring randomly. For example, if fewer women than expected were selected for a particular job, and this disparity measured 2.17 standard deviations, we can ascertain the probability that women by chance would be underselected to this extent or greater. This probability corresponds to the area between 2.17 standard deviations and the end of the bell curve representing the most extreme underselection of women. Standard statistical tables reveal that this probability is only 1.5%.

We can speak of the probability measurement associated with 2.17 standard deviations in another way, however. Although the observed disparity between the actual and expected number of women in this example was an underselection of women, there is a corresponding possibility that women might randomly be overselected such that the difference between the expected number of women selected and the number of women selected due to this random overselection also measures 2.17 standard deviations. The probability of a random deviation from the expected number of women selected with a magnitude of 2.17 standard deviations or larger, resulting from *either* an underselection *or* overselection of women, corresponds to the area under the bell curve between 2.17 standard deviations and *both* extremes of the curves: 3%.

The difference between "one-tailed" and "two-tailed" tests of statistical significance stem from these two different ways of measuring probability. If one decides (as the *Segar* court did) to reject the hypothesis that an observed disparity from an expected result occurred randomly only if the observed disparity falls within the range of the 5% most extreme possible disparities, one must still decide whether the 5% range should be entirely within only one of the tails of the bell curve, or instead should be divided with half of the range in each tail. Five percent of the total bell curve can be found *either* in the range from 1.65 standard deviations from the mean to one extreme end of the bell curve *or* in the area from 1.96 standard deviations to both extreme ends of the bell curve. *Compare* Diagrams 2 and 3, copied from V. Cangelosi, P. Taylor & P. Rice, *Basic Statistics* 173-74 (1979). For this reason, a 5% probability of randomness corresponds to 1.65 or 1.96 standard deviations, depending upon whether one uses a one-tailed or a two-tailed test. (Similarly, 1.65 standard deviations correspond to a 10% probability of randomness under a two-tailed test; and 1.96 standard deviations correspond to a 2.5% probability of randomness under a one-tailed test.) . . .

> Statistical texts frequently recommend the use of a one-tailed test when the only question of interest is the likelihood of a difference in one direction, e.g., when only a positive disparity between two numbers is of interest. This practice supports the use of a one-tailed test in discrimination cases, since the issue is always whether one group is favored over another. A defendant will argue, however, that both minority and majority groups [or men and women] are protected from discrimination and it is therefore inequitable to disregard the

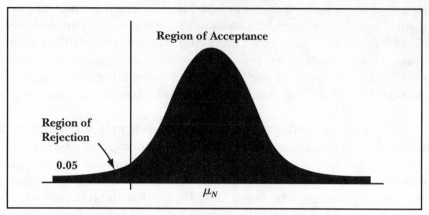

Diagram 2

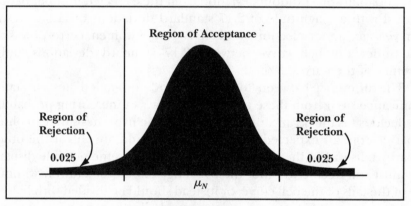

Diagram 3

probability of outcomes that may favor either group. Since there is no clear answer to this question, the most desirable approach is an awareness of the conceptual and practical differences between the two types of tests and a consistent use of the same type of test in similar cases whenever practical. We have used two-tailed tests throughout this book.

D. Baldus & J. Cole, *Statistical Proof of Discrimination* 307-08 (1980) (footnote omitted). In the most recent supplement, however, the authors . . . state a preference for a legal rule that would allow a one-tailed test "if the possibility of intentional discrimination favoring the protected group represented by plaintiff [*e.g.*, women in this case] can be ruled out as defying logic," i.e., the available evidence excluding the statistic in question gives strong support to the conclusion that the system is either nondiscriminatory or disadvantageous to the plaintiff's group." *Id.* at 129-30.

. . . We note that some of appellants' claims of unlawful discrimination involved complaints that women were *overselected* for particular kinds of jobs, *e.g.*, consular cone and downstretch assignments [less prestigious assignments] ... Such claims of discriminatory overselection, however, require a two-tailed statistical analysis ... Indeed, appellants' own statistical expert testified that a two-tailed test was necessary in evaluating the disparity between men and women in assignments to the consular cone because the hypothesis to be tested is whether cone assignments are made without regard to sex.

We also think a two-tailed test of statistical significance should be applied to *all* of appellants' discrimination claims in this case. ... After all, the hypothesis to be tested in any disparate treatment claim should generally be that the selection process treated men and women equally, *not* that the selection process treated women at least as well as or better than men. Two-tailed tests are used where the hypothesis to be rejected is that certain proportions are equal and not that one proportion is equal to or greater than the other proportion. ...

Taken together, as we have said, a two-tailed test and a 5% probability of randomness require statistical evidence measuring 1.96 standard deviations. Consequently, if plaintiffs come into court relying *only* on evidence that the underselection of women for a particular job measured 1.75 standard deviations, it seems improper for a court to establish an inference of disparate treatment on the basis of this evidence alone.[9]

NOTES AND QUESTIONS

1.   There is great deal going on in *Palmer*. Let us attempt to break out the key statistical points. First, the opinion explains why *Castenada*'s choice of two or three standard deviations was not arbitrary. According to the properties of the normal distribution, a finding that is more than two standard deviations above or below (the two-tailed problem, discussed in the next Note) the expected mean would occur by chance less than 5 percent of the time. For three standard deviations, the corresponding probability is less than 1 percent. In other words, the *p*-value for two standard deviations is less than .05, and for three standard deviations, much less than .01. These are the two levels at which *p*-values are most commonly computed, and .05 has long been the threshold for statistical significance for most applications, especially in the social sciences. The choice between .05 and .01, or even some lower value, will depend on how much evidence the researcher will insist on before rejecting the null hypothesis. (Note, however, that the selection of a threshold is a matter of judgment and convention rather than mathematics. For more on this point see David H. Kaye & David A. Freedman, *Reference Guide on Statistics*,

9. In any event, given the language of the Supreme Court in *Castenada* ... we do not believe that we can allow the threshold at which statistical evidence alone raises an inference of discrimination to be lower than 1.96 standard deviations, whether one views this number as signifying a 5% probability of randomness using a two-tailed approach or a 2.5% probability of randomness using a one-tailed approach.

in Reference Manual on Scientific Evidence 121-125 (Federal Judicial Center, 2d ed. 2000).) So the *Castenada* Court was following statistical convention in setting a legal threshold at two or three standard deviations, as well as in using the ambiguous conjunction *or*. And a final point about *Castenada:* The alert reader will have noted that the Court said that the evidence involved the binomial distribution, not the normal distribution discussed in *Palmer*. But the two distributions are very similar with large sample sizes, so the reasoning is equally applicable in both contexts.

2.   The choice between the one- and two-tailed analyses comes down to whether the statistician has a practical concern about deviation from the expected mean in either direction, or only in one. In other words, is it really possible that the selection process might produce *either* an overrepresentation *or* an underrepresentation of the protected group (women, in *Palmer*)? Or does that possibility "defy logic," in the words of Baldus and Cole that the court quotes? If it really is a possibility, then use the two-tailed test; if not, the one-tailed is appropriate. Note that the choice can have serious legal consequences, as *Palmer* illustrates. The court points out that if a one-tailed test is used, the plaintiffs will pass the .05/two standard deviation test of significance. But if a two-tailed test is used they will fail. Can you explain the statistical logic of these consequences? (Note, by the way, that a two-tailed test with a .05 significance threshold is the equivalent of a one-tailed test with a .025 threshold.)

IV.   CORRELATION

Most of the examples thus far have dealt with *differences*. In *Castenada*, it was the difference between the observed and expected representation of Mexican-Americans in jury pools; in *Allard*, a difference between the rates at which older and younger workers were selected for downsizing; and in *Palmer*, between the rates at which men and women received various employment perquisites. There are other contexts, though, in which statisticians and courts are interested in *correlations*. In the case that follows, the question is whether there is a statistically demonstrable correlation between an employment screening test and the job performance that it was supposed to predict.

Hamer v. Atlanta

872 F.2d 1521 (11th Cir. 1989)

CLARK, Circuit Judge

This is an appeal from an order issued by the United States District Court for the Northern District of Georgia determining that a written

examination given by the City of Atlanta for the purpose of promoting candidates in the Bureau of Fire Services from the rank of firefighter to fire
lieutenant was properly validated. . . .

... [I]f business necessity requires employees to perform certain
specified skills, an employer is not guilty of violating Title VII of the
Civil Rights Act if promotions are made pursuant to testing applicants
for those skills by a procedure that is properly validated. 29 C.F.R.
§ 1607.2(C) states:

> Nothing in these guidelines is intended or should be interpreted as discour-
> aging the use of a selection procedure for the purpose of determining quali-
> fications or for the purpose of selection on the basis of relative qualifications, if
> the selection procedure had been validated in accord with these guidelines for
> each such purpose for which it is to be used. . . .

The [Equal Employment Opportunity Commission's] Uniform Guidelines for Employee Selection Procedures ("Guidelines") require a sufficiently high correlation between test scores and performance ratings in
order to establish the criterion-related validity of a promotion exam. In
other words, an employer desiring to use a certain exam must first show
that those performing well on the exam are also given high job performance
ratings and those performing poorly are given lower job performance ratings. If a statistically significant relationship is indicated, then the examination is considered to be valid because a high grade on the examination is
predictive of satisfactory performances. . . .

[C]riterion-related validity is the statistical correlation between performance on the test and objective measures or "criterions" [sic] of performance on the job. This is measured in one of two ways. In a "predictive"
study, all applicants for a position are given the examination. Those applicants selected for the position are allowed to work at the job for a period of
time and their job performance is then measured. Their preemployment test
scores are then compared to their job performance ratings. In a second
method, known as "concurrent" validation, the test is administered to existing employees and their scores are compared to their job performance. It is
this method that was used by McCann Associates in the preparation of the
allegedly unlawful examination.

To prove that a test is criterion-related, a proponent of an exam
must show two elements of correlation. These elements are "practical
significance" and "statistical significance." Practical significance is the
degree to which test scores relate to job performance and is measured
by a "correlation coefficient." Statistical significance is a measure of the
confidence that can be placed on the practical significance; that is, it
expresses the probability that a particular correlation coefficient occurred
by chance. . . .

Statistically, the degree of correlation between two variables (*e.g.*, entrance exam scores and subsequent school grades) is expressed as a "correlation coefficient" on a scale running from +1.0 to −1.0. A perfect positive correlation (*e.g.*, entrance exam scores exactly predict subsequent school grades, with the higher exam scores predicting the best grades) would be expressed as +1.0, and a perfect negative correlation (*e.g.*, entrance exam scores exactly predict subsequent school grades, except in reverse, with the lower exam scores predicting the best grades) would be expressed as −1.0. Where the two variables had absolutely no relationship to each other, the correlation coefficient would be .0. The closer a correlation coefficient is to either +1.0 or −1.0, the "higher the magnitude" of the correlation; and the closer it is to .0, the "lower the magnitude." Mueller, Schuessler & Castner, *Statistical Reasoning in Sociology*, 2d ed., at p. 315. Because a purely random drawing of a sample is liable to produce a correlation coefficient which is somewhat off an absolute .0, the concept of statistical significance becomes relevant. The concept is tied to the statistical theory of probability and is dependent upon the number of people in the sample. Generally, if a correlation coefficient is so low that, on the basis of the sample size involved, more than 1 in 20 random drawings could be expected to produce a correlation at least as great, that correlation coefficient is considered not to be statistically significant, or simply to be the same as a correlation coefficient of .0. On the other hand, if the obtained coefficient could be expected to reoccur no more than once in 20 random drawings, it is considered statistically significant, the statistical indication for which is $p < .05$. Mueller, et al., pp. 394, *et seq.*

Ensley Branch of NAACP v. Seibels 616 F.2d 812, 817 n.13 (5th Cir.), *cert. denied*, 449 U.S. 1061, 101 S. Ct. 783, 66 L. Ed. 2d 603 (1980).

... Dr. Stephen Cole, appearing on behalf of the appellants [the plaintiffs], testified at the district court hearing that he had observed inconsistencies between the test scores of the participating fire captains and the ratings given those officers by their respective shift commanders and battalion chiefs. Dr. Cole stated:

> The point here is that there is very little correspondence with those captains between the test and the supervisory ratings. For those of correlation .33, there is very little association between how well you did on the test and how well the supervisors evaluated your job performance. Of the top 25 candidates identified by supervisors, only seven of them would be identified in the top 25 if the test alone was used.

Dr. Cole also pointed out that the person who ranked first on the written exam was ranked 31st by the supervisors; the person who ranked second on the written exam was ranked 68th by the supervisors; and the person who ranked 20th on the written exam was ranked 79th by the supervisors.

Dr. Cole's conclusion was that ". . . clearly when used as the sole criterion for promotion, the test does not act as a good predictor." ✓

Dr. Cole['s] . . . testimony that the ratings of the subject for job skills did not correlate with their test scores is seriously flawed. Dr. Cole relied on his (plaintiff's) Exhibit 13 which listed (not by name) the 89 subjects, the ratings given by their supervisors, and their test scores. His testimony to the district court concerned only 25 of the subjects which he picked out because their test scores differed greatly from their ratings. For example, the subject who was ranked at the bottom, 89th, was 5th from the top on test scoring. Cole used him and others to contend that the study results were skewed.

It is elementary statistical knowledge that the smaller the sample the more unreliable the result. McCann Associates [the City's test preparation consultant] admitted concern that having only 89 subjects was not as large a group as would be preferred. Dr. Cole shrank the group from 89 to 25 in order to reach a conclusion that the study did not accurately predict that the test would result in demonstrating which firemen would make the best fire lieutenants. The district court correctly rejected Dr. Cole's unscientific approach to the issue.

One of the City's experts was Dr. Chester Palmer, a professor of mathematics at Auburn University. . . . Dr. Palmer concluded that the McCann study and tests met professional standards. *conflicting expert*

Dr. Palmer conducted five separate analyses of the validity of the [test] system used by McCann. Dr. Palmer ran these analyses in an attempt to equalize — that is, to take out the extraordinary influences caused by certain factors, such as a very lenient supervisor/rater who scored everyone rather high or such as the captain (ratee) who was rated 89th by the raters but scored fifth on the test. (This person was rated by only one supervisor rather than the usual two or three, which may account in part for the deviation.) Dr. Palmer's term for such persons was "an outlier." Others might use the term "sport" or "deviant." Dr. Palmer discussed the importance of such factors in making an analysis:

> One of the problems with this kind of study with small "n" is that one person can swing that correlation a large amount. So I tried just to see what would happen if I went back and I ran those charts of the correlations again but I left him out. Okay. Now, I must emphasize I don't have any justifiable reason for leaving him out other than the fact that it looks strange. Okay. That is, I'm not saying that the right thing to do is to leave him out. I can't say that but when you see one person who is that wild, it only makes sense to see what would happen otherwise.

The answer turns out to be quite different. Now, we are back to the back of the chart. In the back of the chart is three more of the correlation tables. You can see in the title that these are labeled in the third line of the title, "88 subjects, one outlier removed." The first one is what the correlations would be for the combined group if you did not include that individual. And we see that now if you read down under the total column we now have two of them that are almost .4. We've got one that's .393 and one that's .398.

So that essentially this one individual will change the correlation from .4 to .3. That's what happens in small groups when there's one person who is sort of off the wall. . . .

Mr. William F. Howeth testified that the exam known as Form A was found to have a correlation coefficient of +.33.[4] The statistical significance was demonstrated to be p<.01, meaning there was less than one chance out of one hundred that the correlation coefficient was the product of chance. This value falls within the range set forth in the Guidelines of .05 or less. 29 C.F.R. § 1607.14(B)(5). Dr. John Veres testified that the correlation coefficient obtained on the study was particularly significant in view of the factors working against McCann. He concluded that ". . . with respect to the guidelines and what I would construe to be the consensus of people in our profession, the criterion related validity study passes muster."

The district court, upon consideration of the credentials of the witnesses, their testimony, and the evidence presented, determined that the experts testifying on behalf of the City of Atlanta were more persuasive and ruled that the test had been properly validated. . . . Because we lack a "definite and firm conviction that a mistake has been committed," we reject the appellants' objections. . . .

AFFIRMED.

NOTES AND QUESTIONS

1. The correlation coefficient is usually written as "r." The concept can be captured by plotting two variables against each other on a simple two-axis graph. If r is close to 0, the points are scattered randomly. As r approaches 1 (or −1), the plot resembles a narrow ellipse. At 1 or −1, the points resolve into a diagonal line.

2. As the court and the various experts noted, simply knowing the correlation coefficient is not enough, because of the possibility of a chance association between test scores and job performance. So, as in other contexts we have examined, the experts assessed statistical significance by calculating p-values. Mr. Howeth, testifying for the City, found that $p<.01$. What was his

---

4. This figure was computed using a statistical technique known as a Pearson Product Moment Correlation.

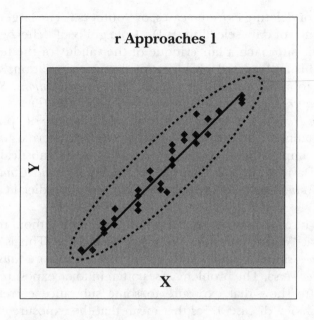

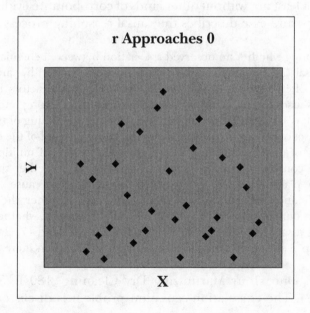

null hypothesis? How would you explain "$p < .01$" in relation to the facts of this case?

3.   Dr. Cole, testifying for the plaintiffs, examined a subset of the fire captains in the validation study and argued that the r for that subset showed "very little association" between test scores and performance. Dr. Palmer, in rebuttal for the City, then endeavored to show how easy it is to manipulate r

by inserting or deleting extreme cases, or "outliers." The larger issue here is the importance of data selection. Is Dr. Cole guilty of "cherry picking" the data, or is his approach a fair critique of the validity of the test? For a discussion of this and related problems of data manipulation, see David W. Peterson & John M. Conley, *Of Cherries, Fudge, and Onions: Science and Its Courtroom Perversion*, 64 L. & Contemp. Probs. 213 (2001).

4.   The *Hamer* court makes rather idiosyncratic use of "practical significance," equating it with degree of correlation. The more usual meaning is "substantive importance," or the real-world value of statistically significant results. See David H. Kaye & David A. Freedman, *Reference Guide on Statistics*, in *Reference Manual on Scientific Evidence* 169 (Federal Judicial Center, 2d ed. 2000).

5.   It is rare for a statistician to discuss correlation without reminding the audience that "correlation does not equal causation." This is not really an issue in *Hamer,* since no one would suggest that a test score *causes* job performance, or vice-versa. The problem arises often in toxic exposure cases. It may be possible to show that exposure to some substance correlates with an increased risk of a disease. Does that mean that the exposure causes the disease? No — at least not without other kinds of corroborative evidence. A recent chemical exposure case describes the causal reasoning process as follows:

> In determining whether an observed association between a chemical and a disease is causal (i.e., general causation), scientists are guided by various factors, which are often referred to as the Hill criteria. These factors include: (1) strength of association (i.e., whether the association is strong and statistically significant); (2) temporal relationship (i.e., whether the timing of the exposure and the onset of disease is consistent with the latency period of the disease); (3) consistency of the relationship (i.e., whether the results of multiple scientific studies are consistent); (4) biological plausibility (i.e., whether there exists a biologically plausible *mechanism* by which the agent *could* cause the disease); (5) consideration of alternative explanations (i.e., whether the association could be accounted for by other factors); (6) specificity (i.e., whether the *specific* chemical is associated with the *specific* disease at issue); and (7) dose-response relationship (i.e., whether an increase in exposure yields an increase in risk).

Magistrini v. One Hour Martinizing Dry Cleaning, 180 F. Supp. 2d 584 (D.N.J. 2002). The correlation-causation problem is discussed in detail in Chapter 7, Medical Causation.

V.   *REGRESSION ANALYSIS*

As *Hamer* demonstrates, the correlation coefficient, *r*, can be a very useful statistic when we are interested in the correlation, or linear

association, between two variables that can have multiple values. But while *r*   ✓
can measure the extent to which two variables move in concert, it leaves ✓
other potentially important questions unaddressed. In *Hamer,* for example,
it might have been helpful to know not only *that* job performance evaluations ⊀
rose with test scores, but *how much* of an improvement in performance was
associated with every one-unit rise in test scores. In addition, many cases
require an assessment of the relationship among more than two variables.

A technique called *regression analysis,* particularly multi-variable or
multiple regression analysis, has been used to address such questions in a
wide variety of cases. Common examples include employment discrimination cases, where the court may be interested in the relationship between
salary and both legitimate (e.g., education, experience, performance) and
illegitimate (e.g., race, sex, age) factors; wrongful death cases, where it is
necessary to build a descriptive model of the decedent's past earnings and
then project those earnings into the future; and antitrust cases, where the
assessment of the relationship between prices and a range of market factors
may be relevant to both liability and damages. While regression analysis is
complicated, examination of a representative case can illuminate the
general principles. The topic will return in more detail in Chapter 8,
Economic Analysis of Liability and Damages.

McReynolds v. Sodexho Marriott Servs.

349 F. Supp. 2d 1 (D.D.C. 2004)

[Class action plaintiffs alleged company-wide racial discrimination in the
promotion of managers. The case was before the court on the defendant's
motion for summary judgment. The plaintiffs relied primarily on "pools analysis," aggregate, company-wide statistics that showed a statistically significant
disparity in the promotion rates of white and African-American employees.
The defendant argued that promotion rates should be broken down by
"RVP," or the Regional Vice President level of company organization, and
contended that "statistically significant results occurred in only 9 of 155 purported RVPs." The defendant also offered a regression analysis.]

In rebutting plaintiffs' prima facie case, which is generally based on a
pools analysis, defendants typically rely on a multivariable regression analysis, which is a wholly different statistical methodology.[23] A regression can

23. "Multiple regression analysis is a statistical tool commonly used by social scientists
to determine the influence that various independent, predetermined factors (so-called
'independent variables') have on an observed phenomenon (the so-called 'dependent
variable'). In disparate treatment cases involving claims of [race] discrimination, plaintiffs
typically use multiple regression analysis to isolate the influence of [race] on employment
decisions relating to a particular job or job benefit . . . The first step in such a regression
analysis is to specify all of the possible 'legitimate' (*i.e.,* nondiscriminatory) factors that are
likely to significantly affect the dependent variable and which could account for disparities in

account for more factors simultaneously than a pools analysis. Hence, regressions are better suited to consider "major variables," which in turn may help to explain the decision-making process. The importance of including the major variables is clear; failure to do so may mask the true cause of a statistical disparity between races. . . .

But what constitutes a major variable for purposes of any given analysis will vary depending on the facts and theory of the case. . . . Because of this delicate balancing act, courts have erred on the side of caution . . . ✓

> While the omission of variables from a regression analysis may render the analysis less probative than it otherwise might be, it can hardly be said, absent some other infirmity, that an analysis which accounts for the major factors must be considered unacceptable as evidence of discrimination. Normally, failure to include variables will affect the analysis' probativeness, not its admissibility.

Bazemore v. Friday, 478 U.S. 385, 400 (1985) (citations and quotation marks omitted). . . .

Defendant relies on Haworth's regression analyses to argue that it has conclusively demonstrated nondiscriminatory explanations for perceived racial disparities so as to preclude any finding of a pattern or practice of discrimination. [Haworth sampled] employees randomly selected across division, salary, grade band ranges and race groups.[25] Her sample included approximately 4,000 of approximately 20,500 salaried exempt employees, of whom 3,800 were African American or white. She then coded for education, considering highest level of education and field of study, and coded for job experience based on occupations defined by the Census Bureau, "capturing experience at all prior positions, as well as the nature of the industry of employment." Certification and licensing information was gathered, and Sodexho tenure was measured by distinguishing between seniority in salaried exempt and hourly employees. With this information, she found, after

---

the treatment of [employees of different races]. By identifying those legitimate criteria that affect the decision making process, individual plaintiffs can make predictions about what job or job benefits similarly situated employees should ideally receive, and then can measure the difference between the *predicted* treatment and the *actual* treatment of those employees. If there is a disparity between the predicted and actual outcomes for [minority] employees, plaintiffs in a disparate treatment case can argue that the net 'residual' difference represents the unlawful effect of discriminatory animus on the allocation of jobs or job benefits." *Ottaviani v. State University of New York,* 875 F.2d 365, 366-67 (2d Cir. 1989) (citations omitted).

25. Plaintiffs challenge her methodology because Haworth's team was only able to code data for an employee where the resume affirmatively listed a trait, such as a higher degree or experience in a given field. Thus, an employee with a certain kind of experience or education, who did not happen to put such information on the resume that was submitted to Sodexho, would not be accurately accounted for. . . . [T]he Court will not reject Haworth's analyses on this basis, although the debate may be relevant at trial.

controlling for education, job experience, prior industry, licensing and memberships, tenure, division, RVP, and grade/band, that no statistically significant patterns emerged that were adverse to African Americans. And to blunt any debate over the meaning of promotion, Haworth re-ran her regression analysis using [the plaintiffs'] definition of promotion, but still found no statistically significant effect of race. Based on these findings, defendant argues it is entitled to summary judgment, for "when a defendant conducts its own regression analysis that measures key variables that plaintiffs' expert had omitted, and where that refined regression demonstrates only statistically insignificant racial disparities, the defendant has more than met its burden of disproving a pattern or practice of discrimination. . . ."

[The results of the regression analysis can be affected by] whether one includes or excludes variables that by all accounts do not fit within the law's definition of "major factors." For instance, Haworth controls for RVP, which defendant concedes is not a major variable and need not be included, as well as licenses and certifications, industry experience, memberships, and "specific unit experiences." Plaintiffs object to the inclusion of these variables as being unnecessary, contrary to good statistical practice, and as having the potential for skewing the study by masking the effect of race on promotions. While the Court is not prepared to categorize all of these variables as "tainted", there is at least a serious question whether RVPs are a legitimate explanatory factor to predict the probability of promotion, or whether they may be masking a discriminatory process, thus qualifying under *Valentino v. United States Postal Service* as an "inappropriate" or "tainted" variable. 674 F.2d 56, 73 n.30 (D.C. Cir. 1982) (citing Finkelstein, *The Judicial Reception of Multiple Variable Regression Studies in Race and Sex Discrimination Cases*, 80 Colum. L. Rev. 737, 738-42 (1980)). This could well be the case, because, following Finkelstein's criteria for inappropriate variables, RVPs could be affected by the employer, are not related to an employee's productivity, and are correlated with group status. *Id.* at 738-39. This would be particularly true, if, as plaintiffs argue, African Americans are clustered or segregated in RVPs not by choice, and if there is a low probability of promotion out of these RVPs regardless of race.

If these variables are eliminated because they are unnecessary, "inappropriate," or "nonsense" variables, *see Valentino*, 674 F.2d at 71 n.21, the results of an expert's regression analyses will necessarily change. For instance, when plaintiffs' expert purports to re-run Haworth's regression analysis, controlling for education and experience, but eliminating these allegedly unnecessary variables and using his definition of promotion, he finds a statistically significant race effect for the class period of at least 2.50 standard deviations. . . .

[T]here can be no doubt that defendant's regression analyses are insufficient to defeat plaintiffs' prima facie case. For, as the above discussion demonstrates, the inclusion or exclusion of non-major variables . . . can have a profound effect on whether a statistically significant race disparity is found. . . . While each side may well have valid criticisms of how the opposing expert executed various methodologies, these highly-credentialed statisticians have reached starkly different conclusions based on re-runs of each other's multiple regression analyses, and the propriety of these different approaches cannot be resolved at the summary judgment stage because they involve issues of credibility and disputed issues of fact.

[The defendant's motion for summary judgment was denied.]

NOTES AND QUESTIONS

1. The court does a good job describing the basic logic of regression analysis. The statistician builds a model of the problem by selecting as *independent variables* those factors which "legitimately" ought to account for the behavior of the outcome we are interested in, which is the *dependent variable*. In *McReynolds,* the independent variables (or "major variables," as the court calls them) are such things as education, experience, tenure with the employer, and certification and licensing. The dependent variable is probability of promotion. Some of the independent variables are measurable in obvious ways: *e.g.,* years of post-high education, years of experience, etc. Others must be assigned arbitrary values: *e.g.,* for college graduates, a business degree might be coded as 0 and a non-business degree as 1. The regression analysis yields a *regression coefficient* (a term not used in *McReynolds*) for each independent variable, defined as the amount that the dependent variable changes for each one-unit change in the specified independent variable, with all the other independent variables held constant. For example, the regression coefficient for years of experience is the change in probability of promotion for each extra year of experience, with everything else held constant. (See Note 2 for some numerical illustrations.) It is possible to calculate whether the various regression coefficients are statistically significant, or, alternatively, are within the realm of expected chance fluctuation of the dependent variable. The ultimate step in the analysis is to assess the suspect, "illegitimate" factor as an independent variable. In *McReynolds,* that factor is race, of course. The question then becomes whether a change in race, with all other independent variables held constant, is associated with [note that we did not say *causes*; see Section C above] a statistically significant change in the dependent variable. That is, is the regression coefficient for race statistically significant? What was defense expert Haworth's answer to that question? How did the plaintiffs' expert respond?

2. To see how regression coefficients are typically presented, examine the following (somewhat simplified) table from Paxton v. Union National

Bank, 519 F. Supp. 136, 163 (E.D. Ark. 1981), a race discrimination class action:

Variable	Mean Value Whites	Mean Value Blacks	Dependent Variable = Earnings Coefficient
Race (workforce = 17.9% black)	0.0	1.0	−$ 4.19
Years of Schooling	13.5	13.1	27.51
B.A. Degree (1 if yes)	0.22	0.11	98.19
M.A. Degree (1 if yes)	0.03	0.00	135.54
Months of Seniority	64.6	28.4	40.80**
Part-time Work (1 if No., i.e. if full-time)	0.06	0.13	126.57
Months of Bank Management Exp.	2.7	0.0	83.44**
Months of Other Management Exp.	6.0	0.0	89.73**
Months of Computer Spec. Exp.	1.1	0.5	77.16**
Months of Accounting Exp.	0.7	0.0	36.23
Months of Collector Exp.	0.8	0.1	88.34**
Months of Professional/ Technical Exp.	2.9	0.3	24.21
R^2			.52
Number of Employees			402

**Statistically significant

3. In reading the *Paxton* table, start with the coefficient for the independent variable *race* (coded, as is customary, as 0/1), which is −$4.19. This means that, holding all other factors constant, changing a hypothetical employee's race from white to black is associated with a $4.19 decrease in monthly earnings. This is not statistically significant, which led the court to conclude, "we find that the earnings of blacks and whites who have similar types of qualifications at the Union National Bank are the same." Which regression coefficients are statistically significant? Note that the absolute size of a coefficient doesn't always predict its significance. An M.A. degree appears to be worth an extra $135 per month. But would you advise bank employees who want to earn more money that graduate school is a good investment? Why or why not? Are there particular kinds of experience within the bank that you would advise them to seek?

4. The choice of independent variables was a major issue in *McReynolds*. The Tenth Circuit has recently discussed the same issue in another employment discrimination case, Carpenter v. Boeing Co.,

No. 04-3334 (10th Cir. Aug. 7, 2006). The class action plaintiffs alleged that Boeing's overtime assignment practices had a discriminatory impact on female employees, with the result that they got far fewer opportunities to work lucrative extra shifts. As you read the excerpt, identify the independent and dependent variables that the expert used, and then ask what the court determined was missing.

> [Plaintiffs] rely on a study by their expert, Dr. Bernard Siskin. Dr. Siskin performed a regression analysis that compared the overtime worked by male and female employees whom he defined as "similarly situated." The Siskin Study examined overtime assignments from April 2, 1999 (the beginning of the liability period for this claim) through June 20, 2002, using Boeing's electronic daily payroll records. For weekday overtime the Siskin Study defined similarly situated employees as those who "[w]orked that day and are in the same job, grade, budget code and shift." Similarly situated employees with respect to weekend overtime were defined as those who "[w]orked Friday and are in the same job, grade, budget code and shift." For each cohort of similarly situated employees, the Siskin Study calculated three measures for men and women: (1) the likelihood of working any overtime; (2) the average number of overtime hours worked; and (3) the average number of overtime hours paid (overtime is paid at either 1.5 or 2 times a normal hour). It then computed a shortfall number for females that described how much greater each measure would be were females represented in proportion to their percentage representation in each cohort. "That is, if females were 25 percent of the cohort, they should be 25 percent of those working overtime and receive 25 percent of the overtime hours and pay."
>
> The Siskin Study concluded that "[h]ourly female employees who are similarly situated to males with respect to job, grade, shift, department, and budget code are consistently and highly statistically significantly less likely to work overtime, to work less overtime, and to receive less overtime pay. This pattern is consistent across time." It observed that "[c]learly, something in the overtime process consistently results in males obtaining more overtime and working more overtime than females." . . .
>
> Boeing concedes that these differences are statistically highly significant. . . . But despite recognizing that the statistics show that men have worked proportionately more overtime than women, Boeing claims that the Siskin Study nonetheless fails to establish a prima facie case. It contends that the Siskin Study does not show that the "something" causing men to work more overtime than women is the manager discretion that Plaintiffs have identified as the challenged employment practice. Boeing's argument appears to be that the "something" is a variable other than those that the Siskin Study included in the statistical model—namely, job, grade, budget code, and shift. According to Boeing, other variables affecting overtime assignments—such as the CBA criteria and potential differences in the rates at which men and women volunteer for overtime—are not controlled for in the Siskin Study and could be responsible for the observed disparities. The district court agreed with Boeing that a statistical study could not establish a claim without considering

such variables and granted Boeing's motion for summary judgment on that basis. [The court of appeals affirmed that judgment in material part.]

5. On the other hand, the *McReynolds* court also cautioned against including independent variables that "may be masking a discriminatory process." The court used the example of RVP "if, as plaintiffs argue, African Americans are clustered or segregated in RVPs not by choice." The argument would be that, while employees' RVP might account for a good deal of the probability of promotion, it is not a "legitimate" explanatory factor, but merely another *effect* of discrimination, like differential promotion rates.

6. This leads to a further issue, which is how much of the variation of the dependent variable the regression model accounts for. This is captured by the "R^2" at the bottom of the *Paxton* table (pronounced "r-squared"; technically, the coefficient of multiple determination). Always a decimal between 0 and 1, it is here .52, which means that this regression model accounts for 52 percent of the variation in the dependent variable *monthly earnings*—and does not account for 48 percent of it. It is hard to generalize about a "good" R^2, since it is easy to boost the number without improving the explanatory power of the model by including independent variables that may be tied to the suspect variable — RVP in *McReynolds,* for example. Nonetheless, where R^2 is very low (well below .5), it is reasonable to ask whether the model may have omitted important and legitimate explanatory variables.

7. No discussion of regression analysis in the law would be complete without a mention of *McCleskey v. Kemp,* 481 U.S. 279 (1987). David Baldus, whose work is cited in the *Palmer* case, and his colleagues conducted a 230-variable regression analysis of the role of race in the administration of the death penalty in Georgia. A 5-4 Court affirmed McCleskey's death sentence. The division among the Justices was less about the validity of Baldus's study than what a regression analysis can prove. Although the majority acknowledged that "the Baldus study indicates that black defendants, such as McCleskey, who kill white victims have the greatest likelihood of receiving the death penalty," it declined "to accept the likelihood allegedly shown by the Baldus study as the constitutional measure of an unacceptable risk of racial prejudice influencing capital sentencing decisions." Looking at the same evidence, Justice Brennan wrote in dissent that, "in light of both statistical principles and human experience . . . the risk that race influenced McCleskey's sentence is intolerable by any imaginable standard." Readers interested in the details of Baldus's very complex analysis should consult the multiple court of appeals opinions at 753 F. 2d 877 (11th Cir. 1985).

8. Despite its wide usage and obvious utility in many legal contexts, it would be wrong to think of regression analysis as a panacea. Some critics have argued that it has been applied inappropriately in some contexts. One of the more prominent of such critics is the statistician David W. Peterson, whose work has provided the basis for two important Supreme Court

decisions, and has been relied on in a third. *See* Hunt v. Cromartie, 526 U.S. 541 (1999) (redistricting); Easley v. Cromartie, 582 U.S. 234 (2001) (same); and Utah v. Evans, 536 U.S. 452 (2002) (validity of census methodology). In the essay that follows (which he generously prepared just for this book), Peterson takes exception to the common misuse of regression analysis in certain kinds of employment discrimination cases. In reading the essay, one bit of additional mathematical background might be helpful: In Note 1 above, we observed that "regression analysis yields a *regression coefficient* . . . for each independent variable, defined as the amount that the dependent variable changes for each one-unit change in the specified independent variable, with all the other independent variables held constant." To be more specific, the regression analysis plots the values of the independent variables as points on a multi-dimensional graph and then finds the line that best fits that set of points. Like every line, it has an equation; here, the equation of this "line of best fit" is the regression equation that yields the regression coefficients for the various independent variables.

A Note Regarding Pay Discrimination

David W. Peterson

One of the earliest employment discrimination cases involving employee pay was brought by the Equal Employment Opportunity Commission (EEOC) against American Telephone and Telegraph Company (AT&T). Though this case was settled in the early 1970s with a consent decree before it could be decided by a court, it established a framework for analysis used in many cases which followed. An economist was employed by the EEOC to examine AT&T's employee pay records for evidence of sex discrimination. Drawing upon human capital theory and a regression framework, he postulated that in the absence of any sex discrimination, the current pay rates of men and women alike should depend on certain factors such as their level of education and work experience, factors which characterize an individual's human capital. He then constructed a prototype formula postulating the manner in which a particular group of these qualities might combine to determine one's proper pay rate. This prototype formula was adjusted in such a way as to fit as well as possible the pay rates and qualifications of the male AT&T employees. When it was subsequently adjusted to fit the pay rates and qualifications of the female employees, he found that the adjustments were very different from those required to fit the males — different in such a way that, according to the adjusted formulas, women were paid less than similarly qualified men. This difference was trumpeted by the EEOC as evidence that AT&T discriminated against women in setting pay.

AT&T responded with an analysis it claimed showed no such thing. Its approach was much the same as that used by the EEOC, though it postulated a different prototype formula for measuring human capital and its relationship to an appropriate pay rate. When AT&T adjusted this prototype to fit first its male employees and then its females, it found that the two adjusted formulas were nearly identical. This, it contended, was evidence that it had not discriminated by gender in setting pay.

Unnerved by the possibility that the court might prefer the EEOC's analysis to its own, and by the vast amount of money it might owe if found guilty, AT&T came to terms with the EEOC before trial. Thus was posterity deprived of the court's opinion in this seminal case.

Nevertheless, the method of analysis found its way soon thereafter into court decisions in other cases, gaining impetus along the way from a 1974 article — written by a law student — in the *Harvard Law Review*. It lingers with us yet in decisions at all appellate levels, a crusted tradition, a hurdle to be cleared every time a litigant pursues or defends against a claim of discriminatory treatment in the setting of pay. It is too bad that this method of analysis does not comport with any legally recognized theory of pay discrimination.

Theories of Discrimination

At the outset, we need to be clear that by discrimination we mean the employer has made illegitimate use of such criteria as employee gender, age or race in setting and applying its policies. We cannot reasonably hold the employer accountable for decisions made by an applicant or employee about what to study in college, or whether to go to college at all, if the employer had no hand in making those decisions. If many men choose to study engineering while many women choose to study nursing, pay disparities resulting from those choices may be part of the fabric of the labor market, a result of general forces governing the supply and demand for skilled labor. In hiring employees from such a market, an employer is not entirely free to pay wages of its own choosing.

We have two basic federal laws governing race and sex discrimination: the Civil Rights Act of 1964 (CRA) and the Equal Pay Act of 1963 (EPA). Working within the framework established by these statutes, courts have come to recognize two distinct theories of discrimination under the CRA, namely disparate treatment and disparate impact. A third theory flows from the EPA.

Disparate Treatment Discrimination

Disparate treatment discrimination occurs when an employer intentionally treats an employee or potential employee differently than it would have, had that person been of different race, color, religion, sex, or national origin. Thus, disparate treatment discrimination involves a decision by the employer, an act in which a choice among alternatives is made. Furthermore, it is an act in which the race, color, religion, sex, or national origin of the victim influences the employer in its choice from among the available alternatives.

DISPARATE IMPACT DISCRIMINATION

In contrast, disparate impact discrimination occurs when an employer applies a policy equally to all employees or potential employees, regardless of their race, etc., but the effect of the policy is to place a disproportionate number of people of one race, etc., at a disadvantage relative to those of another, and there is no valid justification for this policy. For example, a state might wish all of its highway patrol officers to be at least six feet tall, and so disqualify from further consideration all applicants who are of lesser height. Such a policy would probably disqualify a greater proportion of women interested in and otherwise qualified for such work than men, simply because women in general tend to be shorter than men. Unless the state articulates a sound justification for its six-foot height requirement, that requirement is discriminatory under disparate impact theory.

DISCRIMINATION UNDER THE EQUAL PAY ACT

Equal Pay Act discrimination occurs when an employer pays current employees at rates that differ based on and because of their sex. The employees being compared must be performing work which requires equal skill, effort and responsibility, and which is performed under similar working conditions. If the pay differences are attributable to differences in seniority, merit, productivity or any factor other than sex, then they are not instances of sex discrimination under the EPA.

THE AT&T MUDDLE

The trouble with the analysis introduced in the AT&T case (and used almost universally thereafter) is that it does not address any of the three legally recognized forms of discrimination. It does not address disparate treatment discrimination because it does not analyze employer decisions. It does not address disparate impact discrimination because it does not examine any policy the employer has applied uniformly to all. And it does not address EPA discrimination because it does not compare all employees performing the same work under the same conditions.

The AT&T recipe for mixing numbers, detached as it is from any meaningful question concerning discrimination, is show without substance. One could as well ascribe meaning to a recipe that adds your height in inches to the number of doorknobs in your dwelling. The math can be done, but the result is of no practical significance.

A PROPER FRAMEWORK FOR MEASURING AND DETECTING DISPARATE TREATMENT DISCRIMINATION

As three distinct types of discrimination are recognized under federal law, logically there should be three corresponding approaches to measuring and detecting discrimination, one tailored to each of the three theories. While some or all of these approaches ultimately might converge to a single form of analysis, each should start with a premise tied to its particular theory of discrimination. As noted, disparate treatment discrimination occurs when an employer makes decisions about individual employees or potential employees based at least in part on their races, genders and so forth. A suit alleging such discrimination turns on the following questions: Why did the employer make the challenged decisions the way it did? In particular, were its choices based in part on the races, etc. of the people affected?

To help answer such questions, one ideally would examine each of the employer decisions in question, noting the alternatives reasonably available at the time each was made, and in each instance contrasting the employer's choice with its alternatives. If, in instance after instance, the choice made by the employer is disadvantageous to, say, female employees, it is circumstantial evidence that either employee gender or else some factor correlated with employee gender played some role in the employer's choices.

Decisions about employee pay typically occur at the time of hire, when the initial pay rate and initial job duties are set. Other decisions affecting pay occur at the times when annual pay increases are decided, promotions are awarded, or bonuses are set. While such decisions affect the current pay rates of current employees, they also affected the pay rates of past employees. All of these decisions inevitably took place before the present time, and in studying them, it is important not to limit oneself to just those decisions affecting current employees, because they may not typify the whole set of decisions. Many employees who were victims of adverse decisions, for example, may already have left this employer for better opportunities elsewhere.

It follows that no statistical analysis, regression or otherwise, can reveal reliably whether disparate treatment pay discrimination has occurred if it is confined to the study of the current pay rates of current employees. Unfortunately, many employment discrimination disputes appear to have been decided or settled on precisely this basis, the AT&T case being one of the first.

A NUMERICAL EXAMPLE

To illustrate how misleading a traditional regression analysis can be, I created a fictional employer called Bob's College, a small but worthy institution offering studies in just two subjects, mathematics and sociology. It hired its first faculty fifteen years ago, five into each department, all at the assistant professor rank. It continued to hire five people each subsequent year into each department, and, after netting out the people who left for various reasons through the years, the faculty currently stands at 36 in the math department and 23 in sociology. Along the way, faculty members have received merit pay increases in varying amounts as well as promotions. Each promotion carries with it an automatic 10% pay increase, so the decisions affecting pay are simply (i) pay at time of hire, (ii) amount of annual merit pay increase, and (iii) annual decision of whether or not to promote.

While this example is discussed in greater detail elsewhere [citation at the end of this essay], it suffices here to examine only the math department. The current pay rates of current employees are displayed in Figure 1, according to the years in which they were hired. Males are represented by the hollow symbols, females by the solid. Note that the pay rates of people hired early on are generally higher than the rates for people hired more recently.

Note too that the pay rates for the female faculty are generally in accord with the pattern set by the males of similar seniority, and that among the more senior faculty, the pay of women is even somewhat above the pattern for males. A casual look at these data gives no indication that women are discriminated against with respect to their pay.

The AT&T approach to studying pay practices in the math department consists in fitting a pair of regression lines to these data, and comparing them to see if they are statistically significantly different. If they are, that is taken as an indication that sex or some factor related to sex has affected employee pay, and the employer must exonerate itself, if it can, by identifying any such factors and establishing their legitimacy. Regression lines fitted to the data for males shown in Figure 1 do not differ significantly from their counterparts fitted to females, and so an AT&T type analysis would reach the same conclusion as our casual inspection: there is no indication here that women are discriminated against with respect to their pay.

But this analysis fails to examine employer decisions in the full context of their alternatives. Consider the initial pay decisions in the math department, the results of which are depicted in Figure 2. Once again men are represented by hollow symbols, women by solid. Note that there are many more data points in Figure 2 than in Figure 1.

That is because a starting pay decision was made for every faculty member who was hired, not just those faculty who are currently employed. Note too that year after year, the starting pay rates of the women are generally less than the rates for men. This pattern is highly statistically significantly disadvantageous to women, and it cries aloud for some explanation from the employer. Yet, the traditional AT&T analysis missed it completely.

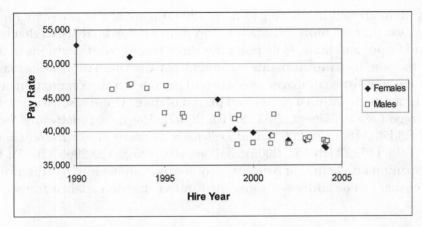

Figure 1. Current Pay Rates of Current Math Department Faculty

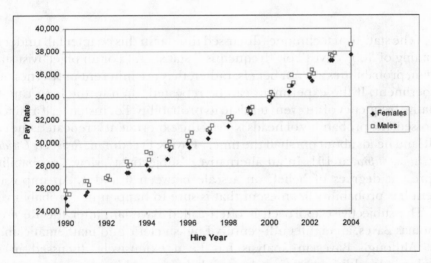

Figure 2. Starting Pay Rates in the Mathematics Department

What happened at Bob's College probably happens elsewhere as well. The people who fell behind, whether as a result of discrimination or not, were inclined to leave their employer. Those who did well, whether by good luck or good work, were inclined to stay on. In any event, employees who stay on are probably not representative of those originally hired, and even if they were, one can infer little or nothing about an employer's starting pay decisions by studying the current pay of just those employees who stay on.

POST SCRIPT

This note is excerpted from David W. Peterson, "Analyst Takes Fresh Look at Pay Discrimination," *Chance*, vol. 19 no. 2 (2006), pp. 7-16. Readers may be interested in the vol. 18 no. 1 (2005) issue of the *Journal of Forensic Economics* devoted more generally to forensic decision analysis. In that issue, David Copus and Jaime Cole point out three recent court decisions indicating that the focus in disparate treatment pay discrimination cases may be shifting away from comparisons of current pay rates to an examination of pay decisions made within a proscribed period of time. These cases are *Nat. R.R. Passenger Corp. v. Morgan*, 536 U.S. 101, (2002), *Morgan v. United Parcel Service*, 380 F.3d 459 (8th Cir. 2004), and *Ledbetter v. Goodyear Tire & Rubber Co. Inc.*, 421 F.3d 1169 (11th Cir. 2005), *cert. granted*, 126 S. Ct. 2965 (2006). In a companion article in that issue, Murray Simpson shows how pay discrimination issues can be addressed using the forensic decision analysis framework.

VI. BAYESIAN STATISTICS

The statistical techniques discussed thus far in this chapter fall under the heading of "objectivist" or "frequentist" statistics. "For an objectivist statistician, probabilities are not beliefs; rather, they are inherent properties of an experiment. If the experiment can be repeated, then in the long run, the relative frequency of an event tends to its probability. For instance, if a fair coin is tossed, the probability of heads is $1/2$; if the experiment is repeated, the coin will land heads about one-half the time." Kaye & Freedman, *Reference Guide on Statistics, supra,* at 151. In an alternative, "subjectivist" view, "probabilities represent degrees of belief, on a scale between 0 and 1. An impossible event has probability 0, an event that is sure to happen has probability 1." *Id.* The subjectivist approach is often called Bayesian, after the Reverend Thomas Bayes, an eighteenth-century English cleric and mathematician.

Although Bayesian analysis has been extensively discussed in the academic legal literature, it is has rarely been used in actual cases, except in the context of paternity testing. The first reading expands briefly on the theory of Bayesian statistics. In the second excerpt, Professor Richard Myers argues for the application of Bayesian analysis to the question of whether an "alert," or positive response, by a drug-sniffing police dog is sufficient to create probable cause to search a car. An example of a Bayesian paternity analysis is presented in Chapter 4, DNA Evidence.

Reference Guide on Statistics

Reference Manual on Scientific Evidence (Federal Judicial Center, 2d ed. 2000)
David H. Kaye and David A. Freedman

Standard errors, *p*-values, and significance tests are common techniques for assessing random error. These procedures rely on the sample data, and are justified in terms of the "operating characteristics" of the statistical procedures. However, this frequentist approach does not permit the statistician to compute the probability that a particular hypothesis is correct, given the data. For instance, a frequentist may postulate that a coin is fair: it has a 50-50 chance of landing heads, and successive tosses are independent; this is viewed as an empirical statement—potentially falsifiable—about the coin. On this basis, it is easy to calculate the chance that the coin will turn up heads in the next ten tosses: the answer is $1/1{,}024$ $[1/2 \times 2 \times 2 \times 2 \times 2 \times 2 \times 2 \times 2 \times 2 \times 2]$. Therefore, observing ten heads in a row brings into serious question the initial hypothesis of fairness. Rejecting the hypothesis of fairness when there are ten heads in ten tosses gives the wrong result—when the coin is fair—only one time in 1,024. That is an example of an operating characteristic of a statistical procedure.

But what of the converse probability: if a coin lands heads ten times in a row, what is the chance that it is fair? To compute such converse probabilities, it is necessary to postulate initial probabilities that the coin is fair, as well as probabilities of unfairness to various degrees. And that is beyond the scope of frequentist statistics.

In the Bayesian or subjectivist approach, probabilities represent subjective degrees of belief rather than objective facts. The observer's confidence in the hypothesis that a coin is fair, for example, is expressed as a number between zero and one; likewise, the observer must quantify beliefs about the chance that the coin is unfair to various degrees—all in advance of seeing the data. These subjective probabilities, like the probabilities governing the tosses of the coin, are set up to obey the axioms of probability theory. The probabilities for the various hypotheses about the coin, specified before data collection, are called prior probabilities.

These prior probabilities can then be updated, using "Bayes' rule," given data on how the coin actually falls. In short, Bayesian statisticians can compute posterior probabilities for various hypotheses about the coin, given the data. Although such posterior probabilities can pertain directly to hypotheses of legal interest, they are necessarily subjective, for they reflect not just the data but also the subjective prior probabilities—that is, the degrees of belief about the various hypotheses concerning the coin specified prior to obtaining the data.

Detector Dogs and Probable Cause

14 Geo. Mason L. Rev 1 (2006)
Richard E. Myers, II

[T]he mere fact of an alert cannot be probable cause, once one considers the effect of Bayes' Theorem, a formula commonly used by medical doctors and scientists for taking proper account of new information, such as that provided by some type of laboratory test. It tells us, through a little calculation, how strong our belief should be that a particular fact or condition exists if we are given a new piece of information to add to what we knew before. Or, in the language of statisticians, what the formula does is allow the user to update their beliefs about certain events in light of new information.[55]

Applying Bayes' Theorem debunks the common fallacy that an alert by a dog with a 90 percent success rate means there is a 90 percent chance that this particular vehicle contains the controlled substance.[56] That couldn't be further from the truth, yet, as the literature and the cases confirm, it is a widely held and intuitive misconception. It should not be surprising that unless the dog is perfect, the test only increases the likelihood that there are drugs there, it does not establish it. We don't expect a 90 percent accurate test to leave us with a 100 percent conviction that there are drugs there. But that 90 percent accurate test increases the likelihood that drugs are there far less than most people think. If the probability was low to begin with, even a really good test will still result in a relatively low number.[57] Imagine that there has been a stop by a deputy sheriff, and while he is writing the driver of the car a ticket, a colleague runs this 90 percent successful dog around the car. The handler has not talked to the other deputy at all about the stop, the reasons for it, the driver's demeanor, story, or other conditions. The dog alerts at the trunk, scratching vigorously as it has been trained to do in the presence of cocaine or marijuana. Knowing nothing else about the driver and her demeanor, what are the odds that the trunk in fact contains an illegal drug? Despite what your instincts may tell you, there is not a 90 percent chance that there will be drugs in the car. It is closer to 16 percent. Surprised? Here's why.

To see how the error rate of dog alerts alters the probable cause calculation, one needs to understand some statistics. Bayes' rule provides a

55. The use of Bayesian analysis in court has been the subject of some controversy, especially where the proponent of evidence wants to use Bayes theorem to show that a particular piece of evidence has extraordinary probative value. See Finkelstein and Fairley, *A Bayesian Approach to Identification Evidence*, 83 HARV. L. REV. 489 (1970); Broun and Kelly, *Playing the Percentages and the Law of Evidence*, 1970 U. ILL. L. REV. 23, Lawrence Tribe, *Trial By Mathematics*, 84 HARV. L. REV. 1329 (1971). For those seeking a more straightforward explanation of Bayes' theorem and how it works, there is an excellent website explaining the application of Bayes Theorem in various contexts which may be helpful for the uninitiated. *See* Eliezer Yudkowsky, *An Intuitive Explanation of Bayesian Reasoning: Bayes' Theorem for the curious and bewildered; an excruciatingly gentle introduction*, available at http://yudkowsky.net/bayes/bayes.html (visited July 12, 2004). Compare Lea Brilmayer, *Second-Order Evidence and Bayesian Logic*, 66 B. U. L. REV. 673, (1986), passim, (discussing the potential limitations on Bayesian Logic in the courtroom).

56. For an earlier, abbreviated discussion of Bayes theorem in the dog sniff context, see Robert C. Bird, *An Examination of the Training and Reliability of the Narcotics Detection Dog*, 85 KY. L.J. 405 (1997).

57. *See* YUDKOWSKY, *supra* note 54.

framework for this analysis. As stated above, Bayes' rule is concerned with updating of beliefs about certain events in light of new information.[58] That sounds technical, so consider the following example. Suppose the police, because of prior experiences, believe that one out of fifty stopped cars will contain drugs. In other words, the police officer's original assessment is that two percent of the cars stopped will possess drugs. (Admittedly, one of the problems with performing this type of analysis is getting a reliable number for the background expectation. Drug usage surveys may provide some help in establishing a useful figure, but there will be considerable disagreement over what figure should be used. This figure is chosen for purposes of illustration only.) Suppose, then, that the dog alerts after the car is stopped. The legal question is whether the dog alert *alone* is enough to justify a search.[59]

This depends on the dog's error rate coupled with the officer's original assessment of guilt. Take first the error rate. The dog might commit two types of errors. First, the dog might fail to alert when there are drugs in the car. Second, the dog might alert when there are no drugs in the car. Assume that the dog is pretty good. He fails to alert in the presence of drugs only 5 percent of the time. Put another way, he has a 5 percent false negative rate. He alerts when drugs aren't present 10 percent of the time. He has a 10 percent false positive rate.

For our purposes, the important number is the false positives. What we want to know is the probability the car contains drugs conditional on (or in light of) the dog alert. Given this information, Bayes rule tells us the chance that the dog alert is correct and the person stopped has drugs. The formula and computation follow:

First, some notation for the mathematically-inclined.

Let P[not alert | guilty] equal the probability the dog commits the first type of error — 5 percent. Relatedly, of course, the dog correctly alerts in the presence of drugs 95 percent of time. So, $P[alert | guilty] = .95$. Let P[alert | innocent] equal the probability the dog commits the second type of error — 10 percent. Hence, $P[not\ alert | innocent] = .90$

Finally, we need the background expectations. Let $P[guilty] = .02$ represent the original assessment of guilt and $P[innocent] = .98$ represent the original assessment of innocence.

---

58. *See, e.g.,* Richard Lempert, *Some Caveats Concerning DNA As Criminal Identification Evidence: With Thanks to the Reverend Bayes,* 13 CARDOZO L. REV. 303, 316-18 (1991), (explaining Bayesian analysis in the context of DNA evidence).

59. Remember that this depends on the stated premise — that we are talking about the value of the alert standing on its own. If we had more information, we could adjust the prior probability upward or downward.

$$P[\text{guilty}\,|\,\text{alert}] = \frac{P[\text{alert}\,|\,\text{guilty}]P[\text{guilty}]}{P[\text{alert}\,|\,\text{guilty}]P[\text{guilty}] + P[\text{alert}\,|\,\text{innocent}]P[\text{innocent}]}$$

$$= \frac{(.95)(.02)}{(.95)(.02) + (.10)(.98)}$$

$$= .162393$$

With a pretty good dog, but a largely innocent population, a dog alert will signal drugs only about 16 percent of the time. The reason is this: Because the officer is stopping mostly innocent people, one has to be more concerned about the false positive error (alerting when there aren't drugs). Because there are more cars without drugs in them, the gross number of searches that result from the error rate will be higher than the gross number of searches that result from correct alerts. Overall, there will be many more searches of innocent people than there will be searches of guilty people.[60]

Now that we have done the math, the constitutional question that follows is: Is a 16 percent likelihood probable cause? Maybe. Perhaps counterintuitively, this too requires some thought. We know from the [U.S. Supreme] Court's decisions that probable cause to search does not mean, as any non-lawyer would think, that it is more likely than not that there are drugs in the car. But how much less still qualifies? The Supreme Court has scrupulously avoided answering that question, choosing instead a range of answers — leaving the touchstone at some unquantified "fair probability."[61] Is a one in eight chance a fair probability? If a 16 percent chance isn't good enough, then there isn't probable cause for the search.[62]

60. Lawyers seem to do particularly poorly with evaluating the value of such a search. See Michael O. Finkelstein and Bruce Levin, *On the Probative Value of Evidence From a Screening Search*, 43 JURIMETRICS 265, 268-69 (2003) ("In biomedical applications, the strengths and weaknesses of screening tests are well understood. For example, it is recognized that even very good blood tests for rare conditions yield many false positives. Nevertheless, a similar appreciation has not been evident in the law."). See also Bird, *supra* note 55, pp. 427-28 (showing that a 98 percent accurate dog, in a population with a 0.5% drug possession rate, will yield 199 searches of innocent people versus 49 searches of guilty people, in a random search of 10,000 people).

61. See Ronald J. Bacigal, *Making the Right Gamble: The Odds on Probable Cause*, 74 MISS. L.J. 279, passim (2004); William J. Stuntz, *Commentary: O.J. Simpson, Bill Clinton, and the Transubstantive Fourth Amendment*, 114 HARV. L. REV. 842 (2001).

62. Unlike many other instances where probable cause is considered a fluid concept, "turning on the assessment of probabilities in particular factual contexts — not readily, or even usefully, reduced to a set of neat legal rules," Illinois v. Gates, 462 U.S. 213, 232, (1983), some lower courts have been establishing a rule for dog cases that the alert of a well-trained dog, standing alone, is enough to constitute probable cause. Because the numbers demonstrate that such an alert is not enough to amount to a "fair probability," the rule has been drawn the wrong way.

(While some believe the caselaw suggests that a one in three chance is probably enough,[63] it is likely that one in six is not.)

NOTES AND QUESTIONS

1. The Myers article might suggest that Bayesian analysis is some kind of legal magic bullet. In fact, as his footnotes indicate, it has had little penetration beyond the theoretical literature, and even there it is controversial. Why do you think this has been the case? Is Bayes' Theorem just too complicated for lawyers and judges? Or is there something about the approach itself that casts doubt on its suitability for use in the law? Recall this from Myers's article: "Let $P[guilty] = .02$ represent the original assessment of guilt and $P[innocent] = .98$ represent the original assessment of innocence"; remember as well his comment that "[a]dmittedly, one of the problems with performing this type of analysis is getting a reliable number for the background expectation." In the view of many statisticians, the difficulties inherent in setting such "prior probabilities" — which play a major mathematical role in the equation — are a fatal flaw. To this point, Bayesian analysis has rarely been used outside of a narrow line of paternity testing cases, one of which, *State v. Skipper,* is reproduced in Chapter 4, DNA Evidence.

2. Assuming for the sake of argument that Myers's Bayesian analysis is persuasive in the drug-sniffing dog context, how do you answer his ultimate question: "Is a 16 percent likelihood [that a car identified by the dog actually contains drugs] probable cause?" More generally, is probable cause something that can or should be reduced to probabilities?

---

63. The Supreme Court has steadfastly resisted reducing probable cause to percentages. "The probable cause standard is incapable of precise definition or quantification into percentages because it deals with probabilities and depends on the totality of the circumstances." *See Maryland v. Pringle*, 538 U.S. 921 (2003). In *Pringle*, three men were arrested after police stopped a car in which all three were riding and found $763 in cash and several glassine bags of cocaine hidden behind the rear seat armrest. Under the circumstances, the Supreme Court held that there was probable cause to arrest any one or all three of the men. When the front seat passenger, Pringle, confessed to ownership of the drugs, and said that the other two men did not know the drugs were there, police released his companions. Some commentators have read *Pringle* as stating that a one in three chance will be sufficient to constitute probable cause. Given the possibility of joint dominion and control in a common criminal enterprise, the better reading of the opinion may be that in the Court's view under the circumstances there was probable cause to find that the men were commonly engaged in selling the drugs, and therefore there was probable cause to arrest any or all of them. That belief was reduced as to the other two men when Pringle confessed.

CHAPTER 4

DNA EVIDENCE

DNA evidence is best known for the role it plays in criminal cases. The prosecution may offer evidence of a "match" (a controversial term that we will explore later in the chapter) between DNA left at the crime scene and the DNA of a suspect, together with an estimate of the probability of such a match occurring if the two samples were in fact from different people. Less often, the authorities identify a suspect by "trawling" through DNA databases (of all convicted felons in a state, for example) in search of a sample that matches the crime scene DNA. But DNA evidence also can be exculpatory: The Innocence Project has secured the freedom of many people who were convicted on other grounds by showing that their DNA did not match samples collected at the crime scene. (For a dramatic example, see Mark Hansen, *Some Testimony from Expert Witnesses in Criminal Trials Is Having Trouble Standing Up to Tougher Scrutiny from the Courts*, ABA J., July, 2005, at 49.)

This chapter presents cases that illustrate all of these uses of DNA in the legal process. We begin, though, with some scientific materials that explain, first, the nature of DNA, and second, the scientific techniques that underlie the various kinds of DNA analysis. We do so because of our belief that it is impossible to become an intelligent user or critic of DNA evidence without having at least a basic grasp of the scientific background.

I. THE SCIENTIFIC BACKGROUND

A. What Is DNA?

Back to the Future: Rethinking the Product of Nature Doctrine as a Barrier to Biotechnology Patents

85 Journal of the Patent and Trademark Office Society 301 (2003)
John M. Conley and Roberte Makowski

. . . DNA (deoxyribonucleic acid) is a very long molecule that is found in every single cell of every living organism. In all organisms other than bacteria, most of the cell's DNA is found in the nucleus (bacteria do not have a nucleus). DNA dictates the functioning of the individual cell by directing the making of proteins at the right time and in the appropriate amount. By cumulative effect, DNA thus controls the growth, development, maintenance, and reproduction of the organism. DNA is made up of subunits or building blocks called nucleotides. Each nucleotide consists of a sugar (deoxyribose, the D in DNA), a phosphate group, and one of four bases: adenine (A), guanine (G), cytosine (C), and thymine (T), commonly abbreviated by their first letter. A DNA molecule resembles a ladder. The sugar and phosphate groups form the two sides and the bases form the rungs, with one base extending out from each side to join in the middle. The bases always join in the same way: A with T and C with G. A-T and C-G are called complementary base pairs. The complementary bases are joined by weak hydrogen bonds; the bonding process is known as hybridization. The relative weakness of the bonds means that they can be easily broken and reformed, allowing portions of DNA to be readily unzipped and zipped back together.

The DNA ladder is in fact a flexible rope ladder, which is usually twisted into a shape resembling a winding staircase — Crick and Watson's famous "double helix."[9] The helical structure permits the very large DNA molecule to be compacted into the nucleus. The total length of DNA in the nucleus of a human cell can be thousands of times longer than the cell diameter. The DNA in the nucleus is organized into units called chromosomes. The number and length of chromosomes are specific for each species of organism. Human beings have 46 chromosomes grouped into 23 pairs in the nucleus of every cell in the body (with the exception of sperm and egg cells, which have 23 unpaired individual chromosomes). These chromosomes contain the human genetic code, or genome. The human genome consists of about 3 billion base pairs; simpler organisms usually have shorter genomes.

The genome consists of the sequence of the four bases — A, T, C, and G. The sequencing of bases is the medium through which DNA stores and ultimately transmits information. The arrangement of these four bases, over a vast number of iterations, thus determines the nature, functionality,

9. James Watson, THE DOUBLE HELIX (1968).

and, often, the health of an organism. In this respect the genome resembles a computer. Both can store enormous amounts of information by the almost endless repetition of very simple operations. In the case of the computer, the operation is binary: a memory location is coded as either 0 or 1. In the case of the genome, it is a four-way choice — A, T, C, or G — repeated over and over, 3 billion times in the human genome. Only some regions (usually a small portion) of an organism's genome have functional significance. These functional regions are called genes.

The main function of genes is to make proteins. Consequently, the process of making proteins is called gene expression. DNA provides the template and the control mechanisms for making proteins. Only certain genes are expressed in certain cell types. For example, genes for the functioning of muscles will be expressed in muscle tissue cells, liver genes will be expressed in liver cells, and so on. When they are needed, genes are turned on by DNA regions called promoters. Proteins are large molecules made up of chains of smaller molecules called amino acids. Proteins are the working molecules of the cell, and all cell activities involve proteins. There are many different kinds of proteins that perform a wide range of functions. Some provide the structure of cells, giving substance to hair fibers and tendons and ligaments; others fight infections as antibodies; others, such as hemoglobin, transport vital substances around the body; others, called hormones, send signals from cell to cell; while others, called enzymes, facilitate biochemical reactions.

Not all of the DNA in the relevant region actually codes for proteins . . .

Over 90% of an organism's DNA is not involved in protein synthesis. In other words, less than 10% of an organism's DNA consists of genes. The function, if any, of the vast majority of this extra DNA is not yet known. It comes in various forms, including non-coding regions, or introns, non-functional gene duplicates called pseudogenes, highly repetitious sequences known as short tandem repeats, and unclassified spacer DNA. The coding regions, or exons, tend to be highly similar across species and between individuals of a given species. However, the non-coding regions [called introns], especially the repetitious stretches of DNA, vary greatly, and it is this variability that permits DNA fingerprinting of individual human beings.

Reference Guide on DNA Evidence

Reference Manual on Scientific Evidence (Federal Judicial Center, 2d ed. 2000)
David H. Kaye and George F. Sensabaugh, Jr.

DNA is a complex molecule that contains the "genetic code" of organisms as diverse as bacteria and humans. The molecule is made of subunits that include four nucleotide bases, whose names are abbreviated to A, T, G, and C . . . [A] DNA molecule is like a long sequence of these four letters, where the chemical structure that corresponds to each letter is known as a base pair.

Most human DNA is tightly packed into structures known as chromosomes, which are located in the nuclei of most cells. If the bases are like

letters, then each chromosome is like a book written in this four-letter alpha-
bet, and the nucleus is like a bookshelf in the interior of the cell. All the cells
in one individual contain copies of the same set of books. This library, so to
speak, is the individual's genome.

In human beings, the process that produces billions of cells with the
same genome starts with sex. Every sex cell (a sperm or ovum) contains 23
chromosomes. When a sperm and ovum combine, the resulting fertilized
cell contains 23 pairs of chromosomes, or 46 in all. It is as if the father
donates half of his collection of 46 books, and the mother donates a
corresponding half of her collection. During pregnancy, the fertilized cell
divides to form two cells, each of which has an identical copy of the 46
chromosomes. The two then divide to form four, the four form eight, and
so on. As gestation proceeds, various cells specialize to form different tissues
and organs. In this way, each human being has immensely many copies of the
original 23 pairs of chromosomes from the fertilized egg, one member of
each pair having come from the mother and one from the father.

All told, the DNA in the 23 chromosomes contains over three billion
letters (base pairs) of genetic "text." About 99.9% is identical between any
two individuals. This similarity is not really surprising — it accounts for the
common features that make humans an identifiable species. The remaining
0.1% is particular to an individual (identical twins excepted). This variation
makes each person genetically unique.

A gene is a particular DNA sequence, usually from 1,000 to 10,000 base
pairs long, that "codes" for an observable characteristic. For example, a tiny
part of the sequence that directs the production of the human group-specific
complement protein (GC) is

GCAAAATTGCCTGATGCCACACCCAAGGAACTGGCA25

This gene always is located at the same position, or locus, on chromosome
number 4. As we have seen, most individuals have two copies of each gene at
a given locus — one from the father and one from the mother.

A locus where almost all humans have the same DNA sequence is called
monomorphic ("of one form"). A locus at which the DNA sequence varies
among individuals is called polymorphic ("of many forms"). The alternative
forms are called alleles. For example, the GC protein gene sequence has
three common alleles that result from single nucleotide polymorphisms
(SNPs, pronounced "snips") — substitutions in the base that occur at a
given point . . . [T]he sequences at the variable sites are shown in Figure 1.

Allele *2: G C A A A A T T G C C T G A T G C C A C A C C C A A G G A A C T G G C A

Allele *1F: G C A A A A T T G C C T G A T G C C A C A C C C A C G G A A C T G G C A

Allele *1S: G C A A A A T T G C C T G A G G C C A C A C C C A C G G A A C T G G C A

**Figure 1. The variable sequence region of the group-specific component gene.
The base substitutions that define the alleles are [underlined].**

In terms of the metaphor of DNA as text, the gene is like an important paragraph in the book; a SNP is a change in a letter somewhere within that paragraph, and the two versions of the paragraph that result from this slight change are the alleles. An individual who inherits the same allele from both parents is called a homozygote. An individual with distinct alleles is termed a heterozygote. Regions of DNA used for forensic analysis usually are not genes, but parts of the chromosome without a known function. The "non-coding" regions of DNA have been found to contain considerable sequence variation, which makes them particularly useful in distinguishing individuals. Although the terms "locus," "allele," "homozygous," and "heterozygous" were developed to describe genes, the nomenclature has been carried over to describe all DNA variation — coding and non-coding alike — for both types are inherited from mother and father in the same fashion.

NOTE

1.   The following illustration, taken from a National Library of Medicine website, summarizes much of the material in the preceding two excerpts:

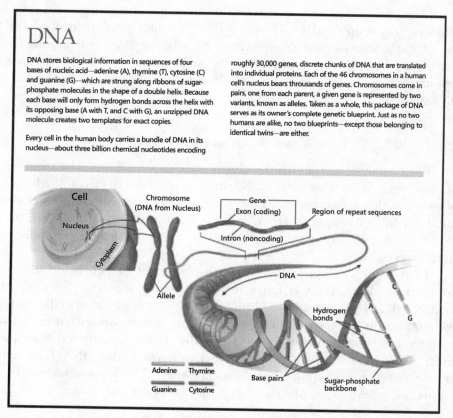

DNA

DNA stores biological information in sequences of four bases of nucleic acid—adenine (A), thymine (T), cytosine (C) and guanine (G)—which are strung along ribbons of sugar-phosphate molecules in the shape of a double helix. Because each base will only form hydrogen bonds across the helix with its opposing base (A with T, and C with G), an unzipped DNA molecule creates two templates for exact copies.

Every cell in the human body carries a bundle of DNA in its nucleus—about three billion chemical nucleotides encoding roughly 30,000 genes, discrete chunks of DNA that are translated into individual proteins. Each of the 46 chromosomes in a human cell's nucleus bears throusands of genes. Chromosomes come in pairs, one from each parent, a given gene is represented by two variants, known as alleles. Taken as a whole, this package of DNA serves as its owner's complete genetic blueprint. Just as no two humans are alike, no two blueprints—except those belonging to identical twins—are either.

Cell
Nucleus
Cytoplasm
Chromosome (DNA from Nucleus)
Gene
Exon (coding)
Intron (noncoding)
Region of repeat sequences
DNA
Allele
Hydrogen bonds
C
A
G
T
Adenine   Thymine
Guanine   Cytosine
Base pairs
Sugar-phosphate backbone

Figure obtained from the National Library of Medicine website, http://www.nlm.nih.gov/exhibition/visibleproofs/education/dna/dna.pdf.

B. The Science of DNA Profiling

The first widely used method of DNA profiling was called either RFLP (restriction fragment length polymorphism) or VNTR (variable number of tandem repeats). The significance of the names is explained in the readings. Later methods have been based on a laboratory technique for replicating DNA called polymerase chain reaction, and are therefore sometimes collectively referred to as PCR methods. They include such specific techniques as short tandem repeat (STR) analysis, mitochondrial DNA (mtDNA) analysis, and single nucleotide polymorphism (SNP) analysis. The case that follows illustrates the judicial understanding of both VNTR and PCR. The subsequent readings and notes examine the science in more detail.

People v. Reeves

109 Cal. Rptr. 2d 728 (Cal. Ct. App. 2001)

[The defendant was convicted of multiple burglaries and sexual offenses and sentenced to 77 years. DNA samples were recovered from two of the sexual offense crime scenes. In affirming the convictions (but not the sentences), the state court of appeals found, under the California *Frye* standard, that the prosecution had used generally accepted methods of DNA analysis.]

1. RFLP Processing and Matching Procedures

RFLP analysis focuses on the highly variable VNTR loci. The variability of these regions "is what makes DNA analysis possible. In effect, the lengths of sets of multiple (usually eight) polymorphic fragments (or VNTR alleles) obtained from a suspect's DNA and from crime scene samples are compared to see if any sets match, and a match is accorded statistical significance."

DNA from a sample and from a suspect must be processed to allow comparison. First, DNA is extracted from bodily material. Second, the "extracted DNA is 'cut' into thousands of fragments at specific points by application of restriction enzymes. The restriction enzymes act as 'chemical scissors' in that they sever the DNA at targeted base-pair sites." Third, in a process called electrophoresis, the DNA fragments are separated according to their base-pair size. "The various sample fragments being tested are placed in separate lanes on one end of a gel slab and an electrical current is applied, causing the fragments to move across the gel. Shorter fragments move farther than longer fragments. Thus, at the completion of electrophoresis, the sample fragments are arrayed across the gel according to size. In addition to the sample fragments, other fragments called size markers, which have known base-pair lengths, are placed in separate lanes on the gel in order to facilitate measurement of the sample fragments." Fourth, through a process called "Southern transfer," the DNA fragments are denatured and wicked from the gel onto a nylon membrane. The fifth and sixth steps allow the DNA fragments to be visualized on X-ray film. Through hybridization, radioactive single-strand DNA probes are applied to the nylon membrane, where they seek out and bind themselves to denatured DNA fragments [split into separate strands] that have complementary base sequences. Then, when the membrane is washed and exposed to X-ray film, a pattern of bands appears depicting DNA fragments at each locus probed. "The location of a band on the X-ray film indicates the distance a fragment traveled as a result of electrophoresis, and hence the length of the fragment. The size-marker fragments also appear on the films, enabling measurement of the base-pair lengths of the sample fragments. The end result of the processing substeps is a picture of a person's DNA pattern (which may be produced by overlaying the four X-ray films)." The X-ray film is called an autoradiograph, or autorad.

Next, scientists compare the autorads to see if the suspect's DNA pattern matches that produced by DNA from the evidence sample. "First, the patterns are visually evaluated (i.e., 'eyeballed') to determine whether there is a likely match. Most exclusions will be obvious, since the patterns will be noticeably different. If there is not an obvious exclusion, the bands in the patterns are subjected to computer-assisted analysis to determine the length of the represented DNA fragments as measured in base-pair units. The measurements are taken by comparing the bands for the sample fragments with the bands for the size-marker fragments of known base-pair lengths."

If the bands at any locus do not match, the suspect is excluded as a possible donor of the sample DNA. However, "if all of the suspect's fragment lengths are the same as the crime scene fragment lengths within the margin of error—i.e., if the band patterns produced by the processing step are identical—a match is declared."

2. PCR Processing and Matching Procedures

PCR is a molecular biology technique that copies or amplifies small pieces of DNA by a process similar to DNA's own self-replicating properties.

It has been likened to a "genetic photocopy machine" and is often employed when the DNA sample available is too small or degraded to produce good results using RFLP.

PCR forensic analysis involves three steps. First, DNA is extracted from cells in the sample. Second, select regions of the DNA are amplified. Scientists have identified these regions, also referred to as genes or genetic markers, as areas that exhibit great genetic variation among the population. One widely used marker is the DQ-alpha gene. On average, only about 7 percent of the population shares the same DQ-alpha type. Like DQ-alpha, the D1S80 locus is used in PCR testing because it contains several alleles and exhibits great variation. Polymarker analysis, which amplifies several loci simultaneously, has also been validated for use in PCR testing. After amplification, in the third and final step of PCR analysis the amplified gene is "typed," through the use of DNA probes, to identify the specific alleles it contains. If the DNA profile thus constructed differs in any way between the suspect and the sample, the suspect is excluded. But if the profiles match, the analyst must next determine how common the profile is in the population.

Reference Guide on DNA Evidence

Reference Manual on Scientific Evidence (Federal Judicial Center, 2d ed. 2000)
David H. Kaye and George F. Sensabaugh, Jr.

VNTR profiling . . . was the first widely used method of forensic DNA testing. Consequently, its underlying principles, its acceptance within the scientific community, and its scientific soundness have been discussed in a great many opinions . . .

1. . . . VNTR profiling begins with the extraction of DNA from a crime-scene sample. (Because this DNA is not amplified, however, larger quantities of higher quality DNA are required.)

2. The extracted DNA is "digested" by a restriction enzyme that recognizes a particular, very short sequence; the enzyme cuts the DNA at these restriction sites. When a VNTR falls between two restriction sites, the resulting DNA fragments will vary in size depending on the number of core repeat units in the VNTR region. (These VNTRs are thus referred to as a restriction fragment length polymorphism, or RFLP.)

3. The digested DNA fragments are then separated according to size by gel electrophoresis. The digest [crime-scene] sample is placed in a well at the end of a lane in an agarose gel, which is a gelatin-like material solidified in a slab. Digested DNA from the suspect is placed in another well on the same gel. Typically, control specimens of DNA fragments of known size, and,

where appropriate, DNA specimens obtained from a victim, are run on the same gel. Mild electric current applied to the gel slowly separates the fragments in each lane by length, as shorter fragments travel farther in a fixed time than longer, heavier fragments.

4. The resulting array of fragments is transferred for manageability to a sheet of nylon by a process known as Southern blotting.

5. The restriction fragments representing a particular polymorphic locus are "tagged" on the membrane using a sequence-specific probe labeled with a radioactive or chemical tag.

6. The position of the specifically bound probe tag is made visible, either by autoradiography (for radioactive labels) or by a chemical reaction (for chemical labels). For autoradiography, the washed nylon membrane is placed between two sheets of photographic film. Over time, the radioactive probe material exposes the film where the biological probe has hybridized with the DNA fragments. The result is an autoradiograph, or an autorad, a visual pattern of bands representing specific DNA fragments. An autorad that shows two bands in a single lane indicates that the individual who is the source of the DNA is a heterozygote at that locus. If the autorad shows only one band, the person may be homozygous for that allele (that is, each parent contributed the same allele), or the second band may be present but invisible for technical reasons. The band pattern defines the person's genotype at the locus associated with the probe. Once an appropriately exposed autorad is obtained, the probe is stripped from the membrane, and the process is repeated with a separate probe for each locus tested. Three to five probes are typically used, the number depending in part on the amount of testable DNA recovered from the crime-scene sample. The result is a set of autorads, each of which shows the results of one probe. If the crime-scene and suspect samples yield bands that are closely aligned on each autorad, the VNTR profiles from the two samples are considered to match.

NOTE

As these readings suggests, the logic of the VNTR/RFLP method is straightforward. A short DNA sequence is repeated a variable number of times at a particular site, or locus, on the genome. Consequently, the length of this segment of the genome varies from person to person. A restriction enzyme can be tailored to cut the DNA sequences that mark the beginning and end of the segment in question. The resulting pieces are called restriction fragments, and they are said to exhibit length polymorphism — hence RFLP. The process is repeated at several loci, and is performed on the suspect's DNA sample, the crime scene sample, and a number of control samples. The National Library of Medicine depicts it as follows:

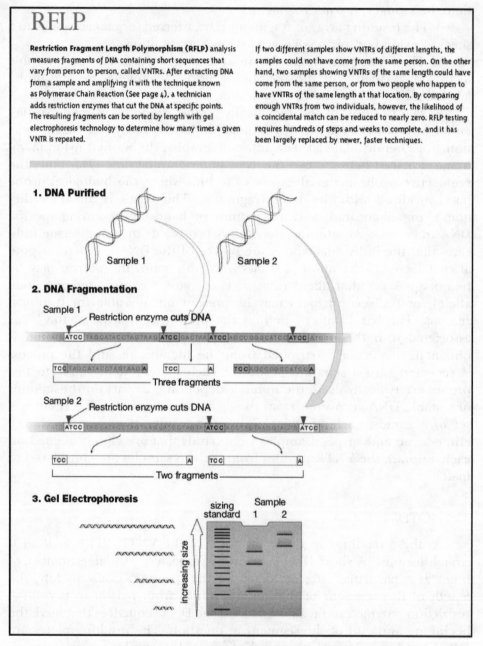

RFLP

Restriction Fragment Length Polymorphism (RFLP) analysis measures fragments of DNA containing short sequences that vary from person to person, called VNTRs. After extracting DNA from a sample and amplifying it with the technique known as Polymerase Chain Reaction (See page 4), a technician adds restriction enzymes that cut the DNA at specific points. The resulting fragments can be sorted by length with gel electrophoresis technology to determine how many times a given VNTR is repeated.

If two different samples show VNTRs of different lengths, the samples could not have come from the same person. On the other hand, two samples showing VNTRs of the same length could have come from the same person, or from two people who happen to have VNTRs of the same length at that location. By comparing enough VNTRs from two individuals, however, the likelihood of a coincidental match can be reduced to nearly zero. RFLP testing requires hundreds of steps and weeks to complete, and it has been largely replaced by newer, faster techniques.

1. DNA Purified

Sample 1   Sample 2

2. DNA Fragmentation

Sample 1
Restriction enzyme cuts DNA

ATCC TAGCATACCTAGTAAC ATCC GACTAA ATCC AGCCGGGCATC ATCC ATCG

TCC TAGCATACCTAGTAAC A   TCC   A   TCC AGCCGGGCATCC A
|————————————— Three fragments —————————————|

Sample 2
Restriction enzyme cuts DNA

ATCC TAGCATACCTAG TAAGA ATCC ATCCTAGTA ATCC AGCTAGTAAGGTAAC ATCC

TCC   A   TCC   A
|————————————— Two fragments —————————————|

3. Gel Electrophoresis

increasing size

sizing standard   Sample 1   Sample 2

Figure obtained from the National Library of Medicine website,
http://www.nlm.nih.gov/exhibition/visibleproofs/education/dna/rflp.pdf.

Each sample is then inserted into one end of an electrophoretic (conductive) gel, and an electric current is applied. A kind of race ensues. The shorter fragments always go faster than the longer ones, so when the current is stopped they will have progressed farther down the gel. The mechanism looks like this:

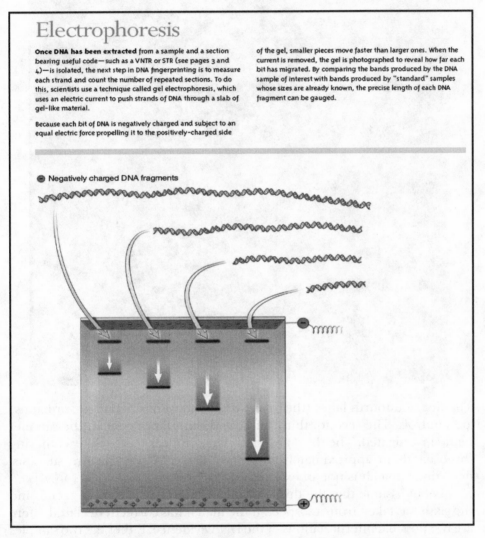

Electrophoresis

Once DNA has been extracted from a sample and a section bearing useful code—such as a VNTR or STR (see pages 3 and 4)—is isolated, the next step in DNA fingerprinting is to measure each strand and count the number of repeated sections. To do this, scientists use a technique called gel electrophoresis, which uses an electric current to push strands of DNA through a slab of gel-like material.

Because each bit of DNA is negatively charged and subject to an equal electric force propelling it to the positively-charged side of the gel, smaller pieces move faster than larger ones. When the current is removed, the gel is photographed to reveal how far each bit has migrated. By comparing the bands produced by the DNA sample of interest with bands produced by "standard" samples whose sizes are already known, the precise length of each DNA fragment can be gauged.

⊖ Negatively charged DNA fragments

Figure obtained from the National Library of Medicine website, http://www.nlm.nih.gov/exhibition/visibleproofs/education/dna/electrophoresis.pdf.

The autoradiograph is essentially a photograph of where the DNA fragments have finished the race. It looks like this:

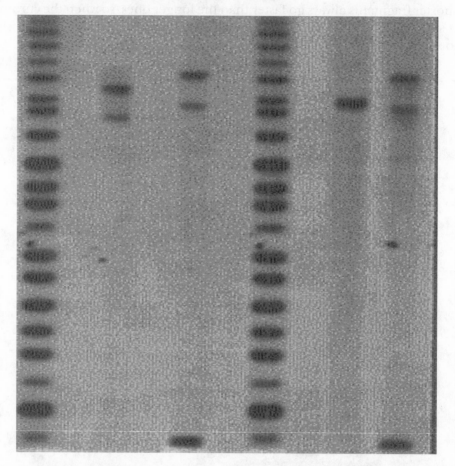

The first and fourth lanes (the ones with the most dark smudges, or bands)
are controls. The second, third, fifth, and sixth lanes contain the samples
being investigated. The third and sixth lanes appear to match, each having
three bands in approximately the same places. As this picture suggests,
declaring a match is not an exact science.

Let us assume that the third sample was found at the crime scene, and
the sixth was taken from a suspect. If the match was correctly declared, there
are two possible interpretations of the DNA evidence: Either the two samples
came from the same person, or they came from people having the same DNA
profile at the three loci that were analyzed. Before deciding between these
explanations, we will want another piece of information: the frequency of
this particular DNA pattern in the relevant population (the definition of
which is a major issue — read on). If the pattern occurs in one-third of
the people who might have left the sample at the crime scene, we will not
be very confident that the suspect was the one who left it. We will be far more

confident if that pattern occurs only one in a billion times. The statistical interpretation of DNA matches is a large and controversial subject that is discussed in Section II. *infra*. As we shall see, one of the most difficult sub-issues is deciding what population to use for the comparative frequencies.

II. *DNA IN THE COURTROOM*

DNA in the Courtroom

In Jane Campbell Moriarty, Ed., Psychological and Scientific Evidence in Criminal Trials
William C. Thompson and Dan E. Krane*

§ 11:5 AN INTRODUCTION TO DNA AND DNA TESTING

In the early 1990s, newer methods of DNA testing were introduced that are faster (producing results in a day or two) and more sensitive (i.e., capable of typing smaller, more degraded samples). The new methods use a procedure called *polymerase chain reaction* (*PCR*), which can produce billions of copies of target fragments of DNA from one or more loci. These "amplified" DNA fragments (called *amplicons*) can then be typed using several methods.

§ 11:6 AN INTRODUCTION TO DNA AND DNA TESTING—

STR TESTS

The late 1990s saw the advent of *STR* (*short tandem repeat*) DNA testing. STR tests combine the sensitivity of a PCR-based test with great specificity (profile frequencies potentially as low as one in trillions) and therefore have quickly supplanted both RFLP analysis and the Polymarker/DQ-alpha test in forensic laboratories.

An *STR* is a DNA locus that contains a length polymorphism. At each STR locus, people have two alleles (one from each parent) that vary in length depending on the number of repetitions of a short core sequence of genetic code. A person with *genotype* 14, 15 at an *STR locus* has one allele with 14 repeating units, and another with 15 repeating units.

Figure 3 shows the results of STR analysis of five samples: blood from a crime scene and reference samples of four suspects. This analysis includes three loci. . . . Each person has two alleles (peaks) at each locus, one from the maternal portion and the other from the paternal portion of the chromosome. The position of the "peaks" on each graph (known as an electropherogram) indicates the length (and hence the number of core sequence repeats) of each STR. As can be seen, the profile of suspect 3 corresponds to

*Reprinted with permission of Thomson/West and the authors.

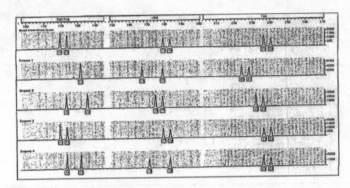

Figure 3. STR Test Results

that of the crime scene sample, indicating he is a possible source. Suspects 1, 2 and 4 are eliminated as possible sources.

A. Declaring a Match

As was evident in both the autoradiograph and the electropherogram reproduced above, there is some judgment involved in deciding whether two bands "match" in a DNA analysis. The first case, California's leading DNA case, considers that issue.

People v. Soto

21 Cal. 4th 512 (1999)

[The defendant was charged with the forcible rape of a 78-year-old woman, and with using a knife in the commission of the offense.]

The victim told Officer Gabrielli she could not identify the rapist because of the mask. She described her assailant as a White male, about five feet nine inches tall and weighing one hundred and seventy pounds, with light or blond hair and an olive complexion, wearing a mask of beige pantyhose. Soto, who is Latino, is 5 feet 10 inches tall and weighs 183 pounds, with a dark complexion and black hair. . . .

The following day the police seized a bedspread (also described as a comforter) from the victim's bedroom after they exposed it to a black light and found fluorescent areas indicating the presence of semen. A blood sample was obtained from Soto; its DNA and that from the semen stains on the bedspread were submitted to the Orange County Sheriff's Department (OCSD) crime laboratory and found to match. Robert Keister, a criminalist in the OCSD crime laboratory, testified at trial that there was a probability of only 1 in 189 million of finding the same DNA pattern in individuals selected at random from the population represented by the OCSD's Hispanic database. . . .

A jury acquitted defendant of both the forcible rape charge and knife use allegation, but found him guilty of attempted rape, a lesser included offense, for which he was sentenced to the middle term of three years in prison. . . .

[In California which follows the *Frye* general acceptance rule in most respects], evidence based upon application of a new scientific technique such as DNA profiling may be admitted only after the reliability of the method has been foundationally established, usually by the testimony of an expert witness who first has been properly qualified. The proponent of the evidence must also demonstrate that correct scientific procedures were used. . . .

C.   INTERPRETING AUTORADS THROUGH APPLICATION OF
"MATCH CRITERIA"

"The second step of DNA analysis is to compare the DNA patterns produced by the processing step in order to determine whether the suspect's DNA pattern matches the DNA pattern of bodily material found at the crime scene. First, the patterns are visually evaluated . . . to determine whether there is a likely match. Most exclusions will be obvious, since the patterns will be noticeably different."

If an exclusion is obvious on any of the autorads, there is a conclusive nonmatch of the samples. Otherwise, "the bands in the patterns are subjected to computer-assisted analysis to determine the length of the represented DNA fragments as measured in base-pair units. The measurements are taken by comparing the bands for the sample fragments with the bands for the size-marker fragments of known base-pair lengths."

Because of inherent limitations in the DNA processing system, it is not possible to obtain exact base-pair measurements of the sample DNA fragments. For that reason, forensic laboratories have developed DNA match criteria based on the variations they have experienced in repeated measurements of DNA from the same source. Those criteria determine the "match window" — or range of sizes — constructed around each band for purposes of declaring a "match." For example, under the FBI's match criterion of plus or minus 2.5 percent, the window around a band that measures 1,000 base pairs is from 975 to 1,025 base pairs. If the window of either band, or a single band, on one sample fails to overlap the window of the corresponding band on another sample, there is an exclusion of any match between the samples. If the windows of both bands, or of the single bands, of each sample overlap, there is a match at the locus disclosed by that probe. [The OCSD crime laboratory arrived at its own match criterion by recording variations in its repeated measurements of the same bands. The OCSD's match criterion of 3.4 percent (plus or minus 1.7 percent) was narrower than the FBI's match criterion of 5 percent (plus or minus 2.5 percent).]

Some conditions adverse to reliability of measurement may call for a determination that a match at that locus is inconclusive. That determination, however, does not invalidate matches at the other loci. There can be a match at multiple loci only if (1) the match criteria are met for all the bands at those loci, and (2) there is no locus at which a match of any band was excluded.

NOTES AND QUESTIONS

1. Inconclusive DNA band comparisons can have a variety of causes, including a sample of crime scene DNA that is too small or is severely degraded. In either case, all of the alleles that are present may not show up. Degraded DNA sometimes migrates farther down the gel than intact DNA. Do you think that these kinds of problems will usually favor the prosecution or the defense? Why?

2. The "match window" concept that the *Soto* court discusses is addressed to the problem of measurement error. Recall that the variable that VNTR or STR testing measures is the length of the DNA found at particular loci on a person's genome. During the test, the length of a DNA fragment determines how far it progresses through the gel. To say that two bands "match" is therefore to say that the two DNA fragments being compared are of the same length. As described in *Soto*, the first step is simply to look at the autoradiograph and see if the bands appear to be in the same place. If so, the next step is to measure the lengths of the two fragments (or alleles). The unit of measurement is not feet or inches, but the number of base pairs (A-T, C-G, etc.) in the fragment. Because the measurement is imprecise, the two units do not have to be exactly the same size to be called a match — there is some leeway on either side of the actual measurement. Under the FBI guidelines that the court describes, for example, a 975-base-pair band is considered indistinguishable from one of 1,025 base pairs. It's a bit like saying that all people between 64.50 and 65.59 inches tall will be referred to as 5'5" because our measurement techniques are inexact.

3. The *Soto* court describes two different match-window criteria: the FBI's plus-or-minus 2.5 percent and the Orange County crime lab's plus-or-minus 1.7 percent. These criteria might strike you as arbitrary, but in fact they are based on laboratory experience. The *Reference Manual on DNA Evidence* describes the FBI's criterion-setting rationale as follows:

> The FBI arrived at this match window by experiments involving pairs of measurements of the same DNA sequences. It found that this window was wide enough to encompass all the differences seen in the calibration experiments. Other laboratories use smaller percentages for their match windows, but comparisons of the percentage figures can be misleading. *See* D.H. Kaye, Science in Evidence 192 (1997). Because different laboratories can have different standard errors of measurement, profiles from two different laboratories

might not be considered inconsistent even though some corresponding bands are outside the match windows of both laboratories. The reason: there is more variability in measurements on different gels than on the same gel, and still more in different gels from different laboratories. *See* Satcher v. Netherland, 944 F. Supp. 1222, 1265 (E.D. Va. 1996).

4.   *Soto* was decided in 1999, at a point in legal history when the basics of DNA analysis had been almost universally accepted by the courts. However, this acceptance was preceded by years of controversy that are often referred to as the "DNA wars." For a thorough review of this controversy, see Thompson & Kane, *DNA in the Courtroom, supra,* at §§ 11:45-11:57. They summarize the history of DNA evidence as follows:

> The reaction in the courtroom to DNA testing has gone through a type of metamorphosis during the past few years. At first, there was widespread acceptance, which gave way to a decline in the admission of the evidence, followed by an admission of the testimony but in a more guarded fashion. Most recently, courts have once again begun to loosen the restrictions on admission of the evidence.

Id. at 11-76.

B.   The Probability of a Random Match — Compared to What?

Once a match has been declared between suspect and crime scene DNA samples, we confront two possible explanations: The suspect left the sample at the crime scene, or someone else did. (There are actually at least two more possible explanations: laboratory error, such as sample switching; and kinship, meaning that the sample was left by a close relative of the suspect who has very similar DNA. These possibilities are difficult to quantify and must be dealt with on a fact-specific, case-by-case basis.) To evaluate the plausibility of the second, exculpatory hypothesis, we need to estimate the probability that we would get a match if someone other than the suspect had actually left the crime scene sample. To do so, we need an estimate of the frequency with which the allele in question occurs in some relevant comparison population. But what population? In the next excerpt the *Soto* court discusses this problem. A second example from Alaska follows.

People v. Soto

21 Cal. 4th 512 (1999)

D.   USE OF POPULATION DATABASES TO ASSESS SIGNIFICANCE OF MATCH

Once a match at multiple loci has been declared, the next step is to determine its statistical significance. Unless a nonmatch between any band of the suspect's DNA and the corresponding band of the questioned sample conclusively eliminates the suspect as the source of that sample, a match of one or more of the suspect's bands with those of the sample places the suspect within a class of persons from whom the sample could have originated. The fact finder's determination of guilt may then turn on the degree of probability that the suspect was indeed the source of the sample. That probability, however, will usually depend, not on the DNA findings alone, but on a combination of those findings together with other, non-DNA incriminating evidence.

The question properly addressed by the DNA analysis is therefore this: Given that the suspect's known sample has satisfied the "match criteria," what is the probability that a person chosen at random from the relevant population would likewise have a DNA profile matching that of the evidentiary sample?[12] That probability is usually expressed as a fraction—i.e., the probability that one out of a stated number of persons in the population (e.g., 1 out of 100,000) would match the DNA profile of the evidentiary sample in question. A greater probability, that is to say, a fraction with a smaller denominator (e.g., 1 out of 10,000), would tend to favor the suspect by increasing the probability that one or more other persons has a DNA profile matching the evidentiary sample.

To assess the probability in question, "the FBI and Cellmark [and the OCSD crime laboratory in this case] calculate how frequently each pair of bands produced by one probe is found in a target population." For this purpose, those and other forensic laboratories use one or more population databases containing measurements of the DNA fragments of several hundred persons at each of the loci reached by the probes. The samples from which those measurements are derived come from such varied sources as blood banks, hospitals, clinics, genetics laboratories, and law enforcement personnel.

Dayton v. State

89 P.3d 806 (Alaska App. 2004)

STEWART, Judge.

This is the second opinion we have issued in this case. In Dayton v. State, 54 P.3d 817 (Alaska App. 2002), we upheld the superior court's decision on

---

12. The evidentiary sample targeted for comparison with the population can be a suspect's sample, a questioned sample, or a combination of both. *Barney* appears to equate the "statistical significance of a match" with "how unlikely it is that the crime scene samples came from a third party who had the same DNA pattern as the suspect." On the other hand, the 1996 NRC Report (supra, pp. 142-144) recommends use of the DNA profile of the questioned sample to calculate the probability of a random match in the pertinent population. It should be kept in mind, however, that at that point in the analysis, the questioned and known suspect samples will themselves already have been declared a "match," and therefore the fragment sizes used in the calculation cannot vary beyond the bounds of the match criterion.

all but one of the claims that Dayton brought on appeal. We remanded this case to the superior court for additional findings on whether a database used for statistical analysis of DNA profile frequencies was the type of data that experts in the field would reasonably rely on. After taking additional evidence, the superior court found that the database met the requirements of Alaska Evidence Rule 703 [which is identical to Federal Rule 703] . . . [W]e affirm Dayton's conviction . . .

Dayton was charged with first-degree sexual assault and first-degree burglary for breaking into S.S.'s house in Huslia and sexually assaulting her. Dayton's first trial ended with a hung jury, but he was convicted at his retrial.

Hayne Hamilton, a forensic serologist at the Alaska Scientific Crime Detection Laboratory (hereafter the "crime lab"), conducted . . . DNA analysis on various samples seized during the investigation. The testing showed that Dayton's DNA was a potential source for the DNA found in sperm collected from S.S.'s vagina. Based on databases that the State had previously developed, Hamilton projected that the frequency of the DNA profile found in the sperm fraction was 1 in 3,500 for North Slope Inupiat Eskimos and 1 in 2,000 for Bethel/Wade Hampton Yup'ik Eskimos. As we noted in our earlier opinion, Hamilton could not calculate a DNA profile frequency for Athabascan Indians because she did not have an Athabascan database. (Dayton is an Athabascan Indian.)

During the first trial, as part of his defense, Dayton argued that the DNA evidence was meaningless without an Athabascan database. Dayton himself testified that he saw someone else having intercourse with S.S. and implied that his brother may have assaulted S.S. The first trial resulted with a hung jury.

After the first trial, the crime lab adopted the short tandem repeat (STR) system of DNA analysis. STR examines thirteen genetic loci . . . The crime lab created a database with genetic samples from Athabascan Indians . . . At Dayton's retrial before Superior Court Judge pro tem Jane F. Kauvar, the State again offered evidence that, based on Dayton's DNA profile and the DNA profile of the sperm collected from S.S., Dayton could not be excluded as the source of the sperm. The statistical analysis of the likelihood that this DNA profile would be repeated randomly in certain groups with existing databases was 1 in 22 billion for North American Caucasians, 1 in 6 billion for African-Americans, and 1 in 413 million for Hispanics. Dayton did not challenge this evidence. In addition, the State offered evidence that STR analysis indicated that Dayton exhibited the DNA profile of the sperm taken from S.S. and the population frequency statistics based on the Athabascan database. Dayton objected to this evidence, arguing that the State had to establish the reliability of the Athabascan database in a hearing outside the presence of the jury before the expert witness could use the database as a basis for providing scientific evidence . . . [Alaska follows the *Daubert* standard for determining reliability.]

However, Judge Kauvar overruled Dayton's objection.

Using the Athabascan database developed by the crime lab, the State's expert testified that the likelihood was 1 in 2.5 million that the DNA profile from the sperm taken from S.S. would be repeated randomly in the Athabascan population. Because Dayton is an Athabascan, the Athabascan genetic frequency data was particularly probative.

Under Rule 703, expert witnesses can rely on facts or data outside their personal knowledge (indeed, facts or data that would not necessarily be admissible themselves) if those facts or data are "of a type reasonably relied upon by experts in the [applicable] field [when] forming opinions or inferences upon the subject [at issue]." The Commentary to Rule 703 states that the rule was designed to allow experts to rely on sources of information that constitute the recognized "tools" of their profession, that is, information that otherwise could not be introduced without "the expenditure of substantial time in producing and examining various authenticating witnesses." . . .

On remand, the State offered Dr. Bruce Budowle, a senior scientist at the FBI laboratory in Quantico, Virginia, as an expert in the creation of DNA databases. Judge Kauvar qualified Dr. Budowle as an expert without objection from Dayton.

Dr. Budowle testified that the Athabascan database was scientifically valid and constituted the type of data that experts who analyze and use DNA databases rely on. He explained that the thirteen STR loci that were examined in the Athabascan DNA database are part of CODIS (Combined DNA Index System, the national DNA data bank) and are the accepted set of genetic markers used nationally and internationally. Dr. Budowle testified that he was a co-author of an article that described the Athabascan database and the Yup'ik and Inupiat databases. The article was published in Forensic Science International, a peer-reviewed publication, after Dayton's retrial. . . .

We conclude that it was not an abuse of discretion to allow testimony that relied on the Athabascan database.

NOTES AND QUESTIONS

1. At the first trial, the state's expert introduced frequency data from two Native Alaskan databases. Why did Dayton object to those frequencies? He apparently thought that the frequency might be more favorable to him if it was based on his own ethnic group, the Athabascans. Why? At the retrial, the state introduced frequencies from four more databases, including Athabascans. In hindsight, did Dayton's lawyer make a good tactical judgment in objecting to the original databases? If you had represented Dayton, how might you have dealt with the DNA evidence at the first trial?

2. Note that Dayton "implied that his brother may have assaulted S.S." How might that implication have helped Dayton, given the facts of this case?

Consider the case of Anthony Dennard Brown. In 1984 a man named Darryl Hunt was in prison for a rape and murder that had taken place in 1984. In 2003 he was freed after new DNA testing showed that his DNA did not match that left at the crime scene. Investigators then screened 40,000 DNA samples in North Carolina's convicted-offender databank looking for a "cold hit." The crime scene sample matched the DNA of Anthony Brown on 16 of 26 alleles. While this was not enough to implicate Anthony Brown, it did get the police interested in his relatives, especially his brother Willard. The police followed Willard Brown and eventually got a DNA sample from a cigarette butt that he had tossed away. Willard's DNA matched the crime scene sample at all 26 alleles; he was charged, pleaded guilty, and is now serving a life sentence. *See* Troy Duster, *Explaining Differential Trust of DNA Forensic Technology: Grounded Assessment or Inexplicable Paranoia?*, J. of Law, Medicine & Ethics, Summer 2006, p. 293, 295. Such "familial searches" and other kinds of "DNA dragnets" are routine in Great Britain; in this country their legality varies from jurisdiction to jurisdiction. In perhaps the most famous example, in 1987 police in Leicester, England obtained voluntary DNA samples from over 4,500 males after the rape and murder of two teenage girls. The man who was ultimately convicted aroused suspicion when he asked a friend to submit a sample in his place. *See id.* at 295-297.

3. The *Hunt/Brown* case also raises the issue of the fairness of "data mining" in criminal databases. Do you see any problems with using such databases to identify suspects through "cold hits"? Does it matter to you how the suspect had gotten into the database? What if, under applicable state law, he had been required to give a DNA sample after being arrested for a non-violent misdemeanor of which he had ultimately been acquitted? Or does the end of solving rapes and murders justify such means? How do you think Darryl Hunt would answer that question?

4. Think about Dayton's position on the proper comparative database from a logical viewpoint. For obvious reasons, defendants usually want the comparative frequency evidence to be drawn from people with whom they share a genetic heritage (even that doesn't always work in the defendant's favor, as Dayton found out). The *phenotypic* (related to an organism's expressed characteristics) categories we call race and ethnicity tend to be indicators of shared genetic heritage, so defendants often argue for comparative databases that sample only their own racial or ethnic group: An Irish-American defendant wants an Irish-American database, an Athabascan defendant wants an Athabascan database, and so on. But is this logical? Aren't we interested in the probability of a match if someone other than the defendant actually left the crime scene sample? Is there any reason to suspect that an Athabascan left the sample? Or a Caucasian, or an Inupiat Eskimo, or a member of any other racial ethnic group? Maybe the answer is that these comparisons are chosen simply because they are most favorable to the defendant, and thus likely to minimize reversals.

C. The Probability of a Random Match—
The Statistics

The *Dayton* opinion reports a number of frequencies (based on different comparative databases) for the DNA profile found at the crime scene ranging from 1 in 2,000 to 1 in 22 billion. The court also notes that the STR technique that the Alaska crime lab uses examines 13 genetic loci. So the reported probabilities reflect, for each of the databases, the frequency of occurrence of a genetic profile that matches the crime scene sample at all 13 loci. A final excerpt from *Soto* explains how such frequencies are calculated.

People v. Soto

21 Cal. 4th 512 (1999)

F.   PROBABILITY OF A RANDOM PROFILE MATCH — THE "PRODUCT RULE"

The final task is to calculate the statistical probability that the DNA profile of any one person, selected at random from the relevant population, would contain all the alleles represented by the measured bands of the evidentiary sample. The most straightforward means of making this calculation is through application of the "product rule." The essence of the product rule is the multiplication of individual band probabilities to arrive at an overall probability statistic expressed as a simple fraction, such as 1 in 100,000 . . . [U]nder the product rule, the frequencies found at each locus are multiplied together to generate a probability statistic reflecting the overall frequency of the complete multi-locus profile. The resulting statistic will oftentimes be very small.[17]

G.   EFFECTS OF POPULATION SUBSTRUCTURE — THE "CEILING PRINCIPLES"

The foregoing application of the product rule to calculate the frequency of a multi-locus profile will produce an accurate result only to the extent that each multiplied frequency is statistically independent from all the others. (See People v. Collins (1968) 68 Cal.2d 319, 328-329 [66 Cal. Rptr. 497, 438 P.2d 33, 36 A.L.R.3d 1176].) Population genetics theory teaches that pairs of alleles at the same locus are statistically independent from each other if they are in "Hardy-Weinberg equilibrium." Hardy-Weinberg equilibrium has been defined as "the condition, for a particular genetic locus and a particular population, with the following properties: allele

17. For example, if the evidentiary sample were to have two alleles at each of four loci, each allele having a frequency of 1 out of 10 (0.1), application of the product rule would produce a frequency of 1 out of 6.25 million (.00000016).

frequencies at the locus are constant in the population over time and there is no statistical correlation between the two alleles possessed by individuals in the population; such a condition is approached in large randomly mating populations in the absence of selection, migration, and mutation."

Alleles at different loci are said to be independent if they are in "linkage equilibrium." Alleles are not in linkage equilibrium if "a specific allele at one locus is non-randomly associated with an allele at another locus."

Generally, the presence of both kinds of equilibrium in a given population depends on the extent to which mating within that population has been at random. If both kinds of equilibrium are not present, application of the product rule in theory may prejudice the suspect by understating the frequency of a profile within particular segments of the population.

Major laboratories that do RFLP analysis, including the FBI and Cellmark [and the OCSD crime laboratory in this case], have developed their own separate population databases for each of several broad racial or ethnic categories such as Caucasian, Black, and Hispanic, the assumption being that mating among members of any one of those categories of the United States population is sufficiently random to justify using them in conjunction with the product rule to calculate the frequency of a DNA profile.[18] . . .

Criminalist Keister testified [for the state] he prepared four autorads in this case, each depicting VNTR fragments at a different DNA locus. The loci examined by the OCSD laboratory were D1S7, D2S44, D4S139, and D10S28, situated on chromosomes 1, 2, 4, and 10 respectively. Keister found that the size differences between the eight bands of the known sample and those of the questioned sample on each of the four loci were 1.01 percent or less, well within the OCSD crime laboratory's match criterion of 3.4 percent.

Keister then determined the statistical probability that alleles numerically indistinguishable from the matched bands would appear in the databases of DNA collected from representative populations. The OCSD had created those databases by obtaining blood samples that the Red Cross collected from its Orange County blood bank and identified as Hispanic, Caucasian, Black, or Asian . . .

Keister testified his initial comparison of the DNA profile of defendant's blood sample was with the OCSD Hispanic database of about 250 individuals, because the frequency in the database from the suspect's ethnic group "will generally be the most frequent number." As noted, defendant's sample had produced eight bands, two at each locus. Keister determined the frequency of each individual band in the Hispanic database from the fixed-bin tables, then used the unmodified product rule to ascertain the statistical probability

18. Conversely, the laboratories do not use a single interracial United States database, presumably because the incidence of random mating between members of the different racial categories is deemed low enough to preclude use of the product rule to calculate an overall frequency statistic for the United States population as a whole.

of finding all combined eight bands in any one person in the population represented by that database.[26] In that manner, he calculated the probabilities of finding defendant's DNA profile in the populations underlying four Orange County databases as follows: (1) Hispanic: 1 in 189 million; (2) Caucasian: 1 in 38 million; (3) Black: 1 in 807 million; (4) Vietnamese: 1 in 177 million. Keister also calculated the probabilities of finding defendant's 8 bands in individuals from 4 populations underlying databases published by the FBI, as follows: (1) Southwest Hispanic (Texas): 1 in 55 million; (2) Southeast Hispanic (Florida): 1 in 2.3 billion; (3) U.S. Black: 1 in 2.4 billion; and (4) U.S. Caucasian: 1 in 3 billion. . . .

It is clear from the evidence in the record, the clear weight of judicial authority, and the published scientific commentary, that the unmodified product rule, as used in the DNA forensic analysis in this case, has gained general acceptance in the relevant scientific community and therefore meets the *Kelly* standard for admissibility [California's *Frye*-based standard].

IV. CONCLUSION

The judgment of the Court of Appeal is affirmed.

NOTES AND QUESTIONS

1. The *Soto* opinion refers to the "unmodified product rule," which involves multiplying the frequencies of individual alleles in order to calculate the frequency with which they all occur together. The unmodified product rule assumes that the occurrence of the different alleles being studied is independent, meaning that the occurrence of one does not make the occurrence of another either more or less likely. Portions of the opinion that are not excerpted discuss a lengthy and somewhat arcane debate over whether the product rule requires modification to reflect what is called "population structure." Thompson and Krane provide a succinct summary of the controversy and its resolution:

> The assumption that the alleles in DNA profiles are statistically independent has been a key point of contention. When DNA evidence was first introduced, a number of experts raised the concern that human populations might be structured, such that certain DNA profiles are particularly common in people of the same ethnic, religious or geographic subgroup. If there is a significant amount of structure in U.S. populations, then the standard method of calculating DNA

26. Keister pointed out in his testimony that the information sought from these calculations is not the likelihood of finding the DNA pattern in the particular individuals who happen to comprise the database, but rather the frequency with which the pattern would appear if one "looked at . . . thousands and thousands of samples" in the population from which the database was derived. The calculations "do not estimate the frequencies of profiles in the current population," but "refer to infinite populations and need not be limited to the reciprocal of the population size."

profile frequencies, which assumes alleles are statistically independent, would be invalid and might greatly underestimate the frequency of a matching profile.

By analogy, suppose that a population survey showed that 10 percent (1 in 10) of Europeans have blond hair, 10 percent have blue eyes, and 10 percent have fair skin. Multiplying these frequencies yields a figure of .001 (1 in 1000) for the frequency of Europeans with all three traits. This estimate is invalid because these traits tend to occur together among Nordics. The estimate of .001 is obviously far too low for Scandinavia, where Nordics are concentrated. Moreover, because Nordics constitute a significant percentage of the European population, the estimate of .001 is also too low for Europe as a whole.[1]

Whether there is sufficient structure in human populations to invalidate forensic statistics was a hotly debated issue in the early 1990s, although empirical research has since allayed much of the concern. In the early 1990s, this debate led courts in several jurisdictions to exclude DNA evidence under the *Frye* standard, on grounds that the method for statistical computation was not generally accepted.[3] A second National Research Council report in 1996 (commonly referred to as NRC II) indicated that the population substructure controversy had subsided and recommended that an alternative corrective factor often referred to as "theta" be applied in product rule calculations for only those loci where an individual possesses two copies of the same allele. "The abundance of data in different ethnic groups within the major races and the genetically and statistically sound methods recommended in this report imply that the ceiling principle and the interim ceiling principle are unnecessary."[4] Most laboratories today follow the NRC recommendations.

Thompson and Kane, *supra*, § 11.37.

2. Independence depends on the relevant population being in "Hardy-Weinberg equilibrium." A common shorthand definition is "random mating," which sounds to many people like a 1960s fantasy. But it is obvious that mating is not random. On the contrary, people pay a lot of attention to genetically based factors when choosing mates — just look at the personal ads and see how many of those seeking mates specify height requirements. What it actually means is that the population is assumed to mate randomly with respect to the genetic loci being studied, a reasonable assumption given that DNA testing focuses on non-coding or "junk" DNA.

1. Any errors caused by population structure are exacerbated when the frequency of individual characteristics is estimated from an inappropriate database. For example, if one relied on a population of Sicilians to estimate the frequency of blond hair, blue eyes and fair skin, among Europeans, one might mistakenly assume each characteristic was found in one person in 100, rather than 1 in 10. Multiplication would then lead to an estimate that only 1 person in one million has blond hair, blue eyes, and fair skin.

3. Com. v. Curnin, 409 Mass. 218, 565 N.E. 2d 440 (1991); Com. v. Lanigan, 413 Mass. 154, 596 N.E.2d 311 (1992); U.S. v. Porter, 618 A.2d 629 (D.C. 1992); People v. Wallace, 14 Cal. App. 4th 651, 17 Cal. Rptr. 2d 721 (1st Dist. 1993); State v. Bible, 175 Ariz. 549, 858 P.2d 1152 (1993).

4. National Research Council, Committee on DNA Forensic Science: An Update, the Evaluation of Forensic DNA Evidence (1996).

3.   The question of how DNA statistics should be presented in court has generated considerable controversy. One general objection to presenting the statistics is that very small probabilities such as those reported at the end of the *Soto* opinion will so overwhelm the jurors that they ignore the rest of the evidence as well as any potential problems with the DNA evidence (see the next section). A related argument is that jurors are prone to misconstruing the probabilities. Footnote 26 in *Soto* is addressed to one aspect of this concern. A common layperson's reaction to such statistics is to say, "One in 3 billion Caucasians? You'd have to go through 3 billion Caucasians to find these alleles? There aren't 3 billion Caucasians — it *must* be the defendant!" What's wrong with this reasoning? Another potential problem is what is sometimes called the "prosecutor's fallacy." The correct phrasing of the match probabilities is "the probability of a match, given that someone other than the suspect is the source of the crime scene sample." This is sometimes treated as if it were equivalent to "the probability of someone else being the source, given the match." Although this may seem like a hyper-technical quibble, the latter phrasing overstates the power of the DNA analysis in a way that may be material. Perhaps the ultimate danger is that jurors will jump erroneously from the probability of a random match, assuming that the crime scene sample did not come from the defendant, to the probability that the defendant is the source: "If there's less than a one percent probability of a random match, then it's more than 99 percent certain that the defendant is the source." In technical terms, this hypothetical juror is expressing a *posterior probability* — a valid approach in some circumstances, but not here (see the discussion of paternity testing in section II.F *infra*). For an example of such reasoning in the case law, see Thomas v. State 830 S.W.2d 546, 550 (Mo. App. 1992) (expert testified that "the likelihood that the DNA found in Marion's panties came from the defendant was higher than 99.99%").

4.   Even if all these problems are very real, what is a court to do? How many judges will have the expertise to monitor the language used by the probability experts? Must we rely on the adversary system to insure a fair presentation, with well-prepared lawyers doing effective cross-examinations and presenting appropriate rebuttal evidence? *Can* we rely on lawyers to do this? One extreme solution is to limit DNA experts to non-numerical verbal descriptions of the evidence. But what should a court allow an expert to say? Is there a point where an expert might properly say, "I am absolutely certain that the defendant is the source of the crime scene sample"? Would non-numerical characterizations of the evidence be likely to be even more misleading than the numbers? *Compare* State v. Buckner, 890 P.2d 460, 462 (Wash. 1995), *aff'd on reconsideration,* 941 P. 2d 667 (Wash. 1997) (improper for expert to say that where random match probability was one in 19.25 billion, "almost four times the present population of the Earth, the match was unique") *with* Commonwealth v. Crews, 640 A.2d 395, 402 (Pa. 1994)

(admitting testimony of FBI expert that he was unaware of any instance "where different individuals that are unrelated have been shown to have matching DNA profiles for three or four probes").

D. Problems with DNA Evidence

The basic science underlying DNA evidence is very solid. When properly done, DNA evidence sets the gold standard for forensic science. This should not imply that it is perfect, however. Almost all of the problems that courts and lawyers confront derive from the human frailties of those who do the analyses. The case that follows presents a typical response to an attack on the proficiency of the laboratory doing the DNA analysis.

People v. Reeves

91 Cal. App. 4th 14, 109 Cal. Rptr. 2d 728 (2001)

[Reeves appealed his conviction for several sexual assaults and burglaries. DNA evidence played a prominent role in the trial. One of his assignments of error related to the failure of the trial court to give adequate consideration to laboratory error rates.]

2. MODIFICATION TO ACCOUNT FOR LABORATORY ERROR RATES

Appellant also claims the DNA evidence should have been excluded because the statistical probability calculations were not modified to take account of laboratory error rates. A laboratory may commit some mistake in sampling or testing that results in an erroneous identification of the suspect—i.e., a false positive. According to defense expert Mueller, the chances of a laboratory making such a mistake range from "1 in hundreds to 1 in thousands," yet that laboratory may declare, based on product rule calculations, that the chances of a random multiple-loci match between the suspect's DNA and that of a sample are 1 in millions or billions. Because the probability of an erroneous identification of the suspect due to laboratory error is much greater than the probability of an erroneous identification due to the commonness of a certain profile, Mueller contends laboratory error rates should be "the dominant statistic for evaluating the weight of a match." Mueller acknowledged that laboratories typically do not publish their "error rates," although they sometimes disclose their proficiency testing results in court cases.

In contrast, prosecution expert Charlotte Word disagreed with the notion that error rates should be considered, in part because the concept of a "rate" implies that errors are recurring at some definite interval. In her analysis, the past experience of a laboratory in other cases is irrelevant to the question of whether it reached a correct result in the current case. Dr. Adams also testified that past errors, or errors from other laboratories, are not relevant considerations. The trial court, essentially agreeing with these witnesses, sustained many objections from the prosecution to defense questions concerning error rates from other laboratories and past errors in DNA testing at the DOJ laboratory.

[The court then considered whether appellant Reeves's objections went merely to the weight to be given the DNA evidence or to its admissibility under California's *Frye* standard.] Here, appellant's only expert offered no opinions about the actual testing performed in this case and conceded he was not qualified to assess the quality of the forensic work. Rather than focusing on possible errors the DOJ may have committed in his case, appellant raises a more general issue: *whether calculations of the statistical significance of a DNA match should factor in or otherwise consider laboratory error rates.* This argument . . . essentially challenges the scientific validity of the DOJ's statistical methodology. Hence, we conclude it is properly considered as an issue of admissibility under *Kelly* [the California *Frye* case].

The next question is whether it is a generally accepted practice in the scientific community to calculate random match probabilities, in RFLP or PCR analysis, without factoring in a laboratory error rate. The record before us suggests that it is.

In a section titled Should an Error Rate Be Included in Calculations? (1996 NRC Rep., *supra*, at pp. 85-87), the 1996 NRC Report listed four reasons why laboratory error should not be combined with random match probability calculations. First, the relevant statistic is not a general error rate for the testing laboratory, or laboratories in general, but whether the laboratory has committed an error in this particular case. But the risk of error in a particular case depends on many variables, and no simple equation exists to translate them into a probability statistic. (*Id.* at pp. 85-86.) Second, a testing laboratory would have to undergo an unrealistically large number of proficiency tests to allow the estimation of a statistically valid probability of error. (*Id.* at p. 86.) Third, although it might be possible to generate a probability statistic by pooling data from the proficiency tests of several laboratories, producing an " 'industry-wide' " error rate, this statistic would unfairly penalize better laboratories. (*Ibid.*) Fourth, an error rate estimated by a laboratory's historical performance on proficiency tests will almost certainly be too high, since errors will be investigated and corrected after they are discovered, and thus errors committed in the past are not likely to recur. (*Ibid.*) The committee concluded: "We believe that a calculation that combines error rates with match probabilities is inappropriate. The risk of error is properly considered case by case, taking into account the record of the laboratory performing the tests, the extent of redundancy, and the overall quality of the results." (*Id.* at p. 87.) Moreover, a suspect's "best insurance" against the possibility of a false match due to laboratory error is the opportunity to have testing repeated at another facility. The committee therefore advised investigative agencies to retain samples for retesting whenever feasible. (*Ibid.*)

[The court then rejected Reeves's argument that the NRC recommendations were controversial in the scientific community. It noted that the critiques Reeves cited had been written by lawyers, not scientists.] In assessing the opinion of the scientific community on a topic, " 'a court is bound to let scientists speak for themselves.' " ...

Appellant offers several detailed arguments criticizing the DOJ's calculation of match probabilities without consideration of a laboratory error rate. However, "our duty is *not* to decide whether [a methodology] is reliable as a matter of 'scientific fact,' but simply whether it is generally accepted as reliable by the relevant scientific community." Because appellant has not presented persuasive evidence of an ongoing controversy in the scientific community, we conclude that the NRC's recommendation is generally accepted, and DNA probability calculations need not be modified to account for a laboratory error rate. ...

Our decision addresses only the necessity of reporting a "summary statistic," i.e., a probability statistic derived when a "laboratory error rate" is combined with a DNA profile's random match probability. We have concluded such a combination is not sanctioned by the weight of scientific opinion. However, we express no opinion on whether a jury can or should receive evidence concerning rates of laboratory error *separate and apart* from the random match probability statistic. Moreover, it should be clear that our decision does not preclude cross-examination on the subject of laboratory error, or the possibility that such errors were committed in a particular case. In general, criticisms about the quality of DNA testing go to the weight of the evidence and hence are appropriate topics for cross-examination.[19]

NOTES AND QUESTIONS

1. The path of the court's reasoning is somewhat circuitous. It initially construed Reeve's objection to the prosecution's failure to factor laboratory error rates into the DNA probabilities as a challenge to the *admissibility* of the DNA evidence. It then rejected that challenge. The court concluded, however, that a defendant could use the error rate data in cross-examining the prosecution's DNA experts (as Reeves had done) in an effort to diminish

19. In fact, that is exactly what happened in this case. Appellant cross-examined criminalist Sims about possible contamination of DNA samples, a mistake in one test, and a possible sizing error on bands at one VNTR locus. In addition, defense expert Mueller estimated that DNA laboratories have error rates ranging from 1 in 700 to 1 in 7,000, and he offered the jury recalculated probability figures using various lab error estimates.

the *weight* that the jury might give to the evidence. How might you use error rate evidence to impeach a prosecution witness?

2.   *Reeves* involved the impact of error rate evidence at trial. Other cases have considered the chronologically prior issue of the discoverability of error rates by criminal defendants under state rules or the constitutional doctrine of Brady v. Maryland, 373 U.S. 83 (1963). The South Carolina case of State v. Proctor, 358 S.C. 424, 595 S.E.2d 480 (2004) is typical in finding that lab proficiency data are discoverable in principle, but then holding that failure to disclose it was harmless error:

> As we understand respondent's argument, he seeks the proficiency test results not to attack the methodology used or results obtained in his particular case, but as the predicate for his expert to derive the SLED [South Carolina Law Enforcement Division] DNA lab's 'lab error rate.' In turn, respondent's expert would use that rate to evaluate the accuracy of SLED's probability estimates. In this case, for example, Lt. Jeffcoat's [the prosecution expert] written report states that the probability of an individual unrelated to the donor matching the DNA obtained from semen evidence was "approximately 1 in 10,000 CAUCASIANS and 1 in 3,700 BLACKS." [Respondent was of mixed Caucasian and Black ancestry.] Further, if SLED's proficiency test results were not perfect, as represented by Lt. Jeffcoat, then they could potentially be used as impeachment evidence. . . .
>
> Where a defendant makes a threshold showing that the evidence he seeks is material within the meaning of *Brady* and [S.C. Criminal] Rule 5, the trial judge should conduct a hearing. Here, respondent made that showing. He presented evidence that defense experts examining proficiency tests from other labs have found errors that demonstrated flaws in the test lab's methodology. Further, he presented evidence that no DNA lab has a "zero error rate" on DNA proficiency exams. Having met this threshold requirement, the trial judge should have examined the material *in camera*. The trial judge's reliance on Lt. Jeffcoat's affidavit in lieu of conducting his own *in camera* examination was error. . . .
>
> For purposes of determining whether respondent was denied a fair trial, we will assume that the undisclosed proficiency tests would have revealed that the SLED DNA lab did not, in fact, have a perfect record. We proceed to consider not just the evidence against respondent at trial, but the context in which the DNA evidence was presented. . . .
>
> At trial, Lt. Jeffcoat testified that the SLED DNA lab used proficiency testing to ensure its analysts were accurate. He was permitted to testify, over respondent's objection, "In every occasion where we have been provided proficiency tests, we've always called the correct match." Assuming that the proficiency test results would have shown this statement to be untrue, Lt. Jeffcoat could have been impeached by those results. While the lieutenant went on to testify that in this particular case, the lab had been able to match four of five probes from samples recovered from the scene to samples given by respondent, the witness did not testify to the probabilities of such a match occurring in a random

population sample. Accordingly, to the extent that respondent sought the proficiency test results in order to calculate the 'lab error rate' and then use that rate to discount the probability match, he cannot demonstrate prejudice from the denial of that information since no 'match' evidence was presented to the jury.

What is it about the "context" of the DNA evidence that persuaded the court that failure to disclose the lab proficiency data was harmless error? What if Lt. Jeffcoat had testified about match probabilities? Having read *Reeves,* how do you think a California court would rule on the *discoverability* of lab proficiency data? (As of this writing, there is no controlling California decision.)

3.   Another potential source of error is mishandling of DNA samples at various points along the chain from collection to analysis. Most of the time, mishandling will help the defense by degrading samples and making a match less likely. A false match could be created, however, if a crime scene sample were mislabeled as a suspect sample. There is also a remote possibility of creating a false match by performing PCR amplification on a suspect sample in a test tube that had formerly held a crime scene sample and had not been properly cleaned. In this form of "carryover contamination," PCR amplification might work more effectively on the crime scene contaminant than the suspect's DNA, leading to a "suspect sample" that has in fact become a second crime scene sample. It is very difficult to determine how common such events are, whether as a result of accident or intentional misconduct. A number of these objections were raised in the *Beverly* case, which is excerpted in the next section.

E.   *Mitochondrial DNA Evidence*

DNA in the Courtroom

In Jane Campbell Moriarty, Ed., Psychological and
Scientific Evidence in Criminal Trials
William C. Thompson and Dan E. Krane*

§ 11:8 An Introduction to DNA and DNA Testing—
Mitochondrial DNA Tests

The tests described thus far examine DNA from cell nuclei (*nuclear DNA*). DNA is also found in *cell mitochondria,* which are *organelles* (structures) in which the process of cellular respiration occurs. Mitochondrial DNA (often designated *mtDNA*) contains *sequence polymorphisms.* In the late 1990s, forensic scientists began testing mtDNA by using a procedure known as *genetic sequencing* to produce a read-out of the genetic code from two polymorphic areas of the *mitochondrial genome.* Forensic scientists

*Reprinted with permission of Thomson/West and the authors.

describe an mtDNA profile by stating how its sequence differs from that of a reference standard called the *Anderson sequence.*

Mitochondrial DNA tests are highly sensitive and can produce results on samples that are not suitable for other DNA tests, such as hair shafts, bone, and teeth. Because mtDNA is present in hundreds or thousands of copies per cell, it often survives much longer than nuclear DNA in old, degraded cellular samples. DNA tests on very old samples, such as the bones of Czar Nicholas II of Russia, have detected and typed mtDNA.

Mitochondrial DNA tests are far less discriminating than STR tests. The frequency of mtDNA profiles is generally put at one in hundreds. Additionally, because mtDNA is inherited maternally, mtDNA tests generally cannot distinguish between individuals in the same maternal line. Hence, sons of the same mother would be expected to have the same mtDNA profile, and this profile would also be found in daughters of the mother's sister and all of their children.

Minor variations are sometimes found in mtDNA profiles of different cells from the same person due to mutations. This phenomenon, known as *heteroplasmy,* complicates the process of determining whether two mtDNA profiles match. The appropriate standards for declaring an mtDNA match, and for estimating the rarity of matching profiles, are issues that have been debated in the courtroom. Mitochondrial DNA tests are expensive and require special laboratory facilities and techniques. At this time only a few forensic laboratories perform these tests and they are used only where other types of DNA testing fail or cannot work. However, future technical improvements may lead to wider use of mtDNA tests.

United States v. Beverly

369 F.3d 516 (6th Cir. 2004)

BOGGS, Chief Judge. Noah Beverly, Douglas A. Turns, and Johnny P. Crockett were indicted for multiple crimes by a federal grand jury, charging them with conspiracy to commit armed bank robbery, in violation of *18 U.S.C. § 371,* committing various armed bank robberies, in violation of *18 U.S.C. § 2113(a)* and (*d*), and possessing firearms during and in relation to these crimes of violence, in violation of *18 U.S.C. § 924(c).* After two evidentiary hearings, a jury trial commenced in which all three defendants were tried together. On February 8, 2000, the jury returned a verdict of guilty on all counts against Beverly and Turns. Crockett was found guilty [on some but not all of the charges].

All three defendants have appealed this verdict. Beverly appeals the introduction of mitochondrial DNA (mtDNA) evidence against him at trial, arguing that the evidence was not scientifically reliable and, even if reliable, its probative value was outweighed by its prejudicial effect. . . .

On May 18, 1995, Warren, Rogers, Beverly, and Crockett robbed the Security National Bank in Springfield, Ohio. . . .

During the robbery, bank surveillance cameras were working and took several photographs. [Two witnesses] were able to identify each other, as well as Beverly and Crockett, in the photos. . . . The photographs also show a man, identified as Beverly, wearing a "Columbia" hat with holes cut in it as a mask. This hat was later recovered from the abandoned stolen car. It was a hair from this hat that was sent to the lab for the mitochondrial DNA test that was ultimately admitted into evidence at trial. . . .

Beverly, against whom mitochondrial deoxyribonucleic acid (mtDNA) testing was used in this trial, argues that the district court erred in admitting expert testimony concerning mtDNA evidence. Specifically, Beverly argues that mtDNA testing is not scientifically reliable because the laboratory that did the testing in this case was not certified by an external agency, the procedures used by the laboratory "sometimes yielded results that were contaminated," and the particular tests done in this case were contaminated. In addition, Beverly argues that even if the mtDNA evidence is determined to be sufficiently reliable, its probative value is substantially outweighed by its prejudicial effect. In this part of his argument, Beverly focuses on the statistical analysis presented, which he claims to have artificially enhanced the probative value of the mtDNA evidence. According to Beverly, Dr. Melton, the government's expert, should only have been allowed to testify that Beverly could not be excluded as the source of the sample in question.

We review the district court's decision to admit expert testimony for an abuse of discretion. *Kumho Tire Co. v. Carmichael,* 526 U.S. 137, 152, 143 L. Ed. 2d 238, 119 S. Ct. 1167 (1999). . . .

1.   MITOCHONDRIAL DNA TESTING IN GENERAL

Before discussing the particular circumstances of this case, it may be helpful to provide some general background concerning mtDNA analysis. Generally speaking, every cell contains two types of DNA: nuclear DNA, which is found in the nucleus of the cell, and mitochondrial DNA, which is found outside of the nucleus in the mitochondrion. The use of nuclear DNA analysis as a forensic tool has been found to be scientifically reliable by the scientific community for more than a decade. The use of mtDNA analysis is also on the rise, and it has been used extensively for some time in FBI labs, as well as state and private crime labs. This technique, which generally looks at the differences between people's mitochondrial DNA, has some advantages over nuclear DNA analysis in certain situations. For example, while any given cell contains only one nucleus, there are a vast number of mitochondria. As a result, there is a significantly greater amount of mtDNA in a cell from which a sample can be extracted by a lab technician, as compared to nuclear DNA. Thus, this technique is very useful for minute samples or ancient and degraded samples. In addition, mitochondrial DNA can be obtained from some sources that nuclear DNA cannot. For example, mtDNA can be found in shafts of hair, which do not have a nucleus, but do have plenty of mitochondria. Nuclear DNA can only be retrieved from the living root of the hair where the nucleus resides.

On the other hand, mtDNA is not as precise an identifier as nuclear DNA. In the case of nuclear DNA, half is inherited from the mother and half from the father, and each individual, with the exception of identical twins, almost certainly has a unique profile. MtDNA, by contrast, is inherited only from the mother and thus all maternal relatives will share the same mtDNA profile, unless a mutation has occurred. Because it is not possible to achieve the extremely high level of certainty of identity provided by nuclear DNA, mtDNA typing has been said to be a test of exclusion, rather than one of identification.

The entire mtDNA sequence, about sixteen thousand base pairs, is considerably shorter than nuclear DNA, which has approximately three billion pairs. Within the mtDNA, two noncoding regions are targeted — Hypervariable-1 (HV1) and Hypervariable-2 (HV2). Each of these regions is about 300 letters in code length and is a region that has a mutation rate five to ten times greater than that of nuclear DNA. Usually there is a one to two percent variance of mtDNA sequence between unrelated individuals. It has been estimated that mutation within the mtDNA control region is one nucleotide difference every 300 generations. National Commission on the Future of DNA Evidence, *The Future of Forensic DNA Testing: Predictions of the Research and Development Working Group* 7, Nat'l Inst. of Justice (2000). *But see* Ann Gibbons, *Calibrating the Mitochondrial Clock,* 279 Science 28 (1998) (discussing research estimating that mutations occur as frequently as every 40 generations). This academic dispute does not affect this case directly. In general, the slower the mutation rate, the more people who will have the same mtDNA pattern, and vice-versa. However the figures presented to the jury were from a database of actual DNA patterns collected by forensic scientists. The mechanics of the analysis involves a process similar to that used with nuclear DNA.

This court has not until now had the opportunity to rule on the admissibility of mtDNA testing. However, mtDNA testing has been admitted into evidence by several state courts and has been upheld on review. *See e.g., State v. Underwood,* 134 N.C. App. 533, 518 S.E.2d 231 (N.C. Ct. App. 1999); *State v. Scott,* 33 S.W.3d 746 (Tenn. 2000); *State v. Council,* 335 S.C. 1, 515 S.E.2d 508

(S.C. 1999); *People v. Klinger, 185 Misc. 2d 574, 713 N.Y.S. 2d 823 (N.Y. Crim. Ct. 2000); Williams v. State, 342 Md. 724, 679 A.2d 1106 (Md. 1996).*

2. MITOCHONDRIAL DNA IN THIS CASE

The district court in this case held a very extensive hearing in order to determine the admissibility of mtDNA evidence at trial. The court determined that the techniques had been established and accepted by the scientific community, accepted by the courts, and had been subject to peer review. Beverly now argues that the district court abused its discretion on the basis of three objections.

Beverly argues that Dr. Melton's laboratory, which had analyzed the sample in this case, has never been certified by an external agency. This point was raised in the pretrial hearing, and, although there is no legal requirement that Dr. Melton's lab be so certified, the district court did question Dr. Melton on this point. Laboratories doing DNA forensic work are accredited through the American Society of Crime Laboratory Directors. However, Dr. Melton's lab, having only been actively engaged in case work for about 11 months at the time of the trial, was not yet able to apply for the accreditation, but was expected to go through the process the following spring. Furthermore, Dr. Melton's own credentials are considerable. Not only has she been working with mtDNA since 1991, she has a Ph.D from Pennsylvania State University in genetics; her thesis investigated mitochondrial DNA as it would apply to forensic applications. In addition, Dr. Melton has published a significant amount of work in this field.

Next, Beverly argues that Dr. Melton's procedures would sometimes yield results that were contaminated, and that furthermore, the sample analyzed in this particular case was contaminated. Testimony given by Dr. Melton and Dr. Kessis, who was Beverly's expert at trial, supported Beverly's general contention, but no evidence demonstrated that any contamination in this case affected the results of the analysis. Dr. Melton testified that "[we] occasionally have what we call sporadic contamination," probably as a result of residue on a piece of equipment brought into the lab. However, Dr. Melton was confident that no contamination of the sample itself had occurred. The reagent blank in the test of the sample itself did not show any indication of contamination, in contrast to a separate reagent blank, used in a different test tube, which was a control in the experiment. Therefore, the actual data relied upon in this case, obtained from the sequencing machine, did not indicate any presence of a contaminant.

Finally, the district court carefully considered during the pretrial hearing the question of whether the relevance of this evidence outweighed its probative value. In particular, Beverly argued that the jury would associate mitochondrial DNA analysis with nuclear DNA analysis and give it the same value, in terms of its ability to "fingerprint" a suspect. The district court, however, decided that this issue was more appropriately dealt with through a vigorous cross-examination, and in fact that was exactly what occurred at trial. Moreover, the court noted the important probative value that this evidence added to the trial. Finally, the court separately considered the scientific reliability of the statistical analysis offered by the government, concluding that:

> The predictive effect of the statistical analysis is based upon a formula which is apparently recognized in the scientific community and used in a variety of scientific contexts, and it has been used specifically here in the analysis of mitochondrial DNA results. The Court concludes that it's an accepted and reliable estimate of probability, and in this case, it led to results, interpreted results, which substantially increase the probability that the hair sample is the hair of the defendant in this case.

Based on the record compiled in the district court's careful and extensive hearing on this issue, there was no abuse of discretion in admitting the mtDNA testing results. The scientific basis for the use of such DNA is well established. Any issues going to the conduct of the specific tests in question were fully developed and subject to cross examination. There was no error in finding that the testing methods, and Dr. Melton's testing in particular, were sufficiently reliable to be admissible. Finally, the mathematical basis for the evidentiary power of the mtDNA evidence was carefully explained, and was not more prejudicial than probative.

It was made clear to the jury that this type of evidence could not identify individuals with the precision of conventional DNA analysis. Nevertheless, any particular mtDNA pattern is sufficiently rare, especially when there is no contention that the real culprit might have been a matrilineal relative of the defendant, that it certainly meets the standard for probative evidence: "any tendency to make the existence of any fact that is of consequence to the determination of the action more probable or less probable than it would be without the evidence." *Fed. R. Evid. 401.* The statistical evidence at trial showed that, at most, less than 1% of the population would be expected to have this mtDNA pattern. Even an article critical of mtDNA stated the most frequent pattern applies in no more than 3% of the population. Erica Beecher-Monas, *The Heuristics of Intellectual Due Process: A Primer for Triers of Science,* 75 N.Y.U.L. Rev. 1563, 1655 n.535 (2000). It would be unlikely to find a match between Beverly's hair and the hair of a random individual. The testimony was that, with a high degree of confidence, less than one percent of the population could be expected to have the same pattern as that of the hair recovered from the bank robbery site, and that Beverly did have the same pattern, and thus could not be excluded as the source of the hair. Finding Beverly's mtDNA at the crime scene is essentially equivalent to finding that the last two digits of a license plate of a car owned by defendant matched the last two numbers of a license plate of a getaway car. It would be some evidence—not conclusive, but certainly admissible. We find the same here.

NOTES AND QUESTIONS

1.   Begin by reviewing the relative advantages and disadvantages from nuclear DNA and mtDNA testing. Assuming both were available, which would a prosecutor generally prefer? Why was mtDNA used in this case?

2.   Note that the potential problems with mtDNA testing are largely the same as those raised in the previous section concerning nuclear DNA testing. Focus specifically on Beverly's contamination argument. Is contamination more likely to help or hurt a defendant? Can you identify circumstances in which it might hurt him?

3.   Finally, review what the *Beverly* court says about the statistical analysis of the mtDNA results, in particular the expert testimony that "less than one percent of the population could be expected to have the same pattern as that of the hair recovered from the bank robbery site, and that Beverly did have the same pattern, and thus could not be excluded as the source of the hair." Based on what you have already read, how do think that the expert arrived at this conclusion? Given the inheritance pattern of mtDNA, might the expert's degree of certainty have been undercut if there was reason to believe that Beverly's brother had also been involved in the robbery?

F.   Bayesian Paternity Analysis

Recall the introduction to Bayesian analysis at the end of Chapter 3, Statistical Inference. It was noted there that Bayes' Theorem has had substantial legal use only in the area of DNA paternity testing. The case that follows discusses this approach in considerable detail. While paternity testing is, in and of itself, normally a civil matter, this case illustrates the fact that it can play a role in the criminal law as well. The statistical analysis in the case is complex, so it might be worthwhile to review the material in Chapter 3 before reading it.

State v. Skipper

228 Conn. 610, 637 A.2d 1101 (1994)

CALLAHAN, J. The dispositive issue in this appeal is the admissibility of the probability of paternity statistic calculated from DNA evidence. The defendant was charged . . . with eight counts of sexual assault. . . . [The victim was a minor with whom the defendant was accused of conducting a lengthy sexual relationship, and who ultimately became pregnant and had an abortion.]

I

The defendant claims that the trial court improperly admitted testimony of the probability of paternity percentage based on DNA testing. We agree and, on this basis, reverse the judgment of the trial court and remand the case for a new trial.

Kevin McElfresh, the state's expert witness and the director of Identity Testing Laboratories of Lifecodes Corporation (Lifecodes), testified at trial regarding the defendant's paternity index. The paternity index is an odds ratio, based on DNA tests, measuring the likelihood that the defendant would produce a child with the same phenotypes[7] as the fetus in question as compared to an unrelated random male. 1 C. McCormick, Evidence (4th Ed. 1992) § 211, pp. 963-64. The paternity index in this case was 3496,[8] indicating that only one out of 3497 randomly selected males would have the phenotypes compatible with the fetus in question. See R. Peterson, "A Few Things You Should Know About Paternity Tests (But Were Afraid to Ask)," 22 Santa Clara L. Rev. 667, 684 (1982).

McElfresh further testified that the paternity index could be converted into a statistic indicating the percentage of the defendant's probability of paternity. In the present case, he testified that he had made that conversion and that the percentage of probability that it was the defendant who had

odds ratio

7. Every person inherits certain traits, such as eye color. "Different versions of a particular trait are known as phenotypes. For the inherited trait of eye color, for example, blue eyes are one phenotype, brown eyes are another." *Plemel v. Walter*, 303 Or. 262, 266, 735 P.2d 1209 (1987). Genes determine the specific set of phenotypes that every person possesses.

8. The paternity index is calculated by doing a battery of tests on blood-tissue specimens. Specifically, DNA was extracted from the victim's blood, the defendant's blood and from tissue from the product of conception. The DNA was then separated according to size by gel electrophoresis. The array of DNA fragments was arranged on a membrane and then exposed to polymorphic probes, which are used to observe the genetic differences between individuals. In the present case, six polymorphic probes, or genetic systems, were used. Each probe or genetic system represented a database of between 500 and 1500 randomly selected African-Americans.

The probes mark DNA fragments so that their lengths can be measured. The result is to give an image of dark bands, called an autoradiograph, that can be read like an X ray. The pattern of bands is called the DNA profile. A visual inspection was then made of the autoradiographs to determine if each included the defendant as a possible biological father based on the DNA profiles. In the present case, the six probes visually indicated inclusion.

Based on the number of genetic systems in which the defendant is included, the paternity index is statistically calculated by applying a theory of population genetics, specifically Hardy-Weinberg Equilibrium. A statistical analysis was done using four of the probes. Each probe result was individually compared to a database of African-Americans to predict the frequency with which each identifying DNA pattern occurs in that population. The results of each test were then multiplied together to determine the probability of finding all of the genetic markers together in one human being. The resulting number is referred to as the paternity index.

fathered the fetus was 99.97 percent. The usual method for calculating the probability of paternity, and the method that McElfresh used in the present case, is Bayes' Theorem. 1 C. McCormick, supra, pp. 962-63. Bayes' Theorem, a mathematical formula in common use by statisticians, is used for the purpose of "showing the effect of . . . new [statistical] evidence on a previously [predicted] probability." Id.; I. Ellman & D. Kaye, "Probabilities and Proof: Can HLA and Blood Group Testing Prove Paternity?" 54 N.Y.U. L. Rev. 1131, 1148 (1979). In the context of determining paternity, Bayes' Theorem postulates the multiplication of the paternity index, i.e., the new statistical evidence, by an assumed prior percentage of probability of paternity in order to obtain a new percentage of probability of paternity.[11] In order to assume a prior probability of paternity, however, it is also necessary to assume a prior probability of intercourse.

In Bayes' Theorem, the prior probability of paternity is not cast as any particular figure. Generally, experts who testify in paternity proceedings choose a number to represent the prior probability. See I. Ellman & D. Kaye, 54 N.Y.U. L. Rev., supra, p. 1149. Most experts, as did McElfresh here, set the prior probability at 50 percent, expressed as odds of one [to one], i.e., fifty-fifty, reasoning that 50 percent is a neutral starting point because it assumes that it is just as likely that the defendant is not the father as it is that he is the father.[12] See, e.g., *State v. Spann,* 130 N.J. 484, 493, 617

---

11. The probability of paternity as computed under Bayes' Theorem may be illustrated as follows:

$$P \times \text{Odds (B)} = \text{Odds (B/P)}$$

P represents the new test evidence or the paternity index. B represents the event that the alleged father is the biological father and Odds (B) designates the prior odds of paternity in favor of this event. Odds (B/P) is the probability of paternity revised in light of the new test result or the paternity index. If the prior odds, Odds (B), are assumed to be fifty/fifty, expressed as odds of one, the probability of paternity will be equal to the paternity index.

12. In the present case, the defendant's paternity index, or the odds of the defendant's paternity as compared to a random male, was 3496 to 1. The assumed prior probability of paternity was fifty/fifty, expressed as odds of one. Using Bayes' Theorem, the probability of the defendant's paternity in the present matter would be calculated as follows:

$$3496 \times 1 = 3496 \text{ (odds of one)}$$

This means that the odds that the alleged father is the biological father are also 3496 to 1. The corresponding probability of paternity is 3496/3497 or 99.97 percent. See 1 C. McCormick, Evidence (4th Ed. 1992) §211, p. 964; R. Peterson, "A Few Things You Should Know About Paternity Tests (But Were Afraid to Ask)," 22 Santa Clara L. Rev. 667, 683 (1982).

We note that no testimony was elicited from the expert indicating that a 50 percent prior probability of paternity was used in calculating the probability of paternity percentage. The expert did testify, however, that "the calculation is that the paternity index divided by the paternity index plus one, gives you the percentage. It's simply a conversion of the paternity index to the percentage. So, it's 99.97 is basically 3500 to 1, which is odds . . . expressed as a percentage." Based on these calculations, a 50 percent prior probability had to have been used because it is only by using a 50 percent prior probability that the paternity index equals the probability of paternity. See R. Peterson, 22 Santa Clara L. Rev., supra, 683, 685; 1 C. McCormick, supra, pp. 963-64.

A.2d 247 (1993). By adopting a prior probability of paternity of 50 percent, the formula operates on the assumption that the defendant and a random male had intercourse with the mother, "making them both equally likely to have fathered the child." R. Peterson, 22 Santa Clara L. Rev., supra, p. 685. . . .

In a sexual assault prosecution, sexual intercourse is an element that must be proven by the state beyond a reasonable doubt. The utilization of Bayes' Theorem by the prosecution, however, permitted the introduction of evidence predicated on an assumption that there was a fifty-fifty chance that sexual intercourse had occurred in order to prove that sexual intercourse had in fact occurred. See *State v. Hartman,* 145 Wis. 2d 1, 426 N.W.2d 320 (1988) (probability of paternity statistic inadmissible in a sexual assault case). The fifty-fifty assumption that sexual intercourse had occurred was not predicated on the evidence in the case but was simply an assumption made by the expert. . . .

In *State* v. *Spann,* supra, in a somewhat complex opinion, the Supreme Court of New Jersey held that it was reversible error to admit expert testimony of the probability of paternity based on an assumption of a 50 percent prior probability of paternity in a sexual assault case without revealing this assumption to the jury. Because the defendant only objected to the implication that the adoption of a 50 percent prior probability was "neutral," the court concluded that a probability of paternity opinion, if admissible at all, is only admissible if the expert states that the calculations leading to that statistic assume a prior probability of paternity of 50 percent.[15] The court noted that it was not confronted with the issue with which we are confronted: the admissibility of the probability of paternity statistic in a criminal case in which the defendant has not conceded the propriety of any prior probability of paternity. Id., 500.

Although the New Jersey intermediate appellate court had concluded that "the State cannot prove intercourse through a formula that assumes intercourse"; id., 496, the Supreme Court stated that that conclusion was incorrect because "the .5 prior-probability assumption . . . says only that the chance that [the] defendant is the father is fifty-fifty, that it is just as likely that he is not the father as that he is. . . ." Id., 496. The court went on to say that the statistic assumes "a substantial possibility, 50%, that he had

---

15. In *State* v. *Spann,* 130 N.J. 484, 499, 617 A.2d 247 (1993), the defendant conceded that "the probability of paternity . . . was admissible if the jury itself found that the prior probability was .5. . . ." In the present case, the defendant does not make such a concession.

The *Spann* court held that although an expert could testify to the probability of paternity statistic if he or she revealed the assumption of a 50 percent prior probability of paternity, the jury would still be required to use its own estimate of the prior probability of paternity based on the non-scientific evidence in the case. Id. Furthermore, the expert would be required to explain what the probability of paternity statistic would be for a range of prior probabilities. For reasons we discuss in footnote 18, we decline to allow the jury to adopt a prior probability.

intercourse with the victim, but not that he positively did." Id., 497; see also D. Kaye, "The Probability of an Ultimate Issue: The Strange Cases of Paternity Testing," 75 Iowa L. Rev. 75, 105 n.153 (1989) ("although the use of the prior probability of 50% . . . does not assume that intercourse definitely took place, it does presuppose a substantial probability of intercourse between the defendant and the mother"). The court concluded nonetheless that "opinions based on Bayes' Theorem . . . are far from universally accepted for forensic purposes, especially in criminal cases. . . . We leave the determination of the admissibility of the probability of paternity opinion to the trial court after a full hearing on the matter." *State* v. *Spann,* supra, 505.

The assumption that there is a substantial possibility that the defendant had intercourse with the victim, however, raises serious concerns in sexual assault cases. It is antithetical to our criminal justice system to presume anything but innocence at the outset of a trial. It is not until the defendant has been convicted that the presumption of innocence disappears. . . .

Without first assuming a prior probability of paternity, i.e., guilt, Bayes' Theorem cannot be applied, and the probability of paternity cannot be computed in sexual assault cases. Because Bayes' Theorem requires the assumption of a prior probability of paternity, i.e., guilt, its use is inconsistent with the presumption of innocence in a criminal case such as this, in which Bayes' Theorem was used to establish the probability of paternity, i.e., that the defendant was the father of the product of conception of an alleged sexual assault. See id., pp. 406-408. Whether a prior probability of 50 percent is automatically used or whether the jury is instructed to adopt its own prior probability,[18] when the probability of paternity statistic is introduced, an

---

18. It has been suggested that jurors be shown a chart illustrating a range of prior probabilities and the resulting probabilities of paternity. See M. Finkelstein & W. Fairley, "A Bayesian Approach to Identification Evidence," 83 Harv. L. Rev. 489 (1970). Permitting the jury to derive its own prior probability to arrive at a corresponding probability of paternity, however, still implicates the presumption of innocence. See, e.g., L. Tribe, "Trial by Mathematics: Precision and Ritual in the Legal Process," 84 Harv. L. Rev. 1329, 1368-75 (1971). "It may be supposed that no juror would be permitted to announce publicly in mid-trial that the defendant was already burdened with, say, a sixty percent probability of guilt—but even without such a public statement it would be exceedingly difficult for the accused, for the prosecution, and ultimately for the community, to avoid the explicit recognition that, having been forced to focus on the question, the rational juror could hardly avoid reaching some such answer. And, once that recognition had become a general one, our society's traditional affirmation of the 'presumption of innocence' could lose much of its value." Id., 1370.

Moreover, allowing the jury to adopt a prior probability and, hence, arrive at a probability of guilt, raises concerns in criminal cases regarding the burden of proof of guilt beyond a reasonable doubt. In adopting a prior probability of guilt and viewing the corresponding probability of paternity on a chart, the jury is left "with a number that purports to represent [its] assessment of the probability that the defendant is guilty as charged. Needless to say, that number will never quite equal 1.0, so the result will be to produce a quantity . . . which openly signifies a measurable . . . margin of doubt. . . ." Id., 1372. "Any conceptualization of reasonable doubt in probabilistic form is inconsistent with the functional role the concept is designed to play." C. Nesson, "Reasonable Doubt and Permissive Inferences: The Value of Complexity," 92 Harv. L. Rev. 1187, 1225 (1979).

assumption is required to be made by the jury before it has heard all of the evidence — that there is a quantifiable probability that the defendant committed the crime. In fact, if the presumption of innocence were factored into Bayes' Theorem, the probability of paternity statistic would be useless. If we assume that the presumption of innocence standard would require the prior probability of guilt to be zero, the probability of paternity in a criminal case would always be zero because Bayes' Theorem requires the paternity index to be multiplied by a positive prior probability in order to have any utility. Id., 406. "In other words, Bayes' Theorem can only work if the presumption of innocence disappears from consideration." Id., 408.

We conclude that the trial court should not have admitted the expert testimony stating a probability of paternity statistic. Moreover, we cannot say with any degree of confidence that a probability of paternity statistic of 99.97 percent, as testified to by the state's expert, would not have influenced the jury's decision to convict the defendant of both sexual assault and risk of injury. Because the admissibility of the probability of paternity statistic involves a constitutional issue, and because we cannot say that the admission of that statistic here was harmless beyond a reasonable doubt, a new trial is required.

NOTES AND QUESTIONS

1. Begin with the court's definition of paternity index: "an odds ratio, based on DNA tests, measuring the likelihood that the defendant would produce a child with the same phenotypes as the fetus in question as compared to an unrelated random male." A more scientifically precise version is: "A number (technically, a likelihood ratio) that indicates the support that the paternity test results lend to the hypothesis that the alleged father is the biological father as opposed to the hypothesis that another man selected at random is the biological father . . . [T]he number can be computed as the ratio of the probability of the phenotypes under the first hypothesis to the probability under the second hypothesis. Large values indicate substantial support for the hypothesis of paternity." Kaye & Sensabaugh, *Reference Guide on DNA Evidence, supra,* at 571. As footnote 8 to the court's opinion indicates

---

Allowing jurors to reach their own prior probability also presents practical problems. See L. Tribe, 84 Harv. L. Rev., supra, pp. 1359-66. We cannot say that merely introducing a chart illustrating a range of prior probabilities for educational purposes without requiring the jury to adopt a specific figure would alleviate our concerns. "Whether the benefits of using this method of statistical inference solely to educate the jury by displaying the probative force of the evidentiary findings would be worth the costs in terms of time-consumption and possible confusion is a close . . . question." 1 C. McCormick, Evidence (4th Ed. 1992) §210, p. 959; D. Kaye, "The Admissibility of 'Probability Evidence' in Criminal Trials — Part II," 27 Jur. 160, 171 (1987). For an exhaustive explanation of the practical problems associated with a chart approach, see L. Tribe, 84 Harv. L. Rev., supra, pp. 1358-68, and R. Jonakait, 1983 U. Ill. L. Rev., supra, pp. 403-405.

(regrettably, much of the scientific heavy lifting in this opinion is done in the footnotes), the "DNA tests" to which it refers are the same as those discussed repeatedly earlier in this chapter.

2.   According to footnote 12, the defendant's paternity index was 3,496 to 1. This ratio compares the strength of one hypothesis (that of the defendant's paternity) to that of another (the paternity of a random male). However, "the judge or jury ultimately must assess a different type of quantity — the probability of the hypothesis [of the defendant's paternity] itself." Kaye & Sensabaugh, *Reference Guide on DNA Evidence, supra,* at 536. This is where the Bayesian analysis comes in. As the court states (this time in footnote 11), this probability of paternity in light of the evidence of the paternity index (a "posterior probability," as it is sometimes called) is calculated by multiplying the *prior* probability of paternity by the paternity index. (The probability of paternity is sometimes expressed as W; W with a prior probability of 50% would be written as W_{50}.) As in many Bayesian analyses, this prior probability proves to be the sticking point. What was the prior probability in *Skipper*? How was it selected? Based on the court's account of the expert testimony in footnote 12, do you think that the state's expert gave a fair presentation of the nature of the prior probability and its role in the computation of the probability of paternity?

3.   Next, consider how the selection of the prior probability leads the court to its legal conclusion. What is it about the Bayesian analysis that is "antithetical to our criminal justice system?" Would any Bayesian analysis of paternity inevitably lead to this same conclusion? Why or why not? The *Skipper* opinion argues that the adoption of any prior probability greater than zero means that "an assumption is required to be made by the jury before it has heard all the evidence — that there is a quantifiable probability that the defendant committed the crime" [which, of course, was having sexual intercourse with the minor victim — not fathering a child]. A critique of the opinion contends, however, that it "fails to explain why or how the presumption of innocence means that the prior probability is zero. Indeed, a prospective juror who professes an absolute, unshakeable belief in the defendant's innocence — which is what a prior probability of zero amounts to — should be excused for cause." David L. Faigman, David H. Kaye, Michael J. Saks & Joseph Sander, *Science in the Law: Forensic Science Issues* 778 (2002). Not all courts have shared *Skipper*'s concerns about the dangers of the paternity probability in criminal cases. *See e.g.,* Griffith v. State, 976 S.W. 2d 241 (Tex. App. 1998) (court agrees with prosecution expert that presumption of innocence does not require zero prior probability and that nonzero prior probability does not amount to an assumption of the fact of intercourse).

4.   The rejection of the Bayesian probability of paternity in criminal cases such as *Skipper* is based in large part on the criminal presumption of innocence. Should it also be rejected in civil cases? Although the use of DNA-

based paternity testing in civil cases has been described as "ubiquitous," Faigman et al., *Science in the Law: Forensic Science Issues, supra,* at 774, some controversy still attends the probability of paternity. Faigman and his colleagues summarize the situation as follows:

> Some states will not allow the [DNA] test results to be admitted to prove paternity unless they are accompanied by the paternity probability, but because of the difficulty of interpreting $W_{50,}$ they require this probability to exceed some threshold such as 0.95. Another state permits the probability to be introduced in all situations, but only if it presented, not as a single number, but as a chart or table of values for a series of probabilities ranging from zero to one. Still other states allow the admission of $W_{50,}$ but require independent proof of intercourse. Most states, however, have not focused on the precise meaning of the "probability of paternity" and the limitations of W_{50}.

Id. at 770 (extensive case annotations omitted). They characterize the criticism of the probability of paternity as increasingly academic, because the available range of DNA tests "can produce posterior probabilities well in excess of 0.99 for virtually *any* plausible prior probability in the ordinary case." *Id.*

    5.   A final point is a reminder of the *Daubert* implications of the controversy in *Skipper.* The case should not be read as casting doubt on the admissibility of the basic DNA testing that underlay the prosecution expert's paternity analysis (the testing described in footnote 8) — assuming of course, that such testing is properly done and presented. Nor does the court seem to be questioning the admissibility of the paternity index. (But what assumptions must it be making? Do any of them relate to the appropriate choice and use of comparative frequency data?) The specific issue is the admissibility of the probability of paternity in the criminal context. Assume that you are a federal judge confronting facts just like those in *Skipper* and that you agree with *Skipper* on the merits. What Rule[s] of Evidence would you cite in excluding the probability of paternity evidence, and why?

CHAPTER 5

EXPERT TESTIMONY
ABOUT
BEHAVIORAL
SCIENCE

Although most believe that psychiatry and psychology are essentially modern developments, English and U.S. courts have been admitting expert testimony about mental health issues for hundreds of years. While behavioral science testimony is often controversial, most courts find it sufficiently helpful to be admissible. Expert testimony based upon behavioral science is frequently admitted in civil and criminal trials, custody disputes, and commitment proceedings.

Historically, the most frequent use of mental health expert testimony was to establish the insanity defense; to help factfinders determine whether a serious mental illness should provide a legal defense to an otherwise criminal act. Mental health expert testimony has been admitted in courts for centuries on the question of competency to stand trial. As the Supreme Court noted in Cooper v. Oklahoma, 517 U.S. 348, 356 (1996), "[t]he prohibition against trying the incompetent defendant was well established by the time Hale and Blackstone wrote their famous commentaries."[1]

---

1. For more on the historical aspects on mental illness in criminal trials, see, Michael L. Perlin, *The Jurisprudence of the Insanity Defense*, (1994); and Jane Campbell Moriarty, Ed., *The Role of Mental Illness in Criminal Trials* (2001)(3 vols).

In contemporary times, there are more varied uses of behavioral science expert testimony than simply insanity and competency. Over the last several decades, courts have admitted much more behavioral and social science evidence in both civil and criminal trials. Most jurisdictions admit "social framework" testimony—often in the form of battered woman and other forms of syndrome evidence—to explain unusual behaviors. Expert testimony about an individual's propensity for future violence is routinely allowed in both the penalty phase of capital cases and in commitment hearings of violent sexual predators. In civil cases, courts allow behavioral science expert testimony to support claims of sexual harassment or other civil wrongs. In domestic relations courts, testimony from psychologists or psychiatrists is often admitted to assist in determining placement of children in custody disputes.[2] Sometimes, courts have taken notice of behavioral or social science presented by parties or amici in briefs to the court.

Despite its widespread admission, behavioral science testimony poses difficult questions: whether the testimony is based on scientifically sound principles; what constitutes adequate qualifications for a testifying expert; what is the appropriate scope of the testimony; and whether the testimony impermissibly interferes with the jury's role in determining credibility.

This chapter considers behavioral science expert testimony and explores the evidentiary issues likely to arise in such cases.

I. EXPERT TESTIMONY ABOUT SYNDROMES, PROFILES, AND FRAMEWORKS

Social Frameworks: A New Use of Social Science in Law

73 Va. L. Rev. 559 (1987)
Laurens Walker and John Monahan

Over the past half-century it has become commonplace for courts and commentators to distinguish two uses of social science in law. Social science is said either to prove "legislative facts" that concern general questions of law and policy, or to prove "adjudicative facts" that pertain only to the case at hand. The choice of procedures to introduce research findings has depended heavily on the assignment of the research to one of these two categories. In this article, we identify a new generic use of social science

---

2. Expert testimony on the subject of repressed memory and eyewitness identification also involves behavioral science. These subjects are considered in Chapter 9, Expert Testimony About Memory.

in law that is emerging from recent cases. In this third use, research findings presented in court are neither legislative nor adjudicative facts themselves. Rather, empirical information is being offered that incorporates aspects of both of the traditional uses: general research results are used to construct a frame of reference or background context for deciding factual issues crucial to the resolution of a specific case. We call this new use of social science in law the creation of social frameworks.

I.   AN EMERGING USE OF EMPIRICAL RESEARCH . . .

B.   ANOMALOUS USES OF SOCIAL SCIENCE

Most of the uses of social science in court fall into either the "legislative fact" or "adjudicative fact" categories. Within the past several years, however, courts have increasingly begun to use research in ways that do not correspond to either of the traditional classifications. There are strong indications that a new, third use of social science in law is emerging. Notable examples can be found in cases concerning eyewitness identification, assessments of dangerousness, battered women, and sexual victimization.

The only evidence that connected the defendant in *State v. Chapple*[13] to the crime of murder was the testimony of two eyewitnesses. At trial, the defense offered the testimony of a research psychologist to rebut the testimony of the state's witnesses. In the offer of proof, the expert testified to published studies on factors such as the speed with which memory decays over time, the effects of stress on eyewitness accuracy, and the relationship between the confidence of a witness in his or her identification and the accuracy of that identification. The trial judge granted a motion to suppress the social science testimony, but the Arizona Supreme Court reversed and remanded the case for a new trial, stating that "there were a number of substantive issues of ultimate fact on which the expert's testimony would have been of significant assistance."

The defendant in *State v. Davis*[14] was also charged with murder, and pleaded guilty. At a penalty trial to determine whether the defendant would be executed or serve a mandatory thirty-year minimum sentence, defense counsel offered the testimony of a sociologist as evidence in support of mitigation of the sentence. The expert, according to the offer of proof, would have testified to published studies and government statistics demonstrating that murderers have the lowest rate of recidivism of all criminals, and that, considering the crime rate among persons of the age the defendant would be when released from prison a minimum of thirty years hence, it was extremely unlikely that the defendant would again be a threat to society. As in *Chapple*,

---

13. United States v. Chapple, 135 Ariz. 281, 660 P.2d 1208 (1983) (en banc).
14. State v. Davis, 477 A.2d 308 (N.J. 1984) (per curiam).

the trial court granted a motion to suppress the testimony, stating that "the statistical approach doesn't tell us anything at all about a given defendant." The New Jersey Supreme Court reversed, however, holding that social science research "may, in effect, encapsulate ordinary human experience and provide an appropriate frame of reference for a jury's consideration."

In addition to eyewitness identification and predictions of dangerousness, apparently anomalous uses of social science research have occurred with respect to the "battered woman syndrome." In *State v. Kelly*,[18] the defendant was convicted of the reckless manslaughter of her husband. She claimed at trial that she was acting in self-defense, fearing that her husband would kill her. The defense presented evidence that the husband had beaten the defendant on many prior occasions. The defense also sought to call a psychologist to testify to the findings of several researchers who had published reports on the state of mind "of other women who had been in similarly abusive relationship[s]." Here, too, the trial judge suppressed the testimony and the state supreme court reversed and remanded the case for a new trial, stating that "the proffered expert testimony may be not only relevant, but critical" to the defendant's case.

Finally, in *State v. Myers*[21] the defendant was found guilty of criminal sexual conduct involving a child. Over the objection of defense counsel, the prosecution had been allowed to present a social science expert witness to testify to behavioral traits "typically" observed in abused children, traits that were also observed in the child complainant. On appeal, the defendant claimed that admitting such testimony constituted reversible error. Affirming the conviction, however, the Minnesota Supreme Court stated that "background data providing a relevant insight into the puzzling aspects of the child's conduct and demeanor which the jury could not otherwise bring to its evaluation of her credibility is helpful and appropriate."

C.   SOCIAL FRAMEWORK AS AN ORGANIZING CONCEPT

The research used in these examples . . . is not pure legislative or adjudicative fact but rather incorporates the essential aspects of both of the established categories. We therefore propose a new category, which we term social framework, to refer to the use of general conclusions from social science research in determining factual issues in a specific case.

NOTE

1.   During the twentieth century, courts increasingly relied on social and behavioral science as part of legal decision making, as mentioned in Chapter 1. In Brown v. Board of Education, 347 U.S. 483 (1954), the Supreme Court overruled Plessy v. Ferguson's ruling that separate but

---

18. State v. Kelly, 478 A.2d 364 (N.J. 1984).
21. State v. Myers, 359 N.W.2d 604 (Minn. 1984).

equal education was constitutional. Citing social and behavioral science articles, the Supreme Court decided in *Brown* that segregated education had a negative psychological impact on children, holding "[w]hatever may have been the extent of psychological knowledge at the time of *Plessy v. Ferguson*, this finding [that segregation is psychologically harmful] is amply supported by modern authority. Any language in *Plessy v. Ferguson* contrary to this finding is rejected." *Id.* at 494-495. The use of social and behavioral science in judicial decisions has fostered much commentary. *See* John Monahan & Laurens Walker, *Social Authority: Obtaining, Evaluating and Establishing Social Science in Law*, 134 U. Pa. L. Rev. 477 (1986); John M. Conley, "*The First Principle of Real Reform": The Role of Science in Constitutional Jurisprudence*, 65 N.C. L. Rev. 935 (1987); Michael Rustad & Thomas Koenig, *The Supreme Court and Junk Social Science: Selective Distortions In Amicus Briefs*, 72 N.C. L. Rev. 91 (1993); and Sarah H. Ramsey & Robert F. Kelly, *Social Science Knowledge in Family Law Cases: Judicial Gatekeeping in the* Daubert *Era*, 59 U. Miami L. Rev. 1 (2004).

2. Can you explain the respective benefits and drawbacks to using social framework testimony?

Behavioral Science in the Age of *Daubert*: Reflections of a Skeptic

73 U. Cin. L. Rev. 867, 867-868 (2005)
Mark S. Brodin

I. INTRODUCTION

From its earliest use in American courts, when one Dr. Brown offered his "scientific" opinion in a Salem witch trial, expert testimony has posed fundamental issues for our system of adjudication. At its most basic the quandary is: How can we utilize specialists to educate a lay jury about matters beyond their ken without at the same time intruding upon the jurors' central role as ultimate factfinder?

In recent years courts and commentators have focused considerable attention on one dimension of this problem assuring some degree of "reliability" regarding the principles and methodologies underlying the expert's testimony before it is heard by the jury. For much of the twentieth century courts followed the Frye decision, which delegated this assessment to the practitioners in the particular field under a "general acceptance" standard. *Daubert v. Merrell Dow Pharmaceuticals, Inc.* and its progeny as well as revised Federal Rule of Evidence (FRE) 702 now assign the trial judge the enhanced role of "gatekeeper," screening expert testimony based on certain reliability criteria. Evidence routinely admitted under the pre-*Daubert* regime from forensic to epidemiological to economic is now subject to close scrutiny and exclusion even before a jury is impaneled. In the age-old contest between judge and jury, the balance has shifted dramatically toward the former.

Daubert's measure of reliability clearly reflects a traditional conception of science, envisioning a model driven by experimentation, replication, and validation. In the context of the "hard" sciences concerning physical phenomena, scientific facts (like the force of gravity) can be validated in these ways. But applying this model to this Article's subject, the social or "soft" sciences, is far more problematic.

The social sciences most often find their way into the courtroom as a tool to account for or predict human behavior. The evidence usually consists of general assertions about classes of persons, such as rape victims, and is offered "to provide a social and psychological context in which the trier can understand and evaluate claims about the ultimate fact."[11] Expert testimony concerning child sexual abuse accommodation syndrome (CSAAS), battered woman syndrome, learned helplessness, and rape trauma syndrome is offered by prosecutors to explain conduct of the alleged victim that might appear inconsistent with abuse. For example an expert may testify to the reasons behind a victim's delay in reporting the events, recantation, or remaining in a relationship with the abuser. Battered woman syndrome evidence may also be offered by the defense for the purpose of establishing that the defendant believed she was in imminent danger, even though the objective circumstances posed no apparent immediate threat justifying self-defense (as where the abuser is killed in his sleep). "Future dangerousness" testimony is offered during the penalty phase of capital cases and in proceedings to commit sexual aggressors.

Derived not from "experimentation but observation," there is serious question as to whether much of this behavioral evidence can meet the *Daubert* definition of reliable science. Nonetheless, this evidence continues to be admitted routinely at trial, often with little critical analysis by the court and sometimes even after the evidence has been discredited in its own field.

In the following cases involving syndrome and profile evidence, consider both the "social framework model" and whether the testimony in question meets the essential reliability requirements.

State v. Chauvin

846 So.2d 697 (La. 2003)

KNOLL, Justice.

This criminal case concerns the admissibility of expert testimony with regard to Post Traumatic Stress Disorder (PTSD) of a sexually abused victim.

---

11. Neil J. Vidmar & Regina A. Schuller, Juries and Expert Evidence: Social Framework Testimony, 52 Law & Contemp. Probs. 133, 135 (1989) [remaining citations omitted].

After a jury trial, defendant was convicted of two counts of indecent behavior with juveniles. . . . We granted the State's application for a writ of certiorari to consider the admissibility of this type of expert testimony as substantive evidence bearing on the credibility of the victim's testimony and the question of the accused's guilt or innocence. . . .

FACTS AND PROCEDURAL HISTORY

[A fifteen-year-old girl, A.C., alleged she was indecently fondled by the 34-year-old fiancé of the aunt of her friend, A.L.]

On this same day, after these incidents, A.C. told A.L. what defendant had done to her. A.L. also told A.C. what defendant had done to her. The next day, A.L. told A.C.'s older sister, Mandy, about these incidents. Detective Ashli Richardson of the Houma Police Department testified that these incidents were reported to the police department approximately four days after they occurred. Detective Dawn Gautreaux testified that a report was made to the Terrebonne Sheriff's Office by the victims on July 26, 1999. At trial, over the objection of the defendant, the State was allowed to introduce the expert testimony of Renee Thompson Ring, a licensed clinical social worker.[6]

The State wanted to use Ms. Ring's expert opinion to establish that A.C.'s clinical symptoms were consistent with a sexual abuse victim; in other words, to use her testimony as substantive evidence of sexual abuse. The trial court allowed Ms. Ring to testify as an expert without conducting a *Daubert* hearing to test the reliability of PTSD in the diagnosis of sexual abuse.

Ms. Ring testified before the jury that she saw A.C. as a patient at "The Haven," "a safe place for persons of sexual assault and domestic violence to come in for individual counseling or group counseling. . . ." She treated A.C. clinically for emotional problems. Based upon objective and subjective symptomatology, she diagnosed A.C. with PTSD. Ms. Ring's testimony described PTSD in layman's terms and the symptomatology that she saw that led her to diagnose A.C. as suffering from PTSD.[7]

---

6. Ms. Ring has a Bachelor's degree in psychology, a Master's degree in social work, and has worked in the field of social work, including internships, for seven years.

7. *Q.* Just from A.C.'s standpoint, what symptomatology did you see that led you to conclude that diagnosis [PTSD] for her?

    A. Primarily, what I saw—well, there was a lot of symptoms that she was manifesting throughout her therapy, both with myself and another counselor. Generally, she was very flat in her affect. . . .

    Q. What other things did you see that clinically were significant to you in regard to symptoms?

    A. A lot of frustration. That's very common too. . . .

    A. A lot of fear; a lot of anxiety, you know. A lot of times persons also with post-traumatic stress find it very difficult to trust. . . .

A . . . they're very shut down, not very open to how they are feeling or what's going on inside of their head. That was another thing that definitely she exhibited that.

Ms. Ring offered her expert opinion in response to the following questions from the State:

Q. Okay. Let me ask you this. The clinical findings, both subjective and objective, that you observed in regard to [A.C.] when you treated her for these problems, were those consistent with a child who had been sexually abused?

A. Yes, the symptoms were that of post-traumatic stress.

Q. Ma'am, I got a question just in general for you. Is there any way that you can predict, based on your experience and education, how a child might react to sexual abuse?

Q. I mean just by the criteria of post-traumatic stress you don't know exactly what symptoms they might have, but there's a general knowledge that they could have this, they could have this, they could have this.

On cross-examination, Ms. Ring was questioned as to whether these same symptoms might be seen in a child that was having problems other than sexual abuse. Ms. Ring responded that one would rule out any other reasons for the disorder and that is how one would make a diagnosis. Also on cross-examination, Ms. Ring acknowledged that the diagnosis was her opinion, and also acknowledged that experts make mistakes.

The jury found the defendant guilty on both counts of indecent behavior with a juvenile. [The court of appeals reversed, alleging a failure to properly apply factors related to reliability of the evidence as set forth in both *Daubert* and *State v. Foret*, 628 So. 2d 1116 (La. 1993)] and [w]e granted the State's writ to further study this problematic issue and after a careful review, we agree with the court of appeal majority and affirm.

DISCUSSION

La. Code Evid. art. 702 sets forth the general rule governing the admissibility of expert testimony in Louisiana:

> If scientific, technical, or other specialized knowledge will assist the trier of fact to understand the evidence or to determine a fact in issue, a witness qualified as an expert by knowledge, skill, experience, training, or education, may testify thereto in the form of an opinion or otherwise.

In *Foret*, we adopted the test set forth in *Daubert*, which "set forth a means for determining reliability of expert scientific testimony and answered many questions as to proper standards for admissibility of expert testimony." . . .

In the matter before us, the majority of the court of appeal relied upon this Court's decision in *Foret* in finding that the trial court failed to perform its "gatekeeping" function by failing to apply the factors enunciated in *Daubert* and *Foret* to test the reliability of the theory of PTSD in the diagnosis of sexual abuse. The appellate majority determined that the State used Ms. Ring's testimony to establish that symptoms of PTSD were consistent with the symptoms of a child who had been sexually abused; that PTSD provided guidelines on what symptoms a child reacting to sexual abuse might have; and that A.C. was suffering from PTSD. Because Ms. Ring did not limit her information to explaining "superficially bizarre" reactions of A.C. and went beyond merely providing a scientific perspective from which the jury could evaluate A.C.'s testimony, the majority held admissibility of her testimony was erroneous. The appellate majority further found that this Foret violation was harmful error with regard to both counts. A.C.'s testimony was the most damaging evidence offered against defendant on count one. The inadmissible expert testimony served to unduly bolster A.C.'s testimony and, in all probability, made it more believable to the jury. Although A.L. was the victim named in count two, the court of appeal found that A.C.'s unduly bolstered testimony corrupted the entire trial. Therefore, finding the erroneously admitted testimony affected substantial rights of the accused and that the defendant timely objected to this testimony, the appellate majority reversed the convictions on both counts, remanding the matter to the trial court for a new trial.

The State argues that the testimony was not so unusual or complex as to require a *Daubert* hearing to test its reliability. Relying upon *Kumho Tire Co., Ltd. v. Carmichael,* . . . the State asserts that the determination of how to test an expert's reliability is in the trial judge's discretion. The record before us shows the trial court held a brief hearing before Ms. Ring testified. The State submits that the trial judge can use his or her own experience and knowledge after hearing briefly what the testimony will be to determine that the testimony is commonly accepted among professionals and thus is reliable and relevant. The State contends that this matter is distinguishable from *Foret,* because Ms. Ring did not testify that A.C. was a victim of sexual abuse nor did she testify as to A.C.'s credibility.

The defendant counters the State's argument by stressing that the trial court is required to prevent undue emphasis from being placed upon expert testimony when no scientific basis for that testimony can be established. Defendant contends the trial court failed to apply the "observations" of *Daubert* and *Foret*. There was no testimony that Ms. Ring's technique had been subjected to peer review; there was no testimony as to the potential rate of error; and there was no testimony as to whether her methodology was generally accepted in the scientific community. Defendant argues the trial court failed to test the reliability, if any, of the theory of PTSD in the diagnosis of sexual abuse.

We must determine under the guidance established in *Daubert*, *Kumho Tire* and *Foret*, whether Ms. Ring's testimony was admissible, and if so, whether the trial court should have first conducted a *Daubert* hearing to test the reliability of PTSD and the diagnosis of sexual abuse. Ms. Ring's clinical diagnosis that A.C. had PTSD was introduced in the State's case-in-chief, for the specific purpose of showing A.C.'s symptoms and/or that her diagnosis were consistent with those of a child who has been sexually abused. The troubling issue raised by Ms. Ring's expert testimony is *res nova* before this Court. In resolving this issue, we have studied scholarly publications and jurisprudence of other states, as well as our own jurisprudence.

[handwritten margin note: case of first impression]

BALANCE OF COMPETING INTERESTS

We begin by noting that child sexual abuse cases are not easy to prosecute. . . . Child sexual abuse is difficult to prove because it most often occurs in private, often the perpetrator is a member of the victim's family, and physical evidence of the abuse is rare. The problems with prosecuting child sexual abuse cases are increased by the fact that most children fail to report the abuse, and, if they do report, there is often a significant lapse in time between the actual occurrence and the ultimate reporting of the abusive incident by the child. . . . Even then, the child may not include details in her revelation and often children recant or alter their allegations of abuse. . . .

Expert testimony can assist a trier of fact in understanding the significance of a child-witness's demeanor, inconsistent reports, delayed disclosure, reluctance to testify, and recantation. . . . An expert witness can explain to jurors that a child-witness's seemingly abnormal behavior — delayed reporting, inconsistent statements, and recantation — is in fact normal for children who have been sexually abused and can also dispel inaccurate perceptions held by jurors, allowing them to better assess a child-witness's testimony. . . . Expert testimony becomes problematic when it infringes upon other interests: for example, when it is unduly prejudicial, when it invades the province of the jury, when it bolsters a child-witness's testimony, or when it leads to a "battle of the experts."

The admissibility *vel non* of this type of expert testimony requires a delicate balance of these competing interests. Our task in this case is to provide guidance to the lower courts that will assist them, on a case by case basis, to balance these competing interests when faced with this difficult issue.

RELIABILITY OF PTSD

With regard to testimony from mental health professionals, it is important to note the distinction between substantive evidence and evidence designed to rehabilitate witness credibility. 1 John E.B. Myers, *Evidence in*

Child Abuse and Neglect Cases, § 5.1, p. 412 (3d ed.1997). Expert testimony in child sexual abuse litigation falls into two categories: (1) expert testimony offered as substantive proof that a child was sexually abused, and (2) expert testimony offered for the more limited purpose of rehabilitating a child's impeached credibility. *Id.*, § 5.12, p. 459. Expert testimony offered as substantive evidence takes several forms, including testimony that in the expert's opinion, the child's symptoms are consistent with sexual abuse. Id., § 5.34, p. 527. When such testimony is offered by the prosecution, the purpose is to prove that abuse occurred.

The fourth edition of the *Diagnostic and Statistical Manual of Mental Disorders* (DSM-IV) of the American Psychiatric Association lists PTSD[10] as an anxiety disorder. Myers, § 5.3 p. 423, citing *American Psychiatric Association, Diagnostic and Statistical Manual of Mental Disorders* 424 (4th ed.1994). The diagnosis was formally introduced into the psychiatric nomenclature

---

10. The American Psychiatric Association characterizes PTSD as having the following diagnostic criteria:
   A. The person has been exposed to a traumatic event in which both the following were present:
      (1) the person experienced, witnessed, or was confronted with an event or events that involved actual or threatened death or serious injury, or a threat to the physical integrity of self or others
      (2) the person's response involved intense fear, helplessness, or horror. . . .
   B. The traumatic event is persistently reexperienced in one (or more) of the following ways:
      (1) recurrent and intrusive distressing recollections of the event. . . .
      (2) recurrent distressing dreams of the event. . . .
      (3) acting or feeling as if the traumatic event were recurring. . . .
      (4) intense psychological distress at exposure to internal or external cues that symbolize or resemble an aspect of the traumatic event.
   C. Persistent avoidance of stimuli associated with the trauma and numbing of general responsiveness (not present before the trauma), as indicated by three (or more) of the following:
      (1) efforts to avoid thoughts, feelings, or conversations associated with the trauma
      (2) efforts to avoid activities, places, or people that arouse recollections of the trauma
      (3) inability to recall an important aspect of the trauma
      (4) markedly diminished interest or participation in significant events
      (5) feeling of detachment or estrangement from others
      (6) restricted range of affect . . .
      (7) sense of foreshortened future . . .
   D. Persistent symptoms of increased arousal (not present before the trauma) as indicated by two (or more) of the following:
      (1) difficulty falling or staying asleep
      (2) irritability or outbursts of anger
      (3) difficulty concentrating
      (4) hypervigilance
      (5) exaggerated startle response
   E. Duration of disturbance (symptoms in Criteria B, C, and D) is more than 1 month.
   F. The disturbance causes clinically significant distress or impairment in social, occupational, or other important areas of functioning. DSM IV 427-429.

in the third edition of the DSM published in 1980. Myers, § 5.3 p. 423, note 75 (citation omitted). According to the DSM:

> The essential feature of Posttraumatic [sic] Stress Disorder is the development of characteristic symptoms following exposure to an extreme traumatic stressor involving direct personal experience of an event that involves actual or threatened death or serious injury, or other threat to one's physical integrity. . . . The person's response to the event must involve intense fear, helplessness, or horror (or in children, the response must involve disorganized or agitated behavior). . . .
>
> Traumatic events that are experienced directly include . . . violent personal assault (sexual assault, robbery, mugging). . . . For children, sexually traumatic events may include developmentally inappropriate sexual experiences without threatened or actual violence or injury. Id.

PTSD is sufficiently recognized in the medical, and particularly the psychiatric, community to be considered as the proper subject of expert testimony.

In many child sexual abuse prosecutions, prosecutors offer expert PTSD-based testimony that the child complainant's behavior is consistent with being sexually abused. . . . Because evidence of PTSD is admissible in other contexts, prosecutors of child sexual abuse cases might attempt to capitalize on PTSD's legacy of admissibility by offering testimony which refers explicitly to PTSD. . . . The expert explains the diagnostic category, and then matches the behavioral characteristics of the child with the PTSD criteria. . . . In its true form, testimony based on PTSD suggests only that sexual abuse may be the cause of the child's behavior, but it does not rule out other traumatic causes of the behavior. PTSD assumes the presence of a stressor and then attaches a diagnosis to the child's reactions to it. PTSD merely is a therapeutic tool; it is not designed to determine sexual abuse. . . .

We recognize that expert testimony regarding PTSD has been admitted in various contexts in Louisiana courts. . . .

Even though PTSD is a catalogued condition of the DSM, and has been admitted into evidence by our courts in various matters, there is no evidence in the record before us that the trial court performed its "gatekeeping" function of determining that the testimony of Ms. Ring was both relevant and reliable as substantive proof that sexual abuse occurred.

Several other state courts have considered the admissibility of expert testimony regarding PTSD in a criminal prosecution for child sexual abuse. Almost every court that has addressed this issue has concluded that PTSD evidence is admissible to explain a victim's behavior that is apparently inconsistent with having been sexually abused if the defense has made it an issue.

As to the more difficult issue of whether evidence of PTSD is admissible to prove sexual abuse, the courts are divided. Some jurisdictions allow PTSD testimony to show that the victim was sexually abused. Other jurisdictions forbid PTSD testimony for the purpose of proving that sexual abuse in fact occurred. In addition, some courts recognize that PTSD is founded upon good science, but conclude it will not assist the trier of fact to determine whether sexual abuse occurred because it is a therapeutic method that was not intended to be used as a forensic tool.

We are concerned about the use of PTSD evidence as substantive evidence that sexual abuse has occurred, when such evidence is not limited to explaining "superficially bizarre" reactions common to victims of child sexual abuse but which are uncommon to the experience of jurors. First, the psychiatric procedures used in developing the diagnosis of PTSD are designed for therapeutic purposes and are not reliable as fact-finding tools to determine whether sexual abuse has in fact occurred. . . . And secondly, the potential for prejudice looms large because the jury may accord too much weight to expert opinions stating medical conclusions which were drawn from diagnostic methods having limited merit as fact-finding devices.

Although PTSD is widely accepted among professionals as an anxiety disorder attributable to some type of trauma, it has not been proven to be a reliable indicator that sexual abuse is the trauma underlying the disorder or that sexual abuse has even occurred. The principal diagnostic criteria for PTSD "include[s] persistent reexperiencing of the traumatic event . . . persistent avoidance of stimuli associated with the trauma and numbing of general responsiveness. . . ." DSM-IV at 463. The diagnostic criteria for PTSD are thus not intended to provide clinical or forensic tools for determining whether child sexual abuse has occurred but for dealing with the aftermath of severe traumatic events that have occurred in a variety of contexts.

The DSM-IV adds the following general observation: "[n]onclinical decision makers should also be cautioned that a diagnosis does not carry any necessary implications regarding the causes of the individual's mental disorder or its associated impairments. . . ." DSM-IV at xxxiii. The psychiatric diagnosis of PTSD was not designed to determine sexual abuse, and the threshold criteria for the diagnosis of PTSD are not specific to child sexual abuse. . . . Furthermore, there are a variety of stressors in a child's life that can produce PTSD-type symptoms, and there is no baseline data about the presence of PTSD-type symptoms in nonabused and otherwise nonstressed children. In short, there is not a sufficient consensus within the mental health community that there are certain behavioral symptoms that can lead a mental health professional to a conclusion of "consistent with child sexual abuse."

LIMITED ADMISSIBILITY OF PTSD

In *Foret*, we concluded that evidence of Child Sexual Abuse Accommodation Syndrome (CSAAS) is of highly questionable scientific validity and fails to unequivocally pass the *Daubert* threshold test of reliability. . . . Similarly, because we find that a diagnosis of PTSD is certainly more general than a diagnosis of CSAAS, the reliability of expert PTSD testimony on causation can be no greater than that concerning CSAAS. . . . If the reliability of expert PTSD testimony on causation can be no greater than testimony of CSAAS as substantive proof that abuse occurred, we find expert testimony of PTSD is inadmissible for the purpose of substantively proving that sexual abuse occurred.

We come to this conclusion because the jury is asked to make the connection between a diagnosis of PTSD and the stressor, child sexual abuse, that is alleged to have caused it. Identification of the stressor is an important component of the PTSD diagnosis. But it is widely accepted that PTSD has not been proven to be a reliable indicator that sexual abuse is the trauma underlying the disorder or that sexual abuse has even occurred. The psychiatric diagnosis of PTSD was not designed to determine sexual abuse, . . . , and the psychological evaluation of a child suspected of being sexually abused is, at best, an inexact science. . . . For these reasons, we find that admission of expert testimony of a diagnosis of PTSD for the purpose of substantively proving sexual abuse fails to pass the *Daubert* threshold test of scientific reliability.

Just as we determined in *Foret*, expert testimony of general characteristics that would explain delays in reporting, recantations, and omissions of details is admissible. In the matter before us, there was no evidence in the record that A.C. or A.L. recanted their allegations. Nor were they young children who were cognitively unable to testify coherently or incapable of providing details. We find Ms. Ring's expert testimony went beyond the limited purpose of explaining the superficially bizarre behavior of a victim of child sexual abuse. We further find Ms. Ring's testimony deprived defendant of a fair trial by imbuing the girls' testimony with an undeserved scientific aura of truth. This testimony impermissibly bolstered the testimony of both girls. There was absolutely no indication that this testimony was necessary to explain to the jury the significance of a child-witness's demeanor, inconsistent reports, reluctance to testify or recantation. Although the defense showed there had been a slight delay between the date of the incidents and the reporting to the police [36 days], expert testimony that Ms. Ring diagnosed A.C. with PTSD did not reliably explain why many sexually abused children delay reporting their abuse.

CONCLUSION

Under these circumstances, we find that the State introduced the expert testimony regarding A.C.'s diagnosis of PTSD for the purpose of substantively proving that sexual abuse occurred. There is no indication that the State attempted to limit this evidence to explain delayed reporting, which could be construed as apparently inconsistent with having been sexually abused. There is no showing that PTSD evidence is reliable and accurate as substantive proof of sexual abuse and therefore, it is inadmissible for this purpose. We hold that this evidence, like CSAAS-based evidence, should be admissible only for the limited purpose of explaining, in general terms, certain reactions of a child to abuse that would be used to attack the victim/witness's credibility. The trial court in its discretion can determine, on a case by case basis, if a particularized hearing is necessary (*Daubert* hearing) to test the reliability of expert testimony on PTSD when it is being offered for the limited purposes discussed above.

NOTES AND QUESTIONS

1.   While most states allow syndrome testimony and find it sufficiently reliable to be admissible for at least limited purposes, some states have disallowed such testimony, finding it to be either insufficiently reliable or too close a comment on credibility — thus encroaching impermissibly on the jury's function. *See e.g.*, Commonwealth v. Dunkle, 602 A.2d 830 (Pa. 1992); and State v. Ballard 855 S.W.2d 557 (Tenn. 1993).

2.   Can juries understand the distinction between expert evidence offered as substantive proof of sexual abuse and expert testimony offered to simply explain superficially bizarre behavior possibly consistent with abuse?

3.   Does this case address the concerns about reliability raised by the commentator at the beginning of the chapter? The court finds that PTSD is not sufficiently reliable to be admitted as substantive evidence. Why does the court decide that aspects of PTSD may be admitted in future cases for a limited purpose? Does that make the testimony any more reliable?

4.   The delay in this case between the incident and reporting to the police was only 4 days. Many courts have held that when the defense argues that long delay is indicative of deception, prosecutors may then introduce expert testimony to explain that delay in reporting is common with victims of abuse. *See* cases collected in Jane Campbell Moriarty, *Psychological and Scientific Evidence in Criminal Cases*, § 8:21.3 (2006). Is this approach fair to the defendant who claims the allegation of abuse is fabricated? Is it a reasonable inference that delay is indicative of deception? Consider Notes 9 and 10 in formulating your answer.

5.   Some commentators argue compellingly that PTSD is based upon a solid scientific foundation and should be readily admitted in cases involving trauma likely to bring about such a condition. *See* Edgar Garcia-Rill & Erica Beecher-Monas, *Gatekeeping Stress: The Science and Admissibility of Post-Traumatic Stress Disorders*, 24 U. Ark. Little Rock L. Rev. 9 (2001). For a

competing argument, see William M. Grove & R. Christopher Barden, *Protecting the Integrity of the Legal System: The Admissibility of Testimony from Mental Health Experts Under* Daubert/Kumho *Analyses,* 5 Psychol. Pub. Pol'y & L. 224, 230 (1999). For further reading on the science of PTSD, see Norman Poythress et al., *Post-Traumatic Stress Disorder — Areas of Scientific Agreement,* 2 *Modern Scientific Evidence* § 11:34 (Faigman et al., eds. 2005–2006). For further reading about violence and its psychological effect on victims, see Mindy B. Mechanic, *Beyond PTSD: Mental Health Consequences of Violence Against Women,* 19 J. Interpersonal Violence 1283 (2004).

6. PTSD was initially raised as part of a defense by Vietnam Veterans charged with crimes after returning home from war. *See e.g.,* United States v. Krutschewski, 509 F.Supp. 1186 (D. Mass. 1981) (raised as a defense to drug smuggling). After that use of PTSD in the courts faded away, litigants began to use it more commonly to explain rape and abuse victims' unusual behaviors. In light of the thousands of veterans returning home from both Afghanistan and Iraq suffering from PTSD, will the disorder likely surface again in the courts as part of a defense to crimes committed by war veterans? As a matter of social framework testimony, how would such evidence be integrated into a defense?

7. Recent studies have begun to look at the prevalence of PTSD in civil cases. *See* Edward J. Hickling et al., *The Psychological Impact of Litigation: Compensation Neurosis, Malingering, PTSD, Secondary Traumatization, and Other Lessons from MVAS* [motor vehicle accidents], 55 DePaul L. Rev. 617 (2006) (studying 158 car crash victims to assess the impact on the victims' psychological functioning).

8. Child Sexual Abuse Accommodation Syndrome ("CSAAS"), a term coined by Roland C. Summit, M.D., consists of some or all of five elements thought to be common to child sexual abuse victims: (1) secrecy; (2) helplessness; (3) entrapment and accommodation; (4) delayed; or (5) conflicted disclosure and retraction. *See* Roland C. Summit, M.D., *The Child Abuse Accommodation Syndrome,* 7 Child Abuse & Neglect 177 (1983). This syndrome was created by Summit as a theory to explain how children adjusted or accommodated to sexual abuse. Summit never claimed CSAAS as a diagnostic tool: "The syndrome does not detect sexual abuse. Rather, it assumes the presence of abuse, and explains the child's reaction to it." *Id.* at 67. Elements of the syndrome have been admitted in the majority of jurisdictions as either proof of abuse or to explain children's behavior. Knowing the limitations of Summit's syndrome, is it properly admitted at trial? As explained in Note 10, subsequent research on CSAAS has failed to substantiate some of its elements. Should jurors be informed of this research?

9. Does the expert testimony at issue reprinted from the case fit within either the construct of PTSD or CSAAS? How close to the defined syndrome must the testimony be to be admitted? Has the court conflated aspects of CSAAS with PTSD? Compare footnote 10 with the elements of CSAAS described above.

10. To date, there has been much written disagreement about the validity of various types of child sexual abuse syndrome evidence, including the aspects of CSAAS that assert that sexually abused children often delay reporting, make tentative or inconsistent reports, and even recant claims of sexual abuse. The defense might typically cross-examine on the issues of inconsistent reporting and recantation because such behaviors are thought to indicate deception. For example, many lawyers would argue to the jury that an alleged victim who later recants is lying about the initial claims. CSAAS testimony answers that argument. But the question has remained: Is recanting truly a feature of abuse? Dr. Mary Ann Mason has written that "there is no consensus in the behavioral sciences that delay, recantation, or inconsistency are indicators of sexual abuse." *The Child Sexual Abuse Syndrome: The Other Major Issue in State of New Jersey v. Margaret Kelly Michaels*, 1 Psychol. Pub. Pol'y & L. 399, 408 (1995). More recently, the authors of a cross-disciplinary article reviewed numerous studies and concluded that there was not empirical support for the claims that large numbers of sexually abused children make tentative reports and recant such claims. The only aspect of CSAAS that received empirical support was the finding that many children delay reporting the abuse. *See* Kamala London, Maggie Bruck, Stephen J. Ceci, & Daniel Shuman, *Disclosure of Child Sexual Abuse: What Does the Research Tell Us About the Ways That Children Tell?*, 11 Psychol. Pub. Pol'y & L. 194 (2005).

11. There is a long-standing disagreement on acceptable proof between some clinical professionals (who treat patients) and some research psychologists (who systematically study behavior in accordance with the scientific method). For many clinicians, their conclusions are often based upon their experience with patients. For research scientists, their conclusions are based upon what is testable and repeatable — in line with the way *Daubert* envisions science. Although *Daubert*'s reliability standard would seem to suggest that research scientists would have greater sway with the courts, the contrary outcome has in fact been true. *See* Brodin, *Behavioral Science in the Age of Daubert, supra,* at pages 869-870. Why might this be?

12. The issue of clinical opinion versus research opinion is particularly at issue in the repressed memory cases, where adults claim to spontaneously recall abuse from their childhood. For a fuller discussion of the debate, see *Final Conclusions of the American Psychological Association Working Group on Investigation of Memories of Childhood Abuse*, 4 Psychol. Pub. Pol'y & L. 933, 934 (1998) (stating that "one of the most consistent observations emerging from our deliberations has to do with the very divergent epistemologies and definitions used by psychologists who study memory and those who study and treat the effects of trauma"). The subject of repressed memory in the courtroom is considered in Chapter 9, Expert Testimony About Memory.

13. While we generally consider syndromes to be a modern form of expert testimony, one of the authors of this casebook has argued that it is

really a very old form of expert evidence, substantially flawed then and still raising concerns in contemporary trials. *See* Jane Campbell Moriarty, *Wonders of the Invisible World: Prosecutorial Syndrome and Profile Evidence in the Salem Witchcraft Trials*, 26 Vt. L. Rev. 43 (2001).

Virtually all jurisdictions admit behavioral science expert testimony in cases where a defendant claims that she killed the decedent in self-defense and there is evidence that the decedent physically abused the defendant.[3] These experts attempt to describe the battering relationship, explain why such victims do not leave their abusers, and provide a general background for juries to evaluate whether the actions of the defendant were both reasonable and warranted. Thorny questions about admissibility of such expert testimony arise when the killing does not occur during a "typical" self-defense posture or when the prosecution seeks to introduce expert testimony to explain why a battered woman might not testify against her batterer. Less frequently, some defendants have tried to introduce expert testimony about battering as part of a duress defense in a criminal prosecution.

In the following case, the government wanted to use expert evidence to prove its case against the batterer; at the time, this was a novel use of the expert testimony.

Arcoren v. United States

929 F.2d 1235 (8th Cir. 1991)

FRIEDMAN, Senior Circuit Judge.

In this appeal from the United States District Court for the District of South Dakota (Porter, C.J.), the appellant (Arcoren) challenges his convictions of two counts of aggravated sexual abuse, . . . , one count of abusive sexual contact, . . . and one count of sexual abuse of a minor. . . . We affirm the convictions of aggravated sexual abuse and abusive sexual contact, and the sentences imposed for those offenses. We vacate the conviction of sexual abuse of a minor, and remand for a new trial on that count.

I.

Arcoren's convictions stem from events occurring on September 17, 1989 at his apartment in St. Francis, South Dakota, which is on the Rosebud Indian Reservation. Viewing the facts most favorably to the government,

---

3. Although women do batter their male partners and battering occurs both between same-sex couples, the majority of reported cases involved male violence against females.

which is the standard on appeal from criminal convictions, . . . there was evidence from which the jury could have found the following:

After attending a dance and doing some drinking, Arcoren, an *A* American Indian, returned to his apartment around 3:00 a.m., accompanied by his nephew, brother, and four young girls — including Charlene Bordeaux (Bordeaux), Arcoren's wife's fifteen-year-old niece. Arcoren's pregnant wife, Brenda Brave Bird (Brave Bird), from whom he had separated two days before, was not in the apartment. Arcoren and Bordeaux went into the bedroom while the others remained in the living room, where they drank *had an affair* beer and played the stereo.

At approximately 5:00 a.m., Brave Bird arrived at the apartment and, after a brief argument with Arcoren, left. Arcoren returned to the bedroom and had consensual sexual intercourse with Bordeaux. Brave Bird later returned to the apartment, discovering Arcoren and Bordeaux in the bedroom. Arcoren forcefully pulled Brave Bird into the bedroom; verbally and physically abused her; prevented Brave Bird and Bordeaux from leaving the bedroom; and, for the next several hours, forced both women to have sexual *what* intercourse with him.

Later in the morning, while Arcoren slept, Brave Bird left the apartment in Arcoren's car, flagged down a police officer, John Two Eagle, and reported the assaults. At his instruction, Brave Bird then went to the hospital for medical treatment, where she told a nurse and attending physician about the beatings and rapes. At the hospital, Brave Bird also described the assaults to Phillip Charles, a criminal investigator with the Bureau of Indian Affairs.

Three days later, Brave Bird testified before a South Dakota federal grand jury, describing in detail Arcoren's violent sexual and physical assaults of both herself and Bordeaux.

After trial, the jury convicted Arcoren of aggravated sexual abuse of Brave Bird . . . of the lesser included offense of abusive sexual conduct toward Brave Bird on Count II. . . .

At trial, Bordeaux testified that she and Arcoren had voluntary intercourse; that after Brave Bird arrived, Arcoren verbally abused and beat Brave Bird, and then forced both herself and Brave Bird to have sexual intercourse with him as the other watched. John Two Eagle, the police officer, testified that when Brave Bird stopped him on the morning of September 17th, she had a swollen face with a cut on the bridge of her nose, blood on her clothing, and was "really upset." According to Two Eagle, Brave Bird stated that Arcoren "had assaulted her most of the night, forced her to stay at the apartment there on the east side of town and raped her and that there was another girl there that was being forced to stay at the apartment by [Arcoren] and that he raped her, too."

Carol Edwards, the receiving nurse at the hospital emergency room, testified that upon arrival, Brave Bird was "crying and upset" and told her that she had been "beaten up twice and she had been raped twice. . . ."

Dr. Teresa Mareska, the treating physician at the hospital, testified that Brave Bird reported being "assaulted by an individual named Tim" and "forced in some sexual activities." Phillip Charles, the Bureau of Indian Affairs criminal investigator who interviewed Brave Bird at the emergency room, testified in great detail about Brave Bird's account of the violent physical and sexual assaults by Arcoren upon Brave Bird and Bordeaux.

When the government called Brave Bird as a witness, she recanted her prior grand jury testimony and denied that Arcoren had beaten and raped her.

After using Brave Bird's grand jury testimony to impeach her trial testimony, the government introduced portions of the grand jury testimony, which were read aloud to the jury by the court reporter, as "substantive evidence." In this appeal, Arcoren has not challenged the introduction of that evidence.

Finally, Arcoren testified on his own behalf. He stated that although he had argued that night with Brave Bird over Bordeaux — during which time Brave Bird's nose was accidentally bloodied — they later made up and then had voluntary intercourse while Bordeaux was asleep. He also testified that the two women were free to leave at any time, and that he "did not make any sexual contact with Charlene [Bordeaux] whatsoever."

II.

As noted, at trial Brave Bird recanted her grand jury testimony. She denied Arcoren raped her, denied that she had seen Arcoren and Bordeaux have sexual intercourse, and stated that the cuts and bruises on her body resulted from an earlier motorbike wreck. When the government confronted her with her contradictory grand jury testimony, Brave Bird stated that she could not remember making the statements or that, where she did recall making them, they were incorrect. She stated that when she made the statements on September 17th accusing Arcoren of raping her, she was angry with Arcoren because "he was with another woman" and not "because he raped [her]."

The government then called an expert witness, Carol Maicky, to testify regarding "battered woman syndrome." She was a psychologist who had worked with battered women for 10 years and with rape victims for 14 years. The government gave the following reasons for offering the evidence:

> Your Honor, there are certain facts which the jury has before it from the testimony which we contend will go unnoticed by a lay jury unless put into a perspective by an expert. We're offering her opinion under Rule 702 to show that these particular facts, while [they] may seem insignificant by themselves when put together against a battered women syndrome would allow the jury to determine the credibility of her in court testimony ... and help them

determine which of the two diametrically opposed sworn statements of Brenda
Brave Bird to believe.

After hearing Maicky's proffered testimony in chambers, the court, over
defense counsel's objection, admitted the evidence. The court ruled that the
evidence was admissible under Rule 702 of the Federal Rules of Evidence
because it was "scientific, technical or other specialized knowledge [that]
will assist the [jury] to understand the evidence or to determine a fact in
issue" and that "the evidence would be more probative than prejudicial."
The court, however, warned that Maicky could not "testify as to the ultimate
fact that a particular party in this case, not the defendant, the party actually
suffers from battered women syndrome. This determination must be left to
the trier of fact."

In her testimony before the jury, Maicky generally described the battered woman syndrome. According to her testimony, which was based on her
knowledge of the literature dealing with the subject and her professional
experience, a "battered woman" is one who assumes responsibility for a
cycle of violence occurring in a relationship, where the abuser (a husband
or boyfriend) has told her that the first violent episode was her fault. Maicky
described the syndrome's general characteristics to include (1) the belief
that violence to the woman is her fault; (2) an inability to place responsibility *b.w.s*
for the violence elsewhere; (3) a fear for her life and the lives of her children;
and (4) an irrational belief that the abuser is omnipresent and omniscient.
According to Ms. Maicky, a battered woman develops coping mechanisms to
deal with the ever-present violence, believing that by doing just one more
thing she can stop the violence.

In accordance with the court's direction, Maicky expressed no opinion
whether Brave Bird suffered from or displayed symptoms of the syndrome.

The district court admitted Maicky's testimony pursuant to Rule 702 of
the Federal Rules of Evidence . . . Rule 702 reflects an attempt to liberalize
the rules governing the admission of expert testimony. See J. Weinstein &
M. Berger, *Weinstein's Evidence*, ¶702[02] at 702-30 (1988). The Advisory
Notes to the Rule comment that "[t]he rule is broadly phrased. The fields
of knowledge which may be drawn upon are not limited merely to the 'scientific' and 'technical' but extend to all 'specialized' knowledge. Similarly,
the expert is viewed, not in a narrow sense, but as a person qualified by
'knowledge, skill, experience, training or education.'" Fed.R.Evid. 702,
Advisory Note.

Rule 702 is one of admissibility rather than exclusion. [Citations omitted.] "[T]he concept expressed by the Rules is sufficiently broad to embrace
psychiatric and psychological testimony from those who possess specialized
knowledge concerning mental aberrations in human behavior, when such
knowledge will help the jury to understand relevant issues in the case."
United States v. Barta, 888 F.2d 1220, 1223 (8th Cir.1989).

The jury in the present case was faced with a bizarre situation. Immediately after the rapes and assaults, Brave Bird had described them to the police officer whose car she flagged down, to the nurse and the doctor at the hospital where she had gone for treatment, and to a criminal investigator from the Bureau of Indian Affairs. Three days later, she described the rapes and assaults in detail in sworn testimony before the grand jury.

Four months later, at Arcoren's trial, she recanted her grand jury testimony. There she stated that she either did not remember statements to the grand jury or that, if she did remember them, the statements were incorrect and that some of them were things she had "made up." At trial, she also changed her explanation for the injuries to her leg she had suffered on September 18, 1989. Although she told the police officer, the nurse and doctors at the hospital, and the criminal investigator that Arcoren had inflicted those injuries when he beat her, at trial she testified that the injuries resulted from a motorbike wreck. She also testified that the reason she stopped the police officer after leaving Arcoren's apartment was because she had been driving 70 miles per hour.

A jury naturally would be puzzled at the complete about-face she made, and would have great difficulty in determining which version of Brave Bird's testimony it should believe. If there were some explanation for Brave Bird's changed statements, such explanation would aid the jury in deciding which statements were credible.

Maicky's expert testimony regarding the battered woman syndrome provided that explanation to the jury. As the witness told the jury, the syndrome is a psychological condition, which leads a female victim of physical abuse to accept her beatings because she believes that she is responsible for them, and hopes that by accepting one more beating, the pattern will stop. Maicky's testimony provided the jury with information that would help it to determine which of Brave Bird's testimony to credit. If the jury concluded that Brave Bird suffered from battered woman syndrome, that would explain her change in testimony—her unwillingness to say something damaging against her husband.

Maicky's testimony thus met the requirement of Rule 702 that "a witness qualified as an expert by knowledge, skill, experience, training or education" may testify with respect to "scientific, technical or other specialized knowledge" that "will assist the trier of fact to understand the evidence or to determine a fact in issue." In permitting Maicky to testify, the district court ruled that she was qualified as an expert based on "a degree in psychology from the University of Michigan which is judicially noticed as a respected university plus the length of time of actual experience that she has had in this general field," and that the evidence would be "relevant and probative for the fact finders, the jury," to aid the jury in "pass[ing] upon the veracity or lack of veracity of the wife."

Apparently this is the first federal appellate case to consider the admissibility under Rule 702 of evidence relating to the battered woman syndrome. A number of state courts, however, have held such evidence admissible in cases in which the syndrome was relied upon to support the defense that the battered woman killed her husband or lover in self-defense. *See, e.g., State v. Hennum,* 441 N.W.2d 793 (Minn.1989). . . . In the *Hennum* case, on which the government relied in the district court as support for the introduction of Maicky's testimony, the Supreme Court of Minnesota stated that a number of courts in admitting the evidence "have held that battered woman syndrome is beyond the understanding of the average person and therefore expert testimony should be allowed." 441 N.W.2d at 798. The court also stated that "the theory underlying the battered woman syndrome is beyond the experimental stage and has gained a substantial enough scientific acceptance to warrant admissibility." Id. at 798-99.

Arcoren does not here challenge either the reliability or the general admissibility of battered woman syndrome evidence. Instead, he urges that introduction of such evidence should be limited to cases in which it is offered to bolster a claim of self-defense. There is no persuasive reason, however, for thus limiting it. The standard under Rule 702 for the admissibility of expert testimony is whether the "evidence will assist the trier of fact to understand the evidence or determine a fact in issue." If the expert testimony serves that end, it is immaterial whether the testimony is presented by the prosecution or by the defense. As a New Jersey appellate court stated, in affirming the admission of battered woman syndrome evidence offered by the prosecution, in a case where the wife was the complainant against her husband, "It would seem anomalous to allow a battered woman, where she is a criminal defendant, to offer this type of expert testimony in order to help the jury understand the actions she took, yet deny her that same opportunity when she is the complaining witness and/or victim and her abuser is the criminal defendant." *See State v. Frost,* 242 N.J.Super. 601, 612, 577 A.2d 1282, 1287 (Ct.App.Div.1990).

This court has held expert testimony admissible under Rule 702 in other circumstances where the expert's specialized knowledge would assist the jury to understand the evidence. This principle is equally applicable to a situation where a psychologist testifies to "mental aberrations in human behavior, when such knowledge will help the jury to understand relevant issues in the case." *United States v. Barletta,* 888 F.2d 1220, 1223 (8th Cir.1989). In this case, Maicky's testimony provided the jury with a basis upon which to understand and evaluate the changes in Brave Bird's testimony.

Arcoren also challenges the admission of Maicky's testimony on the ground that "the jury was in a better position than the government's expert to judge the credibility of Brave Bird." Maicky, however, expressed no opinion on whether Brave Bird suffered from battered woman syndrome or which of her conflicting statements were more credible. Maicky merely provided expert information to aid the jury in evaluating the evidence. Maicky's testimony did not interfere with or impinge upon the jury's role in determining the credibility of witnesses. . . .

The decision whether to admit expert testimony ordinarily lies within the discretion of the trial court and will not be reversed unless there has been an abuse of discretion. . . . In the unusual circumstances of this case, the district court did not abuse its discretion in admitting Maicky's expert testimony regarding battered woman syndrome.

NOTES AND QUESTIONS

1. Battered Woman Syndrome ("BWS"), a term first coined by Dr. Lenore Walker, has become part of the lexicon of modern culture as we have become more aware of the prevalence of battering. BWS is a three-phase cycle of violence, with tension-building, acute-battering, and loving-contrition phases. According to Dr. Walker, the cycle repeats and the victim develops a form of "learned helplessness." The woman lives in a state of constant fear, believing she cannot escape from her abuser. *See generally,* Lenore Walker, *The Battered Woman* (1979) and *The Battered Woman Syndrome* (1984). Dr. Walker is a highly regarded authority and frequent expert witness on the subject of battering. Although BWS is admitted in virtually every jurisdiction, the study has been criticized as poor quality and unsupportable science, beginning with David L. Faigman's oft-cited 1986 critique. *See* David L. Faigman, *The Battered Woman Syndrome and Self-Defense: A Legal and Empirical Dissent,* 72 Va. L. Rev. 619 (1986) (questioning the validity of BWS research and arguing against its admission at trial). For additional critique, *see* Erica Beecher-Monas, *Domestic Violence: Competing Conceptions of Equality in the Law of Evidence,* 47 Loy. L. Rev. 81 (2001); and Alafair Burke, *Rational Actors, Self-Defense, and Duress: Making Sense, Not Syndromes, Out of Battered Women,* 81 N.C. L. Rev. 211 (2002).

2. For alternative approaches to cases involving battered women, see Mary Ann Dutton, *Understanding Women's Responses to Domestic Violence: A Redefinition of Battered Woman Syndrome,* 21 Hofstra L.Rev. 1191 (1993) and Myrna S. Raeder, *The Better Way: The Role of Batterers' Profiles and Expert "Social Framework" Background in Cases Implicating Domestic Violence,* 68 U. Colo. L. Rev. 147 (1997).

3. Courts routinely allow expert testimony about battering when the defendant alleges self-defense and the facts permit such a claim. Many courts, however, have disallowed any expert testimony or historical evidence of battering when the defendant did not kill the abuser in a traditional self-defense posture. *See e.g.,* Commonwealth v. Grove, 526 A.2d 369 (Pa. Super. 1987); and Lane v. State, 957 S.W.2d 584 (Tex.

Crim. App. 1997). There is a great deal of commentary about this use of expert testimony on the subject of battering. *See e.g.*, Holly Maguigan, *Battered Women and Self-Defense: Myths and Misconceptions in Current Reform Proposals*, 140 U. Pa. L. Rev. 379 (1991); V.F. Nourse, *Self-Defense and Subjectivity*, 68 U. Chi. L. Rev. 1235 (2001); Joshua Dressler, *Battered Women Who Kill Their Sleeping Tormenters: Reflections on Maintaining Respect for Human Life while Killing Moral Monsters*, in *Criminal Law Theory: Doctrines of the General Part* 259, 261, 269 (Stephen Shute & A.P. Simester eds., 2002); Kimberly Kessler Ferzan, *Defending Imminence: From Battered Women to Iraq*, 46 Ariz. L. Rev. 213 (2004); and Jane Campbell Moriarty, *"While Dangers Gather": The Bush Preemption Doctrine, Battered Women, Imminence and Anticipatory Self-Defense*, 30 N.Y.U. Rev. of L. & Social Change 1 (2005).

4. Some federal courts have allowed expert evidence about battering to establish either a duress defense or a reduction in responsibility at sentencing. The seminal federal case on this issue is United States v. Johnson, 956 F.2d 894 (9th Cir. 1992), *op. supplemented on denial of rehearing by* United States v. Emelio, 969 F.2d 849 (9th Cir. 1992). Nonetheless, many courts have disallowed expert testimony on battering in cases involving duress. *See e.g.*, State v. Riker, 869 P.2d 43 (Wash. 1994); and State v. B.H., 870 A.2d 273 (N.J. 2005).

United States v. Romero

189 F.3d 576 (7th Cir. 1999)

Before RIPPLE, MANION, and EVANS, Circuit Judges.

TERENCE T. EVANS, Circuit Judge.

This case began in the spring of 1995, when 36-year-old Richard Romero "met" a 12-year-old boy in a "chat room" on the Internet devoted to UFOs and extraterrestrials. The case raises interesting questions about the permissible scope of expert opinion testimony in "child molester" cases.

The boy Romero met, who we'll call "Erich" in this opinion, lived in Mount Prospect, Illinois, a suburb of Chicago. Posing first as a 15-year-old boy, then as his 20-year-old brother, Romero exchanged e-mails and phone calls with Erich throughout 1995 and into 1996. Eventually, in March of 1996, Romero, who lived in St. Petersburg, Florida, at the time, convinced Erich to run away with him. The two boarded a bus in Chicago bound for St. Petersburg. Some quick investigative work by the local police and the FBI foiled the trip, as Romero and Erich were intercepted at the Greyhound bus station in Louisville, Kentucky. This activity led to four federal charges and two jury trials. . . . [A jury convicted Romero of the kidnapping and transportation charges.]

The first issue raised on this appeal is whether Judge Kocoras abused his discretion when he admitted the testimony of the prosecution's FBI expert on child molesters. Before trial, the government filed a notice of its intent to use the testimony of Agent Kenneth V. Lanning, who had spent many years studying the sexual exploitation of children and produced over 20 publications, to talk about the subject of child molestation. The prosecution proposed to have Agent Lanning testify regarding (1) characteristics of "preferential" child molesters and the methods they used to attract and abuse children; and (2) his opinion that Romero is a child molester with an interest in adolescent boys and that Romero had a sexual interest in Erich. Romero filed a motion in limine to exclude Agent Lanning's testimony, arguing that the expert could not offer his opinion about Romero's intent with respect to Erich under Federal Rule of Evidence 704(b) because it would involve the ultimate issue the jury was impaneled to decide. Romero also argued that Lanning's testimony would be unduly prejudicial under Rule 403 because it amounted to impermissible "profiling."

In response to the defense arguments, the government offered that it would limit Lanning's testimony to the methods and techniques employed by preferential child molesters. The prosecution would not ask Lanning to give his opinion about Romero or to comment about his intent or culpability. Subject to these limitations, Judge Kocoras allowed Agent Lanning to testify, noting that the testimony would be highly probative:

> [T]here was not any question really in my mind as to the propriety of his testimony as a general matter [in the first trial], highly relevant and, in fact, in my judgment, superior to, I think, someone who might offer some psychiatric testimony along the lines of characteristics and what people do and do not do given certain characteristics and impulses. Here is a man who studied the field extensively, an acknowledged expert in the field. And I do not think there is any question whatever that his testimony meets all the criteria of the 700 series, and is particularly helpful to the jury because he has had an abundance of training and experience far beyond any lay person, certainly, and far beyond, I think, most experts in the field.

Judge Kocoras thus denied the motion to exclude Lanning's "testimony in general." The judge, however, agreed with the defense concern that Lanning's testimony could possibly invade the province of the jury and usurp their function in determining whether Romero had the requisite criminal intent. For that reason, Judge Kocoras encouraged the defense to object to Lanning's testimony on a question-by-question basis if it seemed that he was going too far.

At trial . . . Lanning testified that his observations arose from his expertise about child molesters in general, not from the specific facts of the case. He then explained his role: "As I understand it, what I am going to do is provide or share the information that I have concerning the nature of certain types of offenders and provide this information to people who would not otherwise be aware and have this kind of knowledge because of their experiences and work."

Lanning then opined that child sex offenders fall on a spectrum from "situational sex offenders," whose activities are based on an accident of circumstance, to "preferential sex offenders," who have a definite preference for sexual contact with children and methodically pursue such contact. He identified four general traits usually exhibited by preferential sex offenders, all of which he had described in published materials long before the Romero case.

First, the conduct of a preferential child molester "is not a temporary, opportunistic kind of thing," but "occur[s] over a long period of time and is extremely persistent." These preferential molesters spend what to the normal person looks like unbelievable amounts of time and energy on their sexual pursuits. They may spend "a lot of time with kids, trying to lower their inhibitions, target them, find out where they are, how they can be maintained, contact with them, develop a method of access to those children." Such offenders can also spend enormous amounts of time on the Internet trying to meet children and develop seemingly innocent relationships with them, and it is not uncommon for an offender to be involved with several children at the same time.

Second, Lanning said that preferential sex offenders have very specific interests and that they focus on certain kinds of children. Sometimes this specificity — for example, "a preference for boys 10 to 15; for girls, 3 to 5, or something like that" — is caused by the offender's unusual arousal patterns. Sometimes the preference is more pragmatic. For example, some offenders "target children who come from dysfunctional families and broken homes" or who suffer from ADD because those children are easier to manipulate.

Third, Agent Lanning explained that preferential sex offenders typically "identify a need in a child and then move forward to temporarily fill that need in the child as part of this process." The offender might seduce the child by expressing an interest in the child's problems at home or a topic of specific interest to the child. He might also try to "mirror" the child's problems, telling the child he understands because he has the same problems. This technique is used to gain the child's trust and confidence so that the child feels the offender is someone who cares about him or her. The offender may also try to drive a wedge between the child and family members or other members of his or her support network to "maximize the child's dependence" on the offender.

Finally, Lanning testified that preferential offenders "engage in fantasy and need-driven behavior." They almost always collect child pornography, and they might also keep records of their encounters with children. They do these things compulsively even though they know their actions increase the risk that they will be caught. Agent Lanning did state, however, that "I am not getting carried away saying that anybody who has [child pornography] in their house" is an active child molester.

After extensive testimony regarding each of these four traits and examples of actions that fit these traits, Agent Lanning wrapped up his direct testimony by explaining again how the jury should use his testimony. He hoped it would help the jury get past popular conceptions of child sex offenders as "strangers who snatch and grab children" by "dragging them into a car," or as parents or stepparents who molest children in the home. He also said that "most people, unless they really focus on this or know somebody this happened to, don't really understand this kind of an offender who does not look like a dirty old man with a wrinkled raincoat" and that "people who are evaluating these facts need to have some kind of understanding or education in these kinds of offenders and how they operate." Lanning emphasized that the jury should look at all the facts and circumstances, not just a few isolated traits, to determine whether Romero intended to molest Erich.

During a vigorous cross-examination, the defense forced Agent Lanning to admit that there is often a large gap between someone who merely collects child pornography and someone who actually molests children. Lanning also admitted that a mere preferential collector of child pornography could exhibit the same "long-term and persistent pattern of behavior" in collecting as a preferential molester who acts out his fantasies. The main difference between the collector and the molester is that the molester would take the additional step of engaging or trying to engage in sexual behavior with children.

The redirect examination of Lanning focused on the question of how to distinguish between a mere collector and a child molester. The prosecution posed a series of hypothetical actions to Lanning and asked him if these actions would indicate someone who would act on his sexual fantasies about children. Not surprisingly, the hypotheticals described actions taken by Romero that had already been produced in evidence: establishing a 9-month relationship with a young (age 12 at the time it started) boy on the Internet; traveling hundreds of miles to meet a 13-year-old; meeting a young boy in a hotel room; spending long hours communicating with multiple young boys; and discussing a sexual interest in children with another adult. Lanning testified that each of these actions would be some indication that the offender in question would act upon his fantasies.

The admission of expert testimony in federal court is governed by the principles of *Daubert v. Merrell Dow Pharmaceuticals, Inc.,* 509 U.S. 579, 113 S.Ct. 2786, 125 L.Ed.2d 469 (1993). . . .

The defense claim that the district court erred in finding that Lanning's testimony in general would be reliable and helpful to the jury is baseless. The testimony was critical in dispelling from the jurors' minds the widely held stereotype of a child molester as "a dirty old man in a wrinkled raincoat" who snatches children off the street as they wait for the school bus. Many real-life child molesters use modern technology and sophisticated psychological techniques to "seduce" their victims.

This court has recognized the value of expert testimony in explaining a complicated criminal methodology that may look innocent on the surface but is not as innocent as it appears. Such modus operandi evidence has proved useful in drug trafficking cases. In the same way, the main thrust of Agent Lanning's testimony described the modus operandi of modern child molesters: devoting large amounts of time to finding and establishing relationships with children; choosing emotionally or mentally disturbed children because of their susceptibility to manipulation; probing the child's needs and interests and then mirroring those needs or attempting to fulfill them; and engaging in compulsive behavior even when that behavior increases the risk of getting caught. This testimony illuminated how seemingly innocent conduct such as Romero's extensive discussions with Erich about UFOs and his troubled home life could be part of a seduction technique. At least one other appellate court has considered expert testimony by Agent Lanning. *See United States v. Cross*, 928 F.2d 1030 (11th Cir.1991). In that case the defendant was in possession of nude photographs of children. He claimed that these photos were innocent "nude studies," and apparently the photos were open to such an interpretation. In describing the habits of pedophiles, Agent Lanning testified that such persons often derive sexual satisfaction from and collect such seemingly innocent materials. This testimony shed light on a critical issue in the case — whether the defendant obtained the photos with the intent to produce child pornography. The Eleventh Circuit held that Lanning's testimony was perfectly permissible for this purpose. See id. at 1050-51. Similarly, there is no question that allowing Agent Lanning to testify in our case was generally proper because his testimony was helpful to the jury in understanding how child molesters operate — something with which most jurors would have little experience.

The defense does raise a couple of legitimate concerns, however, about the scope of Agent Lanning's testimony. First, Romero argues that some of Lanning's testimony violated Federal Rule of Evidence 704(b) because he indirectly opined that Romero intended to molest Erich. The defense also argues that some of Agent Lanning's testimony constituted "group character evidence" in violation of Rule 404. One problem with both of these arguments is that throughout Lanning's long direct and redirect testimony the defense never objected to any question or answer. . . .

Federal Rule of Evidence 704(b) provides that

[n]o expert witness testifying with respect to the mental state or condition of a defendant in a criminal case may state an opinion or inference as to whether the defendant did or did not have the mental state or condition constituting

an element of the crime charged or of a defense thereto. Such ultimate issues are matters for the trier of fact alone.

The defense contends that Agent Lanning invaded the province of the jury when he responded to "hypotheticals" that mirrored the actual actions of Romero. He responded that in his expert opinion the actions described such as cultivating a long-term relationship with a juvenile and traveling hundreds of miles to meet that juvenile tend to indicate an offender who is going to "act out" or go beyond mere fantasy. According to the defense, this testimony is tantamount to Lanning opining that Romero had the intent to molest Erich when he transported him in interstate commerce.

To support its position, the defense relies on *United States v. Boyd*, 55 F.3d 667, 671 (D.C.Cir.1995). In *Boyd* the D.C. Circuit considered the testimony of an expert on drug trafficking who opined that the facts of the case (two men seen looking into a plastic bag that contained crack, then running and discarding the bag when the police approached) showed "possession with intent to distribute." The D.C. Circuit reasoned that Rule 704(b) creates a line that expert witnesses may not cross. Expert witnesses may not opine as to the criminal mental state of a defendant, and the prosecution may not make an end run around this rule by posing an "intent" question as a hypothetical.

In this circuit, however, we have taken a somewhat more lenient approach to this type of testimony. In *United States v. Brown*, 7 F.3d 648 (7th Cir.1993), we considered testimony very similar to that in *Boyd*. Again the defendant was in possession of crack, and the only issue in the case was whether he had the intent to distribute it. When asked what the circumstances of the case indicated to him, the expert responded over a defense objection, "[t]hat this crack cocaine was intended for distribution." *Brown* at 650. When asked why, he pointed to "the fact that there was no paraphernalia, no smoking device found on the individual, and the weapon that was found." *Id.* On appeal, the defense argued that the expert had crossed the Rule 704(b) line. We reasoned, however, that, viewed in context, the expert was "merely suggesting that . . . this crack probably would be distributed rather than used by" the defendant himself. *Id.* at 653. The expert was merely expounding on his earlier testimony that a mere user of crack would usually carry a pipe and would rarely carry such a large supply of crack at one time, whereas dealers usually carry weapons to protect their supply. Thus, the expert's testimony analyzed the facts supporting an inference that the defendant had the intent to distribute "without directly addressing [the defendant's] actual mental state." *Id.*

Agent Lanning does not even approach the Rule 704(b) line drawn in *Brown*. While his redirect testimony addressed some of Romero's actions served up in the form of hypotheticals, he never directly opined as to Romero's mental state when he crossed state lines with Erich in tow. And even if we were to accept the D.C. Circuit's formulation of the Rule 704(b) line, Agent Lanning's testimony does not cross it. The agent's testimony focused primarily on the modus operandi — on the actions normally taken by child molesters to find and seduce their victims. On redirect he explained for the jury what types of actions might distinguish the actual molester from the mere collector of child pornography. His testimony did not amount to a statement of his belief about what specifically was going through Romero's mind when he met Erich. Therefore, we conclude that Agent Lanning's testimony did not violate Rule 704(b) as analyzed in Boyd and Brown.

The second concern the defense raises regarding Lanning's testimony is whether it amounted to impermissible "group character evidence" under Rule 404(a): "Evidence of a person's character or a trait of character is not admissible for the purpose of proving action in conformity therewith on a particular occasion." According to the defense, Lanning described a profile of the character traits of preferential sex offenders who have a propensity to molest children. He opined through the prosecution's hypotheticals that Romero fit the profile. The prosecution therefore successfully presented evidence to the jury of a trait of Romero's character — his alleged propensity to molest children — in order to show that he acted in conformity with that trait. The bulk of Lanning's testimony, however, did not have anything to do with "character." As we have noted before, it is difficult to come up with a comprehensive definition of "character evidence," but in general, it is evidence that "refers to elements of one's disposition, such as honesty, temperance, or peacefulness" which show a propensity to act a certain way in a certain situation. *United States v. Doe*, 149 F.3d 634, 638 (7th Cir.1998) (quotations omitted). Although Agent Lanning used a profile of the four major "characteristics" of a preferential sex offender, he focused primarily on the behavior and actions of such offenders to explain their techniques or modus operandi. He described each of the four "traits" in terms of behavior: long-term persistent efforts to cultivate relationships with potential victims; targeting of children who have emotional or mental problems; efforts to identify a child's needs or interests in order to "mirror" them; and engaging in "need-driven" behaviors even though such actions might get them caught.

Presenting character evidence is an attempt to use a person's personality or psychological propensity to prove what the person did. Testimony that a defendant is hot-tempered might be used to prove that he threw the first punch in a fight. Agent Lanning's testimony did exactly the opposite. It was an attempt to use Romero's actions to prove his psychological propensities — his intentions for Erich. As such, it was not really character evidence at all. To the extent that Agent Lanning discussed the preferences and psychological proclivities of sex offenders, he did so only to elaborate on his behavior-driven analysis of their modus operandi.

We have stated before that we are generally "sympathetic to the core concern underlying the 'group character evidence' argument" — that the jury will conclude that the defendant is guilty based only on his membership in some nefarious group. *Doe* at 638. Rule 404, however, includes no reference to "group character evidence." The rule addresses the problem of the prosecution parading a defendant's acquaintances before the jury to make slanderous remarks, such as "He's a violent, hot-tempered man" or "She's a liar." Such remarks are inadmissible because they are often subjective and unreliable and because a criminal conviction should be based on a defendant's actions, not on his or her general character. Agent Lanning never remarked on Romero's character; he did not know Romero personally. Lanning's testimony was a careful explanation of techniques used generally by child molesters much like the expert testimony regarding techniques used in the drug trade in the cases we have cited. To the extent that Lanning discussed Romero specifically through the prosecution's hypotheticals, he addressed the defendant's actions and how those actions might be interpreted. Lanning's testimony was not evidence of Romero's character. There was no error in admitting it.

NOTES AND QUESTIONS

1. While syndrome evidence generally describes a constellation of behaviors in a victim, profile evidence focuses on the behavior of the accused. *See* Jane Campbell Moriarty, *Prosecutorial Syndrome and Profile Evidence in the Salem Witchcraft Trials*, 26 Vt. L. Rev. 43, 45 (2001) (defining syndrome and profile evidence). Several federal courts have allowed Special Agent Lanning to testify about child sexual abuse, although many courts have shown a great deal of reluctance to admit expert testimony on profiles — primarily because it is often a form of prohibited character evidence. *See e.g.*, Flanagan v. State, 625 So.2d 827 (Fla. 1993) (disallowing sex offender profile both because it fails *Frye*'s general acceptance standard and is impermissible character evidence); Commonwealth v. Day, 569 N.E.2d 397 (Mass. 1991) (reversible error to admit testimony of "child battering profile"). *See also*, Mark S. Brodin, *Behavioral Science in the Age of* Daubert: *Reflections of a Skeptic*, 73 U.Cin. L. Rev. 867, 882, n.66 (2005) ("profile evidence offered by the prosecution regarding the defendant (unlike syndrome evidence regarding the victim) is generally not admissible, as it is viewed as unreliable and runs afoul of the character evidence prohibition against painting the defendant as a particular 'criminal-type.'"). Does the testimony in *Arcoran* constitute syndrome or profile testimony?

2. Although *Daubert* requires that expert testimony be reliable, it also requires that it be relevant. *See* Daubert v. Merrell Dow Pharmaceuticals, Inc., 509 U.S. 579, 589 (1993). How does the expert evidence in *Romero* assist the jury to understand the facts or determine a fact in issue? Did the jury need to

hear the evidence to render a fair verdict? A primary use of framework testimony has been to defeat commonly held misperceptions juries may have to help them render a fair verdict — as FRE 702 provides — to "assist the trier of fact to understand the evidence. . . ." Many courts and legislatures allow framework evidence to be admissible for this purpose. *See e.g.,* Commonwealth v. Dillon, 598 A.2d 963, 969 (Pa. 1990) (Cappy, J., concurring) (discussing the need for expert testimony to counter the myths that battered women are masochistic and could leave their abusers if they wanted). *Accord,* State v. Koss, 551 N.E.2d 970 (1990). Ohio's Rules of Evidence recognize the admissibility of expert testimony "to dispel[] a misconception common among lay persons." Ohio R. Evid., Rule 702(A).

3. Should courts distinguish between profile and syndrome evidence? For an interesting discussion, see Myrna S. Raeder, *The Better Way: The Role of Batterers' Profiles and Expert "Social Framework" Background in Cases Implicating Domestic Violence,* 68 U. Colo. L. Rev. 147 (1997). For a thoughtful discussion of the subject of "group character evidence," see Robert P. Mosteller, *Syndromes and Politics in Criminal Trials and Evidence Law,* 46 Duke L.J. 461 (1996).

4. Was the court correct in its decision that the expert testimony did not constitute "group character evidence"?

5. The defendant in *Romero* alleged the government's expert testimony violated FRE 704(b). That rule, explained in Chapter 2, Expert Evidence: Rules and Cases, provides:

> (b) No expert witness testifying with respect to the mental state or condition of a defendant in a criminal case may state an opinion or inference as to whether the defendant did or did not have the mental state or condition constituting an element of the crime charged or of a defense thereto. Such ultimate issues are matters for the trier of fact alone.

Was the court's interpretation of this rule correct in *Romero?*

6. Were the experts in each *Chauvin* and *Romero* case sufficiently qualified? The expert in *Chauvin,* Ms. Ring, possessed a Bachelor's degree in psychology, a Master's degree in social work, and worked in the field of social work for several years. Is she sufficiently qualified to "diagnose" PTSD?

Mr. Lanning, the expert in *Romero,* is a special agent for the FBI with two Masters' degrees and many years of training. Is Lanning sufficiently qualified to give the opinions he does? Should his employment as a special agent give the court pause when deciding whether he is properly an expert?

Some argue only those with a medical license specializing in psychiatry or those with a Ph.D in psychology should testify about complicated issues of behavioral science. Often, however, courts are remarkably lenient about the qualifications of the experts in the areas of behavioral science, allowing social workers, rape counselors, and even police officers without advanced degrees to testify as expert witnesses about mental processes in rape and abuse cases. *See e.g.*, State v. Griffin, 564 N.W.2d 370, 374 (Iowa 1997) (permitting a social worker to testify about BWS primarily on the strength of her credentials and expertise); State v. Watson, 599 A.2d 385, 386-387 (Conn. App. Ct. 1991) (holding one year's experience counseling battered women after college sufficient to qualify witness as an expert on delay in reporting rape); State v. Hicks, 535 A.2d 776, 777 (1987) (holding witness with Master's degree in social work with five years' experience as a caseworker with sexually abused children qualified to testify that it is common for victims to delay reporting); People v. Turner, 608 N.E.2d 906, 912-913 (Ill. App. Ct. 1993) (permitting police officer with two years' experience working with sexually abused children to testify "it was normal" for abused children to initially deny the abuse); and People v. Gallegos, 644 P.2d 920, 927-928 (Colo. 1982) (permitting police officer to testify that victim's "nervous giggle" during her testimony was an emotional reaction to the stress of testifying and not indicative that she was taking the situation as a joke).

II. EXPERT TESTIMONY ABOUT INSANITY

Questions of sanity arise in criminal cases where the defendant alleges that as a result of his mental illness, he was unable to appreciate the wrongfulness of his otherwise criminal actions. The relationship between mental illness and criminal actions has not been harmonious and although expert testimony about sanity has been admitted in courts for hundreds of years, there has been controversy about such testimony for an equally long time.

Historically, a person insane at the time of the crime could not be found guilty of that crime. Even though a defendant may have intentionally shot a victim, he might be found "not guilty by reason of insanity" if the factfinder determined that the defendant was insane at the time of the killing and that such insanity prevented him from appreciating the wrongfulness of the conduct. Federal courts follow the so-called "*M'Naghten* standard" of insanity from English common law, which provided that "at the time of the committing of the act, the party accused was labouring under such a defect of reason, from disease of mind, as not to know the nature and quality of the act he was doing; or, if he did know it, that he did not know he was doing what was wrong." M'Naghten's Case, 8 Eng. Rep. 718, 722-723, 10 Clark & Fin. 200, 210 (1843).

In the mid-1980s, President Reagan was shot and seriously injured by John Hinckley. Under a less rigid standard than the *M'Naghten* test, the attacker was found not guilty by reason of insanity. This verdict sparked an outrage and Congress very quickly toughened the standard governing insanity, along with enacting various other changes. As part of the Insanity Defense Reform Act of 1986, Congress enacted the following statute, which considers insanity an affirmative defense that must be proved by clear and convincing evidence.[4]

The statute provides:

§ 17. *Insanity defense*

(a) Affirmative defense. — It is an affirmative defense to a prosecution under any Federal statute that, at the time of the commission of the acts constituting the offense, the defendant, as a result of a severe mental disease or defect, was unable to appreciate the nature and quality or the wrongfulness of his acts. Mental disease or defect does not otherwise constitute a defense.

Most states have also adopted this standard that focuses on the cognitive aspect of insanity — whether the defendant has the ability to appreciate the wrongfulness of the conduct. A small minority of states also focus on the defendant's volition, considering whether the defendant was able to "conform his conduct to the requirements of law." This test, the often-termed "irresistible impulse" test, is not allowed in federal courts or in most states.

To prove insanity, defendants call experts in the area of behavioral science to testify. In the following case, consider the role that expert testimony played in the jury's determination of whether the defendant was legally insane and how the court of appeals considered that determination.

State v. Perez

745 So. 2d 166 (La. Ct. App. 4th Cir. 1999), *writ denied,* **768 So. 2d 32 (La. 2000)**

Judge WILLIAM H. BYRNES, III, Judge CHARLES R. JONES, and Judge DENNIS R. BAGNERIS, Sr.

JONES, Judge.

Defendant Salvador Perez (Perez) appeals his conviction of first degree murder, and sentence of life imprisonment. Finding no error by the trial court, we affirm the judgment.

---

4. IDRA also amended FRE 704(b), to disallow an expert to opine whether a defendant "did or did not have the mental states or condition constituting an element of the crime charged or a defense thereto." The purpose of this evidence rule is to prevent behavioral science experts from testifying that a defendant could or could not appreciate the wrongfulness of his conduct. This subject is addressed in the previous case and in Chapter 2, Expert Evidence: Rules and Cases and in the preceding section.

PROCEDURAL HISTORY

Perez was charged by grand jury indictment on September 12, 1996, with first degree murder, [and] [f]ollowing a lunacy hearing on January 30, 1997, defendant was found competent to proceed. . . . Following trial before a twelve-person jury on March 11-14, 1998, he was found guilty as charged. . . . A notice of appeal was filed on the date of sentencing. . . .

FACTS

[Defendant and his son were in Louisiana when Defendant shot a police officer. The defense alleged that Perez was suffering from extreme paranoid psychosis and was hallucinating at the time of the shooting, thinking drug gangs were chasing and trying to kill him. When Perez shot the police officer, he thought (erroneously) that the police were part of the gang coming to kill him. Ample forensic and witness identification identified Perez as the person who shot and killed the officer.]

[THE EXPERT TESTIMONY]

Dr. Kenneth Ritter was qualified by stipulation as an expert in the field of forensic psychiatry. Dr. Ritter, . . . concluded that Perez was competent to proceed . . . [although] diagnosed Perez as a chronic paranoid schizophrenic, finding that he had all the signs and symptoms—delusions, hallucinations, and disorganized thinking. Dr. Ritter testified that it was his opinion that Perez did not understand the difference between right and wrong when he shot Officer Chris McCormick on July 17, 1996. He based his opinion on the fact that Perez had been under the delusion that people were out to kill him, and that he fled from his home in Seguin, Texas to avoid these people. Perez took evasive maneuvers such as sleeping in a Texas park rather than in a motel. He took country roads rather than regular highways. Perez's wife and son said Perez had been suffering from this delusional condition for at least two weeks prior to the murder.

There was information that Perez took his son because he felt that he could trust him, and that he did not trust his wife because he thought that she might be involved. Dr. Ritter testified that Perez was acting delusional when he grabbed his son when he was approached by the security guard at the Fair Grounds, indicating that he was afraid that the security guard would try to take his son. Dr. Ritter testified that when Perez became separated from his son later that day, he believed that someone had kidnapped his son, which could have reinforced his delusional thinking. However, Dr. Ritter did not believe that Perez was malingering.

On cross-examination, Dr. Ritter again testified that he only met with Perez once. Dr. Ritter said that at the time he examined Perez he was in "decent remission" and not having delusions, but did have some signs of disorganized thinking. . . .

Dr. Ritter admitted that he had not examined Perez in a delusional state, stating that Perez had been released from the Feliciana Forensic Facility after responding to medication, which, he said, was a classic situation seen in paranoid schizophrenia. Dr. Ritter admitted that he did not objectively corroborate anything, and that his conclusions were essentially based on the stories of his wife and Perez's adolescent son.

Dr. Raphael Salcedo was qualified by stipulation as a forensic psychologist. He first examined Perez on October 8, 1996. He testified Perez claimed he did not know his date of birth, leading the doctor to conclude that Perez was malingering. Dr. Salcedo was later informed by defense counsel that Perez was behaving oddly. Therefore, Dr. Salcedo evaluated defendant again on May 6, 1997. On this examination Perez was verbalizing and sounded psychotic. Perez said people from Texas were following him; and his thought processes seemed more disorganized. Dr. Salcedo testified at that time he started to have some doubts about the issue of malingering. He recommended that Perez be committed to the Feliciana Forensic Facility (the "FFF"). It was determined by the staff at FFF that Perez was extremely paranoid and had a serious mental illness, and that he was not competent to proceed. Dr. Salcedo testified Perez was treated with an anti-psychotic medication at the hospital. When he and Dr. Ritter examined Perez in December 1997, Perez was found to be displaying some psychotic symptoms, but they were in fairly good remission. Therefore, he and Dr. Ritter found Perez competent to proceed.

Dr. Salcedo testified he and Dr. Ritter then interviewed Perez's wife and thirteen year-old son in an effort to determine whether Perez was sane at the time of the offense. Dr. Salcedo's testimony in this regard generally tracked that of Dr. Ritter. He did add that Perez's wife related that Perez had no history of psychiatric problems or treatment. Dr. Salcedo testified he learned from some unknown source that Perez's father had displayed a similar pattern of late onset psychosis. Dr. Salcedo testified it is unusual for someone Perez's age to develop a psychotic disorder, that most are seen in people in their early to mid-twenties. Dr. Salcedo testified that it was not too difficult to detect malingerers; most people do not know the constellation of symptoms justifying a diagnosis of psychosis. He testified that, based on Perez's educational background and his work experience, he did not think Perez could develop such a classic response to the medication prescribed to him at the FFF — which takes time to begin working in the brain — and also to the onset of the symptoms. Dr. Salcedo testified that is was his opinion that Perez's condition had progressed during the trip to New Orleans and that, with the disappearance of his son, he was so actively psychotic that he was unable to distinguish right from wrong at the time of the offense, and in fact believed he was acting in self-defense. . . . On redirect examination, Dr. Salcedo testified that he did his doctoral dissertation on malingering, and said that it is one of the first things he feels the need to rule out in cases like Perez.

Dr. Jose Pena, qualified by stipulation as an expert in the field of clinical psychiatry, interviewed Perez in December 1997, while Perez was in the FFF, to determine Perez's competency to proceed. Dr. Pena interviewed Perez again on March 8, 1998, days before trial, as to Perez's mental state at the time of offense. It was Dr. Pena's opinion that Perez was suffering from a psychotic disturbance at the time of the offense. Dr. Pena based his determination on his interview with Perez, his wife and son, and for the same reasons as Drs. Ritter and Salcedo. . . . It was Dr. Pena's opinion that at the time Perez shot Officer McCormick he was not able to distinguish right from wrong because of the severe psychotic mental disturbance. . . .

Dr. Guillermo Urrutia, who was qualified by stipulation as an expert in clinical psychiatry, testified that it was his impression that Perez had a delusional disorder of a persecutory type, which, he testified, usually is a disorder that happens in middle or late middle life. Dr. Urrutia interviewed Perez nine months after the crime. He did not think Perez was malingering. Dr. Urrutia went into detail about the things Perez would say, and that he was uncooperative. Perez accused Dr. Urrutia of being an investigator, not a doctor, and said he would not talk to him until his wife got there. Perez said he was driving down I-10 and people were following him and he had to press buttons on the dashboard of the van to deceive them. Dr. Urrutia testified Perez was very confused on the subject of the shooting, which the doctor found consistent with someone who had been in a very panicked state. It was his opinion that Perez did know right from wrong when he shot Officer McCormick. He testified Perez was in a state of panic and was totally psychotic, insane. . . . However, Dr. Urrutia testified he could never pin Perez down to tell him exactly what happened because, the doctor felt, Perez did not remember. Dr. Urrutia admitted that Perez was not experiencing hallucinations.

Dr. David Carrington, who was qualified by stipulation as an expert in the field of forensic psychiatry, was a psychiatrist employed at the Feliciana Forensic Facility. After Perez was sent to the FFF on August 9, 1997, Dr. Carrington testified it was his job to evaluate him and, if possible, treat him and restore him to competency so that he could stand trial. . . . Dr. Carrington found Perez's thought processes quite disorganized. He had a great deal of difficulty relating past events, his history, and had "flight of ideas," jumping from one subject to another, which, Dr. Carrington testified, was not an uncommon finding in someone who has a significant degree of mental illness. Perez related that he previously had been hearing sounds of machinery and music. One week later, Perez's thinking continued to be disorganized, and he continued to hear music and machinery. Perez also said he could communicate with his wife; he could hear her voice in his head. . . . Dr. Carrington testified he did not believe Perez was malingering, something he testified they are acutely aware of at the FFF. Dr. Carrington increased the Haldol dosage after Perez had been at the FFF for three weeks, and as of the fourth week, Perez was free from any hallucinations or disorganization of his thinking. . . .

Dr. Sarah Deland, qualified by stipulation as an expert in the field of forensic psychiatry, testified that she was appointed by the court to a sanity commission along with Dr. Salcedo. It was her opinion that Perez had a significant mental illness, a psychotic disorder similar to schizophrenia. . . . Dr. Deland testified that in a forensic setting, malingering is always an issue to be considered, but that she did not believe Perez was malingering. She testified he presented a classic case of a person suffering delusions of being pursued, persecuted, and threatened. Dr. Deland also testified that the information she received from Perez's wife and son was consistent with the progression of the illness she saw in Perez, and testified they did not strike her as persons attempting to manufacture anything. She testified she did not believe Perez knew right from wrong on July 17, 1996 when he shot Officer Chris McCormick. . . .

Dr. Carlos Kromberger was qualified by stipulation as an expert in clinical psychology. Dr. Kromberger had been awarded a "diplomat" in clinical psychology, granted to approximately four percent of psychologists in the United States. Dr. Kromberger evaluated Perez during several interviews over a period of fourteen hours in April 1997. Dr. Kromberger testified that Perez had IQ scores within the mildly retarded range. However, he testified he saw indications that Perez could function at a higher level; he really had a little bit more understanding than what he was showing on the tests. He testified Perez cooperated but was guarded. Dr. Kromberger did not believe Perez was mentally retarded. Nevertheless, he diagnosed Perez to be suffering from a severe persecutory delusional disorder, although he did not find Perez to be schizophrenic. He testified Perez said he thought people were following him and he was afraid they were going to kill him. He initially thought his wife was in on the plot, and was worried that his son was going to get killed. He told his son that he wanted to go live in Florida, where they had lived until they were wiped out by Hurricane Andrew. Perez told Dr. Kromberger that he shot a dog, and that Perez believed the people approaching him were the ones that had taken away his son. "So he must have been in an acute state of anxiety or fear, very frightened. And when he fired off tragically killing a policeman, he probably didn't have any idea what was going on." Dr. Kromberger testified he did not think Perez knew right from wrong when he killed Officer McCormick. He thought Perez was in an acute psychotic state at the time. He testified he did not know whether or not Perez had a chance to see the officer, "but he certainly didn't know what he was doing." He did not think Perez was malingering.

By this assignment of error, Perez argues that the evidence was insufficient to find that he was able to distinguish between right and wrong at the time of the offense. . . . To be exempted of criminal responsibility [in Louisiana], defendant must show he suffered a mental disease or mental defect which prevented him from distinguishing between right and wrong with reference to the conduct in question. . . . The determination of sanity is a factual matter. All the evidence, including expert and lay testimony, along with the defendant's conduct and action, should be reserved for the fact finder to establish whether the defendant has proven by a preponderance of the evidence that he was insane at the time of the offense. . . . Lay testimony pertaining to defendant's actions, both before and after the crime, may provide the fact finder with a rational basis for rejecting unanimous medical opinion that the defendant was legally insane at the time of the offense. . . .

In reviewing a claim for insufficiency of evidence in an action where an affirmative defense of insanity is raised, this court, applying the standard set forth in *Jackson v. Virginia*, 443 U.S. 307, 99 S.Ct. 2781, 61 L.Ed.2d 560 (1979), must determine whether under the facts and circumstances of the case, any rational fact finder, viewing the evidence most favorable to the prosecution, could conclude, beyond a reasonable doubt, that the defendant failed to prove by a preponderance of the evidence that he was insane at the time of the offense. [Citations omitted.]

In the instant case, all five of the psychiatrists and the one psychologist who examined Perez for insanity at the time of the offense, all of whom testified for Perez, stated that he did not know the difference between right and wrong at the time of the offense.

However, two of those psychiatrists, Drs. Salcedo and Deland, initially diagnosed him on October 8, 1996, less than three months after the crime, as competent to proceed, finding him to be a malingerer because he kept answering that he did not remember when questioned about simple things, such as his date of birth. Dr. Salcedo said Perez had no mental disorder or defect which would render him incompetent to proceed. Dr. Deland wrote the court on February 24, 1997 to state that she and Dr. Salcedo had examined Perez a second time on January 30, 1997, after which she found that he had no symptoms of any mental illness which would affect his competency to proceed. Both doctors later changed their minds. Dr. Salcedo was contacted by defense attorneys who mentioned that Perez was acting oddly. Consequently, Dr. Salcedo said he examined Perez a second time, on May 6, 1997 — almost ten months after the crime — at which time Perez was verbalizing and had classic symptoms of psychosis. Dr. Salcedo recommended that Perez be committed to the FFF at that time. Nevertheless, in his report from that May 1997 examination Dr. Salcedo still wrote that Perez "presented as previously; i.e., as an individual who is at the very least grossly exaggerating any psychopathology which might actually be present." Dr. Salcedo testified at trial, however, that he did not believe Perez had been malingering. Dr. Deland also examined Perez a second time, presumably on May 2, 1997, the date of her second report. She changed her mind because, by that second examination, after spending ten months in parish prison, Perez exhibited signs of psychosis.

Both Drs. Salcedo and Deland believed that Perez did not know right from wrong based on what they learned from him, his wife and son.

Dr. Ritter stated that he only examined Perez on one occasion, December 18, 1997 — exactly one year and five months after the crime — to determine whether he was competent to proceed. Just as Drs. Salcedo and Deland had found on October 6, 1996 (and, apparently, January 30, 1997), Dr. Ritter found on December 18, 1997 that Perez was competent to proceed, stating that he believed Perez was in a remission on that date. However, on February 3, 1998, Drs. Ritter and Salcedo wrote the court a letter, stating that they had examined Perez for both competency to proceed and sanity at the time of the offense, and both found that, although he was competent to proceed, he did not know right from wrong at the time of the offense. Not coincidentally, February 3, 1998 was the date Dr. Ritter, and presumably Dr. Salcedo also, met with Perez's wife and son. Dr. Ritter found that Perez did not know right from wrong based on what he also learned from Perez, his wife and son.

Dr. Jose Pena interviewed Perez in December 1997 to determine his competency to proceed, and interviewed him again on March 8, 1998, days before trial, for the specific question of Perez's mental state at the time of offense. Dr. Pena also interviewed Perez's wife and son via telephone on March 8, 1998. He also reached his conclusion that Perez did not know right from wrong at the time of the offense based on information given to him by Perez, his wife and son.

Dr. Guillermo Urrutia examined Perez in April 1997, nine months after the crime. In his detailed report Dr. Urrutia recounts the supposedly delusional beliefs of Perez, as told to him by Perez. Dr. Urrutia also interviewed Perez's wife and son, and also concluded that Perez could not tell the difference between right and wrong.

Dr. Carlos Kromberger, the only psychologist to testify, examined Perez in April 1997. He found that Perez suffered from a severe persecutory delusional disorder, and that Perez did not have any idea what was going on when he shot the police officer, or knew the difference between right and wrong.

Dr. Carrington, a psychiatrist at the Feliciana Forensic Facility when Perez was sent there on August 9, 1997, did not examine Perez until that date, over one year after the crime. He gave no opinion as to whether or not Perez was capable of distinguishing right from wrong at the time he shot and killed Officer McCormick. However, he found Perez's thinking to be quite disorganized, consistent with a serious mental illness, and said Perez had hallucinations — he heard music and machinery. Perez's disorganized thinking and hallucinations completely disappeared after four weeks on antipsychotic medication. Dr. Carrington did not believe Perez was malingering, a problem of which he said he was acutely aware. But he admitted that

Perez's thirteen months of incarceration before being moved to the FFF could have contributed to the condition Perez was in upon arrival. . . .

All of the physicians who testified that Perez did not know right from wrong based their opinions, in significant part, on information obtained from Perez's wife and son concerning his behavior prior to the shooting of Officer McCormick.

It is undisputed that Perez's fears stemmed from his belief that persons involved in the drug trade were pursuing him and posed a threat to him and his son. However, his son testified that Perez and his wife both believed that friends of Perez's step-grandfather were involved in drug activity. Perez's son further testified that he believed that his father had spurned a request by these persons to become involved in their drug activities. His son testified both parents believed that Perez had thereby made the "drug buyers" mad, and that Perez consequently believed these people were after him. This is a rational explanation for Perez's paranoid behavior — he was fearful because he had spurned drug dealers and they were after him. His fear for his and his son's safety may well have been justified. As for any possible belief by Perez that his wife may have been involved, there is no evidence that he could not have temporarily had a justifiable suspicion of his wife. The medical experts all inferred that Perez's fears were delusional and not based in reality, as illustrated by Dr. Pena when he testified: "[W]hat we have here is a picture in which the symptoms began what appears to be one or two weeks before the incident at a time when there was no reason for the person to begin to act disturbed before anything happened." These assumptions that Perez's fears were not based in reality unquestionably formed the basis for the opinions of the medical experts that Perez did not know the difference between right and wrong at the time he shot Officer McCormick. Where those fears were based in reality, as the record indicates they may well have been, then the opinions of those physicians is called into question. Perez's possible very real fears essentially explain his supposed delusional thinking and paranoid behavior.

All of Perez's actions traveling to New Orleans were consistent with a man fleeing rebuffed drug dealers. . . .

It is true that, in addition to the supposed delusional thinking, the medical experts found disorganized thinking in Perez, which was consistent with some type of psychosis or serious mental illness. This finding too factored heavily in the experts' opinions that Perez did not know right from wrong at the time of the offense. However, all of the findings of disorganized thinking were made following examinations conducted long after — at least nine months — the shooting of Officer McCormick. Charity Hospital records from the night of the shooting note Perez as being oriented, responsive, and obeying commands. Dr. Carrington admitted that Perez's condition at the time he first examined him at the FFF in August 1997 could have been attributed in some part to his thirteen months of incarceration in Orleans Parish Prison. Two of the physicians, Drs. Ritter and Pena, did not even examine Perez until he had been taking anti-psychotic medication and was no longer experiencing either the supposed delusions or any disorganized thinking. This delay from the time of the offense to noting the disorganized thinking undermines the credibility of the medical experts insofar as their opinions that Perez was insane at the time offense.

On another point, it is important to note that, while anti-psychotic medication first prescribed to Perez at the FFF apparently remedied the disorganized thinking, allowing him to proceed to trial, there was no testimony by any of the medical experts that the now competent Perez and his wife no longer believed that friends of Perez's step-father had been involved with drugs; that defendant had spurned offers by these persons to become involved in the drug trade; or that he had consequently been afraid of harm to him and his son. These factors had been the basis of Perez's fears. These first two factors were facts as stated by Perez's wife and son, not delusions, and the resulting fear on the part of Perez may very well have been justified.

Also, Dr. Ritter stated that Perez's son said that while driving on the highway his father was pressing buttons in the van, thinking that for some "magical reason" this would throw off his pursuers. The son said his father told him he did that in hopes that anyone pursuing him would think he was doing something. Perez was obviously attempting to outwit any pursuers, perhaps making them think that he saw them, by pushing buttons the son said were in an upper console, near the rear view mirror. Perez did not think he would throw off his pursuers for some "magical reason," as stated by Dr. Ritter. Yet, Dr. Ritter based his opinion that Perez was incapable of distinguishing right from wrong, in part, on this nonexistent "magical reason" action by Perez. This undermines Dr. Ritter's credibility. The jury could have considered the opinions of Drs. Deland and Salcedo as undermined because they found Perez free from any mental disease or defect after examining him less than three months after the crime; ten months after the crime found him incompetent to proceed; and then, within a month or so of trial, determined that he had been insane at the time of the offense and unable to distinguish right from wrong.

In conclusion, even assuming Perez was not malingering, the opinions of the medical experts are undermined by their obvious belief that he was suffering from delusions of persecution — crucial to their determinations that he did know the difference between right and wrong at the time of the offense — when the record supports the view that he may very well have been justified in his fears. Their opinions are also undermined by the fact that all of their observations of disorganized thinking in Perez, also crucial to their opinions and diagnoses, were made long after the shooting of Officer McCormick, during which time his condition could have worsened. The opinions of Drs. Ritter, Deland and Salcedo could be viewed as also undermined for the aforementioned reasons.

When reviewing evidence for sufficiency, a reviewing court is not called upon to decide whether it believes the witnesses. . . . The determination of credibility is a question of fact within the sound discretion of the trier of fact, and that determination will not be disturbed unless clearly contrary to the evidence. . . .

Considering the facts and circumstances of the instant case, it cannot be said that it would have been clearly contrary to the evidence for the jury to reject the credibility of the medical experts insofar as those experts stated that Perez was incapable of distinguishing right from wrong at the time he shot Officer McCormick. Thus, viewing all of the evidence in a light most favorable to the prosecution, any rational trier of fact could have found that Perez failed to prove by a preponderance of the evidence that he was incapable of distinguishing between right and wrong at the time he shot Officer McCormick.

NOTES AND QUESTIONS

1. Was the court of appeals correct in its decision to reject the unanimous testimony of the mental health experts that the defendant was suffering from paranoid psychosis at the time of the incident and did not appreciate the wrongfulness of his conduct? Would the court have been as willing to dismiss the opinion of several physicians who agreed upon a diagnosis of physical impairment? What accounts for such a difference?

2. In this case, the government did not introduce any expert evidence to rebut the defendant's claim of insanity. In fact, three of the experts were appointed by the court to evaluate Perez. According to reports of the case, the prosecutor in his closing argument said he was not going to waste time talking about the medical testimony. "Doctors, doctors, doctors," he said, according to reporters. *See* Pamela Coyle, *Texas Man Is Guilty of Cop's Murder*, 3/14/98 New Orleans Times Picayune, 1998 WLNR 1161818. Should the defendant be entitled to a directed verdict of not guilty by reason of insanity if the prosecution does not introduce expert testimony to rebut the findings of the defense experts? Why or why not?

3. In the *Perez* case, the court stated that "[l]ay testimony pertaining to defendant's actions, both before and after the crime, may provide the fact finder with a rational basis for rejecting unanimous medical opinion that the defendant was legally insane at the time of the offense. . . ." Other courts agree, permitting factfinders to reject expert testimony in insanity cases in favor of lay witness testimony concerning insanity or competency. *See e.g.*, Garner v. State, 704 N.E.2d 1011, 1014 (Ind. 1998) ("The determination of insanity is a question for the trier of fact, who may elect to credit the testimony of lay witnesses over that of medical experts."); and State v. Gilbert, 951 P.2d 98, 104 (Okla. Crim. App. 1997) ("The determination of whether a

sufficient doubt has been raised regarding a defendant's competency is left to the trial judge. . . . [who] is not required to give controlling effect to the opinions of experts, but may rely on the opinion of lay witnesses and the court's own observations of the defendant.").

4.   The insanity defense, nearly universally disliked by the public, is rarely invoked and almost never successful, contrary to commonly held beliefs. According to Professor Michael L. Perlin, a prolific scholar on the intersection of mental health and law, the insanity defense is used in only about 1 percent of all felony cases and is successful only about 25 percent of the time. *See* Michael L. Perlin, *The Jurisprudence of the Insanity Defense*, 108 (1994) (discussing statistics). Perlin states that insanity defense is shrouded in inaccurate myths:

> It is taken as "common wisdom" that the insanity defense is an abused, over-pleaded and over-accepted "loophole" used . . . to thwart the death penalty; that most . . . are not truly mentally ill; that most acquittals follow sharply-contested "battles of the experts"; that most successful pleaders are sent for short stays to civil hospitals. [E]ach of these myths . . . has been . . . empirically disproved; yet they remain powerful, and show no sign of abating.

Id. at 229-230.

5.   Professor Christopher Slobogin, a well-known commentator on the subject of behavioral science and the law, provides an in-depth explanation about the problem behavioral science has in meeting the *Daubert* standard of reliability. *See Doubts About* Daubert: *Psychiatric Anecdota as a Case Study*, 57 Wash. & Lee L. Rev. 919 (2000). Nonetheless, Professor Slobogin argues compellingly about the legal and policy reasons that favor admission of such evidence, particularly when it concerns the defendant's past mental state. A critical reason to allow expert evidence about insanity and incompetency, Slobogin argues, is that despite its shortcomings, such expert testimony can help juries decide whether a person suffers from a severe mental illness and, if so, to understand to some degree the defendant's thought process. *Id.* at 932-938. For further thoughtful commentary, also see Christopher Slobogin, *Psychiatric Evidence in Criminal Trials: To Junk or Not to Junk?*, 40 Wm. & Mary L. Rev. 1 (1998); and Christopher Slobogin, *The Admissibility of Behavioral Science Information in Criminal Trials: From Primitivism to* Daubert *to* Voice, 5 Psychol. Pub. Pol'y & L. 100 (1999).

6.   The Supreme Court has commented both on the reliability problem of behavioral science and the need for such evidence in questions of legal insanity:

> Psychiatry is not, however, an exact science, and psychiatrists disagree widely and frequently on what constitutes mental illness, on the appropriate diagnosis to be attached to given behavior and symptoms, on cure and treatment, and

on likelihood of future dangerousness. Perhaps because there often is no single, accurate psychiatric conclusion on legal insanity in a given case, juries remain the primary factfinders on this issue, and they must resolve differences in opinion within the psychiatric profession on the basis of the evidence offered by each party. When jurors make this determination about issues that inevitably are complex and foreign, the testimony of psychiatrists can be crucial and "a virtual necessity if an insanity plea is to have any chance of success." By organizing a defendant's mental history, examination results and behavior, and other information, interpreting it in light of their expertise, and then laying out their investigative and analytic process to the jury, the psychiatrists for each party enable the jury to make its most accurate determination of the truth on the issue before them.

Ake v. Oklahoma, 470 U.S. 68, 81 (1985).

7. In Ake v. Oklahoma, 470 U.S. 68, 83 (1985), the United States Supreme Court held that "when a defendant demonstrates to the trial judge that his sanity at the time of the offense is to be a significant factor at trial, the State must, at a minimum, assure the defendant access to a competent psychiatrist who will conduct an appropriate examination and assist in evaluation, preparation, and presentation of the defense." Should the right to expert assistance apply beyond the question of insanity? *Ake* and its implications are considered in Chapter 11, Final Considerations: Ethics, Discovery, Procedure.

8. Many people who are mentally ill are now sentenced to jail, rather than institutions, when they commit crimes. Thus, many of those currently in prisons are mentally ill — according to current statistics, nearly 550,000 of those serving time are mentally ill. For an in-depth look at this problem, see the PBS *Frontline* program, which can be accessed at the following website:

> *http://www.pbs.org/wgbh/pages/frontline/shows/asylums/etc/synopsis.html*

III. EXPERT TESTIMONY ABOUT MENTAL COMPETENCE

Expert testimony about mental health is often admitted to assist a court in determining whether a defendant is competent to stand trial, waive rights, or be executed. The Supreme Court of the United States has held that placing an individual on trial who is mentally incompetent violates the defendant's due process of law. Pate v. Robinson, 383 U.S. 375, 378 (1966); and Cooper v. Oklahoma, 517 U.S. 348, 354 (1996). So too, execution of an insane person violates the Eighth Amendment of the Constitution. Ford v. Wainwright, 477 U.S. 399-410 (1986).

In many cases raising issues of competency, courts consider far more than just the testimony of the expert witnesses. In the following case, consider how the court weighed the testimony of the experts against other factual testimony it received in determining the competency of the defendant, a reputed Genovese crime family member.

United States v. Gigante

987 F. Supp. 143 (E. D. N.Y., 1996)

MEMORANDUM AND ORDER

NICKERSON, District Judge:

Defendant Vincent Gigante and others are charged in an indictment dated May 30, 1990 with committing crimes of labor payoffs, extortions, and mail frauds. A second indictment dated June 10, 1993 alleges that Gigante and others murdered six persons between July 10, 1980 and March 15, 1982, engaged in conspiracies to murder three other persons between June 1982 and 1991, and committed further crimes of labor payoffs and extortion.

Gigante's attorneys moved pursuant to 18 U.S.C. § 4241 for a hearing to determine his mental and physical competency to stand trial.

I

On June 13, 1990, Judge Raymond J. Dearie ordered psychiatric examinations of Gigante pursuant to 18 U.S.C. § 4241(b). On June 20, 1990 he appointed two psychiatrists, Dr. Jonas R. Rappeport and Dr. Daniel W. Schwartz, to conduct psychiatric examinations and report. Thereafter, Gigante was examined by those two doctors and by Dr. Abraham L. Halpern and Dr. Stanley Portnow, two psychiatrists selected by his attorneys.

After examining Gigante and reviewing his medical records, all four psychiatrists made reports and testified that Gigante was not competent to stand trial because he was unable to understand the proceedings against him or to assist in his defense. In reaching this conclusion, the psychiatrists took into account Gigante's behavior and demeanor during their sessions with him and also the hospital reports made from 1969 on by Gigante's treating psychiatrists. In *United States v. Gigante*, 925 F.Supp. 967 (E.D.N.Y.1996) ("*Gigante I*") . . . the court set forth the substance of these reports and of the doctors' accounts of their meetings with Gigante. The examining doctors' diagnoses of incompetence were qualified. All four testified that new information could lead them to change their opinions. Before the hearings both Dr. Schwartz and Dr. Rappeport were asked whether their opinions would change if they were presented with clear and convincing evidence that Gigante had either (1) actively conducted the affairs of the Genovese Family during the time he says he was mentally ill, or (2) planned well in advance of their diagnoses a feigned insanity defense. Dr. Rappeport wrote on March 10, 1991 that such evidence might change his opinion. Dr. Schwartz wrote on March 8, 1991 that such evidence would lead him to conclude that Gigante was malingering and was fit to proceed.

After the psychiatrists testified the court heard testimony from former high ranking Members of organized crime and other witnesses. They gave evidence of Gigante's criminal activities during the years from the 1970s through 1991, evidence that had never been presented to the four examining doctors.

In *Gigante I* the court made various findings of fact . . . based on the evidence presented by these witnesses. The court found that Gigante "occupied high positions in the Genovese Family from at least the early 1970s until September of 1991 and as such performed executive functions." For example, Gigante took an active part in high level meetings and managed the internal organization and external affairs of the Genovese Family. The court also found that during this period Gigante took extreme measures — including a "crazy act" in which he feigned insanity — to conceal his illegal activities.*

Gigante took other unusual steps to avoid apprehension. Concerned about electronic surveillance, he insisted that none of his criminal associates use his name.

The court submitted the Findings to the four psychiatrists, directed them to accept them as true, and asked each to testify as to what extent, if any, the Findings altered their prior assessment of Gigante's competency to stand trial.

---

*[EDS.] In *Gigante I*, 925 F.Supp. 967, 970-971 (E.D. N.Y. 1996), the court noted that the defendant engaged in the following behaviors:

> From 1969 through 1990 Gigante went about once a year to St. Vincent's Hospital in Westchester County (the Hospital) for psychiatric treatment, which his fellow Genovese Family Members Venero "Benny Eggs" Mangano and Dominic "Baldy Dom" Canterino described as a "tune-up." The reports show that Gigante gave the doctors the impression that he was an incompetent, frightened, isolated man, cared for by his elderly mother, and living in a tenement building in lower Manhattan.
>
> Hospital visits were not the only means by which Gigante gave an appearance of incompetency to the outside world. He appeared disheveled on the streets, unshaven and in an old bathrobe and pajamas. He would mumble and babble to himself, and even urinate in the street. On one occasion in the early 1980s when he observed a law enforcement official he walked across the street, knelt down on the sidewalk outside a church, and appeared to pray before a statue. His "crazy act" was common knowledge among those in organized crime.
>
> Gigante took other unusual steps to avoid apprehension. Concerned about electronic surveillance, he insisted that none of his criminal associates use his name. The Genovese associates were instructed in no uncertain terms that they were never to mention Gigante's name. They thus took to referring to him as "that guy" or touched their chin, "Chin" being a nick-name for Gigante. Gigante even sent word to Joseph Gorgone, a Member of the Colombo Family, who had been captured on tape saying Gigante's name, that if Gigante was indicted as a result he would kill Gorgone. After a Member of the Genovese Family learned that Joe Fiore, an associate in the Lucchese Family, had mentioned Gigante's name in a gambling machine transaction, three men from the Genovese Family administered a beating to Fiore.

On May 28, 1996, Dr. Rappeport testified that the Findings "make me think that it is quite possible that [Gigante] is competent to stand trial and that much or all of his mental illness has been malingered." During cross-examination by Gigante's attorney, Dr. Rappeport also said that it is his opinion "to a medical degree of certainty" that Gigante is malingering.

On July 10, 1996, Dr. Schwartz testified that the Findings "convince me that [Gigante] is fit to proceed."

Dr. Halpern testified on May 28, 1996 and July 10, 1996. On May 28, 1996, he stated that the Findings had not changed his opinion that Gigante was incompetent to stand trial. On July 10, 1996, Dr. Halpern reiterated his opinion that Gigante is "incompetent to stand trial." At this time, Dr. Halpern also stated that he could not accept the finding that Gigante was competent and malingering in 1991. He felt that accepting this finding would require him to accept that Gigante is presently competent and malingering, a point that he was unwilling to concede.

On August 22, 1996, Dr. Portnow testified that after reading and accepting the Findings he concluded that in 1991 Gigante "was competent to stand trial." Dr. Portnow said that he believes to a reasonable degree of medical certainty that Gigante has been incompetent to stand trial since 1995. Before reading the findings, Dr. Portnow had attributed Gigante's incompetency to the combined effects of schizo-affective disorder and organic brain disease, but he now believes that Gigante suffers only from organic brain disease, which he said has become more serious since 1995.

Dr. Portnow said that he examined Gigante at his home on April 16, 1996 and at Saint Vincent's Hospital in Westchester (the "Hospital") on August 4 and 6, 1996. During these examinations, Gigante displayed impaired cognition and short-term memory, fabricated stories to hide gaps in his memory, fixated on and repeated certain words, and behaved in a "childlike" manner. Dr. Portnow said that Gigante previously had displayed these symptoms, but that on these three occasions the symptoms appeared generally "much more prominent." It was unclear to the court just how someone incapable of functioning in any area of life, as Dr. Portnow and others had previously described Gigante's condition over the years, could have deteriorated still further. . . .

II

A criminal defendant is mentally competent to stand trial if he has (1) "a sufficient present ability to consult with his lawyer with a reasonable degree of rational understanding" and (2) "a rational as well as a factual understanding of the proceedings against him." The Court of Appeals for the Second Circuit has stated that "some degree of mental illness cannot be equated with incompetence to stand trial." *United States v. Vamos*, 797 F.2d

1146, 1150 (2d Cir.1986), *cert. denied*, 479 U.S. 1036, 107 S.Ct. 888, 93 L.Ed.2d 841 (1987).

Under 18 U.S.C. §4241(d), the court determines competency by a preponderance of the evidence. Although that section does not in terms allocate the burden of proof, the Supreme Court in referring to it has stated in dicta that "the accused in a federal prosecution must prove incompetence by a preponderance of the evidence." *Cooper v. Oklahoma*, 517 U.S. 348, 362, 116 S.Ct. 1373, 1380, 134 L.Ed.2d 498 (1996). . . .

In determining Gigante's mental competency to stand trial, the court considers "a number of factors, including medical opinion." [Citation omitted.]

MEDICAL OPINION

After reading the Findings, Dr. Schwartz testified unequivocally that Gigante is "fit to proceed." Dr. Rappeport testified that he believed that Gigante is malingering and that it is "quite possible" that he is competent to stand trial.

Although Dr. Halpern did not change his original diagnosis of incompetency, the court found his testimony unconvincing. Dr. Halpern made clear during direct and cross-examination that he was unable or unwilling to accept the court's instruction that he was to accept the Findings as true.

The court also does not credit Dr. Portnow's testimony that Gigante is presently incompetent to stand trial. In discussing the factors that led him to conclude that Gigante's condition has deteriorated since 1991, and particularly precipitously since 1995, Dr. Portnow described symptoms substantially identical to those displayed by Gigante since 1970.

Although Dr. Portnow said that the symptoms were more pronounced, other examining psychiatrists agreed that Gigante showed no signs of deterioration. Dr. Halpern testified on May 28, 1996 that he had examined Gigante on the previous evening and found him "essentially the same as he had been on previous occasions." On May 28, 1996, Dr. Rappeport testified that he examined Gigante in 1991 and 1995 and found "no great progression or remission of the symptomatic picture between" those years. Dr. Rappeport also said that Gigante's medical records suggested that since the early 1970s his "symptomatic picture perhaps changed a little, but very little."

Dr. Portnow also emphasized that a SPEC Scan of Gigante's brain and various psychological tests suggested organic brain disease. But Dr. Rappeport did not believe that these results required him to find Gigante incompetent. Indeed, he conceded that Gigante had an "abnormal" SPEC scan, but said his brain damage was not "severe" or "extreme" and "would not say that the brain damage would account for any incompetency."

Based on the foregoing, the court finds the weight of medical opinion to show that Gigante is mentally competent to stand trial.

GIGANTE'S PERSISTENT MALINGERING

The court described in the Findings Gigante's extensive efforts through September of 1991 to hide his criminal activities and to evade prosecution by presenting himself as crazy. The record reveals that in addition to these measures Gigante also sought over the years to mislead his doctors by inventing a false medical history and by concealing from them the true nature of his daily existence.

On April 17, 1959, Judge Bicks of the United States District Court for the Southern District of New York sentenced Gigante to seven years imprisonment for conspiracy to violate the narcotics laws of the United States. The record shows that before Gigante was released from prison in 1964, he never mentioned any history of mental or psychiatric illness.

On March 3, 1960, Gigante stated in a detailed "Report of Medical History" that he had never suffered from "depression or excessive worry," "loss of memory or amnesia," or "frequent or terrifying nightmares." He also said that he had never been a patient in a mental hospital or sanatorium and that he had been rejected for military service in 1952 because of a "bad heart."

On March 6, 1960, Gigante's mother, Yolanda Gigante, filled out a form providing information about his family, childhood, and education. She described Gigante as a "normal," "healthy," and "happy" child. She mentioned a speech impediment and heart murmur, but did not refer to any childhood depression or phobias. She did not say that he had ever been knocked out or suffered severe head injuries as a boxer, or that he had been injured in a car accident.

A classification study dated March 24, 1960 discusses Gigante's childhood, but does not mention depression, phobias, or other psychological problems. This study includes a physical examination and correlated history prepared by Dr. Leon A. Witkin and dated March 15, 1960. The section of this report entitled "Past Medical History" does not allude to any psychiatric problems.

During his incarceration, in the years 1960-1964, Gigante complained of many physical ailments and received regular medical treatment, but never mentioned psychiatric problems or displayed any symptoms of them. The many pages of the prison physicians' reports on Gigante contain no mention of mental illness.

The accounts of Gigante's supervisors in prison do not suggest that he was under any mental disability. On June 23, 1961, E.F. McConnell, Gigante's supervisor at the prison power station, wrote a glowing recommendation for meritorious good time. He described Gigante as a "very good maintenance man" who "can be depended on to complete assigned duties without supervision and to the best of his ability." McConnell said that Gigante tried to learn the jobs of other inmates so that he could fill in for them. On May 29,

1963 M. Musky, the operating engineer of the prison power plant, wrote that Gigante volunteered for difficult and dangerous jobs, including emergency work on top of a boiler. This work exposed him to extreme heat and took place without safety equipment at a height of thirty-five feet. Musky also said that Gigante frequently performed tasks beyond those expected of an inmate.

A Special Progress Report prepared by the Bureau of Prisons and dated February 7, 1964 mentions Gigante's "very good" job performance, his "neat and orderly" personal habits, and his status as a "well known leader of the young, more aggressive Italian American inmates." It also describes Gigante's medical and psychiatric history, noting an I.Q. of 101, a history of pneumatic heart diseases, and abdominal complaints of various sorts. It mentions no psychiatric problems and closes with the observation that "the medical staff found no special abnormalities and it is considered that he is experiencing good health at the present time."

In short, the record shows that Gigante had never displayed any symptoms of mental illness before his release from Lewisburg Penitentiary in 1964. Up to that time, the medical histories provided by Gigante and his family did not mention any psychiatric problems.

The record shows that in 1969 Gigante was indicted in New Jersey Superior Court, Bergen County, on charges of bribery and conspiracy to obstruct justice. The indictment alleged that beginning in 1967 Gigante attempted to bribe members of the New Jersey police force to provide him with information about ongoing investigations and surveillances of him. The record also reveals that Gigante sought psychiatric treatment from Dr. Michael Scolaro in October of 1966, at about the time that he learned of the police investigation.

In 1970 and 1971 Judge Morris Malech of the New Jersey Superior Court, Bergen County, conducted hearings to determine Gigante's competency to stand trial on the bribery charges. Dr. Henry Davidson, Dr. Joseph Zigarelli, and Dr. George Cassidy examined Gigante in connection with this proceeding.

The record shows that Gigante displayed the same symptoms described in the Findings and that he and his family gave Dr. Scolaro and the examining psychiatrists a revised account of his childhood and medical history. Gigante's wife and mother reported that as a child he suffered from "severe temper tantrums, phobia for the dark, truancy at school, obesity, and learning problems" and that at the age of sixteen he was deferred from the army for "psychiatric causes."

Dr. Scolaro was told that Gigante had suffered "psychiatric disturbances since childhood." Dr. Scolaro and Dr. Davidson were both told that Gigante "had been under psychiatric care in childhood" and that these psychiatric issues had figured in his deferral from the military.

Medical reports also show that Gigante and his family concealed from his physicians the true nature of his day-to-day existence. All of Gigante's physicians were aware of his wife and five children living in New Jersey, but apparently none heard of his relationship with Olympia Esposito or the children that it produced.

On the basis of Gigante's behavior and the medical history that he and his family then described, the examining psychiatrists reported in 1971 that Gigante was incompetent to stand trial. On June 11, 1971, Judge Malech found Gigante incompetent because the doctors deemed him "insane" and there were "no other factual proofs presented by other witnesses" so he "could come to no other conclusion."

The record shows that after this competency hearing Gigante and his family continued to misrepresent to his doctors the nature of his life and the extent of his activities. In a letter dated January 4, 1973 to Queens County District Attorney Lombardino, Gigante's treating psychiatrist, Dr. Hugh McHugh, described him as leading a "very narrow existence" with "his entire world being confined to the block where he lives and the church he attends regularly with his mother." Dr. McHugh's 1977 admission note also refers to Gigante's "narrow life in Greenwich Village." In a discharge note dated March 24, 1982, Dr. McHugh referred to Gigante's "narrow sphere of living at home, going to church and going to a small cafe across the street and play [sic] pinball which was his life."

A social work record dated May 7, 1984 shows that Gigante and his family informed the hospital staff that Gigante "functions marginally at home and is cared for by his family."

As the scrutiny of Gigante's condition has increased over the years, he and his family have continued to revise his medical history by adding previously undisclosed incidents of brain trauma. In 1971, Gigante's mother told Dr. Davidson that although he had been a boxer during adolescence, he had never been knocked out. At the same time, Dr. Scolaro said "there never had been any evidence of his having been punch drunk." But in 1991 Gigante's family told Dr. Portnow and Dr. Rolland S. Parker that during his boxing career he suffered numerous injuries to the head and face, including two severe head butts that caused hemorrhaging and swelling. Gigante's family also mentioned, apparently for the first time, that during his childhood he was struck by cars on two occasions. In one of these accidents, when Gigante was eight years old, he was allegedly knocked unconscious.

The behavior described in the Findings and Gigante's dealings with his doctors convince the court that Gigante deliberately feigned mental illness from the late 1960s until at least September of 1991. As he has presented no convincing reason for the court to conclude otherwise, the court finds that the symptoms that Gigante has demonstrated since that time are also the product of his malingering.

Gigante's attorneys say that even if he was competent to stand trial in September 1991, his condition has so deteriorated that he can no longer understand the proceedings or assist in his own defense. In support of this argument, they offer the testimony of Gigante's dentist, Dr. Rubin, and his chiropractor, Dr. Pressman, who said that they observed a steady deterioration in Gigante's condition.

Without objective medical evidence that Gigante suffered some new illness after 1991, the court can only conclude that the symptoms of deterioration observed by Dr. Portnow, Dr. Rubin, and Dr. Pressman are the result of malingering. As Gigante has feigned illness for over twenty years, the reasonable inference from the appearance of any exaggerated symptoms after 1991 is not that his condition has deteriorated, but rather that the imminent threat of prosecution has increased his incentive to malinger. . . .

[The court then holds that Gigante is competent to stand trial.]

NOTES AND QUESTIONS

1. How important was the testimony of the experts in this case to the court's decision finding the defendant sufficiently competent to stand trial?

2. All four psychiatrists testified that they had found the defendant incompetent to stand trial, since they concluded he was unable to understand the proceedings against him or to assist in his defense. Their conclusions were based upon his behavior, demeanor, and hospital reports from 1969 through 1990. However, all four physicians admitted that "new information" could lead them to change their opinions. Indeed, after learning of the factual evidence of Gigante's organized crime involvement, the government's physicians opined that Gigante was competent to stand trial. In light of their willingness to change their opinion based on facts about the defendant—as opposed to further medical testing or psychiatric evaluation—how certain does psychiatry seem as a science?

3. Most defendants who claim to be incompetent to be tried usually involve severe mental illness, such as schizophrenia. In some cases, courts have found that the defendant's mental retardation is sufficiently severe to render him unable to understand the proceedings and assist his counsel. *See e.g.*, United States v. Hoskie, 950 F.2d 1388 (9th Cir. 1991) (finding that the trial court erred in finding the defendant competent where there was evidence that he had an I.Q. of 62; did not understand abstractions like guilt, innocence, or rights; and never progressed beyond a second- or third-grade level. "[h]e was unable to remember his son's name, his age at the time of his father's death, or what grade he completed in school.")

4. Mental retardation has become an important determination in many death penalty cases since the court decided Atkins v. Virginia, 536 U.S. 304, 321 (2002). In that case, the court held that execution of mentally retarded criminals was unconstitutional in light of "evolving standards of

decency." Determinations of mental retardation have become hotly contested in penalty hearings in capital cases since *Atkins.*

5. In the penalty phase of capital trials, defendants may introduce psychiatric or neurological evidence that might not otherwise be admissible during the guilt phase of a trial because such evidence does not meet the standard required for insanity.

6. One newer kind of expert testimony is the use of various forms of neuroimaging, which purport to show brain injury or disease. The defendant in *Gigante* attempted unsuccessfully to use neuroimaging to prove his incompetence. *See* United States v. Gigante, 982 F.Supp. 140, 147-148 (E.D.N.Y. 1997). For cases allowing neuroimaging in penalty phase hearings, see State v. Reid, 213 S.W.2d 792 (Tenn. 2006) and State v. Hoskins, 735 So.2d 1281 (Fla. 1999).

IV. PREDICTIONS OF FUTURE DANGEROUSNESS

Barefoot v. Estelle

463 U.S. 880 (1983)

Justice WHITE delivered the opinion of the Court.

On November 14, 1978, petitioner was convicted of the capital murder of a police officer in Bell County, Texas. A separate sentencing hearing before the same jury was then held to determine whether the death penalty should be imposed. [T]wo special questions were to be submitted to the jury: whether the conduct causing death was "committed deliberately and with reasonable expectation that the death of the deceased or another would result"; and whether "there is a probability that the defendant would commit criminal acts of violence that would constitute a continuing threat to society." The State introduced into evidence petitioner's prior convictions and his reputation for lawlessness. The State also called two psychiatrists, John Holbrook and James Grigson, who, in response to hypothetical questions, testified that petitioner would probably commit further acts of violence and represent a continuing threat to society. The jury answered both of the questions put to them in the affirmative, a result which required the imposition of the death penalty.

On appeal to the Texas Court of Criminal Appeals, petitioner urged, among other submissions, that the use of psychiatrists at the punishment hearing to make predictions about petitioner's future conduct was unconstitutional because psychiatrists, individually and as a class, are not competent to predict future dangerousness. Hence, their predictions are so likely to produce erroneous sentences that their use violated the Eighth and Fourteenth Amendments. It was also urged, in any event, that permitting answers to hypothetical questions by psychiatrists who had not personally examined petitioner was constitutional error. The court rejected all of these contentions and affirmed the conviction and sentence. . . .

III

Petitioner's merits submission is that his death sentence must be set aside because the Constitution of the United States barred the testimony of the two psychiatrists who testified against him at the punishment hearing. There are several aspects to this claim. First, it is urged that psychiatrists, individually and as a group, are incompetent to predict with an acceptable degree of reliability that a particular criminal will commit other crimes in the future and so represent a danger to the community. Second, it is said that in any event, psychiatrists should not be permitted to testify about future dangerousness in response to hypothetical questions and without having examined the defendant personally. Third, it is argued that in the particular circumstances of this case, the testimony of the psychiatrists was so unreliable that the sentence should be set aside. As indicated below, we reject each of these arguments.

A.

The suggestion that no psychiatrist's testimony may be presented with respect to a defendant's future dangerousness is somewhat like asking us to disinvent the wheel. In the first place, it is contrary to our cases. If the likelihood of a defendant committing further crimes is a constitutionally acceptable criterion for imposing the death penalty, which it is, *Jurek v. Texas*, 428 U.S. 262, 96 S.Ct. 2950, 49 L.Ed.2d 929 (1976), and if it is not impossible for even a lay person sensibly to arrive at that conclusion, it makes little sense, if any, to submit that psychiatrists, out of the entire universe of persons who might have an opinion on the issue, would know so little about the subject that they should not be permitted to testify. In *Jurek*, seven Justices rejected the claim that it was impossible to predict future behavior and that dangerousness was therefore an invalid consideration in imposing the death penalty. Justice STEVENS responded directly to the argument:

"It is, of course, not easy to predict future behavior. The fact that such a determination is difficult, however, does not mean that it cannot be made. Indeed, prediction of future criminal conduct is an essential element in many of the decisions rendered throughout our criminal justice system. The decision whether to admit a defendant to bail, for instance, must often turn on a judge's prediction of the defendant's future conduct. Any sentencing authority must predict a convicted person's probable future conduct when it engages in the process of determining what punishment to impose. For those sentenced to prison, these same predictions must be made by parole authorities. The task that a Texas jury must perform in answering the statutory question in issue is thus basically no different from the task performed count-less times each day throughout the American system of criminal justice. What is essential is that the jury have before it all possible relevant information about the individual defendant whose fate it must determine. Texas law clearly assures that all such evidence will be adduced."

Although there was only lay testimony with respect to dangerousness in *Jurek*, there was no suggestion by the Court that the testimony of doctors would be inadmissible. To the contrary, the Court said that the jury should be presented with all of the relevant information. Furthermore, in *Estelle v. Smith*, 451 U.S. 454, 473, 101 S.Ct. 1866, 1878, 68 L.Ed.2d 359 (1981), in the face of a submission very similar to that presented in this case with respect to psychiatric testimony, we approvingly repeated the above quotation from *Jurek* and went on to say that we were in "no sense disapproving the use of psychiatric testimony bearing on future dangerousness." . . .

Acceptance of petitioner's position that expert testimony about future dangerousness is far too unreliable to be admissible would immediately call into question those other contexts in which predictions of future behavior are constantly made. For example, in *O'Connor v. Donaldson*, 422 U.S. 563, 576, 95 S.Ct. 2486, 2494, 45 L.Ed.2d 396 (1975), we held that a non-danger-ous mental hospital patient could not be held in confinement against his will. Later, speaking about the requirements for civil commitments, we said: "There may be factual issues in a commitment proceeding, but the factual aspects represent only the beginning of the inquiry. Whether the individual is mentally ill and dangerous to either himself or others and is in need of confined therapy turns on the meaning of the facts which must be inter-preted by expert psychiatrists and psychologists." *Addington v. Texas*, 441 U.S. 418, 429, 99 S.Ct. 1804, 1811, 60 L.Ed.2d 323 (1979).

In the second place, the rules of evidence generally extant at the federal and state levels anticipate that relevant, unprivileged evidence should be admitted and its weight left to the fact finder, who would have the benefit of cross examination and contrary evidence by the opposing party. Psychi-atric testimony predicting dangerousness may be countered not only as erro-neous in a particular case but as generally so unreliable that it should be ignored. If the jury may make up its mind about future dangerousness unaided by psychiatric testimony, jurors should not be barred from hearing the views of the State's psychiatrists along with opposing views of the defen-dant's doctors.[5]

Third, petitioner's view mirrors the position expressed in the amicus brief of the American Psychiatric Association (APA). As indicated above,

___

5. In this case, no evidence was offered by petitioner at trial to contradict the testimony of Doctors Holbrook and Grigson. Nor is there a contention that, despite petitioner's claim of indigence, the court refused to provide an expert for petitioner. In cases of indigency, Texas law provides for the payment of $500 for "expenses incurred for purposes of investigation and expert testimony." Tex.Code Crim.Proc.Ann. art. 26.05, § 1(d) (Supp.1982).

however, the same view was presented and rejected in *Estelle v. Smith*. We are no more convinced now that the view of the APA should be converted into a constitutional rule barring an entire category of expert testimony.[6]

We are not persuaded that such testimony is almost entirely unreliable and that the factfinder and the adversary system will not be competent to uncover, recognize, and take due account of its shortcomings.

The amicus does not suggest that there are not other views held By members of the Association or of the profession generally. Indeed, as this case and others indicate, there are those doctors who are quite willing to testify at the sentencing hearing, who think, and will say, that they know what they are talking about, and who expressly disagree with the Association's point of view.[7]

6. The federal cases cited by the dissent as rejecting "scientific proof," . . . at n. 9, are not constitutional decisions, but decisions of federal evidence law. The question before us is whether the Constitution forbids exposing the jury or judge in a state criminal trial to the opinions of psychiatrists about an issue that Justice BLACKMUN's dissent concedes the factfinders themselves are constitutionally competent to decide.

7. At trial, Dr. Holbrook testified without contradiction that a psychiatrist could predict the future dangerousness of an individual, if given enough background information about the individual. Tr. Trial (T. Tr.) 2072-2073. Dr. Grigson obviously held a similar view. See T. Tr. 2110, 2134. At the District Court hearing on the habeas petition, the State called two expert witnesses, Dr. George Parker, a psychologist, and Dr. Richard Koons, a psychiatrist. Both of these doctors agreed that accurate predictions of future dangerousness can be made if enough information is provided; furthermore, they both deemed it highly likely that an individual fitting the characteristics of the one in the Barefoot hypothetical would commit future acts of violence. Tr. of Hearing (H. Tr.) 183-248.

Although Barefoot did not present any expert testimony at his trial, at the habeas hearing he called Dr. Fred Fason, a psychiatrist, and Dr. Wendell Dickerson, a psychologist. Dr. Fason did not dwell on the general ability of mental health professionals to predict future dangerousness. Instead, for the most part, he merely criticized the giving of a diagnosis based upon a hypothetical question, without an actual examination. He conceded that, if a medical student described a patient in the terms of the Barefoot hypothetical, his "highest order of suspicion," to the degree of 90%, would be that the patient had a sociopathic personality. H. Tr. 22. He insisted, however, that this was only an "initial impression," and that no doctor should give a firm "diagnosis" without a full examination and testing. H. Tr. 22, 29-30, 36. Dr. Dickerson, petitioner's other expert, was the only person to testify who suggested that no reliable psychiatric predictions of dangerousness could ever be made.

We are aware that many mental health professionals have questioned the usefulness of psychiatric predictions of future dangerousness in light of studies indicating that such predictions are often inaccurate. For example, at the habeas hearing, Dr. Dickerson, one of petitioner's expert witnesses, testified that psychiatric predictions of future dangerousness were wrong two out of three times. H. Tr. 97, 108. He conceded, however, that, despite the high error rate, one "excellently done" study had shown "some predictive validity for predicting violence." H. Tr. 96-97. Dr. John Monahan, upon whom one of the State's experts relied as "the leading thinker on this issue," H. Tr. 195, concluded that "the 'best' clinical research currently in existence indicates that *psychiatrists and psychologists are accurate in no more than one out of three predictions of violent behavior over a several-year period among institutionalized populations that had both committed violence in the past . . . and who were diagnosed as mentally ill*." Monahan, The Clinical Prediction of Violent Behavior 47-49 (1981) (emphasis in original). However, although Dr. Monahan originally believed that it was impossible to predict violent behavior, by the time he had completed his monograph, he felt that "there may be circumstances in which prediction is both empirically possible and

Furthermore, their qualifications as experts are regularly accepted by the courts. If they are so obviously wrong and should be discredited, there should be no insuperable problem in doing so by calling members of the Association who are of that view and who confidently assert that opinion in their amicus brief. Neither petitioner nor the Association suggests that psychiatrists are always wrong with respect to future dangerousness, only most of the time. Yet the submission is that this category of testimony should be excised entirely from all trials. We are unconvinced, however, at least as of now, that the adversary process cannot be trusted to sort out the reliable from the unreliable evidence and opinion about future dangerousness, particularly when the convicted felon has the opportunity to present his own side of the case.

We are unaware of and have been cited to no case, federal or state, that has adopted the categorical views of the Association.[8]

Certainly it was presented and rejected at every stage of the present proceeding. . . .

The judgment of the District Court is Affirmed.

[The concurring opinion of Justice Stevens and the Dissenting Opinion of Justice Marshall are not included.]

Justice BLACKMUN, with whom Justice BRENNAN and Justice MARSHALL join in Parts I-IV, dissenting.

. . . I, too, dissent, but I base my conclusion also on evidentiary factors that the Court rejects with some emphasis. The Court holds that psychiatric testimony about a defendant's future dangerousness is admissible, despite the fact that such testimony is wrong two times out of three. The Court reaches this result — even in a capital case — because, it is said, the testimony is subject to cross-examination and impeachment. In the present state of

---

ethically appropriate," and he hoped that his work would improve the appropriateness and accuracy of clinical predictions. *Id.*, at v.

All of these professional doubts about the usefulness of psychiatric predictions can be called to the attention of the jury. Petitioner's entire argument, as well as that of Justice BLACKMUN's dissent, is founded on the premise that a jury will not be able to separate the wheat from the chaff. We do not share in this low evaluation of the adversary process.

8. Petitioner relies on *People v. Murtishaw*, 29 Cal.3d 733, 175 Cal.Rptr. 738, 631 P.2d 446. There the California Supreme Court held that in light of the general unreliability of such testimony, admitting medical testimony concerning future dangerousness was error in the context of a sentencing proceeding under the California capital punishment statutes. The court observed that "the testimony of [the psychiatrist was] not relevant to any of the listed factors" which the jury was to consider in deciding whether to impose the death penalty. 631 P.2d, at 469. The court distinguished cases, however, where "the trier of fact is required by statute to determine whether a person is 'dangerous,'" in which event "expert testimony, unreliable though it may be, is often the only evidence available to assist the trier of fact." Ibid. Furthermore, the court acknowledged "that despite the recognized general unreliability of predictions concerning future violence, it may be possible for a party in a particular case to show that a reliable prediction is possible. . . . A reliable prediction might also be conceivable if the defendant had exhibited a long-continued pattern of criminal violence such that any knowledgeable psychiatrist would anticipate future violence." Ibid. Finally, we note that the court did not in any way indicate that its holding was based on constitutional grounds.

psychiatric knowledge, this is too much for me. One may accept this in a routine lawsuit for money damages, but when a person's life is at stake — no matter how heinous his offense — a requirement of greater reliability should prevail. In a capital case, the specious testimony of a psychiatrist, colored in the eyes of an impressionable jury by the inevitable untouchability of a medical specialist's words, equates with death itself.

I

[T]he prosecution called Doctors Holbrook and Grigson, whose testimony extended over more than half the hearing. Neither had examined Barefoot or requested the opportunity to examine him. In the presence of the jury, and over defense counsel's objection, each was qualified as an expert psychiatrist witness. Doctor Holbrook detailed at length his training and experience as a psychiatrist, which included a position as chief of psychiatric services at the Texas Department of Corrections. He explained that he had previously performed many "criminal evaluations," and that he subsequently took the post at the Department of Corrections to observe the subjects of these evaluations so that he could "be certain those opinions that [he] had were accurate at the time of trial and pretrial." He then informed the jury that it was "within [his] capacity as a doctor of psychiatry to predict the future dangerousness of an individual within a reasonable medical certainty," and that he could give "an expert medical opinion that would be within reasonable psychiatric certainty as to whether or not that individual would be dangerous to the degree that there would be a probability that that person would commit criminal acts of violence in the future that would constitute a continuing threat to society."

Doctor Grigson also detailed his training and medical experience, which, he said, included examination of "between thirty and forty thousand individuals," including eight thousand charged with felonies, and at least three hundred charged with murder. He testified that with enough information he would be able to "give a medical opinion within reasonable psychiatric certainty as to [the] psychological or psychiatric makeup of an individual," . . . and that this skill was "particular to the field of psychiatr[y] and not to the average layman." . . .

Each psychiatrist then was given an extended hypothetical question asking him to assume as true about Barefoot the four prior convictions for nonviolent offenses, the bad reputation for being law abiding in various communities, the New Mexico escape, the events surrounding the murder for which he was on trial and, in Doctor Grigson's case, the New Mexico arrest. On the basis of the hypothetical question, Doctor Holbrook diagnosed Barefoot "within a reasonable psychiatr[ic] certainty," as a "criminal sociopath." He testified that he knew of no treatment that could change this condition, and that the condition would not change for the better but "may

become accelerated" in the next few years. Finally, Doctor Holbrook testified that, "within reasonable psychiatric certainty," there was "a probability
that the Thomas A. Barefoot in that hypothetical will commit criminal acts of
violence in the future that would constitute a continuing threat to society,"
and that his opinion would not change if the "society" at issue was that
within Texas prisons rather than society outside prison.

Doctor Grigson then testified that, on the basis of the hypothetical
question, he could diagnose Barefoot "within reasonable psychiatric certainty" as an individual with "a fairly classical, typical, sociopathic personality
disorder." He placed Barefoot in the "most severe category" of sociopaths
(on a scale of one to ten, Barefoot was "above ten"), and stated that there
was no known cure for the condition. Finally, Doctor Grigson testified that
whether Barefoot was in society at large or in a prison society there was a
"one hundred percent and absolute" chance that Barefoot would commit
future acts of criminal violence that would constitute a continuing threat to
society. Id., at 2131.

On cross-examination, defense counsel questioned the psychiatrists
about studies demonstrating that psychiatrists' predictions of future dangerousness are inherently unreliable. Doctor Holbrook indicated his familiarity
with many of these studies but stated that he disagreed with their conclusions. Doctor Grigson stated that he was not familiar with most of these
studies, and that their conclusions were accepted by only a "small minority
group" of psychiatrists — "[i]t's not the American Psychiatric Association
that believes that."

After an hour of deliberation, the jury answered "yes" to the two statutory questions, and Thomas Barefoot was sentenced to death.

II

A

The American Psychiatric Association (APA), participating in this case
as *amicus curiae*, informs us that "[t]he unreliability of psychiatric predictions
of long-term future dangerousness is by now an established fact within the
profession." Brief for American Psychiatric Association, as *Amicus Curiae*, 12
(APA Brief). The APA's best estimate is that two out of three predictions of
long-term future violence made by psychiatrists are wrong. The Court does
not dispute this proposition, see ante, at 18-19, n. 7, and indeed it could not
do so; the evidence is overwhelming. For example, the APA's Draft Report of
the Task Force on the Role of Psychiatry in the Sentencing Process (Draft
Report) states that "[c]onsiderable evidence has been accumulated by now
to demonstrate that long-term prediction by psychiatrists of future violence
is an extremely inaccurate process." Draft Report 29. John Monahan, recognized as "the leading thinker on this issue" even by the State's expert
witness at Barefoot's federal habeas corpus hearing, concludes that "the

'best' clinical research currently in existence indicates that psychiatrists and psychologists are accurate in no more than one out of three predictions of violent behavior," even among populations of individuals who are mentally ill and have committed violence in the past. J. Monahan, The Clinical Prediction of Violent Behavior 47-49 (1981) (emphasis deleted) (J. Monahan, Clinical Prediction); see also id., at 6-7, 44-50. Another study has found it impossible to identify any subclass of offenders "whose members have a greater-than-even chance of engaging again in an assaultive act." Wenk, Robison & Smith, Can Violence Be Predicted?, 18 Crime & Delinquency 393, 394 (1972). Yet another commentator observes that "[i]n general, mental health professionals . . . are more likely to be wrong than right when they predict legally relevant behavior. When predicting violence, dangerousness, and suicide, they are far more likely to be wrong than right." Morse, Crazy Behavior, Morals, and Science: An Analysis of Mental Health Law, 51 S.Cal.L.Rev. 527, 600 (1978) (Morse, Analysis of Mental Health Law). Neither the Court nor the State of Texas has cited a single reputable scientific source contradicting the unanimous conclusion of professionals in this field that psychiatric predictions of long-term future violence are wrong more often than they are right.

The APA also concludes, see APA Brief 9-16, as do researchers that have studied the issue, that psychiatrists simply have no expertise in predicting long-term future dangerousness. A layman with access to relevant statistics can do at least as well and possibly better; psychiatric training is not relevant to the factors that validly can be employed to make such predictions, and psychiatrists consistently err on the side of overpredicting violence. Thus, while Doctors Grigson and Holbrook were presented by the State and by self-proclamation as experts at predicting future dangerousness, the scientific literature makes crystal clear that they had no expertise whatever. Despite their claims that they were able to predict Barefoot's future behavior "within reasonable psychiatric certainty," or to a "one hundred percent and absolute" certainty, there was in fact no more than a one in three chance that they were correct.

Indeed, unreliable scientific evidence is widely acknowledged to be prejudicial. The reasons for this are manifest. "The major danger of scientific evidence is its potential to mislead the jury; an aura of scientific infallibility may shroud the evidence and thus lead the jury to accept it without critical scrutiny." Giannelli, The Admissibility of Novel Scientific Evidence: *Frye v. United States*, a Half-Century Later, 80 Colum.L.Rev. 1197, 1237 (1980) (Giannelli, Scientific Evidence).[8]

---

8. There can be no dispute about this obvious proposition:

"Scientific evidence impresses lay jurors. They tend to assume it is more accurate and objective than lay testimony. A juror who thinks of scientific evidence visualizes instruments capable of amazingly precise measurement, of findings arrived at by dispassionate scientific tests. In short,

Where the public holds an exaggerated opinion of the accuracy of scientific testimony, the prejudice is likely to be indelible. . . . There is little question that psychiatrists are perceived by the public as having a special expertise to predict dangerousness, a perception based on psychiatrists' study of mental disease. [Citations omitted.] It is this perception that the State in Barefoot's case sought to exploit. Yet mental disease is not correlated with violence, see J. Monahan, Clinical Prediction, at 77-82. . . . and the stark fact is that no such expertise exists. Moreover, psychiatrists, it is said, sometimes attempt to perpetuate this illusion of expertise, . . . and Doctors Grigson and Holbrook—who purported to be able to predict future dangerousness "within reasonable psychiatric certainty," or absolutely—present extremely disturbing examples of this tendency. The problem is not uncommon. . . .

Psychiatric predictions of future dangerousness are not accurate; wrong two times out of three, their probative value, and therefore any possible contribution they might make to the ascertainment of truth, is virtually nonexistent. . . . Indeed, given a psychiatrist's prediction that an individual will be dangerous, it is more likely than not that the defendant will not commit further violence. It is difficult to understand how the admission of such predictions can be justified as advancing the search for truth, particularly in light of their clearly prejudicial effect.

Thus, the Court's remarkable observation that "[n]either petitioner nor the [APA] suggests that psychiatrists are *always wrong* with respect to

---

in the mind of the typical lay juror, a scientific witness has a special aura of credibility." Imwinkelried, Evidence Law and Tactics for the Proponents of Scientific Evidence, in Scientific and Expert Evidence 33, 37 (Imwinkelried ed. 1981). See 22 C. Wright & K. Graham, Federal Practice and Procedure § 5217, at 295 (1978) "Scientific evidence impresses lay jurors. They tend to assume it is more accurate and objective than lay testimony. A juror who thinks of scientific evidence visualizes instruments capable of amazingly precise measurement, of findings arrived at by dispassionate scientific tests. In short, in the mind of the typical lay juror, a scientific witness has a special aura of credibility." Imwinkelried, Evidence Law and Tactics for the Proponents of Scientific Evidence, in Scientific and Expert Evidence 33, 37 (Imwinkelried ed. 1981). See 22 C. Wright & K. Graham, Federal Practice and Procedure § 5217, at 295 (1978) ("[s]cientific . . . evidence has great potential for misleading the jury. The low probative worth can often be concealed in the jargon of some expert. . . ."). This danger created by use of scientific evidence frequently has been recognized by the courts. Speaking specifically of psychiatric predictions of future dangerousness similar to those at issue, one district court has observed that when such a prediction "is proffered by a witness bearing the title of 'Doctor,' its impact on the jury is much greater than if it were not masquerading as something it is not." *White v. Estelle*, 554 F.Supp. 851, 858 (SD Tex.1982). See Note—*People v. Murtishaw*: Applying the *Frye* Test to Psychiatric Predictions of Dangerousness in Capital Cases, 70 Calif.L.Rev. 1069, 1076-1077 (1982). In *United States v. Addison*, 162 U.S.App.D.C. 199, 202, 498 F.2d 741, 744 (1974), the court observed that scientific evidence may "assume a posture of mystic infallibility in the eyes of a jury of laymen." Another court has noted that scientific evidence "is likely to be shrouded with an aura of near infallibility, akin to the ancient oracle of Delphi." *United States v. Alexander*, 526 F.2d 161, 168 (CA8 1975). See *United States v. Amaral*, 488 F.2d 1148, 1152 (CA9 1973); *United States v. Wilson*, 361 F.Supp. 510, 513 (Md.1973); *People v. King*, 266 Cal.App.2d 437, 461, 72 Cal.Rptr. 478, 493 (1968).

future dangerousness, *only most of the time*," *ante*, at 3398 (emphasis supplied), misses the point completely, and its claim that this testimony was no more problematic than "other relevant evidence against any defendant in a criminal case," *ante*, at 3400, is simply incredible. Surely, this Court's commitment to ensuring that death sentences are imposed reliably and reasonably requires that nonprobative and highly prejudicial testimony on the ultimate question of life or death be excluded from a capital sentencing hearing.

III

A

Despite its recognition that the testimony at issue was probably wrong and certainly prejudicial, the Court holds this testimony admissible because the Court is "unconvinced ... that the adversary process cannot be trusted to sort out the reliable from the unreliable evidence and opinion about future dangerousness.". . . . One can only wonder how juries are to separate valid from invalid expert opinions when the "experts" themselves are so obviously unable to do so. Indeed, the evidence suggests that juries are not effective at assessing the validity of scientific evidence. . . .

There can be no question that psychiatric predictions of future violence will have an undue effect on the ultimate verdict. Even judges tend to accept psychiatrists' recommendations about a defendant's dangerousness with little regard for cross-examination or other testimony. . . . There is every reason to believe that inexperienced jurors will be still less capable of "separat[ing] the wheat from the chaff," despite the Court's blithe assumption to the contrary, . . . The American Bar Association has warned repeatedly that sentencing juries are particularly incapable of dealing with information relating to "the likelihood that the defendant will commit other crimes," and similar predictive judgments. American Bar Association Project on Standards for Criminal Justice, Sentencing Alternatives and Procedures § 1.1(b), Commentary pp. 46-47 (Approved Draft 1968); III American Bar Association, Standards for Criminal Justice, Standard 18-1.1, Commentary pp. 18-16, 18-24 to 18-25 (1980). Relying on the ABA's conclusion, the plurality in Gregg v. Georgia, 428 U.S., at 192, 96 S.Ct., at 2934, recognized that "[s]ince the members of a jury will have had little, if any, previous experience in sentencing, they are unlikely to be skilled in dealing with the information they are given." But the Court in this case, in its haste to praise the jury's ability to find the truth, apparently forgets this well-known and worrisome shortcoming.

As if to suggest that petitioner's position that unreliable expert testimony should be excluded is unheard of in the law, the Court relies on the proposition that the rules of evidence generally "anticipate that relevant, unprivileged evidence should be admitted and its weight left to the factfinder, who would have the benefit of cross-examination and contrary evidence by the opposing party." But the Court simply ignores hornbook law that, despite the availability of cross-examination and rebuttal witnesses, "opinion evidence is not admissible if the court believes that the state of the pertinent art or scientific knowledge does not permit a reasonable opinion to be asserted." McCormick, Evidence 31 (1972). Because it is feared that the jury will overestimate its probative value, polygraph evidence, for example, almost invariably is excluded from trials despite the fact that, at a conservative estimate, an experienced polygraph examiner can detect truth or deception correctly about 80 to 90 percent of the time. . . . [9] In no area is purportedly "expert" testimony admitted for the jury's consideration where it cannot be demonstrated that it is correct more often than not. "It is inconceivable that a judgment could be considered an 'expert' judgment when it is less accurate than the flip of a coin." *Id.*, at 737. The risk that a jury will be incapable of separating "scientific" myth from reality is deemed unacceptably high.[10]

V

I would vacate petitioner's death sentence, and remand for further proceedings consistent with these views.

NOTES AND QUESTIONS

1.   Is Barefoot v. Estelle still good law after Daubert v. Merrell Dow Pharmaceuticals, Inc., 509 U.S. 579 (1993)? The majority in *Barefoot* states "the rules of evidence . . . anticipate that relevant, unprivileged evidence

9. Other purportedly scientific proof has met a similar fate. See, *e.g., United States v. Kilgus,* 571 F.2d 508, 510 (CA9 1978) (expert testimony identifying aircraft through "forward looking infrared system" inadmissible because unreliable and not generally accepted in scientific field to which it belongs); *United States v. Brown,* 557 F.2d 541, 558-559 (CA6 1977) (expert identification based on "ion microprobic analysis of human hair" not admissible because insufficiently reliable and accurate, and not accepted in its field); *United States v. Addison,* 162 U.S.App.D.C., at 203, 498 F.2d, at 745 (expert identification based on voice spectrogram inadmissible because not shown reliable); *United States v. Hearst,* 412 F.Supp. 893, 895 (ND Cal.1976) (identification testimony of expert in "psycholinguistics" inadmissible because not demonstrably reliable), aff'd on other grounds, 563 F.2d 1331 (CA9 1977).

10. The Court observes that this well established rule is a matter of evidence law, not constitutional law. *Ante,* at 3397, n. 6. But the principle requiring that capital sentencing procedures ensure reliable verdicts, see *supra,* at 3393, which the Court ignores, and the principle that due process is violated by the introduction of certain types of seemingly conclusive, but actually unreliable, evidence, see *supra,* at 3393, and n. 7, which the Court ignores, are constitutional doctrines of long standing. The teaching of the evidence doctrine is that unreliable scientific testimony creates a serious and unjustifiable risk of an erroneous verdict, and that the adversary process at its best does not remove this risk. We should not dismiss this lesson merely by labeling the doctrine nonconstitutional; its relevance to the constitutional question before the Court could not be more certain.

should be admitted and its weight left to the fact finder, who would have the benefit of cross examination and contrary evidence by the opposing party. Psychiatric testimony predicting dangerousness may be countered not only as erroneous in a particular case but as generally so unreliable that it should be ignored. If the jury may make up its mind about future dangerousness unaided by psychiatric testimony, jurors should not be barred from hearing the views of the State's psychiatrists along with opposing views of the defendant's doctors." In *Daubert*, the majority remarked that "under the Rules the trial judge must ensure that any and all scientific testimony or evidence admitted is not only relevant, but reliable. . . . In order to qualify as 'scientific knowledge,' an inference or assertion must be derived by the scientific method. Proposed testimony must be supported by appropriate validation — i.e., 'good grounds,' based on what is known. In short, the requirement that an expert's testimony pertain to 'scientific knowledge' establishes a standard of evidentiary reliability." Can you reconcile these competing approaches to expert testimony? For thoughtful commentary on this issue, see Michael H. Gottesman, *From* Barefoot *to* Daubert *to* Joiner: *Triple Play or Double Error*, 40 Ariz. L. Rev. 753 (1998); Paul C. Giannelli, Daubert: *Interpreting The Federal Rules of Evidence*, 15 Cardozo L. Rev. 1999 (1994); and Flores v. Johnson, 210 F.3d 456 (10th Cir. 2000) (Garza, J. , concurring).

2.   Dr. Grigson, one of the government's expert witnesses, has long been dubbed "Dr. Death" for his involvement as a prosecution expert in death penalty cases. In 90 percent of the cases in which he testified, the defendant received the death penalty. "The explanation for his success rate, according to numerous observers, is the combination of his unequivocal, confident diagnoses that capital defendants are incorrigible "sociopaths" who "absolutely" pose a future danger, and his manner of testimony — coming across as a "kindly, gregarious, country-doctor" who is "perpetually grinning." Brent E. Newton, 1 Tex. F. on C. L. & C. R. 1, 22 (1994). *See also* Bennett v. State, 766 S.W.2d 227, 231 (Tex. Crim. App. 1989) (Teague, J., dissenting) (discussing Grigson and his testimony).

3.   The legal determination of dangerousness is implicated in preventative detention of mentally ill people who pose a danger to themselves or others, and preventative detention of sexual predators who the state alleges are unable to control their impulses. The Supreme Court has upheld a statute that allows the continued civil confinement of a sexual predator after his sentence if the person suffers from a "mental abnormality" or "personality disorder" that makes him unable to control his behavior and thus likely he will continue to engage in "predatory acts of sexual violence." *See* Kansas v. Hendricks, 521 U.S. 346 (1997). For commentary on this case, see Michael L. Perlin, *"There's No Success Like Failure/And Failure's No Success at All": Exposing the Pretextuality of* Kansas v. Hendricks, 92 N.W. L. Rev. 1247 (1998); and Eric Janus, Hendricks *and the Moral Terrain of Police Power Civil Commitment*, 4 Psych. Pub. Pol'y & L. 297 (1998).

4.   The intersection of dangerousness and legal decision making has prompted much commentary. *See e.g.,* Erica Beecher-Monas & Edgar Garcia-Rill, *Danger at the Edge of Chaos: Predicting Violent Behavior in a Post*-Daubert *World,* 24 Cardozo L. Rev. 1845 (2006); John Monahan, *A Jurisprudence of Risk Assessment: Forecasting Harm Among Prisoners, Predators, and Patients,* 92 Va. L. Rev. 391 (2006); and Christopher Slobogin, *Dangerousness and Expertise Redux,* 56 Emory L. J. 275 (2006).

5.   In the decades since *Barefoot* was decided, there has been some change in the ability to predict future dangerousness, according to a recent article by Professor John Monahan. Apparently, the subjective judgment employed in clinical prediction is still quite poor — "little has transpired . . . to increase confidence in the ability of psychologists or psychiatrists, using their unstructured clinical judgment, to accurately assess violence risk." Monahan, *supra,* n.4 at 406-407. However, the use of risk assessment instruments, which use multiple predictor variables (including age, gender, psychological and substance abuse disorders, criminal and violence history, family history, and prior victimization) seems to hold more promise for actuarial predictions of future violence. *Id.* at 409. Nonetheless, the jurisprudential considerations surrounding the use of such information in legal decisions have become no less controversial.

6.   Whether predictive ability is poor or not, expert evidence about future dangerousness continues to be admitted in federal and state courts. Could it be that courts believe that some expert testimony is preferable to no expert testimony on this issue?

CHAPTER 6

FORENSIC SCIENCE

I. INTRODUCTION AND EXPLANATIONS

This chapter considers three common forms of forensic science in criminal cases: identification of substances, identification of persons, and determinations of cause and manner of death.[1] The first category consists of identifying and measuring substances. Examples include determining whether and how much alcohol is in a blood sample, testing confiscated white powder to ascertain whether it is heroin, and examining fabric for gunshot residue. This category of forensic science is based upon long-established principles of chemistry and biology and is generally quite reliable, unless there is evidence of fraud, negligence, or mishandling or degradation of a sample.

The second category, sometimes termed "individualization," attempts to link a specific person to a crime scene using blood samples, handwriting, fingerprints, tool marks, shoe prints, bite marks, or hair. The crime lab compares a known sample (generally taken from a suspect or a victim) with samples found at a crime scene or in another location (a defendant's vehicle, for example). DNA evidence is considered the most scientific and reliable of these individualization specialties. Although fingerprints and handwriting

---

1. Crime scene reconstruction is addressed in Chapter 10.

have long been relied upon by forensic scientists and have been admissible for decades, a number of cases have challenged the reliability of these specialties. The exculpation of those wrongfully convicted has also exposed the potential for error in hair, bite mark, and shoe print comparison.

Finally, the chapter delves into determinations of cause and manner of death in which physicians, often board certified in pathology forensic pathology, testify about the results of autopsies. These pathologists may be the Medical Examiner (ME) or Coroner or may be physicians hired to work for the ME's or Coroner's office. In addition to describing their autopsy findings, these physicians testify about what caused the death and the manner of death; that is, whether the death was natural, accidental, a suicide, or a homicide. Sometimes, pathologists and other experts provide testimony that relies on factors outside of the autopsy to help determine the manner of death. This testimony is often critical to both civil and criminal cases but its reliability and value are vigorously debated.

The following article explains some of the concepts of both identification and individualization.

Forensic Science: Grand Goals, Tragic Flaws & Judicial Gatekeeping

44 Judges' Journal, 16 (Fall 2005)
Jane Campbell Moriarty & Michael J. Saks

An important distinction exists in forensic science between identification and individualization specialties. "Identification" specialties typically are derived from conventional basic sciences with well-developed and well-tested principles applicable to answering disputed factual questions in litigation. The parent field most often is chemistry, though sometimes principles are drawn from physics or biology. The goal of these specialties typically is to identify a substance (that is, to determine what something is) and to measure how much of the substance there is. For example, what chemical is a certain powder and how much of it is present? Does a blood sample contain poison and if so, how much? These fields, based on conventional science, are considered highly reliable and are rarely challenged in court unless a new technique is presented or there is evidence of negligence or fraud.

The "individualization" specialties have quite different goals from the identification sciences. The individualization specialties seek to associate an item of evidence found at a crime scene to its "unique" source, "to the exclusion of all others in the world." That is not a goal shared with any conventional sciences and, thus, the methods and principles of these specialties have not been derived from conventional sciences. Indeed, the only science-based individualization specialty is DNA comparison, which does not claim to have a match, but only expresses a probabilistic likelihood of a match.[1]

The methods and principles employed by the individualization specialties — involving the comparison of such things as bitemarks, bullets, fingerprints, footwear, hair, handwriting, and so on — were invented by and for these specialties themselves. . . .

A. Identification

General forensic testing includes the analysis of such liquids as blood or urine in order to determine, for example, blood type and enzymes. This type of testing also analyzes solids, such as clothing or material, to ascertain the presence of gunpowder residue or blood stains on the fabric. The following sections discuss the various methods commonly used in crime labs in the areas of identification.

1. Serology

Laboratories often must first determine whether a reddish brown stain is indeed blood or some other substance and, if it is blood, whether of human origin. After presumptive tests suggest that blood is present, additional confirmatory immunological tests are then performed to determine if it is human. Presumptive tests for blood tend to be very sensitive (needing small amounts of blood to generate a positive result) but are also prone to false positive results (commonly encountered materials unrelated to blood give results that cannot be distinguished from those for blood). In contrast, confirmatory tests rarely give false positive results but require larger amounts of material for testing and therefore more often give rise to false negative results (a tested sample really does contain human blood but the test reports that it does not). . . .

In addition to analyzing blood, serological tests can also be performed to determine the presence or absence of other bodily fluids such as semen, urine, saliva, and other physiological fluids. Semen and blood can be identified with virtual certainty, but other bodily fluids, such as saliva and urine can only be presumptively identified.

2. Chromatography: Function and Uses

Gas and liquid chromatographs are common fixtures in crime laboratories throughout the country and are used to determine whether a sample contains a questioned chemical, such as a poison or a toxin, by separating

1. [EDS.] DNA evidence is discussed in Chapter 4.

the various components in the sample. For example, if death by carbon monoxide is suspected, blood can be run through the gas chromatograph to determine whether it contains carbon monoxide. Similarly, urine can be tested with a gas chromatograph for the presence of opiates or alcohol. Chromatographs can often identify unknown substances, such as a vial of an unidentified liquid, located at a crime scene.

Gas chromatographs function by heating samples until they become gaseous and graphing the time it takes for the various components to turn from liquid to gas. Most components require different lengths of time to convert from liquid to gas and the chromatograph will chart various components accordingly. The results appear as a graph representing both the amount and nature of the substance.

3. Microscopy: Function and Uses

Various types of microscopes are used in crime labs, including the commonly employed stereo-binocular microscope, which provides a magnified image of the object as it actually appears, allowing the viewer to see the three dimensions of length, breadth, and depth.

Microscopes are used to separate small amounts of trace materials that are relevant to a crime scene (such as material in a pant cuff) or to look closely at pieces of larger items to determine whether they contain bloodstains or markings.

While polarizing microscopes allow examiners to study physical and chemical properties of specimens, comparison microscopes are employed to permit examination of two specimens at the same time. By employing an optical bridge, comparison microscopes allow the samples to be seen in a single field and compared. Comparison microscopes are used to look at two fibers, for example, to determine whether they appear to be similar or not. A comparison microscope is also used as part of individualization specialties, particularly in visual hair comparison.

Of a more sophisticated nature are the scanning electron microscopes, SEMs, which produce magnification in excess of 300,000 times — far greater than other microscopes, which generally do not exceed the power of 2,000 times. SEMs use a beam of electrons directed at the item in question. Put simply: When the beam strikes the surface, the interaction generates secondary electron emissions, which create a micrograph of the image that appears in shades of gray, black, and white and permits observations of objects and characteristics that were not visible even with the strongest optical microscope. SEMs can be used to see different layers of paint chips that may be collected from a crime scene, such as a hit-and-run accident, where the car has been driven from the scene but has left behind paint chips as a result of the collision.

B. Individualization

In principle, all forensic individualization specialties assume uniqueness in the markings and objects of interest — fingerprints, handwriting, hair, bite marks, tool marks, etc. These no-two-alike differences are assumed to be the product of random variations in the creation of or changes in the objects. These variations are explained, if at all, by the notion of the multiplication rule in probability theory, which suggests that where different objects vary on numerous attributes, the probability of any two of them sharing the same attributes is extremely small. They assume, further, that while not all features are "individualizing" (some features are "class" characteristics, shared by numerous persons or objects in the class), at least some are unique to the particular object or person. Part of the claimed skill is to distinguish class from individual features, and not to be fooled by subclass characteristics. Judgments of inclusion or exclusion require careful comparisons of features. When marks (or material) found at a crime scene or other relevant place might have been left by the perpetrator or a crime victim, examiners compare the questioned evidence to those known to belong to a suspect or victim to try to determine whether the two can be associated or excluded.

Exclusion is easier to determine than association: If two marks differ in any "unexplained" way, they cannot share a common source. Inclusion requires, first, a judgment that two sets of features are indistinguishably alike and, second, that those similarities are shared by no other person or object. None of these specialties, except DNA typing, possesses a database which permits the calculation of an objective probability of the likelihood that other persons or objects share those same features (known to statisticians as the probability of a coincidental match). In large part, the basic concepts and methods employed in the earliest days of a specialty continue to be used today. Advances that have taken place have occurred in peripheral technologies (*e.g.*, improved photographic techniques, chemicals for making latent fingerprints visible), not in the core theory by which judgments of association or exclusion are made.

II. FORENSIC SCIENCE CHALLENGES IN THE COURTROOM

The most sophisticated form of individualization is found in DNA comparisons, which use well-grounded science to create a DNA profile (DNA is discussed at length in Chapter 4, DNA Evidence) and to calculate the probability someone other than the person in question is the source of the DNA. In contrast, fingerprint, hair, bite mark, shoe and footprints, and handwriting comparison are methods of individualization that rely primarily upon experience and visual comparison to reach conclusions of a "match." These forms of comparison have been used for decades, and have been acceptable for an equally long time in the courts, although many questions have been raised about their validity and reliability. These forms of comparison do not rest on scientific principles, but are the observations and conclusions of technicians who compare a known sample with unknown sample(s).

In the last decade, criminal defendants have questioned the reliability and methodology of the individualization specialties. Consider the majority and dissenting opinions in the following case.

United States v. Crisp

324 F.3d 261 (4th Cir. 2003)

Before WILKINS, Chief Judge, and MICHAEL and KING, Circuit Judges. Affirmed by published opinion. Judge KING wrote the majority opinion, in which Chief Judge WILKINS joined. Judge MICHAEL wrote a dissenting opinion.

KING, Circuit Judge:
Patrick Leroy Crisp appeals multiple convictions arising from an armed bank robbery carried out in Durham, North Carolina, on June 13, 2001. Crisp maintains that his trial was tainted by the Government's presentation of inadmissible expert testimony. His appeal presents a single question: whether the disciplines of forensic fingerprint analysis and forensic handwriting analysis satisfy the criteria for expert opinion testimony under *Daubert v. Merrell Dow Pharmaceuticals, Inc.* . . . As explained below, the prosecution's fingerprint and handwriting evidence was properly admitted, and we affirm the convictions.

I.

[A day after the bank robbery, an informant, Michael Mitchell, contacted the police and provided them with information that Patrick Crisp and Lamont Torain had robbed the bank. He claimed the two had tried to recruit him to participate, but that he had declined. Crisp and Torain were subsequently arrested and were in the same jail. Crisp slid a note ("the Note") under his cell door as Torain passed, which stated as follows:]

Lamont

You know if you don't help me I am going to get life in prison, and you ain't going to get nothing. Really it's over for me if you don't change what you told them. Tell them I picked you up down the street in Kathy's car. Tell them that I don't drive the Probe. Tell them Mike drove the Probe. He is the one that told on us. Tell them the gun and all that shit was Mike's. That is what I am going to tell them tommorow [sic].

Feds.

~~Tell the Feds Mike Drove you away from the bank~~

Patrick.

[Police also secured surgical gloves, a bullet-proof vest, and a sawed-off shotgun from Crisp's girlfriend's belongings. Palmprints and handwriting exemplars were obtained from Crisp. Experts testified that a palmprint found on the Note matched Crisp's prints and that the handwriting was also his.]

Both Mitchell and Torain testified against Crisp at Crisp's trial. . . . Mitchell testified Crisp told him he needed to make some quick money and that he planned to rob a bank. Mitchell told the jury that Crisp then took him to the Central Carolina Bank, informed him that he (Crisp) and Lamont Torain were going to rob it, and asked if Mitchell would participate. The following day, Mitchell, Crisp, and Torain discussed the robbery plan in further detail. Crisp showed Mitchell a bullet proof vest, a sawed-off shotgun, an automatic weapon, a mask, and clothing, all of which Crisp and Torain intended to use in the bank robbery. Mitchell further testified that Crisp had shown him the purple Ford Probe. According to Mitchell, the initial plan was that he and Torain would enter the bank, and Crisp would drive the getaway vehicle. The following morning, however, when Torain came to pick up Mitchell for the robbery, Mitchell begged off, explaining that he had to babysit his children.

Torain described to the jury a slightly different set of events. He asserted that it was Mitchell and Crisp who planned the robbery, and that, originally, it was he who was to drive the getaway vehicle. According to Torain, when Mitchell refused to participate, the plan changed: Torain entered the bank, while Crisp waited in the getaway car.

At trial, Mary Katherine Brannan, a fingerprint expert with the North Carolina State Bureau of Investigation ("SBI"), testified that Crisp's right palm had produced a latent print that had subsequently been recovered from the Note. Furthermore, a handwriting expert, Special Agent Thomas Currin, a "questioned document analyst" with the SBI, testified that Crisp had authored the Note.

Crisp presented an alibi defense. His cousin, Cecilia Pointer, claimed that, on the day of the robbery, her husband and Crisp came to her place of employment at approximately 12:30 p.m., and that the two men then left to submit applications at a temporary employment agency. She testified that they stopped back by her work around 1:00 p.m. or 1:15 p.m.

After the four-day jury trial, Crisp was found guilty of bank robbery, bank robbery with a dangerous weapon, and brandishing a firearm during and in relation to the bank robbery. . . .

conviction

II.

Fingerprint and handwriting analysis have long been recognized by the courts as sound methods for making reliable identifications. *See, e.g., Piquett v. United States,* 81 F.2d 75, 81 (7th Cir.1936) (fingerprints); *Robinson v. Mandell,* 20 F. Cas. 1027 (D.Mass.1868) (handwriting). Today, however, Crisp challenges the district court's decisions to permit experts in those fields to testify on behalf of the prosecution. The fingerprinting expert, Brannan, gave her opinion that a palm print lifted from the Note was that of Crisp; the handwriting expert, Currin, testified that, in his judgment, the handwriting on the Note matched Crisp's handwriting. We review for abuse of discretion a district court's decision to admit or reject expert testimony. . . .

challenge

B.

In seeking to have his convictions vacated, Crisp also challenges the admissibility of the opinions of Currin, the handwriting expert, on grounds that are essentially identical to those on which he relied to make his case against fingerprint evidence. Crisp contends that, like fingerprinting identifications, the basic premise behind handwriting analysis is that no two persons write alike, and thus that forensic document examiners can reliably determine authorship of a particular document by comparing it with known samples. He maintains that these basic premises have not been tested, nor has an error rate been established. In addition, he asserts that handwriting experts have no numerical standards to govern their analyses and that they have not subjected themselves and their science to critical self-examination and study.

1.

While the admissibility of handwriting evidence in the post-*Daubert* world appears to be a matter of first impression for our Court, every circuit to have addressed the issue has concluded, as on the fingerprint issue, that such evidence is properly admissible. . . . [5]

2.

The Government's handwriting expert, Thomas Currin, had twenty-four years of experience at the North Carolina SBI. On voir dire, and then on direct examination, he explained that all questioned documents that come into the SBI are analyzed first by a "questioned document

---

5. Certain district courts, however, have recently determined that handwriting analysis does not meet the *Daubert* standards. *See, e.g., United States v. Lewis,* 220 F.Supp.2d 548, 554 (S.D.W.Va.2002) (finding proficiency tests and peer review meaningless where the evidence showed that handwriting experts "*always* passed their proficiency tests, . . . [and that] peers *always* agreed with each others' results" (emphasis in original)); *United States v. Brewer,* 2002 WL 596365 (N.D.Ill.2002); *United States v. Saelee,* 162 F.Supp.2d 1097 (D.Alaska 2001); *United States v. Hines,* 55 F.Supp.2d 62 (D.Mass.1999).

examiner"; and that the initial analysis is then reviewed by another examiner. Currin discussed several studies showing the ability of qualified document examiners to identify questioned handwriting.[6]

In addition, he had passed numerous proficiency tests, consistently receiving perfect scores. Currin testified to a consistent methodology of handwriting examination and identification, and he stated that the methodology "has been used not only at the level of state crime laboratories, but [also in] federal and international crime laboratories around the world." When he was questioned regarding the standards employed in questioned document examination, Currin explained that every determination of authorship "is based on the uniqueness of [certain] similarities, and it's based on the quality and the skill and the training of the document examiner."

At trial, Currin drew the jury's attention to similarities between Crisp's known handwriting exemplars and the writing on the Note. Among the similarities that he pointed out were the overall size and spacing of the letters and words in the documents; the unique shaping of the capital letter "L" in the name "Lamont"; the spacing between the capital letter "L" and the rest of the word; a peculiar shaping to the letters "o" and "n" when used in conjunction with one another; the v-like formation of the letter "u" in the word "you"; and the shape of the letter "t," including the horizontal stroke. Currin also noted that the word "tomorrow" was misspelled in the same manner on both the known exemplar and the Note. He went on to testify that, in his opinion, Crisp had authored the Note.

3.

Our analysis of *Daubert* in the context of fingerprint identification applies with equal force here: like fingerprint analysis, handwriting comparison testimony has a long history of admissibility in the courts of this country. *See, e.g., Robinson v. Mandell*, 20 F. Cas. 1027 (D.Mass.1868). The fact that handwriting comparison analysis has achieved widespread and lasting acceptance in the expert community gives us the assurance of reliability that *Daubert* requires. Furthermore, as with expert testimony on fingerprints, the role of the handwriting expert is primarily to draw the jury's attention to similarities between a known exemplar and a contested sample. Here, Currin merely pointed out certain unique characteristics shared by the two writings. Though he opined that Crisp authored the Note in question, the jury was nonetheless left to examine the Note and decide for itself whether it agreed with the expert.

---

6. Rather than analyzing the ability of document examiners to correctly identify authorship, the studies to which Currin referred examined whether document examiners were more likely than lay people to identify authorship correctly. In one study, lay participants had a 38% error rate, while qualified document examiners had a 6% error rate.

To the extent that a given handwriting analysis is flawed or flimsy, an able defense lawyer will bring that fact to the jury's attention, both through skillful cross-examination and by presenting expert testimony of his own. But in light of Crisp's failure to offer us any reason today to doubt the reliability of handwriting analysis evidence in general, we must decline to deny our courts and juries such insights as it can offer.

MICHAEL, Circuit Judge, dissenting:

The majority believes that expert testimony about fingerprint and hand-writing identification is reliable because the techniques in these fields have been accepted and tested in our adversarial system over time. This belief leads the majority to excuse fingerprint and handwriting analysis from the more careful scrutiny that scientific expert testimony must now withstand under *Daubert v. Merrell Dow Pharmaceuticals, Inc.,* . . . before it can be admitted. In Patrick Leroy Crisp's case the government did not prove that its expert iden-tification evidence satisfied the Daubert factors or that it was otherwise reliable. I respectfully dissent for that reason. In dissenting, I am not suggest-ing that fingerprint and handwriting evidence cannot be shown to satisfy *Daubert.* I am only making the point that the government did not establish in Crisp's case that this evidence is reliable. The government has had ten years to comply with *Daubert.* It should not be given a pass in this case.

I.

. . . The majority excuses fingerprint and handwriting analysis from any rigorous *Daubert* scrutiny because these techniques are generally accepted and have been examined for nearly one hundred years in our adversarial system of litigation. These circumstances are not sufficient to demonstrate reliability in the aftermath of *Daubert.* To say that expert evidence is reliable because it is generally accepted is to say that it is admissible under *Daubert* because it was admissible under the old rule articulated in *Frye v. United States,* 293 F. 1013, 1014 (D.C.Cir.1923) (allowing expert evidence that had "gained general acceptance in the particular field in which it belongs"). *Frye's* "general acceptance" rule was replaced by Fed.R.Evid. 702, which now requires expert testimony to be "the product of reliable principles and methods." *Daubert,* of course, outlines the factors that are relevant to the determination of reliability. Nothing in the Supreme Court's opinion in *Daubert* suggests that evidence that was admitted under *Frye* is grandfathered in or is free of the more exacting analysis now required. . . .

Nor is fingerprint and handwriting analysis necessarily reliable because it has been subjected to the adversarial process of litigation. In a criminal case like this one, adversarial testing simply means that the defense lawyer cross-examines the government's expert. That, I concede, is important, but it only goes part way. In most criminal cases, particularly those in which the defendant is indigent, the defendant does not have access to an independent expert who could review the analyses and conclusions of the prosecution's expert. Simon Cole, *Suspect Identities: A History of Fingerprinting and Criminal Identification* 280 (2001) [hereinafter Cole, *Suspect Identities*] (noting that defense lawyers rarely challenge fingerprint evidence, in part because they often do not have the funds to hire experts). Lack of money is only one problem. Lack of independent crime laboratories is another. The great majority of crime laboratories are operated by law enforcement agencies. Paul C. Giannelli, *The Abuse of Scientific Evidence in Criminal Cases: The Need for Independent Crime Laboratories*, 4 Va. J. Soc. Pol'y & L. 439, 470 (1997); Paul C. Giannelli, *"Junk Science": The Criminal Cases*, 84 J.Crim. L. & Criminology 105, 118 (1993). More important, criminal defendants do not appear to have access to experts who could challenge the basic principles and methodology of fingerprint and handwriting analysis. Jennifer L. Mnookin, *Fingerprint Evidence in an Age of DNA Profiling*, 67 Brooklyn L.Rev. 13, 38-39 (2001) [hereinafter Mnookin, *Fingerprint Evidence*] (explaining that fingerprint evidence came to be seen as particularly powerful in part because it was so rarely challenged by the defense); Cole, *Suspect Identities, supra* at 280 (reporting that New York City police officers caught fabricating evidence chose to create fingerprint evidence because it was so unlikely to be challenged). Our adversarial system has much to commend it, but it is not a general substitute for the specific *Daubert* inquiry. The system without *Daubert* did not work to ensure the reliability of fingerprint and handwriting analysis. As I point out in parts II.B. and III *infra*, fingerprint and handwriting analysis was admitted with little judicial scrutiny for decades prior to *Daubert*.

Nothing in the history of the use of fingerprint and handwriting evidence leads me to conclude that it should be admitted without the scrutiny now required by *Daubert*. The government, of course, has the burden to put forward evidence "from which the court can determine that the proffered testimony is properly admissible" under *Daubert*. . . . The government utterly failed to meet its burden here.

Handwriting identification evidence has been greeted with more skepticism by courts in the wake of *Daubert*. Some courts have refused to admit it. . . . Other courts have allowed testimony about the similarities between handwriting samples without permitting the expert to testify to conclusions about the authorship. . . . I believe that the government's evidence on handwriting, like its evidence on fingerprinting, does not demonstrate its reliability, and the evidence should therefore have been excluded. Cf. Andre A. Moenssens, *Handwriting Identification Evidence in the Post-Daubert World*, 66 UMKC L.Rev. 251, 276-77 (1997) (noting that if *Daubert* factors were applied to forensic sciences, many expert opinions would no longer be admissible).

I will again run through the *Daubert* factors, considering first whether the technique of handwriting analysis has been tested. The proposition that forensic document examiners can reliably identify handwriting was not established in this case. . . . This case aside, it appears that no one has ever assessed the validity of the basic tenets of handwriting comparison, namely, that no two individuals write in precisely the same fashion and that certain characteristics of an individual's writing remain constant even when the writer attempts to disguise them. The government asserted in this case that because these premises had not been disproven, they must be true. . . . One researcher has attempted to compare the ability of professional examiners to identify handwriting with the ability of lay persons. . . . Even with this study, which is discussed below, the data on handwriting analysis is "sparse, inconclusive and highly disputed." [*United States v. Starzecpyzel*, 880 F.Supp. 2d 1027, 1037 (S.D.N.Y. 1995)]; D. Michael Risinger with Michael J. Saks, *Science and Nonscience in the Courts: Daubert Meets Handwriting Identification Expertise*, 82 Iowa L.Rev. 21, 65 (1996) [hereinafter Risinger & Saks, *Science & Nonscience*] ("Put simply, if courts trust handwriting experts to be experts, little incentive exists to advance the field's knowledge or to test its claims. And so, in the past century virtually no research of that kind has been done."). Moreover, although the government's expert here testified to his success on proficiency tests, the government provides no reason for us to believe that these tests are realistic assessments of an examiner's ability to perform the tasks required in his field (testimony of the government's handwriting expert that he has always achieved a perfect score on proficiency tests) . . . If what little the government said in this case is any indication, the premises upon which handwriting analysis is based have not been exposed to a sufficient amount of objective testing.

The next *Daubert* question is whether handwriting examination has been subjected to peer review and publication. The government did not present any evidence about peer review or critical scholarship in the field. . . . Those within the field have failed to engage in any critical study of the basic principles and methods of handwriting analysis, and few objective outsiders have taken on this challenge. D. Michael Risinger et al., *Brave New "Post-Daubert World"—A Reply to Professor Moenssens*, 29 Seton Hall L.Rev. 405, 441 (1998) [hereinafter Risinger et al., *Reply*] ("No members of the handwriting identification community are rewarded for doing empirical testing and for examining the claims of the enterprise skeptically."). This lack of critical review has hampered the advancement of methodology in the field. Indeed, the field of handwriting analysis, unlike most other technical fields, relies primarily on texts that were written fifty to one hundred years ago. The second *Daubert* factor, peer review and publication, is not satisfied.

The next *Daubert* factor requires a look at the technique's known or potential rate of error. Under pressure from courts, handwriting analysis appears to have been subjected to more testing than fingerprint analysis. . . . In this case, however, the government failed to introduce any evidence about what the error rate might in fact be. The testing that has been done suggests that experts, on average, do better than non-experts at avoiding false positives, that is, in identifying someone as an author who in fact is not. On some tests, however, the best of the non-experts did as well as some of the experts. Even these modest results have been challenged. . . . Moreover, other more challenging studies that more accurately reflect real world conditions show higher rates of error. One study found that as many as nine percent of document examiners misidentified a forgery as being written by the named author, and almost one-quarter of the examiners incorrectly concluded that a disguised writing was written by someone other than the true author. The error rates in the testing that has been reported are disquieting to say the least. In any event, the government did not satisfy the third *Daubert* factor in this case.

The next *Daubert* factor focuses on whether there are standards or controls that govern the expert's analysis. In this case the government's expert asserted that handwriting examiners follow the same methodology, . . . , but he provided no listing of objective criteria that are used to form an opinion. There does not seem to be any list of universal, objective requirements for identifying an author. Risinger & Saks, *Science and Nonscience, supra* at 39 (explaining that because document examiners base their conclusions on their own empirical observations rather than publicly available data, the results are "only as good as the unexaminable personal database of the practitioner[ ] and the practitioner's not-fully-explainable method of deriving answers").

The last factor is whether the technique is generally accepted in the scientific community. The general acceptance of handwriting analysis appears to come only from those within the field. . . . And those within the field have not challenged or questioned its basic premises. More is required to meet the "general acceptance" factor.

The government did not show that there are factors beyond the *Daubert* list that credibly demonstrate the reliability of handwriting evidence. Like fingerprint experts, document examiners have long been allowed to testify in judicial proceedings. . . . But, like the case of fingerprint evidence, there is no reason to believe that longstanding use of handwriting evidence demonstrates its reliability. The testimony of handwriting experts was initially admitted into evidence because courts saw it as no less reliable than that of lay witnesses who claimed to be able to identify the writers of documents. Mnookin, Scripting Expertise, supra at 1763-64, 1784; D. Michael Risinger et al., *Exorcism of Ignorance as a Proxy for Rational Knowledge: The Lessons of Handwriting Identification "Expertise,"* 137 U. Pa. L.Rev. 731, 762 (1989). But that does not make handwriting analysis a reliable science.

Because the government has failed to demonstrate either that its handwriting evidence satisfies the *Daubert* factors or that it is otherwise reliable, I would reverse the district court's decision to admit it as an abuse of discretion. *See Starzecpyzel*, 880 F.Supp. [1027, 1028 (S.D.N.Y.1995)] ("The *Daubert* hearing established that forensic document examination, which clothes itself with the trappings of science, does not rest on carefully articulated postulates, does not employ rigorous methodology, and has not convincingly documented the accuracy of its determinations.").

NOTES AND QUESTIONS

1. Are you more convinced by the reasoning of the majority or dissenting opinion? Why? As a matter of application of Supreme Court law, is the majority or dissenting opinion more faithful to the gate-keeping requirements of *Daubert* and *Kumho Tire*? Does the *Frye* general acceptance test seem to motivate the majority? One concern raised about *Frye* is that it places more weight on the general acceptance by the courts, rather than the general acceptance by the scientific community. Does that critique seem warranted in light of the preceding opinion?

2. The majority in *Crisp* also held that fingerprint comparison met the *Daubert* standard of reliability. Like handwriting, fingerprint comparison has been challenged in numerous courts, with little success. In United States v. Llera Plaza, 2002 WL 27305 (E.D. Pa. Jan. 7, 2002) [*Llera Plaza I*], *vacated*, 188 F. Supp. 2d 549 (E.D. Pa. 2002) [*Llera Plaza II*], Judge Pollak limited the admissibility of fingerprint comparison, holding that:

> The government may present expert fingerprint testimony (1) describing how the rolled and latent fingerprints at issue in this case were obtained, (2) identifying, and placing before the jury, the fingerprints and such magnifications as may be required to show minute details, and (3) pointing out observed similarities (and differences) between any latent print and any rolled print the government contends are attributable to the same person. The defendants may present expert fingerprint testimony countering the government's fingerprint testimony. But no expert witness for any party will be permitted to testify that, in the opinion of the witness, a particular latent print is — or is not — the print of a particular person.

Llera Plaza I, at 18. This opinion "sent shock waves through the community of fingerprint analysts, the FBI, and the Department of Justice." Richard Friedman et al., *Expert Testimony on Fingerprints: An Internet Exchange*, 43 Jurimetrics J. 91 (2002). At the urging of the government, the court agreed to reconsider its original ruling and two months later, withdrew its opinion and issued a new opinion allowing examiners to testify to a match between unknown and known samples based on extensive briefing (but no new evidence). "In short," the judge concluded, "I have changed my mind." 188 F. Supp. 2d at 576. For further discussion about the *Llera Plaza* case, see Simon A. Cole, Grandfathering Evidence: *Fingerprint Admissibility Rulings: From* Jennings *to* Llera Plaza *and Back Again*, 41 Am. Crim. L.

Rev. 1189 (2004). For further discussion about fingerprint evidence, see Robert Epstein, *Fingerprints Meet* Daubert: *The Myth of Fingerprint "Science" Is Revealed,* 75 So. Cal. L. Rev. 605 (2002); and Jennifer Mnookin, *Fingerprint Evidence in an Age of DNA Profiling,* 67 Brooklyn L. Rev. 13 (2001).

3. In 2005, the Massachusetts Supreme Judicial Court addressed a new variant of fingerprint comparison in Commonwealth v. Patterson, 840 N.E.2d 12 (Mass. 2005). In *Patterson,* the examiner claimed to match the simultaneous aggregate print at the crime scene with the defendant — that is, he looked at several partial prints close together, and, by matching them to the defendant's rolled fingerprints, declared a match. Although there was not sufficient detail in any single fingerprint to declare a match, the examiner claimed that by looking at the aggregate of all the prints he claimed were made simultaneously, he could declare a match. To declare this match the examiners would "take into account the distance separating the latent impressions, the orientation of the impressions, the pressure used to make the impression, and any other facts the examiner deems relevant." *Id.* at 632. Although the court approved of fingerprint methodology in general in *Patterson,* it held the government failed to prove that the aggregate comparison method met either the *Frye* or *Daubert* standards. For more on this case, see also The Reliability of Latent Print Individualization: Brief of Amici Curiae Submitted on Behalf of Scientists and Scholars by the New England Innocence Project, Commonwealth v. Patterson, reprinted in 42 No. 1 Crim. L. Bull. 2 (2006).

4. In *Crisp* and other cases involving forensic science, the scientific community is primarily those law enforcement personnel who make their living comparing fingerprints and handwriting, since law enforcement is the only consumer of such skills. Should this concern the courts? In civil cases, courts have remarked unfavorably about science prepared for the courtroom — as in the Bendectin litigation in Daubert v. Merrell Dow Pharmaceuticals, Inc., 43 F.3d 1311 (9th Cir. 1995) (on remand), where the Court of Appeals for the Ninth Circuit stated:

> One very significant fact to be considered is whether the experts are proposing to testify about matters growing naturally and directly out of research they have conducted independent of the litigation, or whether they have developed their opinions expressly for purposes of testifying. That an expert testifies for money does not necessarily cast doubt on the reliability of his testimony, as few experts appear in court merely as an eleemosynary gesture. But in determining whether proposed expert testimony amounts to good science, we may not ignore the fact that a scientist's normal workplace is the lab or the field, not the courtroom or the lawyer's office.

Id. at 1317. However, the court adds this caveat in a footnote:

> There are, of course, exceptions. Fingerprint analysis, voice recognition, DNA fingerprinting and a variety of other scientific endeavors closely tied

to law enforcement may indeed have the courtroom as a principal theatre of operations. . . . As to such disciplines, the fact that the expert has developed an expertise principally for purposes of litigation will obviously not be a substantial consideration.

Id. at, n.5. Why not? Although the Bendectin expert witnesses received money, the forensic science experts' continued employment depends on the continued admissibility of their specialty. It is appropriate to have different standards? If so, why?

5. To date, few courts have excluded individualization evidence, despite some compelling proof that these types of forensic sciences do not meet the *Daubert/Kumho* reliability standards. As mentioned in the *Crisp* case, a few courts have held the proponent did not carry the burden to show such evidence is sufficiently reliable to be admissible in the case of handwriting comparison. *See e.g.,* United States v. Saelee, 162 F. Supp. 2d 1097 (D. Alaska 2001); and United States v. Fujii, 152 F. Supp. 2d 939 (N.D. Ill. 2000) (disallowing expert testimony from a handwriting examiner who compared block letters of a non-native English writer).

6. A number of courts have allowed forensic individualization testimony but have refused to allow the expert to render an opinion as to a conclusion of a match, particularly in the area of handwriting comparison. *See e.g.,* United States v. Hines, 55 F. Supp. 2d 62, 73 (D. Mass. 1999) (testimony of the government's handwriting expert limited to identifying the similarities and dissimilarities of the known writing and the unknown); United States v. McVeigh, 1997 WL 47724, *4 (D.Colo. Trans. Feb. 5, 1997) (same); United States v. Van Wyck, 83 F. Supp. 2d 515, 525 (D.N.J. 2000) (allowing a forensic "stylistics" examiner, who compares such things as grammar, spelling, and punctuation, to testify about his experience and to compare known "markers" in the known sample with the questioned sample); and United States v. Rutherford, 104 F. Supp. 2d 1190, 1194 (D. Neb. 2000); Wolf v. Ramsey, 253 F. Supp. 2d 1323, 1347 (N.D. Ga. 2003) (disallowing forensic document examiner to give conclusions, noting that the expert's "explanation for his conclusion seems to be little more than 'Trust me; I'm an expert.' "). Does this approach resolve the reliability problems of the evidence?

7. In United States v. Green, 405 F. Supp. 2d 104, 109 (D. Mass. 2005), Judge Gertner held that a tool mark witness could testify about points of comparison, but could not testify as to conclusions. Although she thought the proposed testimony did not meet the *Daubert* test, she held it was partially admissible (points of comparison admissible, but conclusion of a match inadmissible) stating:

I come to the above conclusion because of my confidence that any other decision will be rejected by appellate courts, in light of precedents across the country, regardless of the findings I have made. While I recognize that the Daubert-Kumho standard does not require the illusory perfection of a television show . . . when liberty hangs in the balance—and in the case of the defendants facing the death penalty, life itself—the standards should be higher than were met in this case, and than have been imposed across the country. The more courts admit this type of toolmark evidence without requiring documentation, proficiency testing, or evidence of reliability, the more sloppy practices will endure; we should require more.

Is Judge Gertner correct? If so, was her decision the correct one in *Green?* What concerns does this quote reflect?

8. Short of exclusion, are there ways to limit the effects of evidence that does not meet *Daubert*'s reliability standards? For suggestions on limiting the effects of evidence that does not meet the standard, see Jane Campbell Moriarty & Michael J. Saks, *Forensic Science: Grand Goals, Tragic Flaws, and Judicial Gatekeeping,* 44 Judges' Journal 16 (Fall, 2005).

9. For data-based analyses of the effects of the *Daubert* standard, see Henry F. Fradella et al., *The Impact of* Daubert *on Forensic Science,* 31 Pepp. L. Rev. 323 (2004) (analyzing civil and criminal cases); and Jennifer Groscup et al., *The Effects of* Daubert *on the Admissibility of Expert Testimony in State and Federal Criminal Cases,* 8 Psych. Pub. Pol'y & L. 339 (2002).

10. For further in-depth reading about forensic science and its limitations, see generally David L. Faigman et al., *Modern Scientific Evidence: The Law and Science of Expert Testimony* (2005, 2006 Edition); Paul C. Giannelli & Edward J. Imwinkelried, *Scientific Evidence* (3d ed. 1999) (two volumes); and *Forensic Sciences* (Cyril H. Wecht ed., 2000) (multi-volume set).

State v. Hayden

950 P.2d 1024 (Wash. App. 1998)

KENNEDY, Acting Chief Judge.

Eric H. Hayden appeals his conviction of felony murder in the first charge degree, contending that the trial court erred in admitting enhanced-fingerprint evidence after conducting a *Frye*[1] hearing. . . . Finding no error, we affirm.

FACTS

Dawn Fehring, a 27-year-old student, was found dead on the floor of her Kirkland apartment on Sunday, May 14, 1995. She was discovered nude near the foot of her bed with her top bed sheet and T-shirt wrapped around her head

1. *Frye v. United States,* 293 F. 1013, 34 A.L.R. 145 (D.C.Cir.1923).

and neck. Blood stains were found on the carpet near her body and bloody hand prints were visible on the fitted bed sheet covering the mattress. An autopsy revealed that Fehring died from asphyxiation sometime the previous Friday evening and that the source of the blood was two tears on her hymen.

During the ensuing investigation, police interviewed occupants of the other apartments in the building, one of whom was appellant Eric Hayden. Hayden became a suspect when he was unable to account for his whereabouts on the night of the murder and seemed nervous during a police interview. He told police that he had been drinking with friends on Friday evening but was unable to identify the friends. He told his girlfriend that he was too drunk that evening to remember where he had been.

The Kirkland Police Department took the fitted bed sheet to Daniel Holshue, a King County latent print examiner. Holshue cut out the five areas of the bed sheet that contained the most blood and prints. He then treated the pieces of sheet with a dye stain called amido black that reacted with the protein in the blood, turning the sheet navy blue. Next, he rinsed the pieces of sheet in pure methanol to lighten the background, leaving only the protein stains dark blue. Finally, he dipped the pieces in distilled water to set the prints. Still, after these chemical processes were completed, the contrast between the latent prints and the pieces of bed sheet was too subtle for Holshue to identify the minimum of eight points of comparison required to make a positive identification.

Holshue took the pieces of sheet to Erik Berg, an expert in enhanced digital imaging at the Tacoma Police Department, for computer enhancement. Berg took computer photographs, or digital images, of the pieces of sheet and then utilized computer software to filter out background patterns and colors to enhance the images so that the prints could be viewed without the background patterns and colors. Using the enhanced photographs of the latent prints, Holshue found twelve points of comparison on one of the fingerprints and more than forty on one of the palm prints. Thus, he concluded that the prints on the bed sheet belonged to Eric Hayden.

On June 5, 1995, the State charged Hayden by information with one count of felony murder in the first degree. . . . After an 8-day trial, a jury found Hayden guilty. . . . Hayden appeals.

Our Supreme Court recently reaffirmed its adherence to the *Frye* test to determine admissibility of novel scientific evidence. Under this test, scientific evidence is admissible if it is generally accepted in the relevant scientific community, but not admissible if there is a significant dispute between qualified experts as to its validity. Yet, if the evidence does not involve new methods of proof or new scientific principles, then the *Frye* inquiry is not necessary. Full acceptance of a process in the relevant scientific community obviates the need for a *Frye* hearing.

Here, the trial court held a *Frye* hearing to determine the admissibility of the prints identified by use of the enhanced digital imaging process. The

State presented testimony from two experts, Holshue and Berg, who explained the steps they took to ultimately identify Hayden's palm and fingerprint from the fitted bed sheet. The State also provided the trial court with forensic literature regarding digital image enhancement. Hayden did not present any witnesses at the *Frye* hearing and presented no contro-verting literature. Based upon the testimony, the trial court found that the amido black chemical dipping process is generally accepted by forensic scientists and that the enhanced digital imaging process is not novel scientific evidence to which the *Frye* test applies. Nonetheless, the court also concluded that the enhanced digital imaging process passed the *Frye* test.

Hayden does not challenge the trial court's rulings with respect to the amido black chemical dipping process. Neither does he challenge the court's rulings under ER 702, that both Holshue and Berg were qualified as experts and that their testimonies would be helpful to the trier of fact. He only argues that the enhanced digital imaging process has not obtained general acceptance in the relevant scientific community because its use for this purpose is recent and because the computer programs used to enhance the images were not designed for forensic science. He maintains that the procedure used to produce the enhanced prints did not satisfy the *Frye* standard and, therefore, that the trial court erred in admitting the evidence. The State responds that enhanced digital imaging is not novel. It argues further that even if the process is novel, it is accepted in the latent print examiner's scientific community, thereby satisfying the *Frye* standard.

A.   NOVEL SCIENTIFIC EVIDENCE

In 1994, the enhanced digital imaging process was described by Berg, the State's digital imaging expert, as "a totally new process based upon research and development done in the late 1960's and early 1970's for the space program." E. Berg, *Latent Image Processing — A Changing Technology*, The Pacific Northwest International Association for Identification Examiner, Second Quarter 1994. This and other literature presented reflects that the technology used to enhance photographs of latent prints evolved from jet propulsion laboratories in the NASA space program to isolate galaxies and receive signals from satellites. The Tacoma Police Department began using digital imaging technology in forensics in January of 1995.

The State contends that because the underlying scientific theory behind enhanced digital imaging is not new, its application to forensic science does not constitute a novel process; it suggests that it was merely the high cost of the process that prevented law enforcement organizations from using it earlier. Yet, a 1987 article from the FBI Academy's International Symposium on Latent Prints observed:

Latent print examiners across the country react differently when image enhancement of latent prints is discussed. Often, the initial reaction is one of disapproval. The concern is that nonexistent detail is added to the latent print. Image enhancement techniques are not designed to create detail but to improve images for human interpretation.

A.L. McRoberts, *Digital Image Processing as a Means of Enhancing Latent Finger-prints*, Proceedings of the International Forensic Symposium on Latent Prints, FBI, July 7-10, 1987, at 166. Although this article may not be reflective of the current latent print examiner community because it was written 10 years ago, it indicates that skepticism, in addition to high costs, may have contributed to the delay in the use of digital image enhancement in forensic science.

In support of its argument that the process is not novel, the State relies further upon *State v. Noltie*, 57 Wash.App. 21, 786 P.2d 332 (1990), *aff'd*, 116 Wash.2d 831, 809 P.2d 190 (1991). At issue in *Noltie* was the admissibility of enlarged views of a child abuse victim's sex organs obtained using a colpo-scope, a microscope developed and used to diagnose cancer. This court concluded: "We find no basis for Noltie's contention that colposcopy con-stitutes a 'novel' field or scientific technique, even though its use in child abuse cases may be relatively recent." It called the colposcope "a magnifying glass with a fancy name" and concluded that it was not subject to the *Frye* test.

In *Noltie*, this court cited three cases from other jurisdictions that agreed with its holding. *Noltie*, 57 Wash.App. at 29-30, 786 P.2d 332 (citing one Kentucky case and two California cases). In the instant matter, no court has ruled in a published appellate decision on the admissibility of latent prints processed by enhanced digital imaging.

The only published case that mentions this process is *Litaker v. Texas*, 784 S.W.2d 739 (Tex.App., 1990). In *Litaker*, the Texas Court of Criminal Appeals rejected a sufficiency of the evidence challenge to a conviction involving amido black blood treatment and a computer image enhancing process. *Litaker*, 784 S.W.2d at 742. A retired United States Army latent print examiner testified as an expert at trial, matching the enhanced latent print with a known print. *Id*. Because admissibility of this evidence was not chal-lenged in *Litaker*, the court did not discuss the processes in detail. Nonethe-less, Litaker indicates that the enhanced digital imaging process was utilized in at least one court as early as 1990.

Certainly digital photography is not a novel process. Neither is the use of computer software to enhance images. It is only the forensic use of these tools that is relatively new. Although we find the State's argument that the process is not novel to be persuasive, because this is a question of first impression we analyze the admissibility of the evidence under the *Frye* standard.

B.   THE FRYE TEST

Review of admissibility of evidence under the *Frye* test is de novo. Because no Washington court, and no other court in a published opinion, has determined that the digitally enhanced print process satisfies the *Frye* test, this court must examine the record, the available literature and cases from other jurisdictions to determine whether enhanced digital imaging is generally accepted in the relevant scientific community.

To demonstrate that the enhanced digital imaging process is accepted in the relevant scientific community, the State presented the testimony of two expert witnesses at trial and attached five articles from forensic journals to its trial brief. Although Hayden asserts: "[I]t is impossible to conclude that [this] process has obtained general acceptance in the relevant scientific community," he provided no witnesses or documentation to contradict the State's experts at the trial court level and provides no literature or other evidence to this court that contradicts the evidence and literature presented by the State, in spite of the fact that we are not limited to the scientific literature that was before the trial court.

Berg is employed by the Tacoma Police Department as a forensic specialist and had spent the 2-1/2 years prior to this trial specializing in enhanced digital imaging and its application in the field of forensic science. He is the author of two articles on the enhanced digital imaging process: *Latent Image Processing—A Changing Technology,* The Pacific Northwest International Association for Identification Examiner, Second Quarter 1994, and *The Digital Future of Investigations,* Law Enforcement Technology, August 1995.

At trial and in his articles, Berg explained the process of enhanced digital imaging in detail. . . . The advantage of digital photographs, rather than analogue film photographs, is that digital photography can capture approximately 16 million different colors and can differentiate between 256 shades of gray. Digital photographs work with light sensitivity, just like film photographs, except the computer uses a chip and a hard drive in place of the camera's film. At trial, Berg testified that there is no subjectivity in this process.

The digital photographs are enhanced using software that improves sharpness and image contrast. In addition, pattern and color isolation filters remove interfering colors and background patterns. This is a subtractive process in which elements are removed or reduced; nothing is added. At trial, Berg testified that the software he used prevented him from adding to, changing, or destroying the original image. In contrast with "image restoration," a process in which things that are not there are added based upon preconceived ideas about what the end result should look like, "image enhancement" merely makes what is there more usable. . . .

On cross examination at trial, Berg admitted this was the first time he had ever taken a latent print off of a fabric. Still, nothing in the literature presented to the trial court and for this appeal indicates that the validity of the process depends upon the nature of the material upon which the print is found. We have examined the fabric and the digitally enhanced photographs in the course of our review. It is clear even to the untrained eye that the fabric contains a hand print and that nothing appears in the digitally enhanced photograph that was not present on the fabric. Rather, the image of the hand print is merely enhanced by removing background detail unrelated to the points of identification by which the hand print was identified as Hayden's. The evidence in the record supports the trial court's unchallenged findings that the technique utilized by Berg has a reliability factor of 100 percent and a zero percent margin of error and that the results are visually verifiable and could be easily duplicated by another expert using his or her own digital camera and appropriate computer software.

The literature presented by the State indicates that digital image processing has been used as a means of enhancing latent fingerprints by the Los Angeles County Sheriff's Department since at least 1987. See A.L. McRoberts, *Digital Image Processing as a Means of Enhancing Latent Fingerprints,* Proceedings of the International Forensic Symposium on Latent Prints, July 7-10, 1987, at 165-66. Because there does not appear to be a significant dispute among qualified experts as to the validity of enhanced digital imaging performed by qualified experts using appropriate software, we conclude that the process is generally accepted in the relevant scientific community. Accordingly, we reject Hayden's contention that the trial court erred by admitting the challenged evidence and affirm his conviction.

NOTES AND QUESTIONS

1.   Forensic examiners have made other use of digital enhancement. *See* State v. Swinton, 847 A.2d 921 (Conn. 2004) (using digital enhancement with a bite mark print).

2.   At least one other jurisdiction has held that digitally enhanced fingerprints meet the *Daubert* standard of reliability. *See e.g.*, State v. Hartman, 754 N.E.2d 1150 (Ohio, 2001). Do you see any dangers with the use of digital images? For an interesting discussion of the potential dangers of digital images in the courtroom, see Jill Witkowski, Note, *Can Juries Really Believe What They See? New Foundational Requirements for the Authentication of Digital Images,* 10 Wash. U. J. L. & Pol'y 267 (2002).

III.   *DETERMINATIONS OF THE CAUSE AND MANNER OF DEATH*

Coroners and medical examiners testify in both criminal and civil cases about the manner and cause of death. By statute, these experts are often required to provide an opinion about the cause of death and whether the death was from natural causes, or was a result of an accident, homicide, or suicide. They often will hire one or more pathologists as deputy coroners to perform autopsies and other duties required of the coroner or medical examiner. The following sections are excerpted from the Ohio Revised Code regulating coroners:

§ 313.02 Qualifications for Coroner

(A) No person shall be eligible to the office of coroner except a physician who has been licensed to practice as a physician in this state for a period of at least two years immediately preceding election or appointment as a coroner, and who is in good standing in the person's profession. . . .

§ 313.05 Deputy Coroners and Other Personnel

(A)(1) The coroner may appoint, in writing, deputy coroners, who shall be licensed physicians of good standing in their profession, one of whom may be designated as the chief deputy coroner. The coroner also may appoint pathologists as deputy coroners, who may perform autopsies, make pathological and chemical examinations, and perform other duties as directed by the coroner or recommended by the prosecuting attorney.

§ 313.19 Coroner's Verdict the Legally Accepted Cause of Death

The cause of death and the manner and mode in which the death occurred, as delivered by the coroner and incorporated in the coroner's verdict and in the death certificate filed with the division of vital statistics, shall be the legally accepted manner and mode in which such death occurred, and the legally accepted cause of death, unless the court of common pleas of the county in which the death occurred, after a hearing, directs the coroner to change his decision as to such cause and manner and mode of death.

Parties often disagree about the manner of death in both civil and criminal cases. For example, the family of a decedent may sue an insurance company claiming the death was accidental after the insurance company denied benefits alleging the decedent committed suicide. In the last several years, some experts have gone beyond consideration of the physical findings of an autopsy and have testified about manner of death based upon the circumstances of the death.

Baraka v. Commonwealth

194 S.W.3d 313 (Ky. 2006)

Cooper, J., concurred and filed an opinion in which Graves, J., and Roach, J., joined.

Johnstone, Dissented and filed an opinion in which Lambert, C.J., joined.

Opinion of the Court by Justice GRAVES.

Appellant, Binta Maryam Baraka, entered conditional guilty pleas to second-degree manslaughter. . . . The sole issue presented before us is whether the trial court erred when making a pre-trial *Daubert* ruling regarding the medical examiner's theory of "homicide by heart attack." For the reasons set forth herein, we affirm.

Appellant was indicted in Fayette Circuit Court for the murder of Brutus Price. The Commonwealth alleged that stress related to a physical altercation between the victim and Appellant caused the victim to suffer a fatal heart attack. Appellant requested a Daubert hearing concerning the testimony of Dr. Cristin Rolf, M.D., a state medical examiner called by the Commonwealth. At the hearing, Dr. Rolf testified regarding her physical findings and her understanding of the circumstances surrounding the victim's death. She ultimately concluded that the cause of death was heart attack and the manner of death was homicide.

Appellant contends that Dr. Rolf's opinion regarding the manner of death in this case was unreliable and does not assist the trier of fact.

Here, the trial court based its reliability determination on the following evidence: (1) Dr. Rolf testified that "homicide by heart attack" was not a new, novel, or unique theory, but was widely accepted in the scientific community and among Dr. Rolf's colleagues; (2) Dr. Rolf was unaware of any colleagues who did not accept the theory; (3) Dr. Rolf introduced an article which indicated that the theory had been in practice and utilized for over 100 years; (4) Dr. Rolf knew of several other articles regarding the theory and had attended a lecture regarding the theory just a week prior; (5) Dr. Rolf had the education and professional experience to know of general theories regarding death and to make medical opinions based thereon; and (6) Dr. Rolf had performed autopsies on more than 500 heart attack victims. In the face of such uncontradicted testimony, we can find no clear error in the trial court's reliability determination.

Appellant nonetheless takes issue with the fact that Dr. Rolf's opinion was based, in part, on disputed information regarding the circumstances of the victim's death that was provided to her by police. Yet, as explained by the Court of Appeals, there is absolutely nothing improper about basing an expert opinion on "facts and data . . . made known to the expert at or before the hearing." KRE 703(a). Indeed, the facts and data in this case, information regarding the circumstances of the victim's death provided by investigating officers, is exactly the kind of information customarily relied upon in the day-to-day decisions attendant to a medical examiner's profession. . . . It has been long held that such underlying factual assumptions are properly left for scrutiny during cross-examination.

Moreover, it is axiomatic that a determination of the cause and manner which led to a person's death is generally scientific in origin and outside the common knowledge of layperson jurors. . . . Such medical testimony is even more critical in a case such as this where the manner of death is not necessarily clear from the mere physical evidence (as compared to a case where the person was shot or stabbed). We thus find it implicitly reasonable for the trial court to determine that a medical professional's opinion is helpful when determining whether stress from a physical altercation caused the victim to have a heart attack. *See Terry v. Associated Stone Co.*, 334 S.W.2d 926, 928 (Ky.1960) (where medical doctor testified that a worker's heart attack was in part caused by physical exertion immediately prior to the attack, the Court stated "The question being of a medical nature entirely, determined on the basis of qualified expert testimony, it would be absurd for a court of lawyers to reject that conclusion as unsupported by probative evidence."). . . .

The trial court's determination is no less reasonable in spite of the fact that Dr. Rolf's determination necessarily included an opinion that a criminal act was likely committed in this case. The term, homicide, of course, does not presuppose the occurrence of a criminal act, but simply refers to when a person causes the death of another human being. . . . Medical examiners must make such determinations every time they indicate on a death certificate whether a death was natural, accidental, suicidal, homicidal, or undetermined. Such conclusions are an inherent part of the medical examiner's duties and have never been thought to invade the province of the jury. Indeed, the Court of Appeals cited as such in its opinion:

> It is settled law that expert medical testimony expressing an opinion as to the cause of death, based on a hypothetical question embracing the material facts supported by the evidence, does not invade the province of the jury, is admissible in evidence on the issue of cause of death, and although not conclusive on said issue, and even though it does not disprove every other possible cause of death, is sufficient to take such issue to the jury and to uphold a verdict in accordance therewith.

Nordmeyer v. Sanzone, 314 F.2d 202, 204 (6th Cir.1963) (citations omitted).

When the trial court's ruling is viewed in light of these prevailing facts and law, there are simply insufficient grounds on which to base a finding of clear error or abuse of discretion by the trial court.

The opinion of the Court of Appeals is affirmed.

COOPER, GRAVES, ROACH, SCOTT, and WINTERSHEIMER, J.J., concur.

COOPER, J., concurs in a separate opinion in which GRAVES and ROACH, J.J., join. Dissenting opinion by Justice JOHNSTONE.

In Kentucky, expert testimony is admitted at trial when it satisfies a four-part analysis set forth in *Stringer v. Commonwealth*, 956 S.W.2d 883 (Ky.1997), which incorporates, as part of that analysis, the requirements of *Daubert v. Merrell Dow Pharmaceuticals, Inc.*, 509 U.S. 579, 113 S.Ct. 2786, 125 L.Ed.2d 469 (1993). To introduce expert testimony, the testimony must satisfy the following four requirements: (1) the expert witness must be qualified, (2) the subject matter must satisfy the requirements of *Daubert*, (3) the subject matter must satisfy the test of relevancy set forth in KRE 401, subject to the prejudicial versus probative balancing test required by KRE 403, and (4) the testimony must assist the trier of fact. . . .

Because it determines only that the expert testimony in this matter satisfies the requirements of *Daubert*, without any analysis of or reference to the *Stringer* requirements, I cannot join the majority opinion. Furthermore, having considered the record in its entirety, and having thoroughly reviewed the proposed testimony that Dr. Rolf delivered at the suppression hearing, I conclude that it fails to satisfy the requirements of *Stringer*.

During her testimony, Dr. Rolf presented the results of her autopsy of Price's body and explained that Price had suffered from cardiac disease during his life. She concluded that the medical cause of Price's death was a fatal cardiac arrhythmia, and that the manner of death was "homicide by heart attack." In explaining this conclusion, Dr. Rolf testified that she followed the criteria set forth in a 1977 article on "homicide by heart attack," to which she repeatedly referred during the hearing. The article lists the requirements as follows:

(1)   The criminal act should be of such severity and have sufficient elements of intent to kill or maim, either in fact or by statute, so as to lead logically to a charge of homicide in the event that physical injury had ensued.

(2)   The victim should have realized that the threat to personal safety was implicit. A logical corollary would be a feared threatening act against a loved one or friend.

(3)   The circumstances should be of such a nature as to be commonly accepted as highly emotional.

(4)   The collapse and death must occur during the emotional response period, even if the criminal act had already ceased.

(5)   The demonstration of an organic cardiac disease process of a type commonly associated with a predisposition to lethal cardiac arrhythmia is desirable.

Dr. Rolf testified that she believed all of these criteria had been met in this case, and therefore concluded that Price died as a result of "homicide by heart attack."

This conclusion rested on several preliminary findings, which Dr. Rolf discussed extensively during her testimony. First, Dr. Rolf determined that Appellant committed a criminal act of such severity and nature so as to fulfill the first requirement of "homicide by heart attack." In addition to the contusions and abrasions on Price's body indicating a physical altercation, Dr. Rolf based this belief on information in the police reports and a tape recording of the 911 call contained in the police record. On cross-examination, though, Dr. Rolf acknowledged that Appellant's behavior might not be considered criminal if Price had initiated the altercation, and that she did not know for certain how the altercation commenced. Second, Dr. Rolf surmised that Price perceived an implicit threat to his personal safety. She testified that this was simply a common sense conclusion based on her understanding of the circumstances. Finally, Dr. Rolf concluded that the confrontation between Price and Appellant had been highly emotional. Again, she drew these conclusions based on information in the police reports indicating that Appellant and Price had been in a heated and physical argument.

Expert testimony is admissible only when it will "assist the trier of fact to understand the evidence or to determine a fact in issue." KRE 702. Here, Appellant was charged with murder. A person commits murder when "with the intent to cause the death of another person, he causes the death of such person or of a third person." KRS 507.020(1)(a). Though the fact of Price's death was not at issue, serious questions remained concerning Appellant's intent and whether her actions did, in fact, cause Price's death. In other words, causation was the central and determining issue in this case, and testimony as to whether the death was a homicide, accident, or suicide would assist the jury. Accordingly, the jury would need expert testimony concerning cardiac disease in general, and specifically the conditions under which extreme stress could induce a fatal heart attack so that a juror could determine whether another person caused Price's death. Thus, Dr. Rolf could properly testify that the autopsy revealed Price's cardiac disease, that he had died of a sudden cardiac arrhythmia, and that his body had numerous abrasions and contusions indicating a physical struggle.

However, by permitting Dr. Rolf to conclude that the manner of death was "homicide by heart attack" pursuant to the list provided in her journal article, the trial court allowed improper opinions that were beyond Dr. Rolf's area of expertise and that were not needed for the jury's understanding of the evidence. The jury did not require expert testimony to determine whether the altercation between Price and Appellant was highly emotional; testimony from the investigating officers and the 911 recording would have been sufficient evidence upon which the jury could base an informed decision. Likewise, Dr. Rolf's expert opinion was unnecessary to an intelligent determination as to whether Price did or did not perceive a physical threat that would induce stress. This question does not require specialized knowledge beyond the understanding of the average juror. Finally, Dr. Rolf's testimony that, in her opinion, Appellant's actions constituted a criminal act upon which to base a charge of homicide was undoubtedly beyond the area of her expertise; in fact, Dr. Rolf stated more than once her belief that this was "a question for the investigating officers" and that she "wouldn't know" if Appellant's actions during the altercation constituted a criminal act. These types of opinions are inadmissible as expert testimony, as they do not assist the jury in understanding the evidence or determining a fact in issue. The majority disregards this fundamental requirement.

The majority also concludes that Dr. Rolf properly based her testimony on "facts and data . . . made known to the expert at or before the hearing," KRE 703(a), correctly noting that medical examiners regularly receive information from investigating officers that aid their inquiry and influences their medical conclusions. A review of Dr. Rolf's testimony, however, reveals that her testimony was not based solely on such information, but also on non-medical opinion. Dr. Rolf acknowledged that her conclusion that Price's death was a homicide rested, in part, on her assumption that Appellant had committed a criminal act by initiating the altercation. She even conceded that she might not have classified the death as "homicide by heart attack" if, for example, Price had initiated and escalated the conflict that later resulted in his fatal heart attack. Dr. Rolf then admitted that she had "assumed" Appellant had initiated the altercation but could not identify a single police report or record supporting this assumption, or disproving the possibility that Price had started the conflict. These assumptions, necessary to Dr. Rolf's overall conclusion that Price's death was a homicide and not merely a heart attack resulting from a stressful situation, were simply expressions of Dr. Rolf's personal opinion and cannot be classified as facts or data regularly relied upon by medical examiners. By identifying the manner of death as "homicide," Dr. Rolf was implicitly testifying that Appellant had caused the death of Price, despite the fact that this conclusion was not based solely on her expert medical opinion or upon facts and data in police reports.

The most glaring omission in the majority opinion is its failure to consider the "prejudice versus probative" analysis required by *Stringer*. The classification of Price's death as a "homicide" is highly prejudicial in this case, especially when introduced in the form of expert testimony. KRE 403. An autopsy conclusion of homicide signifies that some human action caused injury to the victim and that the victim died as a result. *See* KRS 507.010. ("A person is guilty of criminal homicide when he causes the death of another human being. . . .") As the majority notes, Price's death is unlike a victim who has been shot or stabbed, where it is clear that a human being caused the victim's death. In such situations, an autopsy conclusion that the manner of death was homicide is not particularly prejudicial and is based solely on medical fact. However, the majority fails to take the analogy to its logical conclusion: in a case where the ultimate issue is whether human action caused a death, expert medical testimony that conclusively answers this question but is not based solely on medical opinion is highly improper and prejudicial.

Instead, the majority concludes that this discrepancy renders Dr. Rolf's testimony even more necessary, stating that it is "axiomatic that a determination of the cause and manner which led to a person's death is generally scientific in origin and outside the common knowledge of layperson jurors.". . . . The fact that jurors "usually" need the assistance of expert medical testimony in similar cases does not somehow relieve this Court of its duty to examine the specific facts and circumstances of this case or to review the actual proposed testimony. . . . Nor does the fact that causation of death is at issue somehow open a floodgate to any and all expert medical testimony of whatever nature. Here, Dr. Rolf's autopsy findings confirmed only that Price died of a heart attack; her conclusion that the death was a homicide incorporated not only objective data gleaned from police reports, but also her personal interpretation of that information.[2]

The substantial weight that a jury places on expert medical opinion cannot be ignored, and the potential for prejudice resulting from improper expert testimony is great. Furthermore, this potential prejudice greatly outweighs the probative value of the testimony, precisely because, by her own admission, medical expertise was not needed to reach Dr. Rolf's conclusion that the death was a homicide. Once informed of the circumstances under which severe stress can hypothetically result in a heart attack, a reasonable juror is perfectly capable of determining whether one person's actions were sufficiently stressful and hostile so as to cause the other to suffer a heart attack. The factors that led to Dr. Rolf's conclusion of homicide — the taped 911 call, the police reports — are factors well within the knowledge and understanding of the jury. Dr. Rolf's expert opinion as a forensic pathologist was simply not necessary to reach this conclusion, and to admit testimony that incorporates these types of non-professional opinions as expert is highly prejudicial. Inferences to be drawn from the testimony are a function completely within the jury's province, and the precise conclusions to be drawn from the evidence should never be presented to the jury in the form of expert testimony. By ignoring the "prejudicial versus probative analysis" required by Stringer, both the majority and concurring opinions fail to fully appreciate the impact of Dr. Rolf's testimony as it pertains to the particular facts of this case. When the entirety of Dr. Rolf's testimony is reviewed, it is evident that her testimony incorporated personal opinion, which is never the proper subject of expert

---

2. *See Medlock v. State*, 263 Ga. 246, 430 S.E.2d 754, 756-57 (1993). (Where an expert's findings as to cause of death "would have permitted the jury to find the death-causing injury either accidental or intentional . . . it would [be] impermissible for the expert to state his opinion that homicide was the cause of death.")

testimony and which carries the danger of great prejudice. I find no error in Dr. Rolf's testimony that fatal heart attacks can be induced by high levels of stress, or in her testimony that Price died of a heart attack. I find it highly prejudicial, however, to permit a forensic pathologist to present expert testimony that Appellant did, in fact, induce this stress when such a conclusion is based on nothing more than her admittedly "personal" and "common sense" opinions of the circumstances preceding Price's death.

For the foregoing reasons, I respectfully dissent.

LAMBERT, C.J., joins this dissent.

State v. Guthrie

627 N.W.N.2d 401 (S.D. 2001)

KONENKAMP, Justice

In this appeal, we affirm the defendant's conviction for murdering his wife.

A.

THE DROWNING

At 7:00 a.m. on May 14, 1999, Dr. William B. Guthrie, a Presbyterian minister, called 911 for emergency assistance. Sharon, his wife of thirty-three years, lay naked and unconscious in the bathtub. The first persons to respond found her face down in the empty tub. Guthrie was "on his hands and knees sobbing and asking for help." Two EMTs pulled her out and moved her to a nearby hallway to perform CPR. In their efforts, they became soaked with water. After the ambulance left, Bonnie Dosch, an R.N. who had assisted in attempts to resuscitate Sharon, offered to take Guthrie to the hospital. She helped him put on his shoes and socks.

Sharon regained some heart activity in the emergency room, but never breathed on her own and never recovered any brain function. She expired on May 15, 1999, at age fifty-four. Dr. Brad Randall, a forensic pathologist, performed an autopsy the following day. Gastric and blood serum toxicology confirmed the presence of subtherapeutic amounts of two antianxiety agents, Diazepam and Lorazepam, and a sedative, Oxazepam. From the partially digested condition of the tablets, it appeared they could have been taken within four hours before her drowning. Also present was a toxic and debilitating level of Temazepam, but not a fatal overdose. The level of Temazepam in Sharon's system was enough to render her unconscious. Randall estimated that she ingested "about 20" Temazepam capsules, which could not have been taken accidentally. She drowned "because she was incapacitated from the Temazepam dose." In Randall's judgment, her death was not natural and not accidental, but from the autopsy alone he could not resolve whether it was suicide or homicide. ıssue

[According to the investigation, the Defendant was having an affair at the time of the murder. The police also discovered that the suicide note was composed on a computer in Defendant's home after the date of death. There was also evidence that someone had done research on the home computer on various forms of drugs, one of which was subsequently pre-scribed for Defendant as a sleeping aid prior to the murder. There were also a number of "household accidents" that decedent suffered before her death.]

On April 15, 1999, Guthrie brought Sharon to the clinic with the com-plaint that she could not wake up. She was "completely out of it." Twice he told clinic personnel, "I didn't do anything to her." The examining physi-cian, Dr. Jeff Hanson, could find nothing wrong with Sharon. A urine tox-icology screen revealed no drugs. The screen would not have revealed the presence of Benadryl, however. Guthrie told the doctor that while sleepwalk-ing Sharon might have taken Benadryl and Codeine. Sharon could remem-ber nothing of the incident the next day, but she believed it was her fault: she had overdosed on her allergy medication (Benadryl) and herbal diet pills. She wanted to lose weight before her daughter's wedding. Her excess weight and her husband's consequent disapproval also concerned her. She once remarked, "As soon as I lose weight, Bill is going to take me on a cruise." . . .

[Shortly before her death] Sharon reported to Thompson that her husband said "he had lost the prescription [for the sleeping pills] and asked if [she] would mind calling a second one in for him." Thompson phoned the prescription in at Statz Drug. Guthrie went to K-Mart that afternoon and had one prescription filled. Two hours later, he went to Statz Drug and had the other filled. On May 4, the church computer was again used to search the Internet, this time specifically for "Temazepam." On May 12, Sharon picked up a refill at Statz Drug. The next day, the day before Sharon drowned, Guthrie picked up yet another refill at K-Mart. Now, sixty capsules had been obtained in the period of two weeks.

One of Sharon's favorite drinks was chocolate milk. She drank it every day and usually in the morning. Because Restoril comes in capsules, their contents can be removed by simply twisting them open. The powdery sub-stance inside is tasteless and odorless. The other sleep remedies that the Physician Assistant had discussed with Guthrie, Ambien and Xanax, come in tablet form and thus cannot be as easily dissolved. When the pathologist examined the contents of Sharon's stomach, he thought it unusual that there were no Restoril capsule remnants to be found. He did find pieces of other medications in non-toxic amounts. Law enforcement officers theorized that the contents of approximately twenty Restoril capsules had been placed in Sharon's chocolate milk before she drank it that morning. She would not have been able to detect it. After Sharon's death, a friend who came to clean the home wiped up what she thought was flour on the kitchen counter. Sharon was allergic to flour, but flour was stored in the home. There were still chocolate milk cartons in the refrigerator.

After Sharon's death, Guthrie gave conflicting accounts of the drowning. . . .

The jury trial commenced on January 10, 2000. Whether Sharon's death was murder or suicide was the crucial issue. The State called various witnesses, including law enforcement officers, doctors, a computer specialist, the Executive Presbyter, and the three daughters. On the question of suicide, the State offered Dr. Alan Berman, a clinical psychologist, suicidologist, and the Executive Director of the American Association of Suicidology. A suicidologist, Berman explained, is an expert who through professional training and experience, studies suicidal death "primarily in terms of learning about the character of individuals who are suicidal and those that do [commit] suicide and the circumstances that surround suicidal death." Guthrie objected, arguing that Berman's theories were not scientifically validated.

Berman detailed for the jury the psychological dynamics found in those who take their own lives. Sharon Guthrie exhibited a minimum of predisposing risk factors. Although she had ingested multiple drugs, a circumstance consistent with suicide, she had no history of mental illness, depression, significant physical illness, chemical dependency, or suicidal ideation. She had no personal or family background of suicidal behavior. Her husband had been having an affair, but she almost certainly had known of it for some time. Guthrie later admitted on the stand that he had told her he wanted a divorce the previous January. With her knowledge of her husband's infidelity and plans for divorce, Dr. Berman believed that those circumstances could not likely be credited with triggering suicide. Berman found several contra-indications for suicide risk. Sharon was excited about her daughter's upcoming wedding. With her personality and her self-consciousness about her weight, she would not have wanted to be found naked. He explained that less than 2% of women kill themselves by drowning in the bathtub, and those who do generally lie back in the water as if to sleep. Berman was permitted to go beyond reciting suicide risk factors and whether Sharon met a profile for suicidal persons. Over objection, he testified that in his opinion "Sharon Guthrie did not die by suicide." Likewise, in his report admitted into evidence, Berman stated, "It is my considered opinion to a high degree of certainty that Sharon Guthrie did not die by suicide."

After two weeks of trial and five hours of deliberation, the jury found Guthrie guilty of murder in the first degree. He was sentenced to mandatory life in prison. He appeals his conviction on the following issues: (1) whether expert testimony was properly allowed on the question of suicide. . . .

Dr. Berman's testimony included an account of the common factors for persons at risk for suicide, a comparison of those factors to this case, and finally an opinion that Sharon Guthrie did not commit suicide. Berman performed his psychological autopsy by reviewing various documents, including the death certificate, the coroner's report, medical records, police interviews, and grand jury testimony. He also independently interviewed family members. Berman indicated that he had been previously qualified as an expert in equivocal death cases, that he was familiar with research on the common characteristics or factors in suicides, and that he had published numerous articles on the subject. After a *Daubert* hearing, the court ruled that Berman's testimony was admissible. Guthrie did not counter with comparable expert testimony. Instead, defense counsel called Dr. Michael McGrath, a clinical psychologist, to attack Berman's methodology. McGrath offered no opinion on Sharon's state of mind before her death. . . .

Guthrie contends that the circuit court erred in allowing Dr. Berman to give his theories on suicide and particularly his opinion that Sharon did not die by suicide, as it improperly went to the ultimate issue and thus invaded the province of the jury. South Dakota abolished the ultimate issue rule and replaced it with SDCL 19-15-4: "Testimony in the form of an opinion or inference otherwise admissible is not objectionable because it embraces an ultimate issue to be decided by the trier of fact."

Before admitting expert testimony, the court must address two preliminary points. First, expert opinion must be relevant to the matter in question. . . . To be relevant, evidence need only be probative, not conclusive. Berman's knowledge of suicidal risk factors bore on the question of Sharon's mental state before her death. His testimony was certainly relevant. Second, the opinion must assist the fact finder in understanding the evidence or deciding the issues. [Citations omitted.] To be helpful, of course, expert opinion must offer more than something jurors can infer for themselves. Berman's knowledge of suicidal risk factors met the helpfulness standard by assisting the jurors in evaluating the perplexing circumstances of Sharon's death.

Opinions merely telling a jury what result to reach are impermissible as intrusive, notwithstanding the repeal of the ultimate issue rule. . . . Although Berman was not asked to address Guthrie's guilt or innocence, his opinion approached the impermissible when he told the jury that "Sharon Guthrie did not die by suicide." . . . It left the inference that she was murdered, or perhaps died accidentally, a far less likely deduction in view of the pathologist's conclusions. It is one thing to state that few of the factors typically found in suicide can be seen in this case. It is another thing to declare as scientific fact that based on a psychological profile the death was not suicide. One assists the jury, but allows it to draw its own inferences from the psychological knowledge imparted. The other simply tells the jury what inference to draw. However, we need not decide if Dr. Berman's final opinion was impermissibly intrusive because it was inadmissible under the *Daubert* standard. Daubert v. Merrell Dow Pharmaceuticals, Inc., 509 U.S. 579, 113 S.Ct. 2786, 125 L.Ed.2d 469 (1993).

Under *Daubert,* the proponent offering expert testimony must show that the expert's theory or method qualifies as scientific, technical, or specialized knowledge. . . . (Rule 702). This burden is met by establishing that there has been adequate empirical proof of the validity of the theory or method. Edward J. Imwinkelried, Evidentiary Foundations 287 (4th ed. 1998). In deciding whether to admit expert testimony, a court must ensure that the opinion abides on a reliable foundation. . . . The standards set forth in *Daubert* are not limited to what has traditionally been perceived as scientific evidence. These standards must be satisfied whenever scientific, technical, or other specialized knowledge is offered. . . . Guthrie does not challenge the relevance of this testimony; he contends only that Berman's opinion does not rest on a reliable foundation.

A trial court can consider the following nonexclusive guidelines for assessing an expert's methodology: (1) whether the method is testable or falsifiable; (2) whether the method was subjected to peer review; (3) the known or potential error rate; (4) whether standards exist to control procedures for the method; (5) whether the method is generally accepted; (6) the relationship of the technique to methods that have been established as reliable; (7) the qualifications of the expert; and (8) the non-judicial uses to which the method has been put. . . . *Daubert*'s list of factors may not each apply to all experts in every case. . . .

Guthrie's argument centers on contradictory testimony about whether psychological autopsies have been subject to validity studies. Of course, the law does not require opinion testimony to be above all criticism before it is admissible. Guthrie's expert testified that there were no validity studies in the area. We interpret our rules of evidence liberally with the "general approach of relaxing the traditional barriers to 'opinion' testimony." . . . The type of studies Berman used were on "reliability," which assesses whether a group will reach the same conclusion given the same criteria. On the other hand, a validity study determines whether the conclusion reached is correct. Thus, Guthrie insists that the methodology was not reliable. The law endows the trial court with "the same broad latitude when it decides how to determine reliability as it enjoys in respect to its ultimate reliability determination." . . . As a result, *Daubert* and *Kumho* provide "a fundamentally deferential analysis, leaving little reweighing in the appellate court." 1 S. Childress & M. Davis, Federal Standards of Review § 4.02, at 4-27 (3d ed. 1999). Generally, an expert's opinion is reliable if it is derived from the foundations of science rather than subjective belief.

The *Daubert–Kumho* factors are guides, not inflexible benchmarks. . . . Nonetheless, as the Supreme Court recognized in *Daubert* and again in *Kumho,* the ability to validate a hypothesis lies at the core of a trial court's inquiry. In *Kumho* the Court "openly extended *Daubert* to non-scientific areas such as engineering, and its reasoning would seem to apply to social sciences as well." Childress & Davis, *supra*, § 4.02, at 4-27. Considering Berman's credentials and methodology, allowing the jury the benefit of his psychological knowledge and experience on typical characteristics or profiles of suicidal persons is within the permissible bounds of expert testimony. These characteristics gave the jury valuable insights into the state of the mind of persons contemplating suicide. The circuit court could reasonably find that "relevant reliability concerns" focused on Berman's "personal knowledge [and] experience." . . .

When opposing experts give contradictory opinions on the reliability or validity of a conclusion, the issue of reliability becomes a question for the jury. . . . The trial process is well equipped to deal with contradictory opinions. "Vigorous cross-examination, presentation of contrary evidence, and careful instruction on the burden of proof are the traditional and appropriate means of attacking shaky but admissible evidence." *Daubert*, 509 U.S. at 596, 113 S.Ct. at 2798, 125 L.Ed.2d at 484 (citations omitted). Guthrie fiercely challenged the accuracy of Berman's methods with expert opinion from another psychologist. He chose to offer this type of testimony rather than expertise on suicide. Consequently, we conclude that the trial court ruled correctly on the reliability question, leaving for the jury to decide whether Berman's testimony on the typical characteristics of suicidal persons deserved factual acceptance.

On the other hand, when Dr. Berman's testimony moved from imparting typical characteristics and whether Sharon met a suicidal profile to declaring that based on her profile she did not commit suicide, we face a more difficult question. What empirical proof is there that because certain deceased persons in equivocal death cases bore only a few characteristics of a suicidal profile, that therefore they can be declared to have not committed suicide? What studies exist on error rates and falsifiability for such opinions? Berman provided little data.[9]

---

9. Dr. Berman testified that he authored or co-authored eighty publications "most of which are research articles in peer review journals which are essentially studies of suicidal people relative to non-suicidal people." Nonetheless, only two of those articles dealt with psychological autopsies: one was published in 1986 and discussed the impact of such autopsies on medical examiners who determine the manner of death; the other one was published in 1989 and dealt with the operational criteria for the classification of suicide. In the *Daubert* hearing, he cited two other studies he did not author, but neither of these dealt with the predictive validity or reliability of psychological autopsies in suspected homicide cases. In truth, psychological autopsies are a "relatively new, unrefined, and un-researched clinical technique. . . ." "[I]t is difficult to identify another area of law where psychological and psychiatric testimony with such little empirical foundation or support, and with such little acceptance by the field, is admitted as evidence." "Given the dearth of research investigating the validity and reliability of psychological autopsies, there is good reason to be cautious about introducing expert testimony about psychological autopsies in legal proceedings." James R.P. Ogloff and Randy K. Otto, *Psychological Autopsy: Clinical and Legal Perspectives*, 37 St.Louis ULJ 607, 620, 645-46 (1993). *See also* James T. Richardson, et al., *The Problems of Applying Daubert to Psychological Syndrome Evidence*, 79 Judicature 10-11 (July-August 1995).

mario

We think there is substantial reason to doubt the reliability of suicidal profiles if they are to be used to declare unequivocally that a subject's death was self-inflicted. This testimony has the same pitfalls as syndrome evidence. We have been cautious in authorizing definitive opinions based on psychological syndromes. . . .

A few courts have allowed psychological autopsy evidence in cases where the question before the jury in a homicide prosecution was whether the deceased died from suicide. In those cases, however, the experts did not opine with scientific certitude that the deceased did or did not commit suicide. In United States v. St. Jean, 1995 WL 106960 *2, a case of a husband accused of murdering his wife, an expert testified that the circumstances of the wife's death bore none of the indicators associated with those who commit suicide. *St. Jean* applied *Daubert* and concluded that the psychologist's testimony was reliable and thus admissible under the military rules of evidence equivalent to the federal rules. However, the psychologist's testimony was limited to "the profile of one who is, psychiatrically speaking, suicidal or a suicidal risk." *Id.* at *1. In Horinek v. State, 977 S.W.2d 696, 701 (Tex.Ct.App.-Fort Worth 1998), a case of a police officer charged with murdering his wife, a forensic pathologist-psychiatrist performed a "psychological autopsy" and then testified "that it appeared very unlikely that this individual would be the sort of person to kill herself." But the *Horinek* court did not discuss the *Daubert* reliability standards. See generally Elizabeth Biffl, Psychological Autopsies: Do They Belong in the Courtroom? 24 Am.J. Crim.L. 123 (1996).

Unquestionably, Dr. Berman had special expertise on the mental states of those who commit suicide, but his knowledge was based primarily on observation and experience, not traditional empirical studies. . . . In allowing experts with specialized knowledge to testify, courts applying *Daubert* generally permit these experts to describe the symptoms or behaviors of known victims, report the symptoms or behaviors observed in the victim in the present case, and give an opinion that the victim's symptoms or behaviors are "consistent with" those of known victims. [Citations omitted.] Berman's understanding of risk factors for suicide was relevant, helpful, and admissible, but in the present state of psychological knowledge, a suicide profile alone cannot be used to declare with scientific certainty that a person did or did not commit suicide. Berman's opinion in that respect was inadmissible under the *Daubert* standards. Thus, the trial court abused its discretion in allowing Berman's opinion that Sharon did not commit suicide. . . .

Although Berman's testimony was not properly limited to suicidal profiles or characteristics, the jury could have easily reasoned purely from his profiles and characteristics testimony that Sharon's death was not the result of a suicide based on the absence of sufficient suicidal indicators and the totality of the evidence offered at trial. Certainly, his opinion that Sharon did not die by suicide was not offered as a substitute for a thorough criminal investigation. The jury had the benefit of substantial and independent circumstantial evidence from which to conclude that Sharon's death was a homicide. As such, we cannot say that in the absence of Dr. Berman's opinion on suicide the jury verdict would have been different. . . . Allowing the opinion was therefore harmless error.

NOTES AND QUESTIONS

1. In *Baraka*, the defendant faced a manslaughter case after she quarreled with her father and he died from a heart attack. Without the expert's opinion of "homicide by heart attack," could the prosecution have prevailed? Does the expert possess specialized, reliable knowledge that makes the opinion particularly helpful?

2. Do you agree with the court's decision to limit the expert testimony in *Guthrie*? Should the result be different if a forensic pathologist (rather than a psychologist) testifies? One can argue that part of a pathologist's job in determining cause and manner of death may well include evaluating the circumstances surrounding the death. For a case allowing such testimony, see Horinek v. State, 977 S.W.2d 696 (Tex. App. Ft. Worth, 1998).

3. Even though "ultimate issue expert testimony" is expressly allowed by FRE 704(a) and many state evidence codes, is there a particular danger in allowing an expert to opine whether a death was a homicide or suicide when there is conflicting physical evidence about the manner of death? Is such testimony helpful?

CHAPTER 7

MEDICAL CAUSATION

One of the most common yet most difficult scientific evidence problems that the courts confront is deciding what constitutes adequate proof of the cause of a disease or injury. In a typical situation, a person is exposed to a substance that is thought to be dangerous (a *toxin*) and then gets sick. That person becomes a plaintiff, suing the party on whose premises the exposure occurred (often the plaintiff's employer) and/or the manufacturer of the alleged toxin. The court must then decide on the admissibility and sufficiency (ability to withstand summary judgment) of the evidence the plaintiff offers to prove that the exposure caused his or her illness.

The plaintiff's evidence is usually drawn from one or more of three main categories. *Epidemiology* is the statistical study of patterns of disease. Its goal is to demonstrate statistical correlations between potential causal factors such as exposure to dangerous substances and larger-than-expected occurrences of a disease. In court, epidemiological evidence is usually introduced to prove *general causation* — that is, that the suspect substance *can* cause the plaintiff's illness. The other two categories of evidence are then used to establish *specific causation* — that the substance *did* cause *this* plaintiff's illness. (As we shall see, however, judges are less precise than scientists and legal scholars in distinguishing between the two kinds of causation.) The first, *toxicology*, is the science of poisons. Relying primarily on chemical analysis and animal studies, toxicologists attempt to discover the specific physiological pathways whereby particular toxins cause human disease. The second, *differential diagnosis,* is the reasoning method that doctors use to assess a patient's symptoms, rule in some possible causes and rule out others, and finally decide on an appropriate treatment. (The emerging science of *toxicogenomics,* which could make causal determinations far more precise, is introduced at the end of this chapter.)

In an ideal plaintiff's case, the three forms of evidence complement each other. An epidemiologist says that the alleged toxin has been associated with the plaintiff's disease in large numbers of other cases, a toxicologist testifies about the biochemical process through which the toxin causes the disease, and the plaintiff's physician says, "Based on the plaintiff's symptoms and other cases I have seen and read about, I diagnosed the plaintiff as having been exposed to [the suspected toxin] and treated her accordingly."

Not surprisingly, there are few ideal plaintiffs' cases. Most often, the plaintiff can offer only one or two of the three categories of evidence, typically in a partial or otherwise imperfect form. The court must then decide whether each individual piece of evidence is admissible, and then whether the totality of the evidence is sufficient to support a prima facie case that the suspect exposure caused the plaintiff's illness. If the defendant offers contradictory scientific evidence, the court will have to repeat the admissibility determination. (The sufficiency question will not come up, since the plaintiff bears the burden of proof.)

As you consider the cases and materials that follow, keep two overarching issues in mind. First, even the best evidence of medical causation will only suggest probabilities. There is no analog in these cases to the eyewitness who saw the defendant's car run over the plaintiff. Second, even though the three disciplines that may offer evidence are all "scientific," each has a different primary objective. For epidemiology, the goal is to study patterns of disease to draw statistically-based inferences about causation; for toxicology, to develop and test hypotheses about the physiological pathways through which disease can develop and injury occur; and for clinical medicine, to learn enough to make the patient better as quickly as possible. None of these inquiries exactly parallels the law's objective, which is to decide whether it is more probable than not that a suspected toxin actually caused a particular plaintiff's particular illness.

I. HOW DO YOU PROVE THAT AN EXPOSURE CAUSED AN OUTCOME? EPIDEMIOLOGY, TOXICOLOGY, AND DIFFERENTIAL DIAGNOSIS

In the following two cases, two federal appellate courts describe the causation dilemma. Both cases involved Bendectin, an anti-nausea drug given during pregnancy that has been suspected of causing birth defects.

The second case is the Ninth Circuit's opinion on remand from the Supreme Court's *Daubert* decision.

Turpin v. Merrell Dow Pharmaceuticals, Inc.

959 F.2d 1349 (6th Cir. 1992), *cert. denied,* 506 U.S. 826 (1992)

MERRITT, Chief Judge.

... Causation here is a matter of trying to measure probabilities. It requires a complex series of inferences drawn from scientific experiment and observation and statistical comparisons. For example, the plaintiffs rely primarily on animal experiments from which an inference is drawn that since chemical compounds in Bendectin, if administered at certain levels, cause birth defects in animals, they may cause similar defects in humans. The plaintiffs draw a further inference that Bendectin caused the birth defects in this particular case. These inferences are necessary because physicians who treated Brandy Turpin and other similarly situated children cannot diagnose the cause of these anomalies.

The defendant, too, reasons from the results of scientific studies to a particularized conclusion with respect to these plaintiffs. Merrell Dow relies primarily on statistical studies that purport to show that the incidence of certain birth defects is no higher with women who used Bendectin than with those who did not or, in the alternative, that where statistical associations indicating a possible causal relationship exist, they would not lead a reasonable expert to infer that Bendectin causes birth defects.

The causation proof in Bendectin birth defect cases is offered by expert witnesses who speak in terms of population groups and statistical samples rather than specific individuals. The expert witnesses on each side are often the same, from case to case, and even when different the scientific conclusions and theories are based on the same or similar statistical studies and scientific experiments. The cases are variations on a theme, somewhat like an orchestra which travels to different music halls, substituting musicians from time to time but playing essentially the same repertoire.

Daubert v. Merrell Dow Pharmaceuticals, Inc.

43 F.3d 1311 (9th Cir. 1995)

KOZINSKI, Circuit Judge.

... Two minors brought suit against Merrell Dow Pharmaceuticals, claiming they suffered limb reduction birth defects[1] because their mothers had taken Bendectin, a drug prescribed for morning sickness to about 17.5 million pregnant women in the United States between 1957 and 1982. ...

---

1. Limb reduction defects involve incomplete development of arms, legs, fingers and toes, such as the defects associated with the Thalidomide disaster of the 1960s.

For the most part, we don't know how birth defects come about. We do know they occur in 2-3% of births, whether or not the expectant mother has taken Bendectin . . . Limb defects are even rarer, occurring in fewer than one birth out of every 1000 . . . But scientists simply do not know how teratogens (chemicals known to cause limb reduction defects) do their damage: They cannot reconstruct the biological chain of events that leads from an expectant mother's ingestion of a teratogenic substance to the stunted development of a baby's limbs. Nor do they know what it is about teratogens that causes them to have this effect. . . .

Not knowing the mechanism whereby a particular agent causes a particular effect is not always fatal to a plaintiff's claim. Causation can be proved even when we don't know precisely *how* the damage occurred, if there is sufficiently compelling proof that the agent must have caused the damage *somehow.* One method of proving causation in these circumstances is to use statistical evidence. If 50 people who eat at a restaurant one evening come down with food poisoning during the night, we can infer that the restaurant's food probably contained something unwholesome, even if none of the dishes is available for analysis. This inference is based on the fact that, in our health-conscious society, it is highly unlikely that 50 people who have nothing in common except that they ate at the same restaurant would get food poisoning from independent sources.

It is by such means that plaintiffs here seek to establish that Bendectin is responsible for their injuries. They rely on the testimony of three groups of scientific experts. One group proposes to testify that there is a statistical link between the ingestion of Bendectin during pregnancy and limb reduction defects. These experts have not themselves conducted epidemiological (human statistical) studies on the effects of Bendectin; rather, they have reanalyzed studies published by other scientists, none of whom reported a statistical association between Bendectin and birth defects. Other experts proffered by plaintiffs propose to testify that Bendectin causes limb reduction defects in humans because it causes such defects in laboratory animals. A third group of experts sees a link between Bendectin and birth defects because Bendectin has a chemical structure that is similar to other drugs suspected of causing birth defects.

II. PROVING GENERAL CAUSATION: EPIDEMIOLOGY

First, read an overview of the purposes and methods of epidemiology taken from the *Reference Manual on Scientific Evidence.* Then observe some of those methods put to use in the *Agent Orange* litigation.

Reference Guide on Epidemiology

Reference Manual on Scientific Evidence (Federal Judicial Center, 2d ed. 2000)
Michael D. Green, D. Michal Freedman, and Leon Gordis

I. INTRODUCTION

Epidemiology is the field of public health and medicine that studies the incidence, distribution, and etiology of disease in human populations. The purpose of epidemiology is to better understand disease causation and to prevent disease in groups of individuals. Epidemiology assumes that disease is not distributed randomly in a group of individuals and that identifiable subgroups, including those exposed to certain agents, are at increased risk of contracting particular diseases.

Judges and juries increasingly are presented with epidemiologic evidence as the basis of an expert's opinion on causation. In the courtroom, epidemiologic research findings are offered to establish or dispute whether exposure to an agent caused a harmful effect or disease. Epidemiologic evidence identifies agents that are associated with an increased risk of disease in groups of individuals, quantifies the amount of excess disease that is associated with an agent, and provides a profile of the type of individual who is likely to contract a disease after being exposed to an agent. Epidemiology focuses on the question of general causation (i.e., is the agent capable of causing disease?) rather than that of specific causation (i.e., did it cause disease in a particular individual?). For example, in the 1950s Doll and Hill and others published articles about the increased risk of lung cancer in cigarette smokers. Doll and Hill's studies showed that smokers who smoked ten to twenty cigarettes a day had a lung cancer mortality rate that was about ten times higher than that for nonsmokers. These studies identified an association between smoking cigarettes and death from lung cancer, which contributed to the determination that smoking causes lung cancer.

However, it should be emphasized that *an association is not equivalent to causation*. An association identified in an epidemiologic study may or may not be causal. Assessing whether an association is causal requires an understanding of the strengths and weaknesses of the study's design and implementation, as well as a judgment about how the study findings fit with other scientific knowledge. . . .

A final caveat is that employing the results of group-based studies of risk to make a causal determination for an individual plaintiff is beyond the limits of epidemiology. Nevertheless, a substantial body of legal precedent has developed that addresses the use of epidemiologic evidence to prove causation for an individual litigant through probabilistic means. . . .

Three basic issues arise when epidemiology is used in legal disputes and the methodological soundness of a study and its implications for resolution of the question of causation must be assessed:

(1)   Do the results of an epidemiologic study reveal an association between an agent and disease?
(2)   What sources of error in the study may have contributed to an inaccurate result?
(3)   If the agent is associated with disease, is the relationship causal?

... II.   WHAT DIFFERENT KINDS OF EPIDEMIOLOGIC STUDIES EXIST?

A.   EXPERIMENTAL AND OBSERVATIONAL STUDIES OF SUSPECTED TOXIC AGENTS

To determine whether an agent is related to the risk of developing a certain disease or an adverse health outcome, we might ideally want to conduct an experimental study in which the subjects would be randomly assigned to one of two groups: one group exposed to the agent of interest and the other not exposed. After a period of time, the study participants in both groups would be evaluated for development of the disease. This type of study, called a randomized trial, clinical trial, or true experiment, is considered the gold standard for determining the relationship of an agent to a disease or health outcome. Such a study design is often used to evaluate new drugs or medical treatments and is the best way to ensure that any observed difference between the two groups in outcome is likely to be the result of exposure to the drug or medical treatment.

Randomization minimizes the likelihood that there are differences in relevant characteristics between those exposed to the agent and those not exposed. Researchers conducting clinical trials attempt to use study designs that are placebo controlled, which means that the group not receiving the agent or treatment is given a placebo, and that use double blinding, which means that neither the participants nor those conducting the study know which group is receiving the agent or treatment and which group is given the placebo. However, ethical and practical constraints limit the use of such experimental methodologies to assessing the value of agents that are thought to be beneficial to human beings.

When an agent's effects are suspected to be harmful, we cannot knowingly expose people to the agent. Instead of the investigator controlling who is exposed to the agent and who is not, most epidemiologic studies are observational — that is, they "observe" a group of individuals who have been exposed to an agent of interest, such as cigarette smoking or an industrial chemical, and compare them with another group of individuals who have not been so exposed. Thus, the investigator identifies a group of subjects who have been knowingly or unknowingly exposed and compares their rate of disease or death with that of an unexposed group. In contrast to clinical studies, in which potential risk factors can be controlled, epidemiologic investigations generally focus on individuals living in the community, for whom characteristics other than the one of interest, such as diet, exercise, exposure to other environmental agents, and genetic background, may contribute to the risk of developing the disease in question. Since these characteristics cannot be controlled directly by the investigator, the investigator addresses their possible role in the relationship being studied by considering them in the design of the study and in the analysis and interpretation of the study results. . . .

III. How Should Results of an Epidemiologic Study Be Interpreted?

. . . A. Relative Risk

A commonly used approach for expressing the association between an agent and disease is relative risk (RR). It is defined as the ratio of the incidence rate (often referred to as incidence) of disease in exposed individuals to the incidence rate in unexposed individuals:

$$\text{Relative Risk (RR)} = \frac{\text{Incidence rate in the exposed}}{\text{Incidence rate in the unexposed}}$$

The incidence rate of disease reflects the number of cases of disease that develop during a specified period of time divided by the number of persons in the cohort under study. Thus, the incidence rate expresses the risk that a member of the population will develop the disease within a specified period of time.

For example, a researcher studies 100 individuals who are exposed to an agent and 200 who are not exposed. After one year, 40 of the exposed individuals are diagnosed as having a disease, and 20 of the unexposed individuals also are diagnosed as having the disease. The relative risk of contracting the disease is calculated as follows:

- The incidence rate of disease in the exposed individuals is 40 cases per year per 100 persons (40/100), or 0.4.
- The incidence rate of disease in the unexposed individuals is 20 cases per year per 200 persons (20/200), or 0.1.
- The relative risk is calculated as the incidence rate in the exposed group (0.4) divided by the incidence rate in the unexposed group (0.1), or 4.0.

A relative risk of 4.0 indicates that the risk of disease in the exposed group is four times as high as the risk of disease in the unexposed group.

In general, the relative risk can be interpreted as follows:

- If the relative risk equals 1.0, the risk in exposed individuals is the same as the risk in unexposed individuals. There is no association between exposure to the agent and disease.

- If the relative risk is greater than 1.0, the risk in exposed individuals is greater than the risk in unexposed individuals. There is a positive association between exposure to the agent and the disease, which could be causal.
- If the relative risk is less than 1.0, the risk in exposed individuals is less than the risk in unexposed individuals. There is a negative association, which could reflect a protective or curative effect of the agent on risk of disease. For example, immunizations lower the risk of disease. The results suggest that immunization is associated with a decrease in disease and may have a protective effect on the risk of disease. . . .

Figure 3. Risks in Exposed and Unexposed Groups

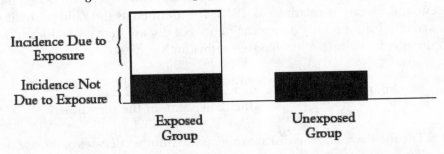

. . . C.   COULD A CONFOUNDING FACTOR BE RESPONSIBLE FOR THE STUDY
            RESULT?

Even when an association exists, researchers must determine whether the exposure causes the disease or whether the exposure and disease are caused by some other confounding factor. A confounding factor is both a risk factor for the disease and a factor associated with the exposure of interest. For example, researchers may conduct a study that finds individuals with gray hair have a higher rate of death than those with hair of another color. Instead of hair color having an impact on death, the results might be explained by the confounding factor of age. If old age is associated differentially with the gray-haired group (those with gray hair tend to be older), old age may be responsible for the association found between hair color and death. Researchers must separate the relationship between gray hair and risk of death from that of old age and risk of death. When researchers find an association between an agent and a disease, it is critical to determine whether the association is causal or the result of confounding.[99] Some

99. Confounding can bias a study result by either exaggerating or diluting any true association. One example of a confounding factor that may result in a study's outcome understating an association is vaccination. Thus, if a group exposed to an agent has a higher rate of vaccination for the disease under study than the unexposed group, the vaccination may reduce the rate of disease in the exposed group, thereby producing an association that is less than the true association without the confounding of vaccination.

epidemiologists classify confounding as a form of bias. However, confounding is a reality—that is, the observed association of a factor and a disease is actually the result of an association with a third, confounding factor. Failure to recognize confounding can introduce a bias—error—into the findings of the study. . . .

V. General Causation: Is an Exposure a Cause of the Disease?

Once an association has been found between exposure to an agent and development of a disease, researchers consider whether the association reflects a true cause–effect relationship. When epidemiologists evaluate whether a cause–effect relationship exists between an agent and disease, they are using the term causation in a way similar to, but not identical with, the way the familiar "but for," or sine qua non, test is used in law for cause in fact. "An act or an omission is not regarded as a cause of an event if the particular event would have occurred without it." This is equivalent to describing the act or occurrence as a necessary link in a chain of events that results in the particular event. Epidemiologists use causation to mean that an increase in the incidence of disease among the exposed subjects would not have occurred had they not been exposed to the agent. Thus, exposure is a necessary condition for the increase in the incidence of disease among those exposed . . . In assessing causation, researchers first look for alternative explanations for the association, such as bias or confounding factors . . . Once this process is completed, researchers consider how guidelines for inferring causation from an association apply to the available evidence. . . .

The factors that guide epidemiologists in making judgments about causation are:

(1) temporal relationship;
(2) strength of the association;
(3) dose–response relationship;
(4) replication of the findings;
(5) biological plausibility (coherence with existing knowledge);
(6) consideration of alternative explanations;
(7) cessation of exposure;
(8) specificity of the association; and
(9) consistency with other knowledge.

. . . A. Is There a Temporal Relationship?

A temporal, or chronological, relationship must exist for causation. If an exposure causes disease, the exposure must occur before the disease develops. If the exposure occurs after the disease develops, it cannot cause the disease. Although temporal relationship is often listed as one of many factors in assessing whether an inference of causation is justified, it is a necessary factor: Without exposure before disease, causation cannot exist.

B.   HOW STRONG IS THE ASSOCIATION BETWEEN THE EXPOSURE AND DISEASE?

The relative risk is one of the cornerstones for causal inferences. Relative risk measures the strength of the association. The higher the relative risk, the greater the likelihood that the relationship is causal. For cigarette smoking, for example, the estimated relative risk for lung cancer is very high, about 10. That is, the risk of lung cancer in smokers is approximately ten times the risk in nonsmokers. . . .

C.   IS THERE A DOSE–RESPONSE RELATIONSHIP?

A dose–response relationship means that the more intense the exposure, the greater the risk of disease. Generally, higher exposures should increase the incidence (or severity) of disease. However, some causal agents do not exhibit a dose–response relationship when, for example, there is a threshold phenomenon (i.e., an exposure may not cause disease until the exposure exceeds a certain dose). Thus, a dose–response relationship is strong, but not essential, evidence that the relationship between an agent and disease is causal. . . .

E.   IS THE ASSOCIATION BIOLOGICALLY PLAUSIBLE
      (CONSISTENT WITH EXISTING KNOWLEDGE)?

Biological plausibility is not an easy criterion to use and depends upon existing knowledge about the mechanisms by which the disease develops. When biological plausibility exists, it lends credence to an inference of causality. For example, the conclusion that high cholesterol is a cause of coronary heart disease is plausible because cholesterol is found in atherosclerotic plaques. However, observations have been made in epidemiologic studies that were not biologically plausible at the time but subsequently were shown to be correct. When an observation is inconsistent with current biological knowledge, it should not be discarded, but the observation should be confirmed before significance is attached to it. . . .

G.   WHAT IS THE EFFECT OF CEASING EXPOSURE?

If an agent is a cause of a disease one would expect that cessation of exposure to that agent ordinarily would reduce the risk of the disease. This has been the case, for example, with cigarette smoking and lung cancer. In many situations, however, relevant data are simply not available regarding the possible effects of ending the exposure. But when such data are available and eliminating exposure reduces the incidence of disease, this factor strongly supports a causal relationship.

H. DOES THE ASSOCIATION EXHIBIT SPECIFICITY?

An association exhibits specificity if the exposure is associated only with a single disease or type of disease. The vast majority of agents do not cause a wide variety of effects. For example, asbestos causes mesothelioma and lung cancer and may cause one or two other cancers, but there is no evidence that it causes any other types of cancers. Thus, a study that finds that an agent is associated with many different diseases should be examined skeptically. Nevertheless, there may be causal relationships in which this guideline is not satisfied. Cigarette manufacturers have long claimed that because cigarettes have been linked to lung cancer, emphysema, bladder cancer, heart disease, pancreatic cancer, and other conditions, there is no specificity and the relationships are not causal. There is, however, at least one good reason why inferences about the health consequences of tobacco do not require specificity: because tobacco and cigarette smoke are not in fact single agents but consist of numerous harmful agents, smoking represents exposure to multiple agents, with multiple possible effects. Thus, while evidence of specificity may strengthen the case for causation, lack of specificity does not necessarily undermine it where there is a plausible biological explanation for its absence. . . .

In re "Agent Orange" Product Liability Litigation

611 F. Supp. 1223 (S.D.N.Y. 1985)

[In this protracted controversy, Vietnam veterans who were exposed to Agent Orange, a defoliant that was widely used in the war, attempted to establish that their exposure caused cancer and other diseases. In this opinion, one of dozens that the case has generated, the district court granted summary judgment against individual veterans who had opted out of a pending class action.]

WEINSTEIN, Chief Judge

. . . Epidemiological studies addressing the effect of Agent Orange exposure on veterans' health have not furnished support for plaintiffs' claims. They have been negative or inconclusive.

The Air Force study is the most intensive examination to date of Agent Orange effects on exposed veterans . . . This study utilized 1,024 matched pairs of men for analysis. Essentially all those who had participated in the fixed wing spraying and who could be located were studied. The conclusion was negative. In summary,

> This baseline report concludes that there is insufficient evidence to support a cause and effect relationship between herbicide exposure and adverse health in the Ranch Hand group at this time. . . .

Two recently-released studies fail to establish any causal connection. A comparison of New York State Vietnam veterans with veterans of that era who did not serve in Vietnam revealed no increased incidence of disease. The authors note that the long induction period involved in some of the diseases suggests the need for further study, but conclude:

> Overall, these studies show no remarkable disease differences between Vietnam veterans and other veterans of that era. To the extent that Vietnam service may be indicative of dioxin-contaminated herbicide exposure, we find no suggested association with cause of death. . . .

The comprehensive three-part Australian study is similarly negative. In 1980, the government of Australia commissioned the Commonwealth Institute of Health to conduct a series of scientific studies of the health of Vietnam veterans and their families . . . Australian forces that served in Vietnam were exposed at least as heavily as United States forces to Agent Orange.

This study sought to determine whether death rates among Vietnam veterans were higher than among comparable non-veterans for all causes of death combined. The study included 46,166 subjects: 19,209 veterans who served in Vietnam or Vietnam waters for over 90 days and did not die prior to two years of service, and 26,957 non-veterans. Information about the study subjects was obtained through death registers, medical certificates, and military and nonmilitary records. The follow-up rate was high, and the authors conclude that the data used was of "high quality."

The study found the death rate among study subjects — both veterans and non-veterans — "statistically significantly lower than expected for Australian males, taking age and calendar year into account." Mortality among veterans was not higher than that among non-veterans in a statistically significant sense, except among Veterans who were members of The Royal Australian Engineers . . . [T]he Report offers several possible explanations for this discrepancy, none of them attributable to Agent Orange.

With respect to specific causes of death, the Report found no statistically significant difference in death rates from cancer among veterans and non-veterans. In particular, the study found that:

> there was no statistically significant difference in the death rates from soft tissue sarcoma or non-Hodgkin's lymphoma. Other studies have indicated that both cancers are possibly caused by phenoxy acetic acid herbicides * * * sprayed in Vietnam.

The study found no statistically significant difference in death rates from a number of other causes of death, including diseases of the skin, of the musculoskeletal system and connective tissue, of the blood, and of the neoplasmic, endocrine, nutritional, metabolic, and circulatory systems. The study attributed a higher veteran mortality rate from diseases of the digestive system to alcoholism.

While cautioning that diseases such as cancer may take longer to develop, the Australian study found no evidence of an excess of deaths among the veterans studied due to "unusual causes." Such evidence — had it surfaced — "*might have suggested* that some deaths of veterans *might have been* caused by a specific toxin or pathogen."

Congress agrees with this generally negative assessment of the effect of Agent Orange exposure . . . [A Report by the House Committee on Veterans' Affairs] concluded that "it is generally agreed that there is insufficient credible scientific evidence that this group of veterans has demonstrated they are experiencing any higher incidence or frequency of medical problems related to their possible exposure to dioxin while in service as to warrant a statutory presumption that such medical problems are related to military service."

Plaintiffs cite a number of studies conducted on animals and industrial workers as evidence of a causal link between exposure to [dioxin] and the development of various hepatotoxic, hematotoxic, genotoxic, and enzymatic responses. None of these studies do more than show that there may be a causal connection between dioxin and disease. None show such a connection between plaintiffs and Agent Orange.

NOTES AND QUESTIONS

1. One of the studies discussed in *Agent Orange* referred to the absence of a *statistically significant* difference in death rates between exposed and unexposed people. The concept of statistical significance is treated in detail in Chapter 3, Statistical Inference. Generally, a difference (or an association) is called statistically significant if it is too large to attribute to chance alone. Significance is calculated by any of a number of standard formulas; the precise one to be used depends on the specifics of the data being analyzed.

2. How would you characterize the various epidemiological studies introduced in *Agent Orange* in terms of the research methods discussed in the *Reference Manual* excerpt? Although the court does not use the precise term, the concept of *relative risk* is implicit in the court's analysis of the studies.

3. Why did the *Agent Orange* court find that the studies it reviewed did not support the plaintiffs' case? What would the results have had to look like in order to support a finding for the plaintiffs?

4. Note the importance of the burden of proof. Despite the absence of strong epidemiological evidence, the Agent Orange controversy went on for years for a number of reasons. Many Vietnam veterans believed on an intuitive level that an abnormal number of them were contracting rare cancers. Many treating physicians thought the same thing, and could find no

common element among the cases except the exposure to Agent Orange in Southeast Asia. In addition, as the case mentions, there was some toxicological evidence that raised suspicions about Agent Orange as a carcinogen. In light of all this, does it strike you as fair to require as a threshold matter that the plaintiffs cite epidemiological evidence? Would it be fair to the defendants to do otherwise? Is your conclusion affected by the court's comment about cancer taking a long time to develop? Should plaintiffs who are sick now have to await the results of epidemiological studies that may be many years in the future?

III. MOVING FROM GENERAL TO SPECIFIC CAUSATION

As the *Reference Manual* reading makes clear, epidemiology sees its objective as proving general causation — that the alleged toxin is capable of causing the plaintiff's disease. Sometimes, as in *Agent Orange,* a plaintiff's case will fail because of the absence of evidence of general causation. But even where general causation is established, the law requires more: evidence of specific causation, or proof that the toxin is likely to have caused this plaintiff's illness. The Ninth Circuit's framing of the problem in this radiation exposure case is typical.

In Re Hanford Nuclear Reservation Litigation

292 F.3d 1124 (9th Cir. 2002)

SCHROEDER, Chief Judge.

These appeals raise fundamental questions concerning how courts should grapple with causation issues in mass tort cases. The appellants are among thousands of plaintiffs who filed suit for damages allegedly arising out of their exposure to harmful levels of radioactive emissions from the Hanford Nuclear Reservation over a period of many years. They filed these actions under the Price-Anderson Act, 42 U.S.C. § 2011 *et seq.,* against E.I. DuPont and other entities who operated the nuclear facility under license agreements with the federal government during the relevant period. . . .

The relevant case law and the record here reflect that plaintiffs' expectations about the parameters of generic causation described in the district court's discovery orders were justified. Causation in toxic tort cases is typically discussed in terms of generic and specific causation. General, or "generic" causation has been defined by courts to mean whether the substance at issue had the capacity to cause the harm alleged, while "individual causation" refers to whether a particular individual suffers from a particular ailment as a result of exposure to a substance. *See In re "Agent Orange"*, 818 F.2d at 165 ("[t]he relevant question ... is not whether Agent Orange has the capacity to cause harm, the generic causation issue, but whether it did cause harm and to whom. That determination is highly individualistic, and depends upon the characteristics of individual plaintiffs (e.g. state of health, lifestyle) and the nature of their exposure to Agent Orange"); *Jones v. Allercare, Inc.*, 203 F.R.D. 290, 301 (N.D.Ohio 2001) ("relevant question in this case will not be whether the products have the capacity to cause harm, but whether the products caused harm and to whom. Thus, the real causation issue in this case is individual, not general, in nature"). *See also Hilao v. Estate of Marcos*, 103 F.3d 767, 788 (9th Cir.1996) (Rymer, J. dissenting in part and concurring in part) (contrasting "generic causation — that the defendant was responsible for a tort which had the capacity to cause the harm alleged — with individual proximate cause and individual damage").

Defendants have not cited a case that articulates a contrary understanding of generic causation. Given this authority, we believe the appropriate understanding of generic causation is the one plaintiffs assert: whether exposure to a substance for which a defendant is responsible, such as radiation at the level of exposure alleged by plaintiffs, is capable of causing a particular injury or condition in the general population.

In order to prevail on their claims, however, plaintiffs must establish both generic *and* individual causation. This means that they must establish not only that the toxic substances released from Hanford are capable of causing the conditions complained of, but in addition, that Hanford emissions were the cause-in-fact of their specific conditions. ...

A.   Using Enhanced Evidence of General Causation to Prove Specific Causation

One approach to bridging the gap between general and specific causation is to permit especially strong evidence of general causation to satisfy the specific causation requirement. A number of cases have focused on one type of epidemiological evidence, relative risk. This is the ratio of the rate of occurrence of the disease in question among those exposed to the relevant hazard to its "background" rate among the unexposed population. Some courts have permitted an inference of specific causation to be drawn when the relative risk — which is, strictly speaking, evidence of general causation — is greater than 2. The next reading explains the logic of this approach. The case that follows (another excerpt from the Ninth Circuit's *Daubert* remand opinion) applies the "doubling of risk" analysis in an especially demanding way.

The Swine Flu Vaccine and Guillain-Barré Syndrome: A Case Study In Relative Risk and Specific Causation

64 L. & Contemp. Probs. 49 (2001)
David A. Freedman and Philip B. Stark

This article discusses the role of epidemiologic evidence in toxic tort cases, focusing on relative risk. If a relative risk is above 2.0, can we infer specific causation? Relative risk compares groups in an epidemiologic study. One group is exposed to some hazard, like a toxic substance; another "control" group is not exposed. For present purposes, relative risk is a ratio:

$$RR = Observed/Expected.$$

The numerator in this fraction is the number of injuries observed in the exposed group. The "expected" number in the denominator is computed on the theory that exposure has no effect, so that injury rates in the exposed group should be the same as injury rates in the control group. Adjustments are often made to account for known differences between the two groups, for example, in the distribution of ages.

The basic intuition connecting relative risk and probability of causation can be explained as follows. Suppose that the exposed and unexposed groups in an epidemiologic study are similar except for the exposure of interest, so that confounding is not an issue. For simplicity, suppose also that the two groups are the same size. To have specific numbers, suppose there are 400 injuries in the exposed group and 100 in the control group. In other words, the observed number of injuries is 400, compared to an expected number of 100. The relative risk is 400/100, or 4. Without exposure, there would be only 100 injuries among the exposed, so 300 of the 400 injuries may be attributable to the exposure and 100 to other factors. Apparently, then, each injury in the exposed group has a chance of 3/4 of being caused by exposure. Likewise, a relative risk of 3 corresponds to a chance of 2/3, while a relative risk of 2 corresponds to a chance of 1/2, which may be the minimum level needed to carry the burden of proof in civil litigation.

The object here is to explore the scientific logic behind these intuitions. Of course, any epidemiologic study is likely to have problems of bias: Uncontrolled confounding appears to be the rule, rather than the exception. When effects are large, such problems may not be material. When relative risk is near the critical value of 2.0, potential biases must be assessed more carefully. Individual differences also play an important role: The plaintiff may not resemble typical members of the study population; effects of such differences need to be considered. This is a salient difficulty in connecting relative risk to specific causation. With a randomized controlled experiment, for example, treatment and control groups are balanced in the aggregate but not at the level of individuals. Thus, even with the best research designs—

where general causation is easily demonstrated — specific causation remains troublesome. . . .

Daubert v. Merrell Dow Pharmaceuticals, Inc.

43 F.3d 1311 (9th Cir. 1995)

. . . Plaintiffs do not attempt to show causation directly; instead, they rely on experts who present circumstantial proof of causation. Plaintiffs' experts testify that Bendectin is a teratogen because it causes birth defects when it is tested on animals, because it is similar in chemical structure to other suspected teratogens, and because statistical studies show that Bendectin use increases the risk of birth defects. Modern tort law permits such proof, but plaintiffs must nevertheless carry their traditional burden; they must prove that their injuries were the result of the accused cause and not some independent factor. In the case of birth defects, carrying this burden is made more difficult because we know that some defects — including limb reduction defects — occur even when expectant mothers do not take Bendectin, and that most birth defects occur for no known reason.

California tort law requires plaintiffs to show not merely that Bendectin increased the likelihood of injury, but that it more likely than not caused their injuries. In terms of statistical proof, this means that plaintiffs must establish not just that their mothers' ingestion of Bendectin increased somewhat the likelihood of birth defects, but that it more than doubled it — only then can it be said that Bendectin is more likely than not the source of their injury. Because the background rate of limb reduction defects is one per thousand births, plaintiffs must show that among children of mothers who took Bendectin the incidence of such defects was more than two per thousand.[13]

None of plaintiffs' epidemiological experts claims that ingestion of Bendectin during pregnancy more than doubles the risk of birth defects. To evaluate the relationship between Bendectin and limb reduction defects, an epidemiologist would take a sample of the population and compare the frequency of birth defects in children whose mothers took Bendectin with the frequency of defects in children whose mothers did not. The ratio

---

13. No doubt, there will be unjust results under this substantive standard. If a drug increases the likelihood of birth defects, but doesn't more than double it, some plaintiffs whose injuries are attributable to the drug will be unable to recover. There is a converse unfairness under a regime that allows recovery to everyone that may have been affected by the drug. Under this regime, all potential plaintiffs are entitled to recover, even though most will not have suffered an injury that can be attributed to the drug. One can conclude from this that unfairness is inevitable when our tools for detecting causation are imperfect and we must rely on probabilities rather than more direct proof. In any event, this is a matter to be sorted out by the states, whose substantive legal standards we are bound to apply. See *O'Melveny & Myers v. FDIC*, 512 U.S. 79, ——, 114 S.Ct. 2048, 2053, 129 L.Ed.2d 67 (1994).

derived from this comparison would be an estimate of the "relative risk" associated with Bendectin. For an epidemiological study to show causation under a preponderance standard, "the relative risk of limb reduction defects arising from the epidemiological data . . . will, at a minimum, have to exceed '2'." That is, the study must show that children whose mothers took Bendectin are more than twice as likely to develop limb reduction birth defects as children whose mothers did not.[16] While plaintiffs' epidemiologists make vague assertions that there is a statistically significant relationship between Bendectin and birth defects, none states that the relative risk is greater than two. These studies thus would not be helpful, and indeed would only serve to confuse the jury, if offered to prove rather than refute causation. A relative risk of less than two may suggest teratogenicity, but it actually tends to *dis*prove legal causation, as it shows that Bendectin does not double the likelihood of birth defects.

NOTES AND QUESTIONS

1. The Ninth Circuit was clearly requiring a doubling of the relative risk, but the details of this requirement are less clear. Is the court saying that a relative risk of greater than 2 is necessary to prove general causation, or specific? Reread the statement that "California tort law requires plaintiffs to show not merely that Bendectin increased the likelihood of injury, but that it more likely than not caused their injuries." Does this suggest that the double-risk discussion that follows is focused on specific causation?

2. In a subsequent Ninth Circuit case, In Re Hanford Nuclear Reservation Litigation, 292 F.3d 1124 (9th Cir. 2002), the court agreed with the plaintiffs "that the 'doubling dose' test plays no part in the initial generic causation inquiry and that they were prejudiced by the district court's decision to apply that standard." *Id.* at 1134. The defendants had cited the *Daubert* remand opinion as support for requiring a doubling of the relative risk to prove general causation. Did the *Hanford* defendants misunderstand *Daubert*? The *Hanford* opinion criticized the defendants' reliance on *Daubert*, but in a roundabout way. The *Hanford* court distinguished *Daubert* on the grounds

---

16. A statistical study showing a relative risk of less than two could be combined with other evidence to show it is more likely than not that the accused cause is responsible for a particular plaintiff's injury. For example, a statistical study may show that a particular type of birth defect is associated with some unknown causes, as well as two known potential causes — e.g., smoking and drinking. If a study shows that the relative risk of injury for those who smoke is 1.5 as compared to the general population, while it is 1.8 for those who drink, a plaintiff who does not drink might be able to reanalyze the data to show that the study of smoking did not account for the effect of drinking on the incidence of birth defects in the general population. By making the appropriate comparison — between non-drinkers who smoke and non-drinkers who do not smoke — the teetotaller plaintiff might be able to show that the relative risk of smoking for her is greater than two. Here, however, plaintiffs' experts did not seek to differentiate these plaintiffs from the subjects of the statistical studies. The studies must therefore stand or fall on their own.

that "the plaintiffs in *Daubert II* had no scientific evidence that Bendectin was capable of causing birth defects (generic causation), and therefore were required to produce epidemiological studies to prove that Bendectin more likely than not caused their own particularized injuries (individual causation)." *Id.* at 1136. Does this make sense? If you have no epidemiological or other scientific evidence to prove general causation, are you likely to have epidemiological evidence that would meet the more demanding specific causation standard? Did the *Hanford* court understand *Daubert?*

3.   So perhaps the *Daubert* court was saying that, at least on the facts before it, a doubling of the relative risk would be necessary to prove specific causation. Should such a showing *always* be necessary? Could both kinds of causation be proved by somewhat weaker epidemiological proof coupled with scientific evidence of another sort? Reread footnote 16 in *Daubert.* The sections that follow examine, respectively, the circumstances under which toxicology and differential diagnosis, standing alone or in concert with epidemiology, can sustain a prima facie case for a plaintiff.

4.   Why are courts often attracted to "2" as a threshold value for relative risk? As Freedman and Stark explain, when the relative risk is greater than 2, it can be plausibly inferred that the suspected agent is *more likely than not* the cause of any given case of disease. This inference appears to bridge the gap between the scientific data and the civil burden of proof. But scientists are sometimes dubious about the law's use of 2 as a make-or-break value. In the same article from which the excerpt is taken, Freedman and Stark review the evidence for an association between the 1970s swine flu vaccine and Guillain-Barre Syndrome. They note anomalies in the rate of reporting of the syndrome as well as individual problems with diagnosis. They conclude:

> The scientific connection between specific causation and a relative risk of 2.0 is doubtful. If the relative risk is near 2.0, problems of bias and confounding in the underlying epidemiological studies may be serious, perhaps intractable. Problems created by individual differences may be equally difficult. Bias and confounding affect the estimation of relative risk from the underlying data. By contrast, individual differences affect the interpretation of relative risk, namely, the application to any specific individual.

Freedman and Stark, *supra,* 64 Law & Contemp. Probs. at 61.

5.   Many of the issues discussed thus far in this chapter appear to be coming together in a new study of health problems experienced after 9/11 by World Trade Center rescue and cleanup workers. According to September 5, 2006 press reports on a Mount Sinai Medical Center Study of nearly 16,000 Ground Zero workers, they had lung function abnormalities at a rate double that of the general nonsmoking population; 70 percent had new or worsened respiratory problems; and 61 percent who had no previous health problems

reported them after 9/11. Yet New York Mayor Michael Bloomberg was reported to have said, "I don't believe that you can say specifically a particular problem came from this particular event." Was the mayor just playing politics, or can you think of some more legitimate reasons for his reaction?

B. The Role of Toxicology

Can toxicology help to prove specific causation? The first reading, from the *Reference Manual on Scientific Evidence*, defines toxicology and introduces its research methodology. It is followed by the second case in the Supreme Court's *Daubert* trilogy, Joiner v. General Electric Company. Although *Joiner* is most often cited for its core holding about the standard of appellate review for the exclusion of scientific evidence, it is also important as a case in which a plaintiff attempted—unsuccessfully—to link a toxic exposure to a disease by means of a combination of epidemiology and toxicology. The questions that follow the case will invite you to think about why this plaintiff failed and what this says about the value of toxicological evidence.

Reference Guide on Toxicology

Reference Manual on Scientific Evidence (Federal Judicial Center, 2d ed. 2000)
Bernard D. Goldstein and Mary Sue Henifin

I. INTRODUCTION

Toxicology classically is known as the science of poisons. A modern definition is "the study of the adverse effects of chemicals on living organisms." Although it is an age-old science, toxicology has only recently become a discipline distinct from pharmacology, biochemistry, cell biology, and related fields.

There are three central tenets of toxicology. First, "the dose makes the poison"; this implies that all chemical agents are intrinsically hazardous—whether they cause harm is only a question of dose. Even water, if consumed in large quantities, can be toxic. Second, each chemical agent tends to produce a specific pattern of biological effects that can be used to establish disease causation. Third, the toxic responses in laboratory animals are useful predictors of toxic responses in humans. . . .

The science of toxicology attempts to determine at what doses foreign agents produce their effects. The foreign agents of interest to toxicologists are all chemicals (including foods) and physical agents in the form of radiation, but not living organisms that cause infectious diseases.

The discipline of toxicology provides scientific information relevant to the following questions:

(1)   What hazards does a chemical or physical agent present to human populations or the environment?

(2)   What degree of risk is associated with chemical exposure at any given dose?

Toxicological studies, by themselves, rarely offer direct evidence that a disease in any one individual was caused by a chemical exposure. However, toxicology can provide scientific information regarding the increased risk of contracting a disease at any given dose and help rule out other risk factors for the disease. Toxicological evidence also explains how a chemical causes a disease by describing metabolic, cellular, and other physiological effects of exposure.

A.   TOXICOLOGY AND THE LAW

The growing concern about chemical causation of disease is reflected in the public attention devoted to lawsuits alleging toxic torts, as well as in litigation concerning the many federal and state regulations related to the release of potentially toxic compounds into the environment. These lawsuits inevitably involve toxicological evidence.

Toxicological evidence frequently is offered in two types of litigation: tort and regulatory. In tort litigation, toxicologists offer evidence that either supports or refutes plaintiffs' claims that their diseases or injuries were caused by chemical exposures. In regulatory litigation, toxicological evidence is used to either support or challenge government regulations concerning a chemical or a class of chemicals. In regulatory litigation, toxicological evidence addresses the issue of how exposure affects populations rather than addressing specific causation, and agency determinations are usually subject to the court's deference. . . .

C.   TOXICOLOGICAL RESEARCH DESIGN

Toxicological research usually involves exposing laboratory animals (in vivo research) or cells or tissues (in vitro research) to chemicals, monitoring the outcomes (such as cellular abnormalities, tissue damage, organ toxicity, or tumor formation), and comparing the outcomes with those for unexposed control groups . . . [T]he extent to which animal and cell experiments accurately predict human responses to chemical exposures is subject to debate. However, because it is often unethical to experiment on humans by exposing them to known doses of chemical agents, animal toxicological evidence often provides the best scientific information about the risk of disease from a chemical exposure.

In contrast to their exposure to drugs, only rarely are humans exposed to environmental chemicals in a manner that permits a quantitative determination of adverse outcomes. This area of toxicological research, known as clinical toxicology, may consist of individual or multiple case reports, or even experimental studies in which individuals or groups of individuals have been exposed to a chemical under circumstances that permit analysis of dose–response relationships, mechanisms of action, or other aspects of toxicology. For example, individuals occupationally or environmentally exposed to polychlorinated biphenyls (PCBs) prior to prohibitions on their use have been studied to determine the routes of absorption, distribution, metabolism, and excretion for this chemical. Human exposure occurs most frequently in occupational settings where workers are exposed to industrial chemicals like lead or asbestos; however, even under these circumstances, it is usually difficult, if not impossible, to quantify the amount of exposure. Moreover, human populations are exposed to many other chemicals and risk factors, making it difficult to isolate the increased risk of a disease that is due to any one chemical. . . .

General Electric Company v. Joiner

522 U.S. 136 (1997)

Respondent Robert Joiner began work as an electrician in the Water & Light Department of Thomasville, Georgia (City) in 1973. This job required him to work with and around the City's electrical transformers, which used a mineral-based dielectric fluid as a coolant. Joiner often had to stick his hands and arms into the fluid to make repairs. The fluid would sometimes splash onto him, occasionally getting into his eyes and mouth. In 1983 the City discovered that the fluid in some of the transformers was contaminated with polychlorinated biphenyls (PCBs). PCBs are widely considered to be hazardous to human health. Congress, with limited exceptions, banned the production and sale of PCBs in 1978. See 90 Stat. 2020, 15 U.S.C. § 2605(e)(2)(A).

Joiner was diagnosed with small cell lung cancer in 1991. He sued petitioners in Georgia state court the following year. Petitioner Monsanto manufactured PCBs from 1935 to 1977; petitioners General Electric and Westinghouse Electric manufactured transformers and dielectric fluid. In his complaint Joiner linked his development of cancer to his exposure to PCBs and their derivatives, polychlorinated dibenzofurans (furans) and polychlorinated dibenzodioxins (dioxins). Joiner had been a smoker for approximately eight years, his parents had both been smokers, and there was a history of lung cancer in his family. He was thus perhaps already at a heightened risk of developing lung cancer eventually. The suit alleged that his exposure to PCBs "promoted" his cancer; had it not been for his exposure to these substances, his cancer would not have developed for many years, if at all.

Petitioners removed the case to federal court. Once there, they moved for summary judgment. They contended that (1) there was no evidence that Joiner suffered significant exposure to PCBs, furans, or dioxins, and (2) there was no admissible scientific evidence that PCBs promoted Joiner's cancer. Joiner responded that there were numerous disputed factual issues that required resolution by a jury. He relied largely on the testimony of expert witnesses. In depositions, his experts had testified that PCBs alone can promote cancer and that furans and dioxins can also promote cancer. They opined that since Joiner had been exposed to PCBs, furans, and dioxins, such exposure was likely responsible for Joiner's cancer.

The District Court . . . granted summary judgment for petitioners because (1) there was no genuine issue as to whether Joiner had been exposed to furans and dioxins, and (2) the testimony of Joiner's experts had failed to show that there was a link between exposure to PCBs and small cell lung cancer. The court believed that the testimony of respondent's experts to the contrary did not rise above "subjective belief or unsupported speculation." 864 F. Supp. 1310, 1326 (ND Ga. 1994). Their testimony was therefore inadmissible.

The Court of Appeals for the Eleventh Circuit reversed. . . .

We granted petitioners' petition for a writ of certiorari, and we now reverse.

II

[The Court held that the Eleventh Circuit had erred by applying "a particularly stringent standard of review to the trial judge's exclusion of expert testimony." Instead, such exclusion should be reviewed under the ordinary abuse of discretion standard.]

III

We believe that a proper application of the correct standard of review here indicates that the District Court did not abuse its discretion. Joiner's theory of liability was that his exposure to PCBs and their derivatives "promoted" his development of small cell lung cancer. In support of that theory he proffered the deposition testimony of expert witnesses. Dr. Arnold Schecter testified that he believed it "more likely than not that Mr. Joiner's lung cancer was causally linked to cigarette smoking and PCB exposure." App. at 107. Dr. Daniel Teitelbaum testified that Joiner's "lung cancer was caused by or contributed to in a significant degree by the materials with which he worked." *Id.* at 140.

Petitioners contended that the statements of Joiner's experts regarding causation were nothing more than speculation. Petitioners criticized the testimony of the experts in that it was "not supported by epidemiological studies ... [and was] based exclusively on isolated studies of laboratory animals." Joiner responded by claiming that his experts had identified "relevant animal studies which support their opinions." He also directed the court's attention to four epidemiological studies on which his experts had relied.

The District Court agreed with petitioners that the animal studies on which respondent's experts relied did not support his contention that exposure to PCBs had contributed to his cancer. The studies involved infant mice that had developed cancer after being exposed to PCBs. The infant mice in the studies had had massive doses of PCBs injected directly into their peritoneums [abdominal cavities] or stomachs. Joiner was an adult human being whose alleged exposure to PCBs was far less than the exposure in the animal studies. The PCBs were injected into the mice in a highly concentrated form. The fluid with which Joiner had come into contact generally had a much smaller PCB concentration of between 0-500 parts per million. The cancer that these mice developed was alveologenic adenomas; Joiner had developed small-cell carcinomas. No study demonstrated that adult mice developed cancer after being exposed to PCBs. One of the experts admitted that no study had demonstrated that PCBs lead to cancer in any other species.

Respondent failed to reply to this criticism. Rather than explaining how and why the experts could have extrapolated their opinions from these seemingly far-removed animal studies, respondent chose "to proceed as if the only issue [was] whether animal studies can ever be a proper foundation for an expert's opinion." *Joiner*, 864 F. Supp. at 1324. Of course, whether animal studies can ever be a proper foundation for an expert's opinion was not the issue. The issue was whether *these* experts' opinions were sufficiently supported by the animal studies on which they purported to rely. The studies were so dissimilar to the facts presented in this litigation that it was not an abuse of discretion for the District Court to have rejected the experts' reliance on them.

The District Court also concluded that the four epidemiological studies on which respondent relied were not a sufficient basis for the experts' opinions. The first such study involved workers at an Italian capacitor plant who had been exposed to PCBs. The authors noted that lung cancer deaths among ex-employees at the plant were higher than might have been expected, but concluded that "there were apparently no grounds for associating lung cancer deaths (although increased above expectations) and exposure in the plant." Given that [the authors] were unwilling to say that PCB exposure had caused cancer among the workers they examined, their study did not support the experts' conclusion that Joiner's exposure to PCBs caused his cancer.

The second study followed employees who had worked at Monsanto's PCB production plant. The authors of this study found that the incidence of lung cancer deaths among these workers was somewhat higher than would ordinarily be expected. The increase, however, was not statistically significant and the authors of the study did not suggest a link between the increase in lung cancer deaths and the exposure to PCBs.

The third and fourth studies were likewise of no help. The third involved workers at a Norwegian cable manufacturing company who had been exposed to mineral oil. A statistically significant increase in lung cancer deaths had been observed in these workers. The study, however, (1) made no mention of PCBs and (2) was expressly limited to the type of mineral oil involved in that study, and thus did not support these experts' opinions. The fourth and final study involved a PCB-exposed group in Japan that had seen a statistically significant increase in lung cancer deaths. The subjects of this study, however, had been exposed to numerous potential carcinogens, including toxic rice oil that they had ingested.

Respondent points to *Daubert*'s language that the "focus, of course, must be solely on principles and methodology, not on the conclusions that they generate." 509 U.S. at 595. He claims that because the District Court's disagreement was with the conclusion that the experts drew from the studies, the District Court committed legal error and was properly reversed by the Court of Appeals. But conclusions and methodology are not entirely distinct from one another. Trained experts commonly extrapolate from existing data. But nothing in either *Daubert* or the Federal Rules of Evidence requires a district court to admit opinion evidence which is connected to existing data only by the *ipse dixit* of the expert. A court may conclude that there is simply too great an analytical gap between the data and the opinion proffered. See *Turpin v. Merrell Dow Pharmaceuticals, Inc.*, 959 F.2d 1349, 1360 (CA 6), cert. denied, 506 U.S. 826, 121 L. Ed. 2d 47, 113 S. Ct. 84 (1992). That is what the District Court did here, and we hold that it did not abuse its discretion in so doing.

NOTES AND QUESTIONS

1. What precisely did the district court hold? Did Joiner, the plaintiff, fail to make a sufficient showing of general causation, specific causation, or both? Note that the mechanism for rejecting the plaintiff's case was finding his expert testimony inadmissible. In toxic exposure cases such as *Joiner*, admissibility and sufficiency are closely intertwined. An expert's opinion is held inadmissible because it fails to make a scientifically reliable case for causation. Then, the absence of admissible expert testimony on causation renders the plaintiff's case insufficient.

2. In the Supreme Court's view, what was wrong with the plaintiff's toxicology studies? Could studies like these ever prove specific causation? Might the reception of these studies have been different if the epidemiology had been stronger? Finally, can toxicological evidence such as animal studies ever support a plaintiff's case all by itself? If, as the Court suggests, it might, what would it have to look like?

3. As a review of the material earlier in the chapter, focus on the four epidemiological studies that the district court rejected. Why did they not provide "a sufficient basis for the experts' opinions"? Again, note that the court found them so unreliable as to be inadmissible on the question of causation. Do you agree that these studies were so flawed that a jury could not be permitted to weigh them?

4. In a dissenting opinion, Justice Stevens argued for a "weight of the evidence" approach to cases such as this one. In his view, it is sometimes appropriate for an expert to base an opinion of causation on a number of studies that trend in favor of the plaintiff, even if none standing alone would be sufficient. Is this consistent with the principles of science as you understand them? Justice Stevens also suggested that the Court's opinion goes beyond evaluating the experts' methodology (as *Daubert* prescribes) and verges on "assess[ing] the validity or strength of [the experts'] conclusions, which is a matter for the jury." Do you agree? Or do you agree with the Court that "conclusions and methodology are not entirely distinct from one another"? Many plaintiffs' lawyers complain that *Daubert* has shifted to judges much decision-making power that formerly resided with juries. Does Justice Stevens' dissent provide evidence that they're right? If so, is that a good or a bad thing?

5. In the strongest plaintiff's case, epidemiology and toxicology come together to make an especially compelling showing of both general and specific causation. Consider the following expert report from Williams v. Grodin, 2003 WL 24337947 (Md. Cir. Ct., Aug. 23, 2003), in which the parents of a deceased baby sued an obstetrician for negligently administering a drug that was believed to cause birth defects. The report discusses "odds ratios," which are first cousins of relative risk. The odds ratio is defined as the ratio of the odds that someone who has the disease (or, here, birth defect) was exposed to the suspect substance to the odds that someone without the disease was exposed. For rare diseases, the odds ratio tends to approximate the relative risk. Note that the odds ratios mentioned in the report, while below 2, are nonetheless characterized as statistically significant (contrast the relative risks in *Agent Orange, supra*). Some further introductory points: Teratology is the study of congenital malformations, or birth defects; a teratogen is a substance that causes such malformations; and a tetralogy is a group of four items — four co-occurring birth defects, in the case of the *Tetralogy of Fallot*.

I, Dr. Stuart A. Newman, hereby swear and affirm the following:

1. I am over the age of 21.
2. My place of business is New York Medical College, Basic Science Building, Valhalla, New York 10595.
3. I am an Embryologist and a Teratologist.
4. A copy of my current Curriculum Vitae is attached hereto.
5. My life's work has been devoted to the study of cells and embryonic development, which includes embryonic malformations and teratogenic substances that affect cells.
6. I have received and reviewed the records in this case, which include the medical records of Victoria Williams and Kara Williams.
7. It is well known that exposure of the fetus to exogenous substances at critical times during the pregnancy may produce teratogenic effects in the fetus and subsequently born child.
8. And as a result of the ingestion of an exogenous substance during the critical time of the pregnancy, congenital malformations may be caused in the fetus.
9. The records in this case indicate that the mother, Victoria Williams, ingested Fertinex during the time the heart was developing in the fetus, Kara Williams.
10. Fertinex would be considered an exogenous substance.
11. I also note that Fertinex was designated as a Category X drug by the Food and Drug Administration (FDA). Category X is defined by the FDA as follows;

    "CONTRADICTED IN PREGNANCY. Studies in animals or humans, or investigational or post-marketing reports, have demonstrated positive evidence of fetal abnormalities or risk which clearly outweigh any possible benefit to the patient."

12. There have been studies performed on Fertinex and gonadotropins (Fertinex is a gonadotropin), which I have reviewed.
13. Studies that have been done on Fertinex and/or gonadotropins indicate the following:

    a. In 2003, a study in maternal drug use and infant cardiovascular defect was conducted. The following are some key points of the study:

    i. The odds ratio for cardiovascular defects of mothers ingesting fertility drugs was 1.81 which is statistically significant . . . ;
    ii. The odds ratio for cardiovascular defects of mothers ingesting chorionic gonadotropin (Fertinex) was 1.77 . . . — statistically significant.

    b. In 2002, a study in the New England Journal of Medicine concluded that the use of assisted reproductive technology appears to double the risk of a child with a major birth defect.

c. In 2002, a study in the New England Journal of Medicine concluded that medications used to induce ovulation may increase the risk of birth defects.

d. In another study, HcG (human chorionic gonadotropin), which is the generic name of Fertinex, given to mice during pregnancy caused malformations in the offspring. In that study, it was discovered that there exists a relationship between the amount of HcG given to the mice and congenital defects in the mice. The more HcG given to the mice, the more prevalent the congenital defects.

14. Because there is a *minimum* of experimental data on Fertinex and gonadotropins and birth defects, it would be inappropriate to state with reasonable scientific certainty that Fertinex was the cause of Kara Williams' birth defects.

15. However, based on my education, training, and experience, and the studies that have been performed on Fertinex and/or gonadotropins, it is my opinion that in light of the fact that there is no other documented exogenous substance which has been shown to be a teratogen ingested by the mother during the development of the cardiovascular system, in view of the facts of the timing of the ingestion of the Fertinex and the development of the cardiovascular system, what is known about Fertinex and gonadotropins, including its category "X" designation, the most likely possible cause of the *Tetralogy of Fallot* suffered by Kara Williams was the ingestion of Fertinex by her mother.

I do solemnly declare and affirm under the penalty of perjury that the matters and facts set forth herein are true to the best of my knowledge, information and belief.

Williams v. Grodin, 2003 WL 24337947 (Md. Cir. Ct., Aug. 23, 2003).

C. Proving Specific Causation Through Differential Diagnosis

Another way to prove specific causation involves the testimony of a physician who treated the plaintiff. Treating physicians sometimes seek to testify about their diagnosis that the suspected toxin caused the plaintiff's disease. Such evidence raises many questions. First, under what circumstances is differential diagnosis testimony admissible as competent evidence of specific causation? Second, what can it contribute to a plaintiff's prima facie case? Is differential diagnosis standing alone ever sufficient to prove either general or specific causation? If not, what kinds of other evidence must it be combined with? Consider these issues as you read two cases that reach different conclusions on the value of differential diagnosis evidence.

Easum v. Miller

2004 Wyo. 73 (Wyo. 2004)

GOLDEN, Justice.

The primary issue in this appeal is the reliability of the differential diagnosis technique for determining general and specific causation in a general negligence action. Differential diagnosis determined that the severe illness suffered by Appellant Jeff Easum (Easum) was caused by numerous electrical shocks that he received while working on his family-owned dairy. In a summary judgment ruling, the trial court determined that this particular differential diagnosis was inadmissible because it was unreliable.

Easum began suffering severe illness shortly after Appellee Clay Miller's company, Prime Power and Communications, LLC (Prime Power), replaced a transformer near Easum's family-owned dairy. An unconnected neutral line was determined to be the cause of stray voltage found throughout the dairy that was administering shocks to Easum as he worked at the dairy. After the neutral line was properly connected, the stray voltage and shocks ceased; however, Easum continued to suffer from his symptoms and was ultimately diagnosed with reflex sympathetic dystrophy (RSD) caused by electrical injury. Easum and his wife (Easums) brought suit against Prime Power for personal injury and property damages.

Prime Power settled with Easums for property damages; however, it moved for summary judgment on other damages. Easums' suit was dismissed by grant of summary judgment based upon a determination that their expert's testimony regarding specific causation was inadmissible as unreliable. The trial court ruled that the expert's differential diagnosis technique insufficiently satisfied reliability standards because the scientific methodology used to determine that low level electric current could cause RSD was inadequate. We reverse and remand for trial. . . .

. . . On February 26, 1999, Prime Power performed electrical work and hung a transformer on an electrical pole near the ranch. Prime Power admits failing to connect the neutral line to the transformer. Before that failure was discovered, however, the dairy cattle were observed reacting in a manner consistent with animals receiving electrical shocks, such as not eating, not wanting to return to the barn, and not cooperating. Easum also experienced numerous shocks. On March 16, 1999, another electrical contracting firm began investigating the problem and discovered the failure to connect the neutral wire. Prime Power returned to the ranch and, after that connection was made, no further electrical shocks were experienced by Easum or observed to be affecting cattle.

Easum first experienced shocks in the dairy on or about March 1, 1999. Between that date and March 17, 1999, Easum experienced numerous shocks while in the dairy milking stalls, the sinks and the tanks. He received the worst shocks when his hands were in water. On March 12, 1999, Easum developed symptoms of nausea, tremors, headache, and extreme fatigue. His illness caused him to stay home the next day, and his symptoms subsided. He returned to the dairy on March 15, 1999, and was again shocked causing his symptoms to reappear immediately. After the electricians connected the neutral wire, the electric shocks were no longer experienced; however, Easum's symptoms continued and worsened.

Before receiving the shocks, thirty-year-old Easum's only known health problem was slightly elevated blood pressure. When his symptoms did not subside, his wife called their family physician, Dr. Wurzel, on March 26, 1999, to discuss whether the effects of electrical shock might be long-term or even permanent. Easum saw Dr. Wurzel on May 21, 1999, and the doctor noted numerous symptoms including fatigue, lack of ambition, tremors, difficulties with fine motor skills, vision blurring, lack of libido, weakness, and increased blood pressure. Later, Easum returned with these symptoms and headaches and swollen, painful hands. Laboratory tests were conducted which indicated some abnormalities. [Easum then saw several medical specialists, none of whom was able to diagnose the precise cause of his symptoms, though they noted that the symptoms had developed after repeated low-voltage electrical shocks. Finally,] Easum was referred to Dr. Hooshmand, a neurologist in Florida, specializing in electrical injury type cases. Dr. Hooshmand has identified electrical injury in thirteen other dairy farmers from different parts of the country suffering similar symptoms as Easum and concluded in all that "stray voltage" was the cause of their medical condition.

Under the direction of Dr. Hooshmand, Easum underwent fourteen days of extensive diagnostic testing. . . . The electroencephlogram test was abnormal, and another specialist, Dr. Weise, reported it to be consistent with electrical injury. The thermography test was also abnormal and determined consistent with tissue responses to electrical injury. From the use of differential diagnosis technique, Dr. Hooshmand concluded that Easum was suffering from Reflex Sympathetic Dystrophy (RSD) and an immune system dysfunction. [Easum's family physician and another specialist] concurred in that diagnosis. Easum was prescribed treatment that is administered and monitored by the latter two doctors and, while he has shown improvement, continues to be afflicted by many of his symptoms.

Dr. Hooshmand concluded that the cause of Easum's RSD was his exposure to low levels of electrical current; however, RSD has no known etiology other than heredity and repetitive strain injury. . . .

The trial court determined that the technique of differential diagnosis is reliable only if the remaining cause is one that is scientifically established and then concluded that the basic research had not been conducted in this case. The trial court stated:

> The scientific method consists of 4 steps: gathering information, classifying those data, forming a theory or prediction of behavior, and testing that theory.

Dr. Hooshmand skipped the first two steps and arrived at a conclusion based upon the common fallacy in reasoning known as "after this, therefore, because of this."

Dr. Hooshmand has treated 13 dairy farmers with similar symptoms. Even with this limited sample, there has been no rigorous collection of data. We are not told the medical histories of the patients, the durations and intensities of electrical exposure, the reactions of others who were exposed, and the incidence of this condition among the general population compared to the incidence among dairy farmers or some other group exposed to low levels of electricity.

The trial court dismissed Easums' case authority supporting the differential diagnosis as distinguishable either because causation was not an issue in those cases or because the causation diagnosis was supported by medical literature, peer-reviewed articles, clinical trials, and product studies. The trial court concluded that the claim of injury from exposure to low levels of electrical current was not based upon science but was only a matter of speculation. Summary judgment was granted for Appellees, and this appeal followed. . . .

DIFFERENTIAL DIAGNOSIS

Dr. Hooshmand presented a medical opinion that Easum's condition was caused by receiving a significant number of electrical shocks over a sustained period of time. Dr. Hooshmand's research in this case was not "conducted independent of the litigation," and was developed "expressly for purposes of testifying." Also, his research was not "subjected to normal scientific scrutiny through peer review and publication." Ordinarily, these *Daubert* factors would indicate unreliability unless good reason existed to explain the absence of independence, peer review and publication. *Clausen v. M/V New Carissa*, 339 F.3d 1049, 1056 (9th Cir.2003). In the case of Dr. Hooshmand, the trial court found it significant that his causation diagnosis was unsupported by medical literature, peer-reviewed articles, clinical trials, and product studies.

Here, medical ethical rules do not permit conducting clinical testing that administers low levels of sustained electrical current to humans to see if RSD results. Dr. Hooshmand examined and treated a patient complaining of symptoms consistent with RSD following sustained exposure to electric shock and, later, that patient filed suit. Similarly, there may exist good reason why an expert's research may not have been published. *Id.* In this case, the apparent reason is that Dr. Hooshmand's research involving the phenomenon of electrical injury to dairy farmers is both recent and singular.

In the absence of these reliability factors, an expert may use an objective source to show that the scientific evidence method has been followed by at least a recognized minority of experts in their field. *Id.* Objective sources may include "a learned treatise, the policy statement of a professional

association, a published article in a reputable scientific journal or the like."
Id. Here, Dr. Hooshmand followed a differential diagnosis method to determine the cause of Easum's condition.

" 'Differential diagnosis' refers to the process by which a physician
'rules in' all scientifically plausible causes of the plaintiff's injury. The physician then 'rules out' the least plausible causes of injury until the most likely
cause remains. The remaining cause is the expert's conclusion." *Hollander v.
Sandoz Pharmaceuticals,* 289 F.3d 1193, 1209 (10th Cir.2002) (citation omitted). The Fourth Circuit describes it this way:

> Differential diagnosis, or differential etiology, is a standard scientific tech-
> nique of identifying the cause of a medical problem by eliminating the likely
> causes until the most probable one is isolated. A reliable differential diagnosis
> typically, though not invariably, is performed after physical examinations, the
> taking of medical histories, and the review of clinical tests, including labora-
> tory tests, and generally is accomplished by determining the possible causes for
> the patient's symptoms and then eliminating each of these potential causes
> until reaching one that cannot be ruled out or determining which of those that
> cannot be excluded is the most likely.

Westberry v. Gislaved Gummi AB, 178 F.3d 257, 262 (4th Cir.1999) (internal
quotation marks omitted). Most physicians use the term differential diagnosis to describe the process of determining which of several diseases is causing
a patient's symptoms while courts use the term more generally to describe
the process by which causes of the patient's condition are identified. *Clausen,*
339 F.3d at 1057 n. 4; see, e.g., *Westberry,* 178 F.3d at 262. . . .

Reliable differential diagnosis alone may provide a valid foundation for
a causation opinion, even when no epidemiological studies, peer-reviewed
published studies, animal studies, or laboratory data are offered in support
of the opinion. *Hollander,* 289 F.3d at 1212 (citing *Westberry,* 178 F.3d at 262).
As the Eighth Circuit has written:

> We do not believe that a medical expert must always cite published studies
> on general causation in order to reliably conclude that a particular object
> caused a particular illness. The first several victims of a new toxic tort should
> not be barred from having their day in court simply because the medical
> literature, which will eventually show the connection between the victims'
> condition and the toxic substance, has not yet been completed. If a properly
> qualified medical expert performs a reliable differential diagnosis through
> which to a reasonable degree of medical certainty, all other possible causes
> of the victims' condition can be eliminated, leaving only the toxic substance
> as the cause, a causation opinion based on that differential diagnosis should
> be admitted.

Hollander, 289 F.3d at 1212 (quoting *Turner,* 229 F.3d at 1209). . . .

RELIABILITY OF DR. HOOSHMAND'S DIFFERENTIAL DIAGNOSIS

Dr. Hooshmand's conclusions established both general and specific causation. He established general causation with evidence that electrical shock can cause harm to humans receiving them and established specific causation by evidence that the electrical shocks received by Easum did in fact cause the onset of his RSD. As our previous discussion indicates, the harm produced on dairy farms by stray voltage is well-established. For many years, Dr. Hooshmand has studied the effects of electrical injury on human patients and concluded that electrical injury can produce disease or disorders in patients. Among his patients were a number of dairy farmers, all of whom received electrical shocks of varying degrees and later suffered illnesses. Dr. Hooshmand believed that the shocks caused the illnesses in those particular patients. Studies show that electric shock can cause trauma to nerve and tissue, and animal studies, usually involving dairy herds, show that very low voltages can have devastating physical effects upon cattle. Dr. Hooshmand properly relied upon studies finding that electrical voltage can seriously harm dairy herds and his own studies as support for the general proposition that electricity, even at low levels, can harm humans. Whether his conclusion is sound presents a jury question; however, reliance upon these studies is not an improper methodology.

Dr. Hooshmand determined that Easum had suffered illness as the result of harm caused by sustained incidences of electric shock and further concluded that Easum suffered from RSD. From this conclusion, the district court determined that no reliable scientific methodology established that low levels of electric current will cause RSD. These last two conclusions, however shaky, present jury questions. The district court's proper focus should have been the reliability of Dr. Hooshmand's opinion that Easum's condition was caused by sustained incidences of electric shock. To make that determination, the focus must be on whether Dr. Hooshmand properly used the technique of differential diagnosis to decide that sustained electric shocks produced illness in Easum.

A differential diagnosis is properly performed when objective tests are used to rule out as many causes as possible. Easum's medical history indicated that he had no symptoms before experiencing shocks and began experiencing symptoms while receiving shocks over a sustained period. Several doctors and Dr. Hooshmand performed numerous objective tests that ruled out other causes of injury and confirmed physical injury consistent with electrical shock. Dr. Hooshmand reviewed Easum's medical history, conducted days of physical examination and testing, relied upon this testing and that of other specialists to eliminate other possible diagnoses, and reviewed electrical injury information and medical studies. Dr. Hooshmand properly evaluated and diagnosed Easum using standard medical procedure and his methodology was based upon valid scientific method. Although the district court believed that the timing between Easum's electrical shocks and the onset of his symptoms discredited Dr. Hooshmand's diagnosis, a temporal relationship remains a factor that can support Dr. Hooshmand's conclusion.

Even though science remains unsure how RSD develops, Dr. Hooshmand has personally conducted research in this area and has had numerous patients with this condition. Dr. Hooshmand does not believe that Easum's condition is unique to dairy farmers and has researched this particular injury to this particular group of patients. Dr. Hooshmand's conclusions may indeed be wrong; however, his methodology is reliable and the accuracy of his conclusions presents a jury question that must be presented at trial.

The district court's order is reversed, and this case is remanded for trial.

Moore v. Ashland Chemical, Inc.

151 F.3d 269 (5th Cir. 1998) (en banc)

W. Eugene Davis, Circuit Judge:

In this toxic tort case, we consider whether the district court abused its discretion in excluding the opinion of a physician on the causal relationship between Plaintiff's exposure to industrial chemicals and his pulmonary illness. We find no abuse of discretion and affirm.

I.

Bob T. Moore was employed as a delivery truck driver for Consolidated Freightways, Inc. ("Consolidated"), a motor freight company. On the morning of April 23, 1990, Moore delivered several drums of chemicals manufactured by Dow Corning Corp. ("Dow") to Ashland Chemical Inc.'s ("Ashland") terminal in Houston. When Moore opened the back door of his trailer, he smelled a chemical odor that caused him to suspect that a drum was leaking. Moore and the Ashland plant manager, Bart Graves, identified two leaking drums and removed them from the trailer. Mr. Graves contacted Dow and requested cleanup instructions and a copy of the material safety data sheet ("MSDS") for the spilled chemicals. The MSDS identified the contents of the leaking drum and health hazards associated with the contents. The MSDS stated that the chemical solution included hazardous ingredients, most notably Toluene. It warned that depending upon the level and duration of the exposure to fumes from the chemicals, irritation or injury to various organs, including the lungs, could result.

After Moore and Graves obtained cleanup instructions, they put the leaking drums into larger salvage drums. Moore and another Consolidated employee then proceeded to place absorbent material on the spilled chemicals, sweep them up, and dispose of them. The men were engaged in this cleanup for forty-five minutes to an hour. After the cleanup, Moore returned to the Consolidated terminal. At trial, he testified that about an hour after finishing the cleanup, he began experiencing symptoms, including dizziness, watery eyes, and difficulty in breathing. However, Moore was able to drop off another Consolidated trailer as requested by his supervisor.

When he completed this delivery, Moore returned to Consolidated's terminal and told his supervisor that he was sick. The supervisor sent Moore to the company doctor. The next day, Moore saw his family physician. After two to three weeks of treatment by the family physician, Moore placed himself under the care of a Dr. Simi, a pulmonary specialist. Dr. Simi released Moore to return to work on the 11th day of June, 1990. After working several days, Moore terminated his employment due to difficulty breathing. On three occasions in the summer of 1990, Moore also consulted Dr. Daniel E. Jenkins, a pulmonary specialist. Dr. Jenkins diagnosed Moore's condition as reactive airways dysfunction syndrome ("RADS"), an asthmatic-type condition. In November of 1990, Moore consulted another pulmonary specialist, Dr. B. Antonio Alvarez, who became his primary treating physician. Dr. Alvarez confirmed Dr. Jenkins's diagnosis and treated Moore for RADS.

Moore reported to his physicians that he had smoked approximately a pack of cigarettes a day for approximately twenty years, and he continued to smoke at the time of trial. He also reported that on April 23, 1990, when he was exposed to the Dow chemical, he had just returned to work following a bout with pneumonia. Moore also related a history of childhood asthma to his treating physician.

Moore and his wife filed suit against Ashland Chemical, Inc., Ashland Oil, Inc., and others, primarily on grounds that Ashland was negligent in insisting that Moore expose himself to vapors created by the chemical spill . . .

After extensive discovery and motion practice dealing particularly with whether Moore's expert physicians, Dr. Jenkins and Dr. Alvarez, would be permitted to testify, the case proceeded to trial before a jury. At the conclusion of the trial, the jury [found for the defendant]. On appeal, a divided panel of this Court concluded that the district court had erred in refusing to allow Dr. Jenkins, one of Moore's experts, to give an opinion on the cause of Moore's illness, and reversed the district court's judgment and remanded the case for a new trial. *Moore v. Ashland Chem., Inc.*, 126 F.3d 679 (5th Cir.1997). We granted rehearing to consider this case en banc and to clarify the standards district courts should apply in determining whether to admit expert testimony.

II.

In this appeal we focus on the trial court's refusal to permit one of Moore's medical witnesses, Dr. Daniel E. Jenkins, to give an opinion on the cause of Moore's illness. Some factual and procedural background is necessary to understand the arguments of the parties.

Moore sought to call two medical witnesses, Dr. Jenkins and Dr. Antonio Alvarez. Dr. Jenkins, a well-qualified medical specialist, was certified by the American Board of Internal Medicine in 1947. He also had special training and taught in the fields of pulmonary disease, allergy, and environmental medicine. Dr. Jenkins saw Moore on three occasions. He examined Moore, performed a series of tests, and reviewed Moore's medical records. He concluded that Moore was suffering from RADS. Based upon his examination and tests, Dr. Jenkins expressed the opinion that Moore's RADS had been caused by Moore's exposure to vapors from the chemical spill at Ashland's facility in April of 1990. We will discuss later in more detail the reasons Dr. Jenkins assigned for his opinion. Generally, he relied upon the MSDS, which warned that exposure to the Toluene solution could be harmful to the lungs, his examination and test results, and the close, temporal connection between Moore's exposure to the Toluene solution and the onset of symptoms.

Dr. Alvarez, who was a former student of Dr. Jenkins, agreed with Dr. Jenkins about the cause of Moore's RADS. Dr. Alvarez was Moore's primary treating physician. In addition to the reasons relied on by Dr. Jenkins, Dr. Alvarez supported his theory of causation with a report of a study on RADS co-authored by Dr. Stuart Brooks that he found in a medical magazine. One case study in the report involved a clerk who was exposed to a Toluene mixture in a small, enclosed room for two and one-half hours. Dr. Jenkins initially stated in his deposition that he knew of no reported literature that supported his causation opinion. During his in limine testimony outside the presence of the jury at trial, Dr. Jenkins, for the first time, pointed to the Brooks study relied on by Dr. Alvarez.

Dr. Jenkins admitted that Moore was his first RADS patient with a history of exposure to Toluene. He had conducted no research on this subject. Dr. Jenkins had previously treated other patients whose RADS he attributed to exposure to chemicals that were known to irritate the airways. However, he conceded that the chemicals involved with these previous patients were stronger and more irritating than the Toluene solution to which Moore was exposed. Dr. Jenkins made no attempt to explain how any of the other chemicals that he believed caused RADS in his earlier patients had properties similar to the Dow Toluene solution.

The district court, after reviewing Dr. Jenkins's deposition and listening to his in limine testimony, decided to exclude his causation opinion. The court did permit Dr. Jenkins to testify about his examination of Moore, the tests he conducted, and the diagnosis he reached. The only feature of Dr. Jenkins's testimony the court excluded was his opinion that the Toluene solution caused Moore's RADS. The district court concluded that Dr. Jenkins had no scientific basis for this opinion, that it was not sufficiently reliable under Fed.R.Evid. 702, and that it would be inconsistent with the court's gatekeeper role under *Daubert* to admit this opinion.

The district court decided to admit Dr. Alvarez's causation opinion even though it was essentially identical to Dr. Jenkins's proffered opinion. The district court was apparently convinced that Dr. Alvarez's opinion linking the RADS to Moore's exposure to the Toluene solution was more reliable than Dr. Jenkins's opinion because Dr. Alvarez had been the treating physician, and also because he had relied from the outset on the Brooks study and therefore had some support from the scientific literature for his conclusion. In view of the verdict, the Defendants do not challenge the district court's decision to admit Dr. Alvarez's opinion. Thus, the propriety of this ruling is not presented to us for review.

The single defense expert, Dr. Robert Jones, was the third medical witness to testify. Based upon his review of the medical records, Dr. Jones concluded that Moore did not have RADS; rather, according to Dr. Jones, Moore suffered from a form of bronchial asthma. Dr. Jones further testified that the evidence in the case was insufficient to allow him to conclude that Moore's exposure to Toluene caused his pulmonary problems. Dr. Jones's conclusion was reinforced by Moore's medical history, which included conditions that Dr. Jones thought were much more likely triggering agents for RADS. These conditions included Moore's history as a heavy smoker for approximately twenty years, his history of asthma, and his recent bout with pneumonia. Dr. Jones also testified that the scientific literature revealed that Toluene and similar substances have a low potential for causing lung injury except when encountered in such high dosages that the person is overcome and passes out.

With this background, we now turn to the issue presented by this appeal: whether the district court erred in excluding Dr. Jenkins's causation testimony. . . .

Dr. Jenkins pointed to the following support for his causation conclusion: (1) the MSDS from Dow warned that exposure to fumes from the Toluene solution could cause injury to the lungs; (2) Moore had an onset of symptoms shortly after his exposure to the Toluene solution; (3) although Dr. Jenkins did not initially rely on the Brooks article, when it was called to his attention at trial by counsel, he did claim to have knowledge of the article and stated that he had relied on it; (4) his training and experience; and (5) his examination and test results.

The district court was entitled to conclude that the above bases for Dr. Jenkins's opinion were individually and collectively inadequate under

Daubert. First, Dr. Jenkins's training and experience and his examination and tests, items 4 and 5 above, were obviously important to his diagnosis. However, Dr. Jenkins gave no reason why these items were helpful in reaching his conclusion on causation. He admitted that he had never previously treated a patient who had been exposed to a similar Toluene solution. Dr. Jenkins was a highly qualified pulmonary specialist, but, as the Seventh Circuit observed in *Rosen v. Ciba-Geigy Corp.*, 78 F.3d 316 (7th Cir.1996), "[u]nder the regime of *Daubert* a district judge asked to admit scientific evidence must determine whether the evidence is genuinely scientific, as distinct from being unscientific speculation offered by a genuine scientist." *Id.* at 318 (internal citation omitted).

With respect to the Brooks article, item 3 above, the authors made it clear that their conclusions were speculative because of the limitations of the study. Also, in the single study involving exposure to Toluene fumes, the level and duration of the exposure was several times greater than Moore's exposure.

The bases for Dr. Jenkins's causation opinion are therefore reduced to the following: (1) the Dow MSDS from which Dr. Jenkins could have gleaned that the contents of the drum were irritating to the lungs at some level of exposure; and (2) the relatively short time between Moore's exposure to the chemicals and the onset of his breathing difficulty.

The district court was entitled to find that the Dow MSDS had limited value to Dr. Jenkins. First, Dr. Jenkins admitted that he did not know what tests Dow had conducted in generating the MSDS. Second, and perhaps more importantly, Dr. Jenkins had no information on the level of exposure necessary for a person to sustain the injuries about which the MSDS warned. The MSDS made it clear that the effects of exposure to Toluene depended on the concentration and length of exposure.

The district court was also correct in viewing with skepticism Dr. Jenkins's reliance on the temporal proximity between the exposure and injury. *Cavallo v. Star Enter.*, 892 F.Supp. 756 (E.D.Va.1995), *aff'd. in part*, 100 F.3d 1150 (4th Cir.1996), contains a helpful discussion of this issue. In that case, the plaintiff alleged that she suffered respiratory illness as a result of exposure to aviation jet fuel vapors. The proffered expert relied substantially on the temporal proximity between exposure and symptoms. The court concluded that this reliance was "not supported by appropriate validation" as required by *Daubert*, and was "ultimately unreliable." 892 F.Supp. at 773. The court observed that although "there may be instances where the temporal connection between exposure to a given chemical and subsequent injury is so compelling as to dispense with the need for reliance on standard methods of toxicology," this was not such a case. *Id.* at 773-74. The court pointed out that the plaintiff in *Cavallo* was not doused with jet fuel and that there was no mass exposure of jet fuel to many people who in turn suffered similar symptoms. In the absence of an established scientific connection between exposure and illness, or compelling circumstances such as those discussed in *Cavallo*, the temporal connection between exposure to chemicals and an onset of symptoms, standing alone, is entitled to little weight in determining causation.

Dr. Jenkins offered no scientific support for his general theory that exposure to Toluene solution at any level would cause RADS. Because he had no accurate information on the level of Moore's exposure to the fumes, Dr. Jenkins necessarily had no support for the theory that the level of chemicals to which Moore was exposed caused RADS.[10] Dr. Jenkins made no attempt to explain his conclusion by asserting that the Toluene solution had properties similar to another chemical exposure to which RADS had been scientifically linked. Several post-*Daubert* cases have cautioned about leaping from an accepted scientific premise to an unsupported one. *See Wheat v. Pfizer, Inc.*, 31 F.3d 340, 343 (5th Cir.1994); *see also Braun v. Lorillard Inc.*, 84 F.3d 230, 235 (7th Cir.1996); *Daubert*, 43 F.3d at 1319; *Cavallo*, 892 F.Supp. at 769. To support a conclusion based on such reasoning, the extrapolation or leap from one chemical to another must be reasonable and scientifically valid. *See Daubert*, 43 F.3d at 1319-20; *Cavallo*, 892 F.Supp. at 769.

In the end, Dr. Jenkins was relegated to his fall-back position that *any* irritant to the lungs could cause RADS in a susceptible patient. Dr. Jenkins cited no scientific support for this theory. None of *Daubert*'s factors to assess whether the opinion was based on sound scientific principles was met. Dr. Jenkins's theory had not been tested; the theory had not been subjected to peer review or publication; the potential rate of error had not been determined or applied; and the theory had not been generally accepted in the scientific community. In sum, Dr. Jenkins could cite no scientific support for his conclusion that exposure to any irritant at unknown levels triggers this asthmatic-type condition. Under the *Daubert* regime, trial courts are encouraged to exclude such speculative testimony as lacking any scientific validity.

The district court was also entitled to conclude that Moore's personal habits and medical history made Dr. Jenkins's theory even more unreliable. Moore had been a moderate to heavy smoker for twenty years. In addition, he had just recovered from pneumonia shortly before his contact with the chemicals. Finally, Moore had suffered from asthma (a condition very similar to RADS) in his youth.

In sum, the district court did not abuse its discretion in finding that the "analytical gap" between Dr. Jenkins's causation opinion and the scientific knowledge and available data advanced to support that opinion was too wide.

10. Given the paucity of facts Dr. Jenkins had available about the level of Moore's exposure to the Toluene solution, his causation opinion would have been suspect even if he had scientific support for the position that the Toluene solution could cause RADS in a worker exposed to some minor level of the solution. Under *Daubert*, "*any* step that renders the analysis unreliable . . . *renders the expert's testimony inadmissible. This is true whether the step completely changes a reliable methodology or merely misapplies that methodology.*" *In re Paoli R.R. Yard PCB Litigation*, 35 F.3d 717, 745 (3d Cir.1994) (emphasis in original).

The district court was entitled to conclude that Dr. Jenkins's causation opinion was not based on scientific knowledge that would assist the trier of fact as required by Rule 702 of the Federal Rules of Evidence.

NOTES AND QUESTIONS

1. First, note that both courts were applying the *Daubert* standard — the state court in *Easum* because Wyoming had chosen to follow *Daubert,* and the federal court in *Moore* because it was required to.

2. Are there important factual distinctions between these two cases, or do the courts simply reach different judgments about the evidentiary value of differential diagnosis? Do you think the Fifth Circuit would have affirmed or reversed the trial court on the facts of *Easum*? Not all federal courts of appeals take the same approach as *Moore. Compare* McClain v. Metabolite Int'l, Inc., 401 F.3d 1233 (11th Cir. 2005) (following *Moore*'s approach) *with* Westberry v. Gislaved Gummi AB, 178 F.3d 257, 262 (4th Cir. 1999) (following "the overwhelming majority of the courts of appeals" to conclude that "a medical opinion on causation based on differential diagnosis is sufficiently valid to satisfy" Rule 702's reliability standard). In *Moore* itself, three Fifth Circuit judges dissented, reviewing contrary cases and arguing that "[t]he majority opinion represents an eccentric additional fragmentation of the *Daubert* picture." 151 F.3d at 280 (Dennis, Parker, and Stewart, JJ., dissenting).

3. For a thoughtful effort to sort out the results of the differential diagnosis cases, see Joseph Sanders & Julie Machal-Fulks, *The Admissibility of Differential Diagnosis Testimony to Prove Causation in Toxic Tort Cases: The Interplay of Adjective and Substantive Law,* 64 L. & Contemp. Probs. 107 (2001). They conclude that differential diagnosis evidence of specific causation is most likely to be admitted when the general causation evidence is of high quality, the witness takes a "rational-processing" or "scientific" approach to analyzing the evidence (as opposed to a "common-sense" approach, which gives great weight to temporal proximity), and the court is committed to jury decision making. How do you think Drs. Hooshmand and Jenkins rated on the first two criteria?

4. In *Easum,* how significant was Dr. Hooshmand's earlier research that indicated that electrical shock can cause harm to humans (including at least some dairy farmers)? Is this evidence of general causation as you now understand the concept? Or should the court have required research showing that electricity can cause *this kind* of harm?

5. Why did the *Moore* court find Dr. Jenkins's causation opinion unreliable? Was his use of the differential diagnosis technique flawed, or was the background scientific data inadequate, or both? If you had been representing Moore, is there anything else you might have asked Dr. Jenkins to do or

consider in developing his opinion? Or, given the facts and the state of medical knowledge recited in the opinion, was this simply an unwinnable case? If so, is that a fair outcome?

6. How important was the evidence of the plaintiff's smoking and his prior respiratory ailments? Why did the court discuss this evidence at some length? Was the trial court correct in considering these facts in determining the admissibility of Dr. Jenkins's opinion? Or are they better viewed as matters to be considered by the trier of fact in deciding what weight to give the opinion?

7. Thinking about the relationship between admissibility and weight leads to a significant policy question: In medical causation cases such as these, are the courts using the law of evidence to alter the content of state tort law? You might reasonably conclude from the two preceding cases that a jurisdiction's approach to admitting differential diagnosis evidence will have an enormous impact on which toxic tort plaintiffs will win and which will lose. Since state supreme courts (like the Wyoming court that decided *Easum*) have the power to change the substance of the common law of torts, perhaps this isn't a problem. But remember that federal courts in diversity cases such as *Moore* do not have such power; on the contrary, they are required to apply state tort law as a constitutional matter. Erie R.R. v. Tompkins, 304 U.S. (1938). Do cases such as *Moore* suggest the potential for federal courts to use the law of evidence to rewrite state tort law? Might the result in any given state be two different tort regimes, one for out-of-state defendants who can remove to federal court, and another for home-state defendants who can't?

8. After comparing these cases, what do you conclude about the proper role of differential diagnosis as evidence of specific causation? Under what circumstances should it be admissible? Can such evidence, standing alone, ever support a prima facie case of general and/or specific causation? If not, what other kinds of evidence should also be present?

D. Toxicogenomics: The Wave of the Future?

A more precise way to analyze toxic tort causation may be on the horizon. A new science called *toxicogenomics* is being used to address the question of whether exposure to a suspect substance caused a plaintiff's illness or injury. Genetic information can be used in two ways. First, it is sometimes possible to demonstrate that a particular plaintiff is genetically more or less susceptible to a disease than the average person, which may be relevant to the causation analysis. Second, some toxins leave a "genetic signature," altering the victim's DNA in ways that may be measurable. This signature may create direct proof that a toxin has affected the plaintiff. The following excerpts review both of these uses, the first at a general level and the second in more detail.

Toxicogenomics: New Chapter in Causation and Exposure in Toxic Tort Litigation

69 Defense Counsel J. 441 (2002)
John C. Childs

A NEW FIELD: TOXICOGENOMICS

A.   WHAT IS IT?

Toxic tort litigation as most trial attorneys know it today is about to undergo a drastic, irrevocable change. Genetic evidence has the potential to revolutionize in this area. The sequencing of the human genome and the creation of DNA (deoxyribonucleic acid) databanks now offer scientists the unprecedented research opportunity to understand the causation of disease. Cellular and molecular testing made possible by recent DNA research analyzes what cellular changes cause disease and looks at the mechanism responsible for the onset of that disease process.

This new scientific field, which has launched a new chapter in the proof of causation and exposure in toxic tort cases, is called toxicogenomics. It is the study of the impact of potentially toxic compounds on gene expression. A gene "expresses itself" by acting on proteins and other body processes in very complex ways to affect how the body grows and develops. Toxicogenomics is the study of the alteration of those mechanisms that leads to conclusions about disease and disease processes. It combines the emerging technology of genomics and bioinformatics to identify and characterize the mechanisms of action of known and suspected toxins.

The premier toxicogenomic tools now are the DNA microarray, also called the DNA chip, which is used for the simultaneous monitoring of gene expression levels, sometimes a hundred to a thousand at a time. The results of these tests offer insights into the relationship between our genetic inheritance, exposure to chemicals and the environment, and the onset of disease.

B.   USE IN LITIGATION

The value of toxicogenomics to toxic tort litigators is quite apparent. For plaintiffs who have insufficient scientific proof that a product was more likely than not to cause cancer, the ability to show that an exposure to the product resulted in a genetic polymorphism or gene sequence difference, which increased cancer susceptibility, could be outcome determinative. Comparing DNA test results from before and after the use of the product provides an opportunity to develop quantitative proof of genetic changes. Before-and-after genetic snapshots will allow plaintiffs to prove that their injuries did not pre-date exposure to defendants' toxins. If these biological changes are specific to a defendant's product, then both causation and exposure have been shown.

Defendants also may be able to use toxicogenomics to buttress their defenses. They could cite the absence of genetic biomarkers as evidence that claimants in fact were not harmed by the chemical in question. Genetic tests performed on plaintiffs may point to a genetic susceptibility to other potentially carcinogenic substances, in addition to the targeted product, and any one of those alternative exposures could have caused cancer. Genetic testing also may reveal that a plaintiff is genetically predisposed to a disease. The defendant could argue that the plaintiff's genes, not the defendant's product, caused the disease.

C. TESTING UNCERTAINTIES

Building a toxic tort case or defense based solely on genetic and molecular testing is still far off. Despite the acceptance of DNA testing in the paternity and criminal areas, it is still very new and its uncertain results are subject to much scientific debate. Genetic research is primarily laboratory testing and is not based on animal or human studies. Consequently, it is done "apart from the human body," either literally or virtually, in a petri dish or test tube. Scientists identify specific genes and proteins that relate to very specific body systems and test those specific systems. However, this is done in isolation from other related body mechanisms and could affect the outcome of and process in a real human being over time. In addition, molecular testing often does not consider the synergistic, additive or environmental influences that might affect the disease outcome.

Genetics and Environmental Law: Redefining Public Health Genetics and Environmental Law: Redefining Public Health

93 Cal. L. Rev. 171 (2005)
Jamie A. Grodsky

A. SEEDS OF CHANGE: MOLECULAR BIOLOGY ENTERS THE SCIENCE OF TOXIC INJURY

Essential to a contextual understanding of environmental genomics are developments born in the 1970s and maturing in the 1980s — the most salient being the application of the tools of molecular biology to the disciplines of toxicology and epidemiology, the linchpins of environmental risk assessment. The widespread application of molecular biology techniques to other disciplines during the 1980s provided new molecular-level insights into important biological processes, including cellular responses to drugs and toxic chemicals.

Specifically, scientists have gained the ability to "peer into cells" to observe the behavior and effects of toxic substances at the molecular level. This capability also has revealed gene mutations and sequence variations that may confer differential human sensitivity to environmental agents. The key to detecting causal relationships and genetic susceptibilities is in the identification of biological markers, or "biomarkers."

Biomarkers essentially are clues or flags signaling events in living systems. Formally, they are defined as "indicators signaling events in biological systems or samples" or "any measurement in or from biological material that defines an exposure or response to that exposure." Hence, biomarkers are indicators of exposure, effect, or susceptibility that are measured in biologic materials, such as tissues or bodily fluids, as opposed to estimates based on levels of foreign compounds in the ambient environment. The biomarker concept was not new in the 1980s. Traditional biomarkers include lead levels in blood and the presence of arsenic, lead, mercury, or the pesticide parathion in urine, indicating exposure to these substances. However, the new biomarkers reveal molecular interactions or events within biological systems, thereby providing much more information than the physical presence of foreign compounds or their immediate derivatives.

The identification of genetic and molecular-level biomarkers has allowed scientists to characterize a number of previously undetectable, intermediate events between chemical exposure and environmentally induced disease. Because classical techniques were insufficient to characterize these intermediate events, traditional toxicology and epidemiology generally were limited to studying the beginning and end of the process—initial toxic exposure and ultimate disease—viewing everything in between as a "black box." The tools of molecular biology effectively opened this black box, revealing a "cascade" of events between exposure and clinical disease.

Those biomarkers that represent events along the causal pathway may give scientists insights into how diseases arise. Hence, certain biomarkers may allow assignment of clearer probabilities of disease risk based on early biological signs of chemical exposure. Specifically, "biomarkers can be used to delineate more precisely how a given ambient toxic exposure causes disease by tracing the 'molecular footprints' as the toxin passes through the body, interacts with critical target molecules . . . and produces the molecular and cellular effects that eventually manifest as [disease]."

1. THE BIOMARKER PARADIGM: OPENING THE "BLACK BOX"

A seminal paper published in 1987 by a scientific committee commissioned by the National Research Council (NRC) synthesized existing studies on the development and use of biomarkers in environmental health research. The paper identified three general types of molecular biomarkers and provided a conceptual model illustrating relationships among them.

The "biomarker paradigm," in which biomarkers identify various stages and interactions on the pathway from exposure to disease, provides the groundwork for understanding dramatic developments in environmental genomics since the 1990s. The three categories of biomarkers are those measuring susceptibility, exposure, and effect.

a.   Biomarkers of Susceptibility

Broadly defined, susceptibility biomarkers are any identifiable genetic variations affecting absorption, metabolism, or response to environmental agents. These genetic variations, generally referred to as "polymorphisms," do not act alone to trigger disease, but confer differential sensitivity to the effects of drugs or chemicals. Such "environmental susceptibility genes" can be contrasted to highly penetrant "disease genes" — such as those for Huntington's disease, cystic fibrosis, and sickle cell anemia — in which a single mutation may be a predictor of disease even in the absence of an environmental exposure. Susceptibility genes are "neither necessary nor sufficient to cause disease. They modify risk." The relationship between genes and the environment has been compared to a loaded gun and its trigger: "A loaded gun by itself causes no harm; it is only when the trigger is pulled that the potential for harm is released or initiated. Likewise, one can inherit a predisposition for a devastating disease, yet never develop the disease unless exposed to the environmental trigger(s)."

Such genetic variations may increase the rate at which carcinogens or other harmful substances are activated, reduce an individual's ability to detoxify harmful compounds, or disable DNA repair mechanisms, tumor suppressor genes, or other protective functions. In this manner, one's genetic complement may affect the toxicity or potency of chemicals. For example, some studies indicate that people with an abnormally slow-acting form of an enzyme that deactivates carcinogens in tobacco smoke, air pollution, and certain cooked foods are at higher risk for bladder cancer. Likewise, smokers who harbor a variant of another gene that enhances the activation of hydrocarbons have been shown to be at greater risk of acquiring lung cancer. . . .

b.   Biomarkers of Exposure

Biomarkers of exposure indicate the amount of a foreign compound that is absorbed into the body. Biological measurements performed on human tissues are vastly expanding the capabilities of classical epidemiology, which has relied primarily on indirect estimates of human exposure derived from chemical levels in the air, water, and other exposure routes. These indirect methods require modeling or monitoring of the ambient environment and significant guesswork as to actual human exposure levels. Moreover, these measurements have severe limitations, as individuals vary in their rates of absorption, metabolism, and excretion of toxic substances; hence, individuals subject to the same ambient exposure may retain different amounts of toxins in their bodies. . . .

c. Biomarkers of Effect

Biomarkers of effect reflect changes in cells or tissues triggered by chemical exposure or changes that are qualitatively or quantitatively predictive of health impairment or potential impairment due to toxic exposure. Biomarkers of effect may measure early biochemical or cellular changes, structural or functional changes in affected cells or tissues, or changes formally recognized as health impairments or clinical disease.

The distinction between biomarkers of effect and biomarkers of exposure, however, is not clear-cut. These classifications may overlap, and may change as our knowledge increases. For example, scientists have classified DNA or protein "adducts" — complexes formed when carcinogenic substances bind to DNA or protein molecules in the body — as either markers of exposure or effect. While some have suggested that biomarkers of effect indicate the moment at which an environmental agent has brought about molecular change, others have limited the definition to changes that portend future disease. For legal purposes, the point at which a biomarker becomes predictive of disease may be a million dollar question (literally), and the process of "validation" aims to solidify the predictive power of early markers.

d. The Continuum Between Exposure and Disease

Perhaps the most important contribution of the biomarker paradigm is the concept of a continuum of effects between environmental exposure and disease. At one end of the continuum is exposure to a toxic substance. The other end represents a manifestation of overt disease, such as a cancerous tumor that may appear years after the initial exposure. The area between the two, once considered a "black box," now includes subcellular biomarkers of exposure and effect. When visualized as points along a horizontal bar, markers will proceed from left to right, with markers of exposure followed by markers of effect. Although these events are most clearly illustrated in the context of cancer, they also may be applied to neurological, immunological, reproductive, developmental, pulmonary, and other environmentally related health impairments.

NOTES AND QUESTIONS

1. To understand the potential effect of toxicogenomics on tort litigation, consider how the science of biomarkers might affect a case such as *Daubert*. Look at the case from the perspective of the plaintiffs' lawyers. Recall

the outcome: ultimate rejection of your scientific evidence, resulting in your inability to make a prima facie case. Ideally, what kind of toxicogenomic evidence might have been most beneficial to you? Now ask the same question from the standpoint of defense counsel in a toxic exposure case such as *Daubert.*

2. As these readings indicate, toxicogenomics still has a long way to go before it figures routinely in litigation. Elsewhere in the article excerpted above, Professor Grodsky identifies a number of challenges facing toxicogenomics as it enters the courtroom and the regulatory arena. These include: (1) How do we engage in the genetic profiling of subgroups while avoiding pseudoscientific racism?; (2) How will the law respond to claims based on genetic changes without current symptoms?; and (3) Will we have to redefine our concept of "health" in genetic terms?

IV. INJURIES ALLEGEDLY CAUSED BY DOCTORS, MEDICAL DEVICES, AND SIMILAR PRODUCTS

A final set of problems under the general heading of medical causation arise when a plaintiff alleges that his or her disease or injury was caused not by some external exposure but by negligent medical treatment and/ or a defective medical device or other similar product. The substantive legal issues can include whether the doctor (or nurse, therapist, etc.) was negligent and/or whether the medical device was defective, whether the negligence/defect was a proximate cause of the plaintiff's injury, and whether that causal influence was superseded by an intervening cause. Underlying these substantive issues, of course, is the question of what kinds of scientific evidence are admissible and sufficient to prove or rebut particular elements of the claim or defense. While this book is not intended as a treatise on the substantive law of malpractice or product liability, the role of scientific evidence in such cases is within our purview. The next case brings together a number of relevant themes in a single fact pattern.

Riegel v. Medtronic, Inc.

2006 U.S. App. LEXIS 1181 (2d Cir. 2006)

KATZMANN, *Circuit Judge.*

This case calls upon us to determine, *inter alia,* the scope of the preemption provision set forth in Section 360k(a) of the 1976 Medical Device

Amendments to the Food, Drug, and Cosmetic Act, 21 U.S.C. §§ 301 *et. seq.* Specifically, we must decide whether Section 360k(a) preempts common law tort claims regarding medical devices that have entered the market pursuant to the Food and Drug Administration's ("FDA") rigorous premarket approval ("PMA") process. . . .

We now join this growing consensus and hold that tort claims that allege liability as to a PMA-approved medical device, notwithstanding that device's adherence to the standards upon which it obtained premarket approval from the FDA, are preempted by Section 360k(a). We therefore affirm the district court's (Kahn, *J.*) summary judgment dismissal of the plaintiffs-appellants' strict liability, breach of implied warranty, and negligent design, testing, inspection, distribution, labeling, marketing, and sale claims as to the Evergreen Balloon Catheter, a PMA-approved medical device. With regard to the plaintiffs' remaining claim for negligent manufacturing — which premised liability on the theory that the particular Evergreen Balloon Catheter deployed during plaintiff-appellant Charles Riegel's angioplasty had not been manufactured in accordance with the PMA-approved standards — we agree with the district court that this claim was not preempted, but that no genuine issue of material fact existed, and thus affirm the district court's summary judgment dismissal of that claim as well. . . .

The Evergreen Balloon Catheter is a prescription medical device that defendant-appellee Medtronic, Inc. developed for patients with coronary disease. Physicians use it during angioplasties to open patients' clogged arteries, essentially by inserting the catheter into the clogged vessel, inflating the catheter like a balloon, and then deflating and removing the catheter. The Evergreen Balloon Catheter entered the market pursuant to the PMA process in the mid-1990s. . . .

On May 10, 1996, plaintiff-appellant Charles Riegel underwent a percutaneous transluminal coronary angioplasty, during which his surgeon used an Evergreen Balloon Catheter. The procedure was intended to dilate Riegel's right coronary artery, which had been found to be "diffusely diseased" and "heavily calcified." The device label for the Evergreen Balloon Catheter specifies that its use is contraindicated for patients who have "diffuse or calcified stenoses." During the procedure, Riegel's physician, Dr. Eric Roccario, first attempted to remove the calcium deposits in Riegel's artery with a rotoblator device, and then unsuccessfully inserted several different balloon catheters. Dr. Roccario ultimately inserted the Evergreen Balloon Catheter into Riegel's artery and inflated the device several times, up to a pressure of ten atmospheres. The device label for the Evergreen Balloon Catheter specifies that it should not be inflated beyond the "rated burst pressure" of eight atmospheres. On the final inflation, the Evergreen Balloon Catheter burst, and Riegel began to rapidly deteriorate. He developed a complete heart block, lost consciousness, was intubated and placed on advanced life support, and was rushed to the operating room for emergency coronary bypass surgery. Riegel survived, but according to his Complaint, he suffered "severe and permanent personal injuries and disabilities."

Riegel and his wife, Donna, subsequently filed [a federal diversity] suit against Medtronic in the Northern District of New York, alleging five state common law causes of action: (1) negligence in the design, testing, inspection, manufacture, distribution, labeling, marketing, and sale of the Evergreen Balloon Catheter; (2) strict liability; (3) breach of express warranty; (4) breach of implied warranty; and (5) loss of consortium. . . .

[After dismissing other claims on preemption grounds, the district court] dismissed the negligent manufacturing claim on grounds that there was insufficient evidence upon which a reasonable fact-finder could conclude that the Evergreen Balloon Catheter had burst because of negligent manufacture, rather than because it had encountered a calcium spicule in Riegel's artery, had been inflated beyond the specified eight atmosphere limit, or some combination thereof. . . .

[After affirming the district court's preemption holding, the court of appeals turned] to the December 2, 2003 order that granted summary judgment to Medtronic on the Riegels' non-preempted negligent manufacturing claim.

The legal framework governing this claim is undisputed. Because the Riegels do not have the actual Evergreen Balloon Catheter that was used during Mr. Riegel's angioplasty, they can prevail only by proving by circumstantial evidence that it must have been defective. As the New York Court of Appeals recently explained, "[i]n order to proceed in the absence of evidence identifying a specific flaw, a plaintiff must prove that the product did not perform as intended and exclude all other causes for the product's failure that are not attributable to defendants." *Speller v. Sears, Roebuck and Co.*, 100 N.Y.2d 38, 41, 790 N.E.2d 252, 760 N.Y.S.2d 79 (N.Y. 2003).

Medtronic, with reference to expert opinions, has argued that the Evergreen Balloon Catheter used during Mr. Riegel's angioplasty burst not because it was negligently manufactured, but rather because (1) it was inflated to 10 atmospheres, even though the label stated that it should not be inflated more than 8 atmospheres; (2) it was inserted into an artery that was "diffusely diseased" and "heavily calcified," even though the label stated that it should not be used in such instances (because calcium spicules can puncture the catheter); and/or (3) Dr. Roccario used metal stents that could have punctured the catheter.

Thus, to overcome Medtronic's arguments and survive summary judgment, the Riegels had to come forward with competent evidence excluding Medtronic's proferred alternative causes as the actual origin of the catheter's rupture. *See Speller*, 100 N.Y.2d at 42 (holding that where the defendants argued that the fire in question had been caused not by their refrigerator's wiring, but rather by the plaintiff's stove, "[i]n order to withstand summary judgment, plaintiffs were required to come forward with competent evidence excluding the stove as the origin of the fire").

We agree with the district court that the Riegels did not come forward with competent evidence excluding Medtronic's proffered causes as the origin of the rupture. It is undisputed that Dr. Roccario, in performing Mr. Riegel's angioplasty, inflated the balloon catheter to ten atmospheres, which is two atmospheres and approximately 29.4 pounds per square inch beyond the maximum rated burst pressure explicitly specified on the device label. The Riegels have argued, through Dr. Roccario's affidavit, that "exceeding the maximum recommended atmospheres of eight (8) to ten (10) atmospheres was not outside the window of [the device's] testing in laboratory settings . . . and inflations to ten (10) atmospheres was based upon my past experience with the product and was called for in the circumstances herein presented in order to attempt to obtain the angiographic appearance that I desired rather than what I was presented with at the time and instead of reintroducing still another balloon." Although it may well be that inflating the balloon catheter up to ten atmospheres was the best decision under the circumstances, this does not indicate that the inflation was not the cause of the catheter's rupture.

It is similarly undisputed that Mr. Riegel had heavily calcified arteries, and that the label for the Evergreen Balloon Catheter contraindicated its use in such an instance. Dr. Roccario has stated that "it is all but routine today at this point in the development of the medical science in question for a PTCA [percutaneous transluminal coronary angioplasty] to go forward under such circumstances." Again, however, this does not mean that in this particular instance, we can exclude the calcified nature of Mr. Riegel's artery as a cause for the catheter's rupture. Indeed, Dr. Roccario himself—while stating that "there was simply nothing about the procedures that I undertook or the medical decisions and choices that I made on May 10, 1996 which in my professional medical opinion in any way contributed to the bursting of this particular Evergreen 3.0-20mm balloon"—has not actually opined that the catheter must have burst as a result of a manufacturing defect.

The only affirmative evidence that the Riegels have adduced in support of their claim that the catheter must have had a manufacturing defect is the report of their expert, engineer Ted Milo, who offered the view that based on the nature of Mr. Riegel's injury, the catheter must have burst not longitudinally, but radially, which — in his view — apparently signified a manufacturing defect. The district court found, however, that Milo's conclusion that the catheter had burst radially was based on "sheer surmise and conjecture rather than on any scientific basis," and therefore found it to be insufficiently substantiated to be admissible as expert testimony. We agree, and thus conclude that the district court did not abuse its discretion in refusing to admit this evidence.

The district court identified serious flaws in Milo's expert opinion. First, Milo did not explain the basis of his conclusion that Mr. Riegel's injury was more indicative of a radial failure than a longitudinal failure. Second, even assuming *arguendo* that the balloon burst radially rather than longitudinally, Milo did not explain why a radial failure could not itself result from the causes that Medtronic proffers here: namely, overinflation of the catheter or by punctures caused by calcifications. Indeed, the district court also pointed out that Milo's own exhibit indicated that even some non-longitudinal failures are caused not by manufacturing defects, but rather by overpressurization or punctures from calcified lesions.[18] The Riegels have not responded to this point on appeal. We also note that in his deposition, when Milo was asked for his response to another expert opinion that "the probable cause of rupture of the balloon catheter was not a manufacturing defect, but rather puncture of the balloon by either a spicule of calcium in the vessel wall or a portion of the previously implanted metal stents," he responded, "I have no opinion."

Although the Riegels argue that Milo's theories should have been evaluated by a jury rather than the district judge, this Circuit has explained that it is appropriate for the district court to determine the admissibility of scientific evidence and to rely only on admissible evidence in ruling on summary judgment. *See, e.g., Amorgianos v. AMTRAK*, 303 F.3d 256, 271 (2d Cir. 2002) (affirming grant of summary judgment after district court had ruled the plaintiff's expert report inadmissible); *Raskin*, 125 F.3d at 66 (stating that "an expert's report is not a talisman against summary judgment"). We believe that the district court was well within its discretion in concluding that Milo's opinion was not an admissible expert opinion and therefore could not serve as a basis for demonstrating a manufacturing defect. An expert opinion requires some explanation as to how the expert came to his conclusion and what methodologies or evidence substantiate that conclusion. *See* Fed. R. Evid. 702 ("If scientific, technical, or other specialized knowledge will assist the trier of fact to understand the evidence or to determine a fact in issue, a witness qualified as an expert by knowledge, skill, experience, training, or education, may testify thereto in the form of an opinion or otherwise, if (1) the testimony is based upon sufficient facts or data, (2) the testimony is the product of reliable principles and methods, and (3) the witness has applied the principles and methods reliably to the facts of the case"). In this case, Milo essentially provided no explanation as to how he had reached his conclusion that the rupture must have been caused by a manufacturing defect, and himself seems to have backed away from this

18. We note that Milo seems to have simply assumed that because Dr. Roccario used a rotoblator to remove the calcium deposits from Mr. Riegel's artery before inserting the Evergreen Balloon Catheter, the device's contraindication for patients with calcified arteries "would no longer be relevant." He did not even address the possibility that some calcium spicules could have remained.

conclusion in his deposition. It was therefore appropriate for the district court to exclude his opinion.

As a result, because there was no competent evidence excluding Medtronic's proffered causes — particularly, encounter with a calcium spicule in the artery and/or the over-inflation of the catheter — as the origin of the rupture of the Evergreen Balloon Catheter, there were no genuine issues of material fact for a jury on this claim. Therefore, we agree with the district court that the Riegels "failed to submit sufficient evidence from which a fair-minded trier of fact [could] reasonably conclude that Plaintiff excluded all other causes of the burst," and affirm the court's December 2, 2003 dismissal of their negligent manufacturing claim.

NOTES AND QUESTIONS

1. As a preliminary matter, consider something that was *not* present in the case: a malpractice (professional negligence) claim against Dr. Roccario. Assume that a malpractice plaintiff must prove (1) that the doctor failed to meet the customary standard of care for his specialty in the place where he practices and (2) that the doctor's failure to meet the standard of care was the proximate cause of the plaintiff's injury. Based on the evidence reviewed in the opinion, would the Riegels have had a malpractice claim against Dr. Roccario? Assuming for the sake of argument that they would have, can you think of any tactical reasons why they might have decided not to assert it? As a practical matter, did the Riegels have to choose between suing the surgeon and suing Medtronic? Do you see any problems with trying to put on a case against both of those defendants in the same trial? Note that the plaintiffs made a different choice in Williams v. Grodin, *supra,* suing their obstetrician for ignoring a Food and Drug Administration "contraindication" and administering a drug thought to cause birth defects.

2. Next look at the case from Medtronic's perspective. It is the sole defendant. The company's executives believe that Dr. Roccario's negligence in implanting the catheter was at least partially responsible for the plaintff's injuries. Can you think of a way to compel the doctor's participation in the case? On similar facts, the Supreme Court held that a defendant bone screw manufacturer was not entitled to Fed. R. Civ. P. 19 dismissal of a negligence claim because of the plaintiff patient's failure to join the doctor who had implanted the screw. The Court did suggest, however, that the defendant might have impleaded the doctor for contribution or indemnity under Fed. R. Civ. P. 14. Temple v. Syunthes Corp., 498 U.S. 5, *rehg. denied,* 498 U.S. 1092 (1990).

3. The most common evidentiary issue in pure medical malpractice cases is whether a given expert is qualified to testify concerning the standard of care in a particular kind of practice. Subissues include whether the expert

is qualified in and/or knowledgeable about the relevant medical specialty and whether the expert has adequate knowledge of the standards that apply in the geographic and demographic (e.g., big city versus small town, teaching versus community hospital) setting where the alleged malpractice occurred. Expert qualification is dealt with in depth in Chapter 2, Expert Evidence: Rules and Cases.

4. Now examine the *Riegel* case as actually filed and focus on the elements of the plaintiffs' claim and the evidence produced by the two sides. As the court's citation of *Speller* indicates, the elements of the claim and the burden of proof with respect to the various elements are matters of state law. According to *Speller,* the most direct way to prove negligent manufacture is to produce "evidence identifying a specific flaw." The Riegels did not have any such evidence, of course, so they attempted to make a circumstantial case (Plan B, as it were). What are the two elements of a circumstantial claim? Did the Riegels offer any evidence in support of the first element? Assuming that some of the Riegels' evidence did tend to prove that "the product did not perform as intended," the case boils down to whether they could "exclude all other causes for the product's failure that are not attributable to defendant[]." The language of *Speller* suggests that this process of exclusion is part of the plaintiff's burden, but it would make no practical sense for a court to require the plaintiff to set up and knock down every conceivable alternative cause while the defendant sat idly by. So Medtronic introduced expert evidence that there were alternative causes, and the Riegels then attempted to rebut that evidence. What did Medtronic's evidence tend to show? What did the Riegels offer in rebuttal? How did the court respond?

5. The Riegels' case ultimately depended on the report of "engineer Ted Milo." The court of appeals' discussion of Milo's report seems to mix questions of admissibility, sufficiency (to overcome a summary judgment motion), and credibility. Given the procedural posture of the case, only the first was really at issue. Why? What was the district court's specific basis for holding the report inadmissible, even at this stage? Do you agree with the Second Circuit that the district court was right? And finally, why did a ruling of inadmissibility lead inevitably to summary judgment against the plaintiffs? As we have seen throughout this chapter, the usual pattern in medical causation cases is that exclusion of the plaintiff's key expert leads to summary judgment for the defendant. Should this incline courts to be more generous to plaintiffs' expert witnesses in such cases?

The summary judgment question also arose in the next case. Although the case involved a motorcycle helmet rather than a medical device, the causation problem confronting the plaintiff was very similar to that in *Riegel*. Note that the case was decided under a state version of Rule 702 that is nearly identical to the pre-2000 Federal Rule.

Howerton v. Arai Helmet, Ltd.

158 N.C. App. 316; 581 S.E.2d 816 (N.C. App. 2003)

This appeal arises from an action instituted by Dr. Bruce Howerton, D.D.S., alleging that his quadriplegic condition, resulting from a motorcycle accident, was caused by a negligently designed helmet. He contends that Arai Helmet, Ltd. ("Arai") negligently designed his helmet without an integrated chin bar which would have distributed the compressive force of his motorcycle collision throughout his chest, thereby preventing the hyper-flexion of his neck and resulting quadriplegia. At trial, upon considering evidence proffered by Dr. Howerton's four expert witnesses, the trial court, applying the reliability standards of *Daubert v. Merrell Dow Pharmaceuticals, Inc.*, 509 U.S. 579, 125 L. Ed. 2d 469, 113 S. Ct. 2786 (1993), concluded that the experts did not offer reliable opinions on causation. Consequently, the trial court granted Arai's summary judgment motion because Dr. Howerton "failed to offer evidence sufficient to raise a material issue of disputed fact as to the element of causation."

On appeal, Dr. Howerton contends the trial court erred by (1) relying upon *Daubert* in determining the admissibility of expert testimony, (2) applying the *Daubert* framework, assuming that it was properly used, and (3) concluding that his unfair and deceptive trade practices' claim failed as a matter of law. After carefully reviewing the record, relevant case law, and arguments of counsel, we hold that (1) North Carolina has recognized and endorsed the use of the *Daubert* framework to the admission of expert testimony, (2) in applying the *Daubert* framework the trial court did not abuse its discretion by excluding the proffered testimony of plaintiff's expert witnesses, and (3) that trial court properly granted Arai's summary judgment motion with respect to plaintiff's unfair and deceptive trade practices' claim, as plaintiff failed to forecast any evidence of proximate cause. . . .

In the trial court, the fundamental issue was whether Dr. Howerton could produce reliable expert testimony that Arai's helmet design was the proximate cause of his quadriplegia. . . .

During his collision, Dr. Howerton wore an Arai open-face helmet. Like a full-face helmet, the Arai helmet had a chin guard. However, unlike full-face helmets, the chin guard was not integral. Instead, the chin guard was attached to the body of the helmet with nylon screws. According to Arai, the nylon screws permitted the chin guard to breakaway during accidents and thereby prevented the chin guard from turning into a lever on the neck. According to Dr. Howerton, this "flexible design," and the corresponding advertising campaign promoting its benefits, was negligent and deceptive. Dr. Howerton claims that if the Arai helmet had been a full-face helmet, the helmet would have prevented his quadriplegia. To support this claim, Dr. Howerton produced, and subjected to deposition, four expert witnesses: Professor Hugh Hurt, Dr. William Hutton, Dr. Charles Rawlings, and James Randolph Hooper.

First, Dr. Howerton offered the expert testimony of Professor Hugh Hurt, President of the Head Protection Research Laboratory of Southern California and Professor Emeritus of Safety Science at the University of Southern California. Arai stipulated to Professor Hurt's expertise in the following subjects: (1) Motorcycle accident investigation and reconstruction, (2) Motorcycle helmet design and construction and related industry standards, and (3) Motorcycle helmet testing and motorcycle helmet performance in accidents and related government industry standards.

In his deposition, Professor Hurt testified that his review and reconstruction of the accident showed that:

[As] a result of the collision, [Dr. Howerton] was thrown over the handlebars, to land on the back of his helmeted head. . . . And in that process, the failure of the flexible chin bar on the Arai helmet allowed a degree of hypermotion of the neck, which produced the injury that he suffered. . . . I think, essentially any other dirt bike helmet with a chin bar, with an integral chin bar, with a rigid chin bar, that Dr. Howerton would not have suffered that critical neck injury due to the unlimited hyperflexion.

Professor Hurt based his causation opinion — that an integrated chin bar would have prevented Dr. Howerton's quadriplegia — on his investigation and reconstruction of three motorcycle accidents. In these three accidents, motorcycle riders wearing full-face helmets did not suffer neck or cervical injuries despite a head landing. In investigating the respective accidents, Professor Hurt noticed a red "u" or "v" shaped mark on the chest of each motorcycle rider. Professor Hurt deduced that these marks were caused when the rigid integrated chin bar on the full-face helmet struck the chest of the rider during the accident. Essentially, when the integrated chin bar struck the chest, the rotation of the rider's neck was limited. According to Professor Hurt, the Arai helmet's breakaway, or flexible, design was defective because it permitted unlimited hyperflexion in the neck and, thereby, created an increased risk of neck injury.

Furthermore, Professor Hurt testified that, without any scientific or engineering evidence, Arai marketed its "flexible helmet design" as a safer alternative to the conventional and rigid designs. According to Professor Hurt, the Arai helmet design created the illusion of being a full-face helmet. Moreover, the consumer was unable to discern the difference, because the only warning regarding the potential hazards of the "flexible chin guard" were visible only to a rider who disassembled the helmet.

After reviewing Professor Hurt's deposition testimony, arguments from counsel, case law, and memorandums of law, the trial court made the following pertinent findings of fact:

19. Professor Hurt could not quantify the extent to which a full-face helmet would prevent forward flexion of the head and neck.

20. Professor Hurt did not test or perform independent research on his hypothesis that full-face helmets equipped with rigid chin bars prevent neck

injuries. He did not subject his hypothesis to peer review by publishing it to his peers.

21. Professor Hurt did not report his hypothesis to the United States government, for whom he conducted extensive studies that included work on motorcycle helmet safety.

22. Professor Hurt was not able to identify any published work by any author that expressly supported his hypothesis and, thus, did not present any evidence other than his unsupported assertions that his hypothesis is generally accepted in the field.

23. Indeed, Professor Hurt's published work did not support — and in fact tends to contradict — his hypothesis that full-face helmets prevent neck injuries. In a University of Southern California report published in 1981, Professor Hurt published data indicating that serious neck injuries occurred more frequently in riders wearing full-face helmets than in riders wearing . . . open-face helmets that were not equipped with chin bars. . . .

Accordingly, the trial court granted Arai's motion to exclude Professor Hurt's causation testimony on the basis of unreliability.

Next, Dr. Howerton offered as an expert in biomechanics Dr. William Hutton, Professor and Director of Orthopedic Research at Emory University School of Medicine. Dr. Hutton inspected plaintiff's helmet and opined that:

When Arai's removable, flexible chin guard touched Dr. Howerton's chest, it should have prevented further flexion and should have transferred a significant portion of the applied force through his chin guard and into his chest. Instead, the bottom screws of the chin guard broke allowing over forty degrees of additional rotation of Dr. Howerton's head and neck. This additional rotation and lack of support from the broken chin guard, permitted additional flexion and compression forces to be exerted on Dr. Howerton's neck. These additional forces resulted in the flexion-compression fractures and movement of the C5 and C6 vertebrae that caused the compromise of Dr. Howerton's spinal cord and the resulting quadriplegia.

Dr. Hutton opined on the issue of causation that the Arai helmet's breakaway feature caused plaintiff's neck to enter into a flexion beyond the physiological limit — "hyperflexion." The hyperflexion magnified the compressive force of the impact, and, in the case of Dr. Howerton, this caused a retropulsion of bone into the spinal canal. Essentially, like Professor Hurt, Dr. Hutton testified that an integrated chin bar would have prevented Dr. Howerton's quadriplegia.

After reviewing Professor Hurt's deposition testimony, arguments from counsel, case law, and memorandums of law, the trial court made the following pertinent findings of fact:

48. Dr. Hutton conceded . . . that he has never researched, tested or published his hypothesis that the degree of retropulsion of bone fragments

is a function of the degree of flexion or hyperflexion involved. He could not cite [] medical or scientific literature in support of this position. Dr. Hutton also conceded that retropulsion of bone fragments can occur in the absence of hyperflexion. Further, he acknowledged that plaintiff could have sustained some degree of retropulsion even if he had been wearing a full-face helmet. Finally, he conceded that he does not know how much retropulsion the spinal cord can withstand before paralysis occurs.

49. Dr. Hutton admitted that he had never dealt with a cervical injury similar to that experienced by plaintiff.

50. Dr. Hutton admitted that he could not identify any literature that supported the conclusion that plaintiff would not have been paralyzed but for the hyperflexion.

51. Dr. Hutton's opinion that plaintiff's injuries were caused by hyperflexion is speculative and based on inadequate data.

52. Dr. Hutton's opinion that plaintiff's injuries were caused by hyperflexion is not reliable. . . . To the extent that his methods represent a technique, it is clear that they incorporate an unacceptably high rate of error.

Accordingly, the trial court granted Arai's motion to exclude Dr. Hutton's causation testimony on the basis of unreliability.

Next, Dr. Howerton offered Dr. Charles Rawlings as an expert in neurosurgery. Dr. Rawlings conducted his residency and received a Doctorate in Medicine from the Duke University Medical Center. Between 1989 and 1999, Dr. Rawlings performed two to three surgeries per month for cervical fractures. At the time of his deposition, Dr. Rawlings was enrolled in Wake University School of Law.

In his deposition, Dr. Rawlings opined that Dr. Howerton did not suffer any cervical injuries until his head rotated forward beyond the normal range of motion. Essentially, like Professor Hurt and Dr. Hutton, Dr. Rawlings' testimony supported the theory that the Arai helmet's flexible design permitted plaintiff's head and neck to rotate beyond physiological limits. With respect to Dr. Rawlings' testimony, the trial court made the following pertinent findings of fact:

41. . . . [Dr. Rawlings] conceded that unless the amount of force is known, it is impossible to distinguish one degree and forty-five degrees of flexion based on radiology films. Dr. Rawlings conceded that he did not know the amount of force involved in the accident. Dr. Rawlings acknowledged that he had no medical basis to opine about whether plaintiff's head was rotated forward in flexion five degrees or forty-five degrees at impact.

42. Even though he did not know the force involved in the accident and could not accurately identify the position of plaintiff's head at impact, Dr. Rawlings opined that plaintiff would not have been paralyzed but for his head rotating beyond that normal anatomical range of motion. He

admitted, however, that there are no objective criteria that can be used to confirm his hypothesis. . . .

Based on these findings, the trial court found that "Dr. Rawlings' opinion that plaintiff injury was caused by hyperflexion is not reliable."

Finally, Dr. Howerton offered James Randolph Hooper as an expert in helmet design. Mr. Hooper was the chief design engineer for a full-face motorcycle helmet developed at the same time Arai was developing its "flexible design" — 1978-1982. Mr. Hooper testified that in 1978 it was well known in the helmet industry that rigid chin bars significantly increased the overall stiffness of the helmet and increased protection from impacts in all axises. Mr. Hooper opined that the Arai's flexible chin guard offered no protection during impact. Furthermore, Mr. Hooper related the details of many accidents in which the rider was (1) wearing a full-face helmet, (2) flipped over the handlebars landing on top of the head, and (3) did not suffer severe neck injury.

During Arai's cross-examination of Mr. Hooper the following colloquy occurred:

> *Q.* Do you contend that you have any sort of expertise so that you can offer an opinion with respect to whether a helmet will prevent a particular type of neck injury?
>
> *A.* No.
>
> *Q.* Is that something you have expertise in?
>
> *A.* No.

After reviewing Mr. Hooper's deposition testimony, arguments from counsel, case law, and memorandums of law, the trial court made the following pertinent findings of fact:

28. Mr. Hooper is not a medical doctor, an accident reconstructionist, an expert in biomechanics, or an engineer. He does not have a college degree.

29. When deposed, Mr. Hooper expressly conceded that he did not have the expertise to opine that a full-face helmet equipped [with] an integrated chin bar would have prevented plaintiff's injury. . . .

32. Mr. Hooper is not qualified to offer the opinion that a full-face helmet would have prevented plaintiff's injury in this case. His opinion that a full-face helmet would have prevented plaintiff's injury was speculative and based on inadequate data. Further, Mr. Hooper did not have a reliable basis to offer any meaningful comparison between his own history of accidents and plaintiff's accident. . . .

. . . [T]he trial court, in its discretion, concluded that the opinion testimony of Professor Hurt, Dr. Hutton, and Dr. Rawlings, on the issue of causation, was unreliable and, therefore, inadmissible. Moreover, the trial court concluded, in its discretion, that Mr. Hooper was not qualified to offer his expert testimony on the issue of causation. Accordingly, the trial court granted Arai's . . . motion for summary judgment because "[in] the absence of reliable expert opinion testimony on the issue of causation . . . [the] plaintiff [] failed to offer evidence sufficient to raise a material issue of disputed fact as to the element of causation."

[The court of appeals reaffirmed that North Carolina had adopted *Daubert* as its standard of admissibility, and then turned to the question of whether the trial court had properly excluded all four causation experts under *Daubert*.]

"The decision on what expert testimony to admit is within the wide discretion of the trial court." Under this standard, "[a] trial court may be reversed . . . only upon a showing that its ruling was so arbitrary that it could not have been the result of a reasoned decision." . . .

First, Professor Hurt testified that Dr. Howerton would not have suffered cervical injuries if his Arai helmet had an integrated chin bar. Professor Hurt testified that he based his opinion on 30 years of experience and, specifically, three motorcycle accidents in which he noticed a "u" or "v" shaped mark on the chests of the respective riders.[9] Professor Hurt deduced from these marks, and the absence of cervical injuries in these riders, that the integrated chin bar prevented hyperflexion of the neck by contacting with the chest.

The trial court, however, found that this testimony was unreliable because Professor Hurt (1) did not test his hypothesis, (2) did not subject his hypothesis to peer review, (3) could not quantify the extent, if any, to which a full-face helmet would prevent forward flexion of the neck, (4) could not identify any literature supporting his hypothesis or demonstrating general acceptance of his hypothesis, and (5) published work that actually contradicted his hypothesis. Based on these detailed findings of fact, which are substantially unchallenged by Dr. Howerton, the trial court excluded Professor Hurt's testimony. . . .

In the case *sub judice*, it is eminently clear that the trial court's decision to exclude Professor Hurt's testimony was neither arbitrary nor an abuse of discretion. The trial court's findings of fact are reasoned, detailed, and address the relevant inquiries required by *Daubert* and its progeny. Although evidence supporting a contrary conclusion does exist in the record, the record is replete with competent evidence supporting the challenged findings of the trial court. Accordingly, plaintiff's assignments of error are

---

9. The trial court, Arai, and Dr. Howerton, note that when asked about the basis of his opinion Professor Hurt replied: "Like Bo knows baseball, Hurt knows motorcycle accidents." The parties debate the significance of this statement, and, whereas Dr. Howerton claims that it was joke, Arai asserts that it demonstrates Professor Hurt's unreliability. In deciding this matter, we have placed little significance on this statement.

overruled insofar as they challenge the trial court's decision to exclude the causation testimony of Professor Hurt.

Second, Mr. Hooper, a proffered expert in helmet design, testified that a full-face helmet with an integrated chin bar would have prevented plaintiff's quadriplegia. However, the trial court found that Mr. Hooper was not qualified to offer an expert opinion on causation because Mr. Hooper expressly conceded that he did not have the expertise to opine that a full-face helmet with an integrated chin bar would have prevented plaintiff's injury. Based on this finding, standing alone, it is eminently clear that the trial court's decision was neither arbitrary nor an abuse of discretion. Accordingly, this assignment of error is overruled.[12]

Third, Dr. Hutton, an expert in the field of biomechanics, testified that when the Arai helmet's chin guard broke during plaintiff's collision, the lack of support from the broken chin guard allowed plaintiff's head to rotate an extra forty-degrees. According to Dr. Hutton, this additional flexion had a magnifying effect on the compressive force of the injury which retropulsed bone into the spinal canal and resulted in quadriplegia. However, the trial court found that this testimony was unreliable because Dr. Hutton (1) never tested, published, nor researched his hypothesis, (2) conceded that retropulsion of bone fragments can occur in the absence of hyperflexion, (3) conceded that plaintiff could have sustained some degree of retropulsion even if he had been wearing a full-face helmet, and (4) could not identify any literature that supported his hypothesis that plaintiff would not have been paralyzed but for hyperflexion. Furthermore, the trial court noted that Dr. Hutton had not subjected his hypothesis to peer review, and that Dr. Hutton's hypothesis incorporated an unacceptable high rate of error. Based on these detailed findings of fact, which are substantially unchallenged by Dr. Howerton, the trial court excluded Dr. Hutton's testimony. Although evidence in the record does support a contrary finding, it is eminently clear that the trial court's decision was neither arbitrary nor an abuse of discretion. Indeed, the record is replete with competent evidence supporting the challenged findings. Accordingly, this assignment of error is overruled. Finally, Dr. Rawlings, an expert in neurosurgery, testified that Dr. Howerton did not suffer any cervical injuries, including his paralysis, until his head rotated forward beyond the normal range of motion. However, the trial court found that this testimony was unreliable because Dr. Rawlings (1) did not test his hypothesis, (2) did not subject his hypothesis to peer review, (3) conceded that there are no objective criteria that could

12. At this point, our analysis could end. Without the testimony of Professor Hurt or Mr. Hooper, Dr. Howerton did not forecast any evidence suggesting that the Arai helmet design was related to hyperflexion. Although the proffered testimony of Drs. Hutton and Rawlings does potentially describe an injury caused by hyperflexion, neither Dr. Hutton nor Dr. Rawlings is qualified to offer an expert opinion pertaining to helmet design. Notwithstanding, we address the trial court's decision to exclude the expert testimony of Drs. Hutton and Rawlings.

be used to confirm his hypothesis, and (4) proffered an hypothesis that was not generally accepted. Furthermore, the trial court noted that Dr. Rawlings conceded that: (1) unless the amount of force in the accident is known, it is impossible to distinguish degrees of flexion, and (2) he did not know the amount of force involved in the accident. Based on these detailed findings of fact, which are substantially unchallenged by Dr. Howerton, the trial court excluded Dr. Rawlings' testimony. Although evidence in the record does support a contrary finding, it is eminently clear that the trial court's decision was neither arbitrary nor an abuse of discretion. Indeed, the record is replete with competent evidence supporting the challenged findings. Accordingly, this assignment of error is overruled.

As Dr. Howerton failed to forecast any admissible evidence on the issue of causation, the trial court properly granted Arai's summary judgment motion with respect to plaintiff's negligence and product liability claims.

NOTES AND QUESTIONS

1. On further appeal (Howerton v. Arai Helmet, Ltd., 358 N.C. 440; 597 S.E.2d 674 (2004)), the North Carolina Supreme Court conducted an extensive review of prior North Carolina scientific evidence cases and rejected the argument that those cases had explicitly or implicitly adopted the *Daubert* standard. Instead, it held that North Carolina courts should make a more flexible inquiry into the reliability of the evidence; it remanded the case for further proceedings under this standard. Focusing on the summary judgment implications of the *Daubert* rule, the court placed great emphasis on its case-deciding potential:

> As a consequence of these stringent threshold standards for admitting expert testimony, we are concerned with the case-dispositive nature of *Daubert* proceedings, whereby parties in civil actions may use pre-trial motions to exclude expert testimony under *Daubert* to bootstrap motions for summary judgment that otherwise would not likely succeed. As expressed in dicta by one federal trial court,
>
> This court notes that inherently, the judge's role in a *Daubert* determination [is] fraught with conflict. In most cases, if the court bars the testimony of one party's expert witness or witnesses, that party is unable to present an essential element of his or her claim, or to proffer a defense. Accordingly, judges are aware that applying *Daubert* heavy-handedly has the effect of lightening one's caseload, as a party stripped of its expert often must dismiss the claims or settle the lawsuit.
>
> Procedurally, this imbalance may be explained because trial courts apply different evidentiary standards when ruling on motions to exclude expert testimony and motions for summary judgment. In a motion for summary judgment, the evidence presented to the trial court must be admissible at trial, N.C.G.S. § 1A-1, Rule 56(e) (2003), and must be viewed in a light most

favorable to the non-moving party. *Caldwell v. Deese*, 288 N.C. 375, 378, 218 S.E.2d 379, 381 (1975). Where there are genuine, conflicting issues of material fact, the motion for summary judgment must be denied so that such disputes may be properly resolved by the jury as the trier of fact. *Kessing v. Nat'l Mortgage Corp.*, 278 N.C. 523, 534, 180 S.E.2d 823, 830 (1971) ("Since this rule provides a somewhat drastic remedy, it must be used with due regard to its purposes and a cautious observance of its requirements in order that no person shall be deprived of a trial on a genuine disputed factual issue.").

Not so in the case of preliminary motions to exclude expert testimony under *Daubert*, which are resolved under Rule of Evidence 104(a). Here, trial courts are not bound by the rules of evidence, are not required to view the evidence in a light favorable to the non-movant, and may preliminarily resolve conflicting issues of fact relevant to the *Daubert* admissibility ruling. N.C.G.S. § 8C-1, Rule 104(a). Taking advantage of these procedural differences, a party may use a *Daubert* hearing to exclude an opponent's expert testimony on an essential element of the cause of action. With no other means of proving that element of the claim, the non-moving party would inevitably perish in the ensuing motion for summary judgment. By contrast, a party who directly moves for summary judgment without a preliminary *Daubert* determination will not likely fare as well because of the inherent procedural safeguards favoring the non-moving party in motions for summary judgment.

In such instances, we are concerned that trial courts asserting sweeping pre-trial "gatekeeping" authority under *Daubert* may unnecessarily encroach upon the constitutionally-mandated function of the jury to decide issues of fact and to assess the weight of the evidence. *See* N.C. Const. art I, § 25. *See also Brasher*, 160 F. Supp. 2d at 1295 (applying *Daubert*, but acknowledging that "for the trial court to overreach in the gatekeeping function and determine whether the opinion evidence is correct or worthy of credence is to usurp the jury's right to decide the facts of the case"); *Logerquist v. McVey*, 196 Ariz. 470, 488, 1 P.3d 113, 131 (2000) ("The *Daubert/Joiner/Kumho* trilogy of cases . . . puts the judge in the position of passing on the weight or credibility of the expert's testimony, something we believe crosses the line between the legal task of ruling on the foundation and relevance of evidence and the jury's function of whom to believe and why, whose testimony to accept, and on what basis."); *Bunting v. Jamieson*, 984 P.2d 467, 472 (Wyo. 1999) (adopting *Daubert*, but nonetheless expressing concern that "application of the *Daubert* approach to exclude evidence has been criticized as a misappropriation of the jury's responsibilities. . . . 'It is imperative that the jury retain its fact-finding function.'" (citations omitted)).

2. Return to the court of appeals' opinion. Review the testimony of the four experts and try to understand why the trial court excluded each one. With respect to each, and assuming that *Daubert* applies, do you see anything that the expert might have done differently, or any alternative way of stating his results, that might have rendered his testimony admissible? Put another way, if these were the best (or only) experts available to the plaintiff, was his case doomed from the outset? Finally, can you

imagine any other kind of expert analyses that might have met the trial court's standards?

3.   Note the importance of the abuse of discretion standard of review, which makes it very difficult to overturn the trial court's admissibility determinations (n.b.: the state supreme court substituted a new legal standard; it didn't find that the trial judge abused his discretion). Indeed, when a *Daubert*-jurisdiction trial judge exercises the care that this one did, his rulings become almost bullet-proof. Given this, and the inevitability of summary judgment if the plaintiff's causation experts are excluded, was the North Carolina Supreme Court correct to worry about the apocalyptic significance of the *Daubert* ruling?

4.   Many North Carolina lawyers suspected that, on remand, the trial judge would make exactly the same rulings under the new standard, and wondered how the state supreme court would respond. (In fact, one justice would have affirmed the court of appeals on the grounds that the trial judge's rulings were easily sustainable under the new standard.) Alas, we will never know, as the case settled before any further proceedings could take place. For an account, see John M. Conley & Scott W. Gaylord, *We Are Not A* Daubert *State — But What Are We?: Scientific Evidence in North Carolina After* Howerton, 6. N.C. J.L. & Tech. 289 (2005).

CHAPTER 8

ECONOMIC ANALYSIS

OF LIABILITY AND

DAMAGES

Experts in economics and finance regularly testify on a wide range of matters. Much of this testimony focuses on proving damages. In almost any kind of case, if the defendant's misconduct has injured the person or the property of the plaintiff, it becomes necessary for the plaintiff to put a dollar value on the injury. For example, if a personal injury prevents the plaintiff from working in the future, her lost earning capacity must be valued; if the defendant has destroyed the plaintiff's business, its value must similarly be determined. In intellectual property (patent, copyright, and trademark) infringement cases, plaintiffs sometimes try to prove either the financial loss that they have sustained or the benefit that has unlawfully accrued to the defendant. In all of these situations, the defendant almost invariably offers a competing valuation.

The law also requires economic valuation in many non-damages contexts. In corporate mergers, for example, dissenting shareholders may have a right to opt out of the merger and have their shares "appraised." Not surprisingly, tax and bankruptcy cases routinely involve the valuation of businesses, stock, and other property. And in antitrust cases, economic evidence is sometimes presented on issues of liability, as when a plaintiff attempts to prove the existence of a price-fixing conspiracy by presenting economic models of its effects.

This chapter will present a sampling of economic evidence cases from several contexts. Sections I, II, and III include valuation cases dealing with working lives, businesses, and intellectual property, while Section IV covers economic models used in antitrust cases. The purpose of the chapter is not to survey the law of damages (or appraisal, or any other body of law), but rather to acquaint the reader with the types of evidence that economists most frequently present, the principles that they customarily follow, and the controversies that their testimony may provoke.

I. THE VALUE OF A WORKING LIFE

When confronting the question of how to calculate an individual's lost earning capacity, economic experts often take the following approach (from Robert E. Hall & Victoria A. Lazear, *Reference Guide on Estimation of Economic Losses in Damage Awards,* in *Reference Manual on Scientific Evidence* 281 (Federal Judicial Center, 2d ed. 2000)):

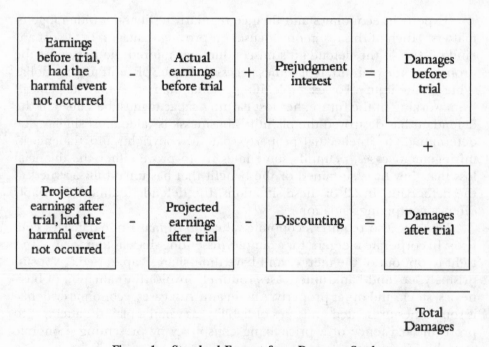

Figure 1.   Standard Format for a Damages Study

As the model suggests, there are two categories of damages to be considered: those that accumulate before the trial and those that will accumulate after the trial. The damages that accumulate before the trial are the more easily determined. The plaintiff is entitled to the amount she would have earned had the injury not occurred. Those damages are then offset by any earnings she actually received. The difference between these two, in most cases, is subject to interest for the period between the plaintiff's injury and when the court actually awards judgment to the plaintiff ("prejudgment interest").

Determination of damages after the trial is more complicated. First, the court must project what the plaintiff would have earned had the injury not occurred. Next, the "projected earnings had the harmful event not occurred" are offset by the earnings that the court determines the plaintiff will actually be able to earn in her injured state ("projected earnings after trial"). Then, in the most complex and controversial step, the damages are often "discounted" in order to translate the award from its future value to its present value. The purpose of this step is to make sure that the defendant pays today only the amount required to produce the plaintiff's lost future earnings at the time they would have accrued.

The following case applies the model, with particular attention to the meaning of "prejudgment interest" and "discounting." Note that "earnings before trial" and "projected earnings after trial, had the harmful event not occurred" were not in issue on appeal, while "projected earnings after trial" were dealt with summarily under the category of "projected ability to mitigate damages."

McCrann v. United States Lines, Inc.

803 F.2d 771 (2d Cir. 1986)

[Plaintiff-appellee McCrann was a merchant seaman who sailed aboard a vessel owned by defendant-appellant United States Lines. He was injured as a result of a fall on an oil-soaked deck. McCrann sued under a federal statute called the Jones Act. The district court found liability and awarded McCrann "$275,544 in compensatory damages for past and future loss of earnings," plus pain and suffering. The defendant appealed.]

KAUFMAN, Circuit Judge:
As any student of elementary economics knows, time has monetary value for some purposes. A dollar in hand today is worth more than a dollar to be paid a year from today, and a dollar a year from today is worth more than a dollar to be received in two years. This basic principle of finance is employed by courts daily in calculating appropriate damage awards, to

ensure that parties receive neither an undeserved windfall nor an unfair penalty. Yet it is remarkable how basic economic concepts can become convoluted by the parties when large sums are at stake.

In the case now before us, we are confronted with two questions concerning the proper means of calculating damages in a personal injury action. The parties challenge the methods employed by the district court to determine the applicable rates for discounting the judgment to present value and for calculating prejudgment interest. Plaintiff contends that the discount rate employed was excessive, while defendant argues that the rate used to calculate prejudgment interest was too high. . . .

Before addressing the contentions of the parties, a brief review of the basic concepts involved in calculating damage awards for lost wages is in order. We begin with the principle that a tortfeasor should be required to put his victim in the same economic position that he would have occupied had he not been injured. *Jones & Laughlin Steel Corp. v. Pfeifer*, 462 U.S. 523, 533, 76 L. Ed. 2d 768, 103 S. Ct. 2541 (1983). When an injury renders a worker unfit to continue in his trade, the court must first calculate his projected salary for each year that he could have worked. Assuming ten more years of gainful employment at $10,000 per year, however, the worker would realize a windfall if he received a judgment of $100,000, since that sum could earn substantial amounts of interest in the bank. Therefore, the court would reduce the judgment by awarding plaintiff the present value of each year's payments. Invested at an interest rate of 6% compounded monthly, $9434 grows to $10,000 at the end of one year, and $8900 grows to $10,000 after two years. Discounting each year's payments and then adding up the total of the discounted amounts, the court would award the present value of the future income stream. In this example, the plaintiff would receive $73,601.[1]

If the award were disbursed at the precise moment of injury, and if the economy were free of inflation, this calculation would represent a fair award of damages. However, neither of these assumptions holds true. Therefore, certain adjustments must be made. Consider inflation first. Just as the defendant would be unfairly penalized if required to pay the full $100,000 today, rather than the discounted sum of $73,601, so would the plaintiff be undercompensated if the court failed to account for the effects of inflation on his award. Therefore, courts will either subtract the estimated rate of inflation from the prevailing market rate of interest before discounting the judgment to present value or account for the effects of inflation in projecting the plaintiff's wages. *Doca v. Marina Mercante Nicaraguense, S.A.*, 634 F.2d 30, 34-38 (2d Cir. 1980), *cert. denied*, 451 U.S. 971, 101 S. Ct. 2049, 68

---

1. Generally, to calculate the value today of $1 payable t years from now, ask how much must be invested today at compounded interest to grow into $1 at the end of t years. We know that at i% compounded interest any principal grows in t years proportionally to $(1 + i)^t$. Thus, by inverting this expression, we arrive at the final answer: The present value of $1 payable t years from now is $\$1/(1 + i)^t$.

L. Ed. 2d 351 (1981). Assuming an inflation rate of 4% and a prevailing interest rate of 6%, the discount rate would be reduced to 2%, and the damage award would now come to $89,826.

Finally, we must account for the additional factor of prejudgment interest. In theory, the tortfeasor incurs his obligation to make the plaintiff whole the instant that the injury occurs. In reality, of course, the plaintiff must wait until the litigation has run its course before realizing a judgment. Since the plaintiff was entitled to the interest income on the damage award from the date of injury to the payment of judgment, courts award prejudgment interest to address the disparity. If a year passed between the moment of injury and the date of judgment, and the prevailing interest rate was 6%, our hypothetical plaintiff would receive an additional $5,479, bringing his final award to $95,305.

Equipped with these basic concepts, we can now turn to the merits of the appeal. The district court determined that McCrann's past and future loss of earnings amounted to $275,444, before discounting or adjusting for inflation. In arriving at this sum, the court took into consideration his salary at the time of injury, his remaining work expectancy of 16 years, and his projected ability to mitigate damages. Judge Lasker then discounted that sum at the rate of 2% per year, relying on this Court's instruction in *Doca* to use 2% absent evidence of a more appropriate rate. Finally he awarded prejudgment interest on the discounted figure* and the $20,000 pain and suffering award, using the average interest rate paid on six-month United States Treasury Bills from November 29, 1979 to February 1, 1986, or 10.397%. The total award came to $420,044.39.

PREJUDGMENT INTEREST

Appellant maintains that the district court erred in selecting a prejudgment interest rate of 10.397%.[+] Specifically, appellant contends that the rate applied to calculate the prejudgment interest cannot exceed the discount rate, which the court set at 2%. This contention, however, is supported by neither logic nor precedent. The prejudgment interest rate is greater than the discount rate in this case for one simple reason: while it is appropriate to subtract the rate of inflation in calculating the discount rate, it would make no economic sense to do the same in figuring the prejudgment interest. When calculating the latter sum, it is wholly proper to award the unadjusted

---

* [This statement implies that the trial court awarded prejudgment interest on the entire discounted damage award. It is unclear from the trial court's reported opinions whether that was actually the case. In any event (and contrary to the Second Circuit's explanation in the preceding paragraph), it is customary to award prejudgment interest only on the pre-verdict component of the damages. *See* Figure 4 *supra* and Note 7 *infra*. — EDS.]

[+] [This interest rate may strike contemporary readers as extraordinarily high. The late 1970s and early 1980s were a period of exceptionally high inflation and interest rates, driven in large part by a series of oil price shocks. — EDS.]

market rate of interest, which includes an inflationary component, since that is the rate at which appellee could have invested the money.

Appellant improperly relies on *Moore-McCormack Lines, Inc. v. Richardson*, 295 F.2d 583, 594 (2d Cir. 1961), *cert. denied*, 368 U.S. 989, 82 S. Ct. 606, 7 L. Ed. 2d 526 (1962), to argue that the discount rate and prejudgment interest rate should be identical. In *Moore-McCormack*, the court stated that the rates ought to be the same, but the case was litigated before the practice of reducing the discount rate by the rate of inflation became universally accepted by the courts. *Id.* at 594; *see, e.g., Doca*, 634 F.2d at 34-38. Even today, it is true that if the plaintiff's projected salary is increased by an inflationary factor in the initial calculation, the discount rate may mirror the market rate and, accordingly, also be identical with the prejudgment interest rate. But where the court employs an adjusted discount rate, as did Judge Lasker, the rates will not be the same. Instead, the prejudgment interest rate will exceed the discount rate by roughly the rate of inflation. . . .

DISCOUNT RATE

At trial, appellee elicited testimony from an economist, who testified that the appropriate discount rate was zero rather than 2%. Conceding that in most cases 2% is a fair discount rate, he argued that in this case that rate should be reduced. The economist maintained that the district court failed to account for wage increases the appellee would have received in the future due to factors unrelated to inflation, such as increased seniority and productivity. Reducing the discount rate to zero, he asserted, would compensate the appellee for this oversight. As he put it, "it would be eminently fair, since we are going 10 years into the future, to assume a wash."

In his memorandum decision, Judge Lasker stated that he found this testimony "unconvincing." Appellee now contends that *Doca*, 634 F.2d at 30, required the district court to accept the uncontroverted testimony of the economist, and that Judge Lasker abused his discretion in employing a discount rate of 2%. We disagree. In *Doca*, Judge Newman made clear that we were not

> requiring the use of an adjusted discount rate, nor specifying that when such a rate is used, it must be set at 2%. Litigants are free to account for inflation in other ways, or, if they use the adjusted discount rate approach, to offer evidence of a rate more appropriate than 2%. But in the hope that disputes about the appropriate rate may be minimized, we simply suggest the 2% rate as one that would normally be fair for the parties to agree upon, and we authorize district judges to use such a rate if the parties elect not to offer any evidence on the subject of either inflation or present value discount.

Doca, 634 F.2d at 40.

We decline to read this language as dictating that courts are bound by the mere existence of evidence in the record concerning the appropriate discount rate, regardless of the credibility of that testimony. Rather, the instruction must be interpreted in light of the primary principle enunciated in *Doca*, making the determination of the applicable discount rate a matter for the trial court's discretion. *Doca*, 634 F.2d at 39, 40. Accordingly, we now reaffirm our holding that courts applying an adjusted discount rate are free to use 2% where the evidence of a more appropriate rate is unconvincing. . . .

In the instant case, the economist's testimony was not illogical. The Supreme Court has noted that a worker's annual wage at the time of injury is but the starting point in estimating lost future wages:

> Even in an inflation free economy — that is to say one in which the prices of consumer goods remain stable — a worker's wages tend to "inflate." This "real" wage inflation reflects a number of factors, some linked to the specific individual and some linked to broader societal forces. With the passage of time, an individual worker often becomes more valuable to his employer. His personal work experiences increase his hourly contributions to firm profits. To reflect [this], he will often receive "seniority" or "experience" raises, "merit" raises, or even promotions. . . . Furthermore, the wages of workers as a class may increase over time. Through more efficient interaction among labor, capital, and technology, industrial productivity may increase, and worker's wages may enjoy a share of that growth.

Jones & Laughlin, 462 U.S. at 535 (footnotes omitted).

While the expert's argument was theoretically plausible, Judge Lasker found it unconvincing here. The economist's testimony was generally confusing and cryptic on this complex issue. Moreover, the economist's exegesis abounded in approximations and failed to cite a single authority. Indeed, the portion of testimony upon which appellee relies consists solely of two paragraphs, imprecise to say the least:

> In the maritime industry, the compounded annual rate of increase has been in the neighborhood of 8 percent and the CPI has been running 3 1/2 to 4 percent, which would leave about 4.5 — 4.4 to 4.5 percent, and currently the real interest rates have been running in the immediate period of time about 4 percent, 3.5 percent to 4 percent real interest rates, and over a long period of time they will average out to around 2 percent. Therefore, I felt that it would be eminently fair, since we are going 10 years into the future, to assume a wash rather than to try to dot the *i* and cross the *t* and add to the earnings perspective wage increases based upon productivity inflation, segregate the real earnings and add just for real earnings and leave inflation out of the picture and then discount.

We conclude, therefore, that Judge Lasker did not abuse his discretion by rejecting the expert's assertions and applying a discount rate of 2%.

Accordingly, we affirm the judgment of the district court.

NOTES AND QUESTIONS

1. The rationale for discounting a future stream of earnings to its present value is nicely captured by the court's introductory remark that "[a] dollar in hand today is worth more than a dollar to be paid a year from today." Why is this true? If the purpose of compensatory tort damages is to restore the injured plaintiff to the situation he would have been in but for the injury, does it seem fair to make the plaintiff accept a discount?

2. What is the proper discount rate? Recall the principle: To compensate the plaintiff for $10,000 he would have earned 10 years from now, the defendant should have to pay him — today — not $10,000, but that lesser amount which, if invested, would produce $10,000 ten years from now. Applying this principle, the court observes early in the opinion, "[i]nvested at an interest rate of 6% compounded monthly, $9434 grows to $10,000 at the end of one year, and $8900 grows to $10,000 after two years." The 6 percent is the discount rate in this hypothetical — the value for the variable i in footnote 1 of the opinion. But where does it come from? Why assume 6 percent, or 2 percent, as in the case, or some other number? The theory is that it is the rate that the plaintiff will actually receive from investing the money. What sort of investment should the court assume that the plaintiff will make — a high-risk, high-yield investment, or a very conservative one, with near-zero risk and a commensurately low yield? (Remember that the defendant benefits from a high rate, since the more the money is assumed to earn, the less the defendant will be ordered to pay up front.) If, as in *McCrann*, the plaintiff is a disabled worker who will have to live off the damages award, should we assume something like U.S. Treasury bills, which are about as close to risk-free as it is possible to get?

3. What about inflation? Inflation, which has been a near-constant fact of life since World War II, erodes the purchasing power of a dollar. Even historically low rates of inflation such as those experienced over the last 10 to 15 years have a measurable impact. At 3 percent annual inflation, in 50 years it will take $4.38 to buy what *one* dollar buys today. *See* Hall & Lazear, *Reference Guide on Estimation of Economic Losses in Damage Awards, supra,* at 300. Wages are usually assumed to rise to compensate for inflation. So if it seems fair to adjust the plaintiff's total award *down* because of the earning power of the up-front money, doesn't it seem equally fair to adjust it *up* to compensate for inflation?

4. Most courts have adopted either of two approaches in accounting for inflation. One, illustrated by *McCann*, is to build inflationary protection into the discount rate. Put yourself in the position of an investor. If you are going to invest some money today, you will want your rate of return (1) to protect you against inflation and (2) to produce some real income — commensurate with the risk you are taking — above and beyond inflation. Market interest rates reflect both of these components: an assumed rate of

inflation and a *real* interest rate, which is the difference between the market rate and the assumed inflation rate. So to account for inflation, a court would subtract the inflation rate from the market rate and use the real rate as the discount rate. (Yet another reminder: Lowering the discount rate gives the plaintiff more up-front money.) Do you see how the *McCrann* court follows this approach in arriving at the Second Circuit's presumptive 2 percent discount rate? What market interest rate does it assume? What inflation rate? An alternative approach is to use the full market interest rate as the discount rate, but to inflate the amounts owed in future years by the assumed inflation rate. To use the numbers from Note 3: To give a plaintiff the inflation-adjusted value of 10,000 of today's dollars 50 years from now, a court that assumed a 3 percent annual inflation rate would award $43,800. Even though the two approaches should usually come out at about the same place, the *McCrann* approach is generally regarded as simpler and is more widely used. *See* Hall & Lazear, *Reference Guide on Estimation of Economic Losses in Damage Awards, supra,* at 300, 315.

5. The court also refers to "wage increases the appellee would have received in the future due to factors unrelated to inflation, such as increased seniority and productivity," and quotes the Supreme Court's reference in the *Jones & Laughlin* case to " 'real' wage inflation." Such wage increases are sometimes called "merit raises," and reflect the belief that many workers get better at their jobs over time, become more valuable to their employers, and thus are deserving of higher pay. Productivity or merit raises can be included in earning capacity projections, regardless of whether inflation is taken into account. The likelihood of productivity raises can also be the basis for a reduction in the discount rate, as is discussed in Note 6.

6. While conceding that "in most cases 2% is a fair discount rate," the plaintiff's expert in *McCrann* argued that it should be reduced all the way to zero. Why? Do you think he was right? Many cases have adopted this approach, which is sometimes called the Total Offset Rule. Here is a detailed explanation of the rationale:

> The general principle underlying the assessment of damages in tort cases is that an injured person is entitled to be replaced as nearly as possible in the position he would have occupied had it not been for the defendant's tort. In the case of impairment of future earning capacity, it is reasoned that a failure to reduce damages to present value would be to place the injured person in a better position than he would have occupied except for the defendant's tort, because the injured person would get all of his future wages long in advance and would be able to invest the lump sum and realize earnings on such investment during the intervening period. For this reason — that money has the power to earn money — it has become the generally accepted rule that damages awarded for future loss of earnings should be reduced to present worth.
>
> In applying the general rule, the Supreme Court of Washington has stated a formula for reducing awards of future earnings to present value

which involves the "rate of interest (which) could fairly be expected from safe investments which a person of ordinary prudence, but without particular financial experience or skill, could make in that locality." [Wentz v. T. E. Connolly, Inc., 273 P.2d 485, 492 (1954).] This formula, although empirical at best, is probably as definite as any that has been devised. But we believe that the rule for reducing awards, including the formula applied by the Washington court, ignores facts which should not be ignored. Annual inflation at a varying rate is and has been with us for many years. There is no reason to expect that it will not be with us in the future. This rate of depreciation offsets the interest that could be earned on government bonds and many other "safe" investments. As a result the plaintiff, who through no fault of his own is given his future earnings reduced to present value must, in order to realize his full earnings and not be penalized by reduction of future earnings to present value, invest his money in enterprises, other than those which are considered "safe" investments, which promise a return in interest or dividends greater than the offsetting rate of annual inflation. But ours is a competitive economy. By their very nature some enterprises backed by investors' money are going to fail with resulting loss to individuals. Thus, instead of being assured of earnings at rates greater than the annual rate of inflation, the injured plaintiff stands a chance of entirely losing his future earnings by unlucky or unwise investments. Since the plaintiff, through the defendant's fault and not his own, has been placed in the position of having no assurance that his award of future earnings, reduced to present value, can be utilized so that he will ultimately realize his full earnings, we believe that justice will best be served by permitting the trier of fact to compute loss of future earnings without reduction to present value. The plaintiff is more likely to be restored to his original condition under the rule we adopt than under the prevailing rule which calls for a discounting of the award for future earnings.

Our conclusion is fortified by another factor which also may not be ignored. This is the factor, relied upon by the trial judge, which involves wage increases that the injured plaintiff might have expected to receive in the future had he not been injured. It is a matter of common experience that as one progresses in his chosen occupation or profession he is likely to increase his earnings as the years pass by. In nearly any occupation a wage earner can reasonably expect to receive wage increases from time to time. This factor is generally not taken into account when loss of future wages is determined, because there is no definite way of determining at the time of trial what wage increases the plaintiff may expect to receive in the years to come. However, this factor may be taken into account to some extent when considered to be an offsetting factor to the result reached when future earnings are not reduced to present value. Thus, if there is any fear that failure to reduce the present value will give the plaintiff more than he is entitled to because of the possibility of his making successful investments of the sum awarded at returns greater than the annual rate of inflation, such fear is obviated by the fact that the award may well be deficient in that it does not take into account probable wage increases that the plaintiff would ordinarily be expected to receive in the future.

Beaulieu v. Elliott, 434 P.2d 665, 670-672 (Alaska 1967). See also Kaczkowski v. Bolubasz, 421 A.2d 1027, 1036-1039 (Pa. 1980) (zero discount appropriate because interest rate and inflation offset each other).

7. Another major issue in the *McCrann* case is the rate of prejudgment interest. Tort law makes the defendant liable from the moment of the injury, but the plaintiff will not get his money until some time after judgment is rendered. The discounting process assumes that, from the judgment forward, the plaintiff will actually invest the damage award. But the opportunity to invest the damages that accrued from injury to judgment *during that period* has been irrevocably lost. Awarding prejudgment interest on pre-verdict damages gives the plaintiff—retroactively—the benefit of having had the money during that period. In setting the rate, why is using the 2 percent discount rate "supported by neither logic nor precedent"? Why does the court choose the full market rate? As you think about these questions, note that the function of prejudgment interest is very simple: to transfer from the defendant to the plaintiff the benefit of having had the money during a fixed period of time in the past.

8. What about post-judgment interest? What's to prevent a defendant from delaying the payment of the judgment as long as possible in order to keep using the money? To combat this problem, most states impose a fairly high interest rate on the amount of a judgment from when it is rendered until it is paid. *See, e.g.*, N.C. Gen. Stat. §24-1 (8 percent).

9. If the plaintiff had not been disabled but instead had kept working, he would have paid income tax on his earnings. Should projected tax liabilities be deducted from an award of lost future earning capacity? Is your answer different with respect to an award of *past* earnings? The approaches that courts have taken to these issues are summarized in the *Beaulieu* case:

> [Defendant] Beaulieu argues that the trial judge erred in failing to deduct from the damages awarded for impairment of future earning capacity an amount representing income taxes that Elliott would have had to pay on future income.
>
> The courts are divided on this question. It is the more general view, supported by a majority of American decisions, that an amount representing future income taxes should not be deducted from the award. As was stated by the Supreme Court of Rhode Island:
>
>> This view has been adopted by the various courts on diverse grounds but primarily on the ground that the quantum of such taxation is of necessity in the realm of conjecture. [Oddo v. Cardi, 218 A.2d 373, 377 (R.I. 1966).]
>
> We adopt the majority rule. Income tax rates, provisions relating to deductions and exemptions, and other aspects of income tax laws and regulations are so subject to change in the future that we believe that a court cannot predict with sufficient certainty just what amounts of money a plaintiff would be obliged to pay in federal and state income taxes on income that he would

have earned in the future had it not been for a defendant's tortious conduct. We hold that a damage award for impairment of earning capacity should not be reduced by an estimated amount representing income taxes that the injured party may be required to pay on future income. In awarding damages to Elliott for impaired earning capacity, the court did not err in failing to take income tax consequences into consideration.

The rule we adopt has no application, however, as to the court's award of past wages in the amount of over $10,000.00. The reason for the rule — inability to predict with sufficient certainty what taxes would have to be paid — does not exist here, because taxes on income earned prior to trial can be easily calculated based on income tax laws and regulations as they existed at the time the wages would have been earned. The court erred in failing to deduct from the award for past loss of wages the income taxes Elliott would have had to pay had he earned the amount awarded prior to the trial.

434 P.2d at 672-673. For a fuller discussion of the various approaches to the tax issue, see Brian C. Brush & Charles H. Breedon, *A Taxonomy for the Treatment of Taxes in Cases Involving Lost Earnings*, 6 J. Legal Econ. 1 (1996).

10.   The amounts that McCrann would have earned but for the injury ($275,544) were not contested on appeal. This will often be the case for a union member or someone else who is subject to lock-step pay increases. But in other circumstances the determination of lost wages is the most difficult issue. The next case provides an example.

Har-Pen Truck Lines, Inc. v. Mills

378 F.2d 705 (5th Cir. 1967)

GOLDBERG, Circuit Judge:

[A truck driver and several corporations were found liable for the wrongful death of Mr. and Mrs. Mills after a load of pipe fell off a truck and crushed their car.] On appeal, defendants admit their negligence and the lack of negligence of the Mills family; they argue that there was insufficient evidence to support the two $100,000 verdicts for wrongful death, that certain expert testimony was erroneously admitted, and that a mistrial should have been granted because of prejudicial statements during final argument by plaintiffs' counsel.

We find no error, and affirm. . . .

III. The defendants claim that the $100,000 verdict for the wrongful death of Mr. Mills was excessive.

The only evidence concerning Mr. Mills's earnings is from Social Security records. This is apparently an incomplete record, showing intermittent earnings from 1956. This evidence shows that Mills's earnings fluctuated. In the last six weeks or so before his death [in July 1963], Mills earned at about the rate of $616 per month. During the last quarter of 1962, he earned at the rate of about $754 per month. Other periods show lesser earnings. In addition, there was testimony by Edward H. Walsh, an associate of Mills during Mills's last employment. Walsh testified that Mills was a competent salesman who could earn $15,000 a year, and that Mills had potential for higher achievement as a manager (at $25,000) and as an executive (at $50,000).

Mills was 48 when he died. The defendants introduced into evidence a mortality table indicating that Mills's life expectancy was 22.5 years; they also introduced an annuity table for computation of the present value of Mills's life. The annuity table discounts at a rate of 7 per cent in finding present value. These tables are suggested by Georgia law, but are not binding on the jury. Using these tables, if Mills's income is figured at the monthly rate of $616, the present value of his life was about $74,385. If the $754 figure is used, present value is $90,997. If the $15,000, $25,000 and $50,000 annual rates are used, the present values, respectively, are about $150,780, $251,300, and $502,600.

Defendants strenuously argue that the $616 and $754 monthly earning figures do not form a reasonable basis for computation because Mills worked only sporadically and his average earnings were much lower. In so arguing, however, defendants ignore the testimony concerning the future potential earning power of Mills. Past earnings are indicative but not conclusive, and defendants would have us stare fixedly at the past with no thought of change in the future. The jury did not have to ignore the possibility of future increases in earnings, when testimony which it could believe supported such a hypothesis. The jury came nowhere near stretching that evidence to the limit. If the jury were restricted to the past for its answers, its computation of loss might have to be purely arithmetic; but the jury may look forward as well as backward, as long as it relies on such relevant and appropriate evidence as is available. In personal injury and death cases, court and jury deal with the inchoate, the intangible, the destroyed potential of tomorrows. To ask the jury to be finite about such a future is neither realistic nor is it a judicially sensible ambition. The future is not finite. We live in a world of probabilities, and the jury need not ignore them. In the main, a jury's calculation of damages must involve some speculation. Our job on appeal is to inquire whether the jury has exceeded the bounds of the probabilities presented by the evidence. . . .

IV. Defendants similarly argue that the evidence was not sufficient to support the jury's award of $100,000 for the wrongful death of Mrs. Mills. . . . Here the distinguishing factor is the presence of the testimony of Chong Soo Pyun, a professor of economics at Mercer University. Professor Pyun testified as an expert on the value of the life of a hypothetical housewife in Mrs. Mills's position had she lived. Without valuing the immeasurables of love, moral guidance, inspiration, encouragement, and the other uncatalog-able aspects of motherhood, Professor Pyun valued the mother's household services from the time of the accident until the youngest child arrived at the age of completing college. From that point on, Professor Pyun assumed that Mrs. Mills could have worked outside her home until she reached retirement age nine years later, at the age of 62. To value household services, Professor Pyun measured "utility producing power" rather than the sum which Mrs. Mills might have earned. He testified:

> The capitalized monetary value of her prospective annual income is nothing but the money that she could have earned, if she had looked for employment. Now her utility producing power before that to the household is much greater than her money income producing power. In other words, if you wanted to hire substitutes for this housewife at the market place, you would have to pay a greater amount of money than the amount that she could have earned. There-fore, in order to compute it, in order to estimate the replacement cost of this housewife's services, we have to estimate the monetary [value] of her services on the basis of the market wage rates for each service which she was performing.

To value the work outside of the home, Professor Pyun chose 24 hypo-thetical occupations which he felt would be open to a woman of Mrs. Mills's age, education, and employment history. The professor randomly chose five of these 24 for computation of an average, and he testified that the error involved in such a choice was at most 5 per cent, which he characterized as standard deviation. Finally, the professor testified that the value of the household services over the 11 year span, reduced to present value by the 7 per cent discount, was $69,852. The value of the outside employment, similarly discounted, was $31,948. The total of these sums is $101,800.

The defendants offered no testimony in rebuttal of Professor Pyun's. They now contest its adequacy on several grounds.

First, the defendants argue that placing monetary value on the household services of a mother is "peculiarly a function of a jury," and that no direct evidence of that value by expert or nonexpert should be admitted, as such admission would invade the function of the jury. . . . But the Georgia courts have expressly sanctioned use of opinion evidence and expert testimony to evaluate services rendered, where that was possible. . . .

From the cases it appears clear to us that the Georgia courts tend to accept whatever probative evidence can be offered, in the attempt to com-pensate for the loss in a just manner. The expert testimony in the present case is a more modern and scientific version of that accepted in Standard Oil Co. v. Reagan, 1915, 15 Ga.App. 571, 84 S.E. 69. Professor Pyun's construct, based on scientific study, investigation, and analysis, was more nearly complete than what was available in the earlier days of Standard

Oil Co. v. Reagan. The brittle, unemotional calculus computed by Pyun was what the sons would have had to pay for services to be rendered by an ersatz mother. Such modern scientific testimony is more reliable than the jury's unbounded musings of yesteryears.

NOTES AND QUESTIONS

1. The evidence on which Mr. Mills's earnings were projected was sketchy at best. Assume that these projections were offered by a qualified industrial economist. Do you think the testimony would meet the *Daubert* standard? What other information might you require? What would be the consequences of rejecting the testimony? The admissibility question was discussed at length in the post-*Daubert* case of Boucher v. United States Suzuki Motor Corp., 73 F.3d 18 (2d Cir. 1996), where the injured plaintiff likewise had an erratic earnings history:

> Where lost future earnings are at issue, an expert's testimony should be excluded as speculative if it is based on unrealistic assumptions regarding the plaintiff's future employment prospects. *See Gumbs v. Int'l Harvester, Inc.* 718 F.2d 88, 98 (3d Cir. 1983) (expert testimony based on assumption that plaintiff would have earned twice his average annual income should have been excluded). . . . Admission of expert testimony based on speculative assumptions is an abuse of discretion. *See Gumbs*, 718 F.2d at 98-99.
>
> In the present case, Dr. Reagles estimated Boucher's lost earnings based on the assumptions (among others) that Boucher would work 40 hours per week, 52 weeks per year, with fringe benefits and regular pay increases, for the rest of his career. Prior to the accident, however, Boucher's sporadic employment had yielded fluctuating low levels of income, with long spells of no income whatsoever. When he was employed, he received few fringe benefits, if any.
>
> The expert's projection thus was based on assumptions about Boucher's employment prospects that represent a complete break with his work history of seasonal and intermittent employment. We cannot say whether Boucher's employment pattern was attributable to low demand for his services, to want of ambition, skills or application, or to bad luck or other causes. In any event, nothing of probative value — such as a change in family responsibilities, or the acquisition of a new set of skills — accounts for the reversal assumed by the expert. . . .
>
> On appeal, Boucher contends that his prospect for full-time employment was a factual matter for the jury to determine, not a ground for exclusion of Dr. Reagles' estimate of his future earning capacity. But the Federal Rules of Evidence require a greater degree of discrimination than that. Since Boucher's expert testimony was not "accompanied by a sufficient factual foundation before it [was] submitted to the jury," *Gumbs*, 718 F.2d at 98, it was inadmissible under Federal Rule of Evidence 702. We hold therefore that the

district court abused its discretion in permitting Dr. Reagles to testify regarding Boucher's past and future lost earnings capacity based on the unrealistic and speculative assumption that Boucher would have been employed on a permanent, full-time basis, year in and year out, had he not been injured.

2. The *Mills* court permitted, without comment, the use of a 7 percent discount rate suggested by an annuity table. The early 1960s were a period of low interest rates and inflation. Does such a rate seem appropriate in comparison to the 2 percent used in *McCrann*? Might the two courts have dealt with inflation in different ways?

3. The "housewife" discussion may strike contemporary readers as quaint, but the problem of valuing the lives of those who do not work for wages outside the home is still very real. Explain Professor Pyun's "utility producing power" approach to valuing Mrs. Mills's services to the family. Would this testimony survive *Daubert* scrutiny?

4. Next, evaluate Pyun's approach to Mrs. Mills's hypothetical employment outside the home under the *Daubert* standard. He talked of random sampling, a 5 percent "error," and "standard deviation." Drawing on what you learned about these concepts in Chapter 3, do you think Pyun was making appropriate use of these terms?

II. VALUING A BUSINESS

In re Radiology Assoc., Inc.

611 A.2d 485 (Del. Ch. 1991)

CHANDLER, Vice Chancellor

[Dr. Kurtz, the plaintiff, is a radiologist who was an employee and shareholder of a corporation that the court calls Radiology. Dr. Papastavros, the founder of Radiology, and some of his colleagues used Delaware corporate law to merge Radiology into a new company called New Radiology. This merger eliminated Kurtz's interest in Radiology in exchange for the "fair value" of his shares. Kurtz was dissatisfied with the compensation — $400 per share — and sued Papastavros and other defendants for breach of contract and breach of fiduciary duty in effectuating the merger. The court found the defendants liable on several theories. In considering damages, the court turned to the question of the fair value of Kurtz's radiology shares as of May 6, 1987, which depended on the value of Radiology itself.]

II. THE FAIR VALUE OF DR. KURTZ'S SHARES

Plaintiff, Dr. Kurtz, challenges the fairness of the merger price. Plaintiff contends that Radiology's fair value was $2300 per share on May 6, 1987, the merger date. Plaintiff's conclusion rests primarily on the testimony of his valuation expert, Anne Danyluk, who is manager of Valuation Services at Coopers & Lybrand's Philadelphia office. Defendants dispute this conclusion and contend that the fair value was $457 per share on the merger date. Defendants' conclusion rests primarily on the testimony of their valuation expert, Charles Stryker, who is a business valuator for the "Benchmark" subsidiary of KPMG Peat Marwick. . . .

A. PLAINTIFF'S VALUATION METHODOLOGY

Plaintiff's expert attempted to value Radiology by using two different methods: (1) a comparable company approach and (2) a discounted cash flow approach. Further, after determining the outcomes from the methods, plaintiff's expert argued that adjustments to the results were necessary in order to account for Radiology's S corporation status; in order to include Radiology's non-operating assets; and in order to alleviate the minority discount implicit in its valuation methods.

1. *The Comparable Company Method*

The comparable company approach attempts to value companies first by finding comparable publicly-traded companies. See Harris v. Rapid-American Corp., 1990 Del. Ch. LEXIS 166, *22-24, Del. Ch., C.A. No. 6462, Chandler, V.C. (Oct. 2, 1990). After identifying a comparable company, this approach calculates the value of the company through the use of earnings and other multiples. See Harris, 1990 Del. Ch. LEXIS 166, *22-25. This Court has affirmed the general validity of this approach. See Harris, 1990 Del. Ch. LEXIS 166, *25-26.

"The first step in doing a comparable companies analysis is to compile a list of comparative companies." Harris, 1990 Del. Ch. LEXIS 166, *22-24. In this case, Ms. Danyluk chose two companies with which she wished to compare Radiology: MEDIQ Incorporated ("MEDIQ") and MMI Medical ("MMI"). The companies chosen for comparison by plaintiff's expert differ significantly from Radiology. First, MMI derives its revenue from the operation of mobile radiological units, from the leasing of such units and from providing maintenance and repair services for radiological equipment. MEDIQ derives only 24% of its revenues from diagnostic imaging services, and MEDIQ provided these services through mobile units. On the other hand, Radiology derives its revenue solely from providing non-mobile radiological services. Further, defendants point out significant differences in revenues, size, profitability, and growth rates:

	Radiology	MEDIQ	MMI
Revenues	$4.8 million	$187.7 million	$28.2 million
Total Assets	$3.4 million	$239.9 million	$30.9 million
Pre-tax Profit Margin	22.4%	7.6%	3.7%
Revenue Growth Rate	7.2%	38.2%	35.5%
Earnings Growth Rate	10.4%	34.4%	13.4%

Finally, MEDIQ and MMI cover much larger geographic areas than Radiology.

The utility of the comparable company approach depends on the similarity between the company the court is valuing and the companies used for comparison. At some point, the differences become so large that the use of the comparable company method becomes meaningless for valuation purposes. In this case, the differences between Radiology and MMI and MEDIQ as to product mix, revenues, profit margins, revenue and earnings growth rates, assets and geographic markets combine to make any comparison with Radiology meaningless.

2. The Discounted Cash Flow Method

The second method Ms. Danyluk used in attempting to value Radiology was the discounted cash flow method.

> In theory, the value of an interest in a business depends on the future benefits discounted back to a present value at some appropriate discount (capitalization) rate. Thus, the theoretically correct approach is to project the future benefits (usually earnings, cash flow, or dividends) and discount the projected stream back to a present value.

S. Pratt, Valuing a Business 25 (2d ed. 1989). The Delaware courts have affirmed the validity of this method of valuation repeatedly.

> The DCF model entails three basic components: an estimation of net cash flows that the firm will generate and when, over some period; a terminal or residual value equal to the future value, as of the end of the projection period, of the firm's cash flows beyond the projection period; and finally a cost of capital with which to discount to a present value both the projected net cash flows and the estimated terminal or residual value.

Cede & Co. v. Technicolor, 1990 Del. Ch. LEXIS 259, *22-25, Del. Ch., C.A. No. 7129, Allen, C. (Oct. 19, 1990). The quality of the projection as to the future benefits over some period and the residual or terminal value is central to the reliability of the underlying methodology of the discount cash flow method. See Harris v. Rapid-American Corp., 1990 Del. Ch. LEXIS 166, *16-18, Del. Ch., C.A. No. 6462, Chandler, V.C. (Oct. 2, 1990).

(a) Projected Revenues and Terminal Value

In Harris, this Court declined to use the discounted cash flow method because the projections on which petitioners relied were too speculative. See Harris, supra, 1990 Del. Ch. LEXIS 166, *18-19. The projections in Harris were rejected because management did not create them and did not have any input with the third party who created them. In this case, Ms. Danyluk used projections prepared by the Delaware Trust Company for its internal purposes of assessing an application for a multi-million dollar loan for an ESOP [Employee Stock Option Plan]. It is not as important that management itself did not create the projections as much as management had input with their creation. That is, although management itself did not do the "number crunching," it had input directly and indirectly (via Radiology's accountant, Barry Crozier, who worked with Delaware Trust in creating the projections). Further, Delaware Trust created the projections for a business purpose (the propriety of a loan) completely unrelated to this lawsuit. Also, Delaware Trust's projections began from fact: they created the projections by making adjustments to and applying a growth rate to historical earnings. For all of these reasons, I believe that the projections are reliable and should be used in applying the discounted cash flow approach.

Ms. Danyluk, however, did not use the exact projections of the Delaware Trust Company. She adjusted the five-year revenue projection of 5% growth annually to 7% annually. Ms. Danyluk did use the 5% growth figure used by the Delaware Trust Company in her terminal year calculation.

Ms. Danyluk justified a change in the five year revenue projection by relying on three factors: historical earnings, an analysis of the industry and an analysis of other projections. The parties argue over exactly what the historical earnings growth rate was. However, the Delaware Trust Company had the information both sides put forth to argue their respective positions available when they made their projections. Thus, Ms. Danyluk's reliance on this factor for adjusting the growth rate upward is without merit since the Delaware Trust Company undoubtedly considered historical earnings in projecting a future earnings growth rate. Similarly, Ms. Danyluk's second factor, an industry analysis, reflects information available to the Delaware Trust Company when they made their projections and information to which they undoubtedly referred in creating the earnings growth rate projections. Finally, Ms. Danyluk relied on the fact that other projections predicted higher growth rates. Ms. Danyluk did not explain who made these projections, how they were different, and why they were different. The concept of "other projections," in my opinion, is too amorphous and insufficient to warrant a deviation from the Delaware Trust Company's projections as to the growth rate.

Since I have adjusted the proper growth rate in the discounted cash flow analysis down to 5%, I also must adjust expenses projected on a percentage of net sales basis (e.g., general administrative expenses and adjusted depreciation).

In determining the projected net cash flows for years 1987 through 1991 and the terminal year, Ms. Danyluk also made an adjustment for officer's salaries. Ms. Danyluk added back as income the distributions made to the doctors as salaries and as part of the general and administrative expenses. However, she does allow a deduction for the reasonable salaries of two administrators adjusted for a nominal raise each year. Defendants argue that the salaries were not earnings.

This Court specifically stated that the distributions were earnings:

> Dr. Kurtz understood that the vast bulk of Radiology's income would be distributed to the shareholders in accordance with their proportionate ownership of stock. Part of these distributions would come to the stockholders in the form of a "salary" that was in actuality a form of return on equity. It is uncontested that the books of Radiology show that for several years Drs. Kurtz [and others] all received income from Radiology representing their proportionate stock ownership.

Any claim by defendants that the salary expenses do not represent, at least in part, a return on equity is wholly without merit. If the salaries do not represent entirely a return on equity, they represent, at least, a partial return on equity. Thus, Ms. Danyluk's calculations which, in effect, treat the salaries as part salary expense and part return on equity is much more appealing than defendants' desire to treat the distributions entirely as salary expenses and general and administrative expenses.

Defendants claim that if I treat some of the salary and general administrative expenses as returns on equity and not expenses, I also must adjust revenue. That is, defendants argue that Radiology bills Papastavros on a cost plus basis. Thus, if I reduce the amount of costs (expenses), I also must reduce Radiology's revenue.

Defendants' argument is without merit. They fail to distinguish the difference between how Radiology treats an item and how Radiology should treat an item. That is, Radiology should treat some or all of the salary distributions as returns on equity. However, this does not mean that Radiology will change its treatment of the distributions as expenses. In fact, Radiology most likely will continue to treat it as an expense and, as such, will bill Papastavros Associates on a cost (including the salary distributions) plus basis. Thus, I make no further adjustment to the treatment of salary distributions.

Having made the adjustments to the projected growth rate, the expenses as a percentage of net sales and "salary" expenses, I am able to determine the projected net cash flows for years 1987 through 1991 and the terminal year. These projections of net cash flow are $744,000 for 1987; $1,218,000 for 1988; $1,301,000 for 1989; $1,388,000 for 1990; $1,480,000 for 1991; and $1,556,000 for the terminal year.

(b) Discount Rate

Having decided what are the proper projected revenues for 1987 through 1991 and for the terminal year, the third element that this Court must calculate in applying the discounted cash flow method is the proper discount rate. The discount rate attempts to reduce the projected future revenues to present value. See Cede & Co., supra, 1990 Del. Ch. LEXIS 259, *92-93.

Ms. Danyluk applied a 14% discount rate. On the other hand, defendants argue that 17% or 16.5% is the proper discount rate. Ms. Danyluk arrived at her discount rate by using the Capital Asset Pricing Model ("CAPM"). [The CAPM approach arrives at a discount rate by estimating the rate of return that a company like Radiology would have to provide in order to raise capital by a combination of equity, or issuing stock, and debt, or borrowing. Using the standard CAPM formula, Ms. Danyluk calculated Radiology's cost of equity to be 21.6 percent. She then estimated Radiology's future cost of borrowing at 6.47 percent, citing Standard & Poors' guide to industrial bonds. The court adjusted this up to 9.8 percent because of tax considerations.]

The final step in the CAPM is to determine the weighted average cost of capital (WACC). The WACC is the weighted average of the cost of debt and equity which represents the average cost of capital. In this case, Ms. Danyluk determined that the cost of debt should carry a 49% weight and that the cost of equity should carry a 51% weight. However, Ms. Danyluk did not use Radiology's debt to equity ratio, which was 21% to 79%, in calculating the WACC. Instead, she used a hypothetical debt to equity ratio of 49% to 51%. Ms. Danyluk's justification for the use of the hypothetical ratio was that the hypothetical ratio reflected the industry average capital structure, that Radiology's deviation from the industry average reflects a hidden value (i.e., underleveraging) in the company, and that the company could and should maximize shareholder value by attaining the optimal capital structure (i.e., the industry average debt to equity ratio). . . .

Even if Ms. Danyluk's hypothetical capital structure represents a debt to equity ratio that is closer to the industry average, defendants argue (and I agree) that the use of the industry average rather than Radiology's actual capital structure was improper. The entire focus of the discounted cash flow analysis is to determine the fair value of Radiology. I am not attempting to determine the potential maximum value of the company. Rather, I must value Radiology, not some theoretical company. Plaintiff has introduced no evidence (e.g., Radiology's debt to equity ratio trends or goals) that implies that Radiology will mimic the industry's debt to equity ratio. Given the lack of evidence as to the applicability of the industry average to Radiology, I will use Radiology's own debt to equity ratio in determining its WACC. Thus, I use 18% ([29.63% × 9.80%] + [70.37% × 21.65%] = 18.14%) as the discount rate in applying the discounted cash flow method. . . .

Given my prior findings as to the growth rate, the net income adjustments and the discount rate, I adjust the terminal value to equal $6,020,000.

3. Adjustments

[The court rejected Ms. Danyluk's adjustments to value for the minority (*i.e.*, non-controlling) status of Kurtz's shares and the fact that Radiology was an S-Corp., which meant that it was not taxed as a corporate entity. It accepted her argument that $1.4 million should be added to Radiology's value to account for such "non-operating assets" as other investments and the cash surrender value of officers' life insurance policies.]

B.   DEFENDANTS' VALUATION METHODOLOGY

Defendants' expert, Charles Stryker, attempted to value Radiology by using one method: the "Delaware Block Method." Even though the Delaware courts have used the Delaware Block Method infrequently [in recent years], the Delaware courts still consider it an acceptable procedure for valuing a company. See Rosenblatt v. Getty Oil Co., Del. Supr., 493 A.2d 929, 940 (1985). The Delaware Block Method actually is a combination of three generally accepted methods for valuation: the asset approach, the market approach and the earnings approach.

1. The Asset Approach

Mr. Stryker's valuation analysis began with a valuation of Radiology's assets. He adjusted the book value of assets to reflect their present value [and made minor adjustments elsewhere]. Mr. Stryker did not add an amount to reflect Radiology's goodwill. He believed that all of Radiology's goodwill belonged to Papastavros Associates [the founding doctor and his original associates] since he believed that patients came to Radiology because of the professional reputation of Papastavros Associates, not the reputation of Radiology's x-ray technicians. . . .

As to the failure to make an addition for goodwill, plaintiff argues that Radiology's expectation of future business was not so much the future business of patients but the future patronage of Papastavros Associates. Clearly, the twenty-one year relationship between the two companies justified this expectation. Thus, I agree that the failure to include an amount for goodwill was inappropriate.

The unjustified failure to include an amount for goodwill affects my decision as to the proper weight of the asset prong of the Delaware Block

Method. First, except for corporations with significant natural resource assets or with significant non-operating assets, the Delaware courts generally have refrained from weighing the asset prong heavily in applying the Delaware Block Method when the earnings valuation method appears reliable. Further, in this case, Mr. Stryker's analysis incorrectly did not include an amount for goodwill. This failure to include such an amount results in his asset value reflecting only the liquidation value rather than the going-concern value of Radiology. The use of liquidation value rather than going-concern value is inappropriate. Thus, I give no weight to Mr. Stryker's asset valuation because Delaware courts generally have not weighed the asset prong heavily and because Mr. Stryker calculated an asset value that more closely reflected Radiology's liquidation value than its going-concern value.

2. The Market Approach

The second prong of the Delaware Block Method valuation analysis is the market value factor. Delaware courts have recognized offers for purchase as valid indications of value for purposes of appraisal. Mr. Stryker's market analysis focused on a sale of Radiology stock and two offers for the purchase of Radiology in calculating Radiology's market value to be $453 per share.

The first factor upon which Mr. Stryker relied in calculating Radiology's market value was the December 1986 sale of Radiology stock. In that transaction, Drs. Papastavros and Piendak sold 22.5% of Radiology stock to Drs. Koniver, Fiss and Mansoory at a price of $400 per share.

The May 4, 1984, offer of Diagnostek, Inc. of Alberquerque, New Mexico was the first offer to purchase Radiology upon which Mr. Stryker relied in calculating Radiology's market value. The net amount of this offer was $4,808,787 or $483 per share.

The "well developed" offer of Wilmington Medical Center to purchase Radiology was the second offer upon which Mr. Stryker relied in calculating Radiology's market value. The net amount of this offer was $4,726.679 or $475 per share.

Mr. Stryker considered the Wilmington Medical Center offer to be "well developed" because it had conducted due diligence and used sophisticated advisers. Also, it had hired an appraiser to value the company. Further, it even retained Coopers & Lybrand to do a business review to support the offer.

Plaintiff argues that this Court cannot use any facet of Mr. Stryker's market valuation analysis because Dr. Papastavros set the pricing parameters of each transaction (the stock sale and the two offers for purchase) and Dr. Papastavros was unaware of the true value of Radiology. It is clear that this Court can give no weight to the $400 stock sale price. Dr. Papastavros set the price for the stock sale. Dr. Papastavros did not have the competency to set a price reflecting Radiology's market value. Further, Drs. Koniver, Fiss and Mansoory blindly relied on the fairness of this price. Thus, this Court cannot justify any reliance on this stock sale price as an accurate reflection of Radiology's market value.

As far as the offers to purchase Radiology, Dr. Papastavros set the initial parameters for the making of such offers. He set the parameters of the price by approaching the two potential offerors with an offer to sell Radiology for $5,000,000. Plaintiff argues that just as the stock sale price is useless as an indication of Radiology's market value because of Dr. Papastavros' involvement so too are the prices of the offers to purchase.

Defendants contend that the offerors' dickering over the $5,000,000 price, even if Dr. Papastavros set it, is an indication of the reliability of their offers as reflections of Radiology's market price. That is, defendants argue that the failure of the offerors to snap up this deal is an indication that, if anything, the $5,000,000 price was too high. However, I cannot get past the fact that Dr. Papastavros set the asking price of $5,000,000. Thus, a person who did not have the ability to determine Radiology's value established the outside limit someone would have to pay to purchase Radiology. The offerors predicated their offers on Dr. Papastavros' asking price and their decision not to buy Radiology for the full $5,000,000, in all likelihood, partially relied on Dr. Papastavros' asking price as an indication of Radiology's value. Thus, I cannot justify any reliance on these offers as an accurate reflection of Radiology's market value. Mr. Stryker's market valuation analysis thus deserves no weight.

3. The Earnings Approach

The final prong of the Delaware Block Method valuation analysis is the earnings value factor. Mr. Stryker based his earnings analysis on the pre-tax earnings of Radiology for the five-year period of 1982 through 1986. In analyzing these earnings, Mr. Stryker gave extra weight to the 1986 earnings because he believed they better reflected Radiology's current earning power. Mr. Stryker capitalized the earnings at a 15% discount rate. His earnings approach valued Radiology at $6,687,000 or $672 per share.

The parties argue over what Radiology's 1985 earnings were. However, I do not need to address this issue because I find the reliance on historical earnings unnecessary in this case where reliable projections are available, whose preparers undoubtedly considered Radiology's historical earnings in making their calculations. I find it intrinsically more appealing to rely on the future prospects of a company, where reliable projections are available, than the historical earnings of the company because the theoretically more correct measure of the entity's value, under an earnings valuation approach, is the present value of its future cash flows or earnings. Correspondingly, I find it unnecessary to address the parties' arguments as to the proper capitalization rate and the proper treatment of Radiology's growth rate because reliance on historical earnings is unwarranted in this case where reliable projections are available. . . .

C.   SUMMARY

I conclude that Mr. Stryker's valuation analysis as to asset value and market value deserve no weight. I give no weight to his earnings valuation principally because of the availability of reliable projections of Radiology's earnings, and secondarily because of my doubts as to the credibility of the information supplied to him.

As far as Ms. Danyluk's analysis, I conclude that her comparable company valuation deserves no weight because of the noncomparability of the companies chosen. Thus, I am left to use Ms. Danyluk's discounted cash flow valuation. However, as discussed earlier, I use only a 5% growth rate and do not use her implicit minority discount adjustment. Also, I do not use her S-Corp. adjustment directly. Therefore, I find the fair value of plaintiff's [250] shares as . . . $271,000 [or $1,084 per share].

NOTES AND QUESTIONS

1.   Because so many American companies are incorporated in Delaware, valuation cases like *Radiology Associates* are quite common and Delaware equity judges (or Vice Chancellors) tend to have a high level of expertise with the various approaches. For a more recent, even more detailed treatment of the discounted cash flow (DCF) method that prevailed in *Radiology Associates,* see Gilbert v. MPM Enterprises, Inc., 709 A.2d 663 (Del. Ch. 1997). For an exhaustive discussion of DCF in the context of valuing stock in a small business corporation, see Gross v. Comm'r of Internal Revenue, 272 F.3d 333 (6th Cir. 2001).

2.   Why did the court reject Ms. Danyluk's use of the comparable companies method? The comparable companies approach is analogous to what real estate appraisers routinely do when they value a property in reference to recent sales of "comparable" properties. Turning to the DCF method, why did the court find the earnings projections of the Delaware Trust Company so persuasive? Why was it appropriate to treat the doctors' "salaries" as part of the corporation's earnings? Note that in a larger, publicly traded corporation, some of the earnings are typically retained and some distributed to shareholders in the form of dividends. The concept of the discount rate is the same as in the wage earner cases, but its application is more complicated. Rather than simply deciding what a plaintiff could expect to earn by investing her damage award safely, the task here is to determine what return this corporation would have to offer in order to attract capital. Corporations raise capital in two ways: by issuing stock, or equity; and by borrowing, usually by issuing debt instruments like bonds. In determining Radiology's future cost of capital, Danyluk applied the Capital Asset Pricing Model (CAPM, pronounced Cap-M) to project the respective costs of equity and debt and then to calculate a weighted average of the two. The court followed the same approach but made a

number of adjustments. CAPM is widely used in business valuation. For a fuller explanation of the calculations involved, see the complete text of the *Radiology Associates* opinion; Hall & Lazear, *Reference Guide on Estimation of Economic Losses in Damage Awards, supra,* at 303; or a corporate finance text, such as William W. Bratton, *Corporate Finance: Cases and Materials* 106-116 (5th ed. 2003).

3.   The unfortunate Mr. Stryker was rejected at every turn. Why did the court think that his asset valuation approach was better suited to determining a liquidation value than a going-concern value? Why was his failure to include goodwill particularly inappropriate to this kind of business? The usual rule of thumb in the market approach is to use only arm's-length, open market transactions. Why did the court reject the purchase offers that Stryker relied on? Finally, what flaw did the court find in Stryker's earnings approach? Did it reject the method itself, or some aspect of Stryker's application of the method?

III.   CALCULATING INTELLECTUAL PROPERTY DAMAGES

Economic and financial experts regularly testify about damages in intellectual property cases. Under federal patent law, "the court shall award the claimant damages adequate to compensate for the infringement, but in no event less than a reasonable royalty for the use made of the invention by the infringer." 35 U.S.C. § 284. The federal Lanham Act provides that a successful trademark plaintiff may "recover (1) defendant's profits, (2) any damages sustained by the plaintiff, and (3) the costs of the action." 15 U.S.C. § 1117(a). The next case was decided under the actual damages section of the Copyright Act, 17 U.S.C. § 504(b), which permits the plaintiff "to recover the actual damages suffered by him or her as a result of the infringement, and any profits of the infringer that are attributable to the infringement and are not taken into account in computing the actual damages." As the court points out, in establishing the infringer's profits, the plaintiff "is required to present proof only of the infringer's gross revenue, and the infringer is required to prove his or her deductible expenses and the elements of profit attributable to factors other than" the infringement of the plaintiff's copyrighted work.

Estate of Vane v. The Fair, Inc.

849 F.2d 186 (5th Cir. 1988)

ALVIN B. RUBIN, Circuit Judge:
The owner of an infringed copyright asks this court to increase the amount of damages awarded it by the district court. . . . We find that the

district court did not err in failing to base the damage award on those profits of the infringer allegedly attributable to the infringement because the infringer did not establish the amount of those profits, if any there were. . . . Accordingly, we affirm.

I.

The Fair, a chain of retail stores, hired photographer Dean Vane to prepare slides showing its merchandise with the stated purpose of using the slides in printed advertising material to be mailed to its customers. Later, however, The Fair hired Vance-Mathews, Inc., an advertising agency, to produce television commercials, which incorporated some of Vane's slides as well as a substantial amount of material from other sources. Several television stations aired the commercials. Vane brought an action based on copyright infringement against The Fair, asserting that his agreement with The Fair involved merely a license to use the slides to produce mailers and that he retained all other rights to the slides provided by copyright law. . . . The court held that The Fair was liable, and it awarded damages in the amount of $60,000, an amount representing the value of the use of the slides in the commercials. The court refused to make a damage award based on profits The Fair had accrued by virtue of the infringement; it found that the evidence was too speculative to support such an award. . . .

II.

. . . [T]he copyright owner need prove only the infringer's gross revenues, while the infringer must prove his deductible expenses and must show which elements of profits are attributable to sources other than the copyrighted work.

Vane attempted through discovery to obtain financial records of The Fair that would enable him to satisfy his burden of proving The Fair's gross revenues attributable to the infringement, but the records were not detailed enough to show the amount received from the sales of particular items shown in the slides. Therefore Vane attempted to establish The Fair's gross revenues, and ultimately its profits, by introducing as an expert witness Dr. Herbert Lyon, Professor of Marketing at the University of Houston's College of Business Administration. Dr. Lyon testified that he had conducted a multiple regression analysis designed to show how much each dollar The Fair spent on television advertising would yield in sales. Dr. Lyon examined monthly data, including profit-and-loss statements and summaries of media costs over a five-year period. He calculated that The Fair sold approximately $25.60 in merchandise for every dollar it spent on television advertising. He multiplied $25.60 by the number of dollars The Fair spent on the infringing television commercials to yield a gross revenue figure, then deducted certain costs to The Fair, including the actual cost that The Fair had paid for the merchandise it sold, transportation charges for getting the merchandise to the stores, a 3% allowance for pilferage, and some other direct operating expenses. After adjusting the resulting figure for inflation, Dr. Lyon concluded that The Fair's profits attributable to its infringement of Vane's slides exceeded $694,000. The district court held that Vane had not brought forth sufficient proof of The Fair's profits and refused to award damages based on Dr. Lyon's calculations.

When financial records sufficiently detailed to show an infringer's sales are not available, expert testimony may be used to develop either such proof or, as Vane attempted, proof of its profits rather than its sales. But it is the trial court's role to evaluate this testimony. The trial court in this case concluded, with ample basis, that the testimony introduced was inadequate to establish The Fair's profits attributable to the infringement.

In conducting his analysis, Dr. Lyon took into account a variety of factors designed to refine his calculations. For instance, his model purported to consider seasonal sales trends, specifically the pre-Christmas boom in sales; the downward economic trend in the Houston area in the early 1980's; and the carryover effect by which an advertisement continues to contribute to some sales long after its initial airing. By taking such factors into account, Dr. Lyon testified, he attempted to produce a model that would analyze with the greatest possible precision the relationship between advertising dollars spent and resulting profits.

Cross-examination, however, brought to light a number of potential shortcomings in this analysis. Dr. Lyon's model yielded only a lump-sum figure for profits attributable to the television commercials that contained infringed material as a whole without accounting for the fact that the infringed material constituted only a fraction of any given commercial. Some portion of the profits may have been attributable to the infringement, but much of the profits must be attributed to non-infringing aspects of the commercials. Testimony at trial showed from three perspectives why the use of an undifferentiated figure does not convincingly establish what profits are attributable to the infringement.

First, the cost of slides used in a commercial is only one of many expenses involved. The single figure for "dollars spent on television advertising" must be composed of lesser expenditures for a variety of goods and services: photographs used in the commercial, fees paid to the producer of the commercial, and air time for showing the commercial, to name a few. If, for instance, 50% of the cost to someone airing a commercial went to television stations to pay for air time, another 30% went to the producer, and 20% went to purchase ten slides used in the commercial, which also used five infringed slides, then it would be wholly illogical to treat the entire profits derived from airing the commercial as attributable to the five infringed slides. Yet this is, in essence, what Vane asked the district court to do. Dr. Lyon testified that he had adjusted the sales figures his model yielded to account for air time and production costs, but neither his testimony nor the computer printouts introduced as an exhibit make clear what this adjustment was. Even if Dr. Lyon's analysis accurately showed the relationship between dollars spent on advertising and profits yielded, it did not show the relationship between the dollars that should have been spent on the rights to use Vane's slides and the total advertising costs. Evidence of this relationship might have provided a basis for showing what portion of the profits the commercials yielded were attributable to the infringement.

Second, the infringed slides appeared during only part of the time the commercials were on the air. Vane testified that the general format of the commercials in question consisted of a "trailer" or introductory film segment setting forth a theme for the commercial, followed by a segment featuring various items of merchandise, concluding with another brief trailer. To the extent that Vane's slides appeared in the commercials, they appeared only in the middle segments, never in the trailers. Moreover, the middle segments that contained infringed slides also contained non-infringed slides. If only eight seconds of a thirty-second commercial contained infringed slides, it would be irrational to believe that all the profits the commercial brought in were due to those slides.

Third, Dr. Lyon's model did not purport to show the relative importance of different elements of the commercials in generating profits for The Fair. On cross-examination, counsel for The Fair asked Dr. Lyon:

> If we take your figures that are given here of some $600,000 that you say are attributable to the TV advertising dollar, do you express any opinion as to what percentage of that should be attributable to Mr. Vane's slides as contrasted to the work product of Vance-Matthews in putting the commercials together?

Dr. Lyon responded:

> No, sir. . . . I'm simply looking at the revenue or gross revenues generated by those ads. I did not look at the ads specifically. I don't think—I mean, I thought of that issue, but I don't think it can be answered.

. . . By pointing to these problems in Dr. Lyon's analysis, we do not suggest that a calculation based on a mathematical formula involving the ratio of fair cost of infringed material to entire cost of commercial, or length of air time of infringed material to length of entire commercial, would be the only means of showing profits. The question will often be highly fact-specific. We merely hold that it was not error for the district court to reject this attempt to show revenues attributable to the infringement as speculative.

NOTES AND QUESTIONS

1.   In analyzing Dr. Lyon's model, recall the discussion of regression analysis in Chapter 3. Insofar as you can tell from the court's very brief summary, what was the dependent value in his regression analysis? What was the independent variable that he was particularly concerned with? What was the regression coefficient associated with that independent variable?

2.   Did the court read the statute correctly? In particular, did it allocate the burden of proof in the way that the statute specifies? The court states, for example, that "Dr. Lyon's model yielded only a lump-sum figure for profits attributable to the television commercials that contained infringed material as a whole without accounting for the fact that the infringed material constituted only a fraction of any given commercial." Given the language of the statute, should this be Lyon's problem? According to a leading copyright scholar, the question of apportioning profits can arise either "when infringing materials become commingled with non-infringing materials" or "when factors other than the use of [the infringing] work are responsible for some of the profits." Marshall Leaffer, *Understanding Copyright Law* 406 (3d ed. 1999). Which of these situations was present in *Vane?* Both, perhaps? In either event, Leaffer concludes, it is the defendant "who bears the burden of proof." *Id.*

IV.   MODELING MARKETS IN ANTITRUST CASES

Antitrust plaintiffs must allege and prove that the defendant has damaged competition in a particular market by engaging in conduct forbidden by the federal Sherman Act and other antitrust statutes. Examples of forbidden practices include monopolization and conspiring with others to fix prices. In most such cases, expert economists offer models of the affected market in order to prove or disprove the alleged misconduct and its effects. The following case considers the admissibility of an economic model that is ostensibly addressed to damages, but also bears indirectly on liability.

In re Industrial Silicon Antitrust Litigation

1998 U.S. Dist. LEXIS 20464 (W.D. Pa. Oct. 13, 1998)

MEMORANDUM

[The plaintiffs alleged that the defendant suppliers conspired to fix the price of ferrosilicon, an alloy of iron and silicon used in making carbon steel.] Before the court is Minerais U.S. Inc.'s motion to preclude the expert testimony of the Steel plaintiffs' expert on damages, Dr. Laurits Christensen. Minerais contends that Dr. Christensen's testimony is unreliable within the meaning of Daubert v. Merrell Dow Pharmaceuticals, Inc., 509 U.S. 579, 125 L. Ed. 2d 469, 113 S. Ct. 2786 (1993). . . .

Federal Rule of Evidence 702 governs the admission of expert testimony in federal court. Rule 702 has three major requirements: (1) the proffered witness must qualify as an expert by knowledge, skill, experience, training, or education; (2) the expert must testify to scientific, technical, or other specialized knowledge; and (3) the expert's testimony must actually assist the jury by providing it with relevant information that is necessary to decide a material fact in dispute. . . .

QUALIFICATIONS

There is no basis in the record to challenge Dr. Christensen's qualifications. Dr. Christensen earned a B.A. degree in Economics from Cornell University. He also holds a Master's degree in Statistics and a Ph.D. in Economics from the University of California at Berkeley. Dr. Christensen taught economics for twenty years at the University of Wisconsin, Madison. He has served as a member of the Board of Editors of the American Economic Review and has published sixty-six articles in the field of economics. Dr. Christensen also has experience as a private economic consultant. The majority of Dr. Christensen's experience is in a non-litigation context; nevertheless, he has been qualified as an expert in a number of cases. . . .

RELIABILITY

Under Rule 702's reliability prong, the court must inquire into the methodology used by Dr. Christensen. This analysis focuses on the principles and methodology used by Dr. Christensen in reaching his conclusions, not on the conclusions that he generates. Daubert, 509 U.S. at 595. The reliability inquiry requires the district court to examine various factors, such as whether the expert's opinion is based on methods and procedures reasonably relied upon by experts in his field rather than on subjective belief or unsupported speculation. Id. at 593-94. An expert's testimony is admissible under Rule 702 as long as the processes or techniques that he used to formulate his opinions are reliable. Id. at 594-95.

DR. CHRISTENSEN'S METHODOLOGY

In reaching his conclusions, Dr. Christensen used an econometric method known as multiple regression analysis. Multiple regression analysis is a statistical technique designed to determine the effect that two or more explanatory independent variables have on a single dependent variable. This method allows the expert to test the causal relationship, if any, between the explanatory independent variables and the dependent variable. There is no dispute that when used properly multiple regression analysis is one of the mainstream tools in economic study and it is an accepted method of determining damages in antitrust litigation. See Petruzzi's IGA Supermarkets, Inc. v. Darling-Delaware Co., Inc., 998 F.2d 1224, 1238 (3d Cir. 1993).

In Dr. Christensen's regression model, the dependent variable was the price that defendants charged for ferrosilicon. Dr. Christensen's model was constructed so that defendants' price was a function of a set of variables related to supply and demand and market conditions relevant to the ferrosilicon industry. Dr. Christensen's model included independent explanatory variables for the following: iron and steel production, capacity utilization in the iron and steel industry, gross domestic product, a price index for electricity, and the import price index of ferrosilicon. In addition, Dr. Christensen's model included a dummy variable to investigate whether plaintiffs sustained damages as a result of defendants' alleged price-fixing.

Dr. Christensen's study included the time before and after the period in which he found damages to exist. He determined that there was a strong relationship between import prices and domestic prices. That is, he concluded that a very large portion of the variation in domestic prices was explained by the variation in import prices. He further concluded that the remaining independent variables contributed nothing or very little to explaining domestic prices. He then examined the movement of defendants' prices in relation to the movement of the Metals Week import price index from 1986 to 1996. Specifically, Dr. Christensen used the movements in the Metals Week import price index to predict what the movement in defendants' prices would have been absent a price-fixing agreement. Dr. Christensen then tested the statistical significance of the difference between the actual prices and the estimated "but for" prices. Dr. Christensen's results are certain with greater than ninety-five percent confidence level.

Dr. Christensen's before and after models, which compare pricing relations during the alleged price-fixing period to the period before and after the alleged violation, is [sic] generally accepted in the field of economics. The regression analysis used by Dr. Christensen is also generally accepted.

Defendants do not dispute the general acceptance and reliability of the methods employed by Dr. Christensen to calculate damages; instead, they contend, among other things, that his model is unreliable because he failed to include certain additional independent explanatory variables.[2] The Supreme Court has made clear, however, that a multiple regression analysis need not include every conceivable independent variable to establish a party's case, as long as it includes those independent variables that account for the major factors that are likely to influence decisions. P.E. Bazemore v. Friday, 478 U.S. 385, 400, 92 L. Ed. 2d 315, 106 S. Ct. 3000 (1986).

2. In response to defendants' criticism, Dr. Christensen included factors suggested by defendants' expert in a subsequent regression analysis. The result was that damages were actually increased.

Moreover, a party challenging the admissibility of a multiple regression analysis must show that the factors it contends ought to have been included would weaken the results of the analysis. Palmer v. Shultz, 259 U.S. App. D.C. 246, 815 F.2d 84, 101 (D.C. Cir. 1987). In other words, a party cannot successfully challenge the admissibility of a regression analysis by simply pointing to a laundry list of possible independent variables that were not included in the study. Rather, the party must introduce evidence to support its contention that the failure to include those variables would change the outcome of the analysis. Id. In this case, defendants merely have advanced their own expert's conclusory opinion to that effect, unsupported by any credible evidence that impugns the scientific reliability of Christensen's methods.

The court is satisfied that Dr. Christensen used reliable, scientifically accepted methodologies in formulating his opinions. Although couched in the appropriate language, defendants' challenges are actually directed at his conclusions, not his methodologies.

RELEVANCY

The final Rule 702 criterion is relevancy. Where the antitrust violation is a price-fixing conspiracy, the measure of damages is the difference between the prices actually paid and the prices that would have been paid absent the conspiracy. Dr. Christensen's model, however, does not tell the jury the actual damages suffered by a given plaintiff as measured by the difference between the actual price that a plaintiff paid and the predicted price it would have paid "but for" the conspiracy. Rather, his model does not depend on or even identify a single purchase price for ferrosilicon or a single predicted "but for" price. The court credits Dr. Christensen's explanation that in a product market with multiple sellers and multiple buyers there is, in reality, a range of prices charged by the various sellers and paid by the various buyers for that product. Concomitantly, there will be a range of predicted "but for" prices.

Dr. Christensen's model, therefore, focuses on whether the average range of prices paid increased during the period of the conspiracy relative to the average range of predicted "but for" prices. Thus, for example, his model concluded that the range of actual prices paid for fifty percent ferrosilicon increased on average by $1.92 per pound over the range of predicted "but for" prices.

Defendants are correct that Dr. Christensen's model does not provide the jury with a "snapshot" of what actual price any individual plaintiff may have paid any individual defendant at any given time during the alleged conspiracy. Defendants advance this criticism as a challenge to the scientific reliability of Dr. Christensen's model; however, defendants' argument actually challenges the relevancy of the model's results. In other words, defendants question whether Christensen's model will assist the jury in determining what any given plaintiff's actual damages were. The court concludes that it will.

To succeed on an antitrust price-fixing claim, plaintiffs must prove that they sustained injury as a result of defendants' unlawful conduct. In re Aluminum Phosphide Antitrust Litig., 893 F. Supp. 1497, 1499 (D. Kan. 1995). Therefore, plaintiffs must establish that defendants' unlawful activities caused at least some of their injury, rather than the injury being wholly attributable to other factors. Id. "Causation of injury may be found as a matter of just and reasonable inference from proof of defendants' wrongful acts and their tendency to injure plaintiffs, and from evidence of change in prices not shown to be attributable to other causes." In re Aluminum Phosphide, 893 F. Supp. at 1499.

Accordingly, an antitrust plaintiff need not prove damages with mathematical certainty, but rather, he need only introduce sufficient evidence of damages to allow a jury to estimate the amount of damages. See In re Lower Lake Erie Iron Ore Antitrust Litig., 998 F.2d 1144, 1176 (3d Cir. 1993). Once causation of damages is determined in an antitrust case, "the actual amount of damages may result from a 'reasonable estimate, as long as the jury verdict is not the product of speculation or guesswork.'" Id.

The court has no difficulty concluding that should the jury find that defendants conspired to fix prices, Dr. Christensen's proffered testimony will assist the jury in determining the amount of damages, if any, that plaintiffs incurred as a result of that conspiracy. Thus, if defendants wish to challenge Dr. Christensen's exert testimony, they must do so by vigorous cross-examination and by proffering their own expert to present contrary evidence. Daubert, 509 U.S. at 598.

NOTES AND QUESTIONS

1. First, make sure you understand Dr. Christensen's regression model. The court lists his "independent explanatory variables" in the second paragraph of the methodology section of the opinion. How did Christensen respond to the defendants' criticisms of his choice of independent variables? What was his dependent variable? What was the "dummy variable" the court refers to in the same paragraph? Is this analogous to the "race" variable in the employment discrimination cases in Chapter 3? Perhaps "let 0 = conspiracy, 1 = no conspiracy"? What is the meaning of the statement in the next paragraph that the "study included the time before and after the period in which he found damages to exist"? Finally, can you infer from the court's account which of the independent variables accounted for the greatest variation in the dependent variable?

2. Christensen's analysis illustrates two related but distinguishable functions of a regression model. First, he attempted to describe the behavior of the price variable during the periods (before and after) when there was no allegation of price fixing. He then used the model *predictively*, filling in the values of the independent variables for the period of the alleged conspiracy

in an effort to predict what the price *should* have been (according to the model, anyway). The difference between the predicted ("but-for") and actual prices comprised an estimate of the damages caused by the conspiracy. Note that Christensen "tested the statistical significance" of this difference. The court characterizes the result as "certain with greater than ninety-five percent confidence interval." What does this mean? It is possible to calculate a 95 percent confidence interval around the predicted value of the dependent variable, and then determine if the actual value falls inside or outside of this interval. Which was the case here?

3.   The relevance of Christensen's analysis to damages is clearly explained in the opinion. But was it also relevant to liability? Recall the court's statement that "[to] succeed on an antitrust price-fixing claim, plaintiffs must prove that they sustained injury as a result of defendants' unlawful conduct . . . plaintiffs must establish that defendants' unlawful activities caused at least some of their injury, rather than the injury being wholly attributable to other factors."

4.   Consider the court's *Daubert* analysis of Christensen's work, especially the following: "Dr. Christensen's before and after models, which compare pricing relations during the alleged price-fixing period to the period before and after the alleged violation, is [sic] generally accepted in the field of economics. The regression analysis used by Dr. Christensen is also generally accepted." Could his regression model have been admitted into evidence even if his techniques were *not* generally accepted? If so, what would the plaintiffs have had to show?

5.   Economic experts do not get a *Daubert* free pass in antitrust cases, as is illustrated by the treatment of the plaintiffs' expert in Concord Boat Corp. v. Brunswick Corp., 207 F.3d 1039 (8th Cir. 2000). At issue was a "market share discount program" that Brunswick, a boat engine manufacturer, offered to boat builders if they would commit to buying a high percentage of their engine requirements from Brunswick:

> The boat builders' primary evidence to establish Brunswick's antitrust liability was presented by their sole expert, Dr. Hall, a professor of economics at Stanford University. He testified that Brunswick had monopoly power in the stern drive market that enabled it to use its market share discount programs to impose a "tax" on boat builders and dealers who chose to purchase engines from other manufacturers. He defined the "tax" as the discount these purchasers gave up by not buying from Brunswick. He stated that Brunswick's program effectively required its competitors to charge substantially lower prices in order to convince customers to purchase from them and forgo the discount. Dr. Hall further testified that the discount programs, combined with the market power Brunswick acquired by purchasing Bayliner and Sea Ray, enabled Brunswick to capture 78% of the stern drive engine market. According to Dr. Hall, other manufacturers could not enter into stern drive engine manufacturing as a result of Brunswick's having such a

high percentage of the market. He concluded that the discount programs were anticompetitive.

In support of the boat builders' damage claim, Dr. Hall relied on the Cournot model of economic theory that posits that a firm "maximizes its profits by assuming the observed output of other firms as a given, and then equating its own marginal cost and marginal revenue on that assumption." 4 Phillip E. Areeda et al., Antitrust Law: An Analysis of Antitrust Principles and Their Application p. 925a (rev. ed. 1998). Dr. Hall postulated that in a stern drive engine market that was competitive, Brunswick and some other firm would each maintain a 50% market share. Under this theory, any market share over 50% would be evidence of anticompetitive conduct on Brunswick's part. Since Brunswick at various points in time had garnered a market share as large as 78% percent, Dr. Hall concluded that it had engaged in anticompetitive conduct and that the boat builders had been overcharged at the moment Brunswick's market share surpassed the 50% threshold. . . .

Dr. Hall used the Cournot model to construct a hypothetical market which was not grounded in the economic reality of the stern drive engine market, for it ignored inconvenient evidence. The basis for his model was a theoretical situation in which some other manufacturer's engine would be viewed as equal in quality to Brunswick's. In this hypothetical market, Dr. Hall assessed an overcharge on each engine sold at any point where Brunswick possessed over the 50% market share he deemed permissible. The overcharge was described as the difference between the actual price paid by the boat builders and the price that would theoretically have existed in a more competitive market. This approach was not affected by the actual price at which Brunswick's engines were sold since the overcharge percentage was applied any time its market share surpassed 50%. As Dr. Hall testified but his opinion did not reflect, Brunswick had achieved a 75% share in the mid 1980s, before it started the market share discounts and before it acquired Bayliner and Sea Ray. See Tr. at 1392.

The model also failed to account for market events that both sides agreed were not related to any anticompetitive conduct, such as the recall of OMC's Cobra engine and the problems associated with the Volvo/OMC merger. Dr. Hall admitted on cross examination that such facts could have been incorporated into his model but that he had not done so. . . .

Dr. Hall's expert opinion should not have been admitted because it did not incorporate all aspects of the economic reality of the stern drive engine market and because it did not separate lawful from unlawful conduct. Because of the deficiencies in the foundation of the opinion, the expert's resulting conclusions were "mere speculation."

What, in the court's view, was the fatal flaw in Dr. Hall's approach? Was it the choice of a method that was inherently unreliable, or the failure to apply that method in a reliable way — or both? Why did the shortcomings that the court identified render his analysis inadmissible, as opposed to merely going to weight? For a discussion of the application of *Daubert* in antitrust cases, see John L. Solow & Daniel Fletcher, *Doing Good Economics in the Courtroom:*

Thoughts on Daubert *and Expert Testimony in Antitrust,* 31 J. Corporation L. 489 (2006). Reviewing *Concord Boat,* Solow and Fletcher contend that Hall's approach, while "novel," "was based on widely accepted economic methodology and had considerable factual support." *Id.* at 500-501. Should that always be enough to satisfy *Daubert?*

6. The case law contains many examples of regression analyses introduced in price-fixing cases. To test your understanding in an even more complex factual situation than *Industrial Silicon,* see In re Polypropylene Carpet Antitrust Litigation, 996 F. Supp. 18 (N.D. Ga. 1997) (assessment of expert report in context of class action certification decision) and 93 F. Supp. 2d 1348 (N.D. Ga. 2000) (motion to exclude testimony of expert economists). And in Petruzzi's IGA Supermarkets v. Darling Delaware Co., 998 F.2d 1224 (3d Cir. 1993), the court considered a multiple regression analysis of prices that was intended to prove, indirectly, that the defendant "fat and bone" suppliers were conspiring to control the market by allocating customers among themselves.

CHAPTER 9

EXPERT TESTIMONY
ABOUT MEMORY

Memory plays a significant role in virtually every trial, from questions about how accidents happen to whether a crime victim is able to recall an attacker's face. As the body of research on the subject of memory has grown, courts and advocates have realized its forensic implications. Nonetheless, the use of such research in trials remains contentious. Recognizing that witness misidentifications are often implicated in wrongful convictions, many courts now admit expert testimony about the shortcomings of eyewitness identification, believing the testimony provides a framework[1] for the jury to better judge the reliability of eyewitness' memory. Other courts disagree, finding such testimony is both unnecessary and confusing to juries.

Courts face a challenging set of scientific, legal, and policy questions when deciding whether repressed and recovered memories should be admitted at trial. At the heart of the controversy is a great deal of disagreement about repressed and recovered memories as valid scientific concepts.

Behavioral scientists have conducted substantial research on children's memories, trying to determine how well children remember (and relate) events and whether children's memories may be altered by coercive and suggestive interrogation techniques. Following the explosion of sexual abuse allegations in the 1980s, many courts have begun to consider the effects of suggestive interrogations.

Creative litigants continue to find new ways to try to introduce expert testimony about memory at trial, as evidenced by the proposed expert testimony in the case of United States v. Libby, 461 F. Supp. 2d 3 (D.D.C. 2006), set forth at the end of this chapter.

---

1. For further discussion on the use of "social framework testimony," see Chapter 5, Expert Testimony About Behavioral Science.

This chapter considers the myriad ways that research on issues related to memory has become expert testimony.

I. THE SCIENCE OF MEMORY: HOW MEMORY WORKS; HOW MEMORIES GET CHANGED

Scientific Study of Witness Memory: Implications for Public and Legal Policy

1 Psychol., Pub. Pol'y & L. 726 (1995)
Gary L. Wells

The legal system relies heavily on human memory. Crime investigations, criminal trials, and many civil trials depend on memory to reconstruct critical events from the past. Getting at the "truth" is often synonymous with establishing the who, what, when, and how of some prior episode. Past events tend to leave traces, and the process of reconstructing events from the past is aided by various types of trace evidence. These traces can be physical, such as a footprint, a blood stain, or a fingerprint. An event can also leave traces of a somewhat different type, namely memory traces. Although these traces can also be said to have a physical property, in the sense that there exists a biological residue for the event somewhere in the brain, they cannot be observed directly by crime investigators or triers of fact. Instead, the memory trace that resides within the human brain is manifested for investigators and triers of fact through verbal testimony. It is probably safe to conclude that courts of law could not function without relying on human memory. Even physical evidence, such as a bloody glove, requires someone to take the witness stand and recall where it was found, by whom, at what time, in what condition, and so on.

The scientific study of human memory was initiated over 100 years ago by Hermann Ebbinghouse (1885/1913), and the scientific study of human memory today remains almost exclusively the province of psychology and related cognitive and neurological sciences.

Why Judges Should Admit Expert Testimony on the Unreliability of Eyewitness Testimony

2006 Fed. Cts. L. Rev. 3
Henry F. Fradella

First and foremost, memory is dependent on perception. We tend to think of perception in terms of our basic senses — sight, hearing, touch, taste, and smell. But perception is really a process — "the total amalgam of sensory signals received and then processed by an individual at any one time." This process is highly selective and is as dependent upon psychological factors as it is on physical senses because it is an "interpretive process." The "actual" sensory data we perceive is "processed in light of experience, learning, preferences, biases, and expectations."

One of the most important factors affecting our ability to perceive is the volume of sensory stimulation. "Perception is highly selective because the number of signals or amount of information impinging upon the senses is so great that the mind can process only a small fraction of the incoming data." This means we focus on certain stimuli while filtering out others. This results not only in incomplete acquisition of sensory data, but also in differential processing (i.e., interpretation) of events. Even when lighting and distance conditions are good for observation, a person may still experience incomplete acquisition if he or she is "overwhelmed with too much information in too short a period of time," a function of differential processing referred to as sensory overload.

Another important factor affecting perception is how humans fill gaps caused by incomplete sensory acquisition. When these gaps are filled, the details often fit logically, but inaccurately. The type of stimuli involved also affects perception. In particular, people are poor perceivers of duration (we tend to over-estimate how long something takes), time (it "flies by" or "drags on"), speed, distance, height, and weight. It is important to keep in mind that people are not aware of their individual variations in the process of perception. In other words, how we perceive and synthesize sensory data are unconscious processes.

B. THE THREE PHASES OF MEMORY

Memory, like perception, is an unconscious process. It is dependent upon three critical stages — acquisition/encoding, retention, and recall/retrieval. All three steps are affected by a number of physical and psychological factors that can taint the accuracy of a memory. Even someone's mood can taint accuracy of a memory. . . .

1.   ACQUISITION PHASE

The first stage in the development of memory is the acquisition, or encoding, stage. During this first stage in the development of memories, sensory data, as perceived by the individual, are encoded in the appropriate areas of the cerebral cortex.

Accordingly, the acquisition of memories is dependent upon perception. Since perception itself is a process dependent on a number of individualized factors, this stage in the process of developing memories is affected by those same factors. Sensory overload is particularly important since it can lead to so many gaps in memory that confabulation — "the creation or substitution of false memories through later suggestion" — can occur.

Perceptual variability aside, there is another important factor that affects memory acquisition. A person's expectations influence the way in which details about an event are encoded. An observer tends to seek out some information and avoid other information, an effect called the confirmation bias. What gets encoded is, therefore, partially dependent on that for which the observer was looking.

2. RETENTION PHASE

The retention, or storage, phase follows the encoding phase in the memory process. During this phase, the brain stores the memory until it is called upon for retrieval. How much data is being encoded and retained obviously affects this phase. The greater the amount of data presented, especially in shorter periods of time, the less that will be retained. The other obvious factor is the retention interval — how much time passes between storage of the memory and retrieval of it. But a third, far less obvious factor than the amount of data or the retention interval, has the most potentially negative effect on memory retention: the post-event misinformation effect. Exposure to subsequent information affects the way in which memories are retained. Therefore, exposure to post-event misinformation can lead to an eyewitness accepting misinformation as if it were an accurate account.

For example, a witness to a traffic accident may later read a newspaper article which stated that the driver had been drinking before the accident. "Post-event information can not only enhance existing memories but also change a witness' memory and even cause nonexistent details to become incorporated into a previously acquired memory." When witnesses later learn new information which conflicts with the original input, many will compromise between what they saw and what they were told later on.

3. RETRIEVAL PHASE

Finally, the retrieval phase occurs when "the brain searches for the pertinent information, retrieves it, and communicates it." This process necessarily occurs when eyewitnesses describe what they observed to police, when they participate in lineup or photo array identifications, and when they testify in court. Time is a very important factor in memory retrieval. As a rule, the longer the time period between acquisition, retention, and retrieval, the more difficulty we have retrieving the memory.

In addition to the passage of time, it has been repeatedly demonstrated that retrieval of memories can be affected by a process known as unconscious transference. In this phenomenon, different memory images may become combined or confused with one another. This can manifest itself when an eyewitness, accurately recalling an innocent bystander at the scene of a crime, incorrectly identifies that bystander as the perpetrator.

Adult Recollections of Childhood Abuse Cognitive and Developmental Perspectives

4 Psychol. Pub. Pol'y & L. 1025 (1998)
Peter A. Ornstein, Stephen J. Ceci, and Elizabeth F. Loftus

SUGGESTIBILITY AND DISTORTIONS OF MEMORY

[M]emory representations are not static but rather are subject to considerable change over time. Details may be lost and information in storage may be modified so as to increase its consistency vis-à-vis underlying knowledge. Moreover, for a variety of reasons, exposure to postevent information, either prior to retrieval or at the time of questioning, has the potential to result in changes in the contents of memory, or at least in participants' reports of what is remembered. At the extreme, it is possible for an individual to "remember" events that might not have been experienced but might have been read about or discussed with others (including therapists). Even the generation of more interpretive detail than was previously reported about an experienced event can be viewed, at least in part, as stemming from postevent interviewing experiences. Thus, many factors can lead to a distortion of one's memory for the past.

THE INFLUENCE OF POSTEVENT MISLEADING INFORMATION

Although there has been considerable interest in suggestibility for more than 100 years (Binet, 1900; Stern, 1910), sustained research on memory distortions began in the 1970s (Loftus & Palmer, 1974; Loftus, 1979). The recent work begins with a simple question: What happens when people experience an event—for instance, a crime or accident—and are later exposed to inconsistent or misleading information about that event? At one level, the answer to this question is clear: The new information can influence recollections of the original event. Indeed, after the receipt of new information that is misleading in some way, people often make errors when they report what they saw. As discussed above in the treatment of the framework for examining memory, the new, postevent information can sometimes become incorporated into the recollection, interfere with the retrieval of the original memory trace, create source-monitoring confusion, and influence participants' reports via social as opposed to mnemonic mechanisms. Moreover, the impact of new information about an event can be quite insidious because witnesses are often not able to detect its influence. Understanding the mechanisms by which revised data about a witnessed event come to be accepted is a central goal of current research.

A great deal of research illustrating that memory can become skewed when people assimilate new data makes use of a simple variation on the traditional retroactive interference paradigm. Participants first witness a complex event, such as a simulated violent crime or an automobile accident.

Subsequently, half of the participants receive new misleading information about the event, whereas the others do not get any misinformation. Finally, all participants attempt to recall the original event. Consider, for example, a study in which participants saw a simulated traffic accident and then received one of two types of written information about the accident. Some participants were misled about what they had seen (e.g., a stop sign was referred to as a yield sign), whereas the others did not receive misleading information. Later, when asked whether they originally saw a stop or a yield sign, those participants who had been given the incorrect information (yield sign) tended to choose it on the recognition test (Loftus, 1979).

By now, this basic finding has been replicated in a wide range of experiments involving a broad variety of materials (see Loftus, 1982), with the result being that the memory performance of participants who were exposed to misleading postevent information was routinely inferior to that of individuals who had not been presented with such information. Indeed, people have recalled nonexistent broken glass and tape recorders, a clean-shaven man as having a mustache, straight hair as curly, stop signs as yield signs, hammers as screwdrivers, and even something as large and conspicuous as a barn in a bucolic scene that contained no buildings at all. In short, misleading postevent information can alter a person's recollection in a powerful, even predictable, manner. In some experiments, moreover, the deficits in recollection following receipt of misinformation have been dramatic, with performance differences as large as 30% or 40% being observed.

NOTES AND QUESTIONS

1. The article selections you just read were written by individuals in the research psychology field, some of whom have been integral to the growing acceptance of psychological research results in trial. Dr. Loftus, author of dozens of books and articles on eyewitness identification and repressed memory, among other issues, has testified in various courts about the factors that may affect memory. For further reading, see e.g., Elizabeth F. Loftus, *Eyewitness Testimony* (1996); and Elizabeth Loftus & Katherine Ketcham, *The Myth of Repressed Memory* (1994). An interesting analysis of the impetus for Dr. Loftus' research is found in John M. Conley & William M. O'Barr, *Just Words: Law, Language, and Power*, 166-169 (2d ed. 2005).

2. Many jurors are understandably convinced by the crime victim who says "I'll never forget that face as long as I live!" But is such a belief warranted? Most research suggests it is not. Two well-accepted principles may affect witness' memories: the effect of stress on memory and the predictable rate at which memory of an event fails. The "Yerkes-Dodson Law" suggests that "when stress levels are too low, people do not pay sufficient attention, and when stress levels are too high, the ability to concentrate and perceive are negatively impacted." Fradella, *supra* at page 419, at 21. Fradella continues:

The Yerkes-Dodson law has a strong effect on people's ability to perceive and remember certain details of an event. Detail significance refers to the minutia of a crime scene, as opposed to its overall significance. When people are concerned about personal safety, they tend to focus their attention on the details that most directly affect their safety, such as "blood, masks, weapons, and aggressive actions." While focusing on these details, they pay less attention to the other details of the crime scene, such as characteristics of the perpetrator (e.g., facial features, hair color and style, clothing, height, weight, etc.), the crime scene, and other important details. This phenomenon manifests itself particularly when a weapon is present. The so-called weapons effect describes crime situations in which a weapon is used and witnesses spend more time and psychic energy focusing on the weapon rather than on other aspects of the event. The weapons effect results in incomplete or inaccurate information about the crime scene and the perpetrator. This effect is magnified when the use of a weapon comes as a surprise to a witness.

The second consideration is the effect that the passage of time has on memory. Memory does not slowly fade, but drops off predictably and rapidly, subject to a number of variables. Fradella explains:

> Both common sense and our own experience inform us about temporal effects on memory. First and foremost, the longer one has to examine something, the better the memory formation will be and the more accurate recall will be. Conversely, the less time someone has to witness an event, the less complete, and therefore less accurate, both perception and memory will be. Closely related to the duration of time for observation is the rate at which events happen. Given the limitations of human perception, when things happen very quickly, memory can be negatively affected. This is true even when an eyewitness has a reasonable period of time to observe an event, since attention is focused on processing a fast-moving series of events, rather than on a particular aspect of the occurrence.
>
> We all know that memory declines over time. Research has confirmed that time delay impacts the accuracy of identification, but to a much smaller degree than might be expected. This may be due to the fact that memory does not fade away in increments over time, but rather fades fairly rapidly immediately following the event — a phenomenon referred to as the forgetting curve. After the initial fade, there is a greater likelihood of confabulation. Such filling and/or alteration of memory by post-event discussions has a much more powerful negative impact on the accuracy of recall than does the passage of time alone.

Id. at 17. Do you think most jurors understand these principles? If not, is expert testimony the best way for jurors to learn about how memory works or are their better, non-adversarial ways to inform the jury?

3. The shortcomings of memory are also implicated where out-of-court identifications are made, particularly with lineups and photospreads. *See*

Gary L. Wells et al., *Eyewitness Identification Procedures: Recommendations for Lineups and Photospreads*, 22 Law & Hum. Behav. 603, (1998); and Gary L. Wells, *Eyewitness Identifications: Systemic Reforms*, 2006 Wis. L. Rev. 615. Dr. Wells, a leading researcher on the subject, participated substantially in the National Institute of Justice study to improve eyewitness identification procedures. The study, organized by former Attorney General Janet Reno, published its results and recommendations, which are available online. *See* Technical Working Group for Eyewitness Evidence, U.S. Dep't of Justice, Eyewitness Evidence: A Guide for Law Enforcement 29 (1999), at *http:// www.ncjrs.org/pdffiles1/nij/178240.pdf.*

4. Another problem relating to memory is confabulation, a process by which an individual unknowingly fabricates information to fill a memory gap. Two of the several causes of confabulated memories are severe drug or alcohol intoxication, during which time the individual may have no memory of a given event. This loss of memory is commonly termed a blackout. To fill the memory gap, the individual attempts to piece together events to help him remember and may be highly susceptible to suggestion during questioning or interrogation. Individuals who confabulate are not aware of the process, which can make them unwittingly unreliable witnesses — they do not know they are not telling the truth. See generally, Jane Campbell Moriarty, *Psychological and Scientific Evidence in Criminal Trials*, §§ 13:17-18 (2006).

5. Confabulation may also occur with hypnosis, where the subject grafts onto her memory suggestions deliberately or unwittingly made by the hypnotherapist. The Court recognized this and other concerns in Rock v. Arkansas, 483 U.S. 44 (1987) (holding Arkansas' per se rule excluding hypnotically refreshed testimony violated criminal defendant's right to testify on her own behalf). The Supreme Court in *Rock* expressed concern that hypnotism could cause errors in memory:

> Three general characteristics of hypnosis may lead to the introduction of inaccurate memories: the subject becomes "suggestible" and may try to please the hypnotist with answers the subject thinks will be met with approval; the subject is likely to "confabulate," that is, to fill in details from the imagination in order to make an answer more coherent and complete; and, the subject experiences "memory hardening," which gives him great confidence in both true and false memories, making effective cross-examination more difficult.

Id. at 59-60. Many states have recognized that hypnosis can interfere with memory and refuse to admit most hypnotically refreshed testimony. Other states allow such testimony. *See generally,* cases collected in Moriarty, *supra* Note 3, §§ 13:36-13:37. For an overview of hypnotically refreshed testimony, see Earl Martin, *A Daubert Test of Hypnotically-Refreshed Testimony in the Criminal Courts*, 9 Tex. Wesleyan L. Rev. 151 (2003).

II. *EXPERT TESTIMONY ABOUT EYEWITNESS IDENTIFICATION*

In United States v. Downing, 753 F.2d 1224 (3d Cir. 1985), the Court of Appeals for the Third Circuit recognized that expert testimony about eyewitness identification may be warranted in certain cases, opening the issue to many federal courts. Since *Downing,* virtually all of the circuit courts of appeals have chimed in on the issue, with the majority of courts allowing such testimony, subject to the discretion of the trial judge finding the testimony both reliable under the *Daubert* test and a good "fit" with the facts in question.[2] Nonetheless, many courts have held that in some circumstances, it is not an abuse of discretion for a trial court to disallow such testimony. A minority of courts, however, continue to categorically disallow such testimony, finding its probative value is substantially outweighed by the likelihood it will confuse or overwhelm the jury.

In the case below, the district court analyzes the specific issues on which expert testimony might be allowed and whether the testimony is "sufficiently tied to the facts of the case." Although this case is more generous in the categories of expert testimony it allows than many other courts would be, it provides a good summary of the various uses of expert testimony on eyewitness identification.

United States v. Norwood

939 F. Supp. 1132 (D.N.J. 1996)

[The defendant was indicted for carjacking, bank robbery, and assault on a bank employee and customers by means of a handgun, among other crimes.]

In *United States v. Downing,* 753 F.2d 1224 (3d Cir.1985), the Court of Appeals for the Third Circuit recognized that Rule 702 may permit "a defendant in a criminal prosecution to adduce, from an expert in the field of human perception and memory, testimony concerning the reliability of eyewitness identifications." *Id.* at 1226. In so holding, the *Downing* Court held that the determination whether to admit such testimony requires an examination of the following criteria:

First, the evidence must survive preliminary scrutiny in the course of an in limine proceeding conducted by the district judge. This threshold inquiry, which we derive from the helpfulness standard of Rule 702, is essentially a balancing test, centering on two factors: (1) the reliability of the scientific principles upon which the expert testimony rests,

---

2. In fact, *Daubert's* discussion of the concept of "fit" is taken from Justice Becker's opinion in the *Downing* case.

hence the potential of the testimony to aid the jury in reaching an accurate resolution of a disputed issue; and (2) the likelihood that the introduction of the testimony may in some way overwhelm or mislead the jury. Second, admission depends upon the "fit," i.e., upon a specific proffer showing that scientific research has established that particular features of the eyewitness identifications involved may have impaired the accuracy of those identifications. . . . In sum, the reliability, the propensity to confuse or overwhelm, and the fit of the proposed testimony must all be considered by a district court before it can be introduced at trial.

In this case, the Defendant seeks leave to introduce the testimony of Michael R. Leippe, Ph.D., concerning the reliability of eyewitness identifications. An in limine hearing on this issue was conducted before this Court. . . .

[The court found the expert, Dr. Michael Leippe, sufficiently qualified. The court also held, based upon the testimony at the in limine hearing, that the proposed testimony was sufficiently reliable under Daubert v. Merrell Dow Pharmaceuticals, Inc., 509 U.S. 529 (1993).]

At the in limine hearing, Dr. Leippe outlined the following specific areas in which he plans to testify at trial: (1) the accuracy of cross-racial identifications relative to same-race identifications; (2) the effect of "weapon focus" on identifications; (3) the effect of stress on identifications; (4) the "forgetting curve," i.e., the effect of time on memory as it relates to identification; (5) the "relation back" phenomenon; (6) the lack of correlation between the confidence a witness expresses in making an identification and the accuracy of the identification; (7) the suggestiveness of the photo array used during the pretrial identification procedures in this case; and (8) exposure duration. . . .*

(1)   CROSS-RACIAL IDENTIFICATION

Defendant first seeks to have Dr. Leippe testify regarding the accuracy of cross-racial identifications relative to same-race identifications. In this case, all of the eyewitnesses are white, while the Defendant is black. Accordingly, Dr. Leippe's testimony on the issue of the reliability of cross-racial identification is "sufficiently tied to the facts of [this] case."

At the in limine hearing, Dr. Leippe testified that expert testimony relating to the reliability of cross-racial identification would be helpful to a jury since, based upon studies, such information is not necessarily within the common knowledge of the average juror.

Courts have found expert testimony of this nature, describing the reduced accuracy of cross-racial identifications as compared to same-race

*[Although the court allowed all of these subjects to be discussed by the expert, this excerpt does not include all of the court's discussion. — EDS.]

identifications, to be helpful to a jury. In *United States v. Smith*, 736 F.2d 1103, 1106 (6th Cir.1984), for example the Court found such testimony to be helpful since it "would not only 'surpass' common-sense evaluation, it would question common-sense evaluation." *Id.* at 1106. [other citations omitted].

Thus, I find that such testimony will prove helpful to the jury in this case.

(2) WEAPON FOCUS

Defendant seeks to have Dr. Leippe testify regarding the effect of "weapon focus" on identifications. At the in limine hearing, Dr. Leippe stated that numerous studies indicate that eyewitness identifications are less accurate when a weapon was present at the crime scene, than when a weapon was not present. Dr. Leippe explained that in situations where a weapon is present, a witness will have a tendency to focus upon the weapon, rather than on the face of the perpetrator.

In this case, it is alleged that one of the perpetrators of the carjacking offense wielded a handgun at the time of the offense. Accordingly, I find that Dr. Leippe's testimony on the issue of "weapon focus" is "sufficiently tied to the facts of [this] case."

Moreover, Dr. Leippe further explained that, while scientific studies have consistently found that witness identifications are notably less accurate when a weapon was present, studies also reveal that many lay people erroneously believe the opposite to be true. Accordingly, I find that Dr. Leippe's testimony relating to the "weapon focus" phenomenon will be helpful to the jury.

(3) STRESS

Dr. Leippe also testified at the in limine hearing as to the effect of stress on eyewitness identifications. Dr. Leippe explained that numerous studies reveal that, while low levels of stress may increase an individual's memory, extreme levels of stress will often impair memory. In this case, it is alleged that two of the eyewitnesses, who were also the victims of the carjacking offense, were under a great deal of stress since a handgun was allegedly brandished by the perpetrator and threats were allegedly made to the victim-eyewitnesses. Therefore, I find that Dr. Leippe's testimony on the effect of stress on the reliability of eyewitness identification is "sufficiently tied to the facts of [this] case."

Dr. Leippe also testified that expert testimony in this area would prove helpful to the jury because, while many scientific studies show that an intense level of stress impairs memory, many lay people assume just the opposite—that memory becomes more acute the higher the stress. In addition, many courts have repeatedly found expert testimony on this issue to be helpful

428   9. Expert Testimony About Memory

to a jury. In *United States v. Sebetich,* 776 F.2d 412, 419 (3d Cir.1985), the Third Circuit held that it was error for the district court to exclude expert testimony relating to the reliability of eyewitness testimony when the eyewitness was under stressful circumstances. In so holding, the Court stated that "[t]here is evidence that stress decreases the reliability of eyewitness identifications, contrary to common understanding." *Id.* at 419. *See also Downing,* 753 F.2d at 1232 ("most people, and hence most jury members, probably believe that stress increases the accuracy of one's perception"); *Stevens,* 935 F.2d at 1397 (district court admitted expert testimony relating to the effect of stress on the reliability of eyewitness identification). Thus, I find that such testimony regarding the relationship between stress and the accuracy of eyewitness identification will prove helpful to the jury in this case.

(4)   FORGETTING CURVE

Dr. Leippe also presented testimony at the in limine hearing relating to a phenomenon known as the "forgetting curve," i.e., the effect of time on memory as it relates to identification. He asserted that studies show that, according to the "forgetting curve" phenomenon, memory weakens at a non-constant rate with the passage of time, with most of the forgetting taking place within the first hours following the event, and certainly within the first few days following the event.

In this case, there was some passage of time between the incident alleged and the eyewitness identifications—one of the victim's identification of the Defendant was made the day after the alleged carjacking, the other victim's identification was made three days after the alleged carjacking, and the Boston Market employee's identification was made eight days after the witness allegedly observed the Defendant in the restaurant. Accordingly, I find that Dr. Leippe's testimony as it relates to the "forgetting curve" is "sufficiently tied to the facts of [this] case."

Dr. Leippe also stated that, while lay persons may understand that memory decreases with the passage of time, most individuals do not realize that memory decreases at a non-constant rate, with much of the memory loss occurring very shortly after the event. In *United States v. Sebetich,* 776 F.2d 412, 419 (3d Cir.1985), for example, the Third Circuit held that it was error for the district court to exclude expert testimony relating to the effect of the passage of time on the reliability of eyewitness identification, finding that such testimony is a proper subject for expert testimony. *See also Downing,* 753 F.2d at 1230-31 (finding that testimony relating to the "forgetting curve," i.e., the fact that memory does not diminish at a uniform rate, may be helpful to the jury in assessing the reliability of eyewitness testimony). Likewise, I find that testimony relating to the "forgetting curve" will prove helpful to the jury in this case.

(5)   RELATION BACK

At the in limine hearing, Dr. Leippe also testified to the "relation back" phenomenon — which states that an initial identification made by an eyewitness may influence that eyewitness's later identifications and perceived memories of the event. Dr. Leippe explained that several studies have shown that once an identification is made from a photo spread, an eyewitness may make an erroneous in-court identification based upon the face initially identified in the photo spread, rather than based upon the face actually seen during the alleged crime.

In this case, the Defendant contends that due to the "relation back" phenomenon, the eyewitnesses may subconsciously incorrectly identify the Defendant in court simply because they identified him earlier in a photo array, and not because they actually remember his face from the alleged incident. Therefore, since all of the eyewitnesses in this case identified the Defendant in a pretrial photo spread, Dr. Leippe's testimony on the issue of the "relation back" phenomenon is "sufficiently tied to the facts of [this] case."

Dr. Leippe further explained that, while jurors may understand the general nature of the "relation back" phenomenon, the average lay person does not comprehend the magnitude of its impact on eyewitness memory.

In *Stevens*, because the eyewitness first identified the defendant from a "wanted board," and then picked the Defendant out from a photo array, the defendant sought to offer expert testimony on the "relation-back" phenomenon. In Stevens, however, the Third Circuit held that it was not an abuse of discretion for the district court to exclude expert testimony describing the "relation-back" phenomenon, finding that in that case, such testimony could be "susceptible of elucidation without specialized scientific knowledge and thus could [be] fleshed out adequately by counsel through probing cross-examination and argument pitched to the common sense of the jury."

Notwithstanding the *Stevens* Court's finding that it was not an abuse of discretion for the district court to exclude such testimony, I find that expert testimony relating to the "relation-back" phenomenon would prove helpful to the jury in this case in assessing the reliability of the eyewitnesses' in-court identifications of the Defendant which were made after earlier pretrial identifications of the Defendant in a photo spread. Although the jury may understand the nature of such a phenomenon, I find that the impact on memory of the "relation-back" phenomenon may be beyond the common knowledge of an ordinary lay person, and therefore, such testimony would be "helpful" to the jury. . . .

For the foregoing reasons, Defendant's motion for leave to introduce expert testimony on the reliability of eyewitness identification will be granted.

United States v. Smith

122 F.3d 1355 (11th Cir. 1997)

Per Curiam:

Defendant Fred Smith appeals from his conviction on a two-count indictment charging him with bank robbery and use of a firearm in violation of 18 U.S.C. §924(c). We affirm.

I. Facts and Procedural History

On January 11, 1993, after 10:00 a.m., a lone individual entered and robbed the Buckhead branch of Merchant Bank of Atlanta. The robber approached the window of teller Diane Hansek, asked for some change, and then pulled out a gun and asked for all her money. Hansek and two other witnesses to the robbery described the robber as a black male with a clean-shaven face wearing a white, snap-brim cap. Hansek described the gun as a revolver with a brown handle and silver barrel, while the other two witnesses described it as a silver-plated automatic. After the robber exited the building, one of the other witnesses ran out the back door and saw the robber drive off rapidly in a reddish-orange car that looked like a Mustang.

To assist in apprehending the bank robber, law enforcement officials sent photographs from the video surveillance camera to Atlanta television stations. The next day, the local FBI office received a phone call from Robert Lun, an inmate in the Atlanta Federal Penitentiary. Lun, who is black, had seen the televised photographs and identified the defendant Fred Smith as the perpetrator of the Merchant Bank robbery.

Smith was arrested on January 15, 1993. At the time of the arrest, Smith identified himself as Victor Eugene Smith and carried a false driver's license in that name. Further investigation revealed that on January 5, 1993, a person using the Victor Eugene Smith driver's license purchased a steel-colored, 9 millimeter semi-automatic Taurus handgun at an Atlanta pawnshop. On January 7, 1993, Smith had purchased an orange 1984 Mercury Capri and had the title put in the name of Victor Smith. The Victor Eugene Smith driver's license was also used on January 11, 1993, to rent room 52 at the Relax Inn in Atlanta. The motel clerk identified Smith as the individual who rented the room.

As a result of a tip to the police, room 52 was placed under surveillance on January 12, 1993, the day after the Merchant Bank robbery. Smith was never seen there, but police observed Terry Walker enter and leave the room several times over the three-day surveillance. Terry Walker was arrested for bank robbery the same day as Smith.

Terry Walker had robbed a SouthTrust Bank branch on Moreland Avenue in Atlanta on January 11, 1993, three hours after the Merchant

Bank robbery. During the SouthTrust robbery, Terry Walker used two "bait" bills, the serial numbers of which were traced to the Merchant Bank robbery. He used a handgun described as silver and nickel-plated. He also wore a baseball cap that was found in a subsequent search of room 52 at the Relax Inn. Terry Walker was convicted of bank robbery in February 1994.

Five weeks after the Merchant Bank robbery, the FBI set up a photographic array and brought in the three Merchant Bank eyewitnesses to identify the robber. Two of the witnesses identified Smith as the robber, but Hansek selected another person's photograph.

Smith was tried in October 1994 for the Merchant Bank robbery and for use of a firearm in violation of 18 U.S.C. § 924(c). The government sought to introduce evidence of three additional bank robberies, including the SouthTrust robbery. The government offered that evidence as proof that Smith, along with Terry Walker, participated in a crime spree. The district court excluded all that evidence, with the exception of evidence related to the SouthTrust robbery. The district court found that the SouthTrust robbery evidence was inextricably intertwined with the Merchant Bank robbery. Moreover, the district court refused to exclude the evidence under Federal Rule of Evidence 403, concluding that the probative value of the evidence was not substantially outweighed by its prejudicial effect.

The government's case in chief included testimony from the three eyewitnesses to the Merchant Bank robbery. The government also called an eyewitness to the SouthTrust robbery. Terry Walker's indictment, judgment and commitment form on the SouthTrust robbery were admitted into evidence. There was also testimony with regard to the Merchant Bank bait bills used at the SouthTrust robbery. The district court also admitted the baseball cap found in room 52 of the Relax Inn, which was the same baseball cap Terry Walker had worn in the SouthTrust robbery.

Defendant Smith offered as his first witness Dr. Brian Cutler, an expert witness in eyewitness identification. Smith made an extensive offer of proof outside the presence of the jury with regard to Dr. Cutler. Dr. Cutler's proposed testimony involved scientific research that showed eyewitness identification could be unreliable under certain circumstances. Dr. Cutler further proposed to testify that several of those circumstances were present in the Merchant Bank robbery: disguise, cross-racial identification, weapons focus, presentation bias in law enforcement lineup, delay between the event and the time of identification, stress, and eyewitness certainty as a predictor of accurate identification.

The district court excluded Dr. Cutler's proposed testimony in its entirety, holding that although the proposed testimony was relevant, it would not assist the trier of fact. Alternatively, the district court held that the probative value of the testimony was outweighed by the possible danger of misleading or confusing the jury.

The jury convicted Smith on both the bank robbery count and the use of a firearm count. The court sentenced Smith to 336 months' imprisonment, and Smith appealed.

II. ANALYSIS

Smith raises two issues on appeal. First, Smith argues that the district court erroneously excluded the expert testimony of Dr. Cutler with regard to eyewitness reliability. Second, Smith argues that the evidence with regard to the SouthTrust robbery was prejudicial and should not have been admitted.

A. EXPERT TESTIMONY REGARDING EYEWITNESS RELIABILITY

Smith argues that the district court abused its discretion in excluding Dr. Cutler's expert testimony regarding eyewitness reliability. This Court has consistently looked unfavorably on such testimony. In *United States v. Thevis*, 665 F.2d 616, 641 (5th Cir. Unit B), cert. denied, 459 U.S. 825, 103 S.Ct. 57, 74 L.Ed.2d 61 (1982), we held that the district court had not abused its discretion in excluding expert testimony regarding eyewitness reliability. Furthermore, we stated:

> To admit such testimony in effect would permit the proponent's witness to comment on the weight and credibility of opponents' witnesses and open the door to a barrage of marginally relevant psychological evidence. Moreover, we conclude, as did the trial judge, that the problems of perception and memory can be adequately addressed in cross-examination and that the jury can adequately weigh these problems through common-sense evaluation.

Id. That attitude of disfavor continued in later cases, where this Court extended *Thevis* and held that expert testimony regarding eyewitness reliability was inadmissible. . . . We found support for that position in the nearly unanimous stance taken by other circuits in affirming the exclusion of such testimony. . . .

Smith asks this Court to reconsider its stance in light of the Supreme Court's opinion in *Daubert v. Merrell Dow Pharmaceuticals, Inc.*, 509 U.S. 579, 113 S.Ct. 2786, 125 L.Ed.2d 469 (1993), and in light of nascent case law more receptive to expert testimony on eyewitness reliability.

Smith contends that the *Daubert* decision "mandate[s] that this Court reassess it's position . . . regarding the admissibility of expert eyewitness evidence." . . .

Smith argues that *Daubert* "lower[ed] the standard for admissibility of expert evidence" and thus opened the door for admitting expert testimony regarding eyewitness reliability. Even assuming that Smith is correct in that characterization of *Daubert*, the question remains as to whether our precedent conflicts with the new standard announced in *Daubert*. We have held that a district court does not abuse its discretion when, after examining the proffered testimony, the court excludes it. . . . Most recently, we have held that expert testimony regarding eyewitness reliability is inadmissible per se. . . . We need not decide whether the post-*Thevis* per se inadmissibility rule decisions conflict with *Daubert*, because we conclude that our holding in *Thevis* is in accord with *Daubert*, and that is all that is necessary to dispose of an appeal in which a district court has excluded the proffered testimony.

The first prong of the *Daubert* test requires that the expert testimony involve scientific knowledge. That requirement is not in contention here. The government has not questioned in this case the scientific validity of expert testimony regarding eyewitness reliability. The district court explicitly held that the proposed testimony is scientific knowledge, and the government does not contest that holding in this case.

The district court based its exclusion of Dr. Cutler's expert testimony on the second prong of the *Daubert* test. The court held that "the proposed testimony . . . will not assist the trier of fact in this case to understand and determine a fact in issue."[1] That holding is in keeping with both *Thevis* and *Daubert*. We held in *Thevis*: "[T]he problems of perception and memory can be adequately addressed in cross-examination and . . . the jury can adequately weigh these problems through common-sense evaluation." We reasoned in *Thevis* that expert testimony regarding eyewitness reliability was not needed, because the jury could determine the reliability of eyewitness identification with the tools of cross-examination. Expert testimony that does not assist the trier of fact can be excluded under *Daubert*. . . . *Thevis* held that expert testimony regarding eyewitness reliability does not assist the jury, and we conclude that that holding is in harmony with *Daubert*. Therefore, it is as true after *Daubert* as it was before that a district court does not abuse its discretion in excluding such testimony.

Smith relies upon an emerging body of case law that he claims looks more favorably on expert testimony regarding eyewitness reliability. As an initial matter, we note that in none of the decisions Smith relies upon has any court embraced the position that expert testimony regarding eyewitness reliability ought to be admitted wholesale in every case. Instead, some courts have held that such evidence would be admissible under "narrow" or "certain" circumstances. . . . Moreover, we have found only one case

---

1. Smith contends that the district court's exclusion of proposed testimony was erroneously based on the notion that it "will invade the province of the jury." Smith argues that the evidentiary rule excluding evidence because it embraces an ultimate issue to be decided by the trier of fact was abolished by Federal Rule of Evidence 704(a). However, a close reading of the district court's holding indicates that the court was concerned with whether the proposed testimony would help the jury, not with whether it would tread on the jury's decisional turf. The district court explicitly stated that one portion of Dr. Cutler's testimony would not be helpful and that another portion was within the "common experience and knowledge of the average lay person."

where a district court was reversed for excluding expert testimony regarding eyewitness reliability. . . .

Of course, defendants who want to attack the reliability of eyewitness recollection are free to use the powerful tool of cross-examination to do so. They may also request jury instructions that highlight particular problems in eyewitness recollection. Smith did in the present case and was successful in getting the district court to instruct the jury about cross-racial identification, potential bias in earlier identifications, delay between the event and the time of identification, and stress.

NOTES AND QUESTIONS

1. Is the rationale of *Norwood* or *Smith* more compelling? Expert testimony about eyewitness identification problems (like other forms of social framework expert testimony) is of a generalized nature: It does not purport to consider how well *this* witness observed and remembered, it considers only what the data shows. While courts are less likely to find the evidence an impermissible comment on credibility due to the generalized nature of the testimony, they may find the testimony is not sufficiently tied to the facts of the case because it does not address the witnesses at issue.

2. There is an instruction many courts give in lieu of allowing expert testimony. See, for example, the Seventh Circuit Court Pattern Criminal Jury Instruction, § 3.08 (1999), which provides:

> You have heard testimony of an identification of a person. Identification testimony is an expression of belief or impression by the witness. You should consider whether, or to what extent, the witness had the ability and the opportunity to observe the person at the time of the offense and to make a reliable identification later. You should also consider the circumstances under which the witness later made the identification. The government has the burden of proving beyond a reasonable doubt that the defendant was the person who committed the crime charged.

Cited with approval in United States v. Carter, 410 F.3d 942, 951, n.2 (7th Cir. 2005). Does this instruction resolve the issue?

3. The court in United States v. Langan, 263 F.3d 613, 621 (6th Cir. 2001), discussed the reasons for excluding expert testimony about eyewitness identification:

> The use of expert testimony in regard to eyewitness identification is a recurring and controversial subject. Trial courts have traditionally hesitated to admit expert testimony purporting to identify flaws in eyewitness identification. Among the reasons given to exclude such testimony are that the jury can decide the credibility issues itself, . . . that experts in this area are not

much help and largely offer rather obvious generalities, . . . that trials would be prolonged by a battle of experts, . . . and that such testimony creates undue opportunity for confusing and misleading the jury. . . .

Are these reasons convincing?

4. The growing recognition that mistaken eyewitness identification is the single largest reason for wrongful convictions has encouraged some courts and many commentators to favor the admission of expert testimony. As leading researchers point out:

> Although there is no way to estimate the frequency of mistaken identification in actual cases, numerous analyses over several decades have consistently shown that mistaken eyewitness identification is the single largest source of wrongful convictions (see Borchard, 1932; Brandon & Davies, 1973; Frank & Frank, 1957; Huff, Rattner, & Sagarin, 1986; Rattner, 1988). Rattner's review of 205 cases of proven wrongful conviction, for example, showed that 52% were associated with mistaken eyewitness identification. Although we cannot be certain that these cases are representative of all cases of wrongful conviction, they provide our best estimate of the proportion of wrongful convictions that are attributable to eyewitness identification error.

Gary L. Wells & Eric P. Seelau, *Eyewitness Identification: Psychological Research and Policy on Lineups*, 1 Psychol. Pub. Pol'y & L. 765, 765 (1995). According to the Innocence Project, erroneous eyewitness identification is the single greatest cause of wrongful convictions, involved in 75 percent of convictions that have been overturned by DNA testing. To find out more about mistaken identification, wrongful conviction, and the science behind the expert testimony, go to: *www.theinnocenceproject.org.*

III. REPRESSED AND RECOVERED MEMORY

State v. Hungerford

697 A.2d 916 (N.H. 1997)

BROCK, Chief Justice.

The State appeals the Superior Court's (Groff, J.) ruling that the testimony of two alleged sexual assault victims is not admissible in criminal prosecutions against the defendants, Joel Hungerford and John Morahan. . . . We affirm and remand.

[Two complainants alleged that while in their twenties, they suddenly recalled being sexually victimized while minors. These prosecutions were brought against the men each claims victimized her.]

Both defendants moved to dismiss the prosecutions, asserting that the complainants' testimony would not be admissible at trial. . . . The two cases were consolidated for purposes of addressing the admissibility of the complainants' "repressed memory" testimony. . . .

The court held a two-week admissibility hearing on the issue of repressed memories. The two complainants testified at the hearing, as did seven psychological professionals. . . . After the hearing and a review of the materials admitted during the hearing, the trial court . . . ruled that the State failed to meet its burden of proving that there was general acceptance of the phenomenon of repressed memories in the psychological community, and, further, that the State had failed to demonstrate that the phenomenon was reliable. The court accordingly ruled the testimony of the complainants inadmissible. This appeal followed. . . .

The State vigorously argues that the processes of repressing and retrieving memories are normal human functions, common to every person's everyday experience, just as forgetting and remembering are; accordingly, the State contends, such evidence is not beyond the average juror's ability to comprehend, and unique treatment is inappropriate. We disagree. Although there are skeptics, it does seem to be accepted in the psychological community that people are capable of repressing or dissociating conscious recollection of all or part of certain traumatic events. See, e.g., Ernsdorff & Loftus, *Let Sleeping Memories Lie? Words of Caution About Tolling the Statute of Limitations in Cases of Memory Repression*, 84 J.Crim.L. & Criminology 129, 133-34 (1993) [hereinafter *Sleeping Memories*]; Pope & Hudson, *Can Memories of Childhood Sexual Abuse Be Repressed?*, 25 Psychol.Med. 121, 121 (1995); Taub, *The Legal Treatment of Recovered Memories of Child Sexual Abuse*, 17 J. Legal Med. 183, 187 (1996). There is, however, a vigorous debate on the questions of how the process of repression occurs, how the process of retrieval occurs, and indeed if in fact retrieval is possible at all. . . . A central and divisive question in this debate is whether a person's memory of an event can be accurate or authentic or "true," having been long lost in the person's subconscious mind and subsequently remembered, either spontaneously or by some method seeking to recover the memory. . . .

The phenomenon of repressing recollection of a traumatic event, and subsequently "recovering" it, may be familiar to or even accepted by parts of the psychological community, but it is far from being familiar to the average juror. . . . Some well-publicized accusations may ensure that many people have heard of the concept of repressed memories . . .; a review of the scientific literature on the subject reveals, however, that ordinary jurors cannot be expected to analyze such claims without the assistance of experts. . . .

The extensive case law from other jurisdictions considering the admissibility of various types of refreshed recollection in civil and criminal cases is helpful to our inquiry. In the loosely analogous circumstance of offered testimony relying upon memory that has been enhanced, refreshed, or recovered by hypnosis, courts generally have divided into four groups: those that categorically accept such testimony, those that categorically reject such testimony, those that will admit the testimony only if rigid procedural safeguards have been met, and those that will admit the testimony only after a "totality of the circumstances" review of the reliability of the particular testimony.

A review of the psychological literature on the subject of memory repression and recovery convinces us that a case-by-case approach, tempered with skepticism, is most appropriate in this context. . . .

We are especially concerned with the influence of therapy on the recovery of memory, as in the instant cases. The process of therapy is highly subjective, with its purpose "not the determination of historical facts, but the contemporary treatment and cure of the patient." . . . This goal, along with the expectations and predispositions of both therapist and patient, tends to distort the "historical truth" of events in the patient's life. . . . Within the environment of therapy, a patient may report memories in response to the perceived expectations of the therapist, . . . or in response to other forces. . . . Observations like the following are troubling:

> [T]he goal of therapy [is to] creat[e] a coherent "narrative truth" that accounts for the events in a patient's life but that does not necessarily make contact with the actual past. The goal is to account for the client's symptoms and allow the client to achieve closure with the past. But the truth of the past is not particularly important; instead, the patient "weaves together" a picture of the past that accounts for his symptoms and allows him to understand his life. Once the past has been reconstructed, however, the past is effectively changed and the original version is lost both for therapy and for all other purposes. The patient's memory will never be the same.

Comment, *Repression, Memory, and Suggestibility: A Call for Limitations on the Admissibility of Repressed Memory Testimony in Sexual Abuse Trials*, 66 U. Colo. L. Rev. 477, 511 (1995). . . .

We do not mean to suggest that all or even a majority of recovered repressed memories are "false." Rather, we merely recognize that the memories are subject to many factors that may affect their reliability, especially, as the trial court found in the instant cases, the uniquely suggestive environment of psychological therapy. . . .

Our approach today reflects our attempt to balance "the legal and emotional needs of survivors of childhood sexual abuse," . . . with our duty to ensure that defendants receive a fair trial and that individuals receive a reliable and fair adjudication of their disputes. . . .

In determining the reliability of a recovered memory, — that is, whether the recovered memory is reasonably likely to be as accurate as ordinary memory — the trial court should consider the following factors: (1) the level of peer review and publication on the phenomenon of repression and recovery of memories . . . (2) whether the phenomenon has been generally accepted in the psychological community . . . (3) whether the phe-nomenon may be and has been empirically tested . . . (4) the potential or known rate of recovered memories that are false . . . (5) the age of the witness at the time the event or events occurred . . . (6) the length of time between the event and the recovery of the memory . . . (7) the presence or absence of objective, verifiable corroborative evidence of the event . . . and (8) the circumstances attendant to the witness's recovery of the memory, i.e., whether the witness was engaged in therapy or some other process seeking to recover memories or likely to result in recovered memories. . . .*

Considering our first factor, the trial court correctly observed that the phenomenon of memory repression and recovery has received extensive attention in psychological publications. The parties presented photocopies of many articles from medical and psychological publications on the issue, and a review of the literature reveals many more. The level of peer review is high. . . . In the case of repressed and recovered memories, the level of submission is high, but the debate over methodology and the meaning of results continues. . . .

The psychological community remains deeply divided on the reliability or accuracy of recovered memories. . . . Despite common support for the phenomenon in the therapeutic setting, scientists rest their rejection of recovery of repressed memories on the absence of confirming laboratory results. . . . Of course, ethically, no complete laboratory study could ever be completed on repression of events as traumatic as sexual abuse.

According to the theory of repression, when a person experiences a particularly traumatic event that is unacceptable to the person's conscious existence, the person may repress the memory of the trauma. . . . Although the memory is not permanently "forgotten," it is unavailable to the person's conscious thought process. . . . True repression or traumatic amnesia ren-dering a person unable to remember any part of a traumatic event are dis-tinguished from ordinary forgetting, . . . incomplete memory, . . . and psychogenic amnesia. . . .

Proponents of widespread repression and recovery of memories of sexual abuse consider several facts to support the phenomenon: the existence of psychogenic amnesia and post-traumatic stress disorder, clinical studies in support of the phenomenon, and the prevalence of patients reporting recov-ery of repressed memories. . . . Discrete memory repression is a different phys-iological phenomenon from psychogenic amnesia, where the victim or witness of an extremely traumatic event temporarily may forget ordinary personal details, such as name and address, in addition to the details of the traumatic event. . . . The typical symptoms of post-traumatic stress disorder also do not support fully the notion of complete memory repression. . . .

*[The court addressed all of these subjects; this excerpt from the case only considers some. — EDS.]

The clinical studies that support the prevalence of recovery of previously completely repressed memories are subject to some criticism in methodology, as the trial court noted in the instant cases. . . . Reviewers raised the following methodological concerns: the subjects were "recruited" by their therapists; it is unclear whether the reported underlying events were confirmed in any way; it is unclear whether the events were "sufficiently traumatic" to have been remembered at every moment; and an affirmative answer to the question conveys insufficient information to conclude that full repression has actually occurred. Finally, the reviewers noted the possibility of suggestion in therapy. . . .

Proponents of the phenomenon of recovering repressed memories also rely on the very existence of a large number of patients reporting recovery of repressed memories as validation of the phenomenon. . . . The stories the patients tell, they argue, are too vivid and too painful to be the product of imagination or fabrication. The emotional troubles these patients have as adults are consistent with the kind of abuse that they remember, and would not be so consistent and so intense in response to a fabricated memory. . . . Apart from its circularity, the argument lends more support to the concept of suggestibility of memory than to the phenomenon of repression. . . . The scientific literature supports the conclusion that, in general, people remember traumatic events well. . . . In fact, experiencing vivid, intrusive thoughts of the event seems to be a more common memory disturbance resulting from severe trauma than repression. . . .

A recent review of the literature, however, caused the reviewer to note that "despite over sixty years of research involving numerous approaches by many thoughtful and clever investigators, at the present time there is no controlled laboratory evidence supporting the concept of repression." . . . The scientific community is extremely divided, at best, on the issue of recovery of completely repressed memories.

A degree of scientific divergence of opinion is indeed inevitable, but the degree of divergence surrounding [recovery of repressed memories] is fundamental and goes to the very validity of the process itself. This kind and degree of divergence is notably absent in other areas of scientific evidence generally deemed admissible. . . . We cannot say that the phenomenon has gained general acceptance in the psychological community.

We turn to the next consideration, whether the phenomenon may be empirically tested. As noted in the foregoing discussion, it would be impossible, ethically, to test repression and recovery of memory of severely traumatic events in a laboratory setting. . . . Almost all studies of the phenomenon to date, accordingly, involve subjects in the clinical or therapeutic context. . . . Further, the studies of memory of childhood sexual abuse involve retrospective self-reporting of prior, typically uncorroborated, sexual abuse. . . . One exception is the study by Linda Meyer Williams, who interviewed 129 women who had been treated for sexual abuse in a metropolitan hospital as children approximately seventeen years earlier. . . . Of these, forty-nine women, or 38% of the sample, did not report the childhood abuse to the interviewer. . . . Williams states that "[a]lthough some of these women may have simply decided not to tell the interviewers about the abuse, additional findings discussed later suggest that the majority of these women actually did not remember the abuse." . . . The "findings" to which she refers include the relative openness of the subjects in answering other personal questions, including other incidents of sexual, physical, or emotional abuse. . . . Another study has concluded that nonreporting of remembered abuse might be explained by "embarrassment, a wish to protect parents, a sense of having deserved the abuse, a conscious wish to forget the past, and a lack of rapport with the interviewer." . . . Considering this similar study, Pope and Hudson concluded that it would be "hazardous to conclude that Williams' 49 'non-reporters' actually had amnesia." . . . Although empirical testing is difficult, and subject to some methodological complaints, it is possible.

It is difficult to estimate the number or rate of recovered memories that are "false." . . . Although some individuals who have recovered memories have since withdrawn their claims, . . . there is no way to track the percentage of such false memories, especially when the phenomenon is still subject to such vigorous debate. . . .

Because the memories in the instant cases were recovered during therapy or while the witness was engaged in therapy, we ordinarily would proceed to examine more closely the circumstances of the therapeutic environment, as discussed earlier. Our review of the memories without regard to the suggestiveness of the therapeutic process, however, convinces us that they do not pass our test of reliability. The phenomenon of recovery of repressed memories has not yet reached the point where we may perceive these particular recovered memories as reliable. . . . The indicia of reliability present in the particular memories in these cases do not rise to such a level that they overcome the divisive state of the scientific debate on the issue.

In a particular case, the court may be satisfied with the state of the scientific debate on the question of recovering repressed memories, and with the general indicators of reliability surrounding a particular recovered memory. If that memory is recovered in the context of therapy, however, we still will be greatly concerned with the suggestiveness of the therapeutic process, and its ability to skew memory and one's confidence in memory. . . . Because we need not engage in that inquiry in the instant cases, however, we shall not.

Affirmed and remanded.

Shahzade v. Gregory

923 F. Supp. 286 (D. Mass. 1996)

HARRINGTON, District Judge.

This matter is before the Court on the Defendant's Motion in Limine to Exclude Repressed Memory Evidence. The defendant in this case is Dr. George Gregory, the plaintiff is Ann Shahzade, the defendant's cousin. For the reasons set forth below, the Court hereby denies the defendant's motion.

The plaintiff in this case alleges repeated episodes of non-consensual sexual touching of her by the defendant from 1940 to 1945, more than forty-seven years prior to her filing a complaint. The plaintiff was between the ages of approximately twelve and seventeen at this time; the defendant is approximately five years her senior. The plaintiff claims that these episodes had been completely blocked out and that she had no memory of them until she recovered so-called "repressed memories" of these touchings during psychotherapy in November of 1990. The defendant admits to some degree of sexual activity between himself and the plaintiff, but there is a dispute with regard to the nature and extent of such activity. The plaintiff now wants to introduce evidence relating to these alleged repressed memories. . . .

The Court acknowledges the appropriateness of an expert in this type of case and concludes that the plaintiff's expert, Dr. Bessel van der Kolk, is not only qualified as an expert in the field of memory, but that he is one of the country's most renowned psychiatrists in this specialty.[1]

For the following reasons, the Court finds the subject matter, repressed memory syndrome, to be reliable and therefore admissible. . . .

The factors to be considered when deciding if proffered testimony is valid "scientific knowledge," and therefore reliable, are: (1) whether the theory has been tested; (2) whether the theory has been subjected to peer review and publication; (3) the theory's known or potential rate of error; and (4) whether the theory has attained general acceptance within the relevant scientific community. . . . After considering these factors, this Court finds that the reliability of the phenomenon of repressed memory has been established, and therefore, will permit the plaintiff to introduce evidence which relates to the plaintiff's recovered memories.

In a case raising the same issue, *Isely v. Capuchin Province*, 877 F.Supp. 1055 (E.D.Mich.1995), the court stated that in order to introduce repressed memory evidence, a witness must "testify as to whether that theory can be, or

---

1. Dr. van der Kolk is currently an Associate Professor of Psychiatry at Harvard Medical School and the Chief of the Trauma Clinic at Massachusetts General Hospital. He has gained international recognition in the field of trauma and memory and is on the Board of Directors for the International Society for Traumatic Stress Studies. Dr. van der Kolk has published many articles on the topic and he is currently writing his fourth book, Memory, Trauma and the Integration of Experience.

has been, tested or corroborated and, if so, by whom and under what circumstances; whether the theory has been proven out or not proven out under clinical tests or some other accepted procedure for bearing it out; and whether the theory has been subjected to other types of peer review. . . . Obviously this part of this foundational element will include testimony as to whether or not the theory of repressed memory is widely accepted in the field of psychology."

Dr. van der Kolk's testimony sufficiently satisfies these foundational factors. Dr. van der Kolk discussed in detail several studies which focused on the concept of repressed memories and ultimately, through their findings, serve to validate the theory. One such study, which Dr. van der Kolk referred to as the Herman and Schatzow study, looked at victims of sexual abuse and found that only approximately one-third of the victims remembered all of the details of the abuse. Another one-third of the victims had a partial memory of the abuse, while the final one-third remembered nothing relating to the abuse. Dr. van der Kolk stated that these figures represent "the sort of figures that every study comes in, regardless of what the methodology is. . . ."

A study conducted by Linda Myer Williams, which Dr. van der Kolk referred to as "the best study on all this," . . . further validates the theory of repressed memories. . . . She conducted extensive interviews with young women who had been sexually abused, and her dissertation detailed the experiences which they had undergone. Seventeen years later, as a research psychologist, Ms. Williams reinterviewed patients who had been the subject of her dissertation to see what impact the earlier sexual abuse had on their later life. She was able to locate about half of her original subjects, and after reinterviewing them, she found that thirty-eight percent of her patients no longer remembered the abuse.

Dr. van der Kolk further testified that the majority of clinical psychiatrists recognize the theory of repressed memories and do not find the theory itself controversial. He further stated that this is not "a new craze among American psychiatrists . . . this is a very old issue in psychiatry." . . . The issue only became controversial when studies on the issue of repressed memories of sexual abuse, as opposed to repressed memories of natural traumatic events or wartime incidents, began to surface. People then began to say, "You're full of nonsense. This doesn't happen." . . . In brief, Dr. van der Kolk testified that repressed memories is not a scientific controversy, but merely a political and forensic one.

Dr. van der Kolk stated that currently the major detractors of the theory are so-called outsiders, "psychologists who do not treat traumatized patients." . . . Although the defendant's expert, Dr. Bodkin, was a clinical psychiatrist, he does not specialize in the field of memory. Nor do his credentials and expertise in the area of memory compare with those of Dr. van der Kolk. Furthermore, Dr. Bodkin did not claim that the theory of repressed memory was invalid, he merely stated that, in his opinion, the 52 studies relating to repressed memories which he critiqued contained methodological deficiencies and therefore could not serve to validate the theory.

According to the expert who testified in Isely, the only controversy among the majority of clinical psychiatrists with respect to the issue of repressed memory "is specifically in the area of elicitation of repressed memories, not with the concept itself." . . . Dr. van der Kolk expanded on this point in recognizing that some memories may not be accurate. "I think there has always been controversies about whether people can trust a patient still. And, particularly, people have always been concerned whether when people tell them something that happened maybe a long time ago that suddenly comes up, whether you can really believe what people, what people tell you." . . . "Translating [a] sensation into a story is still subject to ordinary human distortions that we all are capable of . . . So at the end, just like every other story you hear, you take your subjective self and eventually you decide what you believe — whether you believe what people tell you is true or not, it's how we all make up our minds. So at the end, there really is no scientific proof whether something is true or not unless there is independent corroboration, unless there was somebody there taking a movie." . . . The testimony of the defendant's second expert, Dr. Ofshe, supported this point. The elicitation and accuracy of the recovered memory itself, however, is not the issue currently before the Court. The Court must decide if the theory itself is valid. Dr. Ofshe's testimony did not directly address this issue. It must be also noted that Dr. Ofshe is not a clinical psychiatrist, but rather a doctor of Social Psychology.

The American Psychiatric Association, which is the major professional association for psychiatrists in America, recognizes the theory of repressed memories and believes it to be very common among people who have experienced severe trauma. In an official statement by the American Psychiatric Association relating to memories of sexual abuse, the Association stated that "Children and adolescents who have been abused cope with trauma by using a variety of coping mechanisms. In some instances these coping mechanisms result in a lack of conscious awareness of the abuse for varying periods of time. Conscious thoughts and feelings stemming from the abuse may emerge at a later date."

Diagnostic and Statistical Manual of Mental Disorders (DSM-IV, 1994), which is a widely used manual by psychiatrists to define mental diagnostic categories and is published by the American Psychiatric Association, also recognizes the concept of repressed memories. The term "Dissociative Amnesia," however, is the true technical psychiatric or medical term for the theory and is the term used when defining the condition in the manual. Repressed memories is the popular term. The two terms were used interchangeably in the hearing. The manual states that "Dissociative Amnesia is characterized by an inability to recall important personal information, usually of a traumatic or stressful nature, that is too extensive to be explained by ordinary forgetfulness." . . . "Dissociative Amnesia can be distinguished from normal gaps in memory by the intermittent and involuntary nature of the

inability to recall and by the presence of significant distress or impairment."
. . . The manual goes on to state that "Dissociative Amnesia most commonly
presents as a retrospectively reported gap or series of gaps in recall for aspects
of the individual's life history. These gaps are usually related to traumatic or
extremely stressful events." . . . Particularly relevant to the issue presently
before the Court, the manual recognizes that "In recent years in the United
States, there has been an increase in reported cases of Dissociative Amnesia
that involves previously forgotten early childhood traumas." . . .

The fact that Dissociative Amnesia is included and discussed in such
depth within the DSM-IV is significant, and, speaking as a member of the
American Psychiatric Association, Dr. van der Kolk said that listing Dissociative Amnesia in DSM-IV "means that at this point in time we recognize that
that [Dissociative Amnesia] exists."

Based on the evidence and testimony of Dr. van der Kolk, the Court
finds that the plaintiff has satisfied the four foundational factors which are
to be considered, although not independently determinative, in order to
introduce evidence relating to repressed memories. The plaintiff has presented sufficient evidence through both Dr. van der Kolk's testimony and
various submissions to the Court that (1) the theory has been the subject
of various tests; (2) the theory has been subjected to peer review and publication; (3) that repressed memory, as is true with ordinary memories, "cannot be tested empirically," and may not always be accurate, however, the
theory itself has been established to be valid through various studies . . . and
(4) the theory has attained general acceptance within the relevant scientific
community, namely, that of clinical psychiatrists.

NOTES AND QUESTIONS

1. *Hungerford* and *Shahzade* represent two different approaches to
the subject of repressed memory and in many ways represent the different
beliefs held by some research psychologists (who study memory using tests
designed to generate data) and some clinical psychologists (who primarily
treat patients). In the *Final Conclusions of the American Psychological Association
Working Group on Investigating Memories of Childhood Abuse,* 4 Psychol. Pub.
Pol'y & Law 933 (1998), the group (comprised of both research and clinical
psychologists) set forth points of agreement and disagreement:

we are in agreement concerning a number of key points. Indeed, we agree on
the following:

1. Controversies regarding adult recollections should not be allowed to
   obscure the fact that child sexual abuse is a complex and pervasive
   problem in America that has historically gone unacknowledged.

2. Most people who were sexually abused as children remember all or part of what happened to them.
3. It is possible for memories of abuse that have been forgotten for a long time to be remembered.
4. It is also possible to construct convincing pseudomemories for events that never occurred.
5. There are gaps in our knowledge about the processes that lead to accurate and inaccurate recollections of childhood abuse.

As important as these areas of agreement are, it is equally if not more important to acknowledge frankly that we differ markedly on a wide range of issues. At the core, the clinical and research groups have fundamentally differing views of the nature of memory. These contrasting conceptions of memory have led to debate concerning (a) the constructive nature of memory and the accuracy with which any events can be remembered over extended delays; (b) the tentative mechanisms that may underlie delayed remembering; (c) the presumed "special" status of memories of traumatic events; (d) the relevance of the basic memory and developmental literatures for understanding the recall of stressful events; (e) the rules of evidence by which we can test hypotheses about the consequences of trauma and the nature of remembering; (f) the frequency with which pseudomemories may be created by suggestion, both within and outside of therapy; and (g) the ease with which, in the absence of external corroborative evidence, "real" memories and pseudomemories may be distinguished.

Id. at 933-934. While these points are clearly critical for psychologists, they are equally critical to courts determining whether such evidence is either generally acceptable or scientifically reliable. Which test — *Fyre* or *Daubert* — makes more sense in deciding the admissibility of repressed and recovered memory evidence? As a judge, how would you weigh these competing opinions?

2. The delay in bringing civil and criminal cases grounded on repressed and recovered memory poses thorny jurisprudential questions. A number of courts and legislatures have addressed the statute of limitations problems, including whether the discovery rule should apply and how it should be interpreted. The delays in these cases are often decades long. For example, in *Shahzade,* 47 years passed before she claimed to remember the abuse. What competing policy considerations should be analyzed in making the decision whether to extend the statute of limitations in these cases? For a list of the respective courts' approaches, see cases collected in Dalrymple v. Brown, 701 A.2d 164, 170-171, ns.9 & 10 (Pa. 1997).

3. These two cases highlight another concern about the oft-times uneasy fit between therapy and evidence. What might be helpful for patients might not make reliable evidence. This uneasy fit is one example of the frequently clashing purposes of law and science.

IV. THE EFFECTS OF COERCIVE AND SUGGESTIVE INTERROGATIONS ON MEMORY

State v. Michaels
642 A.2d 1372 (N.J. 1994)

In September 1984, Margaret Kelly Michaels was hired by Wee Care Day Nursery ("Wee Care") as a teacher's aide for preschoolers. Located in St. George's Episcopal Church, in Maplewood, Wee Care served approximately fifty families, with an enrollment of about sixty children, ages three to five. . . .

Wee Care had staff consisting of eight teachers, numerous aides, and two administrators. The nursery classes for the three-year-old children were housed in the basement, and the kindergarten class was located on the third floor. During nap time, Michaels, under the supervision of the head teacher and the director, was responsible for about twelve children in one of the basement classrooms. The classroom assigned to Michaels was separated from an adjacent occupied classroom by a vinyl curtain.

During the seven month period that Michaels worked at Wee Care, she apparently performed satisfactorily. Wee Care never received a complaint about her from staff, children, or parents. According to the State, however, between October 8, 1984, and the date of Michaels's resignation on April 26, 1985, parents and teachers began observing behavioral changes in the children.

On April 26, 1985, the mother of M.P., a four-year old in Michaels's nap class, noticed while awakening him for school, that he was covered with spots. She took the child to his pediatrician and had him examined. During the examination, a pediatric nurse took M.P.'s temperature rectally. In the presence of the nurse and his mother, M.P. stated, "this is what my teacher does to me at nap time at school." M.P. indicated to the nurse that his teacher, Kelly (the name by which Michaels was known to the children), was the one who took his temperature. M.P. added that Kelly undressed him and took his temperature daily. On further questioning by his mother, M.P. said that Kelly did the same thing to S.R.

The pediatrician, Dr. Delfino, then examined M.P. He informed Mrs. P. that the spots were caused by a rash. Mrs. P. did not tell Dr. Delfino about M.P.'s remarks; consequently, he did not examine M.P.'s rectum. In response to further questioning from his mother after they had returned home, M.P., while rubbing his genitals, stated that "[Kelly] uses the white jean stuff." Although M.P. was unable to tell his mother what the "white jean stuff" was, investigators later found vaseline in Wee Care's bathroom and white cream in the first-aid kit. During the same conversation, M.P. indicated that Kelly had "hurt" two of his classmates, S.R. and E.N.

M.P.'s mother contacted the New Jersey Division of Youth and Family Services ("DYFS") and Ms. Spector, Director of Wee Care, to inform them of her son's disclosures. On May 1, 1985, the Essex County Prosecutor's office received information from DYFS about the alleged sexual abuse at Wee Care. The Prosecutor's office assumed investigation of the complaint.

The Prosecutor's office interviewed several Wee Care children and their parents, concluding their initial investigation on May 8, 1985. During that period of investigation, Michaels submitted to approximately nine hours of questioning. Additionally, Michaels consented to taking a lie detector test, which she passed. Extensive additional interviews and examinations of the Wee Care children by the prosecutor's office and DYFS then followed.

Michaels was charged [with multiple counts of child sexual abuse]. . . . The bulk of the State's evidence consisted of the testimony of the children. That testimony referred extensively to the pretrial statements that had been elicited from the children during the course of the State's investigations. The State introduced limited physical evidence to support the contention that the Wee Care children had been molested.

By the time the trial concluded nine months later, another thirty-two counts had been dismissed, leaving 131 counts. On April 15, 1988, after twelve days of deliberation, the jury returned guilty verdicts on 115 counts, including aggravated sexual assault (thirty-eight counts), sexual assault (thirty-one counts), endangering the welfare of children (forty-four counts), and terroristic threats (two counts). The trial court sentenced Michaels to an aggregate term of forty-seven years imprisonment with fourteen years of parole ineligibility.

II

The focus of this case is on the manner in which the State conducted its investigatory interviews of the children. In particular, the Court is asked to consider whether the interview techniques employed by the state could have undermined the reliability of the children's statements and subsequent testimony, to the point that a hearing should be held to determine whether either form of evidence should be admitted at re-trial.

The question of whether the interviews of the child victims of alleged sexual-abuse were unduly suggestive and coercive requires a highly nuanced inquiry into the totality of circumstances surrounding those interviews. Like confessions and identification, the inculpatory capacity of statements indicating the occurrence of sexual abuse and the anticipated testimony about those occurrences requires that special care be taken to ensure their reliability.

Woven into our consideration of this case is the question of a child's susceptibility to influence through coercive or suggestive questioning. As the Appellate Division noted, a constantly broadening body of scholarly authority exists on the question of children's susceptibility to improper interrogation. . . . The expanse of that literature encompasses a variety of views and conclusions. . . .

A.

Like many other scientific and psychological propositions that this Court has addressed in different contexts, . . . the notion that a child is peculiarly susceptible to undue influence, while comporting with our intuition and common experience is in fact a hotly debated topic among scholars and practitioners. The recognition of that notion in a judicial proceeding, therefore, requires utmost circumspection.

Additional factors temper our consideration of whether children are susceptible to manipulative interrogation. This Court has been especially vigilant in its insistence that children, as a class, are not to be viewed as inherently suspect witnesses. We have specifically held that age per se cannot render a witness incompetent. . . . We declined to require or allow, absent a strong showing of abnormality, psychological testing of child-victims of sexual abuse as a predicate to a determination of the credibility of the child-victim as a witness. . . . We have also recognized that under certain circumstances children's accounts of sexual abuse can be highly reliable. . . . Nevertheless, our common experience tells us that children generate special concerns because of their vulnerability, immaturity, and impressionability, and our laws have recognized and attempted to accommodate those concerns, particularly in the area of child sexual abuse. . . .

The issue we must determine is whether the interview techniques used by the State in this case were so coercive or suggestive that they had a capacity to distort substantially the children's recollections of actual events and thus compromise the reliability of the children's statements and testimony based on their recollections.

We begin our analyses by noting, as did the Appellate Division, that the "investigative interview" is a crucial, perhaps determinative, moment in a child-sex-abuse case. . . . A decision to prosecute a case of child sexual abuse often hinges on the information elicited in the initial investigatory interviews with alleged victims, carried out by social workers or police investigators. . . .

That an investigatory interview of a young child can be coercive or suggestive and thus shape the child's responses is generally accepted. If a child's recollection of events has been molded by an interrogation, that influence undermines the reliability of the child's responses as an accurate recollection of actual events.

A variety of factors bear on the kinds of interrogation that can affect the reliability of a child's statements concerning sexual abuse. We note that a fairly wide consensus exists among experts, scholars, and practitioners concerning improper interrogation techniques. They argue that among the factors that can undermine the neutrality of an interview and create undue suggestiveness are a lack of investigatory independence, the pursuit by the interviewer of a preconceived notion of what has happened to the child, the use of leading questions, and a lack of control for outside influences on the child's statements, such as previous conversations with parents or peers . . . - see also, John E.B. Myers, *The Child Witness: Techniques for Direct Examination, Cross-Examination, and Impeachment,* 18 Pac.L.J. 801, 889 (1987) (stating that factors that influence child's suggestibility include: (1) whether interviewer believes in presumption of guilt; (2) whether questions asked are leading or non-leading; and (3) whether interviewer was trusted authority figure).

The use of incessantly repeated questions also adds a manipulative element to an interview. When a child is asked a question and gives an answer, and the question is immediately asked again, the child's normal reaction is to assume that the first answer was wrong or displeasing to the adult questioner. . . . The insidious effects of repeated questioning are even more pronounced when the questions themselves over time suggest information to the children. . . .

The explicit vilification or criticism of the person charged with wrong-doing is another factor that can induce a child to believe abuse has occurred. Similarly, an interviewer's bias with respect to a suspected person's guilt or innocence can have a marked effect on the accuracy of a child's state-ments. . . . The transmission of suggestion can also be subtly communicated to children through more obvious factors such as the interviewer's tone of voice, mild threats, praise, cajoling, bribes and rewards, as well as resort to peer pressure.

The Appellate Division recognized the considerable authority support-ing the deleterious impact improper interrogation can have on a child's memory. Other courts have recognized that once tainted the distortion of the child's memory is irremediable. *See State v. Wright,* 116 Idaho 382, 775 P.2d 1224, 1228 (1989) ("Once this tainting of memory has occurred, the problem is irredeemable. That memory is, from then on, as real to the child as any other."). The debilitating impact of improper interrogation has even more pronounced effect among young children. . . .

The critical influence that can be exerted by interview techniques is also supported by the literature that generally addresses the reliability of children's memories. Those studies stress the importance of proper interview techniques as a predicate for eliciting accurate and consistent recollection. . . .

The conclusion that improper interrogations generate a significant risk of corrupting the memories of young children is confirmed by govern-ment and law enforcement agencies, which have adopted standards for con-ducting interviews designed to overcome the dangers stemming from the improper interrogation of young children. The National Center for the Prosecution of Child Abuse, in cooperation with the National District Attorney's Association and the American Prosecutor's Research Institute has adopted protocols to serve as standards for the proper interrogation of suspected child-abuse victims. Those interview guidelines require that an interviewer remain "open, neutral and objective." American Prosecutors Research Institute, National Center for Prosecution of Child Abuse, *Investigation and Prosecution of Child Abuse* at 7 (1987); an interviewer should avoid asking leading questions; an interviewer should never threaten a child or try to force a reluctant child to talk; and an interviewer should refrain from telling a child what others, especially other children, have reported. The New Jersey Governor's Task Force on Child Abuse and Neglect has also promulgated guidelines. It states that the interviewer should attempt to elicit a child's feelings about the alleged offender, but that the interviewer should not speak negatively about that person. Governor's Task Force on Child Abuse and Neglect, *Child Abuse and Neglect: A Professional's Guide to Identification, Reporting, Investigation and Treatment,* at 31 (1988). Further, multiple interviews with various interviewers should be avoided.

Finally, we can acknowledge judicial recognition of the very same concerns expressed in the academic literature and addressed by the guidelines established by governmental authorities with respect to the improper interrogation of alleged child sex abuse victims. The United States Supreme Court in *Idaho v. Wright,* 497 U.S. 805, 110 S.Ct. 3139, 111 L.Ed.2d 638 (1990), noted with approval the conclusion of the Idaho Supreme Court that the failure to video tape interviews with alleged child victims, the use of blatantly leading questions, and the presence of an interviewer with a preconceived idea of what the child should be disclosing, in addition to children's susceptibility to suggestive questioning, all indicate the potential for the elicitation of unreliable information. . . .

We therefore determine that a sufficient consensus exists within the academic, professional, and law enforcement communities, confirmed in varying degrees by courts, to warrant the conclusion that the use of coercive or highly suggestive interrogation techniques can create a significant risk that the interrogation itself will distort the child's recollection of events, thereby undermining the reliability of the statements and subsequent testimony concerning such events.

B.

The interrogations undertaken in the course of this case utilized most, if not all, of the practices that are disfavored or condemned by experts, law enforcement authorities and government agencies.

The initial investigation giving rise to defendant's prosecution was sparked by a child volunteering that his teacher, "Kelly," had taken his temperature rectally, and that she had done so to other children. However, the overwhelming majority of the interviews and interrogations did not arise from the spontaneous recollections that are generally considered to be most reliable. . . . Few, if any, of the children volunteered information that directly implicated defendant. Further, none of the child victims related incidents of actual sexual abuse to their interviewers using "free recall." . . . Additionally, few of the children provided any tell-tale details of the alleged abuse although they were repeatedly prompted to do so by the investigators. We note further that the investigators were not trained in interviewing young children. The earliest interviews with children were not recorded and in some instances the original notes were destroyed.[1] Many of the interviewers demonstrated ineptness in dealing with the challenges presented by pre-schoolers, and displayed their frustration with the children.

Almost all of the interrogations conducted in the course of the investigation revealed an obvious lack of impartiality on the part of the interviewer. One investigator, who conducted the majority of the interviews with the children, stated that his interview techniques had been based on the premise that the "interview process is in essence the beginning of the healing process." He considered it his "professional and ethical responsibility to alleviate whatever anxiety has arisen as a result of what happened to them." A lack of objectivity also was indicated by the interviewer's failure to pursue any alternative hypothesis that might contradict an assumption of defendant's guilt, and a failure to challenge or probe seemingly outlandish statements made by the children.

The record is replete with instances in which children were asked blatantly leading questions that furnished information the children themselves had not mentioned. All but five of the thirty-four children interviewed were asked questions that indicated or strongly suggested that perverse sexual acts had in fact occurred. Seventeen of the children, fully one-half of the thirty-four, were asked questions that involved references to urination, defecation, consumption of human wastes, and oral sexual contacts. Twenty-three of the thirty-four children were asked questions that suggested the occurrence of nudity. In addition, many of the children, some over the

---

1. As a matter of sound interviewing methodology, nearly all experts agree that initial interviews should be videotaped. . . . We have recognized generally that the existence of a video or sound recording of a statement elicited through pretrial interrogation is a factor bearing on its reliability. . . .

In this case, fully one-half of the earliest interviews at issue here were not audio or video-taped. The record indicates that the DYFS investigator did not begin taping interviews until June 19, 1985. The Court is aware of 39 transcripts of interviews with thirty-four children, or about one-half of those interviewed by DYFS. The rest were apparently unrecorded.

course of nearly two years leading up to trial, were subjected to repeated, almost incessant, interrogation. Some children were re-interviewed at the urgings of their parents.

The record of the investigative interviews discloses the use of mild threats, cajoling, and bribing. Positive reinforcement was given when children made inculpatory statements, whereas negative reinforcement was expressed when children denied being abused or made exculpatory statements.

Throughout the record, the element of "vilification" appears. Fifteen of the thirty-four children were told, at one time or another, that Kelly was in jail because she had done bad things to children; the children were encouraged to keep "Kelly" in jail. For example, they were told that the investigators "needed their help" and that they could be "little detectives." Children were also introduced to the police officer who had arrested defendant and were shown the handcuffs used during her arrest; mock police badges were given to children who cooperated.

In addition, no effort was made to avoid outside information that could influence and affect the recollection of the children. As noted by the Appellate Division, the children were in contact with each other and, more likely than not, exchanged information about the alleged abuses. . . . Seventeen of the thirty-four children were actually told that other children had told investigators that Kelly had done bad things to children. In sum, the record contains numerous instances of egregious violations of proper interview protocols.

We thus agree with the Appellate Division that the interviews of the children were highly improper and employed coercive and unduly suggestive methods. As a result, a substantial likelihood exists that the children's recollection of past events was both stimulated and materially influenced by that course of questioning. Accordingly, we conclude that a hearing must be held to determine whether those clearly improper interrogations so infected the ability of the children to recall the alleged abusive events that their pretrial statements and in-court testimony based on that recollection are unreliable and should not be admitted into evidence.

C.

[W]e find that the interrogations that occurred in this case were improper and there is a substantial likelihood that the evidence derived from them is unreliable. We therefore hold that in the event the State seeks to re-prosecute this defendant, a pretrial hearing must be held in which the State must prove by clear and convincing evidence that the statements and testimony elicited by the improper interview techniques nonetheless retains a sufficient degree of reliability to warrant admission at trial.

NOTES AND QUESTIONS

1. The *Michaels* case also includes an appendix detailing a number of the suggestive interrogations. *See* 642 A.2d at 1385-1392.

2. The *Michaels* case is not the only case to highlight the problem of suggestive interrogation technique in children:

> In one of the earliest cases, the McMartin preschool case, none of the seven accused individuals was convicted of child sexual abuse, despite seven indictments on 208 different sexual abuse and exploitation charges, two trials, and expenditures by the State of California in excess of $15 million. A number of the jurors claimed during a press conference after the trial that they believed that some of the children had been abused, but that they were unable to reach a guilty verdict because of the highly suggestive (videotaped) interviews of the child witnesses.
>
> In the Little Rascals Day Care case, the Court of Appeals of North Carolina unanimously reversed the child sexual abuse convictions of both Bob Kelly and Dawn Wilson, again due to the suggestive questioning of child witnesses.

Stephen J. Ceci et al., Suggestibility of Child Witnesses, in *Modern Scientific Evidence*, § 21:14 (David L. Faigman et al., eds. 2005-2006).

3. There has been a great deal of research and commentary on this subject. *See generally*, Stephen J. Ceci & Maggie Bruck, *The Suggestibility of the Child Witness: A Historical Review and Synthesis*, 113 Psychol. Bull. 403 (1993); John E.B. Myers, *New Era of Skepticism Regarding Children's Credibility*, 1 Psychol. Pub. Pol'y & L. 387 (1995) (challenging the conclusions of Ceci & Bruck); Thomas D. Lyon, *The New Wave in Child Suggestibility Research: A Critique*, 84 Cornell L. Rev. 1004 (1999) (critiquing the work of Ceci & Bruck and other researchers); and Stephen J. Ceci & Richard D. Friedman, *The Suggestibility of Children: Scientific Research and Legal Implications*, 86 Cornell L. Rev. 33 (2000) (responding to Lyon's and Myers' critiques); and Amye R. Warren & Dorothy F. Marsil, *Why Children's Suggestibility Remains a Serious Concern*, 65 Law & Contemp. Probs. 127 (2002).

4. Some courts have framed the issue of suggestibility as a question relevant to the child's competence to testify: Has the child's memory been sufficiently tainted by coercive or highly suggestive interrogation to distort the child's memory and thus undermine the reliability of the child's statements and testimony? *See, e.g.,* Commonwealth v. Delbridge, 855 A.2d 27 (Pa. 2003). Should the issue of coercive interrogation be decided pretrial by a judge in a competency hearing or should the jury hear expert testimony to decide the issue? In Pennsylvania, expert testimony on most "social frameworks" is generally not admissible, so juries are unlikely to hear any expert critique the methods used to elicit statements. Is that a sensible approach? Is the issue simply too likely to mislead juries?

V. NEW CHALLENGES

United States v. Libby

461 F. Supp. 2d 3 (D.D.C. 2006)

REGGIE B. WALTON, District Judge.

[T]he defendant opines that he should be permitted to introduce the testimony of Dr. Bjork "regarding [what he characterizes as] the widely-accepted findings from the science of memory." . . . Having carefully considered the papers filed in connection with this motion, the exhibits, and the testimony presented during the hearing on the motion, the Court must conclude that Dr. Bjork's testimony is not admissible. Accordingly, for the reasons that follow, the defendant's motion to introduce Dr. Bjork's testimony will be denied.

I. BACKGROUND

. . . The defendant is charged in a five-count indictment with obstruction of justice . . . two counts of false statements in violation of . . . , and two counts of perjury. All of these charges arise from a criminal investigation into the possible unauthorized disclosure of classified information — Valerie Plame Wilson's affiliation with the Central Intelligence Agency ("CIA") — to several journalists. . . . Specifically, the charges against the defendant are predicated upon statements that the defendant allegedly made to Special Agents of the Federal Bureau of Investigation ("FBI") in October and November, 2003, . . . and testimony he provided to a grand jury in March 2004. . . . The alleged false statements occurred when the defendant recounted conversations he had in June and July 2003, with news reporters Tim Russert, Judith Miller, and Matthew Cooper to the FBI Agents and to the grand jury.

The defendant has made clear that in his effort to rebut these charges he will argue, in part, (1) that it is the government's witnesses, and not him, who misremembered the facts and the substance of the various conversations detailed in the indictment and (2) that any errors he may have made in describing the events were occasioned by confusion or faulty memory, not any wilful intent to misrepresent the truth. . . . This Court has acknowledged that this "faulty memory defense" is a viable defense to the charges. . . . Accordingly, the memory and recollection of the principal players will undoubtedly play a substantial role in the assessment of the defendant's culpability in the upcoming trial.

To support his faulty memory defense, the defendant seeks to introduce at trial the testimony of Dr. Bjork "to show that it is entirely plausible, given how memory has been found to function, that Mr. Libby or the government witnesses — or both — have innocently confused or misremembered the conversations on which this case turns." Specifically, Dr. Bjork would testify about thirteen scientific principles concerning human memory, including the process by which memory is encoded, stored, retained, and retrieved and various scientific bases for memory errors including "content borrowing," source misattribution, subsequent recall, divided attention, and "retroactive interference." . . .

A. *DAUBERT* ANALYSIS

The government does not challenge the proposed testimony of Dr. Bjork on the grounds that his testimony fails to satisfy the first prong of *Daubert*, noting that it "does not quibble with Dr. Bjork's expertise concerning research into memory, particularly with respect to the reliability of eyewitness identification.[6]

Rather, the government contends that the defendant "cannot meet his burden as the proponent of the evidence of establishing that the testimony will assist the jury in understanding or determining any of the facts at issue in this case." Thus, this is the only question the Court must resolve. For the reasons that follow, this Court agrees with the government. Therefore, Dr. Bjork will not be permitted to testify at trial.

In support of his position that Dr. Bjork's testimony will be helpful to the jury, the defendant asserts that "[r]esearch has shown that jurors are generally unaware of the frequency and causes of honest errors of recollection, and they underestimate the fallibility of memory." . . . In opposing Dr. Bjork's testimony, the government contends that (1) expert testimony on memory issues is permissible only under special circumstances not at issue here, . . . (2) the proposed testimony is within the knowledge and experience of an average juror, . . . the testimony cannot be applied to the facts of this case, under Rule 403, the proposed testimony is likely to confuse, mislead, or unduly influence the jury. . . .

There is no clear case authority, or absolute rule, on when an expert should be permitted to testify on issues regarding memory and perception. Courts have permitted such testimony when the testimony related to eyewitness identifications, repressed memory, and medical conditions that may affect memory. . . . And other courts have excluded such testimony when it related to eyewitness identifications and recollection of past events. . . . In addition, expert testimony relating to memory and perception has been excluded when, for example, effective cross-examination was employed to

---

6. Although a former member of this Court concluded almost twenty years ago that the "psychodynamics of memory and perception" are not sufficiently scientifically reliable to permit an expert to testify on the subject, Robertson v. McCloskey, 676 F. Supp. 351, 355 (D.D.C.1988), this conclusion hardly remains good law [legal and scientific authority citations omitted]. . . .

challenge the credibility and memory of the witnesses. . . . Contrary to the government's position, these cases do not demonstrate that expert testimony on memory and perception is only admissible in certain "special circumstances." . . . Rather, these cases simply stand for the proposition that there is no per se rule for or against the admissibility of such testimony. . . . [T]his Court must . . . determine whether the proffered testimony will be helpful to the jury. For the reasons that follow, it will not be helpful.

To support his argument that Dr. Bjork's testimony will be helpful to the jury, the defendant relies on various studies, which he avers stand for the proposition that "jurors are generally unaware of the frequency and causes of honest errors of recollection, and that they underestimate the fallibility of memory." . . . As further support for his position, the defendant offered the testimony of Dr. Elizabeth Loftus, who detailed her belief, based upon her research and the research of others, that many[7] of the principles which Dr. Bjork would testify to are not commonly understood by jurors.[8] After carefully reviewing the studies provided by the defendant and the testimony of Dr. Loftus, this Court must conclude that those studies are inapposite to what the jurors will have to decide in this case because: (1) the studies examine issues of memory and cognition under substantially different factual situations than the situation here; (2) the research does not demonstrate that jurors will underestimate the fallibility of memory when the matter is addressed in the trial setting though voir dire, cross-examination, closing arguments, and jury instructions; and (3) insofar as the studies relied on by Dr. Loftus purport to demonstrate the failure of jurors to sufficiently understand factors that impact the accuracy of memory, the scientific value of the studies themselves is suspect.

The studies relied upon by the defendant were based upon research that examined prospective juror understanding of factors that could impact the reliability of eyewitness identifications. . . . This Court cannot accept the proposition that the research findings concerning juror knowledge of factors impacting the reliability of eyewitness identification applies equally to juror knowledge of the factors that impact memory and cognition in other

7. Dr. Loftus acknowledged that Dr. Bjork's proposed testimony that "a person is more likely to encode accurately and retrieve accurately information that is important to him than information that is unimportant to him" is a matter of common sense. Def.'s Mot., Ex. A.

8. To support her conclusions, Dr. Loftus relied on principally on six studies. R. Schmechel, T. O'Toole, C. Easterly, & E. Loftus, *Beyond the Ken? Testing Jurors' Understanding of Eyewitness Reliability Evidence*, 46 Jurimetrics J. 177-214 (2006); K. Deffenbacher & E. Loftus, *Do Jurors Share a Common Understanding Concerning Eyewitness Behavior*, 6 Law & Human Behavior 15 (1982); T. Rapus Benton, D. Ross, E. Bradshaw, W.N. Thomas, & G. Bradshaw, *Eyewitness Memory is Still Not Common Sense: Comparing Jurors, Judges and Law Enforcement to Eyewitness Experts*, 10 Appl. Cognit. Psychol. 115 (2006); S. Kassin, V.A. Tubb, H. Hosch, & A. Memon, *On the "General Acceptance" of Eyewitness Testimony Research*, 56 Am. Psychologist 405 (May 2001); R. Wise & M. Safer, *A Survey of Judges' Knowledge and Beliefs About Eyewitness Testimony*, Court Review 6 (Spring 2003); and A. Daniel Yarmey & H.P Tressillian Jones, *Is the Psychology of Eyewitness Identification a Matter of Common Sense?* in Evaluating Witness Evidence 13 (Lloyd-Bostock and Clifford eds.1983.

contexts, such as the memory and recall of conversations. Thus, while the defendant has proffered numerous scientific studies describing how memory functions, the research showing that jurors do not understand these concepts is limited to the application of the concepts in the discrete area of eyewitness identification and its findings have limited, if any, applicability in other respects.

First, the design of these surveys demonstrates their limited value. . . . [one] survey design was based primarily on hypothetical situations involving eyewitness identification and the credibility of eyewitnesses. Other studies have been similarly designed. For example, in one study, participants were shown a video of a mock criminal trial to examine what factors might impact a potential juror's verdict. Different groups were shown different versions of the trial where various witness and identification factors were altered such as the disguise of the robber, the visibility of a weapon, and the amount of violence committed. . . . Other studies have examined the effect of cross-racial identification on an eyewitness's ability to identify an alleged perpetrator, the effect of extreme stress on an eyewitness's ability to identify the alleged perpetrator, and the effect the length of time an eyewitness viewed a criminal act had on his or her ability to identify the alleged perpetrator. In addition, these studies have examined the reliability of show-ups and lineups, and the effect of alcohol intoxication and age on eyewitness identification. . . . Thus, it is clear that based on the design of these studies, the research was focused solely on the impact of various factors on eyewitness identifications. This Court, therefore, has difficulty concluding that the studies provided by the defendant are applicable in any meaningful way to the case at hand, because they do not focus on the precise issues before the Court. . . .

Moreover, the value of these studies is further diminished by the factual basis that would underscore an expert's testimony on eyewitness identification issues and the expert testimony on the principles of memory and cognition that the defendant seeks to introduce. Under the former category, there can be little doubt that the average juror is not regularly, if at all, presented with issues of eyewitness identification of an alleged perpetrator of a criminal offense. Thus, it is highly probable that the average juror would be less familiar with concepts that may impact a witness's identification such as weapons focus, mug-shot-induced bias, or lineup format. . . . However, on a daily basis the average juror is personally faced with innumerable questions of memory and cognition, as everyone in their daily lives is called upon to store, encode, and retrieve information he or she has been subjected to. Although the average juror may not understand the scientific basis and labels attached to causes for memory errors, jurors inevitably encounter the frailties of memory as a commonplace matter of course. . . . Accordingly, the jury does not need a tutorial on the science of "content borrowing," "memory conjunction," or "source misattribution" errors to appreciate that people sometimes experience mistaken memories. The same applies for each of the thirteen areas upon which Dr. Bjork would testify, as the defendant has not established that the principles are either so complex or counter-intuitive that jurors do not understand them. . . . And just as a jury can comprehend the memory errors in the hypothetical above, the defendant here will be able to present to the jury the high pressured and sensitive nature of his work and the volume of information he received daily, to demonstrate that any error he may have made was the product of confusion, mistake or a faulty memory. Similarly, the defendant has an arsenal of litigation tools at his disposal to challenge the recollection of the government witnesses. . . .

And even if the Court could conclude that these research findings establish that jurors do not understand the fallibility of memory in situations like the one currently before the Court, . . . none of the studies provided to the Court show whether the rigors of the normal trial process provides jurors with the knowledge they need to critically assess the merits of the positions presented to them concerning the accuracy of one's memory. . . . One example of the studies . . . ask[s] respondents hypothetical questions, presented in multiple choice format over the telephone, to ascertain how the respondents would interpret a particular piece of evidence. . . . These hypothetical situations make no assessment of whether the respondent's answers might change if exposed to, for example, probing voir dire questions, vigorous cross-examination and closing arguments, and instructions that advise the jury of the factors that may impact on the accuracy of memory. Nor do these studies account for the effect of the deliberation process. Thus, the questions asked in these surveys were posed in a vacuum and did not provide a valid assessment of whether any perceived failure to understand memory errors can be rectified by the normal trial process. . . .

The only literature this Court has located that discusses in any detail whether the normal trial processes will sufficiently elucidate the points the defendant desires to impress upon the jury is a chapter in the book Psychology and Law: The States of Discipline. S. Penrod & B. Cutler, *Preventing Mistaken Convictions in Eyewitness Identification Trials*, in *Psychology and Law: The State of Discipline* 89-118 (Roesch et al. ed., 1999). As noted above, the chapter focuses on eyewitness identification, so its usefulness here is limited. The chapter does, however, have an insightful discussion about whether cross-examination is a sufficient safeguard against mistaken identifications, . . . setting forth three conditions that the authors believe must be satisfied if cross-examination is to be effective: (1) the "[a]ttorneys must have a full opportunity to identify the factors that are likely to have influenced an eyewitness's identification performance in a particular case"; (2) "[a]ttorneys must be aware of the factors that influence eyewitness identification performance"; and (3) "[j]udges and juries must be aware during trial, and consider during deliberations, the factors that influence an eyewitness identification performance." Although this test is premised on cross-examining a witness who has made an eyewitness identification, its principles have application here too.

Here, regarding the first factor, there can be no doubt that the defendant and his attorneys have had a full the opportunity to identify the factors that may impact the credibility of his memory defense. He has already been provided a substantial amount of documentation, including topic overviews of the intelligence briefings he received, all of his personal notes, and his daily schedules. Moreover, the defendant himself has undoubtedly apprised his highly skilled attorneys of the work that was consuming his attention during the times relevant to this prosecution. As to the second prong of the test, the substance of the defendant's current motion and his consultations with both Drs. Bjork and Loftus demonstrate that the defense team is well aware of the factors that influence the accuracy of memory and thus will be in a capable position to effectively raise during cross-examination of the government's witnesses, the direct examination of the defendant himself (if he chooses to testify), and through closing arguments, the factors that impact the accuracy of memory. . . . Thus, satisfaction of the first two factors identified by Penrod and Cutler would suggest that effective cross-examination will provide a sufficient safeguard.

As to the final requirement, this Court has already noted that there is a substantial difference between eyewitness identification factors and the factors relevant to the defendant's memory defense. Thus, while jurors may not understand some of the memory and cognition principles underlying eyewitness identification, it can be assumed that they have a firm grasp of the memory and cognition issues about which Dr. Bjork would testify. And as the Court has already indicated, it is prepared to provide the jury with an instruction that will remind them of the factors they may consider in accessing the accuracy of memory. Moreover, Penrod and Cutler's chapter noted that "leading questions — typically used in cross-examination — may have a salutary effect on juror assessments of eyewitness performance." . . . The same clearly holds true for elucidating the factors that will be relevant to evaluating the testimony that will be presented in this case. And despite the chapter's ultimate conclusion that expert testimony on eyewitness identification "can serve as a safeguard against mistaken identification," the article opines that "a significant problem is that jurors simply do not make use of the knowledge they do possess." . . . Thus, even with expert testimony, the authors seemingly conclude that there is no guarantee that the jurors would apply the information provided to them. Accordingly, based upon these considerations, the Court must conclude that cross-examination, along with other trial procedures, will provide sufficient safeguards (if safeguards are needed at all) to ensure that the defendant's memory defense is properly evaluated by the jury. . . .[3]

Finally, even if this Court could accept the proposition that these research studies support the defendant's proposition that jurors do not have an understanding of memory errors such as the errors that allegedly occurred in this case, which it cannot do, the Court declines to accept the findings of these studies for a more basic reason — the reliability of these studies as applied to this case is questionable. . . .

Based on the foregoing, the Court cannot conclude that the defendant has satisfied his burden of establishing that the expert testimony of Dr. Bjork will be helpful to the jury. Not only are the studies offered by the defendant inapposite to the situation here, but the theories upon which Dr. Bjork would testify are not beyond the ken of the average juror. And as the facts of this case unfold during the trial, the Court has no doubt that aided by the normal trial processes, and the assistance of very capable legal counsel, the jurors will have the ability to collectively draw upon their common-sense understanding of memory and render a fair and just verdict.

B. FEDERAL RULE OF EVIDENCE 403

Even if this Court could conclude that Dr. Bjork's testimony satisfied the requirements of Rule 702, which it cannot, the Court would still exclude the evidence under Rule 403 for several reasons. First, as already discussed, it is reasonable to assume that the jurors selected in this case already have an understanding of the principles about which Dr. Bjork would testify. . . . In addition, the value of the evidence is also outweighed by the "danger of unfair prejudice, confusion of the issues, or misleading the jury." Fed.R.Evid. 403. The jurors will be the ultimate arbiter of the facts, and in this role, they must weigh the credibility of each witness. . . . Permitting Dr. Bjork to testify on even the general principles of memory and cognition "may cause jur[ors] to surrender their own common sense in weighing [the] testimony," . . . and instead cause them to rely too heavily upon Dr. Bjork's testimony. This would amount to an invasion of the jury's province, as the collective wisdom of the jurors, aided by the trial process itself, will more than adequately provide the jury with the means to assess the credibility and

---

3. In fact, in this case, the Court believes that cross-examination will be a powerful tool for the defense to challenge the confidence of the government's witnesses about their memories, just as it was for the government in its cross-examination of Dr. Loftus. For example, the Court has no doubt that the defendant, during the cross-examination of Tim Russert, will challenge the confidence he presumably will ascribe to the accuracy of his recollection of the conversation he had with the defendant, especially since there are no notes (either taken by Mr. Russert or the defendant) memorializing their conversation. Thus, even if there is some value to be derived from Dr. Bjork's testimony, effective cross-examination of the principal players will be far more valuable to the defendant's case than testimony on abstract principles of memory and cognition.

veracity of the witnesses, and testimony concerning scientific principles regarding memory and cognition would only serve to confuse those determinations. *United States v. Edelman*, 873 F.2d 791, 795 (5th Cir.1989) (affirming district court's exclusion of expert testimony under Rule 403 on the grounds that it would confuse the jury).

The defendant's motion to present the testimony of Dr. Bjork must therefore be denied.

NOTES AND QUESTIONS

1. In March, 2007, the defendant in this case was convicted on perjury, obstruction of justice, and lying to the FBI. Do you agree that the jury should not have heard the testimony of the expert in this case? Did the proposed expert make an unfounded leap from the data to the conclusion? Or was the matter simply one on which the jury did not need any expert help?

CHAPTER 10

ACCIDENT AND CRIME SCENE RECONSTRUCTIONS, DEFECTIVE PRODUCTS, AND EXPERIMENTS

Expert witnesses testify in civil trials about defective products, accident causation and prevention, fault for vehicle collisions, and the origin of suspicious fires. They opine on how accidents occurred and how they could have been avoided, how products were designed dangerously and how they could have been designed safely. They interpret vehicle accident scenes and crash sites. In criminal cases, experts also reconstruct accident and crime scenes. They explain to juries how a murder occurred by inspecting and interpreting blood spatter evidence. They testify as to whether a fire was of criminal or accidental origin. In some courts, they render opinions about the profile of the alleged perpetrator, based on an interpretation of the crime scene.

The technology explosion of the last two decades has had a marked effect on how lawyers try cases — notably with expert testimony. Many courtrooms are now wired for various types of technologies and lawyers routinely use computer reenactments of accidents and crime scenes to show to juries. Lawyers now can film sophisticated experiments so experts can explain complex causation issues to juries. Parties may now use computers to recreate accidents, giving rise to a new category of expert testimony: computer-generated evidence.

These reconstructions, re-creations, experiments, and interpretations raise questions about the foundation of experts' opinions, methodology, and qualifications; the accuracy and helpfulness of the re-creations; and the danger of unfair prejudice. This chapter considers all of these concerns.

I. EXPERIMENTS, VIDEOTAPES, AND COMPUTER-GENERATED EVIDENCE

Law in the Digital Age: How Visual Communication Technologies Are Transforming the Practice, Theory, and Teaching of Law

12 B.U. J. of Sci. and Tech. L. 227 (2006)
Richard K. Sherwin, Neal Feigenson, and Christina Spiesel

Here are some scenes from contemporary legal practice:

- In a recent class action against some of the world's largest tobacco companies, plaintiffs' lawyers contended that the defendant companies were being deceitful when they denied knowledge of the addicting properties of nicotine. At trial a simple computer simulation demonstrated how ammonia molecules had been added to cigarettes for the sole purpose of facilitating the rapid intake of nicotine. The color-coded images made plain that the tobacco companies had designed their product as a maximally efficient nicotine delivery system.

- In its highly publicized 2002 prosecution of Michael Skakel for the 1975 murder of Martha Moxley, lawyers for the State of Connecticut used an interactive CD-ROM to display all of their demonstrative evidence throughout the trial, including photographs of the neighborhood and crime scene, diagrams of the locations at which real evidence had been found, and an audiotape of a telephone interview Skakel had given to a journalist in the late 1990s. During closing argument, the prosecution replayed excerpts from the audiotape and simultaneously projected a transcript of Skakel's words onto a screen for jurors to follow. In the closing's most dramatic moment, jurors heard Skakel describe the panic he felt when Martha's mother asked him about her daughter the morning after the murder—and simultaneously saw on the screen a photograph of Martha's lifeless body next to the transcript of Skakel's words.

- For an insider trading case against the investment firm Kidder, Peabody and its former executive and corporate takeover

> wizard Martin Siegel, lawyers for the plaintiff Maxus Corporation (which eventually purchased the target company) prepared a video for closing argument that incorporated animated graphics, archival photographs, excerpts from videotaped depositions, and other materials to show that Siegel had conspired with Ivan Boesky to drive up the target's stock price. Siegel's repeated refusal to testify at his deposition—he took the Fifth Amendment over 600 times—was captured by nine sequential clips of Siegel looking down at a prepared text. As one clip followed another on the screen they took the shape of a three-by-three grid reminiscent of the popular TV game show "The Hollywood Squares." When the grid was complete, the audience both saw and heard the simultaneous Siegels turning the Fifth Amendment right to refuse to testify into a self-protective mantra.

Lawyers, as rhetoricians, have always known that effective persuasion requires speaking in terms that their audiences understand. They are now adapting to a culture in which audiences are accustomed by their everyday work and leisure experiences with television, movies, print media, and computers to rely on multimedia information. Adding to their traditional demonstrative arsenal of maps, diagrams, models, and photographs, lawyers (and the litigation consultants who help them) are now introducing new kinds of visual and multimedia displays. They assemble video previews of the strengths of their cases and show them to opposing counsel in the hope of obtaining favorable settlements. They shoot and edit day-in-the-life movies of accident victims for personal injury cases and compile video montages of murder victims' lives to be used as victim impact evidence in sentencing proceedings. Software programs like Sanction and Trial Director enable them to replay video depositions for judge and jury and simultaneously to display deponents' words on a scrolling transcript. Advocates digitally enhance photographs and create overlays of different forensic images using Photoshop® software. They use computer animations to illustrate expert witnesses' reconstructions of crimes and accidents. To set the scene for eyewitness testimony they can use "virtual reality views"—seamless, 360-degree representations of a scene, composited from digital photographs, with which witnesses can interact, moving in any direction and zooming in or out as desired. To build opening statements and closing arguments around multimedia displays that integrate text, photos, video clips, original graphics, and sound files, lawyers need not rely on the sorts of sophisticated consultants who produced the arguments in the three case examples above. They can do it themselves with PowerPoint®.

The ongoing transformation of law practice by digital visual and multimedia technologies can be gauged in part by the growing numbers of high-tech courtrooms, legal visual consultants, and instructional materials for lawyers. But even more importantly, the proliferation of digital and visual tools is profoundly changing the way litigators approach their jobs. First, the ability to put so much of their thinking into visual form leads lawyers to strategize their cases differently. When lawyers visualize a case, different possible relationships between elements can emerge that remain invisible when those same elements are described only verbally. This is because visual spatial arrangements are different from linear linguistic sequences. For example, one can talk about information channels in a complex corporate hierarchy, but a box-and-line chart showing who communicated with whom can make instantly intelligible the paths of information and influence. Second, the process of assembling and designing the visual presentations to be shown during negotiations, arbitration proceedings, or trials forces lawyers to prepare their cases earlier and more thoroughly than they would otherwise. Advocates must think through their theories of the case in the beginning so that they can plan for, design, and integrate apt visuals at the right spots in their presentations. Third, as scientific and other complex evidence plays an ever-larger role in legal disputes, the move to the visual enables lawyers and their expert witnesses to teach their cases more effectively to judges and juries. By using pictures as well as words, lawyers can present their cases in ways that interact more effectively with their audiences' diverse styles of learning.

Where the Not-So-Wild Things Are: Computers in the Courtroom, The Federal Rules of Evidence, and the Need for Institutional Reform and More Judicial Acceptance

13 Harv. J.L. & Tech. 161 (2000)
Fred Galves

The use of computer generated exhibits ("CGEs") in the courtroom has glided through its first wave of novelty, hyperbole, and even fear, with less roar than many predicted, and increasingly with much more acceptance from those who actually have used CGEs at trial. . . . Some legal scholars, using very colorful imagery, warn against "computerized 'razzle-dazzle' . . . used to Disney-up the evidence." It appears that the view of some is that computer technology will continue to forge ahead on its inexorable conquest of our social institutions, with the law and our courtrooms being just the latest casualties.

Fortunately, it has taken little time for most to witness what an anti-phenomenon, in many respects, the introduction of CGEs in the courtroom actually has been. By July of 1996, a commentator observed that "desktop portable computers now bedeck courtrooms like dandelions in May and, like dandelions, their number, use and application continue to grow." Indeed, any perspective that may have initially prevailed of computerization in the courtroom as a threatening newcomer — unwelcome to a well-established, and perhaps even a technophobic clique — is fading into the view that the incorporation of CGEs in the courtroom is positive, inevitable, and in many ways quite natural.

Although CGEs may be a way to up the ante of advocacy in the courtroom because they allow an attorney to communicate more clearly, powerfully, and efficiently, another compelling reason to incorporate CGEs is that they allow attorneys to keep up with the general advancement of technology in our society — an advancement upon which many lawsuits are based. Over the last few decades, courts have dealt with injuries and infringements stemming from intricate, complex products such as artificial heart valves and their parts, pesticides, asbestos, breast implants, and computer chips. Courts have also been faced with disasters such as bombings, plane crashes, and fires caused by highly technical elements. Thus, CGEs are not solely being introduced to add "sparkle" to cases, or "entertain" or even "dazzle" easily-bored jurors, as much as they are simply necessary to explain the complexities of the case so that the jury can understand the factual issues involved before they attempt the more difficult task of determining how to resolve the challenging factual disputes. . . .

THE SCIENCE IN DEMONSTRATIVE CGE CREATION

Expert witnesses are almost never eyewitnesses to events. Rather, they analyze information gathered after the lawsuit has begun and offer their expert opinions as to what the analyzed information means in order to help the jury understand the evidence. It is at this juncture — the testimony of an expert witness — that Rule 702 and the *Daubert* requirements come into play. However, a critical distinction should be made here. When an expert witness uses a CGE to help explain her verbal testimony to the jury, that CGE is a demonstrative exhibit only. . . . In such circumstances, *Daubert* and Rule 702 should come into play only with respect to the underlying scientific testimony that forms the basis of the expert's testimony, not with respect to the "science" of the display technology being used to illustrate the expert's testimony. . . . The mere fact that the expert witness would use a computer animation to display or illustrate points in her testimony does not make the display technology itself the relevant science that must be analyzed under Rule 702 and *Daubert,* any more than had the expert witness used a chalkboard and pointer or overhead projector and transparencies. Note that the expert witness can be cross-examined on the science presented for the jury's assessment. But the jury is not required to assess the reliability of the display technology itself, only the underlying science it is portraying. Of course, if the underlying science is inadmissible, then the CGE explaining or illustrating that inadmissible expert testimony would be inadmissible as well — not because the CGE display technology is inadmissible, but because the expert's alleged expertise does not satisfy *Daubert*.

RULE 702, *DAUBERT*, AND SUBSTANTIVE EXHIBITS

If a CGE goes beyond illustration of an expert's opinion to become the basis of that opinion, as in a re-creation or simulation based on input data, then the CGE is substantive in nature. It is being offered on its own merits and at that point would become subject to *Daubert* and Rule 702. The standard for the CGE, as well as any underlying scientific knowledge, is the Rule 702 scientific evidence standard under *Daubert*. . . .

MEETING RULE 702 AND THE *DAUBERT* REQUIREMENTS

Making general statements about the admissibility of the science behind substantive CGEs is difficult because admissibility turns on the integrity of the underlying computer program and the underlying science employed by the expert witness. The proponent simply has to make certain that the four Daubert requirements are met.

First, the evidence definitely can be tested. For example, when confronted with re-creations or simulations based on measured input data, the court or opposing counsel could offer random input variables to see how the computer would process that information and how plausible and consistent the results are. In fact, opposing counsel could videotape an actual event and feed the variables for that event into the computer. The parties could then compare the video tape of the actual event with the simulation or re-creation generated by the computer to see how close the computer program is to reality.

Second, computer simulations and re-creations already " [have] been subjected to peer review and publication." Moreover, as this technology continues to proliferate, this hurdle will continue to be less and less of a burden to overcome.

Third, there appears to be developing a "known or potential rate of error," at least for certain kinds of re-creations, such as accident reconstructions. However, because re-creations and simulations tend to be unique, this kind of information may be difficult to obtain.

Finally, although CGEs were seen as novel science in the past, there clearly has been a "particular degree of acceptance" of this technology, especially in the field itself. As such, this would not be that difficult of a hurdle to overcome; modern computer technology probably would meet even the old Frye test.

Kudlacek v. Fiat S.p.A.

509 N.W.2d 603 (Neb. 1994)

On the evening of September 22, 1980, Christopher Kudlacek was a passenger in a Fiat X1/9 driven by Arlan Broome, Jr. Broome testified they were traveling north on 144th Street, by Dodge Street in Omaha, at a speed between 40 and 55 miles per hour. Broome testified that when he saw an animal crossing the road in front of the vehicle, he turned into the southbound lane to avoid hitting the animal, and lifted his foot off the accelerator. When Broome attempted to steer the vehicle back to the northbound lane, the vehicle began to fishtail. The vehicle remained out of control and ultimately slid sideways off the west side of 144th Street down the embankment of a ditch. Broome could not remember what happened after the vehicle left the road. Reconstruction experts testified that after reaching the bottom of the ditch, the vehicle tripped, rolled upside down, launched itself in the air, and struck a group of trees on Kudlacek's side of the vehicle. Finally, the vehicle rebounded from the trees and came to rest right side up. As a result of the impact to Kudlacek's side of the vehicle, the upper portion of the passenger door was crushed into the passenger compartment approximately 19 inches.

Kudlacek sustained several injuries, the most serious of which was a brain injury which left him permanently and totally disabled. Plaintiffs offered the testimony of several medical, as well as automotive, experts to support their claims.

The plaintiffs also called Harley Copp and William N. Weins, Ph.D., to testify as experts on automotive design and handling. Michael Dickinson was the plaintiffs' reconstruction expert. Dickinson presented a computerized simulation of the Fiat X1/9's path during the accident. Weins and Copp testified that they found the Fiat X1/9 was defective and unreasonably dangerous because it made a rapid transition from understeer to oversteer when the driver lifted his foot off the throttle, during sharp cornering or emergency maneuvering, at or near the car's limit of control, making the vehicle uncontrollable. Understeering and oversteering refer to the handling characteristics of the vehicle. Weins explained that a vehicle which does not turn as much as the driver wants is an understeering vehicle. He further testified that understeering is a feature common among American-built cars. In contrast, an oversteering vehicle would turn more than a driver would like, and therefore the vehicle will turn more sharply if it is an oversteering vehicle. Weins testified that in a situation in which the driver has lost control in an understeering vehicle, the vehicle will go forward, whereas an oversteering vehicle which is out of the control of the driver will turn sideways or spin.

During their defense, defendants presented the expert testimony of Edward Heitzman, an automotive engineer. Heitzman testified, in part, on several tests conducted on the Fiat X1/9 as well as on other vehicles. Videotapes were made of all the testing performed. Plaintiffs' objections to the introduction of the videotapes showing the testing of the other vehicles were overruled.

A substantial number of tests were conducted in preparation for the trial of this action. Out of many hours of testing videotape, short selections were made by Heitzman, the defendants' automotive expert, to highlight the results of the various tests. The plaintiffs contend that the defendants failed to establish proper foundation for the introduction of three videotapes which showed the handling and steering tests performed by Heitzman on a Fiat X1/9 and several other vehicles.

When defendants questioned Heitzman about the results of the tests of the other vehicles, plaintiffs objected for lack of foundation with respect to comparative testing. Plaintiffs cite [*Kluender v. Mattea*, 214 Neb. 327, 334 N.W.2d 416 (1983); *Shover v. General Motors Corp.*, 198 Neb. 470, 253 N.W.2d 299 (1977)] in support of their position. This reliance is misplaced. *Kluender* and *Shover* involved foundational questions where the videotape attempted to re-create the accident conditions. Other jurisdictions have found that where the videotape is offered not to re-create conditions similar to the accident, but merely to illustrate certain principles, differences in surrounding conditions are less relevant and do not require the videotape's exclusion. . . . Other courts have allowed the videotape as an illustration where the judge has told the jury that the videotape is only a visual illustration and not proof. . . . When allowing videotapes to be shown, courts have found the lack of similarity to go to the weight of the evidence rather than to its admissibility. . . .

It is clear that Heitzman's videotapes were not meant to re-create the accident, but merely to rebut the plaintiffs' contention that the Fiat X1/9 was unique in its tendency to spin when the throttle was taken off as it reached its limits of handling. Heitzman described his work as measuring, defining, and describing automobile handling. He addressed several questions regarding the handling characteristics of the Fiat X1/9. One question was whether the Fiat X1/9 handled differently from other cars in normal maneuvers at 45 to 65 miles per hour.

In order to answer this question, Heitzman developed several questions to be answered by the testing conducted at the Transportation Research Center (TRC):

> *Q.*   This testing which you did at TRC, what was it designed — what questions was it designed to answer?
>
> *A.*   Well, the first question was will all these cars spin in liftoff — when you acc — at the ragged edge of their capabilities of — of their limit.
> If you lift off, will they — will they spin out?
> Second question is if they're not at the limit of their capabilities, will they spin out?

Q. Uh-huh.

A. The third question is how do — how do they compare in — in their — in their understeer behavior — the transient understeer behavior?

Q. Uh-huh.

A. And then just comparison. We were trying to compare the six cars, and as a — to — to see if any of them differed much from any of the others or if they were all pretty much the same in performance.

A series of tests was done on the Fiat X1/9 and other vehicles at the TRC on June 20, 21, 29, and 30, 1990. Heitzman testified that Weins, plaintiff's automotive expert, was present during the testing on these dates. Heitzman testified that he was the driver in all of the tests and that in addition to the Fiat X1/9, he tested a 1984 Fiero with a four-cylinder engine, a 1987 Fiero GT with a six-cylinder engine, a 1987 IROC Z Camaro, a 1975 Pontiac Trans Am, and a 1979 Datsun 280ZX. A Subaru wagon was also tested, but the results were incomplete due to a malfunction of the vehicle. The results for the Trans Am were also incomplete. The 1984 Fiero was tested because Weins had tested it previously. The 1987 Fiero was tested because it was the latest development by General Motors of the mid-engine concept. The 280ZX and the Trans Am were considered by Heitzman to be high-performance contemporaries of the Fiat X1/9 and were owned by the Broome family. The IROC Z was tested because it was a state-of-the-art V-8 front-engine, rear-drive sedan. In general, these vehicles were chosen because they were all high-performance, sporty vehicles designed to have a larger than usual performance limit as compared with six-passenger vehicles or sedans.

The following tests were performed on the Fiat X1/9 as well as on the other vehicles: a constant radius test, a step response test, a lane change test, and a frequency response test. The constant radius test consists of driving around a circle and constantly increasing speeds and measuring steering wheel angle changes to determine the understeer gradient or the amount of understeer. This test requires increasing the speed of the vehicle until it reaches its limit of control. Since the limits of each vehicle are different, the speed of each vehicle was different. The frequency response test measures the sensitivity of the car insofar as how much it turns when the steering wheel is turned, and the response time. This test was conducted on the Fiat X1/9 at the research runway of the aerospace mechanical science department at Princeton University at the end of 1988. The testing surface at Princeton, as well as the surface at the TRC, was asphalt. The testing surface for the TRC was also very flat and smooth. In a step response test, the vehicle is driven in a straight line at 50 miles per hour and the driver puts in increasing steer until the car's limit of control is reached. The test was performed on all vehicles, with the throttle on and the throttle off, and with the same rate of turn of 200 to 500 degrees per second. The speed at which the vehicles were tested was the same, 50 miles per hour.

To address the foundation question, defense counsel asked Heitzman if the same test protocol was used for each vehicle, if the instrumentation was the same, and if the same surface, same driver, and the same analysis method were used. He was also asked whether the data recordation methodology was the same. Each car was subjected to constant radius tests with drop throttle and no drop throttle. Each vehicle did the J-turn-type testing (step response test with and without throttle). Heitzman testified that the same speeds were used for most of the tests. However, in the constant radius test, he explained, the object is to reach the vehicle's limit and see if it spins when it reaches its limit. Since the limit of control is different for each vehicle, it would be reached at different speeds.

On voir dire, Heitzman conceded that some of the vehicles tested were front-engine vehicles and some were mid-engine vehicles, and the size and pressure of the tires would also vary. Nevertheless, the purpose of the testing was to demonstrate the principle that the Fiat X1/9 reacted similarly to other high-performance vehicles when they reached their limits. The dissimilarity of the test conditions to the accident conditions would go to the weight of the evidence and not to its admissibility. *Gilbert v. Cosco Inc.*, 989 F.2d 399 (10th Cir. 1993).

In *Gilbert*, the defendant introduced tests to refute testimony by the plaintiffs' expert that defendant's design had caused a "springboard effect" in the child-restraint seat manufactured by the defendants. The appellate court stated that when experiments do not simulate actual events at issue, the jury should be instructed that the evidence is admitted for the limited purpose or principles. No limiting instruction was given to the jury. However, the court upheld the admission of the tests because the trial court heard testimony regarding the purpose of the tests, it considered arguments by both sides and the relevancy of the data, and it allowed the plaintiffs' attorney to question the expert to determine relevancy and prejudicial impact. The appellate court also found the credibility of the expert's conclusions was attacked by the plaintiffs' attorney's pointing out inconsistencies and that the jury could consider this in weighing the evidence.

No limiting instruction was provided for the jury in the case before us. However, the trial court also heard testimony regarding the purposes of the tests conducted on the other vehicles. Defendants advised the court that inferences had been created by plaintiffs' expert that if a vehicle spins, it is defective, and that the Fiat X1/9 spins more quickly than American cars. The tests therefore were introduced to show that all cars will start to spin when they reach their limit of control. Plaintiffs' counsel was also able to question Heitzman on the differences in vehicles before the jury. Through this questioning the jury could determine how much weight to give the tests.

Under these circumstances, we cannot say that the trial court abused its discretion in admitting the videotapes depicting tests run on vehicles other than the Fiat X1/9.

COMPUTER SIMULATION

Defendants . . . complain[s] that plaintiffs' expert's testimony regarding a computer simulation of the path of the Fiat X1/9 on the roadway was erroneously admitted. Evidence relating to an illustrative experiment is admissible if a competent person conducted the experiment, an apparatus of suitable kind and condition was utilized, and the experiment was conducted fairly and honestly. . . . It is not essential that conditions existing at the time of the experiment be identical with those existing at the time of the occurrence. Substantial similarity is sufficient.

Other jurisdictions have permitted the use of computer simulations to aid the trier of fact. . . . In *Commercial Union Ins. Co. v. Boston Edison Co.*, 412 Mass. at 549, 591 N.E.2d at 168, the court conditioned the use of computer simulations on several factors:

[W]e treat computer-generated models or simulations like other scientific tests, and condition admissibility on a sufficient showing that: (1) the computer is functioning properly; (2) the input and underlying equations are sufficiently complete and accurate (and disclosed to the opposing party, so that they may challenge them); and (3) the program is generally accepted by the appropriate community of scientists.

We find the simulation meets the requirements necessary to be admissible evidence. Dickinson, the plaintiffs' accident reconstruction expert, generated the simulation of the accident through a computer program called Engineering Dynamics Single Vehicle Simulator. Dickinson testified that this program or model is used regularly by members of the reconstruction group company Failure Analysis Associates, possibly the largest failure analysis firm in the world, and is generally relied upon by experts in the reconstruction field for single-vehicle accident simulation. He also stated the program is used either to reconstruct an entire accident or to evaluate driver-vehicle interaction prior to an impact with an object or another car.

Dickinson described the authentication process used with this model. The dimensions of the Fiat X1/9 were measured in order to accurately represent the various dimensions that were to be input into the model. Those dimensions which were not available through direct measurement, such as the steering angle input and acceleration, were taken from the input data from the track tests as reported by Weins and Heitzman.

Track test data was used by Dickinson for verification purposes. Dickinson compared the J-turn and the constant radius skid-pad tests track tests performed by Weins and Heitzman, respectively, to the computer simulation of those tests in order to have an independent validation of the computer model. These simulations were done to validate the computer model, which was developed through measurement of vehicle properties and comparison to track test data, to show that in an off-throttle step-steer type maneuver, the computer model accurately represents the vehicle, the Fiat X1/9. Once the computer model is validated, an accurate simulation of the accident may be achieved.

In order to simulate the accident, Dickinson testified, he ran simulations using the model developed to compare the track test of the vehicle on the roadway, which allowed him to review the vehicle behavior and the vehicle trajectory and compare those to the marks on the roadway, the road exit speed, the angle at which the vehicle left the roadway, and the elements Broome described to him.

Fiat argues that the simulation was invalid because it was based on actions by Broome that were contrary to Broome's testimony and on factual assumptions which had no support in the evidence. Specifically, Fiat argues that the simulation is invalid because Broome testified that he thought he downshifted and that he attempted to brake at the time of the accident, and those elements were not placed in the computer simulation. We disagree. Broome testified that he thought he had downshifted and that he tried to apply the brakes but was unsure he had succeeded in doing either.

Dickinson explained his decision to not use those elements in the simulation by stating that a reconstructionist evaluates the witnesses' or driver's testimony against the physical evidence and against the simulation. The control elements were developed through runs of the simulation and were performed to best match the physical data that was available from the accident, which included the marks on the road, the road exit speeds, the angle exiting the road, and Broome's testimony of swerving to miss the animal on the road, lifting his foot off the accelerator, and attempting to steer back into his lane. Dickinson explained the simulation did not include braking because there was no evidence on the roadway that Broome succeeded in applying the brakes. Under these circumstances, we find the simulation accurately reflected the accident and was therefore correctly admitted by the trial court.

Muth v. Ford Motor Company

461 F.3d 557 (5th Cir. 2006)

Before Garwood, Higginbotham and Clement, Circuit Judges.
Patrick E. Higginbotham, Circuit Judge:
A jury returned a nearly $9 million judgment against Ford Motor Company for injuries sustained by Barry William Muth, Sr. while traveling in a 1996, four-door Ford Crown Victoria. Ford appeals, challenging the sufficiency of the evidence, evidentiary rulings, and the conduct of the trial judge. We affirm.

I

After finishing a pick-up basketball game, plaintiff Barry W. Muth, Sr. and Julius Wineglass, both Majors in the United States Army, got in a 1996, four-door Ford Crown Victoria and headed back to Escon village, site of a U.S. Army base, in Riyadh, Saudi Arabia. Wineglass was driving with Muth in the front passenger seat, both men wearing seatbelts. Traveling along a four-lane highway, they approached a right-hand curve going approximately ten miles per hour over the speed limit. Loose in the turn, Wineglass lost control of the car and ran it into a three-foot high "Jersey barrier" separating the two sides of the highway. Although the precise movement of the car was disputed, generally the left front wheel climbed the side of the barrier, causing the car to slide along the barrier for a short distance and, ultimately, to flip, landing on its roof and coming to rest about 209 feet from where it initially hit the barrier. Muth sustained a subluxation injury of the C5-C6 vertebrae in his spinal cord, leaving him a quadriplegic with only limited use of his arms and hands. Wineglass received minor injuries and is not party to this litigation.

Muth and his family sued Ford in federal district court, bringing negligence and strict product liability claims. Muth alleged two design defects: first, that the 1996 Ford Crown Victoria contained "inadequate rollover/roof crush protection"; and second, that the 1996 Ford Crown Victoria contained an "inadequate occupant restraint system." During the seven day trial, Muth focused on the roof strength defect, contending that a stronger and economically practical roof would have prevented the injury. Keith Friedman, Muth's expert witness, testified that the roof was defective because it collapsed twelve to fifteen inches on the passenger side. Friedman testified that increasing the thickness of the steel in several parts of the roof structure could have reduced the "roof collapse" to three inches for $9 per car or two inches for $31 per car. Ford did not dispute that a stronger roof would be feasible. Rather, Ford contended that a stronger roof would do little, if anything, to prevent injuries in rollover accidents. According to Ford, during a rollover accident, the body drops toward the ground—in other words, toward the roof. Because a normal seatbelt system allows the body to drop five inches, which is more than the normal three-to-four inches of clearance between head and roof, the only way to prevent injuries in rollover accidents is to use a five-point, NASCAR-style seatbelt with crotch strap, an impossibility in commercial vehicles. In short, Ford contended that a stronger roof would not help prevent head-and-neck injuries in rollover accidents.

Attempting to prove this counterintuitive point, Ford relied on data from two crash tests: an early 1980s series from General Motors using Chevy Malibu sedans ("the Malibu test"); and a 2000-2001 series from Ford using the Controlled Rollover Impact System ("the CRIS test"). Both tests used slow-motion video and high-speed cameras to record the precise movements of cars and dummies during rollovers. Although the district court allowed Ford's expert witnesses to discuss the data and conclusions drawn from the tests, the court excluded the demonstrative evidence — video and photograph — illustrating those results.

At the close of all the evidence, Muth withdrew his negligence claim and only submitted his design defect claim to the jury. The jury answered "yes" to the question of whether there was "a design defect in the Crown Victoria at the time it left the possession of Ford Motor Company that was a producing cause of the injury" and awarded Muth and his family nearly $9 million in damages.

II

Ford objects to the exclusion of demonstrative evidence from the Malibu and CRIS tests.

C

Ford ... objects to the district court's exclusion of demonstrative evidence — video and photograph — from the Malibu test, a rollover crash test conducted by General Motors in the early 1980s using a Chevrolet Malibu, and the CRIS test, a rollover crash test conducted by Ford in 2000-2001 using a 1998-2000 model Crown Victoria. The Malibu test was one of the first attempts to determine the relationship between roof deformation and injury. Improving on the Malibu test, the CRIS test was conducted after the National Highway Traffic Safety Administration sought comments on Federal Motor Vehicle Safety Standard 216, which set requirements on the amount of weight the roof structure in passenger cars must withstand. The CRIS test controlled the position, momentum, and point of impact of the vehicle's first contact with the ground. According to Ford, both tests illustrate how a stronger roof would do little, if anything, to prevent injuries in rollover accidents.

Ford offered the visual evidence from the tests to assist the jury in understanding their expert's testimony regarding the general dynamics of rollover accidents. Muth objected, pointing to several differences between the conditions involved in the tests and the conditions, at least as Muth saw them, involved in the accident. The court excluded the demonstrative evidence, noting that the tests were not conducted "under substantially the same conditions as those that [were] involved in this particular litigation."

We review the exclusion of demonstrative evidence for an abuse of discretion. No one seriously contests that the video and photographs help the jury understand the general dynamics involved in rollover accidents. The evidence illustrates Ford's claim that during rollover accidents, head-and-neck injuries can occur prior to any roof deformation. Importantly here, however, Ford's expert witness testified at length to this conclusion. In other words, the jury heard the evidence; the only question is whether the district court abused its discretion when it forced Ford's expert witness to testify without his visual aids.

When the demonstrative evidence is offered only as an illustration of general scientific principles, not as a reenactment of disputed events, it need not pass the substantial similarity test.[19] Such demonstrative aids, however, must not be misleading in and of themselves, and one such way that a demonstration might mislead is when, as here, the demonstration resembles the disputed accident. Indeed, it is this resemblance which gives rise to the requirement of substantial similarity. As the First Circuit has explained, "Scientific principles, when demonstrated in a fairly abstract way, are quite unlikely to be confused with the events on trial. The more troublesome cases, however, are ones like this one where some principles of some kind may be demonstrated but in a fashion that looks very much like a recreation of the event that gave rise to the trial."[20]

The district court rejected Ford's demonstration as not quite similar enough, yet that same demonstration too closely resembles the disputed accident to effectively present abstract principles without misleading the jury. One of the central disputes in this case concerned the precise movement of the Crown Victoria as it went from an upright position on top of the Jersey barrier to upside-down on the pavement below. To Muth, as the car rolled to the driver's side coming off the barrier, the left wheel struck the pavement briefly, causing the back end of the car to bounce back up and the car to come down on the left front wheel, the car then rolling onto the roof from the driver's side. Ford's accident reconstructionist, in contrast, contended that the car was airborne for twelve feet while coming off the barrier, rolling 90 or more degrees around its lengthwise axis at a rate of 202 degrees per second. The car then hit the pavement with its left front tire, wheel assembly, and fender, the forward movement causing it to pivot around and twist around that point, hitting the pavement first on the front passenger's side of the roof. Ford characterized the CRIS test as essentially depicting Ford's theory of the accident, all the while maintaining that it was offered, not as a reenactment, but only to show general scientific principles. The CRIS test shows a car dropped directly onto the roof over the front passenger seat, consistent with Ford's theory of the accident; Muth contended, however, that the car landed first on its front left side before falling onto the front passenger side. The vehicle in the CRIS test was spun at a rotational speed of 220 degrees per second, consistent with testimony from Ford's expert that the vehicle rolled at a rate of 202 degrees per second as it came off the Jersey barrier; again, Muth disputed this point, contending that the car teetered off the concrete barrier, making only one-quarter of a roll. As we have explained, the

19. *Four Corners Helicopters, Inc. v. Turbomeca, S.A.*, 979 F.2d 1434, 1442 (10th Cir.1992); 1 K. Broun, *McCormick on Evidence* § 202 (2006).

20. *Fusco v. General Motors Corp.*, 11 F.3d 259, 264 n. 5 (1st Cir.1993).

similarities between Ford's theory of the accident and the conditions of the CRIS test heighten the visual evidence's prejudicial effect, and this is sufficient to justify the district court's exercise of discretion in limiting Ford's expert to oral testimony only.

NOTES AND QUESTIONS

1. The substantial similarity test requires a showing that the experiment or testing was conducted under conditions substantially similar to the incident in question. While the conditions need not be identical, they must be sufficiently close to provide a fair comparison. *See* Christoper B. Mueller & Laird C. Kirkpatrick, 5 *Federal Evidence*, § 536 (2006). Many courts distinguish between experiments attempting to re-create the conditions of the event and those intended simply to illustrate the expert's testimony. Those intended as only illustrations of a scientific principle are not required to be substantially similar. In *Muth*, Ford's experiment was both too similar and not similar enough. By comparison in *Kudlacek*, the court held that any dissimilarities in defendant's videotape illustrations went to weight, not admissibility.

2. In Clark v. Cantrell, 529 S.E.2d 528 (S.C. 2000), the court notes the distinction between animation—which is an illustrative aid and simulation—which is substantive evidence: "Courts and commentators distinguish a computer animation and a computer simulation. An animation is used to illustrate a witness's testimony by recreating a scene or process, and properly is viewed as demonstrative evidence. A simulation is based on scientific or physical principles and data entered into a computer, which is programmed to analyze the data and draw a conclusion from it. Courts require proof of the validity of the scientific principles and data before admitting a simulation as evidence." *Id.* at 535, n.2.

3. In Miller v. Bike Athletic Co., 687 N.E.2d 735 (Ohio, 1998), the plaintiff, a high-school football player, was rendered quadriplegic when he collided head-on with another player. The plaintiff's expert was an engineer who opined that the bladders in Plaintiff's helmet were insufficiently inflated to protect against head and neck injuries. To support his theory, the expert conducted a test in accordance with standards established by the National Operating Committee on Standards for Athletic Equipment ("NOCSAE"). The expert mounted the helmet on a head form and then dropped it from varying heights, with the head form aligned so that impact could occur at the sides, back, top, and front. The "severity index" was then calculated from measurements of acceleration to determine the helmet's concussion tolerance. The expert concluded that "[h]ad the helmet been properly inflated, the helmet would have sufficiently absorbed the force of the impact, and the injury would have been avoided." *Id.* at 610.

The defendants argued that the tests in question were not substantially similar to the actual accident, a position with which the trial and intermediate court agreed. The Ohio Supreme Court reversed, stating:

> Under the facts presented here, it is virtually impossible to recreate the conditions under which appellant sustained his injuries. Quite obviously, if we were to hold that a test or experiment must exactly recreate the conditions present at the time an injury was sustained, a plaintiff would rarely be able to overcome an opponent's motion for summary judgment. We are unwilling to require such proof. Instead, we agree with [the rationale from prior cases:] Any dissimilarity between the NOCSAE test and the conditions on the football field at the time appellant was injured goes to the weight of the evidence, not to its admissibility.

Id. at 615-616.

4.   As the authors of *Law in the Digital Age* explain, trials are rapidly changing to make use of burgeoning technology. Much of the high-tech testimony is part of experts' overall testimony. The authors of that article ask the reader to "consider some of the ways in which pictures, in contrast to purely verbal communications, can affect legal decision makers' thinking and judgments."

- Pictures of all kinds, still or moving — from diagrams to documentary photography — tend to have a greater impact than non-visual expressions of the "same" information because pictures tend to be more vivid.
- Visual displays can convey more information than words alone and enable viewers to understand more. For example, spatial arrays, graphs, and diagrams can show relationships between data that would remain obscure if the data remained in tabular notational form. Similarly, computer animated reconstructions of events can represent with clarity and precision small but legally significant changes within a given period of time (such as the relative positions and speeds of vehicles prior to a collision). These factual details might remain difficult for a decision maker to imagine and thus harder to understand if left to verbal descriptions alone.
- Photorealistic pictures tend to arouse cognitive and emotional responses similar to those aroused by the real thing. For example, an IMAX movie of a roller-coaster ride can induce vertigo in viewers who would remain unruffled by a verbal description. . . .
- When people take in pictures that look real, they tend to believe that they have gotten all there is to get. Consequently, they are disinclined to pursue the matter further. This sense of communicative efficacy is even stronger in time-based media such as film, video, and computer animation, which offer the eye rapid visual sequences. These tend to

disable critical thinking because viewers are too busy attending to the picture immediately before their eyes to reflect on those that have gone before. As a result, compared to words, visual communications tend to generate less counterargument and hence more confidence in the judgments they support. . . .

- Finally, pictures, more so than words, convey meaning through associational logic, which operates largely subconsciously through its emotional appeal. Thus, a person may be aware that a picture is strongly linked to an emotional response without knowing or understanding what the connection is. And when the emotional underpinnings of judgment remain outside of awareness, they are less susceptible to effective critique and counterargument.

12 B.U. J. Science and Tech., at 241-245. Do these concerns affect your evaluation of the two decisions you just read?

5. Judge Weinstein, a leading commentator on evidence law, discusses the ubiquity and utility of technology in the courtroom in Verizon Directories Corp. v. Yellow Book USA, Inc., 331 F. Supp. 2d 136, 146 (E.D.N.Y 2004) ("The revolution in communicating [in the courtroom] . . . may sometimes be distracting, but it can strengthen the ability of courts to seek truth. . . . In any complex case, computer-generated presentations are the norm rather than the exception."). If Judge Weinstein and the other commentators are correct that technology in the courtroom will continue to grow, what are the implications for expert evidence?

II. ESSENTIAL CONSIDERATIONS FOR ACCIDENT RECONSTRUCTION: FOUNDATION, QUALIFICATIONS, AND SPECULATION

Kumho Tire Co. v. Carmichael

526 U.S. 137 (1999)

[The portions of *Kumho Tire* addressing general admissibility questions are reprinted in Chapter 2, Expert Evidence: Rules and Cases.]

On July 6, 1993, the right rear tire of a minivan driven by Patrick Carmichael blew out. In the accident that followed, one of the passengers died, and others were severely injured. In October 1993, the Carmichaels brought this diversity suit against the tire's maker and its distributor, whom we refer to collectively as Kumho Tire, claiming that the tire was defective. The plaintiffs rested their case in significant part upon deposition testimony provided by an expert in tire failure analysis, Dennis Carlson, Jr., who intended to testify in support of their conclusion.

Carlson's depositions relied upon certain features of tire technology that are not in dispute. A steel-belted radial tire like the Carmichaels' is made up of a "carcass" containing many layers of flexible cords, called "plies," along which (between the cords and the outer tread) are laid steel strips called "belts." Steel wire loops, called "beads," hold the cords together at the plies' bottom edges. An outer layer, called the "tread," encases the carcass, and the entire tire is bound together in rubber, through the application of heat and various chemicals. See generally, e.g., J. Dixon, Tires, Suspension and Handling 68-72 (2d ed.1996). The bead of the tire sits upon a "bead seat," which is part of the wheel assembly. That assembly contains a "rim flange," which extends over the bead and rests against the side of the tire. See M. Mavrigian, Performance Wheels & Tires 81, 83 (1998) (illustrations).

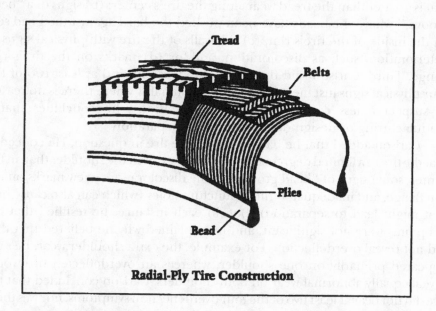

Radial-Ply Tire Construction

Carlson's testimony also accepted certain background facts about the tire in question. He assumed that before the blowout the tire had traveled far. (The tire was made in 1988 and had been installed some time before the Carmichaels bought the used minivan in March 1993; the Carmichaels had driven the van approximately 7,000 additional miles in the two months they had owned it.) Carlson noted that the tire's tread depth, which was 11/32 of an inch when new, App. 242, had been worn down to depths that ranged from 3/32 of an inch along some parts of the tire, to nothing at all along others. He conceded that the tire tread had at least two punctures which had been inadequately repaired.

Despite the tire's age and history, Carlson concluded that a defect in its manufacture or design caused the blowout. He rested this conclusion in part upon three premises which, for present purposes, we must assume are not in dispute: First, a tire's carcass should stay bound to the inner side of the tread for a significant period of time after its tread depth has worn away. Second, the tread of the tire at issue had separated from its inner steel-belted carcass prior to the accident. Third, this "separation" caused the blowout.

Carlson's conclusion that a defect caused the separation, however, rested upon certain other propositions, several of which the defendants strongly dispute. First, Carlson said that if a separation is not caused by a certain kind of tire misuse called "overdeflection" (which consists of under-inflating the tire or causing it to carry too much weight, thereby generating heat that can undo the chemical tread/carcass bond), then, ordinarily, its cause is a tire defect. Second, he said that if a tire has been subject to sufficient overdeflection to cause a separation, it should reveal certain physical symptoms. These symptoms include (a) tread wear on the tire's shoulder that is greater than the tread wear along the tire's center; (b) signs of a "bead groove," where the beads have been pushed too hard against the bead seat on the inside of the tire's rim; (c) sidewalls of the tire with physical signs of deterioration, such as discoloration; and/or (d) marks on the tire's rim flange. Third, Carlson said that where he does not find at least two of the four physical signs just mentioned (and presumably where there is no reason to suspect a less common cause of separation), he concludes that a manufacturing or design defect caused the separation.

Carlson added that he had inspected the tire in question. He conceded that the tire to a limited degree showed greater wear on the shoulder than in the center, some signs of "bead groove," some discoloration, a few marks on the rim flange, and inadequately filled puncture holes (which can also cause heat that might lead to separation). But, in each instance, he testified that the symptoms were not significant, and he explained why he believed that they did not reveal overdeflection. For example, the extra shoulder wear, he said, appeared primarily on one shoulder, whereas an overdeflected tire would reveal equally abnormal wear on both shoulders. Carlson concluded that the tire did not bear at least two of the four overdeflection symptoms, nor was there any less obvious cause of separation; and since neither overdeflection nor the punctures caused the blowout, a defect must have done so.

We further explain the way in which a trial judge "may" consider *Daubert*'s factors by applying these considerations to the case at hand, a matter that has been briefed exhaustively by the parties and their 19 amici. The District Court did not doubt Carlson's qualifications, which included a masters degree in mechanical engineering, 10 years' work at Michelin America, Inc., and testimony as a tire failure consultant in other tort cases. Rather, it excluded the testimony because, despite those qualifications, it initially doubted, and then found unreliable, "the methodology employed by the expert in analyzing the data obtained in the visual inspection, and the scientific basis, if any, for such an analysis." After examining the transcript in "some detail," and after considering respondents' defense of Carlson's methodology, the District Court determined that Carlson's testimony was not reliable. It fell outside the range where experts might reasonably differ, and where the jury must decide among the conflicting views of different experts, even though the evidence is "shaky." In our view, the doubts that triggered the District Court's initial inquiry here were reasonable, as was the court's ultimate conclusion.

For one thing, and contrary to respondents' suggestion, the specific issue before the court was not the reasonableness in general of a tire expert's use of a visual and tactile inspection to determine whether overdeflection had caused the tire's tread to separate from its steel-belted carcass. Rather, it was the reasonableness of using such an approach, along with Carlson's particular method of analyzing the data thereby obtained, to draw a conclusion regarding *the particular matter to which the expert testimony was directly relevant.* That matter concerned the likelihood that a defect in the tire at issue caused its tread to separate from its carcass. The tire in question, the expert conceded, had traveled far enough so that some of the tread had been worn bald; it should have been taken out of service; it had been repaired (inadequately) for punctures; and it bore some of the very marks that the expert said indicated, not a defect, but abuse through overdeflection. The relevant issue was whether the expert could reliably determine the cause of this tire's separation.

Nor was the basis for Carlson's conclusion simply the general theory that, in the absence of evidence of abuse, a defect will normally have caused a tire's separation. Rather, the expert employed a more specific theory to establish the existence (or absence) of such abuse. Carlson testified precisely that in the absence of *at least two* of four signs of abuse (proportionately greater tread wear on the shoulder; signs of grooves caused by the beads; discolored sidewalls; marks on the rim flange), he concludes that a defect caused the separation. And his analysis depended upon acceptance of a further implicit proposition, namely, that his visual and tactile inspection could determine that the tire before him had not been abused despite some evidence of the presence of the very signs for which he looked (and two punctures).

For another thing, the transcripts of Carlson's depositions support both the trial court's initial uncertainty and its final conclusion. Those transcripts cast considerable doubt upon the reliability of both the explicit theory (about the need for two signs of abuse) and the implicit proposition (about the significance of visual inspection in this case). Among other things, the expert could not say whether the tire had traveled more than 10, or 20, or 30, or 40, or 50 thousand miles, adding that 6,000 miles was "about how far" he could "say with any certainty." The court could reasonably have wondered about the reliability of a method of visual and tactile inspection sufficiently precise to ascertain with some certainty the abuse-related significance of minute shoulder/center relative tread wear differences, but insufficiently precise to tell "with any certainty" from the tread wear whether a tire had traveled less than 10,000 or more than 50,000 miles. And these concerns might have been augmented by Carlson's repeated reliance on the "subjective[ness]" of his mode of analysis in response to questions seeking specific information regarding how he could differentiate between a tire that actually had been overdeflected and a tire that merely looked as though it had been. They would have been further augmented by the fact that Carlson said he had inspected the tire itself for the first time the morning of his first deposition, and then only for a few hours. (His initial conclusions were based on photographs.)

Moreover, prior to his first deposition, Carlson had issued a signed report in which he concluded that the tire had "not been . . . overloaded or underinflated," not because of the absence of "two of four" signs of abuse, but simply because "the rim flange impressions . . . were normal." That report also said that the "tread depth remaining was 3/32 inch," *id.*, at 336, though the opposing expert's (apparently undisputed) measurements indicate that the tread depth taken at various positions around the tire actually ranged from .5/32 of an inch to 4/32 of an inch, with the tire apparently showing greater wear along *both* shoulders than along the center, *id.*, at 432-433.

Further, in respect to one sign of abuse, bead grooving, the expert seemed to deny the sufficiency of his own simple visual-inspection methodology. He testified that most tires have some bead groove pattern, that where there is reason to suspect an abnormal bead groove he would ideally "look at a lot of [similar] tires" to know the grooving's significance, and that he had not looked at many tires similar to the one at issue.

Finally, the court, after looking for a defense of Carlson's methodology as applied in these circumstances, found no convincing defense. Rather, it found (1) that "none" of the *Daubert* factors, including that of "general acceptance" in the relevant expert community, indicated that Carlson's testimony was reliable; (2) that its own analysis "revealed no countervailing factors operating in favor of admissibility which could outweigh those identified in *Daubert*"; and (3) that the "parties identified no such factors in their briefs." For these three reasons *taken together*, it concluded that Carlson's testimony was unreliable.

Respondents now argue to us, as they did to the District Court, that a method of tire failure analysis that employs a visual/tactile inspection is a reliable method, and they point both to its use by other experts and to Carlson's long experience working for Michelin as sufficient indication that that is so. But no one denies that an expert might draw a conclusion from a set of observations based on extensive and specialized experience. Nor does anyone deny that, as a general matter, tire abuse may often be identified by qualified experts through visual or tactile inspection of the tire. See Affidavit of H.R. Baumgardner 1-2, cited in Brief for National Academy of Forensic Engineers as *Amicus Curiae* 16 (Tire engineers rely on visual examination and process of elimination to analyze experimental test tires). As we said before, the question before the trial court was specific, not general. The trial court had to decide whether this particular expert had sufficient specialized knowledge to assist the jurors "in deciding the particular issues in the case." 4 J. McLaughlin, *Weinstein's Federal Evidence* ¶702.05[1], p. 702-33 (2d ed.1998); see also Advisory Committee's Note on Proposed Fed. Rule Evid. 702, Preliminary Draft of Proposed Amendments to the Federal Rules of Civil Procedure and Evidence: Request for Comment 126 (1998) (stressing that district courts must "scrutinize" whether the "principles and methods" employed by an expert "have been properly applied to the facts of the case").

The particular issue in this case concerned the use of Carlson's two-factor test and his related use of visual/tactile inspection to draw conclusions on the basis of what seemed small observational differences. We have found no indication in the record that other experts in the industry use Carlson's two-factor test or that tire experts such as Carlson normally make the very fine distinctions about, say, the symmetry of comparatively greater shoulder tread wear that were necessary, on Carlson's own theory, to support his conclusions. Nor, despite the prevalence of tire testing, does anyone refer to any articles or papers that validate Carlson's approach. . . . Indeed, no one has argued that Carlson himself, were he still working for Michelin, would have concluded in a report to his employer that a similar tire was similarly defective on grounds identical to those upon which he rested his conclusion here. Of course, Carlson himself claimed that his method was accurate, but, as we pointed out in *Joiner,* "nothing in either Daubert or the Federal Rules of Evidence requires a district court to admit opinion evidence that is connected to existing data only by the *ipse dixit* of the expert."

Respondents additionally argue that the District Court too rigidly applied *Daubert*'s criteria. They read its opinion to hold that a failure to satisfy any one of those criteria automatically renders expert testimony inadmissible. The District Court's initial opinion might have been vulnerable to a form of this argument. There, the court, after rejecting respondents' claim that Carlson's testimony was "exempted from *Daubert*-style scrutiny" because it was "technical analysis" rather than "scientific evidence," simply added that "none of the four admissibility criteria outlined by the *Daubert* court are satisfied." . . . Subsequently, however, the court granted respondents' motion for reconsideration. It then explicitly recognized that the relevant reliability inquiry "should be 'flexible,'" that its "'overarching subject [should be] . . . validity' and reliability," and that "*Daubert* was intended neither to be exhaustive nor to apply in every case." And the court ultimately based its decision upon Carlson's failure to satisfy either *Daubert*'s factors *or any other* set of reasonable reliability criteria. In light of the record as developed by the parties, that conclusion was within the District Court's lawful discretion.

In sum, Rule 702 grants the district judge the discretionary authority, reviewable for its abuse, to determine reliability in light of the particular facts and circumstances of the particular case. The District Court did not abuse its discretionary authority in this case.

NOTES AND QUESTIONS

1.   What are the specific shortcomings of Carlson's testimony in *Kumho Tire*? Do you think the district court would have abused its discretion if it allowed Carlson to testify? Does application of the *Daubert* factors make sense in a case like this?

2.   The Court notes that "Carlson's conclusions that a defect caused the separation, however, rested upon certain other properties, several of which defendants strongly dispute." In a hearing on admissibility of expert testimony, should the court decide which expert's opinion is more credible?

3.   Carlson testified that the tire was very worn in spots and bald in others. Do you think the district court disbelieved Carlson's opinion that the tire was defective and simply believed the tire was old? If you were to call Carlson as an expert, how would you establish that the method he used was sufficiently reliable? As a more overarching concern, how do experience-based experts prove their methodology is reliable?

Brooks v. Outboard Marine Corporation

234 F.3d 89 (2d Cir. 2000)

Before Van Graafeiland and Katzmann, Circuit Judges, and Jones, District Judge.

Per Curiam:

A tragic accident occurred on June 25, 1996. Theresa Brooks rented a boat from Harry's Bait Shop in Waterport, New York for her 14-year-old son Matthew and his 15-year-old friend Andrew May. Neither boy was old enough to rent the boat or in possession of any certification or license which would allow him to legally do so. After renting the boat, Mrs. Brooks sent the two boys off to fish unsupervised. The owner of the shop also understood that the boys would use the boat unsupervised. Matthew's fishing line soon became entangled with the propeller. The motor was still running but was in neutral so that the propeller itself was not spinning. Matthew wrapped the line around his right hand to get a better grip, and reached into the water to attempt to untangle it. At that time, perhaps due to Matthew's shirt catching on the gearshift, the motor engaged in reverse and Matthew's hand was pulled into the now-spinning propeller and amputated.

William Brooks brought suit on behalf of his son Matthew against the owner of Harry's Bait Shop, Andrew May, and Outboard Marine Corporation ("OMC"), the manufacturer of the motor. Andrew May and Harry's settled with the plaintiff, and the suit continued against OMC under two theories: that the motor was defective and unreasonably dangerous due to the lack of a propeller guard and a defective gearshift mechanism which allowed only minimal pressure to cause the engine to shift into gear.

In February 1998, OMC deposed the plaintiff's expert witness. After the close of discovery on March 31, 1998, the plaintiff requested permission to extend discovery in order to obtain a new expert witness. In the meantime, OMC filed a motion for summary judgment, arguing that the plaintiff's current expert should be precluded from testifying and that summary judgment was proper on the plaintiff's two theories of liability. The motion was referred to the magistrate judge. The plaintiff then filed a curriculum vitae and one-page report of a new expert witness, Robert A. Warren. Mr. Warren's report concluded that either a propeller guard or an emergency motor shut off device, known as a "kill switch,"[2] could have prevented the accident or lessened its severity. After OMC deposed Mr. Warren in June 1998, the plaintiff then filed a response to the pending summary judgment motion. At oral argument, plaintiff's counsel abandoned the "shift mechanism" and "propeller guard" claims, conceding that the only claim on which he would proceed was the new "kill switch" claim. The magistrate recommended denying OMC's motion for summary judgment, finding that it was "premature" because the defendant had not properly responded to the plaintiff's new design defect theory. In addition, the magistrate found it premature to rule on the admissibility of Mr. Warren's testimony, noting that such rulings are usually made on a more complete record. The district court adopted the magistrate's recommendation.

Subsequently Mr. Warren produced a videotape demonstrating how a kill switch works, and also submitted to a second deposition. OMC then filed a second motion, moving pursuant to Fed.R.Evid. 104 for a ruling that Mr. Warren be precluded from testifying and pursuant to Fed.R.Civ.P. 56 for summary judgment. OMC argued that Mr. Warren was unsuited by education or experience to testify about the kind of boat and engine in question, and also that his conclusion that the kill switch would have activated and prevented or lessened the severity of the accident was untested and unsupported by any examination of the actual boat or motor, or the interview of any witnesses. OMC also argued that it was entitled to summary judgment because of certain alleged admissions regarding the kill switch made by Mr. Warren in his deposition.

---

2. A "kill switch" operates by means of a lanyard attached to both the motor and the operator of the boat; when the operator moves more than the length of the lanyard from the motor, as, for example, when the operator is thrown out of the boat, the kill switch automatically shuts off the engine.

The magistrate agreed that Mr. Warren's opinion regarding the kill switch was "unreliable and speculative, and would not assist the jury in its determination of the facts at issue in this case." The magistrate noted inter alia that Mr. Warren had not performed any tests on the actual boat or engine involved in the accident, conducted any interviews with any witnesses, or conducted "any actual testing to determine whether the use of a lanyard-activated kill switch would have disengaged the engine under the circumstances." As a result, the magistrate recommended precluding Mr. Warren from testifying. Without this testimony, the magistrate found that the plaintiff could not make out a prima facie case of a design defect and recommended granting summary judgment. The district court adopted this recommendation over the plaintiff's objections. This appeal followed.

DISCUSSION

We review a grant of summary judgment de novo . . . Brooks makes three principal arguments on appeal. First, he argues that the Supreme Court's recent decision in *Kumho Tire Co., Ltd. v. Carmichael*, 526 U.S. 137, 119 S.Ct. 1167, 143 L.Ed.2d 238 (1999), requires the party challenging the admissibility of its opponent's expert witness to first use its own expert to call the challenged expert's testimony "sufficiently into question." *Id.* at 149, 119 S.Ct. 1167. Only then, contends the plaintiff, can the district court analyze the admissibility of the testimony of the expert witness. This argument is without merit. In *Daubert v. Merrell Dow Pharmaceuticals, Inc.*, 509 U.S. 579, 113 S.Ct. 2786, 125 L.Ed.2d 469 (1993), the Supreme Court instructed that the Federal Rules of Evidence require the trial court to "ensure that any and all scientific testimony or evidence admitted is not only relevant, but reliable." *Id.* at 589, 113 S.Ct. 2786. The subsequent decision in *Kumho Tire* makes clear that this gate-keeping function applies not just to scientific expert testimony as discussed in *Daubert*, but also to testimony based on " 'technical' and 'other specialized' knowledge." *Kumho Tire*, 526 U.S. at 141, 119 S.Ct. 1167 (quoting Fed.R.Evid. 702). The plaintiff's argument that this gate-keeping role disappears when a proposed expert witness is not challenged by an opposing expert witness thus runs counter to the thrust of *Daubert* and *Kumho Tire*. Nowhere in either opinion is there language suggesting that testimony could only be "called sufficiently into question" by a rebuttal expert.

Brooks also argues that the lower court erred in finding that Mr. Warren's testimony was speculative and unreliable. Reviewing this decision under an abuse of discretion standard, . . . it is evident that the district court acted well within its discretion. To note but a few shortcomings of Mr. Warren's testimony: he had never seen the actual boat or motor either in person or in photographs, had never spoken to either of the boys involved in the accident, was unaware of the dimensions of the boat and the placement of the seats in relation to the motor, did not know precisely what happened and where the boys were positioned in the time immediately preceding the accident, and had never attempted to reconstruct the accident and test his theory. The failure to test a theory of causation can justify a trial court's exclusion of the expert's testimony. . . . On appeal, the plaintiff appears to suggest that the videotape represents a test of Mr. Warren's theory, but Mr. Warren made it clear at his second deposition that the videotape was not meant to simulate the actual accident but merely was a "demonstration of how a kill switch would work." As such, it lends no reliability to Mr. Warren's theory.

Having determined that the district court acted within its discretion in excluding Mr. Warren's testimony, the plaintiff has no evidence in the record to support his theory that the motor had a design defect which caused the accident or increased its severity. As a result, summary judgment was properly granted. The judgment of the district court is therefore affirmed.

NOTES AND QUESTIONS

1. The court in this case agreed with the district court that the expert had an insufficient foundation to render an opinion at trial and summary judgment was appropriate. Is the sufficiency of the foundation a question for the judge or the jury? Should the court have allowed the jury to hear the testimony and accord the weight, if any, it deemed appropriate? At a minimum, what should an expert in a products liability case consider in forming an opinion?

2. The court states that "the failure to test a theory of causation can justify a trial court's exclusion of the expert's testimony." Consider this comment as you read other cases.

3. In Zaremba v. General Motors Corp., 360 F.3d 355, 357 (2d Cir. 2004), the driver was killed and passengers injured when their Trans Am, traveling nearly 100 mph, went out of control, rolling over and crashing. Plaintiffs alleged design defects. The court of appeals upheld the trial court's decision to exclude the plaintiffs' alternative design:

> In support of their theories of design defect, plaintiffs intended to call, as expert witnesses at trial, Donald Phillips and Joseph Burton. Phillips, an engineer, would testify as to his reconstruction of the accident and as to an alternative safer design. Burton, a medical doctor and biomechanical expert, would testify that plaintiffs' injuries would not have been so serious if they had been riding in Phillips's alternative design.
>
> GM challenged the testimony by Phillips and Burton as inadmissible, . . . contending that the proffered testimony was not grounded in a reliable methodology. The District Court agreed, holding that plaintiffs had not met their burden of showing that the proffered opinions satisfied Federal Rule of Evidence 702. First, the Court found that Phillips (1) had not examined or tested the Trans Am; (2) had no measurements or calculations to support his theory of how the accident occurred; (3) made no drawing or model

("prototype") of his hypothetical alternative design for a Trans Am; (4) conducted no test of his design; (5) offered no calculations in support of the safety of his design; (6) had not subjected his alternative design to peer review and evaluation; and (7) presented no evidence that other designers or manufacturers in the automobile design community accepted the untested propositions underlying his opinions. The Court concluded that "[e]ssentially the Phillips design has no concrete basis in reality."

With respect to Burton, the Court found that (1) his opinions were speculative because they were based on Phillips's unsupported conjecture of how the accident occurred; (2) Burton could not say with sufficient certainty when during the rollovers and final crash the plaintiffs sustained their injuries, how their bodies moved within the vehicle, or when they were ejected, if ejected in the way Burton described; and (3) Burton was on "even shakier ground" in opining what injuries plaintiffs would have sustained had Phillips's hypothetical alternative design been used.

The District Court concluded that, while Phillips and Burton were "qualified experts in their fields," their testimony was "based on unfounded speculation and [was] unreliable under Daubert principles." After its exclusion of the testimony of plaintiffs' experts, the Court granted summary judgment to defendant.

Do *Brooks* and *Zaremba* suggest that courts are properly drawing the line between inadmissible and "shaky but admissible" evidence? Is the standard too formidable for plaintiffs?

4. In a vehicle accident reconstruction case, Belew v. Nelson, 932 So. 2d 110 (Ala. Civ. App. 2005), one party challenged the opposing party's opinion about the cause of the accident, which rested on a conclusion about skid marks. The expert was a Trooper who testified he saw skid marks. No skid marks were visible in the photographs of the accident scene and the Trooper had testified in a deposition that he did not recall skid marks. Nonetheless, the court held it was proper to admit the testimony, noting "[a]ny weakness in the evidentiary foundation of this testimony was a matter that went to its weight, rather than its admissibility. See Baker v. Edgar, 472 So. 2d 968, 970 (Ala. 1985) ('It is well settled that any challenge to the facts upon which an expert bases his opinion goes to the weight, rather than the admissibility, of the evidence.'")". *Belew*, 932 So. 2d at 116, n.5. Do you agree?

Weisgram v. Marley

169 F.3d 514 (8th Cir. 1999)

Before Bowman, Chief Judge, Bright, and Magill, Circuit Judges.
Bowman, Chief Judge.
Marley Company appeals from the judgment of the District Court, entered upon a jury verdict, awarding damages to Chad Weisgram, individually

and on behalf of the heirs of Bonnie Weisgram, and to State Farm Fire and Casualty Company. We vacate the judgment and remand for entry of judgment as a matter of law in favor of Marley.

I.

On December 30, 1993, at approximately 6:00 a.m., firefighters were called to the town house of Bonnie Weisgram in Fargo, North Dakota, when an off-duty firefighter noticed flames around the front entrance to the home. The front door of the residence was open (although the storm door was closed), notwithstanding the sub-freezing outdoor temperature. Firefighters entered the town house and found Bonnie Weisgram's body lying face down on top of a large, broken mirror, in the upstairs bathroom of the split-entry residence. They also found an open window in Weisgram's upstairs bedroom, which adjoined the bathroom where the body was found. The cover of the smoke detector located in the ceiling of the upstairs hallway had been removed and was found on the carpeted floor of Weisgram's bedroom, where it had been laying since before the fire produced the soot that covered the exposed areas of carpeting. A folding chair was on the floor, folded up, near the detector cover. Upstairs in the living room, an L-shaped sectional sofa was badly damaged by fire in both sections. The back of one section of the sofa was along a metal railing that was open to the entryway and immediately to the right (north) of the entrance at about shoulder level when standing in the entryway; the other section, equally damaged, was along the adjoining (east) wall upstairs. To the left of the entrance, directly in front of the south entryway wall, there was a hole burned through the floor of the entryway. A fifteen-year-old baseboard heater manufactured by Marley had been mounted on that south wall before the fire. There was structural fire damage around the entrance of the town house. The remainder of the residence, including the area downstairs from the entryway, suffered damage from smoke, heat, and water, but no fire damage.

An autopsy determined that Weisgram had died from smoke inhalation, that is, carbon monoxide poisoning, at approximately 2:30 in the morning. There is no dispute that the likely source of the carbon monoxide was the smoldering sofa. Further, Weisgram's blood alcohol level was 0.15, and there was evidence that she had taken a drug that generally is prescribed to relieve pain and as a sleep aid, although it was not clear from the tests whether she took it that night. She was last seen alive at 11:00 p.m. the evening of December 29 by her fiancé, who observed her drink an alcoholic beverage and smoke a cigarette before he left.

[The jury awarded damages to the family of the decedent and Marley filed a motion for judgment as a matter of law (JAML) and a motion for a new trial. Both were denied and Marley appeals.]

We initially consider the plaintiffs' burden of proof in this strict products liability case. In order to prevail under North Dakota law, the plaintiffs were required to prove by a preponderance of the evidence that the heater "was defective in design or manufacture; the defect rendered the product unreasonably dangerous to the consumer; the defect existed when the product left the manufacturer; and the defect was a proximate cause of the [plaintiffs'] injuries."

[W]e hold that JAML should have been granted for Marley. The District Court abused its discretion in allowing certain opinion testimony at trial. Once that testimony is removed from consideration, the evidence properly admitted is insufficient. . . . Marley is entitled to judgment as a matter of law on plaintiffs' claims. . . .

As we explain below, portions of the testimony from three of the plaintiffs' witnesses were unreliable, and the District Court abused its admittedly broad discretion in allowing the suspect testimony. Further, we can say that the errors were not harmless, as they had " 'substantial influence' on the jury's verdict."

A.

We begin with the testimony of Dan Freeman, the Fargo fire captain who arrived with the first fire truck on the scene of the fire at the Weisgram home. He also was the firefighter who did the investigation for the Fargo fire department. Freeman testified that he had considered whether careless smoking might have started the fire in the sofa, but he rejected that possibility because he saw no smoking materials in the home and because he did not think the burn pattern in the sofa indicated that the fire began as the result of careless smoking.[1] He opined that the fire started in the area of the baseboard heater and that "radiated heat . . . ignited the material on the backside of that couch." The sofa was six to eight feet away from the heater at shoulder height and shielded at least partially from any radiated heat or flame by the open front door, which was constructed of insulated steel. The witness then was allowed to testify, over objection, that the fire started because "we had a malfunction of the heater." Notwithstanding Freeman's admission that he was "not an electrical expert" and that he did not "know what happened with the heater," he nevertheless was allowed

1. The testimony of Marley's witnesses advanced this scenario for the cause and origin of the fire: At some time that night, Bonnie Weisgram dropped a lighted cigarette behind a cushion of the sofa, which eventually started a smoldering fire. The smoke detector activated, and Weisgram disabled it. Believing she had doused the fire in the couch, she removed the sofa cushion to the entryway. At some point, she opened the bedroom window and the front door to clear the house of smoke. The cushion and the sofa continued to smolder, producing the smoke and the carbon monoxide that eventually killed Weisgram. Under the influence of the alcohol she had consumed and the sleeping aid she had taken, she was unaware that the fires continued to burn until it was too late. The smoldering cushion in the entryway slowly burned through the floor and eventually caused the flaming fire around the entrance that was spotted at 6:00 a.m.

to testify that he "believe[d] that we had a runaway of that heater." Although Freeman clearly was qualified as a fire cause and origin expert, there is no question that he was not qualified to offer an opinion that the Weisgram heater malfunctioned and he should not have been permitted to do so.

Moreover, Freeman's testimony regarding the events that followed the surmised "runaway" amounted to nothing more than blatant speculation:

> I believe that we ignited nearby combustibles, namely, the, possibly the throw rug or area rug that was on that vinyl floor was very possibly pushed up against that heater. . . . That up against the heater would contain the heat, would trap it, would cause it to build up to the point where you could have had ignition of that cellulose based product [the jute backing on the rug]. . . . In addition to that, the heat build up would start to cause other things to start what we call off gassing. The vinyl floor is going to warm up, the vinyl flooring is stuck to the floor with a glue, a plastic. There are several types on the market but one of them there is an asphalt base type. There is another type . . . ones I have looked into have got products in them that will off gas and ignite such as a naphtha, ethylene glycol. . . . It's a solvent. Basically it's an accelerant. It will off gas [sic] and it will cause vapors to disperse. It will loosen up. Those vapors are going to try to find a way to escape from underneath that vinyl. Normally that would be at the edge of the wall where the vinyl floor meets the wall. I believe the ignition temperature of naphtha is probably somewhere in the neighborhood of 400, 450 degrees. The flash point is considerably lower than that. . . . [B]y flash point I mean it will give off enough vapors to ignite briefly if there is a heat source to ignite.

Now, as a qualified expert in fire investigation, Freeman was free to testify — as he did — that the burn and smoke patterns and other physical evidence indicated that, in his opinion, the fire started in the entryway and radiated to the sofa. Freeman's further testimony, however, was patent speculation, as there was no evidence in the record regarding the location of the throw rug when the fire started, the type of vinyl linoleum on the floor, the glue used some fifteen years prior to secure the vinyl to the underflooring, or the flammability of the vinyl or the glue.[2] While Freeman was qualified to testify that he thought the fire originated in the area of the baseboard heater, we think the court abused its discretion when it permitted Freeman to "run

_____

2. As the individual assigned to investigate the Weisgram fire, Freeman would have been responsible for taking samples of these items for analysis. Nevertheless, he sought only samples of the burned rug from the area around the burn-through in the floor in the entryway (and Freeman had another firefighter retrieve those samples after Freeman left the scene). Freeman had these samples tested for composition and to see whether there was an accelerant present. The only other evidence gathering Freeman did was to take some photographs and to retrieve the burned baseboard heater. It is clear from his testimony that from the very beginning Freeman thought the baseboard heater caused the fire, see, e.g., Trial Tr. of May 20, 1997 (testimony of Dan E. Freeman), at 77-78, 81, which probably explains the limited evidence he collected. State Farm, which also was early on the scene, did not gather any evidence either, as far as we can tell from the record.

away" with his own unsubstantiated theories: that the throw rug somehow blocked the heater, that the rug then ignited, that the heater transferred sufficient heat to the floor so that the adhesive under the vinyl flooring (an adhesive whose composition and other characteristics are unknown) "off gassed," and that the heater radiated enough heat so that those vapors — whatever they were — ignited. Freeman's qualification as a fire investigator did not give him free rein to speculate before the jury as to the cause of the fire by relying on inferences that have absolutely no record support. No foundation was established for Freeman to testify to the extent he did, and the court abused its discretion in allowing the jury to hear this testimony.

B.

Marley also challenges the reliability of the testimony of Ralph Dolence. Within days after the fire, Freeman told Dolence "that we had a fire that appears to have originated in and around an electric baseboard heater" and sent him the remains of the baseboard heater. Dolence testified as a "fire investigator" and "technical forensic expert." As a master electrician in Ohio, he also had experience consulting on electrical fires, although that is irrelevant in this case as there is no contention that the Weisgram fire was electrical. He denied being an "expert electrician" but testified that he was "an electrical expert in electrical things."

Dolence's theory of the fire, not surprisingly, was the same as Freeman's. Dolence never went to the Weisgram town house. As he testified at trial, he drew his conclusions largely from the observations Freeman made at the scene of the fire: "Based on the examination of the heater and the physical evidence that Captain Freeman and I had discussed and the photographs which I interpret as physical evidence, the hole in the floor in my opinion was made by a couple things." Dolence went on to conjecture that a small rug was pushed over two-thirds of the heater, that the heat was "trapped in there and was focused down on to the . . . linoleum," that "volatile vapors from the adhesive come [sic] into the location of the heater," and that "[t]he ignition of those vapors is what caused this fire." And Dolence's basis for his theory? "There is no other explanation. Everything else is ruled out . . . by Captain Freeman." Dolence did no testing to bolster this theory and admitted that he knew of no tests that anyone had conducted to support a similar theory of fire cause and origin. As with Freeman's testimony, there was insufficient foundation for Dolence's testimony; the ostensibly expert opinion testimony he offered was rank speculation.

Dolence noted that the "thermostat or other components" of the heater were destroyed, "in a crumpled mass," and so he did not test them. He nevertheless testified that his theory of how the fire started — runaway heater, off gassing, ignition of vapors — could be true only if the thermostat (designed to shut the heater off at a comfortable room temperature set by the user) failed, followed immediately by the failure of the backup high limit control (designed to shut the heater off when it sensed a temperature of 190 degrees). Therefore, he opined, after fifteen years of operating without incident, both the thermostat and the high limit control suddenly and simultaneously "did not function" to shut the heater off. To be "fair and honest," however, Dolence was compelled to testify that he could not identify what caused the heater to run away and that he had "no idea what caused the thermostat to fail." He also could not determine what caused the high limit control to fail. Finally, he agreed with the proposition that there were no design defects in the heater, in part because, during testing, he could not create a similar overheating episode in the undamaged exemplar Marley heater that had been retrieved after the fire from the adjoining Ferguson town house. He thought there was the possibility of a manufacturing defect in the Weisgram heater, but he had been unable to identify one. Upon examining the contacts[3] of both the thermostat and the high limit control of the Weisgram heater, Dolence testified, "I was bothered by the condition of things I saw on some of this evidence." Therefore he sought the assistance of a metallurgist, but Dolence could offer no opinion of his own about the contacts or what may have caused the presumed failure of the thermostat and the high limit control.

In these circumstances, the District Court abused its discretion by permitting Dolence to testify as an expert witness regarding matters about which he could only speculate. As with Freeman's testimony, there is no reasonable factual basis for Dolence's opinions. Dolence's own testimony attests to the fact that he was offering nothing more than pure conjecture as to whether or not the Weisgram heater was defective. The testimony therefore was unreliable under Rule 702 and should have been excluded.

C.

The metallurgist Dolence contacted was Sandy Lazarowicz. Dolence told Lazarowicz his theory of the fire and asked him to take a look at the Weisgram heater. Lazarowicz examined the thermostat contacts and the high limit control contacts from the heater and studied the same components in the Ferguson heater. He was qualified as an expert in the properties of metals. Admittedly, however, he was not an expert in fire cause and origin, in baseboard heater operation, or in the design or testing of contacts in such a unit.

He testified that the thermostat contacts were defectively designed because they were serrated. The rough surfaces caused arcing and material transfer between the contacts. He theorized that "the continual usage and build up of defects on the surface" of the contacts must have caused them to weld, and that they could not then pull apart (at least not until the heat from

3. When the contacts are closed, that is, touching, the circuit is complete and current flows through the appliance. The circuit is broken — current through the unit is cut — when the contacts are separated, or open.

the fire in the home softened the weld). Thus, he said, there was a closed circuit, the heater did not shut off, and that is why the unit overheated. He formulated his theory knowing practically nothing about the Weisgram heater, or any other baseboard heater for that matter. For example, when he formed his opinions he was unaware of the heater's wattage or the amperage it drew, and therefore could not say if the thermostat contacts could have reached a high enough temperature to melt the metal and to form a weld before the fire. He performed no tests to determine whether it was even theoretically possible that the contacts could get sufficiently hot to weld during operation of the heater. In fact, in his first deposition, Lazarowicz was unable to say for certain that the contacts actually had welded, notwithstanding his examination of them under an electron microscope. Only after closer examination of the contacts from the Ferguson exemplar was he able to see the evidence of welding in the Weisgram contacts. We think the District Court abused its discretion when it permitted this testimony from Lazarowicz.

Further, as we have explained, the heater had a backup system that would prevent it from dangerously overheating even if the heater ran amok because the thermostat failed to shut it off: the high limit control. In order for the heater to be defective in the way the plaintiffs theorize, the high limit control had to fail to shut off the electrical current to the heater at the very same time that the thermostat was failing. Lazarowicz testified that the high limit contacts did not open when the unit was energized (receiving current), but opened only after the fire was well underway. He theorized that this failure may have occurred because the high limit control's temperature sensing mechanism was placed within the unit in a location where it could not detect the actual temperature of the heater.[4] He had metallurgic evidence for the opinion that the contacts did not open while electricity was flowing through the heater (and, in fact, other witnesses noted the same evidence). But he had no metallurgic reason for his conclusion that the device was not properly sensing the temperature, because, of course, that is not a metallurgic issue. Lazarowicz testified that he had performed no tests on the Ferguson exemplar to see if its high limit switch functioned properly, or to determine if in fact there was a defect (in design) in that similar heater. He did not have the necessary experience — either from his work as a metallurgist or from tests performed in connection with this case — to be qualified as an expert who could testify that the high limit control failed because it was defectively designed or manufactured.

---

4. At oral argument, counsel for plaintiffs said the high limit control was not defective and did not fail, but simply did not shut off the heater when it should have. It is not clear to us, then, what the plaintiffs' theory of liability now is. We continue with our analysis, however, under the theory submitted to the jury: strict products liability because of a design or manufacturing defect.

Lazarowicz's opinions amount to no more than "subjective belief or unsupported speculation." Daubert, 509 U.S. at 590, 113 S.Ct. 2786. We conclude that the nexus between his observations of the contacts and his conclusion that the heater was defective is not scientifically sound. He admittedly had very limited experience with electrical contacts in small appliances and no experience with how contacts function in baseboard heaters. "[T]here is simply too great an analytical gap between the data and the opinion proffered." General Elec. Co. v. Joiner, 522 U.S. 136, 118 S.Ct. 512, 519, 139 L.Ed.2d 508 (1997). Therefore, his testimony was unreliable and it was an abuse of discretion to allow it.

D.

We have read very carefully the entire transcript of the trial in this case. Freeman, Dolence, and Lazarowicz were the plaintiffs' only witnesses to testify to the theory of liability on which this case was based: that the baseboard heater was defective in design or manufacture.[5] Neither Freeman nor Dolence was qualified under Rule 702 to testify that the heater was defective, and it was an abuse of the District Court's discretion to allow their testimony to that effect (not to mention their rampant speculation about how the "runaway" heater then might have ignited the fire). Further, Lazarowicz's testimony about the defective thermostat contacts and the placement of the high limit control sensor also was not sufficiently reliable under Rule 702 to have been admitted in evidence. Because these witnesses offered the only evidence of defect, their testimony obviously had a substantial influence on the jury's decision to find Marley strictly liable for damages. Bonnie Weisgram's death in this fire was a tragedy and the damage to the town houses was unfortunate. But if the heater cannot be proven to have been defective when Marley sold it, then under North Dakota law of strict products liability the plaintiffs cannot prevail—even assuming Freeman and Dolence are correct about the off gassing adhesive and the rest of their theory relating to the cause of the fire. Without the testimony at issue, the jury's verdict cannot stand.

The judgment for the plaintiffs is vacated and the case is remanded to the District Court with instructions to grant Marley judgment as a matter of law.

BRIGHT, Circuit Judge, dissenting.

---

5. Dolence testified that the heater was not defectively designed, but that it may have had a manufacturing defect that he simply could not identify. Lazarowicz testified that the defects were in the design of the heater—the serrated contacts on the thermostat and the placement of the high limit control sensor—but he also said there was no design defect in the high limit control. These contradictions from the plaintiffs' own witnesses are yet another indication that the jury reached a finding that the heater was defective only by engaging in speculation.

I dissent. I would deny Marley's motions for a new trial and judgment as a matter of law. The jury verdict has adequate support from properly admitted expert testimony. The plaintiffs' theory of the case relied on the testimony of two properly qualified fire investigators and a properly qualified metallurgist. This testimony provided evidence that the fire originated with the heater and that defects in the thermostat contacts and the placement of the high limit control contributed to the fire. The experts arrived at their conclusions by personally inspecting the evidence from the fire scene using accepted investigative techniques. Although each expert may have testified on matters outside his particular area of expertise, these matters went to the weight and not the admissibility of the testimony. Moreover, the experts' experience lent support to this testimony.

Fire cases differ from most accident cases because fires tend to destroy evidence of causation. As a result, theories about the cause of fires inevitably rest on circumstantial evidence. Arson and insurance cases, as well as product liability cases like this one, require expert evaluations to determine the cause of fires. The courts traditionally permit qualified fire investigators to express opinions on the cause of fires.

For example, in *Talkington v. Atria Reclamelucifers Fabrieken BV (Cricket BV)*, 152 F.3d 254 (4th Cir.1998), a product liability case, the court affirmed a jury verdict for the plaintiffs which rested on the testimony of two fire investigators. The fire investigators discovered the body of a child in close proximity to a cigarette lighter and a sofa. They also conducted a test in which they compared the sofa to a sofa ignited with a cigarette and an open flame. At trial, the investigators testified that the fire occurred because the child ignited the sofa with the cigarette lighter. The court upheld the admission of this testimony. The experts qualified as fire investigators and gave reasoned explanations for rejecting alternative explanations, including the defense theory that a cigarette started the fire.

Similarly, in *Marshall v. Humble Oil & Refining Co.*, 459 F.2d 355 (8th Cir.1972), this court affirmed a jury verdict finding the defendants liable for an explosion in a poorly ventilated gas station storeroom. The plaintiffs contended that the explosion occurred when a spark from an air compressor switch ignited accumulated gas vapors. This theory rested on the discovery of soot in the storeroom after the fire, testimony that the storeroom door was found closed immediately after the explosion, and the fact of the explosion itself. This court held that the plaintiffs presented sufficient evidence of causation even though the compressor switch itself showed no fire damage.

In this case, the jury was required to determine the cause of the fire that killed Bonnie Weisgram in her home. Plaintiffs Weisgram and State Farm argued that a defect in the baseboard heater caused the fire. The court must determine whether the plaintiffs presented reliable evidence of their theory by experts who possessed the necessary qualifications.

The plaintiffs first called Captain Dan Freeman of the Fargo Fire Department. Freeman was the first person to arrive at the fire scene. Freeman testified as a fact witness and to some extent as an expert. Freeman testified that the fire originated in the entryway. Upon arrival, he saw a fire burning on the south side of the entryway. He saw no other fire in the house. After searching for survivors and removing Bonnie Weisgram's body, Freeman began to investigate the cause of the fire. He first considered the sofa as a source of the fire, but discarded that possibility when he inspected the sofa and the surrounding area. The sofa exhibited signs of smouldering combustion but not flaming combustion. Freeman saw no charring on the floor beneath the sofa or damage to the ceiling above the sofa. Furthermore, a piano located within 1 1/2 feet of the sofa remained in good condition. As Freeman continued to investigate, he determined that the fire originated in the entryway and spread to the sofa. The sofa suffered the most damage on its backside, which was exposed to the entryway, and there was charring on the woodwork inches from the backside of the sofa. Freeman testified that a fire strong enough to char the woodwork could have ignited the sofa. Freeman also saw evidence of flaming combustion in the entryway. A two-foot long hole had been burned through the floor underneath the heater and the ceiling above the heater had suffered significant damage.

The plaintiffs next called Ralph Dolence, a professional fire investigator, to testify as an expert witness. Dolence listened to Freeman's description of the fire scene and inspected the heater and photographs of the fire scene. Dolence also inspected and tested an exemplar heater from a nearby house. Dolence testified that the fire originated with the heater. In his opinion, a throw rug pushed up against the heater caused heat to accumulate in and around the heater.[10] The excess heat caused the glue on the vinyl flooring beneath the heater to vaporize and ignite. The fire spread to the walls and ceiling in the entryway and eventually to the sofa in the living room. To support his conclusions, Dolence testified that burn patterns on the heater indicated that it had been partially covered during the fire and that it had been exposed to extreme heat underneath. Dolence also testified that asphalt-based glue used in vinyl flooring has an ignition temperature of approximately 450°. Dolence's testing of the exemplar heater demonstrated that the heater could reach a temperature of 750°.

As their third expert, the plaintiffs called Sandy Lazarowicz, a metallurgist. Lazarowicz had performed failure analysis on the thermostat contacts and had inspected the high limit control. Lazarowicz's testimony provided evidence of defects in the thermostat contacts and the placement of the high limit control that resulted in their failure to shut down the heater at the time of the fire. Lazarowicz testified that the thermostat contacts were welded together at the time of the fire. He testified that serrations on the contact

10. Three frequent visitors to the Weisgram home testified that an entryway throw rug would frequently get pushed up against the heater by the movement of the entryway door.

surfaces and mismatching of the contacts caused electrical arcing and material transfer, which in turn caused the contacts to weld.[11] Lazarowicz also testified that the high limit control did not detect the heat build-up before the fire because it was placed behind a deflector shield.

Freeman and Dolence possessed ample qualifications to testify as experts on the cause of the fire. Freeman was a certified fire investigator and had investigated over 100 fires in addition to completing 400 hours of training in fire and arson investigation. Dolence had been investigating fires for over fifteen years and had directed fire investigation units in two municipalities. While neither Freeman nor Dolence had worked with the type of heater found in the Weisgram home, they both had experience investigating fires caused by heaters and other electrical appliances. Thus, in my view they were qualified to offer opinions on whether the heater caused the Weisgram fire. Dolence possesses particularly relevant qualifications. He is a master electrician who has investigated a number of electrical fires and has written a book on the subject. He was well-qualified to give his opinion that a malfunction in the electrical components of the heater caused the fire. The district court did not abuse its discretion in permitting Freeman and Dolence to testify.

Lazarowicz also possessed sufficient qualifications to testify about defects in the thermostat contacts and high limit control. While Lazarowicz may not have been a specialist in heaters per se, he was a metallurgical engineer and had inspected defective electrical contacts for years as part of his employment. These qualifications made him competent to testify about the post-fire condition of the thermostat contacts and high limit control, which were in essence electrical contacts. The district court did not abuse its discretion in permitting him to testify.

Moreover, even if the plaintiffs' experts lacked specific expertise in heaters, this matter went to the weight and not the admissibility of their testimony. . . .

The majority opinion views the testimony of the plaintiffs' experts as unreliable. Certainly expert testimony must be reliable. Reliability in the context of this case and under Rule 702 relates to the qualifications of the experts, the foundation for their opinions, and their helpfulness to the jury. An expert's opinion should be excluded if it is fundamentally unsupported so that it can offer no assistance to the jury. The plaintiffs' experts based their opinions on personal inspection of the evidence and applying knowledge acquired from training and experience. Their opinions rested on factual

11. Defense experts Michael Phy, Richard Moore, and Vincent Acampora testified that the thermostat contacts showed evidence of electrical arcing and material transfer. Dolence testified that he observed serrations on the surface of the contacts, something he had never seen before even though he had inspected thousands of contacts. Marley's own witness, Richard Moore, likewise testified that he had seen over 1,000 contacts, none with serrations.

support. The district court did not abuse its discretion in determining that their opinions were reliable and could be considered by the jury.

Lazarowicz personally inspected the thermostat contacts and the high limit control. He saw that the surface of the contacts was serrated and that the contacts did not properly connect. He concluded in light of his knowledge and experience that these features contributed to the fire by causing the contacts to weld at the time of the fire. He saw that the high limit control was located behind a deflector shield. He determined, again in light of relevant training and experience, that the high limit control had failed to shut down the heater because the deflector shield prevented it from detecting the heat build-up. When determining whether such evidence is sufficient to support the jury's verdict, the evidence must be viewed in the light most favorable to the plaintiffs, giving them the benefit of all inferences. Lazarowicz's observations of the contact features and the placement of the high limit control provided enough factual support for his opinions to justify submitting the issue of a product defect to the jury.

Freeman and Dolence personally inspected the evidence from the fire scene. Their opinions about the cause of the fire did not lack factual support. The condition of the sofa and the charring in the entryway supported Freeman's and Dolence's determination that the fire originated in the entryway. The charring in the entryway and the hole in the floor supported their determination that the fire originated near the heater. Freeman discovered a partially burned throw rug near the hole. Three frequent visitors to the Weisgram home testified that a throw rug in the entryway was frequently pushed up against the heater. These facts supported the determination that the throw rug was pushed up against the heater and caused heat to build up in the heater. Freeman and Dolence knew that the throw rug and the glue used on vinyl flooring had flashpoints within the range of temperatures produced by baseboard heaters. This knowledge supported their determination that the heat build-up ignited the throw rug and the glue. Dolence knew the heater could not overheat if the thermostat and the high limit control functioned properly. This justified his determination that those parts failed to shut down the heater at the time of the fire.

The plaintiffs' theory of causation depended primarily on circumstantial evidence. However, as discussed earlier, theories of fire causation must rely heavily on circumstantial evidence. There was enough evidence here for a reasonable jury to conclude that the fire originated as Freeman and Dolence testified. The fire investigators saw no other source of heat in the entryway other than the heater and no combustibles were found other than the throw rug and the glue.[12] The district court did not err in submitting the issue of causation to the jury. . . .

12. Freeman had the hole beneath the heater checked for accelerants. None were found.

In sum, the parties presented two reasonable theories about the cause of the fire. The experienced and able trial judge admitted the testimony of the plaintiffs' experts. He also permitted expert witnesses to testify to Marley's theory of the case. A North Dakota jury evaluated the evidence and determined that the plaintiffs should recover damages. As a court, we are only called upon to determine whether the district court abused its discretion in permitting the experts to testify. Had the jury rendered a verdict for Marley, we would not be in a position to say that the district court abused its discretion in admitting the testimony of the defense experts. This controversy represents a typical case to be decided by a jury. This court ought not overturn both the trial judge and the jury. Accordingly, I dissent.

NOTES AND QUESTIONS

1. Were you more convinced by the majority or the dissenting opinion? Why? Is this case a question of qualifications or foundation or both? Is the majority opinion true to the "abuse of discretion" standard?

2. Not all opinions that rely on circumstantial evidence are inadmissible. In DeRosiers v. Flight Intern. of Florida, Inc. 156 F.3d 952 (5th Cir. 1998), the court upheld the decision to admit expert testimony of plaintiff's accident reconstructionist concerning an airplane crash, commenting on the foundation for his opinion. "The record shows that Underwood has extensive experience with instrumentation analysis and electronic equipment. . . . His methodology included extensive review of maintenance records, wreckage, depositions, service manuals, textbooks, and the radar tape. . . . Given the nature of this case — in which direct, physical evidence could yield few clues as to the cause of the crash — the circumstantial evidence Underwood employed was the best information available to reconstruct the accident." *Id.* at 961. Can you distinguish this court's approval of the use of circumstantial evidence to form an opinion from the reasoning in *Marley* that disapproved such use?

3. Cause of fire opinions, as the dissent notes in *Marley,* often pose difficult questions because fire destroys evidence. Should courts be more or less concerned about speculative opinions in cases involving causation of fire? In Pride v. BIC Corp., 218 F.3d 566 (6th Cir. 2000), the decedent went outside to check on a drain pipe and was found thirty minutes later, severely burned. He died from the injuries. Government investigators found no foul play, no leaking gas or any cause for the fire — only pieces of a BIC lighter (decedent was a smoker). Plaintiff's experts, a mechanical engineer, claimed that the lighter was defective and caused the accident. The court excluded the testimony, finding the opinion unreliable, since the expert could not replicate by experiment the explosion and damage he claimed

were caused by the lighter's alleged manufacturing defect. So what was the cause of Mr. Pride's burns?

Scott v. Yates

643 N.E.2d 105 (Ohio 1994)

FRANCIS E. SWEENEY, Sr., Justice.

In this case, we are asked to draw a clear distinction between accident investigation, which involves the collection and recording of information, and accident reconstruction, which involves use of scientific methodology to draw inferences from the investigative data. We decline the invitation to offer hard and fast rules pertaining to this issue. Instead, we confine our discussion to the particular facts at hand. In so doing, we simply find that the police officer testifying here went beyond his scope of expertise. Thus, we determine the trial court abused its discretion in permitting Deputy Hawkins to testify as to which party was at fault. Accordingly, we reverse and remand for a new trial.

To qualify as an expert, the witness need not be the best witness on the subject. The expert must demonstrate some knowledge on the particular subject superior to that possessed by an ordinary juror. A ruling concerning the admission of expert testimony is within the broad discretion of the trial court and will not be disturbed absent an abuse of discretion.

Appellant has no dispute with Hawkins' qualifications to collect data at the accident scene or his ability to testify as to his observations. What appellant urges as error, however, is the admission of Hawkins' opinion as to how the accident occurred. Upon the particular facts in this case, we agree that Hawkins was not qualified to give an opinion on causation.

Here, Deputy Hawkins testified that his highest level of formal education was the twelfth grade. Some time after high school, he attended the police academy for vocational training. There, he spent approximately two weeks on accident investigation.

Hawkins testified he was unfamiliar with the theory of conservation of momentum and consequently did not know how it might affect the post-impact course of motor vehicles involved in a crash. Nor did he know the formula for calculating the speed of motor vehicles, either before or after impact, or what effect speed would have upon the post-impact course of vehicles.

Hawkins testified that there is a difference between investigating an accident, and reconstructing one. He frankly admitted that he was not an accident reconstructionist; that he never had the opportunity to work with an accident reconstructionist; and further, that he had never conducted an accident reconstruction.

Thus, based upon these facts, we conclude the trial court abused its discretion. Because Deputy Hawkins did not possess the necessary knowledge or expertise, his opinion that appellant caused the collision was inadmissible. Accordingly, we reverse the judgment of the appellate court, and remand the cause for a new trial.

WRIGHT, Justice, dissenting.

I respectfully dissent. In my view, there is no way to find an abuse of discretion here, as the officer involved was a veteran accident investigator who testified to nothing more than the point of impact of plaintiff's automobile with that of the defendant.

Under former Evid.R. 702, a witness may qualify as an expert and, therefore, testify as to his opinion if the witness has the requisite "knowlege, skill, experience, training, or education." The majority opinion in this case relies on Hawkins' lack of formal education and simply ignores his specialized training and experience with regard to locating points of impact.

In this case, Deputy Hawkins' experience and training in locating the point of impact between colliding cars gave him "some superior knowledge not possessed by ordinary jurors." While in the police academy, Hawkins' two-week training involving accident investigation consisted of determining who was at fault in an accident, what caused the accident, and which driver to cite for the accident. At the time of the accident, Hawkins had been a police officer and had investigated accidents for twelve years. At the trial, Hawkins testified that he had investigated at least one hundred fifteen accidents per year while working for the Pickaway County Sheriff's Department. More specifically, Hawkins testified that, while with the sheriff's department, he had received specialized training from two supervisors on "point of impact tracking" and the causes of accidents. Hawkins explained that he had been trained to determine the point of impact from such evidence as a car's ultimate resting point after an accident, skid marks, marks through grass, location of debris from the cars, vehicle separation, and other physical evidence such as gouges in the road. In response to a question by the trial judge, Deputy Hawkins expressly stated that his job required him to draw conclusions from accident investigative data concerning "points of impact" about every day.

A trial court does not abuse its discretion unless its decision is "unreasonable, arbitrary or unconscionable." . . . How can anyone seriously suggest that the trial court acted in an arbitrary, unconscionable, or unreasonable fashion in the fact situation posed to it in this case?

Deputy Hawkins testified as to what he observed at the scene. The jury disbelieved the plaintiff and the plaintiff's expert witness and found that plaintiff had crossed the center line prior to impact and was the architect of her husband's death and her own injuries. We should respect the call made by the trial judge and affirm the well-reasoned opinion of the court of appeals.

MOYER, C.J., and A. WILLIAM SWEENEY, J., concur in the foregoing dissenting opinion.

Eskin v. Cardin

842 A.2d 1222 (Del. 2004)

Before VEASEY, Chief Justice, HOLLAND, BERGER, STEELE and JACOBS, Justices, constituting the court en banc. STEELE, Justice:

In this appeal we address for the first time whether biomechanical expert testimony may be admitted in Delaware courts to address the relationship between the physical forces involved in an automobile accident and the cause and severity of an occupant's alleged injuries. In doing so, we take the opportunity to . . . provide guidance to Delaware trial judges who are frequently called upon to consider the admissibility of proffered biomechanical expert testimony.

We hold that trial judges may admit qualified biomechanical expert testimony regarding the physical forces involved in automobile accidents and the effect on the human body those forces may produce where the relevance, reliability and trustworthiness of that testimony is established by the proffer and is not outweighed by the danger of confusion of the issues or misleading the jury. We caution that even competent, qualified biomechanical testimony may not be admissible when that testimony purports to bridge the analytical gap between an engineer's application of constants to, and a physician's artful evaluation of, a specific individual. Competent biomechanical expert testimony may be admissible, however, to impeach factual assumptions made in expert medical testimony, where the medical opinion relies on an injured party's subjective statements about the facts of an accident. Biomechanical evidence may contradict expert medical testimony under some circumstances — e.g., where it purports to quantify the forces exerted on an individual's body during an accident, describe an individual's reaction to the forces involved in the accident, or relies upon principles of physics to rationalize causation, diagnoses, course of treatment or an opinion on permanency. We reaffirm that the long-standing standard of review of abuse of discretion applies to trial judges' rulings on the admissibility of this testimony.

We follow the holding in *Davis* that, absent facts that are supported by competent expert testimony, counsel may not directly argue to the finder of fact that there is a correlation between the extent of the damage to the vehicles involved in an accident and the cause or severity of personal injuries alleged from that accident.

We conclude, in the case *sub judice*, that the trial judge exercised reasonable discretion by granting a Motion *in Limine* to exclude the proffered testimony of a biomechanical expert. Under the particular circumstances of this case, a trial judge could reasonably conclude that the proffered biomechanical evidence, although superficially relevant, was neither reliable nor validated sufficiently to be deemed trustworthy. What relevance it may have had was, accordingly, outweighed by the danger of misleading or confusing the jury.

I.

On December 3, 1998, Robert Chickadel, and Appellee, Barbara Carden, were involved in a motor vehicle collision. Chickadel struck the rear-end of Carden's vehicle. After the first collision, Chickadel backed his vehicle up, stopped, moved forward, and struck Carden's vehicle again. The accident caused physical damage to both vehicles.

Carden went to the emergency room later that day complaining of a burning sensation in her lower back and tingling in her legs. She was treated and released with prescriptions for pain medication, a steroid and a muscle relaxer. On September 14, 1999, after conservative treatment and therapy had failed, Carden had back surgery. After the lawsuit was filed, the Defendant . . . admitted liability. Consequently, the nature and extent of Carden's alleged injuries were the only issues at trial.

Before trial, Carden moved in limine to exclude the testimony of Lawrence Thibault, D.Sc., a biomechanical expert, whose report proffered the following expert opinions:

(1) The forces, or "loading," of this rear-end collision were insufficient under the principles of physics and engineering to have caused the acute lumbar spine disc herniation to this individual plaintiff;

(2) The loading associated with this collision was less than the loadings associated with everyday activities such as walking, bending, and lifting; and

(3) The loading associated with this collision placed this incident in category AIS-1 (minor transient injuries) of the "Abbreviated Injury Scale" ("AIS") developed in a cooperative effort by the American Medical Association, the Association for the Advancement of automotive Medicine, and the Society of Automotive Engineers.

After a hearing, the trial judge granted Carden's motion to exclude the testimony. The trial judge ruled that Thibault could not testify consistently with the proffer because his opinions had no probative value and were not "tied in" with the admissible medical evidence. The trial judge further ruled that *Davis v. Maute* barred introduction of photographs of Carden's vehicle, because they were not supported by expert testimony that was related to an issue at trial. . . .

We recently held, in *Davis v. Maute*, [770 A.2d 36, 40 (Del. 2002)] that "a party in a personal injury case may not directly argue that the seriousness of personal injuries from a car accident correlates to the extent of the damage to the cars, unless the party can produce competent expert testimony on the issue."

Eskin proffered Thibault's testimony to link "the contention of slight damage to a contention tending to minimize the plaintiff's physical injuries." For that type of proffered testimony to be admitted, the proponent must first present reliable, competent expert testimony relevant to the circumstances of the particular case. Admissible biomechanical testimony bridges the gap between the general forces at work in an accident determined by physical forces analysis (whether it be "physics" or "engineering") and the specific injuries suffered by the particular person who was affected by those forces. The testimony must provide definitive evidence that the physics of a particular accident did (or did not) cause a particular injury to a particular individual. A trial judge must closely scrutinize this testimony to be confident that it is trustworthy, i.e., relevant, reliable and validated. Neither here, nor, we suspect, in most cases, will the issue be the competency of an expert or whether the field of "biomechanics" is a recognized scientific or technical field. The words of an expert qualified to opine within a recognized "field" do not automatically guarantee reliable, and therefore admissible, testimony, however. The inquiry will be whether the expert and the "field of expertise" itself can produce an opinion that is sufficiently informed, testable and in fact verifiable on an issue to be determined at trial. The trial judge must be satisfied that the generalized conclusions of the biomechanical expert are applicable to a particular individual. For example, did the expert consider the effect of pre-existing medical conditions and the unique susceptibility of a particular plaintiff to the injuries claimed? Does the "field" of biomechanical engineering adequately test for these highly individualized characteristics and document verifiable statistical results about which an expert within the field can render a trustworthy opinion in a particular case?

Biomechanics is defined as "the mechanical bases of biological, especially muscular, activity; also: the study of the principles and relations involved."

For purposes of simplicity, we define biomechanics as the study of the effects of forces and motion on the human body. Accordingly, we recognize that an individual demonstrating knowledge, skill, experience, training or education in the field of biomechanics may be qualified to testify generally about how the human body will react to the impact of forces exerted upon it during an automobile accident. The use of applied physics by trained engineers aided by computer simulations, control groups and crash test dummies, does create indicia of reliability and may be relevant and ultimately trustworthy in the circumstances of a given case. We must, however, caution that it is the very predictability and consistency of applied physics that makes biomechanical evidence reliable in some circumstances but not necessarily in others. For example, if the crash test dummy or a member of the control group is replaced with an uniquely susceptible driver, those indicia of reliability become a facade.[10] In different circumstances, this Court has held that unless a "special nexus" i.e., a logical connection, is shown between the evidence of common behavior and the facts of the case, the use of such common behavior evidence can be highly prejudicial. Here, the engineering constants that anchor biomechanical principles are analogous to the "common behavior" that requires a special nexus to the facts. Extrapolating from general biomechanical principles to demonstrative evidence that supports or disproves injury to an individual may not be reliable in every case.[12] We, therefore, hold that a trial judge may admit biomechanical expert opinion that a particular injury did (or did not) result from the forces of an accident only where the trial judge determines that the testimony reliably creates a connection between the reaction of the human body generally to the forces generated by the accident and the specific

10. Support for this assertion is found, ironically, in a case also involving Dr. Thibault's biomechanical testimony. *Suanez v. Egeland*, 353 N.J.Super. 191, 801 A.2d 1186, 1193 (*citing Suanez v. Egeland*, 330 N.J.Super. at 194, 749 A.2d 372 (App.Div.2000)) ("These lengthy excerpts from Thibault's testimony show that he did not identify any scholarly literature which shows the reliability of his purported expert opinion that the subject automobile accident could not possibly have caused plaintiff to suffer a herniated lumbar disc. The only specific scientific tests to which Thibault referred were performed either upon cadavers or upon military personnel under controlled conditions quite dissimilar from an automobile accident. Moreover, there is no indication that the persons who performed the tests or others in the scientific community have concluded that they provide a reliable foundation for drawing any conclusions concerning the physiological effects of a low-impact automobile accident upon a middle-aged woman.") *See also* Bruce H. Stern, *Diffusing the Defendant's Biomechanical Engineer Testimony in a Low-Impact Collision Case*, Trial Diplomacy Journal, Vol. 21, 1-7 (1998) at http://www.stark-stark.com/news/articles/ "The majority of low speed accident investigations and studies have used young healthy volunteers with no preexisting spinal deficiencies. West and colleagues used males aged 25-43 who were of normal physical condition for their ages and none of whom had any preexisting spinal deficiencies. Allen used eight healthy subjects, four men and four women, between the ages of 19 and 50 years." (*citing* Szabo T.J., Welcher J.B., Anderson, R.D., Rice M.M., Ward J.A., Paulo L.R. and Carpenter N.J., *Human Occupant Kinematic Response To Low Speed Rear-End Impacts*, SAE Paper 940532 (1994); West D.H., Dough J.P. and Harper G.T.K., *Low Speed Rear-End Collision Testing Used In Human Subjects*, Accident Reconstruction Journal May/June, 1993, 12-28, 22; Allen M.E., Weir-Jones I., Eng P., Motiuk D.R., Flewin K.R., Goring R.D., Kobetitch R. and Broadhurst A., *Acceleration Perturbations of Daily Living—A Comparison to Whiplash*, Spine Vol. 19, No. 11, pp. 1285-1290, 1297 (1994)).

12. "Qualified experts in the field of biomedical engineering or biomechanics are a rare breed. This discipline requires expertise in both mechanical engineering and in medical sciences." Martin A. Conn, *Admissible and Effective Uses of Accident Reconstruction and Biomechanical Evidence*, Journal of Civil Litigation Vol. XIV, No. 4 (Winter 2002-2003) at http://www.morankikerbrown.com/CM/Articles/.

individual allegedly injured or another determinative fact in issue. We now turn to the circumstances of the case sub judice.

When he granted the Motion *in Limine*, the trial judge ruled: "under the circumstances [Dr. Thibault] is out there giving an opinion that doesn't mean anything, doesn't have any probative value one way or the other. It is not tied in with the medical people." Eskin argues that the trial judge misapplied Davis. She insists that neither D.R.E. 702 nor *Davis* requires that biomechanical and medical expert testimony be "tied" together. Essentially, Eskin maintains that the trial judge should have allowed Thibault to testify because he was a qualified biomechanical expert and all that *Davis* requires is "competent expert testimony" consistent with D.R.E 702. Eskin gives the trial judge's understandably brief analysis too little credit. The Court's "tie in with the medical people" reflects far more insight into the issue than the suggested requirement that there be medical opinion confirming or at least consistent with Thibault's view before it can be admitted.

Thibault's proffered opinion was that the physical forces involved in this car accident could not have caused Carden's particular injury. Thibault sought to counter the evidence that the slight forces involved in the automobile accident did in fact cause Carden's injury. His proffered view did attempt to particularize Carden's individual response to the forces at work, by suggesting that no human would have suffered the injury about which she complained (acute lumbar spine disc herniation) given that the minimum "loading" forces at work were consistent with ordinary daily activities such as walking, bending and lifting. Thibault's view, however apparently consistent with others in his "field," made no attempt to take into account the specific personal history of any injured person.

Carden had lower back surgery in April, 1997. In December 1998 she was involved in this automobile accident. She sought medical attention at an emergency room for a burning sensation in her lower back and tingling in her legs. After a regimen of rehabilitation with at least two medical doctors, she sought relief through another back surgery. The physician who performed the surgery opined that the auto accident caused Carden's injury and the course of treatment she had to undergo after December 1998. Carden's physician testified that the accident was 75% responsible for her current condition.[13] Further, the record reveals that Eskin's medical expert agreed that this accident aggravated Carden's pre-existing back injury. Neither physician testified about the forces involved in the accident, nor about how Carden's body may have specifically reacted to those forces. Neither physician relied upon any impeachable assumption about those forces or their effect on Carden's body in forming their opinions that the accident aggravated Carden's pre-existing back injury.

---

13. Carden's doctor explained that the remaining 25% was the result of her pre-existing back problems, including the April 1997 surgery.

The April 1997 surgery both resulted from, and created, a pre-existing medical condition. That highly individualized fact calls into question the reliability of using general biomechanical principles to prove directly that the forces in the accident could not have caused Carden's specific injury. That question is particularly telling here, since both parties' medical experts agreed that this accident aggravated Carden's pre-existing back injury. That fact highlighted the need to examine carefully Thibault's proffer for reliability and to balance its relevance against the danger of confusing or misleading the jury.

Thibault is not a physician and, not surprisingly, he neither reviewed Carden's medical records nor examined her. Thibault did not review any deposition testimony of Carden. He did not question her about the accident itself, or her body position at the time of the collision. His conclusion that her lower back injury could not have been caused by the minor forces involved in the accident plainly did not take into account her particular pre-existing condition and proclivity to further injury. On this record, it is fair to say that Thibault had neither the competency nor the opportunity to consider these idiosyncratic circumstances. No evidence of record suggests that any expert in his field would be competent, or would have taken the opportunity, to do so. Nothing in the record suggests that Thibault or anyone else in the field of biomechanics has performed reliable testing to validate such an opinion if proffered by any expert in this field. As one author has noted: "Sometimes there is a zone of genuine scientific knowledge possessed by a field, but some or many of its members step outside of that zone and make assertions that exceed their field's empirically tested knowledge."[15]

The proponent of the expert scientific or technical testimony must establish its admissibility consistent with the *Cunningham* five step test. Indeed, this is what *Daubert* scrutiny is ultimately all about — to determine whether the testimony is trustworthy. That is, can its reliability be tested to validate it? "Expert testimony" can not be admitted with confidence that it is trustworthy solely because there exists a recognized scientific or technical field in which certain experts are appropriately credentialed. In this particular case, Thibault's testimony, while relevant to the human body generally, could not, without more, shed trustworthy light on the issue of whether the forces of this accident caused Carden's back injury. That is because the proffer did not establish that either Thibault or his "field" had performed tests that would validate the applicability of the general conclusion reached here to a particular "abnormal" human body. His testimony did not identify any percentage deviation from the "norm" or a recurring error rate to compensate for the out-of-the-ordinary person like

---

15. Faigman et al., *Scientific Method: The Logic of Drawing Inferences From Empirical Evidence*, in 1 *Modern Scientific Evidence: The Law and Science of Expert Testimony* § 4-1.1 at 118.

Carden. Accordingly, there could be no assurance that Thibault's conclusion was not more than marginally in error.

For these reasons, the trial judge could properly conclude that there was a danger that the jury would be confused or misled into believing that Carden fell within the "field's" "one-size-fits-all" statistical range.

This risk plainly outweighed the relevance of Thibault's proffered testimony, because his proffered testimony did not create the special connection we require between evidence of common behavior and the facts of a specific case. If admitted, Thibault's testimony, focused on the norm, would have unfairly prejudiced Carden who, all the medical evidence established, did not have a normal, average human body, at the time of the accident. Thibault's testimony did not connect the general biomechanical analysis of the physical forces involved in the accident to the unique medical history that provided the necessary, reliable link to Carden. As one writer has observed: "Scientists draw a sharp distinction between reliability and validity. In *Daubert*, Justice Blackmun took pains to reject that distinction for the law of evidence, and to combine both reliability and validity into what he and many lawyers and judges before him referred to as the reliability of evidence. . . . Validity . . . is the extent to which something measures what it purports to measure."[17]

The jury could fairly rely upon Thibault's testimony to describe the "norm." But that testimony would not validate the norm's applicability to Carden. As a result, Thibault's opinion was not a trustworthy measure of the critical fact at issue: could she have been injured in the collision? Here, we think the trial judge was well within her discretion to acknowledge that Thibault's testimony may have been relevant if what generally happens to the average person were in issue and if Carden fairly represented the average human body. But here, that proffered opinion lacked reliability because there was no evidence that either the expert witness or the "field" had measured the validity of the opinion as it may apply to Carden, given her individual pre-existing deficiencies, or any other potentially "abnormal" human body. The trial judge recognized that: "[w]hile science attempts to discover the universals hiding among the particulars, trial courts attempt to discover the particulars hiding among the universals."[18] The trial judge correctly granted the Motion in Limine.

NOTES AND QUESTIONS

1.   Reconstructing vehicle accidents often proves to be contentious. Questions frequently arise about causation, expert methodology and

17. Faigman et al., *Scientific Method: The Logic of Drawing Inferences From Empirical Evidence*, in 1 Modern *Scientific Evidence:* The Law and Science of Expert Testimony § 4-2.3 at 125-126.

18. David Faigman, *Legal Alchemy: The Use and Misuse of Science in the Law* 69 (1999).

qualification, and the relationship between collisions and injuries. In the preceding cases, which concerns seem to pose the greatest challenge for courts?

2. Many accidents involve questions about whether the accident could have caused the type of injury alleged, as was argued in *Eskin*. As with many areas of expert testimony, there is disagreement both about the required qualifications of the witnesses and the foundation for such opinion. In Marron v. Stromstad, 123 P.3d 992 (Ala. 2004), the defendant wished to introduce James Stirling as an accident reconstruction expert to rebut Plaintiff's testimony suggesting that the accident involved a forceful impact on her car and thus, the accident did not cause her injuries. Plaintiff complained that the witness Stirling "does not have a Bachelor's degree. He has no degree of any kind in engineering. He is not a biomechanic." The court disagreed:

> Stirling's formal training is limited to courses in accident reconstruction, but the record indicates that this coursework was both extensive and highly specialized. Stirling is also a member of several professional societies, is certified by this state as a police instructor in accident reconstruction, and has been working in his field since the late 1970's. By Stirling's estimation, he has assisted in or investigated over 4,500 accidents. The superior court was thus within its discretion in holding that whatever the limitations of Stirling's expertise in determining the force of the accident, "it is a more informed evaluation than could be made by a jury looking at the same evidence without the assistance of an expert." This is fundamentally all that Alaska Rule of Evidence 702 requires.

Id. at 1003. In *Marron*, however, a neurologist testified as well. The field of biomechanics combines both principles of engineering and medicine. Some parties choose to call both an engineer and a physician. In other cases, parties call biomechanical engineers. Is the Alaska court's holding more reasonable than Ohio's about necessary expert qualification for accident reconstruction? Is experience more important than education?

3. Thibault's opinion was disallowed in another case in New Jersey. *See* Suanez v. Egeland, 801 A.2d 1186, 1189 (N.J. Supr. A.D. 2002) ("Thibault is not a physician or medical researcher. His education and training are in the fields of physics and mechanical engineering, with only basic training in anatomy, physiology and pathology. Moreover, Thibault has not himself conducted or observed tests of low-impact collisions on humans. His knowledge of this subject is derived solely from literature in the field.") The New Jersey court also remarked on the lack of scientific foundation for his opinions:

> [h]e did not identify any scholarly literature which shows the reliability of his purported expert opinion that the subject automobile accident could not possibly have caused plaintiff to suffer a herniated lumbar disc. The only specific scientific tests to which Thibault referred were performed either

upon cadavers or upon military personnel under controlled conditions quite dissimilar from an automobile accident. Moreover, there is no indication that the persons who performed the tests or others in the scientific community have concluded that they provide a reliable foundation for drawing any conclusions concerning the physiological effects of a low-impact automobile accident upon a middle-aged woman. Thibault's further reliance upon unidentified articles by unidentified authors in various international journals did not provide any discernable foundation in scholarly literature for his opinion.

Id. at 1193.

III. CRIME SCENE RECONSTRUCTION

Specialists who reconstruct crime scenes piece together evidence to determine whether and how a crime occurred: A trained officer might look at the bloodstain patterns to determine how a homicide victim was murdered; an arson specialist would look at the scene and conduct tests to determine whether a fire was intentionally set or was the result of an electrical malfunction; a firearms expert could testify about gunpowder residue on the hand of the defendant; and some experts testify about the "profile" of the person who killed the victim. As one might expect, some of these specialties are admitted with little challenge — expert testimony that a window was broken from the inside rather than the outside. Other specialties, such as crime scene profiling, for example, are more commonly the subject of courtroom debate.

State v. Moore

458 N.W.2d 90 (Minn. 1990)

[Defendant was convicted of murder.]

Finally, we consider the admissibility of Gary Kaldun's analysis of the blood splatters in the Moore living room. Defendant argues that the trial court committed reversible error by admitting the evidence because the state failed to qualify Kaldun as an expert, failed to establish that results of blood splatter analysis are generally accepted in the scientific community, and failed to demonstrate that the results of the analysis in this case were reliable. Kaldun's analysis of the blood splatter in the Moores' living room allowed him to testify at trial to the position of Debra Moore's body at the time she was shot. This evidence was important to the jury's finding of first degree murder because it made defendant's version of what happened highly unlikely, if not impossible.

As to Kaldun's qualifications as an expert witness, the sufficiency of an expert's qualifications, like proper foundation, rests within the sound discretion of the trial court. . . . Minn.R.Evid. 702 provides that an expert may be qualified "by knowledge, skill, experience, training, or education." Kaldun served as an expert for two different areas of the trial. First, he testified as to the blood types found in the Moore home, then as to the blood splatters in the Moore living room. Kaldun is a serologist with a bachelor's degree in biology and medical technology, had worked at a hospital for six years before joining the BCA in 1980, and is currently the BCA crime scene coordinator. He has had two additional years of training in serology and has attended FBI training for serology, as well as other classes throughout the country. Kaldun had performed 30 to 35 blood splatter interpretations before this case.

Kaldun testified to his general qualifications, but because he did not give any testimony concerning his training in the specific area of blood splatter interpretation, defendant contends that admission of the blood splatter interpretation was an error. The state argues that because Kaldun is a trained serologist who has performed many splatter test interpretations in the past, he is qualified to testify by virtue of his experience in the field.

This court has taken a liberal approach to the question of an expert's qualifications by virtue of experience. . . . Since Kaldun is a trained blood specialist with over 16 years experience, the last 10 with the BCA, and since he has performed between 30-35 blood splatter interpretations, there was sufficient foundation for the trial court to conclude that by virtue of his training Kaldun was an expert in the area of blood splatter analysis. . . .

This court has not had occasion to address the specific issue of whether blood splatter interpretation is a generally accepted scientific technique within the scientific community. We have, though, on at least five occasions, cited the results of blood splatter interpretations in murder and manslaughter cases. . . . In these five opinions we "implicitly accept[ed] the reliability" of blood splatter interpretation insofar as the opinions cited the results of the blood splatter analysis as support for or against a murder or manslaughter conviction. . . .

The proponent of a scientific test has the burden of demonstrating its reliability. At trial, Kaldun gave the following explanation of the blood splatter interpretation technique:

> During bloodsplattering interpretation we look at the actual droplets of blood that have been shed on a crime scene.
> Blood has characteristics that abide by the law of physics when blood is shed, whether it is from a stabbing, bludgeon or gunshot wound.
> When a drop of blood is shed it undergoes certain patterns. If it is dropped straight up and down and lands on a surface, it will leave a perfectly round pattern.

As the angle increases the blood splatter or droplets of blood as they strike something will become longer or narrower.

There is a mathematical correlation between the length and the width of these blood splatters that can be measured. We can then determine what angle they came in at and by using a set of strings and thumbtacks and large protractor we are able to reconstruct the scenes of crimes many times and actually place people where they were at the time they were injured * * * or shot.

In addition to this explanation, Kaldun testified that blood splatter interpretation was a generally accepted technique within the scientific community. . . . Other jurisdictions have not required a substantial foundation to be laid to establish the overall general acceptance of blood splatter interpretation.[6]

The reasoning is primarily based on the fact that the analysis of blood splatters at a crime scene is not an emerging scientific area like DNA testing or electrophoretic typing. . . . Blood splatter analysis is a simple way for crime scene investigators to determine the position of a victim's body by the placement and formation of the blood splatters at the time the wound was inflicted. It is a narrow application of techniques borrowed from established fields. . . . The state sufficiently established that the results of blood splatter analysis are generally accepted in the scientific as well as the judicial community.

General acceptance and reliability have also been proven by such things as: the existence of training programs for blood splatter interpretation; the existence of organizations for the same; the offering of courses and seminars on the subject and the availability of specialized journals on bloodstain interpretation. . . . In the absence of specific proof at trial that the analysis was reliable and generally accepted by the scientific community, other courts have relied, at least in part, on the general acceptance of blood splatter analysis in the United States at large. . . .

Nevertheless, the state is still required to demonstrate the reliability of a particular test in a given case. . . . Of most concern in this case is not the general acceptance of blood splatter interpretation in the scientific community, but the foundation introduced by the state regarding the reliability of this particular interpretation. A proper foundation for a scientific test requires the "proponent of a * * * test [to] establish that the test itself is reliable and that its administration in the particular instance conformed to

6. Courts have held blood splatter interpretation to be reliable and accepted in the scientific community by recognizing the simplicity and reliability of the scientific principles underlying blood splatter interpretation. Once testimony is introduced concerning the basic principles of blood splatter analysis, and the reliability of the underlying principles is recognized, blood splatter interpretation itself is deemed to be generally accepted and reliable. . . . Similarly, some courts have reached the same conclusion by taking judicial notice of the general reliability of the principles underlying blood splatter interpretation. Because the techniques involved in the analysis are based on the well-settled sciences of chemistry and physics, the reliability of the technique may be appropriate for judicial notice. . . .

the procedure necessary to ensure reliability." . . . "The question of proper foundation is largely one for the discretion of the trial court * * *." . . .

At trial, Kaldun testified that he used approximately 20 blood splatters in the Moore living room to calculate the point of convergence for the gunshot wound. Kaldun testified that the tools needed for the interpretation were string, thumbtacks, masking tape and anchors to which the string was tied. The state introduced pictures showing Kaldun performing the tests. On the basis of his analysis of the 20 blood splatters in the Moores' living room, he was able to form an opinion concerning the position of Debra Moore's chest at the time she was shot.

The determination of a proper foundation rests within the sound discretion of the trial court (on the evidence presented) including Kaldun's testimony about the general theory behind blood splatter interpretation and his application of the theory when he conducted the tests, the trial court did not abuse its discretion in concluding there was sufficient evidence that the blood splatter analysis in this case was reliable. Therefore, we hold the trial court did not err in admitting evidence based on the blood splatter analysis.

Romano v. State

909 P.2d 92 (Okl. Cr. 1995)

[Defendant was convicted of murder.]

In his eighth proposition of error Appellant argues Captain Bevel improperly commented that Appellant must have been an active participant in the stabbing. He contends this eviscerated his defense and usurped the fact finding function of the jury as to the ultimate fact of Appellant's guilt or innocence. . . . While expert witnesses can suggest the inferences which jurors should draw from the application of specialized knowledge to the facts, opinion testimony which merely tells a jury what result to reach is inadmissible.

Bevel's testimony was based upon his examination of photographs and bloody clothing. In his testimony Bevel indicated the spatters in the photographs and on Appellant's clothing were consistent with the theory that the wearer of the clothes was in very close proximity to decedent and may have participated in the stabbing. We find this portion of Bevel's testimony is not improper expert opinion on the ultimate issue of Appellant's guilt. Rather, it is admissible expert testimony based on facts or data of a type reasonably relied upon by experts in the field of blood spatter analysis when forming opinions. . . . Moreover, on cross examination defense counsel attacked the imprecision of Bevel's analysis and elicited from Bevel that he did not visit the murder scene, did not talk with the medical examiner, did not make a report of his conclusions, did not determine the heights of decedent or either

Appellant or Woodruff, was unable to say with certainty that Appellant was within eighteen to twenty-four inches of decedent, was unable to state that Appellant actually stabbed decedent, and could find the blood spatter evidence and knife wounds consistent with the theory that Woodruff held and stabbed decedent alone. Defense counsel's attempts to expose the imprecision of Bevel's conclusions on cross examination cured any error which may have resulted. *Fox v. State*, 779 P.2d 562, 571–572 (Okl. Cr. 1989). . . .

The testimony to which Appellant most strongly objects came at the very end of Bevel's testimony just before the State rested. The prosecutor's final questions on re-direct examination and Bevel's answers were:

Q. Now with respect to the medium velocity blood spatter that we see on the right sleeve of this garment, State's Exhibit Number 39, is there anything inconsistent with what you see there with this person being the one doing the stabbing?

A. There is nothing inconsistent with that, no, sir.

Q. Is that what you would expect to see if that person had in fact done the stabbing?

A. Yes, sir.

Q. **In your opinion, sir, based upon your education, training and experience and your observation of State's Exhibit Numbers 39, the shirt and 38 the jeans, was the person wearing these garments a passive observer of this stabbing?**

A. **No, sir.**

[Emphasis in original.]

We find Bevel's first two answers, as set forth above, are proper blood spatter expert opinion evidence. Both answers are reasonable inferences drawn from the application of Bevel's specialized knowledge to the facts of this case.

However, Bevel's last response was error because it overstepped the bounds of proper blood spatter expert opinion and constitutes prejudicial personal opinion. As noted above, Bevel's testimony until the last question and answer presented strong circumstantial evidence that Appellant stabbed decedent. Bevel's final answer removed this last inferential step and the jury's fact finding function by effectively telling the jury Appellant murdered decedent. *Compare with Hogan v. State*, 877 P.2d 1157, 1161 (Okl.Cr.1994), *cert. denied*, 513 U.S. 1174, 115 S.Ct. 1154, 130 L.Ed.2d 1111 (1995); *and Fox*, 779 P.2d at 570 (holding blood spatter experts properly testified as to the location, order and method of killings in cases where the experts did not testify to the defendants' role in the crimes). . . . It is one thing to say a defendant is in close proximity to a violent attack and quite another to state definitely a defendant participated in the attack. When this is done, the expert's opinion is effectively transformed from circumstantial to direct evidence. Because Bevel's opinion overstepped the proper bounds of blood spatter evidence his answer constitutes a personal opinion of Appellant's guilt. Bevel's personal opinion does not assist the jury in concluding Appellant stabbed decedent. Further, admission of Bevel's personal opinion is more prejudicial than probative because it carries the substantial weight and credibility of an expert opinion. . . .

In his ninth proposition of error Appellant claims the entirety of Bevel's testimony is inadmissible. He contends, for the first time on appeal, that blood spatter analysis is not a proper subject for expert scientific testimony because it does not pass the Frye test. He argues this Court has never subjected blood spatter analysis to the Frye test to determine whether such testimony is grounded in scientific proof or is generally accepted by the scientific community. He further argues even if blood spatter analysis is a proper subject for expert testimony Bevel was not properly qualified as an expert and failed to properly examine all available evidence. He finally argues that under the admissibility standard of *Daubert v. Merrell Dow Pharmaceuticals, Inc.,* 509 U.S. 579, 113 S.Ct. 2786, 125 L.Ed.2d 469 (1993), Bevel's testimony is inadmissible because his methodology is faulty.

We held blood spatter analysis is a proper subject for expert testimony in *Farris v. State,* 670 P.2d 995, 997-998 (Okl.Cr.1983), and we have consistently upheld this decision. Appellant's first two challenges are without merit. . . .

This Court explicitly abandoned *Frye* and adopted *Daubert* in *Taylor v. State,* 889 P.2d 319, 328-29 (Okl.Cr.1995). However, we will not apply the *Daubert* analysis retroactively to scientific subjects previously accepted as valid for expert testimony. Because Bevel was qualified to testify as a blood spatter expert, any challenge to his examination of exhibits and methodology goes to his credibility and is properly left to the jury to decide what weight to give his testimony. . . . Because the record in the present case supports the jury's conclusion, we will not substitute our findings for those of the jury. . . . Moreover, defense counsel vigorously attacked Bevel's examination of exhibits and his conclusions, thereby placing his methodology at issue.

NOTES AND QUESTIONS

1.   Courts almost unfailingly admit blood spatter expert evidence. For a detailed review of decisions around the country, see Holmes v. State, 135 S.W.3d 178 (Tex. App. 2004) (taking judicial notice of the validity of blood spatter analysis). Although Holmes reviews numerous decisions finding blood spatter expert testimony reliable, generally accepted, or otherwise admissible, few of the cited cases analyze the area substantively. Most decisions simply admit the testimony based on its historical acceptance by courts. *See also* State v. Fry, 126 P.3d 516 (N.M. 2005) (finding testimony reliable).

State v. Stevens

78 S.W.3d 817 (Tenn.), *cert. denied*, 537 U.S. 1115 (2002)

WILLIAM M. BARKER, J., delivered the opinion of the court, in which FRANK
F. DROWOTA, III, C.J., and E. RILEY ANDERSON and JANICE M. HOLDER, JJ., joined.

WILLIAM M. BARKER, J.

The defendant was found guilty by a Davidson County jury of hiring
eighteen year-old Corey Milliken to murder his wife, Sandra Jean Stevens,
and his mother-in-law, Myrtle Wilson. . . . On automatic appeal to this Court,
we affirm and hold as follows: (1) the trial court did not abuse its discretion
in limiting the testimony of defendant's crime scene expert to his analysis of
the evidence at the crime scene. . . .

FACTS

On December 22, 1997, police were dispatched to the defendant's,
William Richard Stevens's, mobile home in Nashville in response to a 911
call made by the defendant and eighteen year-old Corey Milliken. When the
police arrived, they found the murdered bodies of forty-five year-old Sandra
(Sandi) Jean Stevens, the defendant's wife, and seventy-five year-old Myrtle
Wilson, the defendant's mother-in-law. After further investigation, the
police concluded that Corey Milliken was hired by the defendant to kill
the women and to make the murders look like they were committed in
furtherance of a burglary.[1]

The record reveals that the defendant and Milliken had known each
other for approximately one year. Milliken and his then fifteen year-old
brother, Shawn Austin, lived with their mother and step-father three trailers
down from the defendant. Both boys often worked for the defendant, assisting him in his job of putting underskirting on mobile homes. Austin testified
at trial that his brother had a close relationship with the defendant and that
he and his brother spent a lot of their free time at the defendant's trailer.

Austin testified that in the fall of 1997, the defendant approached
both brothers and asked them if they would kill the defendant's ex-wife,
Vickie Stevens. The defendant instructed them to "get a rifle" and shoot
her when she came out of her trailer. He told them that if she were dead, he
would get full custody of his then nine year-old son, John. He would also get
"her car, her trailer and her land."

However, around Thanksgiving, the defendant changed his mind and
offered to pay Milliken and Austin $2,500 apiece if they would instead kill his
current wife, Sandi Stevens, and his mother-in-law, Myrtle Wilson. The
defendant and his wife were having marital problems, and he knew that
another divorce would "wipe him out." He told the boys that he would

---

1. It is undisputed that Milliken killed the victims. He pleaded guilty to first degree
murder shortly before his trial was set to begin and was sentenced to life imprisonment.

get the money either from the proceeds of Ms. Wilson's life insurance policy or from the proceeds of a yard sale. Austin would act as a "lookout," while Milliken killed the victims in their trailer. The defendant preferred that the victims be shot; however, if the boys could not find a gun with a silencer, Milliken was to kill them using a knife. Austin eventually decided that he did not want to be the "lookout," but agreed to provide an alibi for the defendant. He would not be paid for this participation, and therefore the entire $5,000 would be paid to Milliken.

Although the defendant had not yet set a date for these murders, he took great pains in planning and instructing Milliken on exactly how the murders were to take place. For instance, he told Milliken to kill his mother-in-law first because his wife would not hear anything: she kept her door shut and the fan running in her bedroom. He also told Milliken that on the eve of the murders, the trailer would be unlocked, and the burglar alarm would not be set; as an extra precaution, Milliken would be given a key to the trailer.

The defendant further instructed that after Milliken killed the victims, he was to steal certain items, including some of Mrs. Stevens's jewelry, and then "destroy" the trailer to make it look like a robbery had occurred. In fact, he took Milliken on a walk-through of the trailer, and he specified which items were to be stolen, which items were to be "trashed," and which items were to remain untouched, such as "the TV and the dishes and [his] Star Trek collection." . . .

Officers Gary Clements and John Donnelly of the Metro Police Department were the first officers to arrive at the crime scene. After entering the trailer and finding the two bodies, the officers sealed off the crime scene and then began canvassing the area for witnesses and searching the grounds for physical evidence. Officer Clements soon met Corey Milliken in his trailer and started talking to him. During their conversation, he noticed blood spots on Milliken's t-shirt, blood under his nails, and fresh gouge marks on his cheek and wrist. Officer Clements eventually turned Milliken over to detectives for further questioning. Milliken confessed to committing the murders by himself and provided a detailed description of the murders and the crime scene.

Continuing his search for evidence, Officer Clements soon discovered that the underpinning on a nearby trailer had been pulled loose. When he looked under that trailer, he found a green canvas bag. The contents of the bag included the following: a white, blood-stained Miami Dolphins t-shirt; several pieces of jewelry; an eight-inch long butcher knife or kitchen knife; prescription medication lying loosely in the bag; a thirty-five millimeter camera; and a black camera bag.

Detectives Pat Postiglione and Al Gray, members of the Metro Police Department assigned to investigate the homicides, found no sign of forced entry. In fact, aside from the appearance of a struggle "in and about the bed area" in Ms. Wilson's room, the crime scene looked, for the most part, "staged." For instance, Detective Gray explained that dresser drawers were pulled open, but nothing in them appeared to be disturbed; clothes were taken out of the closet and dumped onto the floor while still on their hangers; and the Christmas presents were unwrapped, but nothing appeared to have been stolen. Even the Christmas tree looked as if it were "gently pushed over," because none of the glass ornaments were broken or scattered on the floor, which would most likely have happened had there been a struggle. He also testified that certain rooms, which "looked like . . . very valuable area[s] of the trailer," remained undisturbed. Both victims were found lying in their beds. Ms. Wilson was wearing a nightgown, which had been pulled above her waist. Her underwear was on the floor. There was a substantial amount of blood on her body, on the bed, and on several items in the room. Dr. Emily Ward, a pathologist with the Davidson County Medical Examiner's Office, performed autopsies on the victims. Her examination of Ms. Wilson revealed that she died from stab wounds and manual strangulation. Although her stab wounds were relatively superficial and did not pierce any vital organs, they resulted in a considerable amount of lost blood.

Mrs. Stevens was completely nude and left in a "displayed" position, that is, lying on her back with her legs spread apart. She died as a result of ligature strangulation. However, there was blood on her knees, indicating that the murderer had killed Ms. Wilson first and then transferred some blood onto Mrs. Stevens.[4]

There were also pornographic magazines placed around her body, as well as a photo album containing nude photos of the victim, presumably taken by the defendant during their marriage. There was no evidence of blood on these items. . . .

The defense presented evidence of Corey Milliken's sexual infatuation with Sandi Stevens. Shawn Austin testified that his brother told him that the defendant had shown him pictures of his wife in lingerie and in the nude, and that the defendant told Milliken that she wanted to have sex with both of them at the same time. The defense theory was that Milliken committed sexual murder as an act of aggression precipitated by an argument with his mother and step-father the night before the crimes. . . .

As evidence that these murders involved a sexual component, the defense introduced the testimony of crime scene expert, Gregg McCrary. Mr. McCrary testified that the display of pornographic magazines around Mrs. Stevens could "best be interpreted as an attempt to further humiliate or degrade" the victim, which "goes to the motive of a sex crime." He defined a sex crime as primarily a crime of violence in which the perpetrator uses sex to punish, humiliate, and degrade the victim.

---

4. Serology tests determined that the blood on Sandi Stevens's body was consistent with that of Myrtle Wilson.

Based upon the proof as summarized above, the jury found the defendant guilty of two counts of premeditated first degree murder and one count of especially aggravated robbery. . . .

I. Nonscientific Expert Testimony

The defendant first contends that the trial court erred when it refused to allow crime scene investigator, Gregg McCrary, to testify to the behavior and motivation of the offender based on his analysis of the physical evidence found at the crime scene. The defense offered Mr. McCrary's testimony to prove that Milliken committed sexually motivated murder as a violent response to a fight with his mother and step-father just hours before the crime.

In a jury-out hearing, Mr. McCrary testified that he had worked as a special agent for the Federal Bureau of Investigation (FBI) for approximately twenty-five years. During that time, he took several graduate courses in criminal justice, and he received a Master's degree in Psychological Services. He served his last ten years with the FBI in the Behavioral Science Unit, investigating cases and conducting research on violent criminal behavior to improve the operational effectiveness of the law enforcement community. He received basic and advanced training in crime analysis, and he also received training in sex crimes investigations, becoming an FBI expert in this field of law enforcement. Moreover, Mr. McCrary testified that as an FBI agent, he participated in the investigation of over a thousand cases, most of which were "sexually violent" homicides. At the time of the trial, he had retired from the FBI and was currently managing his own consulting business in behavioral criminology.

Mr. McCrary had been contacted by the defense to conduct a criminal investigation of the crime scene in this case. He explained that the FBI used criminal investigative analysis to discern the probable motive of the criminal by analyzing the evidence found at the crime scene "primarily from a behavioral perspective, looking at what the offender has done in the commission of the crime to understand the potential motive for the crime as well."

In this case, Mr. McCrary reviewed the crime scene photos, the medical examiner's report, Mrs. Stevens's diary, and a video tape of the crime scene. However, he specifically asked not to be given any information on the suspect so as to be able to provide an objective analysis. Based on his review of this evidence, Mr. McCrary categorized the crime scene in this case as a "disorganized sexual homicide scene." He explained that in a disorganized scene, the victim and location are known to the offender; . . . there is minimal conversation, a minimal interpersonal conflict—contact between the victim and the offender during the course of the crime. It's usually a blitz attack[9] or a sudden violence that's used. The crime scene is quite sloppy and in great disarray. There is minimal use of restraints. The sexual acts tend to occur after death; so, there is post-mortem injury to the victim . . . indication of post-mortem sexual activity. The body is left at the death scene . . . and is typically left in view. There's a good deal of physical evidence that's — that's left at the scene. And, anytime just a weapon of opportunity that the offender uses, and by that, I mean a weapon that is contained at the scene, uses it and, then, it's not uncommon for the offender to leave that weapon either at or near — near the scene.

Mr. McCrary testified that criminals usually commit disorganized violent crimes as a result of some "precipitating stresser, [or] stressful event" in the criminal's life. Such an event invokes a lot of anger in the offender, and that anger — transferred onto the victim — triggers this violent behavior. Moreover, he stated that it was common in disorganized scenes to find evidence of post-mortem sexual activity, including insertion of a foreign object.

In contrast to his description of a disorganized crime scene, Mr. McCrary testified to the characteristics of a typical contract murder crime scene. Usually, the offender spends very little time at the crime scene. A firearm is normally the weapon of choice, and the "kills are quick [and the offender is] out of there . . . right after the murders are committed." However, he testified that the perpetrator in this case spent a fair amount of time at the crime scene "trashing" the place to make it look like a burglary or a "for profit" motive.[10] Mr. McCrary also testified to the possibility that more than one perpetrator committed these murders based on the use of different murder weapons and the lack of blood transference on several items throughout the trailer.

On cross-examination, Mr. McCrary testified that the FBI had conducted a study to determine the accuracy rate of its crime scene analysis. The results of that study yielded a seventy-five to eighty percent accuracy rate. He presented as further evidence of the reliability of crime scene analysis the FBI's increased number of trained agents in this field from seven to forty. Although Mr. McCrary acknowledged that crime scene analysis "is not hard science where you can do controlled experiments and come up with ratios in all this," he said that "the proof [that] there is validation and reliability in

9. According to Mr. McCrary, a "blitz attack" is "an immediate application of an injurious physical force. . . . [T]he attack is sudden. There is no leading up to the attack." He compared this to those situations in which an argument arises between the victim and the offender that starts with pushing, shoving, slapping, and hitting, and may escalate to a homicide. In a blitz attack, however, "there is none of that antecedent behavior. It starts with the immediate attack on the victim without any — any build up or any of that antecedent behavior."

10. Mr. McCrary defined "staging" as "the purposeful alteration of the crime or crime scene by the offender to provide a false motive for investigators, which will take the focus off that particular killer and onto . . . a non-existent offender."

the process is that it's being accepted. It's being used and the demand is just outstripping our resources to provide it."

At the close of the jury-out offer of proof, the trial court found that Mr. McCrary had demonstrated expertise in his ability to analyze the evidence found at the crime scene, and therefore he was permitted to testify to the staging of the crime scene, to any omissions in the police investigation, and to the possibility that the homicides were committed by more than one offender. However, the court refused to admit any testimony indicating an interpretation of criminal behavior, including Mr. McCrary's description of the characteristics of a typical contract murder crime scene and his opinion regarding what motivated the killer in this case. Although the court deemed such evidence to be "specialized knowledge" and a "tremendous asset as an investigation tool in law enforcement," the court determined that such evidence did not comply with Rule 702 "in terms of substantially assisting the [trier] of fact because there is no trustworthiness or reliability." In its order denying the defendant's motion for a new trial, the trial court stated that it was not "convinced that this type of analysis has been subject to adequate objective testing, or that it is based upon longstanding, reliable, scientific principles."

The Court of Criminal Appeals affirmed the trial court's decision and held that the factors set forth in *McDaniel v. CSX Transportation, Inc.,* 955 S.W.2d 257, 264-65 (Tenn.1997), are applicable not only to scientific evidence, but also to "technical" or "specialized" knowledge as well. . . .

Reliability Determination of Nonscientific Evidence

The testimony at issue in this case, however, is not based on scientific theory and methodology, but rather, is based on nonscientific "specialized knowledge," that is, the expert's experience. *See Simmons v. State,* 797 So.2d 1134, 1151 (Ala.Crim.App.1999) ("Crime-scene analysis, which involves the gathering and analysis of physical evidence, is generally recognized as a body of specialized knowledge."). The trial court correctly reasoned that such nonscientific testimony must still meet the fundamental requirements of relevance and reliability. Indeed, nothing in the language of Rules 702 and 703 suggests that scientific testimony should be treated any differently than expert opinions based on technical or nonscientific specialized knowledge.

In this case, the trial court found that Mr. McCrary's testimony failed to pass the McDaniel test of scientific reliability. The defendant argues that the trial court erred in applying McDaniel in this case because McDaniel applies only to scientific testimony. Mr. McCrary's testimony, on the other hand, was based on his extensive experience as a former agent with the FBI, his training in crime scene analysis, and his personal investigation of over a thousand violent crimes. Consequently, the defendant argues, such testimony, which would have substantially assisted the trier of fact to understand what motivated Milliken to commit these crimes, should have been admitted under Rule 702 simply by virtue of the witness's experience, training, and education.

We agree with the defendant's assertion that not all disciplines are amenable to empirical verification but may nevertheless substantially assist the trier of fact. Consequently, we are reluctant to measure the reliability of expert testimony that is not based on scientific methodology under a rigid application of the *McDaniel* factors.*

However, we are equally reluctant to admit nonscientific expert testimony based on an unchallenged acceptance of the expert's qualifications and an unquestioned reliance on the accuracy of the data supporting the expert's conclusions. . . .

[W]hen the expert's reliability is challenged, the court may consider the following nondefinitive factors: (1) the *McDaniel* factors, when they are reasonable measures of the reliability of expert testimony; (2) the expert's qualifications for testifying on the subject at issue; and (3) the straightforward connection between the expert's knowledge and the basis for the opinion such that no "analytical gap" exists between the data and the opinion offered. Subject to the trial court's discretion, once the evidence is admitted, "it will thereafter be tested with the crucible of vigorous cross-examination and countervailing proof." . . .

Inadmissibility of Behavioral Crime Scene Analysis

Turning to the facts in this case, we cannot conclude that the trial court erred in refusing to admit Mr. McCrary's expert opinion regarding the behavior of the perpetrator of these crimes. This type of crime scene analysis, developed by the FBI as a means of criminal investigation, relies on the expert's subjective judgment to draw conclusions as to the type of individual who committed this crime based on the physical evidence found at the crime scene. Although we do not doubt the usefulness of behavioral analysis to assist law enforcement officials in their criminal investigations, we cannot allow an individual's guilt or innocence to be determined by such "opinion

---

*In *McDaniel*, the Tennessee Supreme Court stated:

Although we do not expressly adopt Daubert, the non-exclusive list of factors to determine reliability are useful in applying our Rules 702 and 703. A Tennessee trial court may consider in determining reliability: (1) whether scientific evidence has been tested and the methodology with which it has been tested; (2) whether the evidence has been subjected to peer review or publication; (3) whether a potential rate of error is known; (4) whether, as formerly required by Frye, the evidence is generally accepted in the scientific community; and (5) whether the expert's research in the field has been conducted independent of litigation.

955 S.W.2d at 265.

evidence connected to existing data only by the ipse dixit" of the expert. Essentially, the jury is encouraged to conclude that because this crime scene has been identified by an expert to exhibit certain patterns or telltale clues consistent with previous sexual homicides triggered by "precipitating stressors," then it is more than likely that this crime was similarly motivated. Indeed, Mr. McCrary himself acknowledged that his analysis involves some degree of speculation, and he further negated the sufficiency of his own analysis when he conceded that each case is "unique" and that criminals are often driven by any number of motives.

Moreover, we find that the FBI's study revealing a seventy-five to eighty percent accuracy rate for crime scene analysis lacks sufficient trustworthiness to constitute evidence of this technique's reliability. Although the frequency with which a technique leads to accurate or erroneous results is certainly one important factor to determine reliability, equally important is the method for determining that rate of accuracy or error. In this case, there is no testimony regarding how the FBI determined the accuracy rate of this analysis. For example, was accuracy determined by confessions or convictions, or both? Even then, the absence of a confession does not indicate the offender's innocence and thus an inaccuracy in the technique. Clearly, the accuracy rate alone, without any explanation of the methodologies used in the study, is insufficient to serve as the foundation for the admission of this testimony.

Therefore, because the behavioral analysis portion of Mr. McCrary's testimony does not bear sufficient indicia of reliability to substantially assist the trier of fact, we conclude that this testimony was properly excluded.

NOTES AND QUESTIONS

1. The prosecution has successfully introduced both expert testimony similar to the defense offered in *Stevens* as well as testimony about the motivation of the perpetrator. *See e.g.,* State v. Patton, 120 P.3d 760 (Kan. 2005) (upholding the trial court's decision to admit testimony from an FBI agent that the crime scene appeared staged); and Simmons v. State, 797 So. 2d 1134 (Ala. 1999) (testimony from a prosecution witness that the killer was sexually motivated and that the killer received sexual gratification was admissible).

2. A crime scene profiler testified in an Ohio murder case that the fire in question, which caused the deaths of defendants' two children, "had all the earmarks of being an 'arson for profit.'" State v. Garcia, 2002 WL 1874535, *5 (Ohio App. 8 Dist.) (unreported). The witness arrived at his conclusion by looking at the "totality of the circumstances surrounding a crime, namely, interviewing witnesses, using informants, investigation of the evidence gathered from the crime scene itself, and any evidence related thereto." While the court held such testimony was improperly admitted because it invaded the province of the jury, such admission did not alter

the outcome of the trial due to the other evidence of guilt. Should witnesses be allowed to testify that a crime scene had indicia of arson for profit? Does such evidence invade the province of the jury or is it helpful to them in deciding facts?

3. McCrary and others are described as "profilers"; law enforcement personnel who attempt to construct profiles about certain categories of criminals, particularly serial murderers. Many of these experts have worked at the FBI Behavioral Science Unit. For further discussion about this form of profiling, see Wayne Petherick, *Criminal Profiling, What's in a Name? Comparing Applied Profiling Methodologies,* 5 J.L. & Soc. Challenges 173 (2003); and a publication of the American Psychology Association at *http://www.apa.org/monitor/julaug04/criminal.html.*

4. Although profiling is a fascinating subject that has been the subject of novels and memoirs, some courts have held such testimony lacks scientific reliability. *See e.g.,* State v. Fortin, 745 A.2d 509 (N.J. 2000). In People v. Mertz, 218 Ill. 2d 1, 72-73 (Ill. 2005), the court stated that "[t]he question of admissibility of profiler testimony in criminal cases has been a matter of some controversy; however, recent decisions by state supreme courts seem to come down on the side of exclusion, at least where the evaluative testimony of the profiler is not supported by evidence of reliable databases and methodologies." The court declined to rule definitively on the subject, finding any potential error was harmless. *See also* Kubsch v. State, 784 N.Ed.2d 905 (Ind. 2003) (disallowing crime scene interpretation evidence). Scientific and legal articles have also critiqued profiling. *See e.g.,* David V. Canter et al., *The Organized/Disorganized Typology of Serial Murderer: Myth or Model,* 10 Psychol. Pub. Pol'y & Law 293 (2004); and D. Michael Risinger, *Three Card Monte, Monty Hall, Modus Operandi & Offender Profiling,* 24 Cardozo L. Rev. 193 (2002).

5. In State v. Fortin, 745 A.2d 509 (N.J. 2000), the profiler, Hazelwood, compared the sexual assault/murder in question (Ms. Padilla) with the prior attack of a police officer (Trooper Gardner), noting a number of points of comparison between the methodology of the two attacks (modus operandi) and then described the ritualistic aspects of the crimes — how the perpetrator sought sexual gratification in the commission of these two crimes and described five points of similarity. Using a "linkage analysis," he determined that the likelihood of different offenders was highly improbable.

The Supreme Court of New Jersey held that such "linkage analysis lacks sufficient scientific reliability to establish that the same perpetrator committed" the two crimes. *Id.* at 525. However, the court held that the profilers could testify about similarities between the murder of the victim in this case and the attack in the other case, stating:

> In all fairness, Hazelwood did not purport to cloak his testimony with a mantra of scientific reliability. He candidly acknowledged that linkage analysis is not a

science, but rather is based on years of training, education, research, and experience in working on thousands of violent crimes over an extended period of time. Such methods have great value for purposes of criminal investigation. We therefore believe that one such as Hazelwood has a proper role in a criminal trial based on his experience as an expert in criminal investigative techniques. Such a witness is qualified to discuss similarities between crimes without drawing conclusions about the guilt or innocence of the defendant. Within that ambit, his testimony can be of assistance to the court and perhaps a jury on the issue of admission of other-crime evidence. Of course, Hazelwood would not be permitted to testify on the ultimate issue of whether the person that assaulted Trooper Gardner is the same person that murdered Melissa Padilla.

Id. at 528-529. This distinction between points of comparison and conclusion is similar to the rulings of some courts in the handwriting comparison cases. Does this ruling resolve the concerns about proof of reliability?

6. In some of these profiling cases (and other expert evidence cases), courts have distinguished between evidence that is based upon experience-based knowledge and evidence that is the product of scientific knowledge. *See e.g.,* Simmons v. State, 797 So. 2d 1134 (Ala. Crim. App. 1999). In State v. Patton, 120 P.3d 760 (Kan. 2005), the court stated

[t]he Frye test does not apply to pure opinion testimony, which is an expert opinion developed from inductive reasoning based on the expert's own experiences, observations, or research. The validity of pure opinion is tested by cross-examination of the witness. . . . The distinction between pure opinion testimony and testimony based on a scientific method or procedure is rooted in a concept that seeks to limit application of the Frye test to situations where there is the greatest potential for juror confusion.

Id. at 783. These courts do not require the proponent to prove that experience-based knowledge meets the *Frye* or *Daubert* standards. Do you agree with this reasoning?

CHAPTER 11

FINAL
CONSIDERATIONS:
ETHICS, DISCOVERY,
PROCEDURE

This final chapter focuses on issues that have been raised but not fully developed in other areas of this casebook. First, it considers the ethical implications of expert testimony and the problems of witnesses testifying less than truthfully.

The second section discusses the pretrial discovery obligations to disclose expert information to the opposition and the resulting imposed sanctions where parties fail to comply. The increased focus on expert testimony has likewise heightened the pretrial disclosure requirements.

The third section of this chapter addresses the appointment of experts for indigent defendants. With the escalating importance of scientific and expert testimony at trial, arranging expert assistance for those without funds has become critical for fair trials.

And finally, the book concludes with some thoughts on how the legal system will adapt to the increased importance of expert testimony. Considering the language from *Daubert* and *Joiner* that suggest approaches to expert testimony, the chapter closes with Justice Breyer's hopeful article about the relationship between science and courts. This final section provides an opportunity for students to think more searchingly about the role experts have in the trial of cases.

I. EXPERTS AND LEGAL ETHICS

Expert Witnesses: Ethics and Professionalism

12 Geo. J. Legal Ethics 465, 467 (1999)
Steven Lubet

It will probably come as no surprise that there are lawyers who will attempt to influence the content of an expert's testimony. After all, advocates want to retain experts for one reason only: to help win the case. Given the effort and expense involved, some lawyers will be tempted to see the expert as simply another member of the litigation team. While expert witnesses will obviously have to work closely with the lawyers who engage them, it is important to maintain a sharp distinction between their roles.

As an advocate in the adversary system, it is a lawyer's job to make the best possible argument in support of her client. A lawyer will often find herself advancing a position in the hope that it will work, without necessarily believing that the view is correct. Lawyers do not testify under oath. While they must be truthful concerning facts and accurate in their representations about the content of the law, their opinions and arguments must always be adapted to the needs of their clients. In the classic formulation of the advocate's duty, Boswell reported that Samuel Johnson did not hesitate to raise arguments that he knew to be weak, saying, "... you do not know it to be good or bad till the judge determines it. ... An argument which does not convince yourself, may convince the judge to whom you urge it: and if it does convince him, why, then Sir, you are wrong and he is right."

Experts, however, have no such latitude. As a witness testifying under oath, an expert is not entitled to state a position "which does not convince yourself" in the hope that it may convince the judge or jury. The entire system of expert testimony rests upon the assumption that expert witnesses are independent of retaining counsel, and that they testify sincerely.

Most lawyers understand and accept this on an intellectual level. Still, in the heat of adversary battle, it is not unknown for lawyers to seek to "extend" or "expand" an expert's opinion in just the right direction. This is wrong. It is no more acceptable for a lawyer to attempt to persuade an expert to alter her opinion than it would be to convince an eyewitness to change his account of the facts.

NOTES AND QUESTIONS

1. The Model Rules of Professional Responsibility form the template for most state ethics' codes. The Rules prohibit the use of testimony that the lawyer knows to be false and permit the lawyer to refuse to introduce most evidence the lawyer reasonably believes is false. See Model Rule 3.3(a) "A lawyer shall not knowingly . . . (3) offer evidence that the lawyer knows to be false. . . . A lawyer may refuse to offer evidence, . . . that the lawyer reasonably believes is false." While few lawyers knowingly offer false evidence, what should the lawyer do when she thinks the expert may be inaccurate or the testimony unreliable? How far should advocates go in determining the reliability of their own expert witness' opinions? See generally, David S. Caudill, *Advocacy, Witnesses, and the Limits of Scientific Knowledge: Is There an Ethical Duty to Evaluate Your Expert's Testimony?*, 39 Idaho L. Rev. 341 (2003) and Jane Campbell Moriarty, *"Misconvictions," Science, and the Ministers of Justice*, 86 Neb. L. Rev. 1 (2007).

Yates v. State

171 S.W.3d 215 (Tex. App. 2005)

SAM NUCHIA, Justice.

Appellant, Andrea Pia Yates, was charged by two indictments with capital murder for the drowning deaths of three of her five children. Rejecting appellant's insanity defense, the jury found her guilty. . . . Following the verdict and before the punishment phase of the trial, appellant learned that the State's expert witness, Dr. Park Dietz, had presented false testimony. Appellant moved for mistrial, but the trial court denied the motion. . . . We reverse and remand.

BACKGROUND

[Appellant was the mother of five children. Throughout her childbearing years, she suffered extensively from depression and psychosis. She was hospitalized for psychiatric treatment on more than one occasion, was prescribed medication for her serious mental illness, and attempted suicide. On the morning of June 20, 2001, she drowned her five children and called police to come to her home.]

At trial, ten psychiatrists and two psychologists testified regarding appellant's mental illness. Four of the psychiatrists and one of the psychologists had treated appellant either in a medical facility or as a private patient before June 20, 2001. They testified regarding the symptoms, severity, and treatment of appellant's mental illness. Five psychiatrists and one psychologist saw appellant on or soon after June 20 for assessment and/or treatment of her mental illness. Four of these five psychiatrists and the psychologist testified, in addition to their observations and opinions regarding appellant's mental illness, that appellant, on June 20, 2001, did not know right from wrong, was incapable of knowing what she did was wrong, or believed that her acts were right.[2]

The tenth psychiatrist, Dr. Park Dietz, who interviewed appellant and was the State's sole mental-health expert in the case, testified that appellant, although psychotic on June 20, knew that what she did was wrong. Dr. Dietz reasoned that because appellant indicated that her thoughts were coming from Satan, she must have known they were wrong; that if she believed she was saving the children, she would have shared her plan with others rather than hide it as she did; that if she really believed that Satan was going to harm the children, she would have called the police or a pastor or would have sent the children away; and that she covered the bodies out of guilt or shame.

On cross-examination, appellant's counsel asked Dr. Dietz about his consulting work with the television show, "Law & Order," which appellant was known to watch. The testimony was as follows:

> Q. Now, you are, are you not, a consultant on the television program known as "Law & Order"?
> A. Two of them.
> Q. Okay. Did either one of those deal with postpartum depression or women's mental health?
> A. As a matter of fact, there was a show of a woman with postpartum depression who drowned her children in the bathtub and was found insane and it was aired shortly before the crime occurred.

The second mention of "Law & Order" came during Dr. Lucy Puryear's testimony. Dr. Puryear, a defense expert witness, was cross-examined by the State regarding her evaluation of appellant. The State specifically asked about her failure to inquire into whether or not appellant had seen "Law & Order." Dr. Puryear testified as follows:

> Q. You know she watched "Law & Order" a lot; right?
> A. I didn't know. No.
> Q. Did you know that in the weeks before June 20th, there was a "Law & Order" episode where a woman killed her children by drowning them in a bathtub, was defended on the basis of whether she was sane or insane under the law, and the diagnosis was postpartum depression and in the

---

2. The fifth psychiatrist in this group, Dr. Melissa Ferguson, testified that she had not made a determination regarding appellant's ability to know whether her actions were wrong. However, she testified that appellant made the statement that, in the context that the children would perish in the fires of hell, [their drowning] was the right thing to do.

> program the person was found insane, not guilty by reason of insanity? Did you know that?
>
> A. No.
>
> Q. If you had known that and had known that Andrea Yates was subject to these delusions, not that she was the subject of a delusion of reference, but that she regularly watched "Law & Order" and may have seen that episode, would you have changed the way you went about interviewing her, would you have interviewed whether she got the idea somehow she could do this and not suffer hell or prison?
>
> A. I certainly wouldn't have asked her that question. No.
>
> Q. Would you have — you didn't have to ask her that question, but you could have explored that?
>
> A. If I had known she watched that show, I would have ask[ed] her about it, yes.

In his final argument at the guilt-innocence phase of the trial, appellant's attorney referred to Dr. Dietz's testimony by stating, "Or maybe even we heard some evidence that she saw some show on TV and knew she could drown her children and get away with it."

The prosecutor, in his final argument, made the following reference to Dietz's testimony about the "Law & Order" episode:

> She gets very depressed and goes into Devereux. And at times she says these thoughts came to her during that month. These thoughts came to her, and she watches "Law & Order" regularly, she sees this program. There is a way out. She tells that to Dr. Dietz. A way out.

After the jury had returned a guilty verdict, appellant's counsel discovered that Dr. Dietz had given false testimony. The producer of "Law & Order" spoke to counsel by telephone and said he could not recall such an episode. An attorney representing the producer, after talking to Dr. Dietz and researching the shows, verified to counsel that there was no show with a plot as outlined by Dr. Dietz. Dr. Dietz acknowledged that he had made an error in his testimony.[3]

Appellant and the State entered into the following written stipulation:

(1) Dr. Park Dietz testified on cross-examination that "As a matter of fact, there was a show of a woman with postpartum depression who drowned her children in the bathtub and was found insane and it was aired shortly before this crime occurred."

(2) Dr. Park Dietz would testify that he was in error and that no episode of "Law & Order" and/or "Law & Order: Criminal Intent" as described above was ever produced for the "Law & Order" television series.

---

3. Dr. Dietz's acknowledgment is not on the record. The record is unclear as to whether it was made to the attorney representing the producer or to appellant's counsel.

Appellant moved for a mistrial based on Dr. Dietz's false testimony, and the trial court denied the motion. Appellant then requested that the stipulation be admitted into evidence and read to the jury. The trial court granted this request. In connection with the stipulation, the trial court, in response to appellant's request, made the following statement to the jury:

> Ladies and gentlemen, during the course of this trial there have been occasions when written stipulations have been introduced for your consideration. . . . While those witnesses that give information which is contained in this stipulation do not physically appear here in court to testify, you must consider the matters which they have indicated in the written stipulation as if they actually appeared in court and give it whatever weight you wish to give to it. So the witness does not have to actually appear in court, but the matters contained in the stipulation are offered into evidence as if they had appeared.

The jury returned verdicts on both charges that at least 10 jurors had a reasonable doubt that appellant would commit criminal acts of violence that would constitute a continuing threat to society.

Motion for Mistrial

[A]ppellant contends that the trial court abused its discretion by denying her motion for mistrial when it was revealed that the State's expert witness had presented false testimony. Appellant argues that Dr. Dietz's testimony was essential to the jury's "guilty" verdict and that his testimony relating to the "Law & Order" episode was the most compelling testimony supporting Dr. Dietz's conclusion that appellant knew right from wrong.

The State recognizes that the State's knowing use of perjured testimony that is likely to materially affect the judgment violates the Due Process Clause of the Fourteenth Amendment of the United States Constitution. . . . The State argues that it did not know that the testimony was false, did not use the false information, and the information was not material. We agree that this case does not involve the State's knowing use of perjured testimony. At the hearing on appellant's motion for mistrial, appellant did not complain that there had been prosecutorial misconduct. . . .

Generally, if a witness has testified to material, inculpatory facts against a defendant and, after the verdict but before a motion for new trial has been ruled upon, the witness makes an affidavit that he testified falsely, a new trial should be granted.[4]

. . . We note that this rule does not require that the State have knowledge that the testimony was false. We review the record to determine

---

4. In our case, Dr. Dietz did not make an affidavit that he testified falsely. However, because the State stipulated that Dr. Dietz would testify that his testimony was in error, there is no credibility issue requiring an affidavit. *See Dougherty v. State*, 745 S.W.2d 107, 107 (Tex. App.-Amarillo 1988), *aff'd*, 773 S.W.2d 320 (Tex.Crim.App.1989) (stating that State was bound by its stipulation).

whether the State used the false testimony and, if so, whether there is a reasonable likelihood that the false testimony could have affected the judgment of the jury.[5]

It is uncontested that the testimony of Dr. Dietz regarding his consultation on a "Law & Order" television show having a plot remarkably similar to the acts committed by appellant was untrue and that there was no "Law & Order" television show with such a plot. The State is bound by its stipulation to these facts. . . . However, the State asserts that it is "very questionable whether it can be said that the trial prosecutors used Dr. Dietz' testimony on cross-examination, especially in light of the fact that it played absolutely no role in the development of Dr. Dietz' conclusion that the appellant knew that her conduct was wrong. . . ."

The record reflects that the State used Dr. Dietz's testimony twice. First, the State used the testimony to cross-examine Dr. Puryear, who had seen appellant for several months while appellant was in the county jail, asking Dr. Puryear whether she knew that appellant watched "Law & Order" and whether she knew that there was an episode with a plot line mirroring appellant's acts. In so doing, the State repeated those facts that were common to appellant's acts and the referenced episode, thus emphasizing those facts already stated by Dr. Dietz. Second, the State connected the dots in its final argument by juxtaposing appellant's depression, her dark thoughts, watching "Law & Order," and seeing "a way out." Thus, the State used Dr. Dietz's false testimony to suggest to the jury that appellant patterned her actions after that "Law & Order" episode. We emphasize that the State's use of Dr. Dietz's false testimony was not prosecutorial misconduct. Rather, it served to give weight to that testimony. . . .

We conclude that the testimony, combined with the State's cross-examination of Dr. Puryear and closing argument, was material. The materiality of the testimony is further evidenced by the fact that appellant's attorney felt compelled to address it in his own closing argument.

The State also asserts that Dr. Dietz did not suggest that appellant used the plot of the show to plan killing her children. Although it is true that Dr. Dietz did not make such a suggestion, the State did in its closing argument.

Five mental health experts testified that appellant did not know right from wrong or that she thought what she did was right. Dr. Dietz was the only mental health expert who testified that appellant knew right from wrong. Therefore, his testimony was critical to establish the State's case. Although

---

5. We recognize that *Ramirez v. State* involved the prosecutor's knowing use of false testimony. 96 S.W.3d 386, 393 (Tex.App.-Austin 2002, pet. ref'd). However, when false testimony is a factor in securing a conviction, the effect is the same, regardless of whether the State used the false testimony knowingly or not. *See Trujillo v. State*, 757 S.W.2d 169, 172 n. 1 (Tex.App.-San Antonio 1988, no pet.) (Cadena, C.J. concurring).

the record does not show that Dr. Dietz intentionally lied in his testimony, his false testimony undoubtedly gave greater weight to his opinion.[6]

[Conviction reversed.]

In the Matter of an Investigation of the West Virginia State Police Crime Laboratory, Serology Division

445 S.E.2d 165 (1994)

MILLER, Justice:

This case is an extraordinary proceeding arising from a petition filed with this Court on June 2, 1993, by William C. Forbes, Prosecuting Attorney for Kanawha County, requesting the appointment of a circuit judge to conduct an investigation into whether habeas corpus relief should be granted to prisoners whose convictions were obtained through the willful false testimony of Fred S. Zain, a former serologist with the Division of Public Safety. . . . On November 4, 1993, after an extensive, five-month investigation, Judge Holliday filed his report with this Court, a copy of which is attached as an Appendix to this opinion. . . .

The report chronicles the history of allegations of misconduct on the part of Trooper Zain, beginning with the wrongful conviction of Glen Dale Woodall, who was eventually released after DNA testing conclusively established his innocence. The report further discusses allegations of misconduct and incompetence by Trooper Zain's subordinates during his tenure with the Division of Public Safety. Finally, the report summarizes the findings of James McNamara, Laboratory Director of the Florida Department of Law Enforcement, and Ronald Linhart, Supervisor of Serology in the Crime Laboratory for the Los Angeles County Sheriff's Department, who were selected by Barry Fisher, Chairman of the Laboratory Accreditation Board of the American Society of Crime Laboratory Directors (ASCLD), to conduct an analysis of the policies, procedures, practices, and records of the Serology Division during Trooper Zain's tenure.

The ASCLD report and the deposition testimony of fellow officers in the Serology Division during Trooper Zain's tenure support the multiple findings of fact by Judge Holliday regarding Trooper Zain's long history of falsifying evidence in criminal prosecutions. Specifically, the report states:

"The acts of misconduct on the part of Zain included (1) overstating the strength of results; (2) overstating the frequency of genetic matches on individual pieces of evidence; (3) misreporting the frequency of genetic

6. On the other hand, had the jury known prior to their deliberations in the guilt-innocence phase of the trial, that Dr. Dietz's testimony regarding the "Law & Order" episode was false, the jury would likely have considered him, the State's only mental health expert, to be less credible.

matches on multiple pieces of evidence; (4) reporting that multiple items had been tested, when only a single item had been tested; (5) reporting inconclusive results as conclusive; (6) repeatedly altering laboratory records; (7) grouping results to create the erroneous impression that genetic markers had been obtained from all samples tested; (8) failing to report conflicting results; (9) failing to conduct or to report conducting additional testing to resolve conflicting results; (10) implying a match with a suspect when testing supported only a match with the victim; and (11) reporting scientifically impossible or improbable results."

The report by Judge Holliday further notes that the ASCLD team concluded that these irregularities were " 'the result of systematic practice rather than an occasional inadvertent error' " and discusses specific cases that were prosecuted in which Serology Division records indicate that scientifically inaccurate, invalid, or false testimony or reports were given by Trooper Zain.

In addition to investigating what occurred during Trooper Zain's tenure in the Serology Division, Judge Holliday also explored how these irregularities could have happened. The report notes that many of Trooper Zain's former supervisors and subordinates regarded him as "pro-prosecution." The report further states: "It appears that Zain was quite skillful in using his experience and position of authority to deflect criticism of his work by subordinates." Although admittedly beyond the scope of the investigation, the report by Judge Holliday notes that there was evidence that Trooper Zain's supervisors may have ignored or concealed complaints of his misconduct. Finally, the report discusses ASCLD criticisms of certain operating procedures during Trooper Zain's tenure, which the report concludes "undoubtedly contributed to an environment within which Zain's misconduct escaped detection." According to the report, these procedural deficiencies included:

"(1) no written documentation of testing methodology; (2) no written quality assurance program; (3) no written internal or external auditing procedures; (4) no routine proficiency testing of laboratory technicians; (5) no technical review of work product; (6) no written documentation of instrument maintenance and calibration; (7) no written testing procedures manual; (8) failure to follow generally-accepted scientific testing standards with respect to certain tests; (9) inadequate record-keeping; and (10) failure to conduct collateral testing."

Judge Holliday's report correctly concludes that Trooper Zain's pattern and practice of misconduct completely undermined the validity and reliability of any forensic work he performed or reported, and thus constitutes newly discovered evidence. . . .

[I]n this case, it matters not whether a prosecutor using Trooper Zain as his expert ever knew that Trooper Zain was falsifying the State's evidence.

The State must bear the responsibility for the false evidence. The law forbids the State from obtaining a conviction based on false evidence.[3] . . .

The matters brought before this Court by Judge Holliday are shocking and represent egregious violations of the right of a defendant to a fair trial. They stain our judicial system and mock the ideal of justice under law. We direct Prosecutor Forbes to pursue any violation of criminal law committed by Trooper Zain and urge that he consult with the United States District Attorney for the Southern District of West Virginia. We direct our Clerk to send all relevant papers to both of them. This conduct should not go unpunished.

This corruption of our legal system would not have occurred had there been adequate controls and procedures in the Serology Division. Judge Holliday's report is replete with the deficiencies and derelictions that existed and as were uncovered by the American Society of Crime Laboratory Directors whose team reviewed the forensic data. To ensure that this event does not recur, we direct the Superintendent of the Division of Public Safety to file with the Clerk of this Court a report outlining the steps that are to be taken to obtain certification of the State Police forensic laboratory by the American Society of Crime Laboratory Directors. We direct that this report be filed within sixty days from the date of the entry of this opinion.

"The American Society of Crime Laboratory Directors, a national association, has established a voluntary Crime Laboratory Accreditation Program in which any crime laboratory may participate in order to demonstrate that its management, operations, personnel, procedures, instruments, physical plant, security, and safety procedures meet certain standards. These standards, which are incorporated into an Accreditation Manual, represent the consensus of the members of ASCLD. For example, the two major requirements for ASCLD/LAB accreditation include (1) periodic, internal case report and case note review and (2) proficiency testing in which blind and/or open samples of which the 'true' results are unknown to the examiner prior to the analysis. State police laboratories which have received ASCLD/LAB accreditation include the Illinois State Police, the Arizona Department of Public Safety, the Washington State Patrol, the Missouri State Highway Patrol, the Michigan State Police, the Oregon State Police, the Texas Department of Public Safety, the North Carolina State Bureau of Investigation, the Virginia Bureau of Forensic Sciences, the Florida Department of Law Enforcement, the Wisconsin State Crime Laboratory, and the Indiana State Police."

---

3. In Miller v. Pate, 386 U.S. 1, 87 S.Ct. 785, 17 L.Ed.2d 690 (1967), the State obtained a conviction based on testimony that certain stains on underwear owned by the defendant matched the victim's blood type. In a subsequent federal habeas corpus case, it conclusively was shown that the stains were paint. The conviction was set aside by a unanimous United States Supreme Court.

NOTES AND QUESTIONS

1.   The first trial of Andrea Yates resulted in a conviction. In the retrial, the jury returned a verdict of not guilty by reason of insanity. How important was Dr. Dietz' testimony?

2.   The problem of crime-lab witnesses testifying falsely is gravely serious — since such testimony may affect hundreds of cases, causing wrongful convictions. "Many, if not most . . . wrongful convictions are attributable to scientific evidence presented by prosecutors as trustworthy, and relied on as such by juries, when if fact the evidence was erroneous or fraudulent." Bennett L. Gershman, *Misuse of Scientific Evidence by Prosecutors*, 28 Okla. City U. L. Rev. 17, 18-29 (2003). For more on the subject of wrongful convictions and legal ethics issues, see Jane Campbell Moriarty, *"Misconvictions," Science, and the Ministers of Justice*, 86 Neb. L. Rev. 1 (2007).

3.   The problem of expert witnesses testifying falsely or in a misleading fashion is one that commentators claim is also common in civil cases. Many expert witnesses receive thousands of dollars (if not hundreds of thousands) to testify. Many experts advertise their services, even publishing the outcomes of trials in their ads. Some experts will testify for only one side in cases (e.g., on behalf of physicians in medical malpractice cases or as part of their job with the FBI). A number of experts do not actually practice in the field in which they claim an expertise. Rather, they make their living solely as experts. What concerns should advocates have about these practices?

4.   For further commentary about the ethical considerations of expert witnesses, also see Michael J. Saks, *Scientific Evidence and the Ethical Obligation of Attorneys*, 49 Clev. St. L. Rev. 421, 423 (2001) (discussing some ethical concerns related to poor-quality forensic evidence); Dick Thornburgh, *Junk Science: The Lawyer's Ethical Responsibilities*, 25 Fordham Urb. L.J. 449 (1998); and Justin P. Murphy, *Note, Expert Witnesses at Trial: Where Are the Ethics?*, 14 Geo. J. Legal Ethics 217 (2000).

II.   DISCOVERY ABOUT EXPERT WITNESSES

Both state and federal rules of procedure allow discovery of expert witnesses in civil and criminal cases. While expert discovery in civil cases is more expansive than in criminal cases, the Federal Rules of Criminal Procedure have enhanced the provisions, requiring for greater disclosure by the parties. This section of the chapter contains the federal rules governing discovery and considers the sanctions imposed when parties fail to comply with the rules.

Rule 26 of the Federal Rules of Civil Procedure governs the discovery of expert testimony and provides, in part:

(a) (E) (2) Disclosure of Expert Testimony.

(A) In addition to the disclosures required by paragraph (1), a party shall disclose to other parties the identity of any person who may be used at trial to present evidence under Rules 702, 703, or 705 of the Federal Rules of Evidence.

(B) Except as otherwise stipulated or directed by the court, this disclosure shall, with respect to a witness who is retained or specially employed to provide expert testimony in the case or whose duties as an employee of the party regularly involve giving expert testimony, be accompanied by a written report prepared and signed by the witness. The report shall contain a complete statement of all opinions to be expressed and the basis and reasons therefor; the data or other information considered by the witness in forming the opinions; any exhibits to be used as a summary of or support for the opinions; the qualifications of the witness, including a list of all publications authored by the witness within the preceding ten years; the compensation to be paid for the study and testimony; and a listing of any other cases in which the witness has testified as an expert at trial or by deposition within the preceding four years.

(C) These disclosures shall be made at the times and in the sequence directed by the court. In the absence of other directions from the court or stipulation by the parties, the disclosures shall be made at least 90 days before the trial date or the date the case is to be ready for trial or, if the evidence is intended solely to contradict or rebut evidence on the same subject matter identified by another party under paragraph (2)(B), within 30 days after the disclosure made by the other party. The parties shall supplement these disclosures when required under subdivision (e)(1). . . .

(b)(4) Trial Preparation: Experts.

(A) A party may depose any person who has been identified as an expert whose opinions may be presented at trial. If a report from the expert is required under subdivision (a)(2)(B), the deposition shall not be conducted until after the report is provided.

(B) A party may, through interrogatories or by deposition, discover facts known or opinions held by an expert who has been retained or specially employed by another party in anticipation of litigation or preparation for trial and who is not expected to be called as a witness at trial, only as provided in Rule 35(b) or upon a showing of exceptional circumstances under which it is impracticable for the party seeking discovery to obtain facts or opinions on the same subject by other means.

Rule 16 of the Federal Rules of Criminal Procedure governs discovery in criminal matters and provides, with respect to experts:

(a) Government's Disclosure
  (1) Information Subject to Disclosure
    (F) Reports of Examinations and Tests.
    Upon a defendant's request, the government must permit a defendant to inspect and to copy or photograph the results or reports of any physical or mental examination and of any scientific test or experiment if:
      (i) the item is within the government's possession, custody, or control;
      (ii) the attorney for the government knows — or through due diligence could know — that the item exists; and
      (iii) the item is material to preparing the defense or the government intends to use the item in its case-in-chief at trial.
    (G) Expert Testimony.
    At the defendant's request, the government must give to the defendant a written summary of any testimony that the government intends to use under Rules 702, 703, or 705 of the Federal Rules of Evidence during its case-in-chief at trial. If the government requests discovery under subdivision (b)(1)(C)(ii) and the defendant complies, the government must, at the defendant's request, give to the defendant a written summary of testimony that the defendant intends to use under Rules 702, 703, or 705 of the Federal Rules of Evidence as evidence at trial on the issue of the defendant's mental condition. The summary provided under this subparagraph must describe the witness's opinions, the bases and reasons for those opinions, and the witness's qualifications.

(b) Defendant's Disclosure
  (1) Information Subject to Disclosure
    (B) Reports of Examinations and Tests.
    If a defendant requests disclosure under Rule 16(a)(1)(F) and the government complies, the defendant must permit the government, upon request, to inspect and to copy or photograph the results or reports of any physical or mental examination and of any scientific test or experiment if:
      (i) the item is within the defendant's possession, custody, or control; and
      (ii) the defendant intends to use the item in the defendant's case-in-chief at trial, or intends to call the witness who prepared the report and the report relates to the witness's testimony.
    (C) Expert Testimony.
    The defendant must, at the government's request, give to the government a written summary of any testimony that the defendant intends to use

under Rules 702, 703, and 705 of the Federal Rules of Evidence as evidence
at trial if—

       (i) the defendant requests disclosure under subdivision (a)(1)(G)
and the government complies, or

       (ii) the defendant has given notice under Rule 12.2(b) of an intent
to present expert testimony on the defendant's mental condition.

The summary must describe the witness's opinions, the bases and reasons
for these opinions, and the witness's qualifications.

Musser v. Gentiva Health Services

356 F.3d 751 (7th Cir. 2004)

Before POSNER, KANNE, and ROVNER, Circuit Judges.

KANNE, Circuit Judge.

Plaintiffs Mischelle and Michael Musser, parents of the deceased
Maverick Musser, appeal the district court's grant of summary judgment
in favor of the defendant, Gentiva Health Services, in this medical malpractice case. Because the expert medical testimony proffered by the Mussers in
response to the motion for summary judgment was properly excluded as a
sanction under Federal Rule of Civil Procedure 37(c)(1), and because under
Indiana law a prima facie case in medical malpractice cannot be established
without expert medical testimony, we affirm.

I.   HISTORY

Maverick Musser was born prematurely on January 10, 1998, at a gesta-
tional age of approximately twenty-two weeks. Maverick's premature birth
led to serious health problems. He suffered from a condition known as
bronchopulmonary dysplasia, a chronic lung disease commonly associated
with premature birth. Tragically, Maverick spent his entire life either hospitalized or under twenty-four hour nursing care at his home. Maverick died
on August 18, 1999.

The present appeal arises out of a medical malpractice action
brought under Indiana law against the nursing service, Gentiva, that
provided care for Maverick. [Plaintiffs filed a medical malpractice case
against Gentiva, alleging a breach of duty of care. They did not disclose
or identify any witness as an expert and did not exchange or file expert
reports.]

Gentiva moved for summary judgment . . . arguing that the Mussers
could not present any competent evidence on breach of duty. The Mussers,
in response, . . . presented the deposition testimony of nurses . . . as well as
the deposition testimony of [treating physicians]. . . . The Mussers assert

that, in the aggregate, the fact and opinion testimony expressed by these witnesses raises a genuine issue of material fact as to whether Kinzer breached her duty of care through inattention to Maverick prior to his death and incompetence in attempting to revive him.

Countering the Mussers' response, Gentiva sought to strike the expert testimony of those witnesses. Gentiva pointed out that the Mussers had not identified as medical experts any of the witnesses previously deposed. The district court agreed, granted the motion to strike, and upon the Mussers' inability to show breach of duty, entered summary judgment in favor of Gentiva. . . .

A. THE EXCLUSION OF EXPERT TESTIMONY

For failure to disclose any of their witnesses as experts, the district court sanctioned the Mussers by disallowing any expert testimony to counter the motion for summary judgment. . . .

[W]are guided by Federal Rule of Civil Procedure 37(c)(1), the rule relied upon by the district court in excluding the expert testimony. This rule states in pertinent part:

A party that without substantial justification fails to disclose information required by Rule 26(a) . . . is not, unless such failure is harmless, permitted to use as evidence at a trial, at a hearing, or on a motion any witness or information not so disclosed. In addition to or in lieu of this sanction, the court, on motion and after affording an opportunity to be heard, may impose other appropriate sanctions. Fed.R.Civ.P. 37(c)(1). . . .

Thus, the text of Rule 37(c)(1) guides our inquiry into whether the exclusion decision lacked evidence in the record, was based on clearly erroneous factual findings, or was arbitrary. The rule asks whether the sanctioned party had "substantial justification" for the failure to comply with discovery rules and whether the failure to comply is "harmless." Fed.R.Civ.P. 37(c)(1). . . .

1. Expert Disclosure Under Federal Rule of Civil Procedure 26

. . . [A]ll witnesses who are to give expert testimony under the Federal Rules of Evidence must be disclosed under Rule 26(a)(2)(A);[2] only those

---

2. To the extent that this statement contradicts *Richardson v. Consolidated Rail Corp.*, 17 F.3d 213, 218 (7th Cir.1994) ("A doctor is not an expert if his or her testimony is based on . . . observations during [treatment]; if testimony was not acquired or developed in anticipation of litigation or for trial and if the testimony is based on personal knowledge.") (quotations omitted), we note that Richardson was interpreting the pre-1993 Amendment Rule 26. Richardson relied on language in a case, *Patel v. Gayes*, 984 F.2d 214, 218 (7th Cir.1993), also decided before the 1993 Amendment. More importantly, the text of the current Rule 26(a)(2)(A) references the Federal Rules of Evidence to determine what must be disclosed as expert testimony. Expert testimony is designated as such by its reliance

witnesses "retained or specially employed to provide expert testimony" must submit an expert report complying with Rule 26(a)(2)(B). The commentary to Rule 26 supports this textual distinction between retained experts and witnesses providing expert testimony because of their involvement in the facts of the case: a "treating physician, for example, can be deposed or called to testify at trial without any requirement for a written report." Fed.R.Civ.P. 26, cmt. 1993 Amendments, subdivision (a), para (2). All of these disclosures should be in writing, signed by counsel, and served to opposing counsel [and] . . . should be delivered by the deadline for expert disclosures set by the trial judge under Rule 26(a)(2)(C).

The Mussers properly disclosed all of the witnesses they proffered under Rule 26(a)(1)(A). In fact, each of these witnesses was deposed by Gentiva in the regular course of discovery. The district court, however, did not exclude all of the potential testimony of the Mussers' witnesses; it merely found that the witnesses identified by the Mussers should not be permitted to testify as expert witnesses. The district court explained that the error made by the Mussers was in confusing Rules 26(a)(1) and 26(a)(2): "[d]isclosing a person as a witness and disclosing a person as an expert witness are two distinct acts." (Dist. Ct. Op. at 14.) Thus, the witnesses could still testify as fact witnesses, but they could not testify as experts.

The Mussers, however, contend that they did comply with Rule 26(a)(2)(A) because Gentiva was in fact made aware of the identity and records of all of their witnesses, and Gentiva had an opportunity to depose these witnesses as to their opinions. The Mussers assert that it would be a pointless formality to disclose in writing a list of names of persons already known to Gentiva through prior discovery, this time with the designation "expert witness." The Federal Rules of Civil Procedure, however, demand this formal designation, as discussed above. The district court set a specific date (June 1, 2002) for the disclosure of all of the Mussers' expert witnesses. The Mussers failed to comply with this deadline.

Formal disclosure of experts is not pointless. Knowing the identity of the opponent's expert witnesses allows a party to properly prepare for trial. Gentiva should not be made to assume that each witness disclosed by the

---

on "scientific, technical, or other specialized knowledge." Fed.R.Evid. 702. Occurrence witnesses, including those providing "lay opinions," cannot provide opinions "based on scientific, technical, or other specialized knowledge within the scope of Rule 702." Fed.R.Evid. 701. Thus, a treating doctor (or similarly situated witness) is providing expert testimony if the testimony consists of opinions based on "scientific, technical, or other specialized knowledge" regardless of whether those opinions were formed during the scope of interaction with a party prior to litigation. Cf. O'Conner v. Commonwealth Edison Co., 13 F.3d 1090, 1105 n. 14 (7th Cir.1994) (noting that treating physicians are not exempt from the requirements of Federal Rules of Evidence 702 and 703 because "we do not distinguish the treating physician from other experts when the treating physician is offering expert testimony regarding causation").

Mussers could be an expert witness at trial. The failure to disclose experts prejudiced Gentiva because there are countermeasures that could have been taken that are not applicable to fact witnesses, such as attempting to disqualify the expert testimony on grounds set forth in Daubert v. Merrell Dow Pharmaceuticals, Inc., 509 U.S. 579, 113 S.Ct. 2786, 125 L.Ed.2d 469 (1993), retaining rebuttal experts, and holding additional depositions to retrieve the information not available because of the absence of a report. In sum, we agree with the district court that even treating physicians and treating nurses must be designated as experts if they are to provide expert testimony.[3]

2. The Exclusion of Expert Testimony Under Federal Rule of Civil Procedure 37(c)(1)

The exclusion of non-disclosed evidence is automatic and mandatory under Rule 37(c)(1) unless non-disclosure was justified or harmless.... After determining that the Mussers failed to comply with Rule 26(a)(2)(A), the district court appropriately inquired into whether the Mussers had a "substantial justification" for failing to disclose their expert witnesses, and whether the failure was "harmless" to Gentiva. Fed.R.Civ.P. 37(c)(1). After considering these factors, the district court excluded the testimony.

Disclosing a person as a witness and disclosing a person as an expert witness are two distinct acts. Obviously, opposing counsel will question a witness differently (during a deposition or at trial) if the witness has been designated as an expert, and is also provided the opportunity to challenge the expert's qualifications. In the present case, although Gentiva knew that the nurses and doctors were witnesses, Gentiva was deprived of the opportunity to question them as expert witnesses. Gentiva has clearly suffered a harm. Additionally, the Mussers have shown no justification for their failure to designate expert witnesses, other than their erroneous assumption that disclosing a witness is the same as disclosing an expert witness.

The issue, then, is whether the sanction of the exclusion of all the Mussers' expert testimony was one "that a reasonable jurist, apprised of all the circumstances, would have chosen as proportionate to the infraction." ...

The district court did not abuse its discretion in finding that the Mussers lacked substantial justification. A misunderstanding of the law does not

---

3. We need not reach the disputed issue of whether an individual who serves in the capacity of "treating physician" (or any analogous position) may nonetheless be required to submit a report under Rule 26(a)(2)(B). It is clear that there is some expert testimony in the nature of the treating physician's testimony that does not require a report. But some district courts have suggested that if the Rule 26(a)(2)(A) testimony exceeds the scope of treatment and ventures into more general expert opinion testimony, a report may be necessary. [citations omitted]. In this case, we do not rely on the absence of Rule 26(a)(2)(B) reports from the Mussers' proffered experts in deciding that the Mussers violated Rule 26.

equate to a substantial justification for failing to comply with the disclosure deadline. In Sherrod [v. Lingle, 223 F.3d 605, 610 (7th Cir. 2000)], we
reversed the district court's exclusion of medical expert testimony, even
though the final reports were not filed by the deadline set by the court.
223 F.3d at 612-13. There, however, the experts had been designated
as such, preliminary reports had been filed, and both sides had delayed
discovery such that late final reports were justified. Id. at 613. This is not a
case where the disclosure was late by a trivial amount of time. In fact, the
Mussers never attempted to disclose any witnesses as experts until the
defendants moved for summary judgment. Moreover, that the defendant
could have obtained the undisclosed information through its own efforts
does not provide substantial justification. . . . Given the necessity for
expert testimony in medical malpractice cases under Indiana law, . . . the
Mussers should have known that expert testimony was "crucial" to their
case, and "likely to be contested;" in these circumstances, there is not a
substantial justification for failing to disclose experts. . . . The district
court did not abuse its discretion in finding harm to Gentiva. It was the
district court's opinion that, in this particular case, Gentiva was denied the
opportunity to question the witnesses in their expert capacity. This choice
is not outside the range of reasonable options available to the district
court. . . .

By the time the district court ruled on the summary judgment motion
on January 8, 2003, there was less than three months to the March 24, 2003
trial date. If the trial had proceeded as planned (and there had already been
a four-month delay from the original trial date), Gentiva may have had to rely
on depositions conducted without the knowledge that each of the witnesses
would be used as experts. . . . Had the Mussers submitted their list of experts
on June 1, 2002, Gentiva could have taken new depositions of the Mussers'
witnesses, or taken whatever steps it considered necessary to oppose the
expert testimony offered by these witnesses in the original depositions.
Fed.R.Civ.P. 26(b)(4). It is certainly true that the district court could have
rescheduled the date for trial and allowed more time for depositions and
new motions for summary judgment. . . . But it is not an abuse of discretion
to conclude that the additional costs to Gentiva of preparing a new summary
judgment motion and further delay in extending the trial date are not
harmless.

In affirming this judgment, we are mindful of our warning that "[i]n the
normal course of events, justice is dispensed by the hearing of cases on their
merits." . . . We do not hold that a district court should always exclude
evidence in similar factual scenarios; in fact, well-reasoned cases have
come to the opposite result. . . . We urge district courts to carefully consider
Rule 37(c), including the alternate sanctions available, when imposing
exclusionary sanctions that are outcome determinative. In the present
case, however, we affirm the exclusion of expert testimony as an appropriate
exercise of discretion.

NOTES AND QUESTIONS

1. While dismissal of civil cases may be warranted where parties fail to comply with expert discovery, federal judges infrequently dismiss criminal cases or suppress witness testimony where the prosecution does not comply with F. R. Crim. P. 16. See e.g., United States v. Gonzales, 164 F.3d 1285, 1292 (10th Cir. 1999) (exclusion is disfavored because of the public interest in the full disclosure of critical facts at trial); United States v. Tin Yat Chin, 476 F.3d 144 (2d Cir. 2007) (stating it was "regrettable" and "at a minimum, a sharp practice, unworthy of a representative of the United States Government" to fail to disclose its expert until trial. Nonetheless, the court held that providing an extra day for defense to prepare was sufficient, since defendant had its own expert and made no claim at trial that the one day was insufficient); and United States v. Stevens, 380 F.3d 1021 (7th Cir. 2004) (noting that the appropriate sanction is not necessarily exclusion of the evidence). Although it may be in the public interest not to dismiss the case, is it fair to the defendant? A few courts have excluded the government's expert when the prosecution failed to comply with the Rules. See e.g., United States v. Wicker, 848 F.2d 1059 (10th Cir. 1988); United States v. Buchanan, 964 F. Supp. 533 (D. Mass. 1997); and United States v. Taylor, 71 F. Supp. 2d 420 (D.N.J. 1999).

2. In United States v. Frazier, 307 F.3d 1244, 1269 (11th Cir. 2004), the court held that the Federal Rules governing discovery did not apply to the government's rebuttal expert witnesses. Does such a rule further the oft-stated aim of avoiding "trial by ambush"?

3. How complete must expert reports be pursuant to F. R. Civ. P. 26? In the words of one court:

> [W]hile Rule 26(a)(2)(B) requires a complete statement of all opinions to be expressed and the basis and reasons therefor, along with the data or other information considered by the witness in forming the opinions, it does not require that a report recite each minute fact or piece of scientific information that might be elicited on direct examination to establish the admissibility of the expert opinion under Daubert. Nor does it require the expert to anticipate every criticism and articulate every nano-detail that might be involved in defending the opinion on cross examination at a Daubert hearing. "The purpose of a detailed and complete expert report as contemplated by Rule 26(a) . . . is, in part, to minimize the expense of deposing experts, and to shorten direct examination and prevent an ambush at trial." Klonoski v. Mahlab, 156 F.3d 255, 269 (1st Cir. 1998) . . . and Thibeault v. Square D Co., 960 F.2d 239, 244 (1st Cir. 1992) (disclosure is consonant with federal courts' desire to make trial less a game of blindman's buff and more a fair contest with basic issues and facts disclosed to the fullest practical extent). Failure to include the required information frustrates the purpose of candid and cost-efficient expert discovery — but so would a requirement of too much information.

McCoy v. Whirlpool, 214 F.R.D. 646, 652 (D. Kan. 2003).

4.   Federal Rules of Evidence 701 and 702 were amended in 2000. As part of those amendments, FRE 701 draws a sharper line between expert and lay opinion testimony, specifically allowing only lay opinion evidence that is "not based upon scientific, technical, or other specialized knowledge within the scope of 702." The Advisory Committee notes indicate one purpose of the amendment is to "ensure[] that a party will not evade the expert witness disclosure requirements set forth in Fed.R.Civ.P. 26 and Fed.R.Crim.P. 16 by simply calling an expert witness in the guise of a layperson." The distinction between lay and expert opinion is developed at length in Chapter 2, Expert Evidence: Rules and Cases.

III. APPOINTMENT OF EXPERT WITNESSES

Ake v. Oklahoma

470 U.S. 68 (1985)

Justice MARSHALL delivered the opinion of the Court.

The issue in this case is whether the Constitution requires that an indigent defendant have access to the psychiatric examination and assistance necessary to prepare an effective defense based on his mental condition, when his sanity at the time of the offense is seriously in question.

I

[Ake was arrested and charged with murdering a couple and wounding their two children. He was diagnosed as probable paranoid schizophrenic and committed, having been found incompetent to stand trial. The court found Ake to be a "mentally ill person in need of care and treatment" and incompetent to stand trial, and ordered him committed to the state mental hospital. Six weeks later, Ake was found competent and the state resumed proceedings against him.]

At a pretrial conference in June, Ake's attorney informed the court that his client would raise an insanity defense. To enable him to prepare and present such a defense adequately, the attorney stated, a psychiatrist would have to examine Ake with respect to his mental condition at the time of the offense. . . . [The trial court rejected counsel's request for an appointed psychiatrist.]

Ake was tried for two counts of murder in the first degree, a crime punishable by death in Oklahoma, and for two counts of shooting with intent to kill. [Ake was found guilty and the jury sentenced Ake to death on each of the two murder counts.] . . .

We hold that when a defendant has made a preliminary showing that his sanity at the time of the offense is likely to be a significant factor at trial, the Constitution requires that a State provide access to a psychiatrist's assistance on this issue if the defendant cannot otherwise afford one. Accordingly, we reverse.

III

This Court has long recognized that when a State brings its judicial power to bear on an indigent defendant in a criminal proceeding, it must take steps to assure that the defendant has a fair opportunity to present his defense. This elementary principle, grounded in significant part on the Fourteenth Amendment's due process guarantee of fundamental fairness, derives from the belief that justice cannot be equal where, simply as a result of his poverty, a defendant is denied the opportunity to participate mean-ingfully in a judicial proceeding in which his liberty is at stake. In recognition of this right, this Court held almost 30 years ago that once a State offers to criminal defendants the opportunity to appeal their cases, it must provide a trial transcript to an indigent defendant if the transcript is necessary to a decision on the merits of the appeal. . . . Since then, this Court has held that an indigent defendant may not be required to pay a fee before filing a notice of appeal of his conviction, . . . that an indigent defendant is entitled to the assistance of counsel at trial, . . . and on his first direct appeal as of right, . . . and that such assistance must be effective. . . . Meaningful access to justice has been the consistent theme of these cases. We recognized long ago that mere access to the courthouse doors does not by itself assure a proper func-tioning of the adversary process, and that a criminal trial is fundamentally unfair if the State proceeds against an indigent defendant without making certain that he has access to the raw materials integral to the building of an effective defense. Thus, while the Court has not held that a State must purchase for the indigent defendant all the assistance that his wealthier counterpart might buy, . . . , it has often reaffirmed that fundamental fair-ness entitles indigent defendants to "an adequate opportunity to present their claims fairly within the adversary system," . . . To implement this principle, we have focused on identifying the "basic tools of an adequate defense or appeal," . . . , and we have required that such tools be provided to those defendants who cannot afford to pay for them.

To say that these basic tools must be provided is, of course, merely to begin our inquiry. In this case we must decide whether, and under what conditions, the participation of a psychiatrist is important enough to prep-aration of a defense to require the State to provide an indigent defendant with access to competent psychiatric assistance in preparing the defense. Three factors are relevant to this determination. The first is the private interest that will be affected by the action of the State. The second is the governmental interest that will be affected if the safeguard is to be provided. The third is the probable value of the additional or substitute procedural safeguards that are sought, and the risk of an erroneous deprivation of the affected interest if those safeguards are not provided. . . . We turn, then, to apply this standard to the issue before us.

A

The private interest in the accuracy of a criminal proceeding that places an individual's life or liberty at risk is almost uniquely compelling. Indeed, the host of safeguards fashioned by this Court over the years to diminish the risk of erroneous conviction stands as a testament to that concern. The interest of the individual in the outcome of the State's effort to overcome the presumption of innocence is obvious and weighs heavily in our analysis.

We consider, next, the interest of the State. Oklahoma asserts that to provide Ake with psychiatric assistance on the record before us would result in a staggering burden to the State. Brief. We are unpersuaded by this assertion. Many States, as well as the Federal Government, currently make psychiatric assistance available to indigent defendants, and they have not found the financial burden so great as to preclude this assistance. . . . We therefore conclude that the governmental interest in denying Ake the assistance of a psychiatrist is not substantial, in light of the compelling interest of both the State and the individual in accurate dispositions.

Last, we inquire into the probable value of the psychiatric assistance sought, and the risk of error in the proceeding if such assistance is not offered. We begin by considering the pivotal role that psychiatry has come to play in criminal proceedings. More than 40 States, as well as the Federal Government, have decided either through legislation or judicial decision that indigent defendants are entitled, under certain circumstances, to the assistance of a psychiatrist's expertise. For example, in subsection (e) of the Criminal Justice Act, 18 U.S.C. § 3006A, Congress has provided that indigent defendants shall receive the assistance of all experts "necessary for an adequate defense." Numerous state statutes guarantee reimbursement for expert services under a like standard. And in many States that have not assured access to psychiatrists through the legislative process, state courts have interpreted the State or Federal Constitution to require that psychiatric assistance be provided to indigent defendants when necessary for an adequate defense, or when insanity is at issue.

These statutes and court decisions reflect a reality that we recognize today, namely, that when the State has made the defendant's mental condition relevant to his criminal culpability and to the punishment he might suffer, the assistance of a psychiatrist may well be crucial to the defendant's ability to marshal his defense. In this role, psychiatrists gather facts, through professional examination, interviews, and elsewhere, that they will share with the judge or jury; they analyze the information gathered and from it draw plausible conclusions about the defendant's mental condition, and about the effects of any disorder on behavior; and they offer opinions about how the defendant's mental condition might have affected his behavior at the time in question. They know the probative questions to ask of the opposing party's psychiatrists and how to interpret their answers. Unlike lay witnesses, who can merely describe symptoms they believe might be relevant to the defendant's mental state, psychiatrists can identify the "elusive and often deceptive" symptoms of insanity, . . . and tell the jury why their observations are relevant. Further, where permitted by evidentiary rules, psychiatrists can translate a medical diagnosis into language that will assist the trier of fact, and therefore offer evidence in a form that has meaning for the task at hand. Through this process of investigation, interpretation, and testimony, psychiatrists ideally assist lay jurors, who generally have no training in psychiatric matters, to make a sensible and educated determination about the mental condition of the defendant at the time of the offense.

Psychiatry is not, however, an exact science, and psychiatrists disagree widely and frequently on what constitutes mental illness, on the appropriate diagnosis to be attached to given behavior and symptoms, on cure and treatment, and on likelihood of future dangerousness. Perhaps because there often is no single, accurate psychiatric conclusion on legal insanity in a given case, juries remain the primary factfinders on this issue, and they must resolve differences in opinion within the psychiatric profession on the basis of the evidence offered by each party. When jurors make this determination about issues that inevitably are complex and foreign, the testimony of psychiatrists can be crucial and "a virtual necessity if an insanity plea is to have any chance of success."[7] By organizing a defendant's mental history, examination results and behavior, and other information, interpreting it in light of their expertise, and then laying out their investigative and analytic process to the jury, the psychiatrists for each party enable the jury to make its most accurate determination of the truth on the issue before them. It is for this reason that States rely on psychiatrists as examiners, consultants, and witnesses, and that private individuals do as well, when they can afford to do so.[8] In so saying, we neither approve nor disapprove the widespread reliance

7. Gardner, The Myth of the Impartial Psychiatric Expert—Some Comments Concerning Criminal Responsibility and the Decline of the Age of Therapy, 2 Law & Psychology Rev. 99, 113-114 (1976). In addition, "[t]estimony emanating from the depth and scope of specialized knowledge is very impressive to a jury. The same testimony from another source can have less effect." F. Bailey & H. Rothblatt, Investigation and Preparation of Criminal Cases § 175 (1970); see also ABA Standards for Criminal Justice 5-1.4, Commentary, p. 5-20 (2d ed. 1980) ("The quality of representation at trial . . . may be excellent and yet valueless to the defendant if the defense requires the assistance of a psychiatrist . . . and no such services are available").

8. See also *Reilly v. Barry*, 250 N.Y. 456, 461, 166 N.E. 165, 167 (1929) (Cardozo, C.J.) ("[U]pon the trial of certain issues, such as insanity or forgery, experts are often necessary both for prosecution and for defense. . . . [A] defendant may be at an unfair disadvantage, if

on psychiatrists but instead recognize the unfairness of a contrary holding in light of the evolving practice. . . .

A defendant's mental condition is not necessarily at issue in every criminal proceeding, however, and it is unlikely that psychiatric assistance of the kind we have described would be of probable value in cases where it is not. The risk of error from denial of such assistance, as well as its probable value, is most predictably at its height when the defendant's mental condition is seriously in question. When the defendant is able to make an ex parte threshold showing to the trial court that his sanity is likely to be a significant factor in his defense, the need for the assistance of a psychiatrist is readily apparent. It is in such cases that a defense may be devastated by the absence of a psychiatric examination and testimony; with such assistance, the defendant might have a reasonable chance of success. In such a circumstance, where the potential accuracy of the jury's determination is so dramatically enhanced, and where the interests of the individual and the State in an accurate proceeding are substantial, the State's interest in its fisc must yield.

We therefore hold that when a defendant demonstrates to the trial judge that his sanity at the time of the offense is to be a significant factor at trial, the State must, at a minimum, assure the defendant access to a competent psychiatrist who will conduct an appropriate examination and assist in evaluation, preparation, and presentation of the defense. . . .

B

Ake also was denied the means of presenting evidence to rebut the State's evidence of his future dangerousness. The foregoing discussion compels a similar conclusion in the context of a capital sentencing proceeding, when the State presents psychiatric evidence of the defendant's future dangerousness. We have repeatedly recognized the defendant's compelling interest in fair adjudication at the sentencing phase of a capital case. The State, too, has a profound interest in assuring that its ultimate sanction is not erroneously imposed, and we do not see why monetary considerations should be more persuasive in this context than at trial. The variable on which we must focus is, therefore, the probable value that the assistance of a psychiatrist will have in this area, and the risk attendant on its absence.

This Court has upheld the practice in many States of placing before the jury psychiatric testimony on the question of future dangerousness, . . . at

---

he is unable because of poverty to parry by his own witnesses the thrusts of those against him"); 2 I. Goldstein & F. Lane, Goldstein Trial Techniques § 14.01 (2d ed. 1969) ("Modern civilization, with its complexities of business, science, and the professions, has made expert and opinion evidence a necessity. This is true where the subject matters involved are beyond the general knowledge of the average juror"); Henning, The Psychiatrist in the Legal Process, in By Reason of Insanity: Essays on Psychiatry and the Law 217, 219-220 (L. Freedman ed., 1983) (discussing the growing role of psychiatric witnesses as a result of changing definitions of legal insanity and increased judicial and legislative acceptance of the practice).

least where the defendant has had access to an expert of his own, ... In so holding, the Court relied, in part, on the assumption that the factfinder would have before it both the views of the prosecutor's psychiatrists and the "opposing views of the defendant's doctors" and would therefore be competent to "uncover, recognize, and take due account of ... short-comings" in predictions on this point. . . . Without a psychiatrist's assistance, the defendant cannot offer a well-informed expert's opposing view, and thereby loses a significant opportunity to raise in the jurors' minds questions about the State's proof of an aggravating factor. In such a circumstance, where the consequence of error is so great, the relevance of responsive psychiatric testimony so evident, and the burden on the State so slim, due process requires access to a psychiatric examination on relevant issues, to the testimony of the psychiatrist, and to assistance in preparation at the sentencing phase.

NOTES AND QUESTIONS

1. In Caldwell v. Mississippi, 472 U.S. 320 (1985), the defendant unsuccessfully sought the appointment of a criminal investigator, a fingerprint expert, and a ballistics expert. The Supreme Court upheld the denial, claiming that there had been no showing of the reasonableness of the request. The Court found that the defendant "offered little more than undeveloped assertions that the requested assistance would be beneficial." *Id.* at 323, n.1. Thus the Court declined to decide, "as a matter of federal constitutional law what if any showing would have entitled a defendant to assistance of the type here sought." *Id.*

2. Although some courts originally limited the applicability of *Ake* to psychiatric experts in insanity cases, the vast majority of courts have read *Ake* and *Caldwell* to require the appointment of other types of experts, provided a particularized showing of need can be met. *See e.g.*, Husske v. Commonwealth, 476 S.E.2d 920, 925-926 (Va. 1996) and cases cited therein.

3. The Criminal Justice Act, 18 U.S.C. § 3006(A), allows counsel for an indigent defendant the right to hire an expert without prior approval in an amount not to exceed $500. If costs will exceed that amount, counsel may spend up to $1,600 with the court's approval. This provision assists defendants in obtaining expert assistance but the cost limitations may impair a defendant's ability to find an appropriately qualified expert. For further discussion about the reasons for and implications of such economic limitations, see Darryl K. Brown, *Rationing Criminal Defense Entitlements: An Argument from Institutional Design*, 104 Colum. L. Rev. 801 (2004).

4. For an in-depth analysis about the need for appointed expert testimony in modern criminal trials and the judicial limitations, see Paul C. Giannelli, *Ake v. Oklahoma: The Right to Expert Assistance in a Post-Daubert, Post-DNA World*, 89 Cornell L. Rev. 1305 (2004).

IV. PROPOSALS FOR STRUCTURAL CHANGE

The *Daubert* trilogy has ushered in a new era of expert evidence. Unlike earlier generations, today's lawyers must be adept at understanding the scientific and technical foundations of their experts' testimony. The system now requires far more of lawyers and of judges with respect to expert and scientific expert testimony. Will courts and litigants be able to manage these challenges? Consider the following readings in deciding how to accommodate this new world of expert testimony. Has our reach exceeded our grasp or is Justice Breyer's encouraging outlook warranted?

Daubert v. Merrell Dow Pharmaceuticals, Inc.

509 U.S. 579 (1993)

... Faced with a proffer of expert scientific testimony, then, the trial judge must determine at the outset, pursuant to Rule 104(a), whether the expert is proposing to testify to (1) scientific knowledge that (2) will assist the trier of fact to understand or determine a fact in issue. This entails a preliminary assessment of whether the reasoning or methodology underlying the testimony is scientifically valid and of whether that reasoning or methodology properly can be applied to the facts in issue. We are confident that federal judges possess the capacity to undertake this review. ...

[A] judge assessing a proffer of expert scientific testimony under Rule 702 should also be mindful of other applicable rules. Rule 703 provides that expert opinions based on otherwise inadmissible hearsay are to be admitted only if the facts or data are "of a type reasonably relied upon by experts in the particular field in forming opinions or inferences upon the subject." Rule 706 allows the court at its discretion to procure the assistance of an expert of its own choosing.

General Electric Co. v. Joiner

522 U.S. 136 (1997)

Justice BREYER, concurring.

The Court's opinion, which I join, emphasizes *Daubert's* statement that a trial judge, acting as "gatekeeper," must " 'ensure that any and all scientific testimony or evidence admitted is not only relevant, but reliable.' " ... This requirement will sometimes ask judges to make subtle and sophisticated determinations about scientific methodology and its relation to the conclusions an expert witness seeks to offer — particularly when a case arises in an area where the science itself is tentative or uncertain, or where testimony about general risk levels in human beings or animals is offered to prove individual causation. Yet, as amici have pointed out, judges are not scientists and do not have the scientific training that can facilitate the making of such decisions. . . .

Of course, neither the difficulty of the task nor any comparative lack of expertise can excuse the judge from exercising the "gatekeeper" duties that the Federal Rules of Evidence impose — determining, for example, whether particular expert testimony is reliable and "will assist the trier of fact," Fed. Rule Evid. 702, or whether the "probative value" of testimony is substantially outweighed by risks of prejudice, confusion or waste of time, Fed. Rule Evid. 403. To the contrary, when law and science intersect, those duties often must be exercised with special care.

Today's toxic tort case provides an example. The plaintiff in today's case says that a chemical substance caused, or promoted, his lung cancer. His concern, and that of others, about the causes of cancer is understandable, for cancer kills over one in five Americans. . . . Moreover, scientific evidence implicates some chemicals as potential causes of some cancers. . . . Yet modern life, including good health as well as economic well-being, depends upon the use of artificial or manufactured substances, such as chemicals. And it may, therefore, prove particularly important to see that judges fulfill their Daubert gatekeeping function, so that they help assure that the powerful engine of tort liability, which can generate strong financial incentives to reduce, or to eliminate, production, points toward the right substances and does not destroy the wrong ones. It is, thus, essential in this science-related area that the courts administer the Federal Rules of Evidence in order to achieve the "end[s]" that the Rules themselves set forth, not only so that proceedings may be "justly determined," but also so "that the truth may be ascertained." Fed. Rule Evid. 102.

I therefore want specially to note that, as cases presenting significant science-related issues have increased in number, . . . judges have increasingly found in the Rules of Evidence and Civil Procedure ways to help them overcome the inherent difficulty of making determinations about complicated scientific, or otherwise technical, evidence. Among these techniques are an increased use of Rule 16's pretrial conference authority to narrow the scientific issues in dispute, pretrial hearings where potential experts are subject to examination by the court, and the appointment of special masters and specially trained law clerks. . . .

Accepting *Daubert*'s Invitation: Defining a Role for Court-Appointed Experts in Assessing Scientific Validity

43 Emory L. J. 995 (1994)
Joe S. Cecil and Thomas E. Willging

In Daubert v. Merrell Dow Pharmaceuticals, Inc. the Supreme Court urged federal judges faced with a challenge to scientific testimony to

undertake "a preliminary assessment of whether the reasoning or methodology underlying the testimony is scientifically valid and of whether that
reasoning or methodology properly can be applied to the facts in issue."
In response to concerns raised by Chief Justice Rehnquist, Justice Blackmun,
writing for the majority, expressed confidence in the ability of federal judges
to undertake such a review, noting that, among other thing, judges "should
also be mindful" of the authority to appoint experts under Rule 706 of the
Federal Rules of Evidence.

In offering this aside the Court joined a long list of recent proponents of
court-appointed experts. The Court's invitation to consider court-appointed
experts is likely to receive greater attention as the demanding requirements
for admissibility of such evidence established in Daubert are applied to the
growing volume of scientific and technical evidence. This article speaks to
judges, attorneys and others who wish to consider using court-appointed
experts by describing the experiences of judges who have appointed experts
and suggesting procedures and techniques for improving the use of such
experts.

A. RULE 706 OF THE FEDERAL RULES OF EVIDENCE

Rule 706 of the Federal Rules of Evidence specifies a set of procedures
governing the process of appointment, the assignment of duties, the reporting of findings, testimony, and compensation of experts. . . .

The trial court has broad discretion in deciding whether to appoint a Rule
706 expert. Although it has been suggested that "extreme variation" among
the parties' experts is the primary circumstance suggesting that such an
appointment may be beneficial, courts frequently appoint experts because
of the complexity of the issues or the evidence. Furthermore, the trial court
retains discretion to refuse to appoint an expert despite extreme variations in
the parties' expert testimony. Such experts should be appointed when they are
likely to clarify issues under consideration; it is not an abuse of discretion for a
trial court to refuse to appoint an expert under Rule 706 when "additional
experts would . . . add more divergence and opinion differences." Appellate
courts on occasion have reminded judges of this authority. Where a trial court
has been unaware of or unclear on its authority to appoint a neutral expert
under Rule 706 or its inherent power to do so, a reviewing court may order the
trial court to exercise its discretion and decide whether appointment of a
neutral expert is justified in the circumstances of the case. . . .

B. INHERENT AUTHORITY TO APPOINT A TECHNICAL ADVISOR

The court's authority under Rule 706 to appoint an expert to offer
testimony represents a specific application of its broader inherent authority
to invite expert assistance in a broad range of duties necessary to decide a

case. The most striking exercise of this broader authority involves appointing an expert as a technical advisor to confer in chambers with the judge regarding the evidence, as opposed to offering testimony in open court and being subject to cross-examination. Although few cases deal with the inherent power of a court to appoint a technical advisor, the power to appoint remains virtually undisputed, tracing a clear line from the 1920 decision of the Supreme Court in Ex parte Peterson to the recent decision of the United States Court of Appeals for the First Circuit in Reilly v. United States. Generally, a district court has discretion to appoint a technical advisor, but it is expected that such appointments will be "hen's teeth rare," a "last" or "near-to-last resort." General factors that might justify an appointment are "problems of unusual difficulty, sophistication, and complexity, involving something well beyond the regular questions of fact and law with which judges must routinely grapple." The role of the technical advisor, as the name implies, is to give advice to the judge, not to give evidence and not to decide the case.

Introduction

Reference Manual on Scientific Evidence (Federal Judicial Center, 2d ed. 2000)
The Hon. Stephen Breyer

In this age of science, science should expect to find a warm welcome, perhaps a permanent home, in our courtrooms. The reason is a simple one. The legal disputes before us increasingly involve the principles and tools of science. Proper resolution of those disputes matters not just to the litigants, but also to the general public — those who live in our technologically complex society and whom the law must serve. Our decisions should reflect a proper scientific and technical understanding so that the law can respond to the needs of the public.

Consider, for example, how often our cases today involve statistics — a tool familiar to social scientists and economists but, until our own generation, not to many judges. Only last year the U.S. Supreme Court heard two cases that involved consideration of statistical evidence. . . .

But science is far more than tools, such as statistics. And that "more" increasingly enters directly into the courtroom. The Supreme Court, for example, has recently decided cases involving basic questions of human liberty, the resolution of which demanded an understanding of scientific matters. In 1997 we were asked to decide whether the Constitution contains a "right to die." . . . Underlying the legal question was a medical question: To what extent can medical technology reduce or eliminate the risk of dying in severe pain? The medical question did not determine the answer to the legal question, but to do our legal job properly, we needed to develop an informed — although necessarily approximate — understanding of the state of that relevant scientific art. . . .

The Supreme Court's docket is only illustrative. Scientific issues permeate the law. Criminal courts consider the scientific validity of, say, DNA sampling or voiceprints, or expert predictions of defendants' "future dangerousness," which can lead courts or juries to authorize or withhold the punishment of death. Courts review the reasonableness of administrative agency conclusions about the safety of a drug, the risks attending nuclear waste disposal, the leakage potential of a toxic waste dump, or the risks to wildlife associated with the building of a dam. Patent law cases can turn almost entirely on an understanding of the underlying technical or scientific subject matter. And, of course, tort law often requires difficult determinations about the risk of death or injury associated with exposure to a chemical ingredient of a pesticide or other product. . . .

The search is not a search for scientific precision. We cannot hope to investigate all the subtleties that characterize good scientific work. A judge is not a scientist, and a courtroom is not a scientific laboratory. But consider the remark made by the physicist Wolfgang Pauli. After a colleague asked whether a certain scientific paper was wrong, Pauli replied, "That paper isn't even good enough to be wrong!" Our objective is to avoid legal decisions that reflect that paper's so-called science. The law must seek decisions that fall within the boundaries of scientifically sound knowledge.

Even this more modest objective is sometimes difficult to achieve in practice. The most obvious reason is that most judges lack the scientific training that might facilitate the evaluation of scientific claims or the evaluation of expert witnesses who make such claims. . . .

Furthermore, science itself may be highly uncertain and controversial with respect to many of the matters that come before the courts. Scientists often express considerable uncertainty about the dangers of a particular substance. And their views may differ about many related questions that courts may have to answer. What, for example, is the relevance to human cancer of studies showing that a substance causes some cancers, perhaps only a few, in test groups of mice or rats? What is the significance of extrapolations from toxicity studies involving high doses to situations where the doses are much smaller? Can lawyers or judges or anyone else expect scientists always to be certain or always to have uniform views with respect to an extrapolation from a large dose to a small one, when the causes of and mechanisms related to cancer are generally not well known? Many difficult legal cases fall within this area of scientific uncertainty.

Finally, a court proceeding, such as a trial, is not simply a search for dispassionate truth. The law must be fair. In our country, it must always seek to protect basic human liberties. One important procedural safeguard, guaranteed by our Constitution's Seventh Amendment, is the right to a trial by jury. A number of innovative techniques have been developed to strengthen the ability of juries to consider difficult evidence. Any effort to bring better science into the courtroom must respect the jury's constitutionally specified role — even if doing so means that, from a scientific perspective, an incorrect result is sometimes produced.

Despite the difficulties, I believe there is an increasingly important need for law to reflect sound science. I remain optimistic about the likelihood that it will do so. It is common to find cooperation between governmental institutions and the scientific community where the need for that cooperation is apparent. Today, as a matter of course, the President works with a science adviser, Congress solicits advice on the potential dangers of food additives from the National Academy of Sciences, and scientific regulatory agencies often work with outside scientists, as well as their own, to develop a product that reflects good science.

The judiciary, too, has begun to look for ways to improve the quality of the science on which scientifically related judicial determinations will rest. The Federal Judicial Center is collaborating with the National Academy of Sciences in developing the academy's Program in Science, Technology, and Law. This program will bring together on a regular basis knowledgeable scientists, engineers, judges, attorneys, and corporate and government officials to explore areas of interaction and improve communication among the science, engineering, and legal communities. This program is intended to provide a neutral, nonadversarial forum for promoting understanding, encouraging imaginative approaches to problem solving, and conducting studies.

In the Supreme Court, as a matter of course, we hear not only from the parties to a case but also from outside groups, which file briefs — thirty-page amicus curiae briefs — that help us to become more informed about the relevant science. . . . Such briefs help to educate the justices on potentially relevant technical matters, making us not experts, but moderately educated laypersons, and that education improves the quality of our decisions.

Moreover, our Court recently made clear that the law imposes on trial judges the duty, with respect to scientific evidence, to become evidentiary gatekeepers. . . .

Federal trial judges, looking for ways to perform the gatekeeping function better, increasingly have used case-management techniques like pretrial conferences to narrow the scientific issues in dispute, pretrial hearings where potential experts are subject to examination by the court, and the appointment of specially trained law clerks or scientific special masters. Judge Jack B. Weinstein of New York suggests that courts should sometimes "go beyond the experts proffered by the parties" and "appoint independent experts" as the Federal Rules of Evidence allow. Judge Gerald Rosen of Michigan appointed a University of Michigan Medical School professor to testify as an expert witness for the court, helping to determine the relevant facts in a case that challenged a Michigan law prohibiting partial-birth abortions. Judge Richard Stearns of Massachusetts, acting with the consent of the parties in a recent, highly technical genetic engineering patent case, appointed a Harvard Medical School professor to serve "as a sounding board for the court to think through the scientific significance of the evidence" and to "assist the court in determining the validity of any scientific evidence, hypothesis or theory on which the experts base their testimony."

In what one observer describes as "the most comprehensive attempt to incorporate science, as scientists practice it, into law," Judge Sam Pointer, Jr., of Alabama recently appointed a "neutral science panel" of four scientists from different disciplines to prepare testimony on the scientific basis of the claims in the silicone gel breast implant product liability cases consolidated as part of a multidistrict litigation process. This proceeding will allow judges and jurors in numerous cases to consider videotaped testimony by a panel of prominent scientists. The use of such videotapes is likely to result in more consistent decisions across courts, as well as great savings of time and expense for the individual litigants and the courts.

These case-management techniques are neutral, in principle favoring neither plaintiffs nor defendants. When used, they have typically proved successful. Nonetheless, judges have not often invoked their rules-provided authority to appoint their own experts. They may hesitate simply because the process is unfamiliar or because the use of this kind of technique inevitably raises questions. Will use of an independent expert, in effect, substitute that expert's judgment for that of the court? Will it inappropriately deprive the parties of control over the presentation of the case? Will it improperly intrude on the proper function of the jury? Where is one to find a truly neutral expert? After all, different experts, in total honesty, often interpret the same data differently. Will the search for the expert create inordinate delay or significantly increase costs? Who will pay the expert? . . .

A number of scientific and professional organizations have come forward with proposals to aid the courts in finding skilled experts. The National Conference of Lawyers and Scientists, a joint committee of the American Association for the Advancement of Science (AAAS) and the Science and Technology Section of the American Bar Association, has developed a pilot project to test the feasibility of increased use of court-appointed experts in cases that present technical issues. The project will recruit a slate of candidates from science and professional organizations to serve as court-appointed experts in cases in which the court has determined that traditional means of clarifying issues under the adversarial system are unlikely to yield the information that is necessary for a reasoned and principled resolution of the disputed issues. The project also is developing educational materials that will be helpful to scientists who are unfamiliar with the legal system. The Federal Judicial Center will examine a number of questions arising from such appointments, such as the following:

- How did the appointed experts perform their duties?
- How did the court, while protecting the interests of the lawyers and the parties they represent, protect the experts from unreasonable demands, say, on their time?

• How did the court prepare the experts to encounter what may be an unfamiliar and sometimes hostile legal environment?

The Private Adjudication Center at Duke University is establishing a registry of independent scientific and technical experts who are willing to provide advice to courts or serve as court-appointed experts. Registry services also are available to arbitrators and mediators and to parties and lawyers who together agree to engage an independent expert at the early stages of a dispute. The registry has recruited an initial group of experts in medicine and health-related disciplines, primarily from major academic institutions, and new registrants are added on a regular basis. As needed, the registry also conducts targeted searches to find experts with the qualifications required for particular cases. Registrants must adhere to a code of conduct designed to ensure confidence in their impartiality and integrity.

These projects have much to teach us about the ways in which courts can use such experts. We need to learn how to identify impartial experts. Also, we need to know how best to protect the interests of the parties and the experts when such extraordinary procedures are used. We also need to know how best to prepare a scientist for the sometimes hostile legal environment that arises during depositions and cross-examination. . . .

In this age of science we must build legal foundations that are sound in science as well as in law. Scientists have offered their help. We in the legal community should accept that offer. We are in the process of doing so. This manual seeks to open legal institutional channels through which science — its learning, tools, and principles — may flow more easily and thereby better inform the law. The manual represents one part of a joint scientific-legal effort that will further the interests of truth and justice alike.

NOTES AND QUESTIONS

1. The article by Joe Cecil and Thomas Willging reflects the result of a multiyear study of court-appointed experts and provides an in-depth analysis of the issues as well as suggestions for the future use of appointed experts. For another in-depth analysis of court-appointed experts, see Ellen E. Deason, *Court-Appointed Expert Witnesses: Scientific Positivism Meets Bias and Deference,* 77 Ore. L. Rev. 59 (1998).

2. Not all agree with the use of court-appointed experts. *See e.g.,* Sophia Cope, *Comment, Ripe for Revision: A Critique of Federal Rule of Evidence 706 and the Use of Court-Appointed Experts,* 39 Gonz. L. Rev. 163 (2003-2004).

3. For an analysis of the use of science panels in the *Silicone Breast Implant Cases,* see Laura Hooper, Joe S. Cecil, & Thomas E. Willgeng, *Assessing Causation in Breast Implant Litigation: The Role of Science Panels,* 64 AUT-Law & Contemp. Probs. 139 (2001).